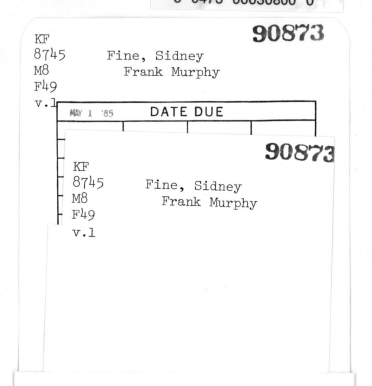

90873

KF
8745
M8
F49
v.1

Fine, Sidney
    Frank Murphy

MAY 1 '85   DATE DUE

90873

KF
8745
M8
F49
v.1

Fine, Sidney
    Frank Murphy

FRANK MURPHY

Frank Murphy

FRANK MURPHY

the detroit years

by
Sidney Fine

Ann Arbor   The University of Michigan Press

*Published with the assistance of a grant from
the Horace H. Rackham School of Graduate Studies
of The University of Michigan.*

To Gail and Deborah

Preface

Not only was Frank Murphy one of the more interesting personalities on the American scene for a thirty-year period following World War I, but few Americans have had so varied a career or been associated with so many great events. As United States attorney, Detroit criminal-court judge, mayor of Detroit, governor-general and high commissioner of the Philippines, governor of Michigan, attorney general of the United States, and justice of the United States Supreme Court, Murphy generally found himself where the action was, and he left his impress on major developments in American life during the three decades that preceded his death in 1949. The intersection between the man and the era has persuaded me to cast this biography, unlike other Murphy biographies, in the life-and-times mold. The present volume focuses on Murphy's Detroit years, especially his service on Detroit's celebrated Recorder's Court (1924–30) and as Detroit's depression mayor (1930–33). A second volume will encompass Murphy's New Deal years as governor-general and high commissioner of the Philippines (1933–36) and as governor of Michigan (1937–38), and the concluding volume will deal with his career in Washington as attorney general of the United States (1939–40) and as a United States Supreme Court justice (1940–49).

It is a pleasure to acknowledge the assistance that I received in writing this book. My research and the publication of the book were facilitated by research and publication grants from the Horace H. Rackham School of Graduate Studies of the University of Michigan. My colleague Bradford Perkins read the entire manuscript and made numerous suggestions for its improvement. Robert M. Warner, J. Fraser Cocks, Mary Jo Pugh, Cathryn F. Abernathy, and William H. McNitt of the Michigan Historical Collections provided me with research services that went far beyond the routine. My manuscript research was also aided by Philip P. Mason and Warner W. Pflug of the Archives of Labor History and Urban Affairs of Wayne State University, James M.

Babcock, Bernice C. Sprenger, Alice C. Dalligan, and George W. Southworth of the Burton Historical Collection, James E. O'Neil, William J. Stewart, and the staff of the Franklin D. Roosevelt Library, David C. Mearns and the staff of the Library of Congress, Joseph D. Howerton, Jane F. Smith, and Donald Mossholder of the National Archives and Records Service, and Howard C. Rice, Jr., of the Firestone Library of Princeton University.

Brigid Murphy, Irene Murphy, Eugene Gressman, and Eleanor Bumgardner Wright deserve special mention for all that they have done over the years to augment the Frank Murphy Papers and to supplement that collection with collateral manuscript collections. Sharon Keyes, Joan Cuddihy, Raymond Moley, Alex Baskin, and Michael Staebler permitted me to examine material in their possession relevant to Murphy's life and career. William H. O'Brien granted me permission to examine the candidate files in the Detroit Citizens League Papers, and Francis A. Allen, then dean of the University of Michigan Law School, made the Department of Law Faculty Records available to me. Unless otherwise noted, the photographs reproduced in the text were generously made available to me by the Michigan Historical Collections. The persons who graciously permitted me to interview them and who responded to my letters seeking information about Frank Murphy are listed in the bibliography. Charles W. Johnson, Richard T. Ortquist, Jr., Madeline Shapiro, Ronald Mulder, and Thomas L. Jones performed one or another research chore for me. My wife, Jean Fine, contributed to the writing of this book in too many ways to mention.

SIDNEY FINE

Contents

I

"Darling Mama"

Although Frank Murphy knew relatively little about his family's genealogy, he was not inclined to discourage reports that his paternal Irish grandfather or great-grandfather had been hanged by the British and that he descended from martyrs in "the cause of freedom." The story of the martyred ancestors has become a part of the Murphy legend, but like so much of that legend there is no documentary evidence to support it. There is actually a dearth of information about Murphy's ancestry, and no one has succeeded in tracing it back beyond his paternal and maternal grandparents.

What is known is that Frank's paternal grandfather, William Francis Murphy, and his wife, Margaret Laval, both of County Mayo, migrated to Canada in 1847. They acquired some land near Guelph, Ontario, and lived there for ten years. In 1857 they moved to Guelph, where William entered the dairy business and became quite prosperous. When Margaret Murphy died, apparently in 1881, her husband retired from business. He died in 1892, at the age of ninety-four; he was described in an obituary as "always a good neighbor and obliging friend."[1]

William and Margaret Murphy had two sons, John F. and William, and two daughters. John F., who was Frank Murphy's father, was born on June 17, 1849, just outside Guelph, and resided in Canada for almost thirty years. He was caught up in the Fenian activity in June, 1866, when he was a lad of only sixteen. According to his own account, he was sent to Buffalo by Fenian authorities and there found a force of about thirty thousand Fenians. He recrossed the border in a party of 650 men who were under the erroneous impression that they were the advance guard of a larger army. While foraging for cattle to feed the anticipated invaders, they ran into the Queen's troops, and a skirmish ensued. John, who discreetly remained behind a tree, remembered the encounter as a "terrific brush" that resulted in the withdrawal of the Queen's soldiers. The Fenians were soon captured, however, and John was jailed. When he was tried, it became evident, as John reported, that his cohorts and he "had been roped into the affair"; and because of his age, the fact that he was a Canadian, and the respectability of his family, he was acquitted.[2]

John Murphy eventually began the study of law in a judge's office and passed the necessary examinations to practice law, but his Fenian past appears to have been an obstacle to his entry into the profession in Canada. He therefore matriculated at the University of Michigan in 1879, received his law degree in 1881, and then worked briefly in the Detroit law office of Colonel John Atkinson. When there was a call from Sand Beach, Michigan, for a lawyer, Atkinson advised John Murphy to respond. He arrived in Sand Beach at the end of 1882 or the beginning of 1883 and remained there for the rest of his life.[3]

Sand Beach, located near the tip of the so-called Thumb district of eastern Michigan where Saginaw Bay joins Lake Huron, was apparently first settled in 1838. Incorporated as a village in 1882, it was described shortly thereafter as "the most important town" in Huron County. Initially, lumbering and the manufacture of shingles were the chief business activities in the Sand Beach region, but farming then became the predominant occupation, and the community came to depend on the trade of the surrounding farm area. The leading business establishment in Sand Beach was J. Jenks and Company, which engaged in a variety of enterprises. It built a large flour mill in the town in the early 1880s, reputedly the first mill to roll winter wheat in the United States, and the community soon boasted that it was the location of the "Largest Specialty Starch Plant in the World."[4]

In the 1890s Sand Beach was the home of six churches, two hotels, and an opera house, and it claimed to have "the best graded school and the best school-building in the county." It had 1,273 inhabitants in 1894 and 1,556 in 1910. In 1899 its name was changed to Harbor Beach—its present name—and it was incorporated as a city eleven years later.

Of Sand Beach's 1,273 inhabitants in 1894, 878 were native born and 395 foreign born. Only 281 were second-generation Americans; one or both parents of the remainder were of foreign birth. Although we cannot be sure, Canadians apparently constituted the largest foreign-born group in the community. There were a fair number of Germans and Poles and a few Irish in the town.

There was no parochial school for Catholic children in Sand Beach, and mass was celebrated in private homes until a frame church was erected in 1882 for the fifty or so Catholic families in the community. Sand Beach did not have a resident priest until the beginning of the twentieth century, and a more substantial church building of brick and stone was not dedicated until 1917. The church was given its name, Our Lady of Lake Huron, by Frank Murphy's mother, and the Murphy family donated its main altar.[5]

One of four attorneys in the town when he began practicing in Sand Beach, John Murphy developed a "very large" practice and acquired a reputation as "a skilled and versatile trial lawyer." Among his clients were the Père Marquette Railway Company and the Huron County Savings Bank, and he was involved in important litigation involving lumber interests in the area. When John Murphy came to Sand Beach, he had few worldly goods, but he became at least moderately wealthy and was able to move into a substantial home and to acquire additional property.[6] It was simply not true, as later reported, that the Murphy children grew up in a home that knew poverty, one in which their mother stretched meager funds "to feed hungry mouths."[7]

In addition to the law, John Murphy devoted himself to politics, and he became "one of the wheel horses" of the Democratic party in Huron County, serving for many years as its chairman. He held the post of deputy collector of customs at Sand Beach during the first Cleveland administration, served two two-year terms as circuit-court commissioner, and was twice elected prosecuting attorney of Huron County, but he was defeated in efforts to gain the latter post on five different occasions. Although friends considered him "an able and fearless prosecutor" and "a terror to the evil doers," a Republican source characterized him as "the oiliest, smoothest and most enthusiastic campaign liar who so far has shown up in these parts." John Murphy helped to keep the Democratic party in Huron County together during the long Democratic drought that began in Michigan in 1894, and he was understandably elated when Woodrow Wilson was elected in 1912. Two years later John Murphy was an unsuccessful candidate for Congress.[8]

John Murphy departed rather widely from the Paddy stereotype of the Irish-American and reflected rather "the . . . ambitious second-generation Irish American who was knocking at the gates of the political parties, the professions, and business." It has been said that "behind the flaming intransigence of the Irish nationalist . . . there was nine times out of ten an ambitious Horatio Alger figure."[9] John Murphy was certainly an Irish-American nationalist, but this did not deter him from the pursuit of wealth and middle-class respectability.

In one respect John Murphy did fit the Paddy stereotype: he had an excessive fondness for alcohol. A one-time Harbor Beach resident when asked whether John Murphy had ever appeared drunk in public, replied, "It has been said that he would never be seen in any other way." John Murphy's drinking habits understandably imposed a strain on the entire family. His wife and daughter supported the prohibition movement, and his famous son hated to think that his adored mother had "to put up" with her husband's drunken sprees.[10]

Soon after arriving in Sand Beach John Murphy fell in love with Mary Brennan, and on January 14, 1885, they became man and wife.[11] Mary Brennan's parents, Robert L. Brennan and Mary Mara, from Templorum in Kilkenny County, migrated in 1849 to Whitehall, New York, where Mary and a brother were born. The family moved on to North Grosvenor Dale, in Connecticut, where a third child was born. After several additional moves, the family settled in 1867 in Michigan, in Huron County, and ultimately in Sand Beach. Mary Brennan worked in her brother's music store in Sand Beach, possibly gave voice lessons, and sang in the choir of the Catholic and Baptist churches.[12]

Mary Brennan Murphy was a slender woman with black hair, blue eyes, a fair complexion, and "finely cut" features. She was a very pious woman, reserved in manner, and altogether devoted to her family—"just a sweet lady," to use the words of a Harbor Beach resident of the time. The wife in the Irish family has been described as "the brains, the manager, the savings bank, the realist for the notional and unrealistic husband." Although Mary Murphy did not fit the description in every respect, she was, in her way, a very strong woman, and she clearly occupied the central position in the Murphy household. As one of her sons remarked, "You see[,] inside our family circle, mother was the head of the family. She was a frail woman, who didn't talk much, but she saw things through. When she came to a decision, it was just about right. And we accepted it as such." "The boys and I," Mrs. Murphy's daughter recalled, "never did a thing in our lives without talking it over and always doing what darling mama told us to do."[13]

Frank Murphy was the third of the four children born to John and Mary Murphy. Frank's older brother, Harold, was born on June 12, 1886; his sister, Margaret Mary (Marguerite), on June 22, 1888; and his younger brother, George, on January 20, 1894. Frank was born on April 13, 1890, in the two-room house behind his father's law office where the family lived until they moved into the Victorian frame house next door a few years later. The child was named William Francis Murphy and was baptized eight days later according to the rite of the Roman Catholic church. From an early age, William Francis preferred to use the name "Frank," and since he hated to think of his mortality and advancing years, he decided that he had been born in 1893 rather than 1890. All the Murphys, as a matter of fact, were rather imprecise when it came to reporting their birth dates.[14]

"Any biography of my brother . . . ," George Murphy wrote a few years after Frank's death, "would be vacuous without knowledge of the soul inspiring character of his love for home and family." The Murphys were, indeed, a very close-knit family, "one of the Irish families," a commentator noted, "which have such intense family loyalty that its children stick together far into adult life—often never marry." Frank did not marry, and his brothers and sister postponed matrimony until quite late in life. The Murphys were not only close knit, but, as one of their neighbors remembered, they "sort of . . . stood apart" from the other families in Harbor Beach. The fact that John Murphy was a university man, was well-read, and was better off financially than the average made the Murphy family somewhat "different" in the town, and it may be that John Murphy's drinking habits inclined the family to turn inward upon itself. ". . . all I want to live for . . . ," Harold Murphy once wrote his brother George, "is our own crowd. . . . To be frank about it, To Hell with the rest of the crowd."[15]

Although the Murphy children were obviously not perfect, it was important for all of them to see one another as nearly so. A friend wrote Marguerite that she thought it "an honor to be allowed to witness the holy love that exists between yourself and your dear brothers. It is such an unselfish love. . . ." Harold Murphy was far from a success in life, if one is to judge by conventional American standards, but Frank, who thought that the members of his family were "almost all too good to be true," remarked that there was "no more refreshing person." "In many ways," Frank once wrote Harold, "you are the greatest of the

Murphys because you seem to have conquered life and kept yourself in perfect physical condition." His brother George, Frank thought, was "the only person I envy much. His character is so superior and erect." "I worship George," Frank said to an associate.[16]

Although Frank, on rare occasions, could see a fault in Marguerite, he was more likely to think of her as "the most loyal sister and the best girl I ever knew." She was "more precious than any jewel," "dearer than life itself," and he "wouldn't want to go on without her." In turn, Marguerite's admiration for Frank was absolutely boundless. "What's a husband compared to a darling brother," she wrote him when she was approaching thirty. "I don't care what other girls may possess," she once remarked, "they may be beautiful or wealthy or all that sort of thing but they haven't got what I've got *because I've got you.*" In Marguerite's opinion, there was no greater man in the world than her brother Frank. "If only I could find a few little faults in you," she wrote him, but "I can't." Her brothers shared Marguerite's high opinion of Frank. A Detroit Recorder's Court judge who knew the Murphys doubted that he had ever seen "such a relationship of what almost amounted to a worship on the part of the other members of the family toward Frank."[17]

In their study of the Irish rural family, Conrad M. Arensberg and Solon T. Kimball have stressed the close and continuing relationship between mother and son. It has also been observed that whereas the father in the Irish family is respected, the mother is "exalted." What has been said to be true of the Irish in general was especially true of the Murphy family, for however close the relationship of Frank Murphy to his brothers and sister, "the most sacred detail of his life" was his relationship to his mother. A Detroit newspaper reporter who interviewed Frank when he was thirty-one years old referred to his devotion to his mother as "a thing so beautifully sacred that any attempt to describe . . . that tender bond of rare understanding, would be nothing short of profane."[18]

Cultural analysts who stress the impact of the Oedipus complex on the Irish character would no doubt find confirmatory evidence for this hypothesis in the life of the Irish-American Frank Murphy. Like most male children, as an infant Frank developed a strong emotional attachment to his mother, but unlike most sons it may be that he never entirely freed himself of his Oedipal fantasy. Whereas most sons eventually tend to identify with their fathers, Frank Murphy never ceased to identify strongly with his mother.

Perhaps he sensed that it was his mother who was the dominant parent, perhaps John Murphy's drinking bouts and his wife's reaction to them weakened the son's attachment to the father, perhaps the son was aware that there was something special in his mother's love for him, something above and beyond the affection that she felt for her other children.[19]

Just as the happiest moments of his youth, at least in his recollection, were those that he spent with his mother, so after Frank Murphy left home in 1908, it was to his mother alone that he addressed his daily letters. "I write to you for you alone are my best girl," he noted. The salutation in these letters was invariably "Darling Mama," and the letters always closed with a copious number of *x*'s. Although it is perhaps not surprising that as a youngster Frank would wake up in the night, crying for his mother, this also occurred when he was in his late twenties and in his thirties. Writing to his mother about such an occurrence in 1918, he concluded, "Tonight if I could sit near you or brush your hair or stroke your forehead or just feel your presence I would be in paradise."[20]

When Frank was overseas during World War I, his mother's letters to him "seemed to be the hinge on which my life swung." Shortly before he left the states he wrote her not to be lonely, for "I will be home with you in a few days and we will walk and talk just like the lovers we are." After he arrived in France, he wrote that he would love to bring his mother there. "What a honeymoon that would be." They would take walks together, "and how happy we would be. You are my girl and whenever I wander down a lover's lane I want to be with you."[21]

Frank's letters to his mother from abroad were really love letters—"I wonder if you really know how I love you and long for you"; "Tonight I want you very much"; "I love you more than anything else in life"; "I am as feverish for you as the desert traveler is for a refreshing brook"; he would be in "paradise" if he could "get off the boat and see your sweet face and really know I could get my hands on you." It was not unusual, of course, for a lonely son to write tenderly to his mother while he was overseas, and the mode of expression was less restrained in 1918 than it is today, but whatever allowances one makes there was a passion in Frank's letters to his mother from abroad that one would not normally find in the letters of a twenty-eight-year-old son to his mother. Although Frank thought that his letters of the time to his mother were "ordinary," his love for her, as he wrote, was "anything but ordinary."[22]

As Frank prepared to return from Europe, he made it clear that it was his mother he must see first, and he threatened to "raise an awful row" if anyone came to meet him without her. Living in Detroit once he became a civilian again, he was always lonely for his mother—"I am hardly ever otherwise"—and his "very happiest and best days" were the ones that she spent with him in Detroit or that he spent with her in Harbor Beach.[23]

As long as his mother lived Frank never freed himself from his dependence on her. He could not "enjoy anything completely" without her, and, as he wrote her, "I suppose I will never get over the tremendous desire to have you around to put me through an[y] slight indisposition which overtakes me." It is not surprising that Frank "never lost the feeling of emptiness" that his mother's death brought to him.[24]

A friend of the Murphy family recalled that Mary Murphy was convinced that all of her children were "people apart." Within the circle of loved ones, however, it was apparent that Mary Murphy had a special fondness for her second son. "Sometimes," she wrote Frank, "when I think how Perfect you are I don't know what to think. I never knew a boy as perfect as you. There are none. What would any mother give to have a boy like you. I am not worthy."[25]

When his mother died, it was necessary for Frank to find a surrogate for her. The logical choice, of course, was Marguerite. "We all need you," he told Marguerite just after Mary Murphy's death. "The home and the love and devotion in our family that Mama gave to us and so cherished will become part of the past unless you take her place. You must appreciate the responsibility that is yours and meet it." Marguerite accepted and tried to play the role that her mother's death had thrust upon her, and she eventually came to think of herself as Frank's " 'little mother.' "[26]

Mrs. William Walker, the wife of a Detroit caterer, also became a mother substitute for Frank Murphy during the decade after his mother's death. She took the Murphy children under her wing in 1924 and "mothered" them through the years. In the 1940s Sharon Murphy, Harold's daughter, became still another mother substitute for Frank. "Sharon," Frank observed, "is Mama all over." "Mother was different from others," Frank wrote Sharon's mother. "Sharon is. . . . None of us on earth are alike but mother and Sharon are so unlike the usual mold."[27]

That Frank Murphy never married was intimately related to

his strong feelings about his mother and the fact that, in his eyes, no girl could successfully compete with Mary Murphy, her son's invariable standard of comparison. As we shall see, there were other factors involved, but one may guess that, almost to the end of his life, Frank could not bring himself to marry because he saw this, in some way, as a betrayal and renunciation of his mother and as an unwanted loosening of the bonds of affection that tied him so closely to her.

When Frank was in occupied Germany in December, 1918, he attended a Christmas Eve celebration in a small theater and was asked to suggest a song for the occasion. His choice should not be a surprise: "I want a girl just like the girl that married dear old Dad." A quarter of a century later he wrote his sister-in-law, "I guess that comparing girls that I knew with mother's shy charm and reach for beauty has caused me something of a lonely life." Noting to a girl friend in the midst of what appeared to be a torrid romance in the 1920s that he began his daily letters to his mother with the word "Darling," he asked forgiveness of the young lady if he should on "some unsteady occasion" address her that way; as a matter of fact, he wrote, he had had to destroy more than one letter that he had begun in that fashion.

The letters that he sent the young lady were full of references to his mother and the competing demands of the girl friend and Mary Murphy on his time and affection. On one occasion he gave the young lady some of his mother's letters to read; the girl friend drew the proper conclusion from this incident—"I *at last* realize I shall never have the monopoly of you. . . ." Her friends and her mother all had told her, she observed some months later, that it was best for her to forget him since he cared only for himself and his mother. When the affair seemed to be breaking up some years later, Frank wrote the lady friend in an anguished letter, "You were like Mother—that is the zenith of accomplishment so far as I am concerned." It is not susceptible to documentary proof, and, in any event, it would be a considerable oversimplification, but a Freudian might suggest that Frank's entire career was "colored by the displacement of energy from the frustrated desire to obtain exclusive possession of the ideal mother." The deflection of his energy into politics and humanitarian endeavors would strike some as in part sublimation.[28]

Frank loved his father, but the son could not overlook John Murphy's drinking. "You have no idea what a wet blanket that throws upon me," Frank wrote his mother on one occasion. He liked to think, however, that when his father did "unpleasant things," he had not been his "true self," and Frank wanted "to forget all about those things. I can't imagine a finer father." After Mary Murphy died, John Murphy came to occupy a more important place in Frank's life than he had before, and his son became unrestrained in expressing his affection for his father.[29]

It may be that his father's "sickness" was one of the factors contributing to Frank's compassion for the frailties of his fellow man. After all, if someone as noble as his own father could be flawed in this way, should not one have sympathy for the shortcomings and weaknesses of lesser men? It was from his father, also, that Frank learned about law and politics, and it was John Murphy who impressed upon Frank the importance of oratory. He listened to his father plead cases in court, carried wood for the stove in John Murphy's law office, and read Blackstone there. John Murphy read the Declaration of Independence and the Constitution to Frank when he was a small boy and "indoctrinated" his son with Jeffersonian philosophy. Frank rode along in his father's horse-and-buggy when John Murphy campaigned in the Seventh Congressional District, and on one such occasion the father read the Cross of Gold speech to his son. Bryan was the greatest orator that Frank had ever heard, he reported many years later, but his father, who had a deep, sonorous voice and was known as the "Demosthenes of the North," ranked next to the Great Commoner in Frank's opinion. Before he left home Frank decided that he wanted to become an orator like his father.[30]

Although Frank's interest in a public career was probably influenced to some extent by his father's active participation in politics, the son, in the end, did not follow the same political path as John Murphy, and it is simply not true, as has been alleged, that Frank learned political independence from his father. When John Murphy became active in Democratic politics in Huron County, he was associated with what was then the majority party in the county, even though Sand Beach itself was a Republican community.[31] After 1894, when Huron County became solidly Republican, John Murphy remained an organization Democrat. Frank inherited his father's Democratic politics, but the son seems to have been offended by the tactics used by the party politicians whom he observed as an idealistic adolescent in his father's office,[32] and Frank's distinguishing political characteristic, in the end, would be his reluctance to play machine politics, as his father had.

Frank's lifelong interest in Irish nationalism almost certainly owed a great deal to John Murphy. He was "brought up," Frank later recalled, "on the history of Irish struggles for independence," and he remembered that at age seven he was already reading about Irish landlords and Irish liberty. When he was a small boy, he was asked on one election day whether he was a Republican or a Democrat, and his reply was, "I am an Irishman." A classmate remembered that in school he "made a little bit of being an Irishman," singing Irish songs and reciting Irish poetry.[33]

It was John Murphy who impressed upon his sons the importance of earning and saving money. "You know I want to make money," John wrote to Frank on one occasion. "It's the staff of life." "It is in the Murphy's to save," Harold Murphy thought. He saw this "everyday," he noted, and if one failed to save he was "not fit to live." As Marguerite wrote Frank, it always pleased their father to learn that Frank had "made some money."[34]

In religion, John Murphy's advice to his children was " 'Stay close to the faith but stay away from the organization.' " Anticlericalism was definitely part of Frank Murphy's heritage—John Murphy and Mary Brennan were married by a justice of the peace, and the marriage was not solemnized in a Catholic church until eight or nine months later[35]—but John Murphy nevertheless underscored for his children the obligations of their faith. "You must be impressed always," he wrote his daughter, "with the sentiment that you are here on earth for the sole and only purpose of constantly serving God and afterwards to enjoy Him during all eternity in Heaven. He suffered for us—we must suffer for others—that is the lesson of the Passion." John Murphy's advice was: "Follow the 'Passion,' it is sweeter to give than to receive."[36] This was counsel that Frank Murphy took to heart.

Although Frank's religious views were to some extent influenced by his father, it was his mother who was most intimately involved with his religious development and with whom most of his religious memories were associated. The Lord's Prayer was the first prayer that he learned "to lisp," and he remembered how patient his mother had been in teaching it to him. Frank's "tenderest memories" were of the Lenten season when his mother led him by the hand to church every afternoon. At night during Lent she gathered the family together, and they knelt in prayer—Frank recalled that he was "frightfully stuffy" and prayed with "Jesuitical zeal"—and she led them in counting the Rosary and reading the Litany. His mother attended church on weekdays as well as on Sunday, and her son sometimes sat and watched her as she prayed. "I did not know what it was all about then," he later remarked, "but it left an unforgettable and beautiful impression on me."[37]

Frank became an altar boy at the age of seven. The priest thought him "mischievous and untalented," and Frank "very distinctly" recalled having been given "an awful slap" by the good father on one occasion. When he was confirmed at twelve, the children in the class pledged not to drink alcohol until they attained their majority, but Frank promised his mother—one can guess the reason—that he would never imbibe alcohol—and he never did. "I made all my principles that day which have so governed my life," Frank wrote his niece many years later.[38]

Although the parish priest in Harbor Beach wanted the town's Catholics to separate themselves from the rest of the community in religious matters, a resident of the town at the time recalled that the Murphys were "never like that." Because Mrs. Murphy wanted her children to respect creeds other than their own, she took them to "the community celebrations and Christmas services" in the Baptist and Methodist churches. The pastor of the Baptist church and John Murphy were close friends, and Marguerite played the organ at Baptist social functions just as her mother had sung in the Baptist choir.[39] There was never anything narrow or intolerant about Frank Murphy's devotion to his faith, and he formed close friendships with a number of Protestant ministers.

In later years Frank insisted that his mother had taught him not just religious tolerance but tolerance in general and that she had done so "in a very shrewd, practical way." The parents enjoyed a friendly relationship with Herman Jacobs, perhaps the only Jew in Harbor Beach, and Mary Murphy made it a point to tell her son what a fine man Jacobs was. She also made complimentary references, Frank recalled, about the occasional black encountered in the town. Frank told Louis Brandeis many years later that, as a boy, he had thought about the part that he should play as an adult and had concluded that, like Sir Galahad, "I would thrust my lance at intolerance."[40] Distant memory may very well reflect present needs and present concerns, and when Murphy made these remarks he was very conscious of his reputation as a civil libertarian, but it would nevertheless be a mistake to dismiss what he said as unalloyed fiction.

It has been said that middle-class homes are "hothouses of ambition," that children in such homes are held to high standards of achievement, and that this "provides the tension between indul-

gence and deprivation so congenial to the accentuation of power."
In a survey of a small town of three thousand inhabitants in upper
New York state, Arthur J. Viditch and Joseph Bensman found that
children in middle-class and professional homes constituted an
"important part of a social mobility calculus." Parents in these
homes, projecting their own mobility strivings onto their children,
stressed "personal achievement" and rewarded accomplishment in
the hope that achievement would become "a firmly fixed motive
in the child."

Putting the matter in psychiatric terms, Philip Slater has suggested
that if the mother encourages her son "in subtle ways" because
of the inadequacies of the father, the son "will work out his Oedipal
strivings on a socio-economic stage. It is this Oedipal fantasy, in
fact," Slater comments, "that sustains the upwardly mobile individual as he ruthlessly cuts away all mundane community bonds and
loyalties that threaten to hold him down."[41] The general, of course,
does not always explain the particular, and it is impossible to
demonstrate that these generalizations about achievement and
"Oedipal strivings" apply to the Murphy family, but there is
nevertheless a certain plausibility to the hypotheses, and there is
no doubt that there was a marked stress on achievement in the
Murphy household.

Mary and John Murphy wanted success for all their children,
but they regarded Frank as the child destined for greatness. "Mother
always pushed Frank," his brother George recalled. "She was so
sure he was going to go far." In a letter to George in which she
advised him to "do everything" to advance himself, Mary Murphy
noted that Frank, who was then a law student, "must work hard
for if he should fail now it would be dreadfull [sic]." "If he
does anything, I want to know it and that is that he has done
well. I don't want to know anything else," John Murphy asserted
about the same time concerning Frank. When Frank ascended to
the United States Supreme Court, Marguerite observed, "Papa and
Mama had a great mission to carry out and they *knew it.*"[42]

Although Mary Murphy occasionally talked of her son's becoming
a priest, it is doubtful that Frank ever gave the matter serious
thought. It is more likely that law and a career in the public service
became his goals at a rather early age. Not only did he have the
model of his father before him, but it is also evident that professional
families contribute a disproportionately large number of children
to the public service.[43]

Devoted as he was to his parents and especially to his mother, success for Frank Murphy became very much involved with pleasing Mary and John Murphy and living up to their expectations for him. "I measure everyone of my acts by what I know you would have me do," Frank wrote his mother at the end of 1918. "I shall strike for the heights on which I rest in their eyes [his parents]," he declared just a year before he committed himself to a public career. It may very well be that by the time he graduated from high school, the "heights" for which Frank had decided to strike was the presidency of the United States itself. It had been Frank's "dream since Boy-hood to receive the Democratic nomination for the Presidency," Harold Murphy wrote a friend when it became evident that his brother would fall short of his goal.[44] Other boys, of course, have had the same ambition, but few have devoted as much effort to its realization as Frank Murphy did.

As Frank Murphy recalled it, he had "about as happy a boyhood as it is possible to have." He was a joyous and fun-loving youth and had a very amiable disposition—he was a "sunbeam," his sister remembered; "no wonder we called you 'sunny Frank.'" Since Harbor Beach was a small town in a rural setting, Frank "led the life of a country boy." He drove the cows to pasture and milked them in the barn in the morning and evening. He swam and fished in the summer, hunted in the woods in the autumn, and skated and went ice-fishing in the winter. As often happens in such surroundings, he found a certain excitement in observing nature that was to remain with him throughout his life.[45]

A "kind of a hero worshipper," young Frank particularly enjoyed reading biographies. When he was in grade school, his father gave him a book of Lincoln stories, and it was Lincoln who became Frank's greatest hero. At age twelve he read a book about Booker T. Washington, and he made Washington the subject of his first school oration. When Frank was in high school, the ideal "hero" in American eyes, judging from the periodical literature of the time, was no longer the independent entrepreneur but rather the politician who was committed to "collective social action," gloried in "the strenuous life," and was independent of bosses and machines in his political behavior.[46] We do not know if Frank was exposed to this literature, but the shape of his career suggests that he may have been influenced by the model of the hero that was being projected.

Since John Murphy objected to idleness, Frank took his first summer job, working in an ice house, when he was ten. Another summer he worked in the sugar-beet fields—"arduous, grinding work," as he remembered it. He was also employed in a chemist's office, and worked as a bus boy and a newsboy. After he entered high school, he began working summers in the great starch plant in Harbor Beach, and this experience apparently left an indelible impression on him. He worked hard, ladling liquid starch into troughs, piling crates of the liquid onto trucks, and toiling in rooms where the temperature reached 140°. What he especially remembered was the long hours—7:00 A.M. to 6:00 P.M., with a break for lunch—and the regulation of the workers' lives by the factory whistle. "It was a slave's life," he recollected, "those long hours and the living by whistles." His experience in the starch plant was something to which he referred again and again in later years, and it seems likely that his lifelong interest in the problems of the workingman had its origin in the several summers that he worked in Harbor Beach's premier business establishment. Frank conveniently forgot, however, that he had refused to join his fellow workers in a strike against the starch plant because he did not wish to forego his earnings.[47]

Frank's education was entirely in the public schools, the only kind of schooling available in Harbor Beach. High school, which began in the ninth year, was a pleasurable time for Frank. Then a gangly, freckle-faced lad with a mop of curly red hair, he was thought to be "cute" by the girls, with whom he enjoyed a few "small romances," and his fun-loving, easy-going ways appealed to all his classmates. It was Frank who suggested the motto for his class, "Climb tho the Rocks be rugged,"[48] a precept that he reiterated in later years.

Frank was a good but by no means a brilliant student—his grade average was approximately 82.5.[49] Frank's favorite teacher was Esther Burr Lincoln, who taught ninth-grade English. Mrs. Lincoln, who found the students in those halcyon years "so thoroughly nice that the discipline is practically nothing," later recalled "the idealism which ran like a golden thread" through Frank's themes. She also remembered his "first case—'legal,' not 'girl.'" The ninth-grade class had decided to try a lad who was alleged to have stolen a turkey. Frank served as prosecutor or defense attorney—she could not remember which—and she recalled how he sternly addressed a witness: "'Mr. Carson, do you understand the nature of an oath?'"[50]

Frank enjoyed considerable success in extracurricular activities as a high school student. He was quarterback on the football team, centerfielder on the school's baseball team, and a distance runner on the track team. He was also one of the organizers of the Crescent Society, a debating, literary, and musical group. As a debater, Frank "could talk circles around anybody," one of his classmates recalled. He rehearsed his speeches in front of his mother, and he remembered that these had been "some of the most enjoyable and profitable moments" of his life.[51]

Frank, the president of his ten-student graduating class, delivered the "Oration" on Class Day, June 24, 1908.[52] His subject was "Character." Full of the high-blown and undiscriminating rhetoric of the high school senior, the address reflected the confidence of those confident years. It rang the changes on some of the popularly accepted beliefs of the time and also provided an indication of some of the values that must have been stressed in the Murphy home.

What would happen to the members of the class in the future, the class orator sententiously observed, would depend on their "characters," for it was the lesson of history that "nature awards the highest positions of life to men and women of nobility of character." In the speaker's opinion, "the only foundation for sound character" was "abundant reverance [sic] for God. . . . The religious element is always essential to a perfect character." If religion was the principal foundation for a sound character, "morality, industry, and sleepless integrity" were "the guardian angels of character[,] and with them near us," Murphy remarked, "we are safe and will be trusted."

It was one of the faults of the age, Murphy asserted, to judge men by their reputation rather than their character, but "when the crisis comes, when government is threatened, when society is menaced . . . character is scrutinized and only he whose character is spotless is selected to lead. . . ." Frank pointed to Washington and Lincoln as men to whom the nation had turned because of their characters. Murphy ended with a comment on the success theme. "There is no royal road to honor in this country," he declared; "we all have a chance; and with a stanch [sic] character we cannot fail to have success."[53]

There was never any question in the Murphy household that Frank would pursue his college education at the University of Michigan. When Frank went to the railroad station in the fall of 1908 to depart for Ann Arbor, he was accompanied by "all the regular lads" from the town. He promised himself now that he was leaving the sheltering protection of his home that he would continue to lead a temperate life. "It wasn't that I wanted to be a goody-goody boy or anything like that . . . ," he noted a few years later. "But I figured I'd run the race from scratch. I cherished certain definite aims in life. I figured I'd need a lot of independence and self reliance and they depend on self-control and a firm will. In short I figured I'd go further in attaining my aims if I steered clear of the stimulating influences of alcohol and tobacco." [54] Although these remarks have all the earmarks of press copy, especially so since they were made at a time Frank was a candidate for public office, there is every reason to believe that their author was speaking the truth. Frank Murphy learned certain rules of behavior during his formative years in Harbor Beach and set certain objectives for himself, and he lived by these rules and pursued these objectives with single-minded intensity for the remainder of his life. [55]

Although Frank Murphy returned to Harbor Beach after 1908 only for vacations, he always regarded the town as home, and it was there that he felt most at peace with the world. "I ache for home," he wrote in 1925. "It is everything to me and I look out to it now to help me. . . . Nothing else counts." Also, although Murphy enjoyed many of the delights of city life and came to be identified as a public servant with the city and its problems, his boyhood in Harbor Beach had made him "partial to places uncongested," and in his heart of hearts he always preferred the small town and the countryside to the big city. "I hate living in cities," he wrote his mother ten years after he had left Harbor Beach. "The chance to stay in the quiet and tranquil spots hits me right." He told a Detroit reporter a few years later that a boy who grew up in a small town was more apt to " 'go straight' " than a city child was because the small-town lad lived in a "more wholesome environment," had "more wholesome amusements," and enjoyed "more wholesome occupations." "I love small towns," he asserted two years before his death. [56]

When Frank graduated from high school, his mother presented him with a Bible, and he promised her that he would read in it daily. He seems to have kept this promise, and in any event he never allowed the Bible to be very far from him. Not only did he find in it "much wisdom and beauty, much solid food for the soul and poetry," and "that discipline which is a necessity for human nature," [57] but it was also a constant reminder to him of the ties that bound him to his "Darling Mama."

II

"Years of the Purest Gold"

Frank Murphy later described his arrival at the University of Michigan in the fall of 1908 as "one of the few great moments of my life." His father, who accompanied Frank to Ann Arbor, took his son to see a particular building on the campus and told him to remember that John Murphy had "carried a hod up a ladder to build that building." "It was a sort of ordination that my father gave me on the spot," Frank recalled. ". . . my father laid his hands on my heart and literally ordained me to a social priesthood" with his story.[1] It cannot be determined if this dramatic event actually occurred, but it is evident that Frank Murphy liked to see his career as a "social priesthood," and, whether apocryphal or not, the story at least tells us something about its author.

The six years that Frank Murphy spent in Ann Arbor, first in the Department of Literature, Science, and the Arts and then in the Department of Law, were among the happiest of his life. They were, he told a reporter a few years later, " 'happy days'—days full of gratifying accomplishment of pleasant tasks, days fraught with rare good fellowship, and friendships that have lasted and endured." As Frank was about to end his student days, George described his brother's years in Ann Arbor as "years of the purest gold," and Frank himself wrote his mother at about the same time: "No wonder I love Ann Arbor and this college. My life here is simply one grand thing after another."[2]

When Frank matriculated, the University of Michigan was nearing the end of the long and distinguished presidency of James Burrill Angell and was "well into its Golden Age." It was an era marked by "intense university spirit," a time when intercollegiate athletics and extracurricular activities were a very important part of the university scene and "university life" was "all-encompassing." "For a four-year period," Howard H. Peckham has written in his history of the university, the students "could be frenzied athletic fans, earnest fraternity members, extravagant dressers, admirers of honorary societies, singers of sentimental college ballads, shouters of college yells, and devotees of class activities."[3]

As a student at the University of Michigan, Frank Murphy was all of the things that Peckham indicated a student of that era might be. In his unquestioning acceptance of everything that the university had to offer both inside and outside the classroom, Murphy was the exact opposite of the alienated college student of the 1960s and 1970s. He thus spiritedly participated in the high jinks that were then a part of the freshman and sophomore years, and he was intent on preserving all the traditions of freshman-sophomore rivalry. His close friend Edward G. Kemp later remarked that one of his earliest recollections of Frank Murphy was hearing him deliver "an earnest harangue" to fellow sophomores regarding the indoctrination of freshmen into "some of the deeper mysteries of higher education."[4]

Murphy was attracted to the social life of the university as much as he was to the high jinks. He was a member of the social committee of the sophomore class of the literary department, and he served as the toastmaster at the class smoker. In his junior year he was on the publicity committee for the all-literary department interclass dance, and he became the spokesman for the men of green in preparation for the St. Patrick's Day dance. When it was discovered that all but one member of the committee for the latter affair were "Dutch," the "micks" became suspicious, and " 'Red' " Murphy organized twenty-five "brawny Irishmen" into the "Irish Dragoons" to ensure that there would be no insult to the shamrock.[5]

In later years Murphy made quite a point of his refusal to join organizations lest they limit him to a particular group of associates or to a particular point of view and separate him from "the human family," and he no doubt enjoyed reading legendary accounts that he had declined to join a fraternity in college because the one he had in mind had denied membership to one of his Jewish friends. Actually, Murphy happily joined the Sigma Chi fraternity and was one of its most loyal and enthusiastic members. "My days in the Chapter," he later wrote, "were as sweet as any in my life." Murphy twice served as head of the chapter, he was chairman of the committee that completed the structure in which the fraternity was to be lodged, and he traveled to Ohio and Indiana in behalf of the national organization to drum up support for petitions from institutions that wished to establish chapters. Three years before his death he accepted a life membership in Sigma Chi and made note of his "deep affection" for the organization.[6]

Quite apart from his active participation in fraternity life and social affairs on campus, Murphy took part in an unusually large number of extracurricular activities. He was off and on one of the editors or a reporter on the staff of the *Michigan Daily,* the largest college newspaper in the nation, was elected a trustee of the Student Lecture Association, played the male lead in a campus dramatic production, competed in a campus singing contest, and was active in the affairs of the Michigan Union. [7]

The Michigan Union movement, without precedent on American campuses, dates from the year 1903 and was designed as the "unifying force and coordinating agency" for students at Michigan. Murphy served on the Union membership committee beginning in his sophomore year and in 1913 was the chairman of a special student committee that looked into the status of similar organizations on other campuses. In 1914 the Union launched a campaign to erect a new building, and as a campus orator of some reputation, Murphy was invited by the Grand Rapids University of Michigan alumni to speak on the subject at an alumni dinner. [8]

In his address Murphy stressed the ideals of democracy and service that were so much a part of the rhetoric of progressivism and that were to become such insistent themes in his own career. The Union, he contended, was "a school to exalt the culture of comradeship" and had done more than any other campus institution to break down the barriers between fraternities and independents. "It might be likened," he declared, "to a huge melting pot into which are poured the members of the fraternities, the faculties and the independents; and out of which they come Michigan men," men "imbued with the idea of equality of opportunity, real democracy." Murphy asserted that the university student in 1914, unlike the student of the past, was expected to do something for his university. The world was calling for "service, civic pride, citizenship," and that was precisely what the Union was helping to develop in the Michigan student. [9]

Murphy failed to distinguish himself in two areas of extracurricular activity—politics and athletics. Despite his later success as a vote-getter and despite a campus legend that he put together a powerful campus political machine, Murphy was regularly defeated in his quest for office outside his own fraternity. He tried out for the literary department's freshman football team, but he did not make the squad, probably because, at 135 pounds, he was too light. This failure, however, did not diminish his interest in football in even the slightest degree. He "at last broke into the game," to use his own words, as a "state interscholastic referee," and he was about as enthusiastic a fan of Michigan football as there was on the campus. He sometimes followed the team when it played away from Ann Arbor, and he became an ardent admirer and close friend of Michigan's famed football coach, Fielding H. Yost—Murphy later described himself to Yost as "one of your boys, never good enough to make the first team." It is not hard to believe, as reported, that Murphy regarded Grantland Rice's "When Yale was king of the conquered East and Michigan ruled the West" as "the greatest poem ever written."[10]

When a giant football rally was held in Hill Auditorium on November 14, 1913, Murphy spoke for the student body and, according to the student newspaper, delivered "a stirring speech." Since alumni from "all over the states" were to attend the rally, Frank had written his mother that he would try "to make a great speech," and he thought that if he succeeded in this effort, it would give him "a great reputation all over."[11] The future, it is evident, was never far from Frank Murphy's thoughts.

Murphy's active participation in extracurricular affairs led to his initiation into several campus honorary societies. At the end of his sophomore year he was initiated into Griffins, and he was also "embalmed and admitted to the innermost pyramid" of Sphinx, the highest nonacademic honor that could be accorded an underclassman. At the end of his junior year, his last in the Department of Literature, Science, and the Arts, he was initiated into both Druids and Michigamua. It was as a Michigamua initiate that he was given the name "Wild Mustard."[12]

One of Murphy's college friends used to chide Frank in later years that as a college student he slept with copies of Bryan's speeches and the Bible under his pillow.[13] Whether the story is true or not, Murphy was much interested as a student in both state and national politics and also took his religion seriously. Caught up in the fervor of the progressive movement, he became chairman of the publicity committee of the Osborn Club, established at the university in June, 1910, to support the campaign for the governorship of Michigan of Chase Salmon Osborn, a Republican but a progressive. In 1912 John Murphy supported Champ Clark for the Democratic nomination for the presidency, but Frank backed the victorious Woodrow Wilson and served as the press agent for the Wilson organization of University of Michigan students. After Wilson's nomination, both father and son campaigned in the New Jerseyan's behalf. Since Frank assumed that voters were unlikely to attend a political meeting addressed by a mere university student, he put out handbills for his appearances that referred to him as the "Honorable Frank W. Murphy of New York." It is possible that after Wilson's victory John Murphy was offered a foreign post as a reward for his long service to the party and his hard campaigning for the Democratic ticket, but what he desired was a postmastership for his son Harold. "Now we are going to line up to the pie counter" was Harold's reaction to the Democratic victory.[14]

That Frank's political ambitions went far beyond lining up at the "pie counter" for the rewards of victory became evident to some of his college friends and to some of his instructors as well. Thus Joseph R. Hayden, who was an assistant in history during Murphy's last year in the literary department and who became Murphy's vice-governor in the Philippines, wrote a faculty colleague in 1934: "The time may come when the prediction that Frank made as a student [that he would become president] will be fulfilled by the event." Murphy's immediate objective, of course, was to become a lawyer, but he told his friends that his interest in the law was not to make money but to aid and defend the unfortunate.[15]

As Frank wrote his mother, he attended mass "nearly every Sunday of my college life." One of his classmates recalled that Frank used to round up "religious slackers" on Sundays and holy days and take them to mass, and a Protestant classmate remembered that Frank spent hours on end seeking to convert him. Despite this proselytizing effort, however, it was typical of Murphy that he saw good in creeds other than his own. He did not regard it as inconsistent with his Catholicism to become a captain in a financial campaign to raise funds for a Protestant medical mission in Arabia, and he served as official in charge of social work in the local YMCA cabinet. He later said that more important than anything he learned in class was a speech delivered in Ann Arbor by Bishop Charles D. Williams in which the Episcopalian cleric endorsed the principle of industrial democracy as the means of lessening the conflict between labor and capital and contended that a nation could not long survive if any group within it felt itself insecure and treated unjustly. That statement, Murphy claimed, was "a trumpet blast" to his soul.[16]

While a student in the literary department Murphy was enrolled in the "combined literary and law course" that had been instituted at the university in 1903-04. Murphy passed all his courses except the second semester of Elements of Political Economy in his sophomore year, in which he received a "condition" and no credit (the possible grades at the time were "passed," "conditionally passed," and "not passed").[17] In May of the second term of his junior year he contracted diptheria, and the illness seems to have prevented him from completing the semester's work and earning credit for his courses. The seventy-four credits that he had received when he entered the Department of Law in the fall of 1911 fell short of the minimum of ninety hours in the literary department that were required for him to complete the combined curriculum in law and letters, with the result that he never received a B.A. Indications to the contrary in the published record are simply inaccurate.[18]

One sample of Murphy's academic work as an undergraduate survives, a paper entitled "Politics and the Laborer" that he wrote for his sociology course in 1911. The paper is of more than ordinary interest because not only does it reflect some of the ideology of progressivism, but it also correctly forecasts Murphy's later role as a champion of the workingman. "It is because I have lived and worked with the common, ordinary . . . laborer and . . . feel that I know his wants and needs, that I have ventured upon this problem," Murphy wrote in explaining his choice of topic. "I love the subject," he stated. "I want to make it my life's work. If I can only feel, when my day is done, that I have accomplished something towards uplifting the poor, uneducated, unfortunate, ten hour a day, laborer from the political chaos that he now exists in, I will be satisfied that I have been worth while." By this criterion, Frank Murphy at the end of his illustrious career had every reason to believe that he had indeed been "worth while."

Murphy's paper revealed his acceptance of many of the tenets of middle-class progressivism: the distrust of the conventional politics of patronage and organization as contrasted with a politics that disinterestedly served the common weal; the stress on environment as the cause of behavior; and the paternalistic obligation of the more fortunate citizens to "uplift" their less fortunate brethren. Murphy indicated that he had observed in his father's office how politicians would "coin schemes" simply to gain votes or to place voters under obligation without the politicians' realizing that they were "doing wrong" and were not "uplifting the condition of the community."

Like so many progressives, Murphy deplored the influence of the saloon interest in politics. He was inclined, in the fashion of middle-class progressives, to see the liquor problem in its relationship to the working class and particularly the foreign-born workingman. "It seems," he wrote, "that in the case of most any nationality the liquor interests are prominent." Since almost the only recreation for the Polish laborers in Harbor Beach was to drink and to play the slot machine in the saloon, politicians took advantage of "the good fellowship spirit" by buying beer for those present in return for their votes.

Murphy noted that the three hundred "Polanders" whom he had supervised as a foreman in the starch plant in Harbor Beach seemed like "nothing more than dumb pieces of machinery." They were uneducated, "coerced" by their bosses, and "weak from social and moral conditions" and hence were unable to exercise their "political duty as citizens" to vote for those seeking to improve the community rather than only "personal benefits." It was these "unfortunate laborers," who were almost "defenceless [*sic*]" against politicians, whom Murphy desired to "uplift." The best way to aid them, he observed, was "to get down to the seed of it" and to deal with their social conditions. Their excessive working hours had to be shortened, their contacts with the outside world increased, and their "moral standards" raised, and they had to be taught to appreciate that their individual needs were "common needs, public needs," that could only be satisfied legitimately as the needs of all were satisfied. Reformers were in error who sought "to correct the political machinery without the ultimate purpose of securing the welfare of the people."

In describing the type of political personality who was most likely to appeal to the workers, Murphy provided a significant clue to what would become his own style of political leadership. "I have found," he wrote, "that the only way that political opinion can reach the laborer is through a personality which seizes the imagination. They look up to the man who has been good to them. The man who attracts them seems to be the simple man of gifts. And I have also discovered that the wise politician ministers directly to life and social needs."[19]

Murphy's instructor, the distinguished sociologist Charles Horton Cooley, gave Murphy a B+ on the paper and commented, "The observations are interesting, the reflections not too deep."[20] One can readily agree with this judgment of the quality of Murphy's effort—similar judgments were later made of much of Murphy's handiwork—but as an historical document that reflects its time and forecasts its author's career, the paper rates an A+.

When Frank Murphy entered the Department of Law, the requirements for admission were either a high school or college diploma or the satisfactory completion of a special examination, "a certificate of character," and a minimum age of nineteen. In an effort to raise standards—Michigan had been getting some "dull, unintelligent students"—and in conformity with the practice of the nation's leading law schools, the law faculty had recommended at the end of January, 1908, that applicants for admission should be required to have completed at least one year of preparatory work beyond high school. The Regents of the university at first rejected this recommendation but then reversed themselves in 1910 and decided that one year of preparatory work would be a requirement for admission effective with the academic year 1912-13 and that a second year should be added "within a reasonable time after 1912." The decision of the Regents encouraged Henry M. Bates, who had become dean of the law department in 1910 and was anxious to restore the department to its former eminence, to believe that his school would "make rapid progress . . . in the matter of raising . . . standards of work . . . , and in building up a strong Faculty."[21]

The three-year course of study introduced in the academic year 1896-97 and in effect when Murphy entered the law department consisted of a combination of required and elective courses. As of the fall of 1911 the faculty was in the process of shifting from the lecture and textbook method of instruction to instruction "by means of the free discussion of legal principles as disclosed in reported cases." Dean Bates thus informed a University of Chicago law professor whom he was trying to lure to Ann Arbor, "I am personally teaching cases upon the inductive method, and find no great difficulty in making it go."[22]

In the 1911-12 *Announcement* of the Department of Law, the faculty expressed its belief that "students are best trained for the practice of law by studying it not as mere dogma and collection of precedents, but with a broader view of its origin, development and function." "What you search after [here]," Bates observed, "is 'What is the law?' and 'What ought it to be?,' and not 'How can you find material which may be strained into supporting the theory necessary to the success of your client's case?'" At Michigan, as elsewhere, this was also a time when teachers of the law were concerned about public affairs and were anxious not only to reform their profession but also the nation as a whole. The law professor, Dean Bates declared in 1913, was "fortunate" to possess "the opportunity for conspicuous service in the cause of social justice." Murphy's commitment to the progressive point of view was undoubtedly strengthened by the instruction that he received in the

Department of Law and his association with men like Bates.[23]

Writing to his father shortly after he began his first semester in the law department, Murphy reported that his record in recitations up to that time had been "perfect." In the midst of the second semester, he wrote home that he was "getting on well" in his studies and had performed more satisfactorily than the majority of his classmates had.[24] The transcript of Murphy's record for his first year in the law department indicates, however, that the future United States Supreme Court justice was having serious academic problems. Of the eight courses that he took during the first year, he passed only four and received the grade of "conditionally passed" and no credit for the others (contracts, criminal law, agency, and real property). In 1912–13, the first year that a new letter-grade system went into effect, Murphy improved his performance considerably. He was able, by reexamination, to convert his "conditionally passed" grades in contracts and criminal law into B's and his "conditionally passed" grade in agency into a C, and he earned a B in all his other courses.

Because his record during his first year and the consequent need to reelect some of his courses left Murphy short of the requisite hours of credit, he was required by the faculty to attend summer session to make up his deficiency. He received B's in the two courses that he elected in the summer session of 1913, and then in his senior year he received two B's, eight C's, a D ("barely passable") in trial practice, and an E, which was a failure, in mortgages. The latter grade left Murphy two hours short of the seventy-two hours of credit required for the LL.B., but he was rescued by faculty action at the eleventh hour. He had petitioned in February, 1914, to receive partial credit for the first-year course in real property, for which he had originally received no credit, because of a readjustment that the faculty had made in the property courses, but the petition had been tabled. At the faculty meeting of June 22, 1914, however, the professor who had taught the course reported that under the existing marking system Murphy would have received a grade of D in the course. The faculty, accordingly, awarded Frank two additional hours of D, and he was able to graduate the next day.[25]

When Murphy was attorney general of the United States, Dean Bates was quoted as saying that Frank was the "best student I ever had"; but, in view of Murphy's record in the law department and the fact that he had received only a C in Bates's course on wills, it is not surprising that Bates, who admired Murphy's "good qualities," had a poor opinion of his former student's legal abilities. When Murphy moved up to the Supreme Court, Professor Edwin C. Goddard, who had given Frank a "condition" in an agency course, refused to stretch the truth and simply recalled "the very live and active student" who had since become so famous. The assertion, however, by one of Murphy's biographers that Murphy was "something of an embarrassment to his alma mater" and that there was "a distant relationship" between Justice Murphy and the Michigan law school is an exaggeration.[26]

As graduation day approached, Murphy wrote his sister that his senior year had been giving him "even more pleasure than any of the others because everyone speaks to me and everyone is very kind to me." By then a renowned campus orator, Frank was invited to speak at so many farewell banquets that he described himself as "fairly . . . brimming over with tears."[27]

Murphy delivered "the best speech I ever made" on Cap Night, the night the freshmen were finally allowed to burn their freshman caps. Speaking to a vast throng that jammed Hill Auditorium, Frank complained that Michigan "spirit, sentiment, and tradition" had suffered at the hands of that generation of students. He pleaded with the underclassmen "to rejuvenate the old spirit, the old red blood, the old devotion to this institution." Just as middle-class progressives put country above class, so Murphy urged the students to place loyalty to the university ahead of loyalty to fraternities and other organizations. "A student without sentiment, without love for his college as far as college life is concerned," Frank grandiloquently declared, "is like a man without a country."

In addition to his call for a rejuvenated school spirit, Murphy stressed the importance of maintaining a "democratic atmosphere" at Michigan, a quality of the Ann Arbor institution that Murphy proudly thought was envied by other great universities. Michigan, he said, "stands to other universities as America stands to other nations."[28]

The affection for Michigan expressed in his Cap Night speech remained with Murphy for the rest of his life. "I love and worship the place," he wrote his mother in 1917. He returned to Ann Arbor in future years to speak at other Cap Nights, to address pep rallies before football games, to attend football games, or simply to relax. When, on the unanimous recommendation of the Law School faculty, Murphy was invited to accept an honorary degree of Doctor of Law in 1939, he informed President Alexander Ruthven that "the University has been one of the finest and most inspiring things in my life. Wherever I have lived and worked, nothing has meant more to me than to be known as a Michigan alumnus, nor has there been anything in my work more satisfying than the thought that such success as may have come to me might have reflected some credit on the University."[29] As those who knew Murphy were aware, his words were from the heart.

As a student at Michigan, Murphy formed friendships and associations that were of considerable significance for his future career. Edward G. Kemp, who became Murphy's closest friend and political adviser, Norman H. Hill, later Murphy's secretary in Detroit, Manila, and Lansing, James K. Watkins, whom Mayor Murphy appointed police commissioner of Detroit, Josephine Gomon, Murphy's assistant secretary and principal speech writer when he was mayor, Frank Picard, a Murphy ally in Democratic politics in Michigan, and Harry Mead, who managed many of Murphy's campaigns for office, were all students with whom Murphy was associated in one way or another during his years in Ann Arbor.

In a curious reversal of roles, Ed Kemp, who became the silent and self-effacing partner of the Murphy–Kemp team, was distinctly the "bigger" and more politically successful of the two men on the campus. Kemp was elected to the student council, whereas Murphy was defeated, and although Murphy lost out when he sought office in the Michigan Union, Kemp was elected its president. When both men contested for seats on the Board in Control of Student Publications in 1913, Kemp came in first, and Murphy ran ninth in a field of nine. At the annual stag dinner of the junior class of the literary department, both Kemp and Murphy offered toasts: the toast of the quiet and scholarly Kemp was "Words"; that of the orator Murphy was "Thou Art a Scholar, Speak to It."[30]

Not only did Murphy form important friendships as a University of Michigan student, but University of Michigan alumni rallied to his support in some of his early political campaigns. His University of Michigan years, in more ways than one, were truly "years of the purest gold" for Frank Murphy.

III

"In a Fighting Mood"

I

Biographers of Frank Murphy have generally dismissed in a few words the period of his life when he worked in a Detroit law office and served in the United States Army, but Murphy's activities and behavior during these years are important for an understanding of his character and personality and for the manner in which they helped to shape his subsequent career. The life of an individual, however, rarely follows a single path, even though he may see it that way retrospectively, as Murphy did, and so it should not be altogether surprising that the Murphy story during these years diverges in at least some particulars from the course that his career would ultimately follow.

II

After graduating from the University of Michigan Frank Murphy practiced law with his father for a short time and then became very much involved in the 1914 political campaign in Michigan. He worked for the Democratic State Central Committee in the gubernatorial campaign of Woodbridge N. Ferris, and he served as treasurer of the Ferris for Governor Club. Although his political duties kept him in Detroit, he allowed the Democratic party to put his name forward as a candidate for the office of prosecuting attorney of Huron County, a post that his father had held when the political balance in the county had been more favorable to the Democrats. Murphy's candidacy was nothing more than a sacrificial offering, and his defeat was entirely predictable.[1]

Following the election Murphy accepted a position with the Detroit law firm of George F. Monaghan and Peter J. Monaghan at an initial salary of five dollars per week. Frank later recalled "the joy and enthusiasm" that were his during the "happy days" with the Monaghans. The practice of the firm was "on a spectacular up-climb," matching the prodigious growth of Detroit itself, the work was "varied and substantial," and the interest of the Monaghans in the newest member of their firm was "friendly and paternal."[2]

Frank began his work for the Monaghans by drafting pleadings and trying minor cases. After he had been with the firm less than two months, the Monaghans raised his salary to ten dollars a week. This "tickled" Frank, he wrote his mother, not only because he could "live alright now" but also because the raise meant "something" since, according to Murphy, the lawyers in most big law firms did not receive any pay during their first six months of service.[3]

Murphy was quite correct in his assumption that his raise meant "something." The Monaghans were very much impressed with Frank's talents, particularly his skill as a trial lawyer, and they demonstrated their high regard for him by raising his salary regularly and involving him more and more in the firm's important litigation. He won one case after another—Peter Monaghan told Frank at one point that he would be "spoiled" if he did not lose a case soon—and by 1917 he had acquired a reputation in some circles as "probably the most brilliant young attorney in the city." Early in 1917 Percy Grose, "a crackerjack of a lawyer," made Frank "a splendid proposition" to join Grose's firm, but when Frank discussed the matter with the Monaghans, they told him that they would soon take him into the firm as a third partner, and they immediately raised his salary to $2,000 per annum. In his last year as an attorney before he enlisted in the Army in May, 1917, Frank earned $4,000 in salary and fees, a considerable income for a young man who had begun his legal career in Detroit two and one-half years earlier at a salary of $5 a week.[4]

Frank threw himself into his work and was immensely pleased with his success. After George Monaghan told him that the firm knew that whatever legal work he did would be done well, Frank wrote his mother, "I have confidence in myself and mark my word, I will be a noted lawyer yet." Always anxious to get ahead and finding what he was doing "deeply interesting," Frank worked on his cases "day and night" and with all the strength that he could muster. "There is only one way to win lawsuits," he noted, "and that is . . . [to] fight vigorously and alertly from start to finish." He especially enjoyed contesting lawsuits against the top attorneys in the city. "When one beats a big lawyer," Frank remarked, "he feels as though he has done something."[5]

Murphy handled a variety of cases in the years that he was associated with Monaghan and Monaghan—slander, libel, divorce, real estate, negligence, wills, highway robbery, and even murder. The highway robbery case resulted in a great victory for Murphy. In his argument to the jury, he contended that the offense should be construed as larceny from the person, for which the maximum sentence was five years, rather than highway robbery, which carried a maximum penalty of life imprisonment. The prosecuting attorney told Murphy that he had his "nerve" even to suggest this, but after ten minutes of deliberation the jury accepted Murphy's argument. The prosecutor was "wild with anger," but the judge complimented Murphy on his conduct of the defense.[6]

Murphy represented the plaintiff in a libel case that was carried to the Michigan Supreme Court and allegedly involved the largest sum sustained in this type of litigation in Michigan up to that time. The plaintiff, an attorney and a politician, sued the Polish-American Publishing Company for libel because of articles published in the *Polish Daily* that had criticized him for allegedly describing himself as a German and a Lutheran when he was actually a Pole and a Catholic. Murphy won a judgment for his client of $10,000 (later reduced by the trial judge to $5,000) for loss of professional income and $5,000 for injured feelings. Citing a variety of alleged errors, the defendant appealed the case from the Wayne County Circuit Court to the Michigan Supreme Court, which affirmed the judgment in a unanimous verdict. Murphy is said to have won "the admiring attention of the Wayne County bar" for his victory.[7]

One of Murphy's negligence cases involved a thirty-five-year-old woman who charged that her nerves had been affected as the result of an injury she had sustained on a streetcar of the Detroit United Railway Company (DUR). The DUR first offered to settle for $2,500 but then raised the figure to $5,000 after Murphy had made his opening statement in court. After another day or so in court the company settled for $6,500.[8]

The Monaghans had several large companies as clients, and Murphy found himself defending these concerns against one charge or another. In one case, he defended the Crowley-Milner Company, a leading Detroit department store, against the allegation that one of its drivers had caused the death of a young boy. Murphy, who actually hated "to see people like they are [the plaintiffs] lose," felt that the sympathy of the jury was against the defendant, but he believed that if he could win under these circumstances, it would be "a splendid thing" for him. His witnesses "fell down terribly and made a mess" of his case, but he put up "a strong fight" in his final argument, a role in which he excelled, and came out of the case with a hung jury. The case was retried, and this time Murphy won, which "deeply pleased" the Monaghans.[9]

Although he never referred to the fact in later life and his biographers make no mention of it, Murphy, as a lawyer in the Monaghan firm, was arrayed on the side of management in its efforts to maintain the open shop in Detroit. "We have several big strikes on to break," Murphy remarked on one occasion,[10] and the man who was to become identified with organized labor and its struggle for recognition and material gain found himself defending restraints upon picketing and the use of the injunction in labor disputes.

In a case tried in the Wayne County Circuit Court in April, 1916, George Monaghan and Murphy charged that three members of Typographical Union No. 18 had unlawfully interfered with the business of the plaintiff, the Joseph Mack Printing Company, by violating an injunction that had been issued during the course of a strike against the printing firm. The defense counsel insisted that all that was involved in the picketing was "peaceful persuasion," but George Monaghan, after citing an Illinois decision to the effect that there could be "'no such thing as peaceful picketing,'" maintained that in the instant case the picketing had not been peaceful. Although there was actually little evidence that the accused had done much more than engage in "spirited arguments" and make threatening gestures, three unionists were nevertheless found guilty of contempt. Twenty-four years later Frank Murphy, perhaps remembering his part in the Mack case, argued in his first opinion as a United States Supreme Court justice that peaceful picketing, at least under certain circumstances, was a form of speech and was consequently protected by the First Amendment.[11]

The Monaghan firm, as counsel for the Employers' Association of Detroit, the spearhead of the open-shop forces in the city, also became involved in a prolonged strike that the Pattern Makers' Association initiated in February, 1916, against job shops that had not agreed to the eight-hour day and the forty-four hour week. "The Monaghan Employers' Association law firm," the Detroit *Labor News* complained, "was kept busy preparing injunctions, gathering evidence and serving them." Five pattern makers were found guilty of contempt in August, and by the time a truce had been reached in October forty court cases were pending against the unionists. The truce broke down, and the strike did not come to an end until January, 1917. [12]

During the first twelve weeks of his service with Monaghan and Monaghan, [13] Murphy supplemented his income as a lawyer by teaching night school to immigrants three nights a week at a rate of three dollars per night. Of Detroit's 465,766 inhabitants as of 1910, 156,565 were of foreign birth, and more than 20 percent of those who were ten years of age and over were reportedly unable to speak English. Since the Americanization Committee of the Detroit Board of Commerce believed that education was "the greatest factor in the fusion of immigrant races," it sponsored night school classes in English for the foreign born at public schools throughout the city. In the school year 1914-15, 3,509 immigrants were enrolled in the program, 310 of them at the Macmillan School, where Murphy was one of the teachers. The Macmillan School was in the Delray district, an area that had once been populated largely by Hungarians but into which Armenians, Poles, Italians, gypsies, and blacks had begun to move after 1910.

Murphy's students were primarily Armenians, and it was his job to introduce them to the mysteries of the English language. After a month of teaching he wrote his mother that he was "getting on wonderfully," that the attendance in his class was better than that of other instructors, and that after class six or seven of the students—his "private body guard," he called them—walked with him to the streetcar that took him back to the apartment that he shared with Ed Kemp and James K. Watkins. The students, apparently, were instructed to practice their English by writing letters to their instructor, and some of their efforts survive: "I go to the Night School. I like my techer"; "Do you think my deare freend my second letter is beast than first. and I promise you. I shall try always to progress." The way Murphy was regarded by the students and the affection that they had for him were summed up by the student who wrote his former teacher some months after the course had been concluded: "I know you my broder." [14]

Murphy's experience as a teacher in Delray was the beginning of his education in the life of the big city. "I learned more then," he said a few years later, "about social problems, about poverty, about the vicissitudes that breed lawlessness, than I could have learned in any other way. I grew to have an understanding of the cares and vexatious riddles of *the submerged majority*." According to a Murphy acquaintance, one night after Murphy returned from his class, he reported that while holding on to the arm strap on the crowded streetcar, he had "'heard a voice'" telling him that he must spend his life trying to help the unfortunate multitudes of the teeming city.[15] His work in the starch plant and his brief service as a night school teacher in a poor neighborhood in Detroit were two of the shaping influences of Murphy's life, but the lessons derived from these experiences had to compete, for the time being, with other and more conventional ambitions like "making big money" and having "a large [law] practice."

In the fall of 1915 Murphy returned to teaching, this time as an instructor in elementary law at the law school of the University of Detroit. "It is going to be very hard work," he wrote his mother. He taught four hours per week in the academic year 1915–16, but he found this too burdensome, and so he limited his weekly teaching the next year to only one hour.[16]

Murphy's work as a lawyer and teacher did not prevent him from dabbling in politics and leading an active social life. He thus enlisted in the campaign that his father and Harold had been conducting ever since the 1912 election to secure Harold the Harbor Beach postmastership. Writing "I will continually pull strings," he called on Democratic political leaders in Michigan who might be helpful in patronage matters, and then in the spring of 1916 he journeyed to Washington with his father to talk to Assistant Postmaster General Daniel Roper. Frank was dazzled by Washington. "It is glorious," he wrote his mother. "Congress, the Senate, the Supreme Court, it is all beyond description." As he looked down into the well of the House, "there was a mighty feeling arose within me, a desire to get in there once and make them listen to me." As for the postmastership, the long struggle for the position came to a successful conclusion at the end of April, 1916. "It is a load off my shoulders," Frank noted. "For months I have had that blasted post-office on my mind."[17] The episode obviously did nothing to enhance Murphy's enthusiasm for the politics of patronage.

Shortly after his return from Washington Murphy served as assistant secretary of the state convention of the Democratic party. He also formed a friendship during this period with his father's friend Judge William F. Connolly, the Democratic national committeeman from Michigan, and Murphy seems to have performed occasional secretarial services for the judge. Although Murphy's political ties at the time were with the Democratic organization, his negative reaction to Tammany Hall indicated that he would in the end depart from the pattern of the Irish politician in America. His father, Murphy remarked, thought that Tammany was "the real goods," but "I don't think so much of that institution." [18]

The direction of Murphy's social thought at the time and the likelihood that he would eventually espouse an advanced program of social reform is suggested by his comments on a speech on socialism that Scott Nearing delivered in Detroit in January, 1917. Nearing's "viewpoint," Murphy wrote home, "appealed to me greatly. I fear it would not take much to make a socialist out of me. Real socialism places human beings and human rights above property, money and property rights. It is true that the distribution of this world's goods is certainly unfair." [19]

Although Murphy had supported Woodrow Wilson in 1912, Theodore Roosevelt, who more than any other figure personified "the ideal life" for his countrymen in the decade before World War I, also "fired" Frank's imagination, and Roosevelt, in Murphy's eyes, became a heroic figure second only to Lincoln. Roosevelt at the end of the nineteenth century had urged Americans to abandon the soft life and to espouse "the life of strife" as the way to attain national greatness. Looking to physical exercise as the means by which the individual could gain health and relieve anxiety, he took enormous pride in his own ability to meet and to overcome physical adversity. "The men among us who have stood foremost in political leadership . . . ," Roosevelt observed, "have been of stalwart frame and sound bodily health." These words struck home to Murphy, and just as his adulation of the brooding, kindly Lincoln symbolized the compassionate, tender side of Murphy's nature, so his devotion to Roosevelt revealed a less well-known bellicose and jingoistic strain in Murphy. Like Roosevelt, whom Murphy described as "the great American, fresh, strong, virile physically and mentally and always ready to fight even with odds all against him," Murphy became a devotee of the strenuous life; and, like Roosevelt, he gloried in the successful struggle against adversity and saw physical fitness as an essential ingredient of political success. [20] Possibly because of the intensity of his ties to his mother, Murphy was somewhat anxious about his masculinity, and he may have compensated for this by rhetoric and behavior that indicated how tough, aggressive, and virile he really was. [21] This became very evident in his reaction to American participation in World War I.

The obverse of Murphy's emphasis on the strenuous life and physical fitness was his concern about his health, a concern that bordered on hypochondria. Murphy's worries about his physical well-being date back to his college days and his bout with diptheria. In the succeeding months and years his letters to his mother were full of references to his health and complaints about one sort of physical problem or another. In the summer of 1916 he had to undergo a hernia operation, and the stay in the hospital convinced him that he had been neglecting his health. Striking the martyr pose that came so easily to him throughout his life, Frank wrote his mother that he had "been a fool for working like a madman at law" and that he had gone "to pieces" as a result. "I shall never so exhaust myself again," he vowed, but soon he was being troubled by insomnia, which he attributed to "nervousness" resulting from overwork, and he complained that his heart "jerked" whenever he became excited.[22]

Murphy found relief from his work and the tension that it sometimes produced in visits to Harbor Beach ("Home means more to me than most boys") and Ann Arbor ("Isn't it strange how content I always am out here?") and in a rather active social life. Throughout his adult life Murphy, although the champion of the lowly and the unfortunate, delighted in the company of the rich and the wellborn, and many of his male and female friends were drawn from wealthy and socially prestigious families. The small-town, middle-class young man of Irish-American background, it seemed, aspired to the social recognition that only the upper class could bestow. The pattern was set during Murphy's first years in Detroit. There were lunches or theater parties at the Detroit Athletic Club and the "exclusive" University Club, "wonderful times" in Bloomfield Hills and Grosse Pointe, and dates with the "very rich" Margaret Stroh, the brewer's daughter, and other young ladies of wealth and imposing social background. Marriage, though, was one of the thoughts farthest from Frank's mind—"The subject is not particularly interesting to me," he wrote his mother.[23]

III

Judging from his letters to his mother, Frank Murphy gave relatively little thought to the war that broke out in Europe in the summer of 1914 until the German declaration of unrestricted submarine warfare at the end of January, 1917, heightened the prospects that the United States itself would become a belligerent. In a Cap Night speech of June 2, 1916, however, Murphy reflected some of the concern that was being expressed in America about hyphenated Americans and the need for national loyalty and solidarity. Making note of the disloyalty of "certain hyphenated citizens who prate about other lands," the Irish-American Murphy asserted that the United States expected those whom it had protected to give their "first love" to her.[24] Actually, since he worked for a firm that was regarded as pro-German and that defended Albert C. Kaltschmidt, a Detroiter ultimately convicted of having engaged in a variety of criminal activities of a pro-German nature, Murphy himself was briefly suspected of pro-Germanism by the United States government.[25] His Irish lineage, as a matter of fact, influenced Murphy to sympathize with Germany before the United States entered the war, but of his loyalty to the United States there was not the slightest doubt.

When Germany made her declaration of unrestricted submarine warfare, Murphy realized that most Americans were now "bitter" against her, but he did "not share that feeling." Germany, as he saw it, had offered England peace, but England wanted to crush her enemy. Germany's position was "easy" for him to understand. "With them," he commented, "it is a question of life and death and they are going to struggle with all their resources to preserve their life. I'm for them."[26]

Once diplomatic relations between the United States and Germany had been severed, Murphy became more critical of Germany, but since he believed in "forgoing [sic] everything in order to avoid the horrible consequences of war," he was "dead set against the war" up to the moment of President Wilson's war message to Congress. On the night of April 1 Murphy attended a peace meeting in Detroit, but when Wilson on the following day asked for a declaration of war, all doubts were resolved for Murphy. Wilson, Murphy declared, had done all that was possible to avoid war, and "now that it is upon us we ought not to whimper under it but meet it like men." Clearly reflecting the radical change in mood evoked by the president's message, Murphy now categorized the opponents of the war among whom he had sat the night before as "revolutionists." "It shows," he wrote, "what dirty dogs there are in this country who are trying to embarrass the president in the moves that he is making because he believes them to be for our good."[27]

"All we talk about is war," Murphy wrote home soon after Congress declared war on Germany, and like so many of his friends he became anxious to attend the Reserve Officers Training Camp at Fort Sheridan, Illinois. In deciding that he must serve, Murphy was influenced not only by his desire to do his duty "like a man" but also by his continuing concern about his health and its effect upon his career and his belief that the Army would provide him with an all-expense paid opportunity to regenerate himself physically. "My health to me," he informed his mother, "is the only thing that might be a big obstacle in my future success. With a strong body I am afraid of nothing."[28]

Dutiful and devoted son that he was, Murphy did not wish to enroll at Fort Sheridan without receiving the prior consent of his parents. The delay that resulted because of their initial opposition threatened for a time to prevent him from attending the first training camp and caused him, for one of the few times in his life, to be angry with his parents. He told them that he had "made a complete fool" of himself for their sake, and, reflecting what must have been a deep-seated concern, he complained that he had passed up "the last chance I will ever have to make a man of myself physically." As it turned out, a vacancy developed among the Sheridan applicants, and Murphy was invited to attend the first camp.[29]

The trainees at Fort Sheridan, thirty miles north of Chicago, entered the camp as civilians and, if qualified, received commissions after three months of training. The Detroit *Free Press* observed that the approximately seven thousand enrollees in the first camp were men "of more than ordinary education and training in many ways," and Murphy, who arrived at the camp on May 18, glowingly reported, "The best men in the land are here." So many University of Michigan men were present—Ed Kemp, Harry Mead, and James K. Watkins were all there—that Murphy thought it was "just like returning to college."[30]

Murphy described the discipline at Fort Sheridan as "rigid." "It is work, work, work," he wrote, "and everything must be right on the dot." There were "no frills" at the camp—the trainees made their own beds, washed their own clothes, and shaved in cold water. "It is not a pink tea gang running things," Murphy observed. "They only want red-blooded virile young Americans here. It is great." All in all, Murphy found the training to be "a delightful experience" and thought that the work was doing him more good physically than "anything that ever happened to me." "I feel like a fighting cock," he wrote George after having been in camp about ten days.[31]

In addition to his regular duties at Sheridan, Murphy was given an opportunity to exercise his legal talents. He was permitted to take some testimony in Chicago for Monaghan and Monaghan, and he was assigned to prepare the case against a lieutenant charged with manslaughter for having accidentally killed a sergeant on the rifle range. The officer had been exonerated by a board of inquiry, but the commanding general ordered the man to be tried by a court of high officers. Although the assumption at Sheridan was that this was being done simply to satisfy the War Department, Murphy believed that the officer had been "extremely negligent," and he intended "to follow that conclusion as strongly as I can." His argument must have been persuasive, for the officer, in the end, received a dishonorable discharge from the Army.[32]

Having performed exceptionally well at Sheridan—the summary estimate of him on his efficiency report was "Fine mind, thorough, and will make an excellent officer"—Murphy was commissioned a first lieutenant, infantry, Officers Reserve Corps, effective August 15, 1917. As one of a select group of officers from among the graduates of the various training camps ("the picked of the picked"), he was sent from Sheridan to Harvard University for a brief course of instruction in trench warfare. He was then assigned to the 340th Infantry, 85th Division, at Camp Custer, about four miles from Battle Creek, Michigan. Here he served as acting battalion adjutant for a time and then as adjutant of his brigade. He received instruction in the use of grenades, took some special work in bombing that was a continuation of his Harvard training, and, like other officers, was required to take a four-week course in the French language. He also lectured on the "trench warfare stuff" and in the hand-grenade school. His superiors thought that he demonstrated "considerable ability" as an instructor, and he himself once remarked, "the men are all breathless during my entire talk." In the initial evaluation of his qualifications at Custer, Murphy received the "highest" rating for intelligence, a "high" rating for physical qualities, leadership, and general value to the service, and a "middle" rating for character; but five months later his rating for intelligence was reduced to "high," his rating for character to "low," and his general value to the service to "middle." Evidence is lacking to explain this decline in Murphy's rating.[33]

The regimen at Custer, which seems to have been rather grim, attracted the attention of the press after a particularly grueling hike by the 340th Infantry on February 16, 1918. The men had been ordered the night before to leave their ears uncovered, and although it turned out to be a bitterly cold, snowy, and windy morning, the order remained unchanged. The men hiked through the snow for about four hours with only a fifteen-minute rest period. They had covered about fourteen miles when they came to an icy stream about two hundred yards wide. Colonel James Parker, the commanding officer of the regiment, "started pell mell through the water," and the entire regiment dutifully followed. The ice-cold water came up over the knees of the marchers, their feet and legs were soaked and numbed, and their underwear froze to their limbs. The march then continued for three or four additional miles until the men reached the camp. One of the marchers had to be placed in the base hospital, and scores of others suffered the effects of frostbite.

Detroit newspapers reported that the march was the sole topic of conversation at Custer and quoted YMCA officials as stating that the men had come together in the YMCA huts in what resembled "protest meetings." Murphy, who had participated in the march, conceded that it had been a "tough hike," but he defended Parker as "severe but fair" and declared that he was "for" the colonel "to the limit."[34]

In the Army, as in Detroit, Murphy enjoyed his comforts, but at the same time, like his hero Theodore Roosevelt, he reveled in his ability to endure hardship. While at Fort Sheridan and Camp Custer Murphy delighted in his visits to country clubs, fine hotels, and the homes of the affluent, but he also liked to point out how much he enjoyed the arduous and strenuous side of the soldier's life. "We have hardships and discomforts galore," he wrote, "but that is one reason why I like it. Anybody can enjoy life in luxury, ease and free from struggles, but it takes a man with red-blood in his viens [sic] to enjoy life like this." He professed to like the "fierce weather" of the winter of 1917–18, and he concluded when spring came that he preferred military life to civilian life because the latter was "tepid" and the former was "virile." In a classic expression of his belief in the virtues of the strenuous life and the struggle against adversity, he wrote his mother before he left the service, "Do you know this Mama Dear, that I shall never want things easy again? Give me the rough, red-blooded way from now on. I don't want the odds my way in any race. I want the odds to be against me if the race isn't even and I shall expect to win, too. I find that the real zip in life is not in winning but in fighting, not in going easily with the current but in beating back the breakers. I'm a tough guy . . . if tough means battling." [35]

In addition to the usual duties of an officer at Camp Custer Murphy served as an official at football games in which the Custer team played, a speaker at civilian gatherings, and an assistant judge advocate. In his speeches Murphy revealed the extent to which he had absorbed the prevalent themes of wartime America— the barbarity of the Germans, the war as a crusade for democracy, and the need for 100 percent Americanism. When he spoke in Ann Arbor at a meeting called to raise money for the Student Friendship War Fund of the YMCA, Murphy, who now believed that the Germans were "like devils" and wanted to rule the world, "lambasted German intrigue and deceit" with such effect that Professor William H. Hobbs, a notorious wartime advocate of 100 percent Americanism, "nearly rose out of his seat and there was fire in his red face." Murphy described the YMCA hut as "the place where everyone rubs elbows, . . . where creeds and race differences are levelled and the seeds of democracy sown," and he predicted that "a new race of men" would return from the war, "strengthened by the wholesome democratic atmosphere of the association." [36]

In a speech in Marshall, Michigan, Murphy, reflecting the spread-eagle, heart-on-the-sleeve patriotism that was characteristic of the era, "poured out . . . my thoughts about my country and the war. I appealed to them all to manifest by some act each day that their hearts were filled to the full with love for America." The superintendent of schools in Marshall was so much impressed with the talk that he arranged for Murphy to address the city's high school students. The war was "the result of evil," Murphy told the students, but America's being in the war was "not wrong. Our motives can not be questioned." The first objective of American participation was "to defend and protect our wonderful country"; the "second, but equally important" goal was "to champion the cause of humanity." [37]

Early in January, 1918, Murphy spoke in Detroit at a Knights of Columbus meeting designed to promote the organization's war-fund campaign. Proclaiming what he described as "good American principles," Murphy urged his listeners to inspire the kind of 100 percent loyalty among those at home that had already been achieved among the troops. Although he himself, he said, was "an Irish-American," he never again wanted to be described that way but only as an "American." Reflecting the demand for national solidarity, Murphy asserted, "Nationalities among us have been obliterated.

Religions have been merged. . . . We have only one division among all of us now, the division of courage." Chase S. Osborn, who also spoke at the gathering, described Murphy's speech as "one of the most stirring addresses" that he had ever heard.[38]

The last important speech that Murphy delivered while he was at Custer was to the Michigan State Bar Association in Kalamazoo. Although the subject assigned to him was "Court Martial," he referred to this only briefly and instead gave a jingoistic address that proclaimed the superior fighting abilities of the American Army and counseled against a premature peace. Peace could come, Murphy declared, only when "the Hun" had been "conquered forever." "This," he declared, ". . . is the demand which the fighting forces make to those back home."[39]

Murphy's most important work at Custer was his intermittent service as an assistant judge advocate. He received his first legal assignment late in October, 1917, when he was appointed to be one of the judges for his brigade in court-martial proceedings. Early in 1918 he was appointed to defend a captain who had been summoned before an efficiency board for possible dismissal from the service. Murphy thought it "a rather hopeless case," but, at his best as a trial lawyer, he made a great impression on the board, and the defendant was acquitted. This created "a commotion" in the camp and caused nearly every officer who got into trouble to request that Murphy be assigned to the defense.[40]

"I am having a 'land-office' law business these days," Murphy wrote his mother just after his victory in the inefficiency case, but his career as a defense attorney at Custer had actually come to a close. Major Francis L. Sward, the trial judge advocate of the division, had been so impressed with Murphy's performance as a defense counsel that he decided to appoint Frank his assistant. Murphy was now on the side of the prosecution, and he did not particularly enjoy the change of roles. He later acquired a reputation as a "soft" judge who tempered justice with a great deal of mercy, and his reaction to his new assignment foretold that this would be so. "I would much rather defend the poor fellows who are in trouble than prosecute them," he wrote. "To me there is deep satisfaction in giving help and relief to the trouble[d] and depressed. I would rather do that than any task I know. To make a sad person glad is real joy to me and that is why I would rather be defending unfortunate fellows . . . than trying to convict them." Military law, furthermore, impressed Murphy as being "very severe," and he was concerned about the drastic punishments that were meted out for offenses that were regarded as minor in civilian life. It may be that Murphy's opinions regarding military justice when he served on the United States Supreme Court were influenced by his experience with courts-martial in World War I.[41]

The most important case in which Murphy participated as a prosecutor was that of Ralph H. Windhorst and Captain Ralph A. Pillinger, which Murphy described as "the biggest military case in the country." Pillinger, a construction quartermaster, had been given the assignment of erecting an addition to the base hospital and constructing other buildings at Custer, and he had engaged Windhorst as his civilian agent to negotiate with the suppliers. It was now alleged that Windhorst had instructed Battle Creek dealers to add what amounted to a 10 percent commission charge to their bills and that this surplusage had ended up in his and in Pillinger's pockets.

Murphy was placed on special duty to work on the Pillinger case in the middle of April, 1918. The government, he wrote home, wanted Pillinger convicted, and "it is up to me to put it across. I don't intend to lose." Since Windhorst was to be tried in federal district court, Murphy went to Detroit to collaborate in the conduct of this phase of the case with John E. Kinnane, the United States attorney for the Eastern District of Michigan. Kinnane was much impressed with Murphy and probably decided right then and there that he would like to have the young man on his staff. The trial ended "most successfully," as Murphy saw it, when Windhorst was found guilty of conspiring to defraud the government and was sentenced to two-years imprisonment and a $10,000 fine.

The military trial of Pillinger, which was conducted at Camp Custer, was one of the first of its kind during the war and consequently attracted a good deal of attention. Important military personages were present for the trial, and two reporters were permitted to observe the proceedings. Sward directed the prosecution with the aid of Murphy, and a lieutenant and a civilian attorney were in charge of the defense. After the defense had presented its case, Murphy made the opening argument for the prosecution and characterized Windhorst and Pillinger as "a couple of cheats and co-conspirators against the government." The court found against Pillinger and sentenced him to twenty-years imprisonment.[42]

Although Murphy had devoted his full energies to securing a conviction, his "heart . . . went out" to Pillinger once the court had made its decision. A peculiar mixture of toughness and softness, Murphy hoped that he would now be relieved of his judge-advocate duties. "I find that it is very trying," he wrote, "and I want to get into the fields again." Murphy was soon returned to his regular duties, but his "military life in the fields" continued to be interrupted by occasional legal assignments.[43]

Murphy was delighted when he learned that he would be sent overseas with his division, and he hoped that he would receive an assignment at the front—"He prefers the line," was the comment of Murphy's rating officer. Murphy sailed for France on July 23 on the S.S. *Vestris.* "Farewell to New York and the land I love best," he recorded in his shipboard diary as the vessel made ready to depart. The *Vestris* anchored at Halifax on July 26 near a transport of Canadian soldiers, and there was a "thunderous exchange of applause and welcome." The next day the *Vestris* left Halifax in a convoy of ten ships. "Feel in a fighting mood—all of us," Murphy wrote in his diary, "bring on your submarines." On August 5 he awakened to find the *Vestris* surrounded by a "speedy fleet of British Destroyers" assigned to escort the troop ship through the danger zone. The men slept with their clothing on that night and the next, and then on August 7 they caught their first glimpse of France as the ship approached Le Havre. "Excitement along the shore," Murphy wrote in his diary. "Vive! La France."[44]

The *Vestris* pulled into Le Havre on August 8, and in a letter to his mother that day, Murphy revealed his innermost thoughts about his country, his family, and himself. "Tonight," he wrote, "I will say my prayers with deep feeling. . . . I will ask that I be guided in the right always and that I will have the courage to refrain from any act or conduct that Papa and you would not have me engage in. I want to be manly while in France and I want to act the part of a true chivalrous American. I may not be much of a soldier but with God's help I can be as decent as anyone and true to my sweet Mother and Father. I want to play the game true to both of you, and my country too."[45]

On August 9 Murphy set foot "on the good soil of France with deep satisfaction." He seems to have learned just then that he had been nominated by the Democrats some weeks previously as a candidate for Congress from Michigan's Seventh Congressional District. Murphy withdrew himself from consideration immediately. It would be "a grave mistake," he wrote to his family, for a soldier in uniform, particularly one serving abroad, to run for political office. "The thought is repulsive to me," he added, but at the same time he asked his family to send him all the political news, for he had not lost interest in politics simply because he was in the service.[46]

From Le Havre Murphy went by train to Veaugues, about 125 to 150 miles from the front. During the approximately two weeks that he was billeted in this "attractive small town" Frank had ample opportunity to record his impressions of France and its people. He was so much taken with the beauty of the French countryside, its flowers, and the scent of its fields that he doubted that he would ever again be able to live in a city. Murphy was as impressed with the French people as he was with their land. In the cliché-ridden language that was all too characteristic of his thought, he described them as "the most modest and meek sort imaginable," "peace-loving," and dedicated to "the art of living." There were, by contrast, some "ugly, well-fed, hoggish looking" German prisoners near where he was stationed, and Murphy was of the opinion that the faces of these "big sloppy fellows" did not "radiate the life spiritual."[47]

Toward the end of August Murphy moved to the Château de Pessilières, about eight to ten miles south of Veaugues. Two other officers and he took up quarters in the castle itself while the enlisted men were comfortably billeted in the little village outside the walls of the estate. "The fondest of my boyhood dreams of chivalry and adventure has come true," Murphy wrote in describing the castle. He thoroughly enjoyed his quarters, but he characteristically remarked to his mother, "I don't feel right here in this castle. At this particular time the mud and slime of a dug out would be much preferable. . . . It's a terrible war—Isn't it?"[48]

After a few days at the Château de Pessilières Murphy was detailed to nearby Jalogne to serve as commanding officer of the headquarters company of a classification camp (the 85th Division was being converted into the 4th Depot Division) that was being established near Cosne to classify men for service at the front. Murphy described the men assigned to him as being "of a very superior type. They are [the] choicest in the Division and real Americans. There is no foreign element amongst them."[49] The wartime concern about the hyphenated American had obviously affected a man to whom notions of this sort eventually became anathema.

While the classification camp was under construction, Murphy lived "like a king" in the Château de Tracy, and his men were quartered over the wine sheds and cellars of the champagne-producing estate. The buildings surrounded a courtyard, which Murphy supposed would be "an ideal place" for the men "to mix and have sings." One can hardly imagine thoughts of this kind occurring to an American officer serving in Europe in World War II.[50]

Murphy moved to Cosne early in October, and now he was only a few miles from the front and could "scent [the] battle" and hear "the boom of the big guns." On October 15 he was promoted to captain. The ambitious Murphy was pleased with the promotion, less because of the rank itself, he wrote home, than because it was a sign that he was "going ahead." His men, who were as fond of him as he was of them, gave him three cheers when they heard the news.[51]

Shortly after the recommendation for his captaincy had gone forward, Murphy was informed by the division adjutant that he no longer was "to appear before any court-martial as counsel" nor was he to "be detailed as Judge Advocate of any court." It became part of the Murphy legend that this decision was reached because Murphy had been so successful in defending soldiers against whom charges had been brought that his presence in a case almost automatically determined its outcome. He had, as a matter of fact, enjoyed a good deal of success in appearances before courts-martial, but his legal career in the Army had been terminated not for this reason but because of an unfortunate statement that he had made before a general court-martial as defense counsel for an accused officer. "It is . . . the contention and theory of the defense," Murphy had stated, perhaps forgetting that he was not in a civilian courtroom, "that this case is brought to trial only as the result of gross and wanton negligence on the part of those who investigated the case." Since the trial had been ordered by the division commander "after full consideration" of reports made by the regimental commander of the accused and the division inspector, Murphy's remarks were judged to be "both untrue and highly insubordinate," and he was deemed to have "grossly abused the privilege of a counsel." "It is apparent," he was informed, "that the double function of the lawyer and the officer are not compatible in your case."[52]

Murphy's stay in the Cosne area was disturbed by the news that Germany had initiated negotiations for an armistice. Consistent with the argument in his speech to the Michigan Bar Association, Murphy, in reacting to this news, lined up with the advocates of unconditional surrender, like Senator Henry Cabot Lodge, rather than with President Wilson and the proponents of a liberal peace. "America," Frank wrote, "will live to regret the day that she accepts any peace other than one of complete victory." The only "good or permanent peace" would be one dictated by the Allies on the battlefield. A negotiated peace, by contrast, would simply "permit the venomous German government to escape punishment for what it had done and permit it to recuperate for similar conduct in the future." "This is no time for diplomacy," Murphy concluded.[53]

Although Murphy's opposition to a liberal and what he regarded as a premature peace undoubtedly reflected his sincere appraisal of the international situation, it was also inextricably intertwined with his personal desire to see action at the front before the war came to an end. "I will never be happy if that privilege is denied me," he had written. Tenderhearted when it came to the suffering of others, he agonized about sending men to the front, but he did not have the same concern about a combat role for himself, possibly because he saw himself as a child of destiny whose "good guardian angel" would not fail him, even at the front. The Americans, the best and most dashing of the fighting men in Europe in Murphy's view, were preparing for "a series of drives" that would "smash" the Germans—"smash them between the eyes"—and Murphy desperately wanted to be a part of that effort.

Murphy's promotion to captain brought with it a transfer to the 310th Training Headquarters and Military Police, but his division was still simply supplying troops to other units, which was not Murphy's idea of how to fight the war, and so he did "everything in my power" to secure a transfer to "a Fighting Division." When he learned on November 7 that he had been transferred to the 39th Infantry, 4th Division, a battle-tested unit that had fought in the Meuse-Argonne campaign and was scheduled to attack south of Metz with the Second Army on November 14, he "yelled with joy." He knew how his parents would react to this news, but, he told them, "I would be a traitor to my country and myself if I hadn't fought to get to the Front after my preachings at home and my own ideas of service." He wanted to make his parents proud of him, and the way to do that, he vaingloriously asserted, was to "leap over-the-top."[54] The Theodore Roosevelt side of Murphy's character had patently come to the fore as the possibility of combat finally loomed before him.

As he proceeded to the front, Murphy wrote his mother, "I am happy . . . for tonight I sleep in a barn—rats—lice for companions, six miles back of [the] Front." His only concern now was that the war would end without his having tasted combat. "I sure will be wild if peace is declared before I get a chance to fight," he had written when he first learned of his transfer. This, however, was precisely what happened since he arrived at the front just hours before the Armistice took effect on Nomember 11, and he was not presented to his new command until the next day.[55]

Murphy was happy that his country had been victorious—"No fellow ever loved his country more than I do"—but he was nevertheless distraught that "Fate" had "dealt" him "an uppercut and called off the war." He had been "beaten out of" the great opportunity to lead troops in combat, and his fear of returning home and to his career with what he anxiously thought would look like "a cheap war record" had been realized. "Someday," he mused at the end of the year, "Fate must repay me for this."[56]

The 4th Division, as part of the IV Army Corps, was assigned to join other American forces in occupying the Coblenz sector of Germany. "The great march into the land of the Hun," to use Murphy's phrasing, began on November 20, 1918. From then until November 23 the American troops marched at a grueling pace through No Man's Land and into Lorraine, where they rested for the remainder of the month. The 39th Infantry marched thirty miles on November 21 and averaged twenty-five miles a day. Men fell out of line "in large numbers" as swollen, blistered, and bleeding feet took their toll. Although Murphy found it necessary to have his feet wrapped in adhesive tape, he stood the march very well. Attributing his durability to his abstemious personal habits, Murphy was "proud" that his "clean limbs and body" were asserting themselves.[57]

The American troops were hailed as liberators in Lorraine—"Bands played and girls danced, while old folks wept," according to the historians of the 4th Division. Food was in short supply in the province, and Murphy observed men and women rummaging for crusts in the garbage of the Americans. He shared his own food with "the fine type of German family" in whose home in Gross Hettingen he was billeted.

On Thanksgiving day Murphy attended religious services in a Catholic church and heard a Protestant minister preach the sermon. "There we were," he wrote in a revealing reflection of the ecumenical character of his own strong faith, "huddled into the church close together, Protestant and Catholic, Jew and Gentile but above all Americans. We all worship the same God, wear one uniform and adore one country and creeds mean little to us." At the end of the service the men stood and sang "America."[58]

On December 2, as the march eastward resumed, the 39th Infantry entered Luxemburg. The next day, as the bands played, Murphy's men, "their chests arched like pigeons" as he had instructed, marched toward the bridge over the Moselle River that linked Luxemburg and Germany. "At exactly 11:07 this morning," Murphy noted that day, "my faithful right foot implanted itself firmly on German soil and deep was the satisfaction and gladness that filled me at the time." Once again it was an exceedingly difficult and arduous march for the Americans. Murphy and his men tramped through town after town until they reached Hönningen, just northeast of Coblenz, on December 16. The hills of southern Germany, Murphy found, were "charming to look at but fiendish to climb," especially so since the men had to perform the feat wearing heavy packs and sometimes in the rain. Murphy's right toe came through his shoe, and some of his men had to march on stone roads in their bare feet. As he pridefully noted, Murphy was the only captain in his battalion who walked every mile of the way, never seeking relief on horseback. From the beginning of the march into Lorraine, the 4th Division had covered over two hundred miles in fifteen marching days. It had been necessary during the march to evacuate 2,197 men to division hospitals. The march was completed on December 17, when the division took up its assigned position southwest of the Rhine, an area of "steep hills and deep valleys."[59]

Murphy found the country through which he had marched "magnificent," but the "tragic area of the front" made a deep impression on him. "I shall never forget the scenes of war's devastation," he remarked. "I passed through Villages, forrests [*sic*], churches even hillsides blown to atoms. Crosses, crosses, crosses everywhere marking graves. . . . Horses dead with their four legs pointing straight up mark all the fields where the battles raged. It's an awful sight."[60]

Two companies of the 39th Infantry occupied the tiny town of Hönningen, and Murphy, as commanding officer, was, as he put it, the "High Mogul" of the village. "In the past," the politically ambitious Murphy wryly noted, "I have had dreams of ruling cities in our good land but never have I imagined that I would be boss in a town of Germany." Like other officers in charge of civil affairs, Murphy enforced the regulations of the Supreme Commander regarding Germany. Although it was American policy to interfere as little as possible in the internal affairs of the German population, no one could leave Hönningen without

Murphy's consent, and his word was law in the town. The inhabitants, he reported, "bow[,] salute and doff their hats" to me, and the Burgermeister "almost turns a flip-flop every time he sees me coming."[61]

Murphy, who had originally stereotyped all Germans as evil, by this time had come to have rather ambivalent views about the German people. They were, of course, "pig-headed" in that they had been unable to see that "America would be their downfall," but they were not "bad people." Bad people, after all, the sentimental and romantic Murphy thought, could not sing in church as the Germans did, "for music cannot come from evil." They had, however, been "betrayed by treacherous[,] selfish leaders," and Murphy was not about to forget the "hoggishness" of these leaders and what they had done in the war. He found the religion of the Rhineland Germans "mighty wholesome," and he was favorably impressed with the stable and sturdy quality of German home life; but he feared that the Germans had militarism in their blood, and although he admired the discipline of the German people, he recognized its potential for evil. He was especially troubled that the Germans "do not show the slightest regret for all the death, desolation and sorrow they have caused." It appeared to him that "German militarism, ego and conceit had so warped the soul of the German people that the questions of the war cannot be morally measured by them."

Murphy thought that the average German was "much more capable in the ordinary tasks of life" than the French were, and he believed that the Germans, because of their greater fecundity, would recover more rapidly from the wartime loss of manpower than their French and English rivals would. "These people of Germany," Murphy astutely warned, "are people to be reckoned with seriously. They always will be powerful under their present habits, and present community of action."[62]

Murphy was transferred to Weibern on December 28, and the next day Colonel F. C. Bolles, the commanding officer of the 39th Infantry, summoned Murphy to Kempenich and made him battalion adjutant. In addition to his duties as adjutant, Murphy was appointed to serve as Interior Judge of the Kempenich area, a role in which he displayed that same combination of occasional toughness but far more characteristic tenderness that marked his performance as a Recorder's Court judge in the 1920s.[63]

Football intruded on Murphy's life at Kempenich just as it had at Custer. "The Generals," Murphy thought, "seemed to have gone nutty on this football proposition." Despite the protests of Colonel Bolles that his adjutant's services were required at regimental headquarters, Murphy was sent to Bad Bertrich to set up a divisional football team—the division wanted to win the AEF title, and "everything," Murphy noted, "is being set aside to do it." As part of his new assignment, he had to journey to AEF headquarters at Chaumont, and he was so "wrought up" by what he saw on this trip back through the area of the front in France that he was persuaded to support the demand that Germany be compelled to "pay in full financially and in every other way" for her wartime deeds. He feared that Germany had "almost won the war for she has left great portions of her hated rival stricken to the ground while all in Germany is fresh and strong and well preserved."[64]

A few weeks later another football assignment provided Murphy the opportunity to travel through Belgium. Wherever he went he saw pictures of Woodrow Wilson, and he was much impressed by the manner in which the American president, then at the height of his world influence, was viewed by the common people. "The reverence the masses of the people have for him," Murphy commented, "measures up to adoration. . . . The only harsh things we hear about our president come from our own people."

Murphy saw much evidence of "poverty and want" in the war-devastated portions of Belgium, but he thought that in Brussels Americans had "gone a little too far" in providing relief to a "people who are conducting themselves . . . with frivolity we would never think of at home during war time." Later, as mayor of Detroit during the Great Depression, Murphy criticized President Herbert Hoover for a lack of generosity in dealing with the desperate relief problem of the nation, but now Frank wondered if the American Relief Administration that Hoover headed was not taking the relief needs of Belgium more seriously than the Belgians themselves were. "And," he asked in words that would often be heard after another world war, "have we not started a bad precedent in acting as fairy-godmother to a war stricken country without first knowing all the facts? Sometimes I think these people here believe we are boobs. I believe in charity. I want to relieve all suffering possible. But it is possible to be indiscreet even in charity."[65]

After a brief time Murphy found life in Kempenich "absolutely dead," and he became increasingly dissatisfied with his assignment. Although it was "great stuff playing the role of the conqueror," he concluded that he "would rather be a constable in a good Yankee town than being over here." He was becoming anxious to return to his profession, and the advancement of his career was very much on his mind. "I must not let the grass grow under my feet," he wrote. He attempted to secure a transfer to the United States to take part in the Victory Loan drive, but in the end an opportunity presented itself to him in Europe that changed his mind about an immediate return to his native land.[66]

At the instigation of the YMCA, an educational program had been established for the AEF in Europe that was very substantially expanded following the Armistice. As part of this program, special arrangements were made with France and Great Britain that resulted in the enrollment of about eight thousand officers and men in French universities and about two thousand in British universities. Late in January, 1919, Murphy wrote his mother that he thought the opportunity to study at Oxford for a few months "would mean worlds to me in my profession." He filled out the necessary forms and on March 2 was placed on detached service and ordered to report to the Commandant, American School Detachment, in England, for classification and registration.[67]

Insisting that he wanted to learn "some real law" while on the school detail, Murphy was at first undecided whether to enroll at Oxford, Cambridge, or the Inns of Court, but when he learned that he could attend Trinity College in Dublin, his Irish blood began to assert itself. He decided in the end to study at the Inns of Court from March 18 to April 15 and then to enroll at Trinity for some law courses that concluded on June 6 and a liberal arts program that continued for an additional two weeks. In explaining his choice of Trinity, Murphy, in a remark that provides an insight into the kind of Supreme Court justice he would be, observed that he was attracted to the Irish university because the "idealism and beautiful humaneness" of "Irish scholars and Jesuits" made them "the superiors . . . of other scholars more exacting in analytical thinking."[68]

Murphy's decision to go to Trinity was tied in with his feelings about his identity as an American of Irish descent. Like most third-generation Irish-Americans, Murphy was a thoroughly assimilated American, but he did not forget his Irish heritage, and, at the very least, he would always maintain a symbolic relationship to the land of his grandparents. Returning to the theme that he had taken up in his Knights of Columbus address in Detroit, he explained that he was "no Irishman—not even an Irish-American. I am purely American and nothing else." But whereas he had called for an obliteration of nationalities at the height of the war, he now proclaimed that his "adoration" of his country and his "loyalty" to it were "not in the slightest lessened by the deep sympathy" that he had for Ireland. "I would be a poor sort of American," he asserted, "if I closed my heart completely to the land of my forefathers. The good Irish blood in me makes me a good American because Irish blood is true and loyal above all else."[69]

Whatever his sympathies for Ireland, Murphy could not be classified as a professional Irishman in his attitude toward England. Although England, in his opinion, had been "wretchedly wrong" in her treatment of Ireland, he was convinced that England and the United States must be "pardners [sic] in international matters. English speaking people should stick together," Murphy thought. "Life on the continent has taught me that."[70]

Murphy, who attended Lincoln's Inn, was impressed with "the dignity and majesty" of the Inns of Court even though he doubted that students there actually learned as much about the law as students did in major American law schools. Murphy journeyed to Ireland in the middle of April, but before beginning his studies at Trinity he visited Killarney, which affected him as "an inspiring religious service would," and Blarney Castle, where, as his political opponents no doubt later suspected, he kissed the Blarney stone not once but twice. In Dublin Murphy lived away from Trinity since he wished to meet people and learn all that he could about Ireland. He thought his course on international law "splendid," but his other courses were "not so profitable" even though they did help him to renew his acquaintanceship with "many fundamental principles of law."[71]

While a student in England and Ireland Murphy was much interested in the peace negotiations taking place in Paris and in the reaction to the peace treaty in the United States. He was "disgusted with the cheap political tricks" that he thought the Republicans were "pulling on the president," such as Lodge's Round Robin, and he believed that "a few selfish men" were "doing America great harm in Europe." By this time Murphy had abandoned his support of a dictated peace and massive German reparations in favor of the Wilsonian position that "permanent peace" could not be achieved by "crucifying Germany." Wilson's "great vision and power to translate into action his ideals no matter what the cost,"

Murphy commented, "stamps [*sic*] him as one of the rare men in statecraft of all time."

Murphy agreed with some of the conferees in Paris that Bolshevism was "the real trouble in Europe." He regarded the Bolsheviks as "a cut-throat crew," and he hoped that the Americans would "get a chance to hit them a lick. We'll stop them if the chance comes our way." Unlike many other foes of Bolshevism, however, he was concerned about the conditions that made its rise possible. Bolshevism, he believed, could come to power in a country like Germany, where it appeared to be a threat early in 1919, only because it grew out of "unhappiness and depression." It was not so much poor people who were to blame for Bolshevism but rather "the selfish and indolent rich. They are crying out against it all the time without realizing that their greed and social tyranny is [*sic*] creating and multiplying it."

Since he could not "subscribe to the doctrine that peace should be arrived at by what the enemy deserves," Murphy was dissatisfied with the terms of the Versailles Treaty as presented to Germany on May 7, 1919. The provisions of the treaty appeared to him to "go beyond our affirmed principles on entering the war and as a basis of peace," and he concluded that Wilson either had had little to do with the treaty or had been forced "to yield his principles." Murphy hoped, nevertheless, that Germany would accept the treaty. Perhaps the injustices of the peace could be "righted" by the League of Nations, which Murphy, like Wilson, thought was "the great question before all of us at present. If it is cast aside we will soon be in another war." [72]

Murphy found Ireland to be "full up with warm hearted kindly people." The more he saw of the Irish people the more he loved them. Faith in independence, he thought, was "the great joy" in their lives, and Murphy fully sympathized with their yearnings in this regard. "My heart," he wrote, "really aches for the Irish," and he did not know how they were able to endure English "terrorism," the shackling of the country by "the powerful English military system," and the "complete controll [*sic*] by the English of political and industrial matters." If he were an Irishman, he remarked, "you can bet I would rebel."

Murphy, however, thought it unfortunate that the Irish in their struggle for independence had engaged in lawless and disorderly acts. Although later, as governor of Michigan during the General Motors sit-down strike, he tolerated an illegal form of protest for a time, he declared himself while in Ireland to be "solid against any kind of lawlessness as protest." He marvelled, though, that, under the circumstances, there was not more crime in Ireland and that the Irish had not turned into "cut throats and murderers."[73]

In his free time in Dublin Murphy gathered up and read "all the good books" that he could find on Irish history and the struggle for Irish independence. British authorities had their eye on Murphy because he not only collected books on the independence issue but also attended Sinn Fein meetings and befriended such Sinn Fein leaders as Michael Collins and Harry Boland. Murphy was later to report that he had been shadowed by the Black and Tans and had been warned by a British officer to spend more time at Trinity and less at protest meetings. It was typical of this man of so many contradictions, however, that just as he was likely to be found in the society of the rich and wellborn in Detroit, so he hobnobbed in Dublin mainly with the castle aristocracy and enjoyed the company of the English and English sympathizers who, as he put it, held Ireland in "shackles."[74]

Murphy, who was so often in his career at the scene of great events, was in Dublin when the American Commission for Irish Independence arrived in the city. The members of the Commission—Frank P. Walsh, who had headed the United States Commission on Industrial Relations, Michael J. Ryan, the former city solicitor of Philadelphia, and Edward F. Dunne, former mayor of Chicago and former governor of Illinois—had been selected by the Third Irish Race Convention that met in Philadelphia in February, 1919, to seek British permission for Eamon DeValera, Arthur Griffith, and Count George Plunkett, the representatives of the Dail Eireann, to proceed to Paris to plead for Irish self-determination or, failing that, to present the Irish case themselves. Colonel Edward House secured the British prime minister's consent for the three Americans to travel to Ireland, and they arrived in Dublin from Paris on May 3. Some American officers thought the visit of the delegation an "open offense" to America's English ally, but Murphy was "not troubled with the same pang of conscience." Frank, who knew Dunne's son and had talked with the father while at Fort Sheridan, visited Dunne several times in Dublin and had a midnight meal with the three commissioners.[75]

Murphy reported that the Sinn Fein and nine-tenths of the Irish were "riotous with joy" over the presence of the American delegates and gathered by the hundreds every night at the house where the commissioners were staying, only a few doors from Murphy's own quarters, to cheer and to sing rebel songs. "It sounds grand," Murphy wrote. When a "huge reception" was held for the delegates at Mansion House, the official residence of the Lord Mayor, Murphy was one of several American soldiers who attended.[76]

When the American delegates left Dublin on May 11, a crowd of four to five thousand persons gathered at their residence and then marched behind the cars that carried the Americans to their ship. Their stay in Ireland, however, had proved to be "a source of great embarrassment" to both the British and American governments, and Lloyd George used this as an "excuse" to refuse to meet the commissioners in Paris or to grant passports to the three Irish representatives so that they might proceed to the peace conference. The three Americans did meet with the United States Peace Commissioners, but Wilson refused to push their demands at the peace conference.[77] The cause of Irish independence was far from dead, however, and Murphy became one of its zealous advocates when he returned to the United States.

Thanks to the support of John Kinnane and William F. Connolly, Murphy, early in May, 1919, was offered the position of first assistant United States attorney for the Eastern District of Michigan. He saw the appointment as an "exceptional" opportunity for a young man and "very much of an intangible asset," and so, after some hesitation about ending his profitable association with the Monaghan firm, he decided to accept the offer.[78]

Before leaving Ireland Murphy, who had already burned candles and prayed in "practically every renowned Cathedral in Europe" but who thought that he could "stand much improvement spiritually," went to Lough Derg for his "first big religious pilgrimage." Perhaps reflecting the " 'unusual devotion of the Irish people . . . to physically punishing religious pilgrimages' " as a way of demonstrating their love of God, Murphy described the arduous three-day pilgrimage as "one of the most enjoyable experiences" of his life. Spiritually refreshed, he left Ireland at the beginning of July, returning to the United States on July 18. He was sent to Camp Dix in New Jersey, then to Camp Grant in Illinois, and was officially discharged on August 6, 1919.[79]

Murphy's wartime experience, quite apart from what it reveals about the contradictory elements of his character, was of no little significance for his future career. His role in the Windhorst-Pillinger case led to his appointment as a federal attorney and the beginning of his career in the public service, and his status as a veteran would help him to gain election as a Recorder's Court judge and as mayor of Detroit.

Some eighteen years after the war Murphy remarked that his interest in military life and military strategy had not "abated." He remained a captain in the Officers Reserve Corps until 1929,[80] and, despite his years and his position on the Supreme Court, when the United States entered World War II, he made a determined but futile effort to command troops in battle and thus to compensate in some measure for the frustration that he had experienced in seeking combat status in World War I.

IV

"I Have Had Success"

I

Frank Murphy took his oath of office as first assistant United States attorney for the Eastern District of Michigan on August 9, 1919. He was one of three assistant attorneys in the office of United States Attorney John E. Kinnane, who had been appointed to his post on August 8, 1916. Kinnane was also assisted by four clerks and a special assistant attorney appointed on January 6, 1920. A Democrat, Kinnane resigned his office at the end of 1921 and was replaced at the beginning of the next year by Earl W. Davis, a Republican. [1]

When Murphy began his career as a federal attorney, the work load of the attorney's office was increasing at a rapid rate. The number of criminal cases initiated in the fiscal year 1918-19 was 384, but the figure rose to 556 in 1919-20 and 585 in 1920-21; the number of civil cases instituted increased from 30 in the fiscal year 1919-20 to 162 in the succeeding fiscal year. In part, the increase in the case load was due to the Harrison Narcotic Act of 1914 and new regulations governing the drug traffic, but the major cause was the advent of national prohibition.

Because of its proximity to Canada, Detroit became a major bootlegging center in the prohibition era. Most of the liquor from Canada came in across the Detroit River. Speedboats from Canada carried their cargoes under cover of darkness to the down-river communities of River Rouge, Ecorse, and Wyandotte, where the bootleggers devised elaborate mechanisms to receive their illegal product. Since the Detroit River is almost seventy miles long but only one-half mile wide, the speedboats did not find it difficult to elude the United States Coast Guard and the United States Customs Border Patrol, the so-called "Prohibition Navy." Within the Eastern District of Michigan a substantial number of blind pigs, speakeasies, and roadhouses attested to the heavy consumer demand for alcohol. The Detroit area also had more than its share of gangsters, rivaling Chicago as one of the toughest cities in the nation.[2]

The Eastern District had only a single federal judge, Arthur Tuttle, to hear the mounting number of cases initiated in the region in the early years of the prohibition experiment. Under the circumstances, it is not surprising that the civil and criminal dockets of the court became clogged with unfinished cases. There were 118 criminal cases pending at the close of the fiscal year 1918–19, 262 on July 1, 1920, and 465 on July 1, 1921. The number of civil cases pending jumped from 36 on July 1, 1920, to 109 on July 1, 1921. In Murphy's first year in the United States attorney's office, 155 of the criminal cases initiated were for internal-revenue law violations and 91 for violations of the Prohibition Act. The remainder involved the postal laws (60 cases), counterfeiting (35 cases), customs legislation (16 cases), the Mann Act (6 cases), the Food and Drug Act (2 cases), draft evasion (5 cases), and miscellaneous offenses (186 cases). In 1920–21, 195 of the 585 criminal cases initiated, exceeding by far all other types of cases, were the result of the prohibition law. Of the 162 civil cases initiated that same year, 60 were instituted under the Prohibition Act and 69 under the customs laws.

Of the 165 civil cases terminated in a four-year period ending July 1, 1921, the judgment favored the United States government in 144 cases, the government lost three cases, and 18 cases were compromised or dismissed—"a good record" according to the federal examiner who investigated the attorney's office at the end of 1921. The government gained convictions in 1,163 of the 1,470 criminal cases terminated in the same period, 26 cases ended in acquittals, and 281 were quashed, nol-prossed, or otherwise disposed of, a record again described as "good" by the Department of Justice's examiner. Of the 207 jury trials in the four-year period, the government gained convictions in 181, a rate "above the average" for federal trials at that level.[3]

The government's excellent record in winning convictions in the Eastern District of Michigan was partly due to Frank Murphy, who apparently won all but one of the cases that he prosecuted, his lone defeat coming as the result of a hung jury. Characterized by the federal examiner as "a young man of considerable ability," Murphy was so effective in addressing a jury that when word went out that he was to make his argument, employees in the Federal Building would flock to the courtroom to hear him perform.[4]

Given his official position, it is not surprising that Murphy insisted that all the laws on the statute books must be observed by all the people all the time. Similarly, he contended that public officials charged with administering the law must "strictly enforce all laws" and were recreant to the trust imposed in them if they failed to enforce a particular statute because they did not think it a wise law or because it was unpopular.[5]

Murphy was an extremely tenacious and zealous prosecutor of the evildoer, but the "soft side" of his nature, the Lincoln in him, also manifested itself while he served as a federal attorney just as it had when he was an assistant judge advocate in the Army. On his first appearance in federal court as a United States attorney, he recommended clemency for two youths of nineteen, both first offenders, who were to be sentenced for auto theft. "I am glad," Frank wrote home, "that my first performance as prosecutor was to recommend leniency." After winning a verdict against a group of hardened criminals more than two years later, Murphy remarked, "I hate seeing the unhappiness of others." When a counterfeiter whom he had prosecuted received a three-year sentence, Murphy discovered that the criminal's family was destitute. He bought supper for the members of the family and arranged for one of the denominational charities to look after them. The experience led him to conclude that "society is inconsiderate and sometimes ruthless in taking the bread-winner of a flock away to expiate his wrong while his dependents—innocent—pay the penalty. To me it is strange," he declared, "that all these ages have flown [by] without society becoming conscious of its duty in this regard," a dereliction to which public authorities are just beginning to turn their attention.[6]

Murphy's initial days in office were principally devoted to a study of two problems stemming from World War I: inflation and conspiracy to defraud the government in the purchase of salvageable war materials. In the same month that Murphy took office the Washington *Post* described the high cost of living as " 'the burning domestic issue' " of the nation. Responding to the public's concern about high food prices, Attorney General A. Mitchell Palmer announced on August 5, 1919, that the Department of Justice would seek " 'to hunt down the hoarders of and profiteers in food,' " and he ordered the federal attorneys to enforce the provisions of the Lever Act that made the hoarding of necessities a crime. "This is business of prime importance which demands your immediate personal attention," Palmer advised Kinnane and the other federal attorneys.

Palmer's instructions led to a nationwide campaign against hoarders in which the Eastern District of Michigan played a particularly active role. "So far as we are concerned," Murphy wrote his mother, "we are not going to talk but go after the high cost of living with sincerity and purpose." A short time thereafter Kinnane advised Palmer that the Detroit office was "devoting practically its entire energies to this work. . . . "

Deciding to "strike at once," Kinnane and Murphy ordered a force of federal officials to seize several million eggs and 300,000 pounds of butter being held in storage in the Detroit area. The next month Murphy led a raid against the Detroit Refrigerator Company and seized 30,000 pounds of poultry allegedly being illegally hoarded by Swift and Company. Consistent with procedures being followed across the country, the seized foods were sold at prices yielding but a modest profit to their owners. Kinnane's office also secured numerous indictments against food dealers, allegedly guilty of profiteering or hoarding, and the Federal Fair Price Committee established in the district sought to fix the price of milk in Detroit; but Judge Tuttle blocked action in all these cases by declaring the Lever Act unconstitutional. The Detroit cases were argued before the United States Supreme Court in the fall of 1920, and all of them had to be nol-prossed early the next year when the Court declared the food section of the Lever Act unconstitutional.[7]

The "extremely important" war-fraud case to which Murphy was assigned almost as soon as he took up his new duties[8] turned out to be the single most significant case with which he was associated as a federal attorney. That Kinnane assigned a neophyte assistant to so important a case attests both to the high opinion the federal attorney had of Murphy and to the fact that the case resembled in some ways the Pillinger-Windhorst case in which Murphy had participated in 1918.

The case in question originated a few months before Murphy joined Kinnane's staff. On May 1, 1919, Major Lester J. Waterbury, attached to the Finance Division of the Ordnance Department, met with Captain Soterius Nicholson, the chief disbursing officer of the Ordnance Board in Detroit, and urged him to "cultivate" the friendship of Lieutenant Bolivar T. Reamy, the chairman of the Committee on Sale of Material of the Ordnance Department's Salvage Board in Detroit. Waterbury advised Nicholson that Grant Hugh Browne, a New York broker who was prominent in financial and sporting circles, was anxious to purchase some of the material that Reamy was authorized to sell and hoped that Reamy would look favorably on his bid for same. Nicholson approached Reamy with this information, and Reamy, his suspicions aroused, reported the matter to military intelligence, which passed on the details to Department of Justice officials in Detroit. Reamy was instructed to permit the plot to develop.

Browne arrived in Detroit at the end of May and met with Reamy and Nicholson in the Statler Hotel. Department of Justice agents tailed Browne while he was in the city and installed a dictograph in his hotel room to record his conversations with Reamy and Nicholson. Browne indicated his desire to buy twenty-two thousand tons of steel forgings and billets, worth about $650,000, for about $310,000, and proposed to meet the requirement for three bids by arranging for Burt Harris and Monroe L. Bardach, dealers in junk, and Frederick C. Collins, the Greek vice-consul in Detroit, to submit dummy bids for the same material at figures below the Browne bid. Harris was allegedly to dispose of the material through the Greek government or private interests in Greece, but according to a fanciful New York *Times* account, the material was ultimately to be transferred to the German Kaiser to enable him to overthrow the German government or to fight the Allies. Browne assured Reamy that he would be "taken care of," it being understood that Reamy and Nicholson would each receive $5,500 for his participation. Reamy accepted the arrangement in writing and confirmed it by wire.

On June 3 Browne met with Harris and Bardach in New York and assigned his contract for the material to them for $22,000. Shadowed by Department of Justice agents, Nicholson met Browne in Rochester at midnight on June 4, and Browne handed him $5,000 in $100 bills. Nicholson returned to Detroit, where he gave Reamy $2,000 and advised him that Waterbury was to receive $1,000 of the $5,000 plus $500 more from Browne. Nicholson was arrested almost immediately thereafter, with his share of the money still in his possession. Browne arrived in Detroit on June 6 and was promptly arrested and the papers in his possession seized, all without a warrant. Harris appeared in Detroit the next day, met Reamy to arrange for shipping the material, and was then arrested, Department of Justice agents having recorded his conversation with Reamy. Bardach was arrested in Albany, and Waterbury was arrested when he returned to the United States at the end of July after completing a European assignment. Nicholson made a full confession of the plot that proved to be of "great value" to the government in prosecuting the case. The plotters were ultimately indicted for conspiring to defraud the government, conspiring to bribe, and offering a bribe.

Kinnane reported to the Department of Justice that Browne had talked of making additional purchases in the Detroit ordnance district, where there was about $30 million worth of disposable material. In subsequent accounts of the affair it became common, as a result, to refer to the Browne case as a conspiracy to defraud the government of $25 to $30 million, but the actual crime was of far more modest proportions.[9]

Kinnane characterized the ten defense attorneys in the case as "the greatest array of counsel . . . ever assembled in a court" in Detroit. Included among them were such well-known lawyers as Thomas Felder, Levi Cook, William C. Manchester, George Monaghan, and Judge Alfred Murphy. Aware of the attention that the case was receiving, Frank Murphy wrote his mother that he wished he could try the case "alone."[10]

The trial began on December 2, 1919, and from then until January 2, 1920, Murphy and Kinnane presented the government's case in a courtroom that was constantly crowded with spectators. The government's case depended on persuading the court to accept the dictograph records and Nicholson's confession as evidence, and Kinnane and Murphy met with success in this regard despite persistent objections by defense counsel that the government's evidence had been obtained illegally and was therefore inadmissible. Kinnane charged in his final argument that the position of the defense was, "The Government got us, but didn't get us fair," and he expressed pleasure that "wit and strategy this time were not all on the side of the criminals."

The defense began presenting its case on January 3, 1920, and then, after two weeks, secured a suspension of the trial because of Nicholson's illness. The trial did not resume until February 25 even though Kinnane was convinced that Nicholson was "shamming" and that his alleged illness was part of a defense plot to "kill the case by indefinite delay." In his final argument, Felder, who was Browne's attorney and who was himself convicted five years later for conspiring to obstruct justice, charged that the government had "deliberately enticed" his client "to come to Detroit that he might be trapped in a carefully laid plot to involve him in a fraudulent scheme." Felder insisted that government agents had violated "the most sacred provisions" of the

Constitution in apprehending Browne and seizing the documents in his possession. Like Felder, the other defense attorneys also stressed the entrapment theme and, among other things, contended that there had been neither fraud nor conspiracy to commit fraud since the government had sold similar material at even lower prices than Browne had offered to pay.[11]

In making the opening argument to the jury for the government, Murphy took up the entire six-hour session of the court on February 27. There was general agreement that his eloquent presentation was "damaging" to the defense. "Making his first big effort as assistant district attorney," the Detroit *Times* reported, Murphy "pleased his friends and amazed his opponents with the way he handled the evidence at his disposal." Felder, although urging the jury to disregard Murphy's "prejudicial appeal," said that he had practiced law for thirty years and in forty-one states and had never heard " 'an abler opening argument,' " and Levi Cook, who was Nicholson's attorney, described the effort as "brilliant" and was at some pains to counter it. "I never imagined," Murphy proudly wrote, "I would draw the fire of these lawyers in such a way."

Reviewing the development of the "conspiracy" from the beginning of the plot to the arrest of the accused, Murphy contended that the evidence proved that Browne had been "the directing mind," and he lambasted Nicholson and Waterbury for taking advantage of their uniforms to steal war material from their country in "a time of peril." Murphy rejected the defense's claim that the government had enticed the accused to commit the crimes with which they had been charged, and insisted rather, "Of their own volition, they concocted and conspired their plans. It was not the duty of Government officials to warn them in a fatherly way of their error."[12]

After the prosecution and the defense had concluded their arguments, the jury members retired to the jury room, where they knelt in prayer and beseeched divine guidance. After nine hours of deliberation they found Browne, Waterbury, and Nicholson guilty of conspiracy to defraud the United States government and conspiracy to bribe an Army officer—Judge Tuttle had previously thrown out the attempted bribery charge as being covered by the conspiracy charge—but Bardach, Harris, and Collins were acquitted. The next day Tuttle sentenced Browne to two years in prison and Waterbury to an eighteen-month term. Both men were then admitted to bail pending an appeal, but the United

States Circuit Court of Appeals for the Sixth Circuit held on July 17, 1923, that the proceedings had been free of reversible error.[13]

Before sentencing Nicholson, for whom the jury had recommended clemency, Tuttle summoned the captain, Cook, Kinnane, and Murphy to the judge's chambers to hear a complaint by Cook that Murphy had visited the accused during his illness and secured information from him about a coded telegram he had sent to Waterbury that had not been mentioned in his confession but which had proved to be the "missing link" in the prosecution's case. Nicholson, Cook maintained, should not have been convicted since he "was made a witness without notice to us, without notice to him."

Although it turned out that Murphy had visited Nicholson several times, Murphy insisted that he had done so not to discuss the case but because he had wished to ascertain the seriousness of Nicholson's condition and because he sympathized with the accused. Nicholson had referred to the telegram during one of these visits, Murphy stated, but the accused, Frank noted, had previously mentioned the wire on the witness stand, to the surprise of the government, and it was for this reason that he had been recalled for cross-examination, not because of his conversation with Murphy. Tuttle, who did not believe that Murphy had been guilty of any impropriety, thereupon decided on a fine of $1,000 for Nicholson.[14]

Judge Tuttle described the Browne case as "the most remarkable ever tried in the Eastern District of the Federal Court" both in terms of the legal talent brought together in the courtroom and the persistence of the defense. The record of the testimony ran to more than four thousand pages, there were more than four hundred exhibits, and sixty witnesses had been called to the stand. Friends of two of the defense attorneys later claimed that "the grinding exaction and bewildering ramifications" of the trial had contributed to their physical breakdown and premature death.[15]

Kinnane and Murphy were lauded by high government officials for their successful prosecution of the Browne case, the only major World War I fraud case that led to a conviction. The important part that Kinnane played in the case was soon forgotten, however, and history proclaimed Murphy the sole victor. There is no doubt that the case enhanced Murphy's reputation, and he capitalized on that fact, but it is possible to see the affair in quite another light, as part of Murphy's education in the ways of the prosecution in criminal trials. Although the government had been upheld throughout, the case, to say the least, presented some interesting issues from a procedural standpoint—the role of Lieutenant Reamy, who had been cautioned by Department of Justice agents, " 'Don't let this look like a frame-up' "; the use of the dictograph; the manner in which Browne had been arrested and the documents in his possession seized; the use of the conspiracy charge; the crucial importance to the prosecution of the Nicholson confession; and the revelation of the Nicholson telegram. No justice of the United States Supreme Court in the 1940s was more concerned than Frank Murphy about the procedural rights of defendants in criminal cases, and one may surmise that the Browne case was at least a partial explanation of that concern. [16]

The Browne trial was conducted at the height of the Red Scare in the United States. In view of Murphy's reputation as a civil libertarian and the fact that Detroit was one of the principal targets of the Department of Justice's dragnet attack on alien radicals, it is remarkable that none of Murphy's biographers has bothered to ascertain whether Murphy succumbed to the national hysteria of the era and what part, if any, he played in the Palmer raids in Detroit and the events that followed.

While serving abroad in 1919, Murphy, it will be recalled, had described the Bolsheviks in less than flattering terms and had expressed the hope that the American forces would "get a chance to hit them a lick." He remained of the same mind after taking his oath as federal attorney and became so aroused about the Red "menace" that he informed his parents that, if not for them, he would have accepted a commission in the Polish army "to fight the Bolshevists." The objective of the Palmer raids was to apprehend and deport alien radicals as defined by the immigration legislation, and Murphy, at least at the time of the November raids, endorsed this approach to the problem. "I sympathize deeply with down-trodden people and people of the lower classes," he wrote in a xenophobic letter to his mother a week after the initial raids in Detroit. "I am with them in all of their struggles for social and industrial uplift. But I have no sympathy with the foreigner who comes to this country and conspires to overthrow the government we Americans have set up for ourselves and want to live under. We must wipe out selfish foreigners trying to upset our government. If there is something wrong with our present system let Americans correct it intelligently. I can [see] nothing to the Bolsheviks' work in this country but greed and selfishness—a terrible desire to get what others have."[17]

The object of the November raids of the Department of Justice, in Detroit and elsewhere, was the Union of Russian Workers (URW), a nationwide anarchist organization composed of autonomous local branches with an estimated total membership of about four thousand Russian immigrants. The manifesto of the URW advocated revolution and anarchy, but the organization as of 1919 "served chiefly as a social club for the lonely and an educational institution for the ambitious," and there was no evidence that it had engaged in subversive activities.[18] On the night of November 7 and during the next day Department of Justice officials arrested about 450 URW members in simultaneous raids in twelve cities. In Detroit, which an overwrought Detroit *Free Press* described as "a hive of radicals," federal agents, under the direction of Arthur L. Barkey, head of the Bureau of Investigation in the city, seized 50 URW members on November 7. The next night federal officials and Detroit police arrested 250 persons attending a play being given by the local URW branch, but only 25 of these individuals were held. More alleged radicals were apprehended in Detroit than in any other city during the November raids.[19]

"We are having a serious time with Bolsheviks and radicals in Detroit," Murphy, who knew as little about the URW as Department of Justice officials in Washington did, wrote a few days after the Detroit raids. He appeared at the arraignment of the thirty "most dangerous" detainees and arranged to have their bail set at the high figure of $10,000 each. The "Bolsheviks," to use his inaccurate designation, initiated habeas corpus proceedings to free their comrades, and it was Murphy's responsibility to oppose this effort. It was his intention, he wrote home, to have the accused deported to Russia. Ultimately, 55 of those arrested, including a few from other Michigan cities, were ordered held for deportation. On January 11, 1920, too late for them to join the 249 deportees who sailed for Russia on the *Buford* on December 21, 1919, 35 of the Detroit prisoners were sent to Ellis Island to await deportation. Two-thirds of them were eventually freed.[20]

By the time the Detroit radicals seized in November were sent to New York, the Department of Justice had staged another series of raids against alleged alien radicals, this time on a far more massive scale than in November. It does not appear that Murphy played any direct part in this second series of raids because he was absorbed at the time in the prosecution of the Browne case. The raids, which took place on January 2, 1920, and during the next few days, were directed against the Communist party and the Communist Labor party. Assisted by police in many areas, Department of Justice agents seized more than four thousand suspected radicals in thirty-three major cities. Many of the suspects were arrested without warrants, searched illegally, and treated with brutality. Citizens were arrested along with aliens, non-members of the two parties along with members. Those arrested were all too often placed in overcrowded and unsanitary detention centers, and even the mistakenly arrested were sometimes held for several weeks. [21]

In Detroit, Department of Justice agents, assisted by city and state police, seized more than eight hundred suspected radicals. "We have absolutely broken the backbone of the established anti-government organizations here," Barkey exultantly announced. Barkey and his aides worked overtime examining the suspects and were "especially rough in the handling of the men" as compared to federal officials in other cities. Citizens and nonradicals—there were hundreds such—were released, but the others were eventually turned over to immigration authorities for possible deportation.

The conditions under which the suspects were held were absolutely barbaric. Eight hundred persons were imprisoned for from three to six days in a dark, windowless, narrow corridor running around the central areaway in the Federal Building. They slept on the bare floor and shared a single drinking fountain and a single toilet. They were "shoved and jostled" by the police and were not permitted to communicate with relatives or counsel. "All the time," according to a Detroit *News* reporter, "there was a state approaching chaos in the offices of the Department of Justice," which did not even have a list available of those being held. [22]

After a few days the prisoners were removed from the heat and stench of the Federal Building to various police stations in the city, except for 130 to 140 suspects who were taken to the Municipal Building. Here, where the prisoners were kept seven days, the conditions were as "abominable" as they had been in the Federal Building. The detainees were kept in a police "bull pen" designed to hold petty offenders for a few hours. It was a cellar room, twenty-four feet by thirty feet, with one window, a stone floor, and wooden benches. "These conditions," Mayor James Couzens told the Common Council, "are intolerable in a civilized city," and he demanded that the suspects be transferred to a proper place of confinement. Private citizens joined in the protest and eventually formed a citizens' committee to protect the rights of the prisoners.[23]

In 1927 Murphy stated at a Sacco-Vanzetti protest meeting that "the appetite for tyranny always grows," and he used the Red Scare in Detroit as an example. He complained about the indiscriminate arrests that had been made, the flouting of constitutional safeguards, and the conditions under which prisoners had been held. An old college friend recalled many years later that Murphy had "stood forth as a shining knight to protect these helpless, illegally jailed individuals" and that his "anger was beautiful to behold," but the small amount of contemporary evidence that is available does not put Murphy in so favorable a light. He seems to have considered "anarchistic" acts and "anarchistic" utterances as equally culpable, and nothing that had happened lessened his apparently high regard for Barkey and Palmer. In recommending Barkey for a position with the Holy Name Society in 1921, Murphy wrote that Barkey was "a man of the sturdiest character" whose "fairness and dependability" had "won the confidence of all the United States Court officials." As we shall see, Murphy's candidate for the presidency in 1920 was A. Mitchell Palmer.[24]

As Washington officials saw it, the federal attorney's office in Detroit was less zealous in enforcing the prohibition law than it was in apprehending alien radicals, real or suspected. Criticism of Kinnane and his staff in this regard led the Department of Justice to conduct a special investigation of the federal attorney's office at the end of 1921. The examiner concluded that Kinnane's office had been guilty of neglect in the institution and prosecution of prohibition cases, had been careless in answering correspondence regarding such cases, and had lost the confidence of the federal prohibition director for Michigan, the collector of internal revenue in Detroit, and the Anti-Saloon League. Although Kinnane was able to offer a defense for at least some of the charges against him, it does appear that he was less than enthusiastic about the all-out enforcement of the prohibition legislation.[25]

The federal examiner who investigated Kinnane's office reported that Murphy had said that he favored the "vigorous prosecution of the prohibition laws," which was an accurate statement of his position on the subject at that time. Murphy was far from being a zealot about prohibition, but he deplored the consequences of alcoholic consumption. Referring in June, 1920, to a murder committed by an individual under the "influence of alcohol," he remarked, "One more tragedy—irreparable can be laid at the door of whiskey—the cursed stuff."[26]

Murphy was especially indignant at the evasion of the prohibition law by the well-to-do—he noted that he spent more time fighting "the so-called law-abiding class" than combating criminals—and he attributed the alleged crime wave of the 1920s to "the shameful example" that those who had reached "the summit of our social life" set for the "less fortunate classes." If one part of the Constitution could be violated with impunity, he argued, the same would soon hold true for other parts, and anarchy would prevail. Similarly, if law-enforcement officials winked at the violation of one law because the "best" citizens did not approve of it, they would soon be winking at other violations as well. It would be better to repeal the law, he thought, than to apply it to some and not to others. Repeal, ultimately, was the position that Murphy espoused, but he was hopeful while a federal attorney that public sentiment could be educated to support the prohibition legislation.[27]

Murphy thought that the most effective way to enforce prohibition was to concentrate on the "big fellows"—"the big dealers must be wiped out," he stated. Among the "big dealers" in the Eastern District of Michigan the most important was Sam Margolies, "the first big-time bootlegger and racketeer in Detroit in the post-prohibition era." Sam and his brothers Louis and Jake leased the St. Dennis Hotel after the Volstead Act went into effect, and they became rich by violating the prohibition law. They were raided from time to time and finally forced to close, but they simply moved to a new Detroit address; and when this too was padlocked, they opened a roadhouse in Grosse Pointe, near Mt. Clemens. This was their "most ambitious venture," and it became "the center of suburban night life" in the Detroit area.

"The death knell of the Margolies brothers roadhouse activities was sounded in federal court today," the Detroit *Times* optimistically proclaimed in a front-page story on September 4, 1921. Louis and Jake pleaded guilty on that day to a liquor violation, and Sam, whom Murphy characterized as "the worst of the three," pleaded guilty to the possession of narcotics. Louis and Jake were each fined $1,000, but Murphy, who had worked on the

Margolies cases for four months, insisted on a jail term for Sam, and he was sentenced to thirteen months in Leavenworth. Murphy claimed that he had been approached by politicians and " 'other influences' " to " 'go easy' " on the Margolies brothers and that efforts had been made to block and delay a trial. "We made up our minds," however, Murphy declared, "that the Margolieses were to go out of business as roadhouse keepers" and that Sam would have to "take his medicine."[28]

Murphy announced that the federal prosecution of the Margolies brothers was the beginning of a campaign to close down roadhouses that were selling liquor. There were, indeed, efforts along this line, but it was impossible to dry up Detroit, and the Margolies brothers themselves were back in business before 1922 had come to an end.[29]

Other than the Browne case, no case took up so much of Murphy's time while he was a federal attorney or attracted so much national attention as the River Rouge condemnation case, the largest of its kind ever tried in the federal court of the district up to that time. The case arose as the result of the appropriation of funds by Congress for the widening and deepening of the River Rouge to improve the port of Detroit. The principal beneficiary of the project was the Ford Motor Company, since the improvement would make it possible for ships to carry ore directly to Ford's great Rouge plant. Ford guaranteed the government that the land along the river's banks would be made available for the needed work; but when the company found it difficult to purchase or secure the condemnation of the affected riparian properties, it was required to post a $2 million bond with the federal court, deemed sufficient to cover any condemnation awards that might be made. In the end, the federal court had to determine the value of fifty-one parcels of land along the river.[30]

Although the case was initiated on November 1, 1919, Murphy was not assigned to it until November 6, 1920. The final arguments were made on January 24, 1921, and Murphy, who opened for the government, believed that he did "well." The property owners in the case valued their land at $1.5 million, but the jury awarded them only a little more than $470,000, which Murphy thought was "a singular victory" for the government.[31]

Although the government was pleased with the verdict as a whole, it nevertheless appealed the awards for sixteen of the land parcels to the Circuit Court of Appeals for the Sixth Circuit, which affirmed fifteen of the awards on December 5, 1922. Murphy, who was in private practice by then, had been engaged by the government as a special assistant in the case. The case was ultimately taken to the United States Supreme Court, which concluded that the trial judge had erred in his instructions to the jury and remanded the case to the district court for further proceedings.[32]

Not all Murphy's work as an assistant federal attorney was concerned with such issues of national interest as inflation, the Browne and Rouge cases, the Palmer raids, and the effort to enforce the Volstead Act. Much of his time was taken up with more conventional matters of law enforcement like auto thefts, counterfeit, extortion, obscenity, embezzlement, mail fraud, and mail robbery.[33]

An embezzlement case that Murphy handled involved a former lieutenant in the quartermaster corps who was charged with having set fires at Fort Wayne in the winter of 1920–21 to conceal an alleged shortage of $54,700 in his accounts. Since sixteen witnesses had provided the accused with "a perfect alibi," Murphy knew that the odds were against him, but, believing the former officer guilty, he decided "to make a last ditch fight of it." He "braced" himself as he began his final argument and "started in slowly. A hush came over the court room," he wrote home, "that did not leave it until I concluded. . . . I have never been in better form." The jury sat for more than six hours, but it was unable to reach a verdict. Judge Tuttle thereupon dismissed the case, Murphy's only failure in the courtroom as a federal attorney.[34]

The mail robbery case in which Murphy took part was the most dramatic courtroom case in which he participated as a federal attorney. Four "hardened criminals," Casper ("Big Sam") Mangiarocine, Nicholas Lambrecht, Alex ("Little Mac") McLean, and James ("Jimmie the Gun") Logan, were accused of having robbed a mail wagon of $25,000. McLean and Logan confessed their guilt and offered to testify against their cohorts, and soon there were rumors that an effort had been made in prison to poison the two men to prevent them from taking the witness stand. All spectators at the trial were searched for weapons, and Murphy got McLean to confess on the witness stand that the prisoners had planned a jail break. After three days of "strenuous contest," Murphy, according to one newspaper account, made "a stirring appeal" to the jury. "I have won once more," Frank was able to report to his family. Mangiarocine and Lambrecht were found guilty and received mandatory twenty-five year sentences, and the two prisoners who had turned state's evidence received ten-year sentences.[35]

As the statutes permitted, Murphy practiced law privately to a very limited extent while he was a federal attorney. Early in 1920 one of Detroit's "most brilliant criminal lawyers" guaranteed Murphy $10,000 per year if he would join the lawyer in private practice, but Murphy, who had a salary at the time of $3,000, decided that he did not "want that kind of work." After the Republican victory in the presidential election of 1920 he must have known that he was not likely to hold his position much longer, but he was "somewhat puzzled" as to which of several attractive propositions to join private law firms he should accept.[36]

In the end, Murphy decided to "hit it off alone" in law practice in a partnership with Ed Kemp. "It will sharpen me and steel me for the better things that will confront me in after years," Murphy wrote in explaining his decision. Although it would mean harder work than if he were to join an established firm, that did not disturb him. "Independence does not come cheaply," he observed, "but I am willing to pay the cost. It is worth having. Many a brilliant life has not measured up to its true proportions because of compromising affiliations grown upon it."[37] As always, Murphy had his eye on the future, and in law, as later in politics, he decided that, for him, the wise course was to "hit it off alone" rather than to join an established organization.

Murphy resigned his position as of March 1, 1922.[38] When he officially advised Judge Tuttle of his decision, Tuttle replied, "My opportunity to live close to you and know you intimately during the past few years will make me know that when you come to court, your client, whoever he may be, will be well represented." Kinnane later remarked that Murphy had been "a fearless prosecutor" and "a match for the best lawyers who practiced in the Federal court" and that he had been "ever mindful of the legal rights of others, particularly the poor and unfortunate." Others with whom Murphy had been associated also commented on his dedication to his job, his ability, and his sense of justice.[39] Murphy, at the very least, enjoyed sufficient success as a federal attorney to sustain his ambition for higher office. He also learned a good deal about the law from the point of view of the prosecutor, and this was an important influence on his behavior as a criminal-court judge and a Supreme Court justice. Finally, he enlarged his reputation in the community, which stood him in good stead when he sought to ascend another rung on the political ladder.

II

The announcement that Frank Murphy and Edward G. Kemp were forming a partnership for "the general practice of law" heralded the formal beginning of "a very remarkable partnership" that continued, in one form or another, officially or unofficially, as long as Murphy lived. Kemp was born in St. Clair, Michigan, on January 22, 1887. While at the University of Michigan, he distinguished himself both in the classroom and in extracurricular activities, and his classmates, misjudging his lack of ambition, picked him as the man in the class most likely to succeed. While still a student, he served as a secretary to Chase S. Osborn, and, after securing his law degree, he worked for two years as an assistant to Michigan Supreme Court Judge Franz Kuhn. Like Murphy, Kemp enrolled at Fort Sheridan, and he was commissioned a lieutenant in the field artillery. He served overseas and, following the Armistice, took advantage of the AEF's educational program to study at Lincoln's Inn and Oxford. After returning to the United States, he joined the law firm of Angell, Turner and Dyer.

Kemp was a Methodist and a Democrat, but, unlike Murphy, he was a conservative Democrat, and he served as a conservative foil for the more liberal Murphy. The two men complemented each other nicely, "because," as one who knew them both well later observed, "Ed Kemp had sort of a steady, hard-working, stabilizing influence that was very good for Murphy [,] who was spiritual, somewhat volatile; so their partnership filled in each other's differences." Osborn, reporting what he alleged to be "the general opinion" of those who knew both men, put it somewhat differently: Frank Murphy, Osborn wrote Kemp, has "all kinds of charm . . . but . . . you have the greater intellect." On another occasion, Osborn wrote Kemp, "I do not see how he [Murphy] can get along without you," and neither did Murphy.[40]

Murphy and Kemp were "busy with clients" even before their new office could receive "a real christening." Murphy described the new firm as "our baby. We pet and fondle it, and with the greatest interest care for its most trivial need." When all the furniture had been moved into the office, Murphy's "first official act" in his "new professional abode" was to write a letter to "my darling mother." Then he sent a brief note to the young lady who had helped the partners to furnish the office. "Thus," he wrote in the sanctimonious and self-righteous way that annoyed some people, "I baptize this work-shop and in so doing resolve that I shall be unbending in my ideals and firm in my lofty purposes."[41]

Although Murphy anticipated a difficult beginning for Murphy and Kemp, a prospect that he found "inspiring"—"I want the stoney [*sic*] and the stormy way," he asserted—the firm was a considerable success from almost the first moment. By early April, 1922, Murphy and Kemp already had so much law business that Murphy was complaining that he could not take care of it properly; and after a busy week at the end of August, Frank reported, "The firm treasure box is bursting with the unfilthy lucre chucked therein." He was elected to the Recorder's Court in April, 1923, but did not take office until January 1, 1924, and during the nine-month interval Murphy and Kemp, not surprisingly, were "swamped with work day and night." "The strain of things here at present is terrible," Frank noted at the end of October. "I am rushed constantly and I don't know how much longer I can stand it." When a Detroit newspaper some years later commented that Murphy's law practice had been nothing out of the ordinary, an attorney who had been closely associated with Murphy and Kemp found the comment vastly amusing. Murphy, the attorney correctly observed, had had "the fastest growing law business in Detroit" and had made "a great deal of money." There is every reason to believe that, had he remained in private practice a few years longer, Murphy, who was "an exceptionally able trial lawyer," would have risen to the top of the Detroit bar.[42]

As was characteristic of him throughout his life, Murphy was rather ambivalent about the money that came with his success as a lawyer. He pretended as a public figure that he was uninterested in money and that he was poor in worldly goods, but money was a subject for which he had an abiding concern, and he was not, during most of his life, a poor man. The most accurate generalization on the subject, it would seem, is that Murphy valued "the unfilthy lucre" a good deal, but he valued political success and recognition by his fellow man even more.

Murphy began to save while he was overseas, noting to his mother that he was hoarding money "just like a miser." As an attorney, he made frequent and admiring references to the large fees that he earned. "Low as my spirit is," he observed on one occasion, "it rises on thought of the prima donna fee I am to get." It was characteristic of him, however, to be troubled about feelings of this sort. He wondered if he would develop into "a Shylock. . . . In the past," he declared, "that is one hunger I have not experienced. . . . It may just be that now it will get into my blood. Luxury, gambling, money, all such softening stuff get into the blood when once you get on intimate terms with them."[43]

Of the cases with which Murphy was associated in private law practice, one, the aforementioned Rouge case, was ultimately taken to the United States Supreme Court, and at least two, the McGraw will case and the Lewen murder case, were carried to the Michigan Supreme Court. Murphy described his selection as a special assistant to represent the federal government in the Rouge case as "the most important event of my thus-far insignificant career." He earned at least $5,500 for his part in the litigation.[44]

In the McGraw will case, which was not resolved until after Murphy had ascended to the Recorder's Court bench, Murphy and Kemp "established some new law" in Michigan with regard to wills. At issue was the will of Howard McGraw, the scion of an old Detroit family, who had divorced his wife, a former chorus girl, but had not altered the will that made her his sole beneficiary. The deceased's brother and sister, represented by Murphy and Kemp, contested the will on the grounds that the divorce "wrought an implied revocation" of the will, but the trial court ruled in favor of the divorcee, who insisted that her former husband and she had remained on friendly terms and had been planning a future together. The McGraws appealed the decision, and the state supreme court, arguing that there had been "an implied revocation of the will," reversed the lower court and ordered a new trial. As the Detroit *News* observed, the supreme court had decided "a notable case, not by comparing court decisions but by sounding their own consciences for what might be the wishes of a man . . . who is dead."[45] In his later public career, Murphy was inclined to act on the principle that a public official should be more concerned with what was "just" than with the letter of the law, and the McGraw case fitted in nicely with this view of things.

Like the McGraw case, the Lewen case reached the Michigan Supreme Court after Murphy had given up his law practice. Mrs.

Sara Elizabeth Lewen, owner of the exclusive Madame LaGrande millinery shop, had been found guilty in June, 1921, of the murder of Donald Max Ernest, a six-year-old boy who had been spirited away from his father's home and found beaten and strangled to death in what was described at the time as "the most revolting murder in the history of the Detroit police department." The trial took place before Recorder's Court Judge William Heston, and Mrs. Lewen, who was assigned an attorney by the court, was found guilty on the basis of circumstantial evidence and sentenced to life imprisonment.

Some socially prominent clubwomen in Detroit, believing Mrs. Lewen to be innocent, concerned about the atmosphere of hysteria that had surrounded the case, and unhappy at the manner in which the trial had been conducted, secured the aid of Murphy and Kemp in appealing the Recorder's Court decision to the Michigan Supreme Court. The appeal was successful, the supreme court reversing the lower court on March 5, 1924, and ordering that Mrs. Lewen be given a new trial. The opinion of the court contained what amounted to a rebuke of Judge Heston, who had sustained the hammering tactics of the prosecution throughout the trial. In his final argument, the prosecuting attorney had stated that although Mrs. Lewen had lived in Detroit for five years, the defense had not produced a single witness to vouch for her reputation. Mrs. Lewen's attorney had immediately objected to this remark, but the judge overruled him and said nothing about the matter in his instructions to the jury despite the fact that the controlling case on the point forbade the prosecutor to go outside the record in his argument. Although the second Lewen trial ended in a second conviction, Murphy's role in the appeal enhanced his reputation as a crusader. By the time of the second trial, Murphy was himself a Recorder's Court judge, a fact that was not unrelated to the tribulations of Sara Elizabeth Lewen.[46]

One of the cases handled by Murphy and Kemp brought Murphy into conflict with the Detroit *News*. When Ruth Maude Devoy Scripps sought a divorce from James E. Scripps II, son of the publisher of the Detroit *News*, she engaged Murphy and Kemp as her attorneys. The trial began on December 21, 1923, shortly before Murphy took up his duties on the Recorder's Court. Mrs. Scripps made "sensational charges of refined cruelty" against her husband, but the judge was unconvinced; he granted James an absolute decree of divorce and denied Mrs. Scripps the separate bill of maintenance that she had sought. One of Murphy's lawyer friends reported that Murphy "absolutely defied" the Scripps family in taking the case and that the *News* never forgave him for this.[47] The *News*, as a matter of fact, was never among Murphy's journalistic admirers, but its opposition to him antedated the Scripps divorce case.

The Murphy with a highly developed ethical sense and the Murphy who sympathized with the deviant individual were in evidence during the brief history of Murphy and Kemp. Soon after the firm was established, Murphy was engaged to represent a brokerage house that was in trouble with the Michigan Securities Commission for using "improper methods" in the buying and selling of securities. Murphy "made it plain" to the heads of the house that he would not agree to represent them unless they agreed, if "saved [,] to conduct their business ethically and in conformity with the desires" of the commission.[48]

In the summer of 1923 Murphy helped to secure the readmission to the Detroit bar of an attorney who had refused to register for the draft in World War I and, as a consequence, had served a year in prison and been disbarred. Despite his own desire to "leap over-the-top" in the war, Murphy had a good deal of sympathy and respect for the lawyer who had "followed his conscience." "We haven't advanced so much," Murphy commented. "We punish those who [*sic*] frequently we should reward for courage and honesty. . . . In my opinion, the profession needs men who are willing to suffer for their conscience. Also ten years hence we may say he was right about the war."[49]

Murphy could be "upset" and unable to sleep because a worried mother called him about a son whom he was representing. When once, after "a mean bitter fight" in court, he was able to secure the return of a baby to its mother, he found the result more satisfying than "winning a corporation suit netting me any amount of money." He took a party of his society friends through police headquarters and night court on one occasion because "seeing the jails and some of the misery of the people down underneath sometimes has a wholesome effect on those of the upper-crust."[50]

As Murphy's career as a private attorney drew to a close, he was satisfied with what he had achieved, and, to be sure, he had every reason to be. "There has been," he wrote his mother, "variety and interest in the work, I have had success, brought happiness to many people and incidentally made a lot of money."[51] Frank was referring in his letter to the preceding few weeks, but what he wrote accurately summarizes the history of Murphy and Kemp.

III

Politics was a continuing concern of Frank Murphy in the years that he served as a federal attorney and was engaged in the private practice of law. Murphy's politics remained the politics of organization, and his closest political associates were still men of the Democratic organization, notably Judge Connolly and Congressman Frank Doremus, "a machine politician" from Detroit who had "an unsavory reputation as a vote trader with the local Republican organization."[52]

As an organization Democrat, Murphy enlisted in the campaign of A. Mitchell Palmer for the Democratic nomination for the presidency in 1920. Since Connolly was anxious for the Democrats of Michigan to get behind Palmer, Murphy agreed to serve as secretary of the Palmer-for-President committee in the state. The Michigan primary was one of two state primaries that Palmer entered, but despite the support of the Democratic organization and his active campaigning in the state, he suffered a crushing defeat in the April balloting, running fifth in a field of five.

Since the results of the Michigan presidential primary were not binding on the state's delegates to the Democratic convention, many of the party regulars, including Murphy, went to the convention with the intention of supporting Palmer as long as he had a chance for the nomination. Palmer, however, was a "hopelessly beaten" candidate by the time the convention opened, and Murphy knew it. "Our man," he wrote from San Francisco, "has the least chance, and he is the ablest candidate." Michigan gave Palmer twelve of its twenty-eight votes on the first ballot. When Palmer quit the race, his Michigan delegates switched to the victorious James S. Cox.[53]

Soon after the Democratic national convention Murphy became even more deeply involved in politics as the Democratic candidate to succeed Doremus in Michigan's First Congressional District. Murphy thought that his chances of victory were "practically zero" since he believed that his opponent, George P. Codd, a Wayne County Circuit Court judge and a former mayor of Detroit, was perhaps the "strongest vote-getter" in the city, but Murphy agreed to run "simply to please" Connolly and Doremus. This was the first time that the two men had asked him to do anything for them, and since Cox wanted the Democrats to make an effort to hold the district, Murphy felt that he could not refuse. "I am going to make the best of this situation which I have not sought," he wrote his mother. "Even if I am overwhelmingly defeated and Cox wins I will be in a splendid position."[54] Murphy clearly saw his candidacy as a necessary investment in his political future.

Murphy had the support of the Democratic organization, the American Legion, the younger University of Michigan alumni, and the Detroit *Times*, which described him as "young, fiery, upstanding," "the class of the younger Democrats," and a "speaker of power." Murphy offered himself to the voters as "a progressive Democrat" who was "eager to advance a sane program of social justice, without which any scheme of post-war readjustment is going to end in a crashing failure." His platform, essentially a vapid restatement of middle-class progressivism, branded Warren G. Harding as "a reactionary" and pledged Murphy, if elected, "to fight . . . the forces of reaction, special privileges and . . . [invisible] government."[55]

Although Murphy did not mention the League of Nations in his platform, he stood foursquare behind Wilson on this issue. When the Republican national headquarters issued a statement to the contrary, Murphy wrote the director of publicity of the Democratic party, "I am for the League of Nations heart and soul as I have always been, and anyone who says I am not is wrong. I am not going to change my mind on such a question for the sake of political expediency. No matter if I stand alone, I want it known that I stand for the league as written."[56]

Murphy campaigned for the Democratic national ticket as well as in behalf of his own candidacy, but he found the Democrats "ducking for cover" everywhere. The prospect for his own victory seemed so slight that Murphy abandoned his campaign in the final few days before the election. Woodbridge Ferris, the Democratic candidate for governor of Michigan, predicted that most Democrats would be "buried out of sight" on election day, and he was absolutely correct: Murphy was overwhelmed by Codd (84,783 votes for Codd to 19,129 for Murphy), and the national and state tickets went down to resounding defeats, although by lesser margins than Murphy.[57]

Although Murphy at one point remarked that he thought the 1920 election had "permanently cured us of politics," he remained very much concerned with political affairs. The local political scene, however, was very distressing to him since the Democratic organization in Detroit simply disintegrated after 1920. The party was lacking in everything that a party needs—vigorous leadership, a popular following, organization at the precinct level, and money. The national political outlook was no more pleasing to Murphy than the prospects at the local level were. He lamented Republican control in Washington—Hamilton's "greatest mischief . . . was the creation of the Republican party," he thought—and he was concerned that the United States was "following the scheming of the old world" and was no longer the "leader of the world's moral forces."[58]

Murphy was almost as interested in the politics of Ireland as in American politics. When Eamon DeValera visited Detroit in October, 1919, as part of his American tour to press the fight for Irish freedom, Murphy attended the luncheon at which the First Minister spoke. It was to DeValera's credit, Murphy thought, that he was of "the extreme school" since "a conservative leader" could not help Ireland very much. DeValera spoke to a crowd of ten thousand at a rally that night, and Murphy's former employer, George Monaghan, read a Friends of Irish Freedom resolution to the throng calling upon the United States to recognize the Irish Republic, withhold a loan to Britain until she withdrew troops from Ireland, and reject the League of Nations. Murphy very much regretted the anti-League position of DeValera and the leadership of the Irish cause in the United States. He did not believe that the Covenant of the League endangered Irish hopes for independence, and, in any event, he thought the League should be judged in terms of its potential benefits to mankind and the United States, which he considered immeasurable, before its effects on Ireland were considered. ". . . we are Americans first," he remarked.[59]

Murphy was a frequent speaker at meetings in Detroit in behalf of the Irish cause. "Speeches, speeches speeches until I could free Ireland in my sleep," he declared after one "ghastly week" of oratory in March, 1922. Murphy sought to explain to a girl friend why he believed that he had "to follow the path as I see it before me" on the Irish question. "I have found," he wrote, "that the world is made up mostly of people who believe one thing and then act in a way that speaks of other beliefs because they are afraid. One should determine first the right of a cause and then unflinchingly follow it. This principle has governed me in my Irish attitude. And I am consistent, for my views and principles on self-government, imperialistic and militaristic aggression I would apply in just the same spirit anywhere as I do in the case of Ireland."[60] Murphy received the opportunity to act on these views when he became governor-general of the Philippines in 1933.

Confused, like many Irish-Americans, about events in Ireland as the struggle for Irish independence reached its climax, Murphy sided with DeValera in the bitter conflict that developed within Ireland after negotiations with the British resulted in a treaty late in 1921 that gave the Irish virtual independence. The Dail Eireann accepted the treaty, but DeValera fought on against it, which resulted in a bitter civil war. Initially, at least, Murphy thought that DeValera's opposition would encourage "the truest nationalism" in Ireland and was in the best interests of a future Irish republic. He thought that "the fratricidal war" was "but the death throes of tyranny. Soon it will be calm."[61]

Murphy resumed his teaching at the University of Detroit Law School during this period, offering a course in criminal law, and he began to teach a course in criminal law at the Detroit College of Law as well. The night law schools of Detroit and other large American cities were filled with upwardly mobile members of the nation's immigrant-nationality groups. In winning the respect and affection of his students as he did, Frank Murphy thus began to forge ties with the ethnic communities of Detroit through individuals who came to play leadership roles in these communities. Although the American Bar Association and the Association of American Law Schools, seeking to raise professional standards, saw as "their common enemy: the night law schools and the immigrants who crowded into them," Murphy's experience as a teacher in these schools was of no little importance for his future political career.[62]

Murphy participated actively during these years in both Catholic and American Legion affairs, and this too was significant for his political career. He became the chairman of the speaker's bureau of the Holy Name Society, served for a time as the president of the Diocesan Junior Holy Name Society, chaired a committee created to encourage the naturalization of foreign-born Catholics in Detroit, and worked with a committee of the League of Catholic Women that was concerned with naturalization and voter registration. In addition, he served on the board of trustees of the Ford Republic, a self-governing reform school for boys, more than half of whom were Catholic.[63]

Murphy was elected senior vice-commander of the Charles A.

Learned Post of the American Legion, the largest post in the Detroit area, after lack of time had persuaded him to resist efforts to make him the commander. He encouraged a Veterans' Political League that sought the election of qualified ex-servicemen, was active in Legion efforts to find jobs for veterans, attended Legion conventions, participated in Armistice Day parades, and supported the efforts of Michigan veterans to secure a state bonus. If Murphy was offended by the ultraconservatism and red-baiting of the Learned post, he made no mention of that fact.[64]

Murphy's devotion to his career and his active role in community affairs did not prevent him from leading a busy private life. He continued to make frequent trips to Ann Arbor, and his interest in Michigan football was unabated. He was, as a matter of fact, "an enthusiastic lover of athletics" in general, both as a participant and as a spectator. "I am all for going into athletics heavily," he had written his mother toward the end of his service overseas. He later informed a girl friend that he was "getting disgustingly healthy. . . . Each morning I kick the room to pieces with flip-flops, walking on my hands, and daily dozens." Shortly thereafter he bought a complete gymnasium outfit and made arrangements with the chief of police to exercise at police headquarters every day. Murphy, it must be remembered, believed that physical well-being was a political asset and that "to be a good citizen and a good thinker a man must be in good physical condition."[65]

Empathizing easily with performing artists, Murphy developed a love for the theater during this period of his life, and the Bonstelle Theater in Detroit became one of his favorite haunts. He also managed to find a little time for reading, preferring biography, religious studies, and books dealing with oratory, crime, and Irish affairs. "Someday when I have a hearth of my own," he wrote a girl friend, "I shall read, read much and long."[66]

Murphy continued to enjoy the dances at the country clubs and the social affairs of high society. He professed to a certain uneasiness about the pleasure that he derived from hobnobbing with the rich in their clubs since he made it a point not to join such organizations himself. "I enjoy going to Club's occasionally [*sic*] with my friends," he noted, "but I don't feel square about it. . . . Should one who objects to clubs accept benefits through another [?] I'm a hog!" Murphy answered his question by deciding to remain a "hog."[67]

Among Murphy's widening circle of acquaintances during these years, three persons were of particular importance for his personal development and subsequent career: Mrs. William A. McGraw, Joseph Mulcahy, and Byron Foy. Mrs. McGraw was one of several Detroit clubwomen of a reformist bent who became associated with Murphy in the early postwar years. George Murphy later remembered that she was Frank's "first teacher on the subject of Government's responsibility for the general welfare of the people." When George visited Frank during this period, they sometimes went together to talk to Mrs. McGraw about social issues.[68]

Mulcahy was a newspaper man who came to Detroit in 1921 to edit the Detroit *Times* after having served as managing editor of the New York *Evening Journal.* He was very much impressed with Murphy and saw in him a man with a bright political future.[69] The fortunes of Frank Murphy and the Detroit *Times* would soon be intertwined.

Murphy roomed with Byron Foy during a considerable portion of the years 1919-23. When Foy married Walter Chrysler's daughter Thelma in December, 1924, Murphy was the best man at the wedding, and he later became the godfather of Joan Foy. The relationship between Murphy and the Chrysler family was to be a very close one in the years to come.[70]

It became evident during the early postwar years that Frank Murphy was very attractive to the opposite sex and that female companionship was very important to him. The subject of marriage, however, remained for him a "distasteful" one. It has already been suggested that Murphy's failure to marry was intimately connected with his relationship to his mother, but his absorption with himself and his career was also a factor. As Norman Hill expressed it, Frank "figured maybe he travels best who travels alone."[71]

Frank's girl friends over the years realized how important his career was to him and what a barrier it was to marriage. One of them wrote him that he had made "great strides alone," and she feared that she might stand in his way. "I love you for the very singleness of purpose that shuts me out," another lady friend wrote him. His work, she observed, "is 99% of you," and she advised him to go "back to your monastery" and to write her not about the two of them but about the "vision that holds your eyes and heart." ". . . you don't adore anybody but your career," still a third female admirer noted. Frank was not unwilling to concede the point, at least to a degree. "I am one of those who is too engrossed with himself to take out much time for expressing appreciation," he wrote a girl friend in trying to explain what she thought was a lack of ardor. "I did the best I could with my temperament and ambitions to get on," he told her on another occasion with regard to the same matter.[72]

In a sense, Frank loved people in the mass more than he loved particular individuals. "Your greatest love always was and always will be the people, and the part you play in their destiny," a girl friend wrote him. "Any woman you love will have a second place." She thought that "nobody, nobody at all" was "vital" to his "life and happiness" and that love would "never be anything but an episode" in his life. "You are like a blazing light flooding over darkness. . . . but noone [sic] can kindle a candle from you." "What a big heart you have for the unfortunate multitudes!," another girl friend wrote Frank while she wondered if his heart was big enough to include her.[73]

Murphy's friend and campaign manager, Harry Mead, asked Frank on one occasion why he did not marry a wealthy young lady who seemed interested in him, and Frank replied that it was because she "smokes and she drinks." Many of Frank's lady friends were drawn from the debutante class, but as a society journal remarked, "Frank thinks the debbies are naughty, dislikes their fags, says they're too modern, does not approve of even a mild cocktail." "Frank loves the teas and the dinner parties," the same journal observed, "but he's just as elusive as the little March hare."[74]

Sheer physical attraction explains part of Murphy's appeal to his legion of female admirers. He was of medium height (5' 11") and slender in build and had keen blue eyes, a rather large mouth, and "a long beautifully modeled head" with thick, curly auburn hair. "When he fixes those big hazel [?] eyes on a femme," one young lady remarked, "he is really a fascinator." One girl friend found him "slim and strong and terribly alive—handsome, too," and another referred to his "sweet, spiritual face and saddish smile." "You have such a gorgeous body," was the observation of another of Frank's female admirers.[75]

Almost without exception Frank's girl friends were attracted by what they believed was his idealism and his nobility of purpose. They said that they knew no other man who had "such a set of high Ideals and standards" and who strove so constantly for "something higher and finer." He was the one person, a feminine admirer thought, who really lived up to civilization's requirement for "perfection in human behavior—religious—social—political—and personal." He always talked "like a Galahad," another girl friend told him, but "as a matter of fact that is exactly what you are and why I look up to you." He was the only man whom she had met in many years whom she could "admire as well as love."[76]

Murphy also had "a way of looking" at a woman that made her think, "I'm the one he really wants to see." Once Murphy became an important man, the ability to make a woman he was with believe that he was concentrating on her alone was especially flattering to his female companions. Women were also attracted by Murphy's gentle and courtly manner, his "chivalrous Irish streak," what some saw as modesty and shyness, and what one described as his "infinite but weary strength." His very elusiveness when it came to committing himself fully to a woman was a source of his appeal. ". . . it is a strange paradox," one woman wrote him, "that a man like you is exactly the kind to inspire the very thing you are incapable of giving. All your life," she correctly predicted, "women will love you—not because of what you give, but because of what you withhold. I would rather have a smile from you than the kiss of another man."[77]

Although Murphy never married, he obviously craved the affection of the opposite sex, and he was always more comfortable with women than with men. Frank had been intensely loved by his mother while he was growing up, and he continued to require the love of females as an adult.[78] The affection that women bestowed upon him gave him a sense of self-assurance and perhaps helped to relieve doubts about his masculinity resulting from his dependence on his mother. He loved to talk to an admiring woman, he obviously enjoyed the gossip about his numerous romances, and he liked to be reassured by words of love and the symbols of affection. He thus urged one of his girl friends to say nice things to him. "You know me," he wrote. The surest way for a woman to stimulate his ardor was to draw away from him. It would then become evident how much he needed her affection.[79]

Among the many women drawn to Frank Murphy in the post-World War I years, two were of special importance to him: Hester Everard and Ann Harding. The glitter of high society and the excitement of the theater always had a great appeal for Murphy, and many of his lady friends over the years, including Miss Everard and Miss Harding, were drawn from these circles.

Frank seems to have met Miss Everard in 1918 when he was sent to Detroit from Fort Custer to aid in a Liberty Loan drive. Hester's father, who died in 1913, had been the president of the Detroit Sulphite Pulp and Paper Company and an important figure in the pulp industry in Michigan. When Hester's mother died in 1928, she left an estate that was valued at more than $500,000.[80] Hester fell in love with Frank soon after their initial meeting, and for twelve years they enjoyed and suffered through a tempestuous romance that was marked by intervals of bliss amidst longer periods of recrimination and accusation and the anguish of what appeared to one or the other of them to be unrequited love. Hester complained constantly that Frank did not write to her often enough when she was away from Detroit, and she thought that his visits to her in her summer home in northern Michigan were too infrequent. She was understandably jealous of the other women in Frank's life, she sometimes thought him too self-centered, and it distressed her to think that she was the pursuer and he the pursued. She also could not help but realize that her real competitor for Frank's affection was Mary Murphy.[81]

Frank was lonely for Hester when she was away from him, was clearly pained and "miserable" whenever he felt neglected by her, and tended to be extra-thoughtful toward her when she became cross with him. In the early years of their romance he found it difficult to "let loose with the honeyed words" in writing to her because of "a forced restraint" that he said "possess[ed]" him. When Hester, who had already complained about his lack of ardor, wrote him in the summer of 1923 that others thought that he did not really care for her, Frank responded that those who said this were "wrong" and that neither her friends nor she realized "how profound is my liking for you." He had "never known any girl so good, so unselfish and so lovely and gracious about all things" as she. She was, as a matter of fact, "the best friend" that he had "ever been blessed with." He conceded that he had not been as "frank" with her about his thoughts as she had a right to expect, but he did not really know why this was so. He was, in any event, upset about the whole matter and would consequently have to return to "home and mother."[82]

By the summer of 1925—his mother had passed on by then—Frank was finding it easier to "let loose with the honeyed words" in writing to Hester, and he was even using the salutation "Darling," once reserved only for his mother. "Tonight," he wrote at the end of the summer, "I would wait on you, stand in adoration of you and gently squibble upon you soft blarney." When in January, 1926, Hester was about to depart for Europe, Frank composed some poetry for the occasion, addressed "To All The World":

> Be good to dear Hester who carries this note
> Written and sealed by a Judicial bloke
> Who loves and adores her where'er she may roam
> Treat her most tenderly—sweet little gal—
> She's fashioned most slenderly and is my best pal
> I want her back home.[83]

There seems to have been talk of an engagement between Hester and Frank in the fall of 1926—there would be talk of other engagements with other girls at other times—but it ended in another one of their many tiffs. Hester then suggested, presumably in jest, that they agree not to see one another for five years, and Frank, then a judge, wrote in a semijocular rejoinder that he could not sign such an agreement since it was "contrary to sound public policy. It seems unfair to deprive the public of the spectacle of combat we have accustomed it to. Furthermore the privilege of announcement [of] our engagement has become a property right and cannot be signed away by two mere persons whose only concern is their hearts and happiness." The engagement was soon forgotten, but the bonds of affection were not severed, and the next year Frank was telling Hester how fortunate he was to "love and be loved by such as my family and my Hester."[84]

Hester took long trips abroad in 1929 and 1930, and Frank was stung to the quick by what he regarded as "a studied separation." He wrote Hester a long letter in which he referred to "licking his wounds" and "the heartaches and unhappiness" that she had caused him. He wondered if she no longer loved him but was not "cruel enough" to say so. He poured out his heart to her and even told her, paying her the highest compliment of which he was capable, that she was like his mother. He would not write more, he asserted, because he was "too hurt. . . . my feelings I guess are too much for me. . . . you deserted me." It is not clear who deserted whom, but the romance soon came to an end, to be replaced by an enduring friendship. Later, Frank looked back nostalgically on their relationship. As he sailed for the Philippines in June, 1933, he wrote Hester, married by then and no longer a threat to his bachelorhood, that he would "give it all up"—it is the last thing he would have done—"if once more I could go back on the slope of a gentle hill at Gull Lake [in southwestern Michigan], there in the perfume of June with you reading verses."[85]

Murphy met the stunningly beautiful Ann Harding in 1922, when the "flaxen haired and cameo faced" actress, later to gain fame as a screen star, was performing at the Bonstelle Theater in Detroit. He kindled a spark in her that flamed from time to time over the years, and she saw in him a heroic quality and an idealism that was lacking in other men she knew and that she did not find in her unhappy first marriage. Like Hester, she never fully understood Murphy, and she discovered, as other women did, that love and marriage were not among his favorite subjects of conversation. She sometimes found solace in her feeling for Murphy, but he seems to have caused her more pain than pleasure, and one of his friends remembered her as "the weeping blond."[86]

IV

After winning an important lawsuit in 1922, Murphy pondered the meaning of the kind of success that he had attained in private practice as compared to the success that might come from public service. ". . . what is there clever about winning a lawsuit?" he asked in a wonderfully self-revealing letter to Hester. "Supposing I win ten thousand of them. What do I contribute to the betterment of the human family?" Murphy characterized the "modern business and professional success" that people admired as "piffle. We all have a wrong sense of values. Cleverness in business and [the] professions is almost completely without virtue. There are many men in Detroit who are financial successes who are total losses in character, intellect and lofty purpose. We contribute nothing by the silly effort that the crowds recognize as success. It is all rot." As for himself, he wanted "to be engaged at some adventurous task with a principle at stake. I would rather live that way a year than eke out existence 60 years in superficial business success."[87]

Shortly after he wrote the above words, Murphy decided to run for public office. He won his election, resuming a career in the public service that lasted for the rest of his life. Other men have also devoted themselves to the public service, but few have done so with the singleness of purpose and the "passion" that Murphy brought to his career. For him, government service was "a life's vocation," and he regarded it "in the light of a ministry." Its purpose, as he defined it, was the service of one's fellow man and the building of "a happier society." "We are not here for ourselves alone," he said; "we are here to do things for those around us. . . ." The educated man and the man blessed with good fortune, as Murphy saw it, had a particular obligation to serve. "We owe a debt about which our eagerness to pay must never abate," he wrote; "the endless paying of that debt is an inward satisfaction that outweighs any advantage in other honorable pursuits."[88]

As a pacifist who admired the "martial type of character," William James was anxious to discover a "moral equivalent of war" that would preserve the "manly virtues" normally associated with the battlefield. In his famous essay on the subject, James proposed public service as the substitute for war and concluded that if society could "inflame the civic temper" and make men "blush with indignant shame" when their community was "vile in any way whatsoever," it could preserve the nation's "ideals of hardihood" without the necessity of waging war.[89]

Murphy, who was as impressed with the martial virtues as James, found his "moral equivalent of war" in public service, as James had prescribed, and he burned with the "civic passion" of which James spoke. Murphy assessed his role as a public servant, naturally enough and with a good deal of truth, in terms of disinterested service to the people and especially the less fortunate among them, but the advancement of his own career was also an essential motivating factor for Murphy. ". . . few in Public Affairs," Benjamin Franklin had observed, "act from a meer View of the Good of their Country, whatever they may pretend; and tho' their Actings bring real Good to their Country, yet men primarily consider'd that their own and their Country's Interest was united, and did not act from a Principle of Benevolence."[90]

V

"A New Detroit Is Arising"

I

For a decade beginning in 1923 Frank Murphy's career as a public official was intertwined with the politics of Detroit, and it was as a Detroiter that he vaulted into national prominence. Murphy's "dreams of ruling cities in our good land"[1] were realized in Detroit, but he served an important apprenticeship as a criminal-court judge before he became the city's mayor.

Although Detroit was already "a thriving industrial and commercial community" in the 1890s, its most spectacular growth occurred in the first three decades of the twentieth century as the automobile industry attracted people to the city from all over the world and gave Detroit its distinctive character as a city on wheels. Detroit's population, only 285,700 in 1900, soared to almost one million by 1920 and reached 1,568,662 in 1930.[2]

In the pre-World War I era Detroit's city government was of the weak mayor–city council variety, two aldermen being elected on a partisan ballot from each of the city's twenty-one wards. The dominant influence in the city government, described by one source as "easy going, inefficient, and, in a petty way, corrupt," was exercised by the so-called Vote Swappers League, a bipartisan group that reflected the preponderant power in municipal affairs of the liquor interests and the Detroit United Railway Company. The Vote Swappers League controlled elections in the city by controlling the precinct election inspectors, who were elected on a partisan basis.[3]

The effort to transform the old political order in Detroit was spearheaded by the Detroit Citizens League, founded in 1912.[4] The League was typical in every way of the good-government civic organizations that flourished in the United States in the progressive era.[5] Its leadership was distinctly upper class, its membership, predominantly Anglo-Saxon middle class; its religion was Protestant; and its goal was clean and efficient government. Working

91

in close relationship with the Protestant churches of Detroit, the League sought to destroy the liquor interests, introduce nonpartisan elections, adopt the city-manager plan or, failing that, augment the power of the mayor, and reduce the ward-based political strength of the ethnic and lower-class elements by providing for the at-large election of the city's aldermen.

In a relatively short period of time the League attained most of its legislative goals. The Scott-Flowers Act of 1915 provided for the nonpartisan administration of elections in Detroit, prohibition came to Michigan in 1917, and a charter approved by the city's voters in 1918 provided for nonpartisan municipal elections in the odd-numbered years, the strengthening of the power of the mayor, and the selection of a nine-man Common Council on an at-large basis.[6]

The movement to reform the institutions of municipal government in the progressive era embraced the municipal court systems as well as the executive and legislative organs of government; and here too the watchwords were efficiency, economy, specialization, and centralization.[7] In Detroit, jurisdiction in criminal cases at the beginning of the twentieth century was divided between the Police Court and the Recorder's Court.[8] The three-judge Police Court was essentially a misdemeanor court and the two-judge Recorder's Court was a felony court, but this implies a precise division of functions between the two courts that did not really exist. Persons convicted of misdemeanors in the Police Court had the right of appeal to the Recorder's Court, and the Recorder's Court did not take up felony cases until the preliminary examination had been conducted in the Police Court or the accused, having waived the preliminary examination, had been arraigned. Neither court had a presiding judge who could direct the flow of work, there was scant opportunity for judges to specialize in particular types of cases, and the division of responsibility between the two courts guaranteed delay in the administration of justice.

Reform elements were particularly critical of the Police Court, which the *Journal of the American Judicature Society* described as "the mean little court with small salary, short and uncertain tenure, close political attachment, sordid, inefficient, partisan. . . ." Some observers attributed the lawlessness of Detroit to an inefficient criminal-court system and complained about an unholy alliance of criminal elements, professional bondsmen, "shyster" lawyers, and judicial personnel.[9]

Working with Judges William M. Heston and Thomas Cotter

of the Police Court, the Detroit Citizens League, and particularly its secretary and counsel, Pliny W. Marsh, pressed for the unification of Detroit's two criminal courts and the designation of a presiding judge with the power to classify court business and to assign his colleagues to special judicial calendars. The Citizens League persuaded the state legislature to enact a new judicial statute for Detroit in 1919 that met at least some of the League's objectives. The law abolished the Police Court, increased the membership of the Recorder's Court to seven, and gave the enlarged court "exclusive and original jurisdiction" over all prosecutions and proceedings arising out of crimes committed within the city of Detroit as well as over ordinance violations and condemnation suits. The act, which had to be approved by the voters of Detroit, gained their support by a margin of three to one in a referendum held on April 5, 1920.

The governor of the state appointed five judges to bring the Recorder's Court up to full strength pending the next regularly scheduled election of its members. He selected the three Police Court judges and also designated Marsh and Harry B. Keidan, a former Wayne County assistant prosecutor who had been a leading advocate of the new court. The appointment of Marsh, Keidan, Cotter, and Heston meant that a majority of the seven-man court was committed to the implementation of Detroit's new criminal-court plan.[10]

Detroit's unified court, which began to function on April 20, 1920, was the "first . . . in the history of criminal jurisprudence" in the United States to have original and exclusive jurisdiction over all criminal cases. Its presiding judge, who was selected by his colleagues to serve a one-year term, determined the assignments of the other judges, set cases for trial, heard motions for new trials in misdemeanor cases, and arraigned defendants in felony cases. Instituting another procedural change, the reorganized court established a night court to obviate the necessity of jailing alleged misdemeanants arrested late in the day or at night.

The 1919 statute provided for the establishment by the court of a "psychopathic department." Although by this time psychiatric services were common in juvenile courts and were available in a few criminal courts, the psychopathic clinic created by the Recorder's Court was the first permanent clinic for adult felons established by an American court. Individual judges or the probation department determined which defendants should be referred to the clinic for examination, and judges were free to follow or ignore the clinic's recommendations.

The reorganized court "overhauled" its probation facilities, substantially enlarging the probation staff and unifying its four divisions—men, women, domestic relations, and adjustment—into a single department. Within two years the number of persons placed on probation had tripled. The reorganized probation unit of the Recorder's Court was later described by the *Journal of the American Judicature Society* as "the best probation department in the country."[11]

In its first two years the reorganized Recorder's Court received the most attention for the speed with which it disposed of cases and for the allegedly beneficial effect that this had on the Detroit crime rate. The court disposed of 55,807 cases during its first year as compared to 40,429 cases by its predecessors in the preceding year. There were 2,200 untried felony cases as of April 20, 1920, but only 32 such cases two years later. On March 31, 1920, there were 173 Recorder's Court prisoners in jail, 47 percent of whom had been there more than twenty-five days; on March 31, 1922, there were 83 such prisoners, and only 7 of them had been there more than twenty-five days. The criminal courts of Detroit disposed of only 2 percent of the felony cases initiated between April 20 and December 31, 1919, within a one-week period, but the new court disposed of 38 percent of such cases in a one-week period during a comparable time in 1921 and 66 percent in 1922.[12]

Unlike those progressives who looked upon the system of criminal justice as primarily a means of rehabilitating the criminal and achieving desired social reforms, the Detroit Citizens League and the majority judges of the reorganized Recorder's Court believed that the principal function of criminal jurisprudence was to deter crime by punishing the criminal. This meant not only an effort to eliminate unnecessary delay in the administration of justice but also the meting out of "almost uniformly severe" sentences. In imposing sentences, Judge Keidan reported for the court in 1921, "the consideration of the safety of the community was paramount to that of the individual committing the crime." The effect upon the length of sentences resulting from this philosophy was dramatic: in 1919 the average sentence imposed by Detroit's criminal courts in felony cases was eight months to three years; in 1920 the average sentence was eight to nineteen years. Since there was, concomitantly, a substantial reduction in the reported number of major crimes committed in Detroit—the crimes of robbery, burglary, and larceny declined an astonishing 64 percent from 1919 to 1921—the Recorder's Court was hailed in some circles as having "solved" the crime problem in the city.[13]

Judicial reformers praised the reorganized Recorder's Court in extravagant terms. The early history of the court, the *Journal of the American Judicature Society* proclaimed, constituted "the most dramatic chapter in the entire history of city government in the United States." George Worthington, an official of the American Social Hygiene Association concerned with legal measures, characterized the establishment of the court as "the most revolutionary and one of the most farsighted pieces of court reorganization that has occurred in the history of criminal courts in this country."[14]

The Detroit Recorder's Court was clearly one of the two or three most distinguished criminal courts in the United States, but it failed in some essential respects to meet the criteria of centralization and specialization so dear to the hearts of judicial reformers, and too much, certainly, was claimed for the court by its supporters. Although it enjoyed exclusive criminal jurisdiction in Detroit, it was not really a "unified whole" but was rather "an aggregate of individual courts," and its presiding judge, unlike the chief justice of the Chicago Municipal Court, lacked clear authority to superintend the work of the court and to classify and distribute cases. Judges of the Recorder's Court, also, although exclusively concerned with criminal justice, did not specialize in particular types of criminal litigation, as many reformers thought desirable. Advocates of the new court, moreover, went too far in alleging that it had solved the problem of crime in Detroit—it obviously had not—and the court's efforts to cope with the professional bondsman and the shyster lawyer were not as successful as some of its enthusiasts proclaimed. Most important, advocates of judicial reform were too much bemused by the procedural aspects of reform and too little concerned with the character of the judge himself as the crucial factor in the determination of the quality of criminal justice.[15]

The introduction of nonpartisanship into the structure of Detroit's government had profound consequences for the style of city politics in general and for the political career of Frank Murphy in particular. Nonpartisan politics diminishes the influence of traditional political organization and enhances the importance of personality, civic organizations, pressure groups, and the press.

A candidate for office in a nonpartisan regime has to develop his own following and organization and must seek to capture the public fancy. A candidate for a seat on the nonpartisan Recorder's Court thus had to cultivate at least some of the major voting blocs in the city to be elected or reelected, and he was tempted to do something of news value to gain publicity. As Raymond Moley pointed out, the candidate for a nonpartisan judicial office was obliged to practice "the politics of nonpartisanship" if he wished to attain electoral success.[16]

Among the civic groups that played a role in Detroit's nonpartisan politics, the Citizens League was the most important. An organization with between three and five thousand members, its policies were determined by its executive board, which was generally composed of men drawn from the upper reaches of the social and business worlds of Detroit. The League was a zealous supporter of nonpartisanship, and because of the part that it had played in the establishment of the new Recorder's Court and because of its continuing concern with law and order and the strict enforcement of the laws against vice, drinking, and gambling, it took a special interest in the affairs of Detroit's criminal court. The League's research was largely confined to the area of personnel; its monthly publication, *Civic Searchlight,* not only contained short articles dealing with the problems of local government but also, at election time, rated candidates for office as "preferred," "qualified," or "not recommended." The Citizens League was interlocked, or at least enjoyed a friendly relationship, with other civic organizations such as the Detroit Bureau of Governmental Research, created in 1916 to investigate local problems and to disseminate information concerning them.[17]

In the absence of partisan elections the press normally enjoys greater influence in political affairs than when the mode of politics is partisan. The Detroit *News,* which had the largest daily circulation in Detroit, stressed local issues and usually shared the point of view of the Detroit Citizens League on these issues. The very conservative Detroit *Free Press* was less closely linked than the *News* to civic organizations like the Detroit Citizens League, but it nevertheless tended to see most issues from the same conservative, business-minded perspective. The third Detroit daily, the Detroit *Times,* purchased by William Randolph Hearst in 1921 at a time when its circulation was a miniscule twenty thousand, was much less interested in local politics than the *News* and *Free Press,* and it was less a defender of the status quo in city affairs. It sought to appeal to the lower middle class and the workingman by aggressively championing selected issues and candidates, one of whom would be Frank Murphy.[18]

In Detroit as elsewhere there was a conservative thrust to nonpartisan politics. The stress was on good government, efficiency, and business management, not on social services for the people, and candidates who reflected this point of view generally received the support of the civic organizations and the *News* and the *Free Press.*[19]

Detroit's remarkable expansion in the 1920s and the changing mix of its population had their effect on Frank Murphy's career just as the nature of the city's political institutions did. According to one historian, Detroit in the 1920s was "the boom city of all boom cities." Its population grew more than 50 percent in the decade, its physical size increased almost 75 percent, approximately 236,000 buildings were erected, and the meetings of the Common Council were largely devoted to providing needed services—sewers, water, light, gas, sidewalks, streets—for a growing city. The cost of these services was indicated in the increase of Detroit's net bonded debt from $26.6 million in 1920 to $255.4 million in 1930 and the per capita bonded debt from $26.85 to $162.83 in the same years. The city's tax levy jumped from $25.5 million in 1920 to $76 million in 1930; its per capita tax was $26.84 in 1920 and $53.44 ten years later.[20]

In 1920, 29 percent of all Detroiters were foreign born and an additional 35 percent were native-born whites of foreign or mixed parentage. Among the city's almost 290,000 foreign-born whites in 1920 were 58,547 persons of Canadian birth, 56,624 of Polish birth, 30,238 of German birth, and 27,278 of Russian birth (largely Jews). Detroit's 40,838 blacks in 1920 constituted about 4 percent of the city's population. By 1930 the percentage of foreign-born whites had dropped to 25.4 and the percentage of native-born whites of foreign and mixed parentage to 32.1, whereas the percentage of blacks in the city had risen to 7.6 (120,066). Canadians, Poles, and Germans remained conspicuous among the foreign born. Although northern Europeans continued to hold the skilled jobs in Detroit's factories, the working class had become increasingly Slavic and southern European in origin by 1930. The ethnic groups of Detroit settled in their own subcommunities, and they established their own newspapers, churches, and voluntary organizations.[21]

There were fewer than six thousand blacks in Detroit as late as 1910, but the black population increased sevenfold in the next ten years as the lure of jobs and a supposedly more hospitable social environment attracted blacks to Detroit from the rural areas of western Georgia, western Alabama, and Tennessee. In the next five years the black population of Detroit increased 100 percent.

The vast majority of Detroit's blacks lived in segregated neighborhoods from the moment of their arrival in the city. In the middle of the 1920s about two-thirds of them lived in the East Side Colored District, as it was known, and the remainder in scattered black enclaves elsewhere in the city. Members of the Detroit Real Estate Board were forbidden to sell homes to blacks in exclusively white neighborhoods, and restrictive covenants were widely used after 1910 to limit the areas where blacks might live. The pressure of an increasing black population on the very limited space available to blacks in Detroit, particularly on the city's East Side, made housing one of the most serious problems faced by the blacks of Detroit. Housing was "the crux of the race problem" in every big city in the 1920s, but housing conditions were "generally worse" in Detroit than in other major cities of the nation.[22]

As some blacks, beginning in 1917, sought to escape the limited confines of Detroit's black ghetto and to find more satisfactory housing in white neighborhoods, they met with hostility and, occasionally, outright violence. In Detroit as in many other cities the transformation or threat of transformation of a neighborhood from white to black, Protestant to Catholic, or old immigrant to new immigrant predisposed lower and middle-income whites in the neighborhood who felt their status threatened to react favorably to the organizational appeal of the Ku Klux Klan. The Klan also appealed to Protestants who were troubled about the increasing number of Catholics in the city—there were more than 350,000 Catholics in Detroit when Harding became president. Reflecting their concern, anti-Catholic elements vainly sought to persuade the electorate in 1920 to ban parochial schools in Michigan.[23]

The first Kleagle of the Klan arrived in Detroit in 1921, and by early 1923 the Klan had twenty-two thousand members in the city. In the 1924 mayoralty election, the Klan threw its support to Charles Bowles, who, although he had placed third in the primary, competed in the final election as a "sticker" candidate. In a remarkable display of electoral strength Bowles garnered 106,679 votes in the election as compared to 116,807 votes for the winner, John W. Smith, a Catholic. More votes may actually have been cast for Bowles than for Smith since the bulk of the seventeen thousand votes that were discarded because the ballots had been improperly marked had apparently been intended for the sticker candidate.

Bowles again sought the mayoralty in 1925 and again received the support of the Klan, which also backed five aldermanic candidates. In what the New York *Times* characterized as "the most remarkable political campaign in Detroit's history," Smith bested Bowles by twenty-nine thousand votes, but one-time Klansman Phillip A. Callahan was elected to the Common Council. This, however, was a distinctly minor triumph for the Klan, and its strength began to ebb soon after the election.[24]

The Ku Klux Klan was but one manifestation of the reaction of white Detroit to the influx of blacks. Because of overcrowding in the black ghetto, poor housing, lack of adequate social and recreational facilities, the high proportion of single men and women, the difficulty that some rural southern blacks encountered in adjusting to urban life, and, according to the Detroit Urban League, the large number of blacks who came to Detroit to engage in "vicious enterprizes [*sic*]," the crime rate among blacks was well above the average for Detroit. At the same time, the system of criminal justice in the city was applied to blacks with particular harshness. Blacks were more likely to be arrested than whites, their homes were more likely to be invaded by the police without search warrants, and they were more likely to be convicted once arraigned. The Mayor's Committee on Race Relations reported in 1927 that "in many cases" blacks were "treated with undue severity, not to say brutality" by Detroit's police and that the attempted arrest of blacks had led to a "needless loss" of black lives. Between January 1, 1925, and June 30, 1926, twenty-five blacks were killed by the Detroit police as compared to three such deaths in the same period in New York, where the black population was more than double that of Detroit. Race prejudice in general rather than the Southern origin of some police officers appears to have been the major cause of police violence in Detroit.[25]

Although their numbers were increasing, blacks were essentially an inert political force in Detroit in the 1920s. As recent migrants from the rural South, they lacked a tradition of political participation, a great many of them were poorly educated, and they were without effective leadership. Only twenty-six thousand of the eighty thousand eligible blacks were registered to vote in

1929, and less than one-third of the number registered actually voted in the municipal election that year. Insofar as blacks voted in partisan elections they were likely to cast a Republican ballot.[26]

In open-shop Detroit organized labor, like the black community, was a political and economic force of minor consequence in the 1920s. Only a few thousand Detroit workers were members of the unions affiliated with the Detroit Federation of Labor (DFL), and these unionists were almost entirely craft workers of one sort or another—members of the building trades, musicians, motion-picture operators, and typographers. The unions of the American Federation of Labor had succeeded in organizing a few craftsmen in the automobile industry, but they had failed altogether to unionize the unskilled and semiskilled production workers who constituted the bulk of the labor force in the industry. Detroit, as a matter of fact, had attained a reputation as "the graveyard of organizers."[27]

Automobile magnates joined with descendants of the old families and with families whose fortunes had been made before the advent of the motor vehicle to form the upper stratum of Detroit's social order. The automotive executives of the 1920s were not, on the whole, men with a highly developed social conscience. "There are few cities," Reinhold Niebuhr, then a pastor in Detroit, remarked in 1926, "in which wealth, suddenly acquired . . . is so little mellowed by social intelligence." Niebuhr was troubled not only by the Detroit establishment's lack of social concern but also by its assumption that more vigorous enforcement of the law was the answer to urban crime. The cities had a crime problem, Niebuhr thought, not so much because the police were lax as because "great masses of men in an urban community" were "undisciplined and chaotic souls, emancipated from the traditions which guided their fathers and incapable of forming new and equally potent cultural and moral restraints."[28]

Whatever the ultimate cause of crime in Detroit in the 1920s, the crime rate was proximately affected in a material way by both the automobile and prohibition. The criminal court in Detroit, like criminal courts elsewhere, was burdened—overburdened, one should say—with cases stemming from violations of the traffic laws and the prohibition legislation.[29] Cases resulting from the regulation of motor vehicles, speeding, and reckless driving constituted the bulk of the ordinance cases that came before the Recorder's Court throughout the 1920s—24,780 of 28,003 ordinance cases in 1924 and 43,132 of 47,447 ordinance cases in 1929 stemmed from violations of the traffic laws.[30] To cope with the flow of traffic cases, it became necessary in Detroit and elsewhere to revise court procedures that had been devised for the pre-automobile era.

Detroit voted wet in referenda in 1916 and 1919, and throughout the 1920s there was widespread violation of the prohibition legislation in the city. Because the city government realized that it was impossible to eradicate the liquor traffic, it sought, in effect, to regulate the trade by tolerating the existence of "reasonable" blind pigs. As it turned out, official Detroit "tolerated" a good deal, probably because there was no real alternative. In a 1923 survey of "bootlegging and murder," the Detroit *News* concluded that there were at least ten thousand blind pigs in Detroit, that ninety-seven persons had been killed in the city since 1919 because of the illegal liquor traffic, and that the entire United States Army would be unable to enforce the prohibition legislation in Detroit.

The New York *Times* reported in 1928 that the smuggling, manufacturing, and distribution of liquor was Detroit's second most important industry measured by the value of its product. The liquor industry was said to employ fifty thousand persons, and the annual value of its product was estimated at $215 million, a figure exceeded only by the automobile industry. The *Times* asserted that there were twenty-one thousand liquor establishments in "Our 'Rum Capital,'" comprising open saloons, blind pigs, stills, alley breweries, home-brew plants, and alcohol plants. Two years later Walter W. Liggett, in a widely publicized article entitled "Michigan—Soused and Serene," concluded that Detroit was "the wettest and widest open town in the country."[31]

There was a steady increase in arrests for drunkenness in Detroit in the 1920s, from 6,590 in 1920 (6.6 per one thousand population) to 28,804 in 1928 (19.6 per one thousand population). The burden imposed on the police of appearing in court as witnesses in cases of arrested drunks became so great that the superintendent of police decided at the end of 1926 that the police would henceforth apply the "Golden Rule" and take to court only those drunks who had been disorderly or appeared guilty of some offense beyond mere intoxication. The remaining drunks were to be sent home or simply detained until they sobered up. The new policy caused a dramatic decline in the number of drunks appearing in the Recorder's Court. Whereas 15,696 of the court's 34,331 misdemeanor cases in 1925 and 13,784 of 28,775 such cases in

1926 were characterized as "drunks," the number fell to 12,431 of 25,859 cases in 1927; 5,769 of 27,293 cases in 1928; 5,320 of 26,529 cases in 1929; and 3,693 of 18,041 cases in 1930. Despite the new policy, the percentage of successful prosecutions also declined in Wayne County toward the end of the decade, partly because of a new state law that became effective in August, 1929, making prison terms mandatory for those convicted in liquor cases: only 23 percent of the liquor cases disposed of in the Recorder's Court and the Wayne County Circuit Court in the last six months of 1929 led to convictions as compared to a 60 percent record of convictions in the first half of 1927.[32]

Although the illicit liquor traffic and gangsterism were intimately associated in Detroit as in other big cities, there were reportedly twenty-five to thirty thousand "gangsters" in Detroit in 1930 who were not involved in bootlegging. Liggett found early in 1930 that murder was "almost literally an everyday occurrence" in Detroit, that there were numerous kidnappings, and that there had been 170 "bomb outrages" stemming from the rackets during the preceding three years. There were a great many gambling and bookmaking establishments in Detroit, it allegedly had "a large colony of drug addicts," and vice conditions in the city in the middle 1920s were characterized as "worse by far than in any other city in the United States." "Vast areas in the district contiguous to the downtown business center," according to a reporter, "swarmed with prostitutes and underworld small fry."

When the American Social Hygiene Association made a survey of vice in Detroit in the first half of 1926, it discovered that 570 disorderly houses were operating openly within a one-mile radius of City Hall and that another 141 houses were operating there covertly. The Association reported that a force of investigators twice as large as the number it had employed in Detroit had been unable to find that many disorderly houses in New York City. The Association's report characterized the number of prostitutes appearing before the Recorder's Court as "tremendous": between December 1, 1925, and June 1, 1926, according to the Association, 3,213 women were hailed before the court on charges of accosting or soliciting or common prostitution.[33] A seat on the Recorder's Court obviously provided a graphic view of the underside of life in Detroit.

II

Several reasons have been advanced to explain why Frank Murphy decided in February, 1923, to become a candidate for a seat on the Detroit Recorder's Court. It has been suggested that Murphy ran at the invitation of one or more of the incumbent judges. The reorganized court was controlled by a majority bloc of four judges— Keidan, Cotter, Marsh, and Heston—who kept the presiding judge-ship in their own hands, monopolized the distribution of judicial patronage, and discriminated in the award of assignments against the other three judges—Edward J. Jeffries, John Faust, and Charles L. Bartlett—because they allegedly were opposed to the reforms introduced by the new court and did not share the majority's view of how to deal with the problem of crime. Even the Detroit Citizens League, an ardent supporter of the "Big Four," as the dominant bloc on the court came to be known, eventually conceded that the majority judges "drove with a little too firm a hand" and had not behaved tactfully in dealing with the minority judges.

Among the minority judges the dominant figure was clearly Jeffries, who some law-and-order advocates believed had more sympathy for criminals than for the victims of crime. The beetle-browed Jeffries, who had been a "general" in one of the Pacific Coast contingents of Coxey's Army, served as a Detroit alderman, and sought several times to become the city's mayor, was an ardent reformer and friend of organized labor. His career had been punctuated by one acrimonious controversy after another, but he reputedly had "the largest personal following of any man in Detroit." A very proud man, Jeffries regarded the behavior of the majority judges toward the minority as "arrogant, brutal, impudent, insult-ing," and it may be that he, as well as Judge Faust, who was associated with Murphy in Legion affairs, urged Murphy to run as an opponent of the Big Four.[34]

Other Detroiters who resented the brand of justice dispensed by the Big Four later claimed that they had helped persuade Murphy to run. The Reverend William L. Stidger, the pastor of St. Mark's Methodist Church, asserted that he had been anxious to break up the majority bloc because of its lack of sympathy for labor and the poor and had appealed to Murphy to run as the means of accomplishing this result. Murphy himself later lent credence to Stidger's account,[35] but if it was the Big Four's unfriendliness to labor that motivated Murphy to run, it is hard to understand why he all but ignored the subject in his campaign addresses.

According to Thomas F. Chawke, one of Detroit's most eminent criminal lawyers of that era, some of Detroit's criminal lawyers first suggested to Murphy that he become a candidate for a Recorder's Court post. Much concerned about the heavy sentences being imposed by the court, particularly by Heston and Marsh, and also about the high percentage of convictions in jury trials, these lawyers were anxious to have some outstanding attorneys seek positions on the court and hopefully defeat at least two of the majority judges. Murphy appeared to them to be an attractive candidate, and Chawke recalls that he discussed the matter with Murphy, who was appalled at the heavy sentences that some of the judges were imposing on first offenders.[36]

Some civic-minded and socially prominent Detroit clubwomen also urged Murphy to run, largely because of their opposition to Heston. They regarded Heston as incompetent and dogmatic and were perturbed by his behavior in the Lewen case and his seeming opposition to their efforts to secure the establishment of a women's division in the Detroit police department. Some of these women, it will be recalled, had persuaded Murphy and Kemp to appeal the first Lewen decision, and they also discussed with Murphy the advisability of his becoming a candidate for the Recorder's Court in the hope that he might contribute to Heston's defeat.[37]

The most frequently advanced explanation for Murphy's decision to enter the 1923 race is that the Detroit *Times* instigated the candidacy as a means of increasing its circulation. The *Times* had been feuding with the majority judges and, according to the usual version, believed that it could successfully exploit the issue by supporting an attractive challenger, namely Frank Murphy.[38] This thesis requires modification, however, since the *Times* did not begin to focus on Murphy's candidacy until almost three weeks after he had filed for the position. It was apparently Joe Mulcahy, the managing editor of the *Times,* who personally urged Murphy to run, and only after the campaign got underway did the *Times* throw its full resources behind him.

Nettled by the *Times*'s criticism of some of the judges, Judge Heston, a former all-American football player at the University of Michigan, had stormed into the offices of the newspaper late in 1922 and threatened "to sling Mulcahy many stories into the street below" if the *Times* persisted in its attacks. "Red Mike" Mulcahy, a "kind of . . . wild-eyed Irishman" who was not apt to run away from a fight, refused to alter the *Times*'s editorial line and began to look about for a promising candidate who might challenge the Big Four's control of the court. He turned to his good friend Frank Murphy, sensing that he had the makings of a successful politician. Murphy, no doubt, understood that if he became a candidate he would receive the *Times*'s support. Once he provided evidence of his forensic abilities and charismatic appeal, the *Times* was only too happy to champion the candidate whom its managing editor had already embraced as his own.[39]

Although the various accounts of Murphy's decision to run for the Recorder's Court all help to explain the reasons why he was being urged to make the race, they shed little light on why he agreed to become a candidate. We know that he was anxious to return to the public service, but since the bar tended to be so "contemptuous" of criminal practice that the average judge preferred to try civil rather than criminal cases,[40] one may ask why the idea of serving on a court that dealt exclusively with criminal cases appealed to Murphy. The Recorder's Court, however, was not just any criminal court; it was, as we have seen, one of the most distinguished and best publicized municipal courts in the United States, and it is safe to assume that the ambitious Murphy was as aware of this fact as he was of the possibility that the publicity normally given to criminal cases might contribute to the advancement of his career.

It would be a mistake, though, to conclude that Murphy was moved by ambition alone in seeking a Recorder's Court judgeship. The human drama that daily unfolded in a criminal court had a strong appeal for Murphy. "It is a weakness of mine," he later wrote, "to love those who are more or less of a problem," and there is no doubt that he empathized with and felt compassion for the human flotsam and jetsam that regularly paraded before a criminal-court judge and that he was anxious to do what he could to lighten their burdens. "To me," it will be recalled Frank had written, "there is deep satisfaction in giving help and relief to the trouble[d] and depressed. I would rather do that than any task I know."[41]

Persuaded that he had a good chance of winning, Murphy decided early in February, 1923, to file as a candidate in the primary election for the Recorder's Court scheduled for March 7. In responding at the outset of the race to a questionnaire from the Detroit Citizens League, Murphy stated that he favored a "unified" court, a "permanent full session night court," further development of the psychopathic clinic, and emphasis on the gathering of statistics in the work of the probation department. He also advocated the study of "all criminal unfortunates" before the court so as to determine the causes of crime and the proper punishment of criminals and so that the "criminal tendency in prospective criminals may be treated and preventive measures taken." He was opposed, at the same time, to "cliques, groups, and combinations in the Judiciary" because "they provoke counter-groups, destroy respect for the court, breed suspicion, and are by nature unjudicial and offensive to justice."[42] The position Murphy took in his response to the Citizens League was the position to which he adhered throughout the campaign: he favored the reorganized court and the reforms that it had introduced, but he was opposed to bloc control of the court; and he was less concerned about the severity of the sentences the court imposed than he was about the causes of crime and the individualized treatment of the criminal.

That the Big Four would be the dominant issue in the campaign became evident at the very outset of the contest when it was announced that Judges Keidan, Cotter, Marsh, and Heston would conduct their campaign through a single committee. Although this strategy was apparently unique in the history of Detroit politics, a spokesman for the four judges declared that since they constituted "a working majority" of the court, the friends of law enforcement believed that the retention of all of them was essential. Six days later the Detroit *Times* entered the lists against the Big Four. The issue, the *Times* stated, was control of the court. Judge Bartlett, who was running without opposition for the post of recorder,[43] which was voted on separately, was "playing a lone hand" in the campaign, but it was "understood," the *Times* indicated, that Jeffries, Faust, Christopher Stein, a former Police Court and Recorder's Court judge and a Jeffries ally, and Murphy had joined forces with the intent of breaking up the bloc. The defeat of any one of the Big Four, the *Times* stressed, would end the bloc's control of the court.[44]

"We have combined for a principle," the Big Four proclaimed to the electorate. The majority judges insisted that it was they who were responsible both for the new judicial statute and the success of the reorganized court, and they contended that the defeat of any one of them would imperil all that the court had accomplished. This was also the line followed by the Detroit Citizens League, the Detroit *News,* the Detroit *Free Press,* and the Detroit *Saturday Night,* a weekly newspaper that spoke for and to the city's upper-income groups.[45]

The majority judges and their supporters were inclined to describe the contest that was underway as one between the forces of decency and the underworld, between the children of light and the children of darkness. "Criminals, their associates and their sympathizers" have opposed us, Judge Keidan declared. William P. Lovett, the secretary of the Detroit Citizens League, informed the city's Protestant ministers that "many of the powerful under-world elements" were seeking to defeat the majority judges and that the March 7 vote would "register the strength or weakness of the moral forces of the city."[46]

Like the minority judges, Murphy made bloc control of the court the major theme of his campaign addresses. He did not make a personal attack on any of the Big Four, and he conceded, as Jeffries would not,[47] that they had "accomplished much that was good," but he declared that it was "a matter of principle" with him to oppose group control of the court. "When cliques walk in," he summarized, "justice walks out."

Speaking as a professor of criminal law in two law schools and as a student of the history of the law, Murphy contended that he was unaware of any effort "to corner justice" that was comparable to the campaign of the Big Four. Supported by "certain special interests," the majority judges, he charged, had "pooled their political fortunes" in 1920 and for reasons apparently "more political than judicial" had chosen to administer justice by the bloc method. This arrangement not only violated "the sanctity of the judiciary" but was "pliable by hidden forces," and Murphy advised the electorate that "a political machine of reactionary and intolerant forces . . . controls your court."

Judges, Murphy asserted, should be knowledgeable, "free," and "fearless"—"And let them be human." They should seek support on the basis of individual merit, not on the basis of their identification with some group. "I am on no 'slate,'" he declared. "I believe in no clique or faction; if elected, I want to owe no obligation to any one but the people of the city." He promised, if victorious, to preserve the gains already achieved by the court but noted that he wished to reduce the term of the presiding judge to one or two months.[48]

The journalistic supporters of the Big Four, undoubtedly because they did not regard him as a formidable candidate, paid relatively little attention to Murphy during the primary campaign. Support came to him from a variety of sources. He ranked fifth among the nineteen candidates and ahead of Marsh, Heston, and Cotter in a poll of attorneys conducted by the Detroit Bar Association, he received the backing of some of his former law students now practicing law in the city, and Judge Jeffries and prominent Detroit clubwomen urged his election.

Veterans and the leadership of the DFL, who remained among his staunchest political friends, rallied to Murphy's side in the primary. Murphy's strong ties with the University of Michigan were also of benefit to him as Fielding H. Yost and several prominent Michigan alumni endorsed his candidacy. Before Murphy began his full-scale attack on the Big Four, he also received the approbation of the Detroit Citizens League, which characterized him as "well qualified" and as a supporter of the "court system."[49]

More important than any other assistance that Murphy received was the backing given him by the Detroit *Times.* The major focus of the *Times* in the primary was on the Big Four, but it also gave Murphy a good deal of favorable attention. It played up the endorsements he was receiving, many of which it had probably solicited, and talked of the manner in which his campaign had "aroused the city." As the voters went to the polls, the *Times* characterized Murphy as the "leading opponent" of the Big Four.[50]

Since the *Times* was providing him free publicity, Murphy did not find it necessary to raise a substantial campaign fund. Some of his friends, however, created a Murphy for Recorder's Court Committee and sought to collect "a modest fund" to defray his expenses, which turned out to be a mere $255.[51]

Since Judge Bartlett was running unopposed for the post of recorder, only six court seats were actually at stake in the primary. Keidan, Cotter, and Marsh placed among the top six of the twelve candidates who survived the primary, but since Jeffries topped all the candidates, Faust and Stein ran second and fifth respectively, and Heston came in seventh, the *Times* interpreted the results as a "rebuke" to the Big Four. Murphy placed eighth, ahead of all nonincumbents except Stein. The *Times* asserted that Murphy had made a "splendid" showing for one who was "inexperienced in political campaigns" and—God save the mark— "of such a naturally retiring nature."[52]

Murphy conducted a vigorous campaign following the primary, speaking to business and labor gatherings, women's organizations, school rallies, and black and ethnic groups. As during the primary, the Murphy for Recorder's Court Committee sought to raise funds in Murphy's behalf, netting a minimum of $1,460 after March 7. Most of the money was contributed by attorneys like Tom Chawke, civic-minded women like Mrs. McGraw, and prominent Democrats.[53]

In his addresses after March 7 Murphy largely repeated and amplified the arguments that he had used in the primary campaign.

He continued to emphasize his opposition to bloc control, and when his opponents said that he himself was part of a bloc that was dominated by Jeffries, Murphy replied that, if elected, he would be "in perfect isolation politically from any of the judges."[54]

More than in the primary campaign, Murphy now identified himself with those who stressed the reformative rather than the deterrent aspects of criminal justice. "I don't believe at all in excessive punishment or brutal punishment," he declared. It was necessary, he argued, for a criminal court to show "adequate respect . . . not only for the rights of society but for the proper regeneration of the delinquent individual." Since most offenders were "not normal persons," crime should be studied just as the doctor studies disease. Crime was "the result of heredity, environment, bad social conditions and too many and too harsh laws," and courts could work toward "a successful solution of the criminal problem" only if they developed a "scientific administration of the criminal law" and provided for the "intelligent treatment" of the offender.[55]

Murphy complained that too much attention was paid by judges to "little" offenders and not enough to such major culprits as "political grafters, exploiters of the poor, [and] profiteers." "The friendless and penniless," he observed, citing his experience as a federal attorney, "have less than an equal chance of justice in our courts." Since he favored "evenness" in the application of the law, he urged the enactment of an ordinance providing for a public defender, an idea to which he remained wedded for the rest of his life.[56]

As in the primary, Murphy's most important ally in his campaign for election was the Detroit *Times*. In a remarkable display of the power of the press, the *Times* completely abandoned even the pretense of objectivity and functioned as a propaganda organ committed to the defeat of the Big Four and the election of Frank Murphy. In attacking the majority bloc, the *Times* concentrated on Heston and Marsh, who even a friendly source conceded were "not as capable as judges of the municipal court ought to be," and largely ignored Keidan and Cotter, both highly respected in legal circles. Day after day the *Times* "exposed" shortcomings in the judicial record of Heston and Marsh and sought to link these symbols of rectitude and law and order with professional bondsmen, or worse. "They have reached after straws and magnified mole-hills into mountains almost daily," William Lovett complained of the *Times*. Lovett, who appreciated the "sled-length" support the League and the Big Four were receiving from the other Detroit newspapers, which also, incidentally, were guilty of many misstatements, thought that "the newspaper angle" was "the most striking feature in this whole campaign."[57]

The obverse of the *Times's* reiterated criticism of Heston and Marsh was its massively favorable treatment of Frank Murphy. It used cartoons, feature stories, editorials, and its news columns to "raise" Murphy, as the Detroit *Saturday Night* remarked, "to something like angelic status." "One would imagine to read the Times," a friend wrote Murphy, "that you controlled the paper," and, as a matter of fact, Murphy did meet regularly with Mulcahy and the *Times* staff to help plan the newspaper's strategy and to decide on the content of its editorials. On March 25 the *Times* devoted a full page to an interview with its favorite candidate, whom it described as a "lawyer, soldier, orator, teacher, idealist in principle and sturdy progressive in thought." The next day, in a cartoon captioned "The Crusader," it pictured Murphy as a knight in armor racing to the rescue of "Miss Detroit," who was being shackled by the Big Four.[58]

Once again, as in the primary, attorneys in Detroit ("every lawyer of Detroit will vote for Frank Murphy"), Legionnaires (Murphy "is fair, he is fearless, he is judicial"), the DFL, clubwomen ("that splendid young man"), men who had served with him in the Army ("ever a true and fearless leader"), his former associates in the federal attorney's office ("he possesses all the qualities of an ideal judge"), his former law students, and University of Michigan alumni all endorsed Murphy. Catholics and various ethnic groups also rallied to his support. The Reverend William J. Murphy wrote Murphy that he would see to it that everyone in church on Easter Sunday received a Murphy card. He would try to get in touch with the Sisters of St. Joseph; Father Herr, he thought, would influence the Felician Sisters; and perhaps someone could turn out the two hundred Monroe Sisters on election day. Polish, Greek, Swiss, and other ethnic organizations endorsed Murphy, and, as we shall see, the black electorate gravitated in his direction.[59]

The establishment forces in Detroit, as represented by the Detroit Citizens League, the Council of Churches, and the newspapers other than the *Times,* continued to portray the election contest as a struggle between " 'the better element' " in the city and the " 'worst elements.' " The defeat of any one of the Big Four, it was feared, would give control to Jeffries, who was portrayed in the blackest of terms. Some supporters of the majority bloc conceded that Murphy would make a competent judge, but they tended to see him as a respectable front for evil forces opposing the four "good" judges. In an editorial captioned "Frank Murphy as a Smoke Screen," the Detroit *News* thus charged that the " 'Silver Tongued Boy Orator,' " who had the "reputation of being a clean, capable young man," was "being used to cloak an attempted comeback" of the forces of evil that had been routed by the reorganized court.[60]

Reversing its earlier endorsement, the Detroit Citizens League now placed Murphy in the "not recommended" category because he was allegedly aligned with "the reactionary group" that was seeking to wrest control of the court from the Big Four. Reacting angrily to the League's change of position, Murphy delivered a withering attack on the organization that saw itself as the embodiment of civic virtue. The League, he charged, was "falsely and wilfully" misrepresenting his position because he threatened "the political security of two of the weakest links of the Big Four chain," one of whom, Marsh, was himself intimately connected with the League. The League had once been "the community leader in a great moral cause," but it had "degenerated into a mere shell of its former self, interested solely in perpetuating its own political advantages and in keeping its political puppets in office." It was "controlled by a mere handful of men" and had become "Detroit's invisible government."[61]

In an effort to persuade supporters of the Big Four to go to the polls on April 2, the *News* and the *Free Press* sought to capitalize on middle-class anxiety about crime and the racist prejudices of white voters by charging that "underworld characters" were "herding" blacks to the election commission to register for the upcoming election. The effort was allegedly being directed by Jerry H. Brock, a black "pawnbroker and gambler," and its object was supposed to be the delivery of twenty thousand "underworld" votes to Jeffries, Stein, Murphy, Faust, and one other candidate. One of Brock's lieutenants told reporters, according to the *News*, that Jeffries had passed the word that Murphy was "a good man." Jeffries, the aide said, "tells us what to do, and we do it. He is our friend."[62]

The *News* and *Free Press* insisted that a high percentage of the new black registrations were fraudulent, and the two newspapers as well as the city clerk predicted that arrests were imminent. In the meantime, the "good people" of Detroit were urged to register and vote lest "the undesirable element" gained control of the court and brought the underworld back into power. In the end, however, the charge of large-scale registration fraud turned out to be a "myth" concocted by the *News* and *Free Press* to "stampede the voters"; of 18,808 registrations checked by detectives in the "tenderloin" districts, only sixty were marked for challenge by election officials.[63]

Some "respectable" black leaders, reacting defensively to the newspaper campaign, maintained that the blacks whom Brock was allegedly registering were from "the lowest stratum of the Detroit Negro population" and did not represent "the better element"; but W. Hayes McKinney, president of the Detroit chapter of the National Association for the Advancement of Colored People, indignantly rejected the press charges as "a malicious aspersion" on the integrity of twenty thousand black voters. Blacks, he declared, did not have to be "organized" to oppose judges like Heston who were "consistently unfair" to blacks.[64] There is every reason to believe that the sensational charges about black voters boomeranged against the Big Four. Although the *News* maintained that it was not talking about "the decent type of Negro homemakers and workers," the racist character of the press allegations could not have been lost on black voters. Frank Murphy may now have appeared to them as a potential friend who, like Jeffries, would deal humanely with blacks should he be elected.

Murphy reacted to the effort to link him to the underworld with indignation and a sense of injured innocence. "I am not connected in any way with any underworld leader," he stated publicly. He would be glad to receive black votes, he asserted, but "I know no Negro leaders, and I have never been approached by any," and he insisted that he was not involved in any effort to arrange for their registration. He wrote the editor of the *News* that the episode was "very painful to me because it has always been a hope of mine to have my name associated only with the good and lofty things in the community." He delivered a stinging attack on "dirty campaigning" and predicted that the voters would "punish the fomenters of class feeling, race enmity and religious prejudice."[65]

Just as the *News* and *Free Press* sought to persuade the "good people" to go to the polls and vote for the Big Four by raising the specter of a black underworld vote, so the Detroit Citizens League, working closely with the Detroit Council of Churches, sought to muster the Protestant vote for Heston, Marsh, et al.

"The whole result," the League advised Protestant ministers as the election drew near, "depends on whether the church people can get the church voters to go to the polls. . . ." This was also very much the view of Dean Warren L. Rogers, the president of the Detroit Council of Churches, who advised the pastors of the city that the election was "strictly a moral issue" and that nothing at all was "more important . . . for the Church and for the Kingdom of God in this city, and righteousness" than the support of "the four good Judges."[66]

On Easter Sunday, April 1, the day before the election, copies of the *Civic Searchlight* that contained the Detroit Citizens League's appraisal of the Recorder's Court candidates were distributed at the doors of practically all of Detroit's Protestant churches. In their sermons, the ministers of these churches, excepting such opponents of the Big Four as the Reverend Mr. Stidger, stressed "the moral issue in the campaign," which was understood to mean support of the Big Four. This was "probably the first time in the history of the city," the Detroit *News* noted, that any great number of clergymen had felt so strongly about an election that they had referred to it in their sermons on such an important religious occasion.[67]

The climax of Murphy's campaign came on the night of March 31 when he addressed a crowd of forty-five hundred at Detroit's Light Guard Armory. The meeting had ostensibly been arranged by Murphy's supporters among the veterans as a rebuke to the "scurrilous attempt" by the *News* and the *Free Press* to slander Murphy, but the *Times* was obviously very much involved in the planning of the event. One hour before the rally fifty buglers stationed at different positions in the downtown area sounded a call to the meeting, and a Veterans of Foreign Wars band played in the downtown streets and then marched to the armory.

"Never before in the history of Detroit," the *Times* said of the meeting, "was there such a demonstration. It was as if the shackles had been dropped from a hand-bound people and the very rafters vibrated with the mad joy of their pent-up feeling." There was "bedlam" when Jeffries appeared in the hall, and when Faust walked in with Murphy, "as a body the crowd came to its feet, cheering, shouting, screaming, madly hysterical." There were speeches by Jeffries, Faust, Stidger, and others, and the crowd hissed whenever there were references to the Big Four or the *Civic Searchlight*. Then Murphy rose to speak, and the audience came to its feet. "Somewhat overcome with emotion and with voice low and slightly atremble," he began his address; his voice grew louder and firmer as he warmed to his subject. Murphy's theme was "The Danger of Bloc Controlled Justice," and he not only rang the changes on ideas that he had expounded in a hundred campaign speeches, but he now also made a blunt attack on the forces of the establishment that opposed his candidacy. "The city is at white heat," he said, "and well it might be." He had gone among the humble of Detroit, and it was their great desire "to free this city from the shackles of judicial tyranny." As for his opponents, "They may have wealth," he declared, "they may have great industries; they may have powerful molders of public opinion . . . , but we are stronger because we are right and they are wrong."

The "little criminals" upon whom the majority judges concentrated their attention, Murphy continued, were "spewed up from social conditions that the upper crust largely cause," and the "underworld would be less," he insisted, "if there was a better upper world among these church people and some other people." As a judge, he would punish those who deserved punishment, but he would not prate about what he had done to "my unhappy brothers," and he would try to make Detroit a better community. "I will try to have a temple of justice, not a butcher shop."[68]

On election day, at the close of a contest that has been described as "one of the bitterest in the City's history," the Detroit *News* reported that stench bombs had been hurled into seven voting booths in districts where there had been a heavy vote for the Big Four in the primary. In a front-page box the *News* urged voters not to be "scared Away from voting by the stench bombs of the Underworld."[69] The election results, however, were not at all pleasing to the *News* and other Big Four supporters. Murphy, providing impressive evidence of his ability as a campaigner, topped all candidates for the six contested seats with 78,347 votes, and Faust (71,758), Jeffries (71,389), Keidan (70,993), Cotter (70,042), and Stein (60,600) were the other winners. Heston and Marsh ran seventh and eighth respectively and were eliminated from the court.

An analysis of the election returns indicates that Murphy appealed to voters throughout the city; that Murphy, Jeffries, Faust, and Stein, the leading opponents of the Big Four, fared best in those wards with a high percentage of persons of foreign birth or foreign and mixed parentage; and that the Big Four received their heaviest vote in wards with a relatively high percentage of native-born whites of native parentage. In terms of the percentage of the vote cast for all candidates that he received, Murphy ran best (15.872) in Ward 7, a ward in which less than 10 percent of the residents were native-born whites of native parents (as compared to 31.69 percent for the city as a whole), about 37 percent were foreign born (as compared to 29 percent for the city as a whole), and which contained the highest percentage of blacks (22.45) of any ward in the city (as compared to 4.1 percent for Detroit as a whole). Murphy made his worst showing, relatively, in Ward 4, a ward in which less than 1 percent of the inhabitants were black, 77.48 percent were native-born whites, slightly more than 50 percent were native-born whites of native parents, and less than 22 percent were foreign born. Keidan, Cotter, Heston, and Marsh, by contrast, ran one, two, three, and four respectively in Ward 4, but only Keidan, who finished sixth, was among the top six vote getters in Ward 7. Wards 2 and 6, which were also strong Big Four wards, were demographically very much like Ward 4.

In addition to Ward 7, Jeffries, Murphy, Stein, and Faust were the top four vote-getters in Wards 3, 5, 9, 11, 13, 18, 19, and 20. In only one of these wards were more than 25 percent of the inhabitants native-born whites of native-born parents; and in Wards 5 and 9, in which the four made their best relative showing, the percentage of inhabitants who were native-born whites of native-born parents was 8.32 and 11.97 respectively, far below the city-wide average. In none of the six wards (3, 5, 7, 9, 11, 13) in which Murphy fared best in terms of the percentage of the total vote cast for all candidates that he received was the percentage of the inhabitants who were native-born whites of native-born parents as high as 23; in five of the wards the percentage did not exceed 19. Deviating from the norm were the results in Wards 15, 17, and 21, where Murphy received more votes than any other candidate even though the percentage of native-born whites of native-born parents in these wards exceeded the city-wide average, the percentage of the foreign born was below the city-wide average, and there were few blacks.[70]

In their classic study of city politics Edward C. Banfield and James Q. Wilson have argued that the cleavages in the contemporary city tend "to coalesce into two opposed patterns" that reflect two different conceptions of the public interest. They distinguish between the Anglo-Saxon, Protestant, "middle-class ethos" that favors "good government," honesty, efficiency, impartiality, and strict enforcement of the laws against vice, and the "immigrant ethos" that is more or less tolerant of vice and is less concerned with good government in the middle-class sense than with government in terms of the favors that it bestows. The adoption of the city charter in Detroit in 1918 had signified the triumph of the middle-class ethos over the immigrant ethos, but in the Recorder's Court election of 1923, an election that in some ways starkly revealed the two contrasting conceptions of government and public service, the "immigrant" and lower-status groups, who supported Murphy, Jeffries, Faust, and Stein, defeated the "middle-class," good-government forces arrayed behind the Big Four. "The old Detroit . . . ," the secretary of the good-government Detroit Citizens League wrote a friend the day after the election, "is disappearing and a new Detroit is arising. What it will be, nobody knows."[71]

Frank Murphy received a very heavy vote in "immigrant" areas in 1923, and the political aspirations of Detroit's ethnic groups were increasingly centered on him, but because of his great personal appeal and the fact that his conception of what constituted good government coincided in some essential respects with that of the Protestant middle class, he also won the support of many old-stock voters who found men like Jeffries and Stein altogether unacceptable. It was Murphy's ability to appeal not only to those whose attitude toward the public service derived from the immigrant ethos but also, although to a lesser degree, to those who viewed government from a middle-class perspective that made him such a formidable figure in Detroit politics in the 1920s and 1930s.

"The Big Four bloc has been destroyed," Murphy declared in his victory statement. The *Times,* its candidate triumphantly elected, its circulation rising, was understandably jubilant. Behind the defeated bloc, it observed, had stood the Michigan Manufacturers' Association, "'Big Business,'" the Detroit *News,* the Detroit *Free Press,* the Citizens League, and various religious and commercial organizations; against the bloc had stood only the Detroit *Times.* The *Times,* it stated, "made the contest and victory possible."[72]

Publicly, the principal opponents of the Big Four sought to minimize the results of the 1923 election, although the Detroit *Saturday Night* defined "a Detroit Optimist" as "one who believes that the new municipal bench will function as well in the reduction of crime as the old bench functioned." Privately, William Lovett conceded that the League had suffered its "first serious defeat" and that "the splinters of the [Big Four] bloc" were "all over

Frank Murphy and his mother, Mary Brennan Murphy.

Frank Murphy and his mother, ca. 1900.

Frank, ill with diptheria in
Ann Arbor, and his father,
John F. Murphy, 1911.

Murphy and Fielding H. Yost, director of
Intercollegiate Athletics, in the University
of Michigan Stadium, 1930. (Photo by the
Detroit *News*)

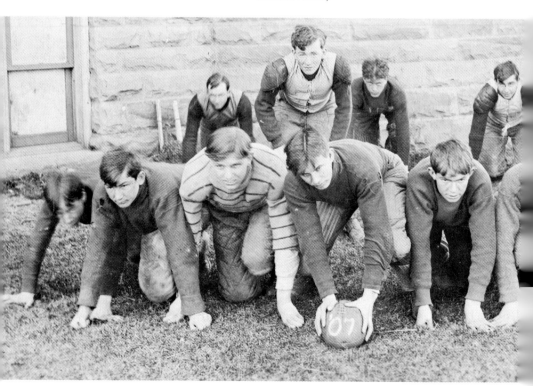

Quarterback Murphy of Harbor Beach High School, 1907.

Captain Murphy, his mother, and his sister Marguerite.

Above left, Captain Murphy, England, 1919.

Murphy at Fort Sheridan, 1917.

The Murphy family, 1923 or 1924. *Left to right:* Mary Brennan, Frank, John F., George, Harold, and Marguerite.

FRANK MURPHY

FOR CONGRESS

FIRST DISTRICT

Candidate Murphy, 1920.

First Assistant United States Attorney Murphy, in court, ca. 1920.

Ann Harding, 1931.
(Photo by the Miami *Daily News)*

Frank Murphy, ca. 1920.

"The Crusader." (Detroit *Times*, March 26, 1923)

"An Abuse of the Sacred Writ." (Detroit *Times*, March 20, 1924)

The judges of the Detroit Recorder's Court, ca. 1928. *Front, from left to right:* Charles Bowles, Christopher E. Stein, Edward J. Jeffries, Murphy, John V. Brennan, Arthur H. Kilpatrick. *Rear, from left to right:* Charles L. Bartlett, W. McKay Skillman, Thomas M. Cotter, Donald Van Zile.

town." "We have met the enemy and we are theirs," he wrote one of his correspondents, and he expected "an entirely new deal in the court." There was general agreement that because of his "immense" vote, the future of the court rested to a large degree with "the 'boy politician'" Frank Murphy, the youngest man ever to have been elected to the Recorder's Court.[73]

In the days immediately following the election, letters and telegrams poured in on Murphy, his phone rang constantly, and his right hand was "crippled from squeezes and shakes." When he spoke at St. Catherine's Church shortly after his victory, a large crowd turned out, and the audience stood up and cheered when the speaker arrived. "They [the Catholics] seem very proud of me," Murphy wrote his family, and indeed they were. For the self-centered Murphy what was happening to him at any moment generally was fraught with unusual significance, and so it was with his election victory. "All agree," he stated, "it is the biggest thing politically ever done in Detroit."[74]

Murphy visited Harbor Beach shortly after the election, and the entire town, it seemed, turned out to welcome him. The bitter campaign, however, had taken its toll of him—"It was a ghastly experience," he wrote Hester. He became ill while in Harbor Beach and then had to enter Harper Hospital in Detroit for treatment of a very serious sinus infection that had been aggravated by a cold contracted during the campaign. He underwent two operations in May, was "critically ill" for a time, and was troubled by a sinus condition for the remainder of his life.[75] This was not the last time that a period of emotional strain for Murphy, aggravated by the intensity of his desire to succeed and his fear of failure, led to physical and nervous exhaustion and was followed by a breakdown in his health or, at least, the need to escape the battlefield for a long period of rest and recuperation.

Since the newly elected Recorder's Court judges did not take their seats until January 1, 1924, Murphy returned to his private law practice after he had recovered from his operation. The Detroit *Times* happily recommended him to anyone needing "a hard-working industrious attorney."[76] At the end of November Murphy accepted an invitation from Mayor Frank E. Doremus to serve on a five-man board of arbitration that was to fix the rates charged by the Detroit City Gas Company. Each of the arbitrators received $10,000 for his services, half paid by the city, half by the gas company. Murphy let it be known that he had not expected payment for his services, which is doubtful, and he implied that he would use his fee for a charitable purpose, but there is no evidence that he actually did so.[77]

By the time Murphy took his seat on the Recorder's Court, the judges had already begun to respond to the decision of the voters in the April 2 balloting. Shortly after the election the judges decided to reduce the term of the presiding judge from one year to two months, and they later selected Jeffries as the presiding judge for the first time since the unified court had been established.[78] Men like William Lovett could not help but wonder what other changes would occur in the court after January 1, 1924.[79]

VI

"Temple of Justice"

I

American historians have paid but scant attention to the history of the criminal courts in their land despite a public interest in crime that, on occasion, has bordered on the obsessive, the substantial number of persons who are annually charged with the commission of one crime or another, and what the historical record of the administration of criminal justice reveals about human behavior. Not surprisingly, then, although Frank Murphy served on the Detroit Recorder's Court for more than six years, from January 1, 1924, to August 26, 1930—he was reelected in 1929—his biographers have all but ignored this phase of his career.[1] Murphy himself, by contrast, correctly described this period of his life as his "'era of formation,'" the time when his social and political philosophy "crystalized" and his personal habits became fixed.[2]

When Murphy took his seat on the Recorder's Court bench on January 2, 1924, the "simple, gray and ivory" courtroom, with its marble flooring, marble wainscoting, and mahogany furnishings, was "packed" with "friends and admirers" of the new judge. In his address to the group, Murphy, reflecting the optimism of the time, proclaimed his belief that progress is "continuous and ever forward." "I want to do what is right here," he asserted in conclusion. "That is all I want to do. I want this court, my friends, to be a court of character. . . . I want it completely free from favoritism and special privilege, and that sort of thing which always destroys a tribunal of justice. . . . I know that I shall frequently drop into error, no matter how hard I shall try to avoid them. I trust and pray that when this occurs it shall be on the side of mercy."[3]

John and Mary Murphy and brother George attended the ceremonies opening Frank's court, and "mama," as Marguerite wrote a relative, "came into her own glory." "It means far more to me," Frank characteristically wrote his parents the next day, "that I brought some happiness to you two than the Judgeship itself."[4]

The cases in Murphy's court ranged from murder to the violation of ordinances specifying the size of a garbage pail. Frank had to deal with traffic and ordinance cases and to preside over condemnation suits, but the distinguishing feature of his court, as of any criminal court, was the "vast range of crime and sin" represented by the "human driftage" before the bench. " 'The spangled parade of life passes here,' " a distinguished student of the criminal courts of that era observed, " 'gaudy and gay, drab and mean. The push of ambition, the drums of crime, the blare of pretension, the keen quiet of tragedy, all of these are integral parts.' "[5]

Moved by "the drama of human weakness" and believing that man is his brother's keeper, Murphy found his service on the Recorder's Court deeply satisfying. As compared to a civil court, he thought, there was "infinitely more action and human interest, opportunity for progressive improvement, and deep social significance" in the work of a judge on the Recorder's Court. Not only did Murphy find his tasks "very interesting and a great education in human psychology" but also "a source of pleasure" and "comforting," for here he could "administer justice tempered with mercy" and "in a very personal way . . . could lighten the load, heal a wound and take a broken life and start it on a fresh path up life's hill once more." "In that vineyard," he wrote Judge Thomas Cotter, "there is the best chance of all to be just and kindly and understanding." Murphy once told his court stenographer that he would have preferred a career in social work, and the Recorder's Court certainly provided an outlet for his social-mindedness. "The social aspects of the work . . . ," he remarked toward the end of his service on the Detroit bench, "has [sic] ever intrigued me."[6]

Throughout the years that Murphy served on the Recorder's Court supporters of the old Big Four like the Detroit Citizens League lamented what they regarded as a decline in the quality of the court's performance. The League, always more concerned with "efficiency" than with the "human factors" in the administration of criminal justice, complained that the efficiency of the court had waned, that it had become "politicized" and catered to "labor voters," and that vice and crime conditions in the city were "appalling" because the court was "too liberal" in its interpretation of the laws. William P. Lovett informed the Citizens

League executive board at the end of 1928 that "no problem in Detroit" was "in greater need of solution" than that of the Recorder's Court.[7]

Since the praise of the Big Four had centered so much upon the speed with which they disposed of cases and their contribution to the alleged reduction of the crime rate in Detroit, it is in these same two areas—if one permits the supporters of the Big Four to define the ground rules—that the claimed decline in the court's effectiveness should have manifested itself after 1923. Critics of the post-1923 court were surely on firm ground in their contention concerning a decline in efficiency in the disposal of cases: in 1921, for example, 66 percent of all felony cases were disposed of within one week and 97 percent within eight weeks, whereas in 1926 the comparable percentages were 10 and 59; and the percentage of felony cases pending at the end of the year was higher in every year from 1924 through 1929 than it had been in the years 1920-23. Despite these facts, however, according to the *Journal of the American Judicature Society,* the Recorder's Court after 1923 remained "remarkably efficient as compared with any other metropolitan court machinery"; there was some improvement in the court's efficiency after 1925, when three new judges were added to handle the mounting case load (two additional judges were added in 1929 to deal with traffic and ordinance cases); and the number of cases pending that were *ready for trial* as of June 1, 1930, was the smallest since the unified court had been established. As Raymond Moley, an authority in the field, has cautioned, however, statistics regarding the disposal of cases tell one nothing about the manner in which these cases were settled, nor do they measure the "justice" of particular dispositions.[8] Also, the statistics, at best, reflect on the court as a whole and not on the behavior of any particular judge in his own courtroom.

The Wayne County prosecuting attorney complained in 1927 that the Recorder's Court judges believed that they had to "cater to underworld votes," and the Detroit Citizens League was so concerned about this matter that it pressed for a state investigation of crime in Detroit. Actually, despite an increasing population, there was a reported 42.54 percent decrease in Detroit between 1923 and 1928 in the four major crimes of robbery, breaking and entering business places, breaking and entering dwellings, and larceny from the person, and the *Journal of the American Judicature Society* thought that this was as good a measure as was available of both police and court efficiency.[9] It should also be noted that the court, with Murphy playing a key role, underwent a "renascence" in 1930 and, in the process, met many of the objections of its critics.[10]

Murphy, it will be recalled, had pledged himself, if elected, to remain "in perfect isolation politically from any of the judges." He was given an opportunity to demonstrate his independence at the outset of his service when Jeffries sought his new colleague's support for a proposal to "clean-out" certain court employees, including, apparently, the able heads of the probation department and the psychopathic clinic. Murphy turned aside the request by suggesting, instead, an investigation of the two units as well as of the clerk's office, and Judge Faust and he were designated to conduct the probe. The investigation convinced Murphy of the technical competence of the individuals concerned, and in the end there was no significant change in the court's professional personnel. In another indication, this time symbolic, that he would be his own man, Murphy selected as his court stenographer the same individual, Hilmer Gellein, who had served Pliny Marsh in that capacity. None of this, however, is to suggest that Murphy was at odds with the "Jeffries-Stein crowd," to use the Citizens League's phrase, for on a good many issues he agreed with these men. Murphy, actually, seems to have served as "a connecting link between the old court and the new," between men like Keidan and Cotter on the one hand and Jeffries and Stein on the other.[11]

At their first meeting in 1924 the judges agreed to reduce the term of the presiding judge to a single month. Murphy strongly supported this action, but he reversed himself on the subject before his service on the court came to an end. Although the experience of other municipal courts provided uncertain guidance on the subject, critics of the post-1923 court favored the selection for a six-year term of a chief judge with "full supervisory authority" over the court. As it was, they complained, the presiding judge was not the "responsible head" of the court but only "a weak chairman of a committee of the whole" who was unable to "administer or control" the affairs of the court. This, they alleged, had reduced the court to "a state of inexcusable inefficiency," as was evidenced by the loss of some of the court's files, the cashing by the clerk's office of several thousand dollars worth of fake witness-fee vouchers, and the forfeiture in the early months of 1927 of some $50,000 in bail bonds.[12] To meet these shortcomings of the court, the Detroit Citizens League pressed for state legislation in 1927 providing for the election of an eleventh Recorder's Court judge who would serve as the presiding judge and would have a good deal of executive power, but the measure failed of enactment.[13]

By 1929, Murphy himself had become disturbed about the "lack of system" in the management of the court and had come to favor the appointment or election of a "strong presiding judge." After a first effort failed early in 1929, he persuaded his colleagues in June, 1930, to create an "executive committee" of two judges to deal with court administration, and monthly meetings of all the judges began to be held for the same purpose. At the end of the year, after Murphy had left the court, the executive committee recommended that the routine administration of court affairs be vested in a single executive judge, an idea that Murphy had previously advanced, so that the presiding judge, who continued to serve for only one month, could devote his full time to assigning cases for trial, conducting trials, and hearing miscellaneous motions. This reform was agreed to by the judges, and it helped the court to cope with its administrative problems more effectively than it had been able to do in the preceding several years.[14]

In the brief remarks that he made when he ascended the bench, Murphy reiterated his belief that the probation department and the psychopathic clinic were indispensable adjuncts of the court and could not operate effectively unless their personnel were selected strictly on the basis of merit and their affairs conducted "solely on the basis of efficiency and science." That Murphy "kept the faith" was attested to by the professional personnel of the two divisions, who agreed that Murphy's "attitude and vote" regarding these two agencies "frequently . . . saved a difficult situation in the interest of the public and non-political administration of the court." ". . . it is awfully important your being here," a probation official wrote Murphy. "A consistent liberal has such an influence."[15]

Probation, Murphy contended, helped to open "the door of hope for the youthful and first offender" and not only saved the taxpayer money but also resulted in "the salvaging of humanity" and helped to reduce crime. Since probation, however, was a "form of social service, above all others" that required "scientific research" and "sympathetic study by independent, qualified, trained investigators," it had to be administered by officials selected without regard to political considerations. Murphy therefore suggested early in 1926 that applicants for positions in the probation department should be examined by a board designated by the judges, with the judges to make the final choice from among the persons ranked highest by the selection committee. A version of this plan was adopted by the court before the year was out, and the Detroit *Times* hailed the first seven persons selected according to the new procedures as "the first non-political appointments in the court's history."[16]

Murphy was as determined to keep politics out of the psychopathic clinic as he was out of the probation department. Since he believed that criminal-court judges should apply the findings of science rather than invoking "vague traditional conceptions and unfortunate political considerations," Murphy took a special interest in the work of the clinic. Its director later wrote Murphy that "many of the techniques and profitable ideas" then being employed in the clinic "could be attributed to suggestions you made while you were here."[17]

Murphy was not only in tune with the progressive thought of his era regarding the use of probation and psychiatry in the administration of criminal justice, but he was also in the vanguard among criminal-court judges in seeking reform of the bail system. The evils of this system were familiar enough, in Detroit and across the land. Pressed for time and lacking the machinery to make anything more than a cursory investigation, a judge might accept a bond secured by property that was nonexistent, mortgaged to the hilt, or pledged as security for a dozen other bonds. Professional bondsmen—"bond sharks"—preyed on "the inexperienced and the ignorant" and, since there was no uniform schedule of fees, charged what the traffic would bear. The poor man, unable to supply bail, remained in jail, whereas the well-financed criminal escaped confinement. Prisoners were generally ignorant of the procedures required to secure a bond, with the result, as one Detroit court official noted, that they were "left to the unregulated and unsupervised mercies of unofficial informants. . . ." Pending trial, many prisoners who could safely have been released on their own recognizance were held in jail, sometimes for long periods, simply because they were impecunious.[18]

Murphy understood that more would have to be done to deal with bail and bond abuses than simply to drive professional bondsmen from the court building—the remedy of the Big Four. Early in 1926, after seeking advice both inside and outside Detroit, Murphy submitted a comprehensive and intelligent plan to the court for the regulation of the bail-bond business. He acted on the premise, often forgotten in his day, often forgotten today, that the only purpose of bail is to secure the appearance in court of the accused and that it must not be used as a pretext to ensure the confinement of a defendant until the day of his trial.

Murphy's principal suggestion was the establishment of a properly staffed bond bureau as an adjunct of the court. No bond would be presented to a judge until it had been investigated by the bureau, which would also establish a fee schedule for bonds and would maintain a list of bondsmen who had agreed to comply with these rates. A representative of the bureau would make a daily visit to the jail to advise the prisoners of the facilities of the bureau and to provide them with the opportunity to submit applications for bonds. Since Murphy was aware that many prisoners remained in jail for long periods because there had been no time at their arraignment for a judge to investigate their reliability, he also proposed that a bureau representative be present when defendants were arraigned and that he conduct an investigation that same day of all defendants for whom bail had been fixed and who were without funds to pay the fee for a bond. On the basis of this information, the judge could admit the accused to bail on a personal bond the next morning if that seemed appropriate.

Murphy was also concerned about the disposition of prisoners arrested at night when the ordinary facilities for release were not available. It was a police decision whether or not to release such prisoners pending their appearance in court the next morning; and since officials, "influential friends," and professional bondsmen might attempt to influence that decision, "all sorts of abuses, improper practices and favoritism" resulted. Murphy therefore suggested that the bond bureau, in these circumstances, be empowered to accept deposits, in lieu of bonds, from those charged with misdemeanors, the deposits to be scaled in accordance with the nature of the alleged offense. This would protect citizens from unnecessary imprisonment and would protect the police department against "the constant efforts of influence, privilege and corruption."

When Murphy's bond-bureau proposal was presented to the court, Judge Charles Bartlett hailed it as "the best plan thus far offered to the Recorder's Court"; but the court took no immediate action on the recommendation. At the end of 1930, however, the judges agreed to establish a bail-bond bureau as an adjunct of the court, which was the heart of the Murphy proposal. The new plan was soon hailed as a phenomenal success.[19]

Successful to a large degree in his efforts to reform the bail-bond system, Murphy failed to secure the implementation of other reforms that he championed while on the court. Among these, the one that interested him the most was the appointment of a public defender as a court functionary. Most states recognized the right to counsel of the indigent accused by providing for the assignment of lawyers by the court where necessary, but only ten states (including Michigan) provided for compensation by the state in all such cases; nineteen states provided for compensation only in capital cases. The system was a defective one at best since the courts generally assigned either young and inexperienced attorneys or "old shysters"'to defend the indigent. Four states and, in addition, four cities had provided for public defenders by the time Murphy became a judge, and he lent his support in 1925 to the effort to add Michigan to the list, but the state legislature was unresponsive.[20]

Toward the end of his tenure on the Recorder's Court Murphy began to stress the high cost of the assignment system as compared to the public-defender device. Partly because the legislature in 1927 had removed the previous ceilings on fees—$250 in a murder case and $100 in other cases—the assignment costs for the Recorder's Court zoomed to about $90,000 per annum in 1928 and 1929, more than double the cost in Murphy's first year on the court. Murphy contended that three competent public defenders could perform the same service at one-third the cost, and he charged that certain attorneys, jail deputies, and police officers had combined to bilk the public of thousands of dollars in assignment fees in what was reaching the "proportions of a public scandal." Although he failed to win the necessary support for the adoption of a public-defender system, the judges agreed to a schedule of fees for assignments that reduced the average stipend by 28 percent and that was expected to save the taxpayers $40,000 per year without impairing the quality of legal service provided.[21]

As a candidate in 1923 Murphy had favored the expanded use of the night court instituted by the Big Four, but he apparently acquiesced in the abandonment of this court shortly after he took his seat. He thought a night court "desirable," he asserted, but only if "the ideal conditions of co-operation" prevailed between police authorities, citizens, and the court, and he did not think that the Detroit court had conformed to that ideal. Under the law, the police were required to bring misdemeanants before a magistrate without delay, but since the police had not always complied with this requirement when defendants were seized at night, Murphy charged that there had been "a scramble on the part of vice leaders and others to get their cases over to the night court." The result, he alleged, was that the night court had proved to be "a dismal failure."[22]

The requirement that the police bring a prisoner before a magistrate "without unnecessary delay" spawned a band of "shyster" writ attorneys in Detroit who made their living tracking down prisoners and securing their release on writs of habeas corpus for a fee of anywhere from fifteen to thirty-five dollars. Sometimes the attorneys presented writs with as many as twelve to fifteen names on them. Soon after he became a judge, Murphy charged that the "ancient and sacred" writ of habeas corpus was being "cheapened" by this practice and that the reputation of the court was being damaged as a result. He believed in the "liberal construction" of the writ, he said, but he was disturbed that it had become "a weapon of the organized lawless and not of the oppressed or distressed of the community." Under the circumstances, he announced, he would not insist that the writ be returnable in less than twenty-four hours, the normal practice, unless the case was "meritorious." At the same time, he warned the police against making unnecessary arrests for harassment purposes, a tactic commonly employed by the police in Detroit and elsewhere.

As a matter of fact, the police were not altogether innocent parties in the alleged "cheapening" of the writ of habeas corpus in Detroit. To frustrate the writ attorneys and to detain prisoners whom they wished to hold beyond the legal period, the police devised the technique of the "trip 'around the loop,'" moving prisoners from one precinct station to another, perhaps to all fifteen of them, just ahead of attorneys who were seeking the prisoners' release. These prisoners often were not booked and were simply held incommunicado. A knowledgeable student of police behavior stated at the end of the decade that "few greater horrors have existed in this country than Detroit's Loop at the height of its glory."[23]

In 1928 the Recorder's Court judges met with the Wayne County prosecuting attorney to discuss the alleged abuse of the writ of habeas corpus. It was agreed that the police would normally not have to respond to the writ, even though it was supposedly returnable "forthwith," until twenty-four hours had elapsed. This meant, in effect, that there was to be "judicial tolerance for an extra day of unlawful detention" and that the court as a whole would henceforth follow the practice that Murphy had already adopted in his own court. There was "a certain understanding" that, in return for this concession, the police would treat their prisoners without "undue brutality," and judges like Murphy "dwelt upon this gain."[24]

The efficiency with which the court operated and the state of its docket were at issue throughout the period that Murphy served on the court. As it became clear at the end of 1924 that legislation would soon be introduced in Lansing to increase the number of judges on the Recorder's Court both because of its mounting case load and to obviate the necessity of building another county jail to accommodate the increasing number of prisoners awaiting trial, Murphy indicated that what was required was neither more judges nor another jail but "intelligence, common sense and discrimination in the handling of criminal problems with the present equipment." So much of a judge's time was taken up with "superficial and minor violations of the law," Murphy remarked, that he was not free to dispose of "serious criminal problems." Perhaps, Murphy advised, a separate court or bureau should be created to deal with minor offenses.[25] This sensible suggestion went almost unnoticed.

The bill that emerged from the legislature provided, in effect, for three additional Recorder's Court judges to be appointed by the governor to serve until the next court election. The Recorder's Court judges had agreed after some haggling to support legislation for two additional judges, and the author of the bill, Senator George Condon, had acceded to this arrangement but had then failed to implement its terms. Murphy was very much opposed to the legislation, ostensibly because he believed that the issue was the "character" of the court rather than its "size," but it may be that he shared the fear of the Detroit *Times* and Jeffries that the appointment by the governor of three new judges would mean three additional judges in the Keidan-Cotter camp and a five-five division on the court.

The Condon bill required the approval of the Detroit electorate before it could go into effect, but the Common Council decided not to place the measure on the April 6 city ballot, most likely because there had been insufficient time for the voters to consider the merits of the proposal. When Condon angrily charged that the Council had acted at the behest of the "ruling clique" of the court, Murphy loftily retorted, "If there is one court in the land free from group control or a faction among the judges, it is this court."[26]

The issue of three additional Recorder's Court judges once again became a matter of public controversy in September, 1925, and from then until the voters resolved the question at the polls on November 3, it was front-page news in Detroit. In addition to pointing out that the increase of the city's population by about 300,000 persons since 1919 in itself justified the expansion of the court's membership, the advocates of an enlarged court cited overcrowded jail conditions as evidence of the need for more criminal-court judges. Although it had been designed for 189 prisoners, there were normally 275 to 300 prisoners awaiting trial in the county jail; as of the beginning of September, 1925, the number was 517, the highest in the jail's history. Of these prisoners, 354 were awaiting trial in the Recorder's Court; the remainder were being held for other jurisdictions. In addition to the Recorder's Court prisoners, 500 defendants had been released on bond while they awaited examination, and this congestion of the docket, the Detroit *News* asserted, resulted in the "defeat of justice."[27]

The proponents of the three-judges bill also contended that the "slow operation of the courts" and the "uncertainty of punishment" had provided an "impetus" to crime in Detroit. Ignoring the fact that it was primarily prohibition and traffic violations that were clogging the court machinery and that the number of major crimes in the city seemed to be falling rather than rising, the *News* chose to believe that there was an "extraordinary outbreak of crime" in the city, that the Recorder's Court had "broken down under the strain," and that the reputation as an "easy city" that it was helping to give Detroit had attracted criminals to the area.[28]

With the exception of the Detroit *Free Press*, the same establishment forces that had supported the Big Four in 1923—the Detroit *News*, the Detroit *Saturday Night*, the Detroit Citizens League, and the Detroit Board of Commerce—were now the zealous advocates of the three-judges plan. It sounded like 1923 all over again when the *News* editorialized that the opposition had "the hearty support and cooperation of every crook, gunman, thief, hi-jacker, bootlegger and professional bondsman in Detroit." On the other hand, many of the opponents of the Big Four in 1923—the

Detroit *Times,* the DFL, and Judges Jeffries and Murphy—were
now arrayed against the three-judges bill. In a very real sense,
the entire contest over the enlargement of the court was a symbolic
struggle between the group that had been defeated in 1923 and
was now seeking to regain prestige and the victors in 1923, who
were anxious to defend their victory and the status quo.[29]

Intent on disproving the need for additional judges, Murphy,
as presiding judge in October, 1925, made a determined effort
to reduce the jail population and to cut down on the number
of cases awaiting trial. After the probation department had investigated the jail situation at his request, Murphy placed a major
share of the blame for the overcrowded conditions on the police
and the prosecutor's office. Sometimes, Murphy noted, the police
and the prosecutor simply forgot about the prisoners in the jail.
Although, according to Murphy, the procedure should not have
taken more than five days, he found men languishing in jail
for up to four weeks who had pleaded guilty when arraigned
on warrants but who were now simply waiting to be arraigned
on the information, which the prosecutor's office had been slow
to prepare. Murphy also discovered that it was not uncommon
for those who had pleaded not guilty to felony charges to remain
in jail for two months or more while the police and prosecutor
drew up the information. Some prisoners, of course, were in
jail simply because they could not afford bail even though there
was little reason to believe that they would not otherwise appear
for their preliminary examinations or trials. Murphy had uncovered
a situation that continues to plague the administration of criminal
justice.

Working closely with the prosecutor's office and the superintendent of police, Murphy began to cope with the " 'lost prisoner
epidemic.' " Aided by the probation department staff, he sought
to determine which prisoners could afford bail and which could
not, and he began releasing some of the latter on their personal
recognizance. He also urged the prosecutor to move for the
dismissal of bail cases in which the evidence was flimsy or the
witnesses were no longer available. As a result of Murphy's
initiative, the Recorder's Court jail population was reduced from
350 to 230, less than the average for the preceding several years,
and the number of felony cases awaiting trial, exclusive of
prohibition cases, was cut to a little more than five hundred.
The court's clerk asserted toward the end of October that Detroit's

criminal court was "ahead of any in the country as far as having the criminal situation in hand is concerned." The *Times* thought that Murphy had "riddled the arguments" for the three-judges bill and had singlehandedly "solved the court problem for Detroit," which accorded with Murphy's own estimate of the situation.[30]

The proponents of the enlarged court, not surprisingly, were not as impressed with Murphy's efforts as the *Times* and Murphy himself were, and there were allegations that Murphy was attempting to solve the jail problem by releasing dangerous criminals on their own recognizance. Even the respected Keidan wondered whether the court was "going to jeopardize the lives and properties of residents of the community by turning loose dangerous men just . . . to save the cost of three additional judges."[31]

The final decision on the three-judges plan rested with the voters of Detroit, and they approved the proposal on November 3 by the extremely narrow margin of 744 votes. This was undoubtedly the correct decision in view of the increase in the city's population and the court's case load—Detroit had fewer criminal-court judges per capita than any major American city—but the solution of the criminal-court problem also required the use of the sensible methods that Murphy had employed to reduce the jail population and to cut the time between arrest and trial.[32]

In addition to the increase in the membership of the court,[33] some procedural changes were also introduced while Murphy was on the court that expedited the administration of criminal justice. In December, 1925, Murphy and Keidan devised a new method of impaneling juries that was intended to forestall delays that had occurred in the jury selection process. Whereas the procedure had been for the court to use a single large panel of veniremen and for the entire panel to be assigned to one judge until a jury had been drawn for the trial in that court, the panel was now split into units of fifteen veniremen, each unit was assigned to a different courtroom, and the remaining veniremen were kept in reserve. This permitted the simultaneous selection of several juries, whereas before the selection of a jury for one courtroom had to be delayed while a jury was being picked for another courtroom.[34]

A significant change in procedure was introduced in 1927 when the Michigan legislature, in revising the state's Code of Criminal Procedure, followed the practice of five other states and stipulated that a defendant in a felony case could waive his right to a jury trial and opt to have the case tried by a judge alone. Misdemeanor trials in Michigan were already held without a jury unless the defendant demanded one either before his hearing or in appealing his conviction, but juries had heretofore been required in all felony cases. In addition, the revised code, in accordance with the long-standing recommendation of leading jurists, provided that if the defense in a criminal trial intended to make an "alibi" or a plea of insanity the basis of its case, it had to notify the prosecution in advance and provide the names of its witnesses.

During the first year the new waiver option was in effect the median time for the completion of a felony case was 31.78 days for cases tried by the judge alone as compared to 33.28 days for cases tried by juries. Judges and prosecuting officials were pleased with the revised code, and Murphy noted in March, 1928, that he had been able to try as many as twelve felony cases a day without a jury as compared to a maximum of three cases a day with a jury.[35]

In the months that Murphy served as presiding judge after the approval of the three-judges bill, he sought by one means or another to reduce the jail population and to clean up the court's docket of bail and jail cases. He continued to release defendants on their own recognizance when he thought this was warranted, to set bail at low sums in other instances, and to insist that the police and the prosecutor be ready for trial at the designated time to ensure that justice would be "swift and certain." In June, 1926, he arranged to have defendants wanting to plead guilty brought before him at once and their cases kept off the docket; in March, 1927, he worked out a plan with the court clerk, the docket clerk, and the prosecutor's office to provide for the trial of major felony cases within two weeks; and in August, 1929, he ordered every case pending called for trial.

When Murphy completed his term as presiding judge in March, 1927, there were only 108 Recorder's Court prisoners in the county jail, and only six of them had been imprisoned for as much as six days. The next year, in November, Murphy reduced the total number of bail and jail cases awaiting trial to 157, a record that the docket clerk hailed as far surpassing "anything we experienced in the last 10 years." Murphy's conclusion on the basis of his court service was that, normally, no more than three weeks should elapse between an arrest and the imposition of the sentence and that this could be achieved if the judge, the police, and the prosecutor's office cooperated and the judge resisted adjournments occasioned by "influence or neglect." "The law's delay," he wrote, "is a scandal and evil and is not in the interest of anyone."[36]

Murphy's performances as presiding judge were praised by the Detroit *Times,* the clerk of the court, the prosecutor, and the police. Although there would continue to be allegations, largely unsupported, that he was "throwing potential criminals back upon the streets" and coddling felons—"Every thing points to the fact that you and the thugs are very close friends. Hope you get what is coming to you," an anonymous correspondent wrote him after he completed one of his terms as presiding judge—there is no doubt that the excellent condition of the Recorder's Court docket in 1930 was at least partly due to Murphy's exertions and the procedures that he had helped to devise.[37]

The work load of the court, as we have seen, was materially affected by the large number of cases stemming from the violation of traffic laws and ordinances, a phenomenon that court systems throughout the country were not prepared to meet. The procedure of the Recorder's Court as of January 1, 1924, was for a different judge to deal with traffic cases each month, a practice that led to delays, postponements, and differing interpretations of the law. It was obvious that some better method had to be found to cope with this problem, and the judges experimented with various techniques until the decision was made to establish a separate traffic and ordinance division of the court. By the beginning of 1929 Murphy, like some of the other judges, had become concerned about the "casual consideration of traffic crimes" and the lack of data available to the judges in dealing with traffic violations, and he had concluded that the establishment of a separate traffic court was the most intelligent way to meet these problems.[38]

In November, 1929, the voters of Detroit approved a state law adding two judges to the Recorder's Court to preside over a new "traffic and ordinance division" that was given original and exclusive jurisdiction over all traffic offenses arising under state laws and city ordinances and over the violation of all other city ordinances as well. The new division, which as the first "independent" traffic court in the United States maintained the record for innovation of the Recorder's Court, began to operate on

January 2, 1930. Although technically a part of the Recorder's Court, it functioned essentially as an independent court, popularly known as "The Traffic Court."[39]

II

". . . the administration of criminal justice," Raymond Moley has observed, "is a government of men, not laws."[40] In the final analysis, it was less the procedures that were followed and the court machinery that was devised than it was the character and ability of the judges themselves that determined the quality of justice dispensed in the courtrooms of the Recorder's Court of Detroit.

Murphy insisted on absolute quiet and the observance of the rules of good behavior in his courtroom—court employees called him " 'Father Murphy' " partly for this reason. Although he was very considerate of the attorneys appearing before him, he did not like lawyers to delay a trial by dilatory tactics or to "translate the trial of the issue into a staged theatrical skit, so as to distract the jury from the consideration of the issue." Murphy's charges to the jury were generally very carefully worked out; a long-time observer of the court has described some of them as "classic."[41]

A Detroit *Free Press* reporter has left us a picture of Murphy presiding at early sessions court and looking over the "human wreckage" that the police had gathered during the night for his judicial ministrations. "It was an interesting clinical study—men and women, young and old, drifters, prostitutes, drunks, petty thieves, wife-beaters; an ethnological potpourri." The police had little interest in who these people were and what had brought them there, but Murphy, the reporter noted, "likes to study the wreckage. Sometimes he seeks to salvage fragments of it by granting a parole, exercising judicial clemency or handing out advice." A semiliterate Detroiter who had visited Murphy's courtroom on two occasions in March, 1927, wrote to congratulate the judge "on the way you handle the peoples That comes before you. you seem to consider that the unfortune are Human just as the fortunate." Murphy sometimes complained that presiding over early sessions court was taxing and "irritating work"—there might be two hundred cases in a single day—but it was the role he played in this court, the opportunity to "bring light to the awful procession of sorrows" before him, that he probably found most satisfying while he was a Recorder's Court judge.[42]

Murphy's behavior as a judge, his reaction to the defendants before him, and the sentences that he meted out were necessarily influenced by his view of crime and criminal behavior. Proclaiming "the growth of crime" to be "the paramount problem of the hour," Murphy, in 1928, characterized the "almost universal lawlessness" in the United States as "a national disgrace and a national menace." He regarded the existing machinery for the administration of criminal justice as inadequate to cope with the problem and as a "dismal" and costly failure. "Politics," he feared, "have been substituted for science, intolerance for intelligence and waste for economy in crime handling," and what was needed was a thorough investigation of the entire problem. Such a study, Murphy thought, should determine whether the length of time between arrest and conviction had any effect on the amount of crime, whether the detention or the release on bond of the accused affected the number or type of crimes, whether certain personality types were associated with certain types of crimes, and whether there was any relationship between the physical, mental, social, and economic history of the criminal and the kind of crime that he committed.[43]

Murphy was concerned about the large number of persons arrested as compared to the number actually taken to court. In Detroit, for example, the police arrested 69,926 persons in 1925, but legal proceedings were initiated against only 37,213 of this number, 8,845 of whom were then acquitted. The high percentage, as compared to England and Canada, of persons arrested who were either released or acquitted after being taken to court indicated, Murphy thought, that innocent persons were being arrested or the guilty were escaping punishment, and either explanation meant that a "crime producing situation" existed. Murphy was pointing to a basic shortcoming in the system of criminal justice that remains unchanged to the present day.

Murphy thought that the large number of arrests by the police that did not lead to judicial processing almost certainly was evidence of an "abuse of authority." He was inclined to believe, moreover, that the police were trigger-happy, and he wondered, for example, how many of the forty-nine persons slain by the police in 1926 had been killed unnecessarily. He thought that the police spent too much time on "trivial inconsequential matters" rather than directing their efforts against "the organized lawless," and he was appalled at the number of police who were themselves tried as lawbreakers. At the same time, Murphy was troubled that there was "a feeling abroad that the government and its agencies have a right to deal with and handle the citizen more or less cavalierly. . . . We are often a little slothful and drowsy about this precious right we call liberty," Murphy remarked; "so long as we individually are not hurt, we look with indifference upon the chains forged for our fellows. . . . We forget that it might be our turn next to feel the heel of injustice upon our necks."[44]

Murphy thought that the more careful selection of police officers was one means of coping with the problem of police misbehavior. Police recruits, he recommended, should be required to pass psychiatric tests as well as physical examinations. He believed that the training and discipline of the police also had to be "greatly improved" and that the police had to be educated to respect the rights of citizens and to avoid illegal arrests and illegal searches and seizures. The courts too, Murphy pointed out, should not be viewed as "mere agencies for the punishment of law-breakers," for they had an equal responsibility "to protect the rights and liberties of citizens from invasions in any quarter. . . . In the temple of justice, due need of honor is to be paid to the majesty of the law; but, there too must abide a virile, vigilant concern for that liberty for whose secure protection governments and laws are instituted among men."[45] As Recorder's Court judge, mayor of Detroit, and justice of the United States Supreme Court, Murphy demonstrated that the criteria for the behavior of the police and the criminal courts that he had set forth were not just rhetoric.

His years on the Recorder's Court, Murphy later wrote, gave him both sympathy for and understanding of làwbreakers and convinced him that many of them were "good men" who had been "led astray through a combination of circumstances for which they are by no means entirely responsible." Although he was willing to concede that hereditary factors played a part in crime, Murphy's explanation of crime, as he had made evident in the 1923 Recorder's Court campaign, was essentially environmental. ". . . the problem of crime," he declared in somewhat overblown rhetoric, "is interwoven with social and economic conditions. . . . The squalor of the cradle in the unlighted, unheated attic of the city slum is where we must begin our study of crime, for it is there that crime is spawned and nurtured into evil deeds; and those who would solve the problem of crime will do well to seek its causes at their source, and strive to apply the remedy at the beginning rather than at the end of a sordid life story."[46]

An advocate of reformative justice, Murphy deplored the "unreasoning clamor" in Michigan in the 1920s for "the punitive administration of criminal justice," manifested in the demand for capital punishment, the use of the whipping post, and the imposition of statutory limitations on judicial discretion. The purpose of judicial punishment, as he saw it, was to reform and to regenerate the criminal, and he did not believe that crime could be deterred by severe punishment. He was not suggesting that criminals should be coddled, but severity alone, he remarked, "too often crushes out what good there is left in the criminal, and generates in him a rancor and a hatred and a fear."[47]

Early in 1927 "a terrifying succession of holdups, daylight robberies, shootings and murderous raids by gunmen" led the Detroit *News,* the Detroit *Free Press,* and the Detroit *Saturday Night* to call for a return to capital punishment, which had been abolished in Michigan in 1846, and bills to this effect were introduced in the state legislature. The Detroit *Times,* which opposed capital punishment, thereupon arranged a radio debate on the subject between Harry M. Nimmo, the acidulous editor of the Detroit *Saturday Night,* and Frank Murphy, who by then was one of the best-known foes of capital punishment in the state. Since a Detroit policeman had been murdered a few days before the debate, Murphy was warned by one of his correspondents that he would be making "the greatest error of his life" in attacking capital punishment. Murphy later wrote this person that the effect of his "very offensive letter" had been "to move me to my best effort."[48]

The capital punishment debate, which was heard by a large audience across the state, was carried by radio receivers into the chambers of the state legislature in Lansing. Nimmo insisted that capital punishment deterred homicides, and he ridiculed those who thought that criminals were really sick people and consequently saw hospitalization as the cure for crime. "Examining heads," he remarked with obvious reference to men like Murphy, "has become a passion among the reformers and redeemers who hope to save society by saving the crook first. . . . Have we gone mad with mush?," he asked.

"Thou shalt not kill!," Murphy responded, was an imperative from Mt. Sinai and had been "the cornerstone of civilization" since that time. Now, however, it was proposed to make Michigan a " 'killer.' " The restoration of capital punishment, Murphy pointed out, would obviously not serve the purposes of reformative justice— "You will not reform any man by hanging him"—and, citing an impressive array of statistics to demonstrate that the homicide rate was little affected by the type of penalty imposed, he contended that capital punishment could not be justified as a deterrent either. If advocates of the death sentence really believed that it was a deterrent, Murphy asked, "why do they not go the length of their logic and demand that the clock be turned back and that we restore burning, drawing and quartering, breaking on the wheel, crucifixion, suffocation, stoning, sawing asunder, flaying alive, burning alive, impaling, the drinking of molten lead . . . ?"[49]

Murphy and Nimmo were both invited to address the legislature after their debate, and both were deluged with mail. Some of Murphy's correspondents disagreed with his idea of "humane treatment for thugs," but mostly his speech drew praise. "I think you have expressed in beautiful language the sentiments of every liberal-minded son of Adam . . . ," a Detroit *Free Press* reporter, disagreeing with the publisher of his paper, wrote Murphy. "You have won the fight from every angle of attack—facts, history, reason, philosophy, progress." Although his friend Selden Dickinson chided Murphy that he was "all wet" on the issue and was "a sentimental Mick with your head in the clouds," Dickinson nevertheless thought that the talk was the "most effective thing" that Murphy had done. When the capital punishment bill died in the legislature a few weeks after the debate, some observers thought that this was a personal victory for Murphy.[50]

When, in 1927, the Michigan House of Representatives approved a bill to restore the whipping post, Murphy lambasted the measure as "a return to barbarism." "It is a further effort," he declared, "to substitute passion and hate for reason and science in the administration of penal justice." The bill died in the senate, but the state legislature, in revising the Code of Criminal Procedure that same year, increased the penalties for multiple offenders in felony cases and limited the discretion of judges in placing criminals on probation, provisions that were not at all pleasing to Murphy.[51]

Murphy's belief in reformative justice led him to stress "the individualization of penal treatment" as "the most important truth that needs to be learned today." The sentence that a judge imposed, he contended, should be "for that man, and for the cause of that man's crime," an enlightened position when one considers that the criminal law was "a rather crude affair." If sentences were to be individualized, Murphy realized that judges would have to be fortified with a good deal of information about the life history of the individual criminal and "all the influencing circumstances." He thought that every person convicted of crime should be referred for a complete medical, psychiatric, and social investigation before the judge pronounced sentence upon him. Much of the investigatory work could be performed by probation officials and psychiatrists, but, in addition, Murphy proposed that a court statistician be appointed in each criminal court to coordinate the information provided by various agencies and to compile a record of changing social and economic conditions in the community as well.[52] Although this recommendation for the appointment of a court statistician was not followed in Detroit, Murphy, as we shall see, found other means of implementing his views concerning sentencing and the individualized treatment of felons.

While writing his book on the nation's criminal courts in the late 1920s, Raymond Moley sat on the bench for a day with Judge Murphy and was "struck . . . by his somewhat excessive sympathy for the characters who came before him." Murphy came to be known as a "soft judge," a characterization that stemmed from the compassion he so obviously felt for those whom he had to sentence. "You know how little I want anyone to suffer or go to prison," he wrote Marguerite early in 1926. "I don't want that to happen to rich or poor." On one occasion Murphy sentenced a group of gunmen to prison for from ten to thirty years. He recognized that they were "genuinely vicious and bad" and had to be confined for the safety of the community, but he nevertheless wrote Hester, "I believe I suffered more than anyone save their mothers over it [the sentence]. . . . I'm no good for this sort of thing." He referred later to hearing confessions on the Recorder's Court and "expiring a little each time" he had "to take part of another man's life from him." The Supreme Court, he wrote while he was an associate justice, "is not without its hours of anguish, but the burden is lighter on one's mind than duties in the Recorders [*sic*] Court."[53]

Whenever possible, Murphy placed first offenders on probation, and even persons with a record were sometimes accorded the same treatment. In 1926 two blacks were convicted in Murphy's court on a charge of simple larceny for stealing food. Murphy placed the offenders on probation after pointing out that the wages the two men earned were below what economists considered to be a living wage. "Fortunately," the Detroit *Labor News* commented, "there was one up on the bench with sufficient

vision to see beyond the bare testimony in the case and . . .
to seek out the facts" that had led to the crime. Another time
Murphy placed six offenders on probation after first speaking
to them in a paternal way—"It was as if a kindly but really
grieved father was admonishing his wayward child." Although
one of the men had already served an eleven-month sentence
for auto theft, Murphy nevertheless decided that the influence
of his home would have a better effect on him than prison would.[54]

It is easy to find other examples of Murphy's alleged "softness"
and sentimentality. He wrote Hester one day that he had been
"merciful" that morning since he had returned a man to his wife
and children after he had languished in jail for three months while
awaiting trial; Murphy knew that the accused was a good man
because his boys loved him. Murphy imposed a thirty-day sentence
on another man who had been in court on five occasions for failure
to support his wife, but when the offender's eleven-year-old son
spoke up and said that the family would starve if the father, who
had allegedly found a job, were placed in prison, Murphy vacated
the sentence. "I want mercy," Murphy wrote his brother George.
"I don't believe in the other [punishment] much and I do a great
deal in mercy."

Murphy was inclined to give the accused the benefit of the doubt,
to assume that life had been "unkind" to them and that they were
"weak" rather than "vicious." He often met privately with a felon
before sentencing him so that the offender would not be shocked
when the sentence was announced in the courtroom. Murphy once
spent three hours with a convicted murderer and his wife before
he imposed a life sentence on the felon.[55]

Despite his compassionate behavior, it would be a mistake to
think of Murphy as having "gone mad with mush," to use Harry
Nimmo's phrase. The Detroit Citizens League, which took a strict
law-and-order approach to the problem of criminal justice, found
Murphy's rulings hostile to the police in many instances but
nevertheless concluded in 1929 that his sentences in felony cases,
like armed robbery, were "adequate" and sometimes "heavy," and
it also characterized his record in typical misdemeanor cases as
"satisfactory." Where the League thought Murphy "lenient" was
in his treatment of prohibition and sex cases, and there is no doubt
that the Catholic Murphy did not approach cases of this sort in
the "moralistic" manner that the Citizens League and many Protestant clergymen in Detroit did. "Some Catholic cultures," Daniel
Bell has written in words that apply on the whole to Murphy,

"worldly in their wisdom and tolerant of human frailties, do not look with horror at gambling, drink, or even easy going sexual conduct; disapproval is tempered with a sense of the inevitability of sin, and salvation is of the other world, not this. . . ." Unlike the moralists, Murphy thought that the nation had gone too far in regulating personal conduct, and when he talked of "absurd laws" and "bad laws," he was generally referring to measures like the prohibition statutes. More than religion, however, was involved in Murphy's reaction to offenses in the area of moral behavior: what the law categorized as crime, Murphy thought was sometimes better diagnosed as illness or social maladjustment, and the remedy, he consequently believed, was to be found outside rather than inside a court of law.[56]

Unlike some of his judicial colleagues, Murphy was disinclined to send drunks to jail and normally gave them the alternative of paying a fine to escape imprisonment. When the state legislature in 1927 made a prison sentence mandatory for prohibition violators, Murphy was sharply critical of the action. Imprisonment, as he saw it, was a "meaningless" way to deal with someone who harmed only himself by his behavior. While he was presiding judge in October, 1925, Murphy released on their own recognizance all prisoners jailed on liquor charges who were family men.[57]

Murphy's attitude regarding prohibition offenses was nicely illustrated in two cases coming before him during his first year on the bench. A man arrested for drunkenness was taken before Judge Stein one day and fined five dollars; the same individual was arrested on a similar charge later in the day and this time was brought before Murphy, who suspended the sentence on the grounds that five dollars was a sufficient fine to pay for the liquor offenses of a single day. A few months later Tommy Teahan made his eightieth appearance for drunkenness in Recorder's Court, but when he promised to behave in the future, as he always promised to do, Murphy placed him on probation for one month. Teahan, Murphy wrote Hester, was a "happy, harmless and hopeless Irishman" whom she would simply "adore."[58]

Murphy believed that it was "unmerciful" to punish drug addicts by sending them to jail, and he failed to see how this benefited either the addicts or society. The problem, in Murphy's opinion, was more a medical than a legal one, and he thought that public institutions should be established to treat addicts for their malady. As for gambling, when the police in 1925 arrested eleven blacks for " 'frequenting' " a gambling place, Murphy rebuked the officers for paying so much attention to "this small fry" and admonished them, if they were serious about enforcing the antigambling laws, to concentrate on the "big flourishing gambling dens where you know commercialized games take place constantly instead of going out of your way to break up some little back alley dice game." He had to find the eleven men guilty, but he suspended their sentences.[59]

Murphy did not like to hear prostitution cases, thinking that this was more appropriately a task for a social worker—the "victims of social maladies," he believed, should receive "social treatment." He was quite "lenient" in dealing with prostitutes and was obviously one of the targets when the Detroit Council of Churches criticized the Recorder's Court for " 'using the technicalities of the law' " in vice cases.

Murphy thought that in dealing with prostitution law-enforcement officials should direct their main effort not at the prostitute but rather at the owners of disorderly houses and the men who frequented these establishments. When the police soon after he ascended the bench arrested several prostitutes who were "window tapping," Murphy wanted to know why the prosecutor and the police had selected "the most superficial and ineffective" approach to the problem instead of padlocking the disorderly houses, prosecuting their proprietors, and arresting the male customers. Murphy consistently criticized the police for using the customers of prostitutes as witnesses in vice cases but then failing to bring charges against these men, and he agreed with the National Women's party that legislation should be enacted making both parties guilty in prostitution cases. Laws that set a double standard of justice, he asserted, are "unjust and eventually become a vicious influence against law enforcement."[60]

A consistent advocate of the view that a judge should tailor the punishment to fit the criminal, Murphy, from the beginning of his service on the Recorder's Court, took full advantage of the facilities of the probation department and psychopathic clinic in an effort to individualize the sentences that he imposed and to decide which prisoners were good probation risks. It was not, however, until the end of 1929 or the very beginning of 1930 that Murphy, acting on the idea that he had advanced in his plea for a court statistician and influenced by developments in Mexico and possibly by a 1927 suggestion of Governor Alfred E. Smith, formally put into effect a new sentencing procedure for felony cases in his court.

As before, Murphy referred felons to the probation department and psychopathic clinic for "complete examination and research." The information thus gathered was placed on a form, with entries made in each case for the economic status of the felon, previous offenses on his record, his physical condition, hereditary factors, psychiatric factors, and environmental factors (family situation, domestic situation).[61]

The next stage of the new sentencing procedure involved the distinctive feature of the Murphy plan, the use of a sentencing board consisting of Murphy and the heads of the probation department and the psychopathic clinic. The establishment of the board was designed "to minimize the effect of judicial temperament in passing sentence" by giving the judge the benefit of expert counsel at the decision-making stage of the sentencing procedure. The sentencing board met with the prisoner, and on the basis of the information that was by then available decided, within the limits defined by the law, on the proper sentence for the felon and for society as well. Murphy, of course, did not have to follow the advice of the other members of the board. "This is the only human and intelligent way to sentence felons," he announced. "It means neither severity or [sic] leniency but a calm and scientific inquiry which is fair, not only to the defendant but to the public."[62]

The manner in which Murphy's sentencing plan was implemented is illustrated by two cases, one involving rape, the other armed robbery. The examination of the felon convicted of statutory rape revealed certain character problems associated with his use of alcohol. The sentencing board decided that the rapist, who had a dependent family, should be placed on probation, the condition being that he was forbidden to drink. The armed robber was one of two youths of nineteen, neither of them a habitual criminal. One of the two entered a not-guilty plea, stood trial before one of Murphy's colleagues, and received a twenty-to-forty year sentence. When the other youth pleaded guilty in Murphy's court, Murphy's sentencing procedure convinced him that the criminal behavior of the young man was unlikely to recur, and so he sentenced the offender to two years in the reformatory.[63]

The Murphy "crime clinic" attracted a good deal of attention outside Detroit. It was the subject of articles in the *Nation* and *Literary Digest,* was lauded by a writer in the Cleveland *Press,* and was hailed by *Survey* as "the greatest contribution to criminology that has been made in 25 years." "The press of the country," Murphy wrote Hester, "is paying tribute to a sincere effort I am making to eliminate hate and vengeance in handling the thousands of unfortunates in the sorrowful procession through the nation's courts." Murphy informed Dean Henry M. Bates that the sentencing plan was eliciting comment from "judges, prison wardens and college professors in various parts of the country." The interest of prison wardens was natural enough since a logical corollary of Murphy's plan was the segregation of prisoners by type of offense. Murphy, as a matter of fact, urged Governor Fred W. Green to appoint a commission of criminologists and sociologists to examine Michigan's prisoners with a view to their ultimate segregation. Green thought that the idea was sound, but he advised Murphy that funds were lacking for its implementation.[64] It remained for Frank Murphy to put the proposal into effect when he himself became Michigan's governor.

VII

"True Justice Does Not Recognize Color"

I

Once on the bench Murphy did not forget his campaign assertions that the friendless, the weak, and the poor received something less than equal justice in the courts. Murphy's critics, however, contended that his commitment to "evenness" in the application of the law was tempered by an undue solicitude for the underdog and that even if he was correct in his view that judges like William Heston leaned too far in one direction in the application of the law, Murphy could be accused of leaning too far in the other.

That the friendless had found a friend in Judge Murphy there was no doubt. One of their number who had watched Murphy in operation wrote the judge, "I taken notice to the way you treat peoples, both white and black. And the smile you wear in performing your duties. the rich man always Did get justice in court for his money gets it for him. but when you See a poor man that is down and out come into court and is given a Square deal as you gives a man, then it is time to take notice and Say, that there is still justice in the courts."[1] This, we can be sure, was the verdict of many unfortunate defendants who appeared in Murphy's court.

In terms of his subsequent career, Murphy's application of his brand of equal justice in cases involving organized labor and blacks was of greatest significance. The Detroit Federation of Labor (DFL), which complained about the treatment of organized labor by some Recorder's Court judges, was entirely satisfied with the performance of Judge Murphy. In 1925 two unionists were brought before Murphy on assault charges stemming from a clash between union pickets and company agents during the course of a strike against the C. B. Sheppard Company by the

145

Metal Polishers Union. Murphy, playing a role far different from the one he had played while working for Monaghan and Monaghan, acquitted the two men and observed that he knew from experience that employers often charged workers with violence in labor disputes even though the employers themselves were the guilty parties. He accused the prosecutor's office of behaving in an unneutral manner in strikes, asserting that this created the "dangerous" impression that "the state is on the side of the employers." Perhaps it was this admonition that led the prosecutor's office soon thereafter to bring charges of "felonious assault" against the employment officer of C. B. Sheppard and a company "thug" for attacking union pickets. "Labor men in general," the organ of the DFL declared, "are pleased to have a judge with such a clear vision and the courage to state his view upon the bench."[2]

During a strike of Waiters and Waitresses Local Union No. 705 against a Detroit café in 1929, a plainclothesman arrested Sarainne Loewe, a union organizer, because she took exception to some remarks he had made to unionists standing near the café. When a passerby objected to what he regarded as the police officer's "rough handling" of Miss Loewe, the plainclothesman arrested him on a charge of interfering with an officer. Miss Loewe and her defender were brought before Judge Murphy, who dismissed the charges against both of them and called the passerby a "hero." Sarainne Loewe became a lifelong supporter of Frank Murphy.[3]

Murphy was convinced not only that the Detroit police were more likely to arrest blacks than whites and to engage in illegal searches of black homes than white ones but also that the judges and juries of the Recorder's Court were unconsciously prejudiced against blacks.[4] Whatever the quality of justice dispensed to the black man in other courts, Murphy was determined that blacks would receive equal justice in Judge Murphy's court. The now famous Sweet trials of 1925 and 1926 presented Murphy with a golden opportunity to act on this determination before an audience that was far larger than the throng of spectators who daily crowded his courtroom.

The Sweet trials stemmed directly from the efforts of some Detroit blacks to escape the black ghetto and to find more satisfactory housing elsewhere in the city. When Dr. Alexander L. Turner moved into his newly acquired home on Spokane Avenue in June, 1925, it was against a backdrop of at least three attempts by whites earlier in the year to intimidate and terrorize blacks who had had the temerity to seek housing in white neighborhoods. "Several thousand" whites welcomed Dr. Turner to his new home with a hail of stones and bricks. They broke every window in the house and tore the tiles from the roof. After "one stormy day" of tenancy Dr. Turner sold the property and fled the neighborhood.

The next month Vollington Bristol, a black undertaker, moved into a house that he had built just on the boundary line of a West Side black district. As whites besieged the house, blacks began to collect near the property, and the police intervened. Stones were thrown at the house, and several hundred shots were fired as the blacks allegedly shouted, "'Shoot the cops.'" The police confiscated more than a score of weapons and arrested twenty-four blacks. A day or so later John W. Fletcher moved into a house in a white neighborhood and was greeted by the now familiar assemblage of white rock-throwers. This time shots were fired from the house, and a fifteen-year old youth outside the dwelling was wounded in the thigh. The police arrested Fletcher, but he was not indicted, allegedly because he had friends "high in power" in the city. Fletcher, however, decided to find a home somewhere else in Detroit.[5]

In a public statement on July 12, Mayor John W. Smith, apparently equating white mobs with blacks who were asserting their constitutional right to live where they pleased, blamed the recent spate of racial disturbances in Detroit on "thoughtless individual[s] of both races" but nevertheless asserted that he expected every policeman to enforce the law "impartially" and without distinction as to race or color. The report of Smith's statement in the Detroit *Free Press* was followed by a brief notice of a meeting called for July 14 by the Waterworks Improvement Association. Residents of the area were urged to attend "in self defense" and were asked, "'Do you want to maintain the existing good health conditions and environment for your children? Do you want to see your neighborhood kept up to its present high standard?'"[6] The reason for the meeting was the news that a house in the neighborhood, on the corner of Garland and Charlevoix, had been purchased by a black.

The buyer of the home at 2905 Garland was Dr. Ossian Sweet, who claimed, perhaps in jest, to be "the only man in America named after a fourth-century Irish warrior-lord." Sweet, "a well set up, broad-shouldered, quiet, firm-jawed, dignified man, with tired eyes," had been born in Orlando, Florida, and educated at Wilberforce and Howard University, where he received his M.D. He set up practice in Detroit in 1921 and the next year married Gladys Mitchell, the daughter of a well-off black family that lived in a white neighborhood. The Sweets went to Europe in 1924; Ossian studied pediatrics and gynecology in Vienna and radiology in Paris. Mrs. Sweet gave birth to a girl while in Paris but was denied admission to the American Hospital for the delivery because of her color.

After returning to Detroit, the Sweets, in June, 1925, purchased a house in a lower middle-class neighborhood of small entrepreneurs, salaried clerks, and factory workers. The neighborhood was on the decline, and the "economically insecure" residents, many of them of Polish, German, or Swedish extraction, feared that the entry of a black family would adversely affect property values. Dr. Sweet purchased the Garland Street property from Edward and Marie Smith—unbeknownst to the neighbors, Ed Smith, who was light-skinned, was a black. Sweet knew Dr. Turner and also was aware that Mrs. Smith's white neighbors had threatened "to 'get' her and 'get' " the purchaser of the house as well.[7]

When the Waterworks Improvement Association held its organizational meeting, one speaker recounted how the improvement association to which he belonged had succeeded in forcing Dr. Turner from his home, and there was talk about driving the Sweets from 2905 Garland. At a later meeting of the Waterworks organization, a realtor reportedly warned, " 'we'll load this nigger's goods on the same van that brings them out and send them back where they came from.' "[8]

Although Dr. Sweet knew that the situation was "ominous," he nevertheless decided to move into his house. He did so, he later indicated, perhaps exaggerating his original purpose, "only because my group had been chased all over town and there didn't seem to be anyone left who was willing to take the lead in the great fight to secure a decent place in which to live." " 'I felt,' " he declared, " 'that I could never respect myself if I allowed a gang of hoodlums to keep me out of it [the house].' "[9]

Dr. Sweet moved into his house on the morning of September 8, 1925, not looking for trouble but prepared to defend himself should trouble arise. In addition to his wife, Ossian was accompanied by his brother Otis, a dentist; his brother Henry, a law student at Wilberforce; John Latting, a friend of Henry; Joe Mack, who drove Dr. Sweet's car; Norris Murray, a handyman friend of Mack's; and William E. Davis, a black federal narcotics agent. The Sweets moved the few pieces of furniture that they owned into the house and also took with them enough food for several days, six revolvers, two rifles, one shotgun, and perhaps two thousand rounds of ammunition.

A crowd began to gather around the property in the evening that was large enough to frighten some of the people inside the dwelling. A total of eleven policemen were on hand, and Inspector of Detectives Robert A. McPherson entered the house to advise Dr. Sweet that the police were there to protect him. "Nothing eventful" happened that night although there was some "jeering" and a few rocks were apparently thrown at the house after midnight.[10]

By morning, all had returned to normal.[11] Dr. Sweet left the house to buy some furniture and invited three insurance agents, Leonard C. Morse, Charles B. Washington, and Hewitt Watson to join the group in 2509 Garland, bringing the total number of persons in the house to eleven. Gladys was preparing dinner when at about 8:00 p.m. something hit the house, and, according to Ossian, one of the men, looking outside, shouted, " 'The people, the people—we've got to get out of here.' " The size of the crowd outside became a critical issue later, with Dr. Sweet initially claiming that it rose to two thousand persons and others placing the figure as low as fifteen to twenty, but it would seem that about five hundred persons had gathered near the Sweet property. Eleven policemen were once again on duty outside the house, and so many people were driving to the scene that the police found it necessary to assign two additional men to divert traffic from Garland in the vicinity of the Sweet house.

The people attracted to the scene stationed themselves across the street from the Sweet home; there is no convincing evidence that anyone actually trespassed on the Sweet property. This is not to suggest that the temper of the crowd in the area was irenic. A passing automobile in which two blacks were riding, for example, was stoned and its front window broken while the crowd shouted, " 'There goes a Negro! Catch him. Stop him!' "

After stones began to hit the Sweet house, Ossian got a gun and went to his room. Soon a stone crashed through a window in the doctor's room. Sweet became very agitated, and there was "pandemonium" in the house. "Everybody ran from room to room," Dr. Sweet later testified. "I made a dozen trips up and down the stairs. It was a general uproar." A taxi drove up to the house carrying Otis Sweet and William Davis. Ossian opened the door for the two men, and as they rushed into the house, he heard the crowd screaming, "'They're niggers, get them.'" The mob surged forward. "It looked like a human sea," Dr. Sweet recalled. Stones continued to hit the house, and another front window was broken. Then, suddenly, shots rang out from several parts of the house—perhaps fifteen to twenty shots in all. Directly across the street from the house, forty-year old Leon Breiner, the father of two, shouted, "'My God, I'm hit,'" and fell dead from a bullet in the back. Twenty-two-year-old Eric Hougberg, standing near Breiner, sustained a bullet wound in the thigh.

Inspector Norton N. Schuknecht, the head of the police detail outside the Sweet home, entered the house after the shooting and demanded to know "'what in Hell are you fellows shooting about?'" "They are destroying my home," Dr. Sweet recalled having told the inspector, "and my life is in imminent danger." As Schuknecht remembered it, Dr. Sweet spoke only of the threat to his property, not to his life. The doctor showed the inspector the broken window in his room, and Schuknecht, not yet knowing of Breiner's death, stated that he had not been aware that stones had been thrown and that he would put a stop to this sort of thing. He left, but soon other police entered the house, and the eleven occupants were arrested and taken to police headquarters. The police searched the house and found ten guns, a large quantity of ammunition, fourteen shells that had been discharged from weapons of five different calibers, and cigar stubs, tobacco ashes, burnt matches, quilts, and chairs near the windows on the second floor where some of the men had apparently stationed themselves.

At police headquarters the defendants learned for the first time that they were being held on suspicion of murder. They were denied counsel when they requested it and were separately and vigorously questioned from shortly after 10:00 P.M. until 3:00 or 4:00 A.M. They were not abused physically, but some "harsh words," to quote Otis Sweet, were used by the interrogators, and Ossian said later that all the defendants would have been killed had it not been for one sympathetic lieutenant. "'Doctor, what business do you have moving into a white neighborhood where you are not wanted?,'" Ossian was asked. When approximately the same question was put to Mrs. Sweet, she replied forthrightly, "'I think it is my perfect right to move where I please.'" The defendants told stories at variance with one another, and Dr. Sweet, nervous and overwrought, obviously did not tell the truth. Only Henry Sweet would admit having fired a weapon—he had shot twice, he stated, the first time into the air, the second time "intending for my shot to go just above the top of the heads."[12]

It fell to Judge Murphy on September 10, on the recommendation of the prosecutor's office, to sign two criminal warrants for each of the defendants, one on the charge of "feloniously" and "wilfully" murdering Breiner and the other on the charge of assaulting Hougberg with the intent of murdering him. When the prisoners were arraigned on September 12, Judge John Faust set bail at $5,000 for each of them on the assault charge but denied bail to all the defendants on the murder charge, and so they remained in the Wayne County jail.[13]

The preliminary examination of the defendants was held before Judge Faust from September 16 to September 18. The police and other witnesses testified for the state that the shooting had been unprovoked and that there had been no more than a few people outside the Sweet house. "There were no unusual crowds, no disturbances and no provocation prior to the shooting," Schuknecht stated. Attorneys for the defendants moved to have the charges against their clients dismissed, but Faust denied the motion.[14]

Murphy became the presiding judge of the Recorder's Court on October 1, and two days later the attorneys for the respondents petitioned him to admit the defendants to bail. Murphy admitted Mrs. Sweet to $5,000 bail on the murder charge, and she was then able to leave the Wayne County jail, but it is not surprising in view of the nature of the charges against them that he denied the motion with regard to the other defendants. The defense attorneys then moved to quash the information and to have their clients discharged on the grounds that the preliminary examination had failed to show probable cause that they had killed Breiner or had conspired to do so, but Murphy denied the motion, thus leaving the issue for a jury to decide.[15]

As presiding judge, Murphy assigned the Sweet trial to himself. He told a friend that his colleagues on the bench wanted no part of the case, fearing that it was "dynamite" because of the hysteria prevailing in Detroit and failing to realize that it was "the opportunity of a lifetime to demonstrate sincere liberalism and judicial integrity." However other judges may have viewed the matter, there is no doubt that Murphy appreciated the possible importance of the case to his own career. Shortly before the trial began Moses L. Walker, the vice-president of the Detroit branch of the NAACP, wrote the national office that he had been confidentially advised that Murphy expected to run for mayor in two years and would "use this case to win the Negro vote. . . ." Walker reported that "a dear friend" of the Murphy family had said that the case provided Frank with " 'the opportunity to make known to Detroit and the Country, his positive stand against prejudice, and [to] build for himself a tower of strength among the Negroes as well as the better whites of Detroit.' " [16]

The Sweet case quickly took on national significance both because the National Association for the Advancement of Colored People (NAACP) decided to involve itself in the affair and because of the counsel that it engaged to defend the accused. A few days after the Sweets were arrested, Walter White, the NAACP's assistant secretary, journeyed to Detroit to appraise the situation. As he left New York, White wrote a friend that he was on his way to Detroit, "where a group of five thousand [?] Nordic gentlemen have been demonstrating their biological and mental superiority by attacking the home of a colored physician who was too prosperous 'for a Negro.' The police force kept their hands off and the mob got the surprise of its life when the colored doctor opened fire . . . , killing one of the heroes and wounding another. Then the police got busy and slapped the doctor, his wife and children [*sic*], and his friends in jail, refusing not only to permit bail but even to let counsel see them. Thus the Nordic is glorified!" [17]

White discovered in Detroit that the defendants' use of firearms had "served to alienate [the] sympathy of the decent white people to a degree" and that sentiment even among blacks was that the accused had fired too soon. White, moreover, formed a very poor opinion of the three black attorneys who were defending the accused. He described Julian W. Perry, who was Ossian's attorney, as "a man . . . [who] commands no respect as far as I can see either as a man or an attorney." Cecil L. Rowlette, whom Perry had brought into the case, struck White as "a blustering, noisy, pompous individual with a very inflated opinion of his own ability." White thought that Charles H. Mahoney, whom the Liberty Life Insurance Company had engaged to defend its three agents, was "by far the best lawyer and the most reliable of the three," but White's opinion was that all three attorneys were "trying to gobble all the fees and credit."

White concluded that it was essential for the NAACP to retain "an eminent white attorney" if the case were to be won. He sought to appease the black attorneys by arguing that to bring in a white attorney was no reflection on their competence but that what was at stake was "bigger than Detroit or Michigan even" since the case was "the dramatic climax of the nation-wide fight to enforce residential segregation." White approached several white attorneys in Detroit, but all were unwilling to participate.[18]

In the end, the NAACP decided to allow the defendants themselves to decide if white counsel should become associated with the case. White knew that a majority of the accused, believing that "the best legal talent available should be obtained to break-down a case that has been wickedly though very subtly and skillfully manufactured by the Police Department with and by the aid of the Prosecutor's Office," favored the employment of white counsel, and so, as White saw it, "It is just a little longer way around but the same results will be accomplished."[19]

The white attorney whom the NAACP invited to take the case was none other than Clarence Darrow, the most celebrated criminal lawyer in the United States. An NAACP delegation visited Darrow in New York and ascertained that he was "much interested." Darrow thought it essential that a white Detroit attorney be brought into the case, and he also wanted the NAACP to engage Arthur Garfield Hays, the famed civil-liberties lawyer who had worked with Darrow in the recently concluded Scopes trial. White and Arthur Spingarn, the chairman of the NAACP legal committee, journeyed to Detroit and conferred with the black lawyers and also with Frank Murphy, who was elliptically described as "very much interested." Darrow had originally asked for $50,000 for his services, but when he was told that the NAACP simply could not afford that sum, he agreed to serve for the modest fee of $5,000. Hays was to be paid $3,000; Walter Nelson, the white Detroit attorney whom Darrow recommended, received $2,000; and each of the black attorneys was paid $1,500. Darrow accepted the assignment, he later wrote, because he realized that "defending negroes, even in the North, was no boy's job, although boys were usually given the responsibility."[20]

Darrow's decision to enter the Sweet case, which "caused a sensation" in Detroit, changed the nature of the defense. The black attorneys had favored separate trials for each of the defendants since they thought that separate trials would reveal discrepancies in the testimony of prosecution witnesses that could then form the basis of appeals and might also cause the state to weary of the whole affair before all the defendants had been tried.

Darrow, however, preferred a collective trial because, the black attorneys correctly thought, he wanted to try the case "from a sociological standpoint."[21]

Since Darrow needed time to prepare his defense, he asked Murphy on October 16 for a continuance of the case until October 30. Murphy granted the request but was insistent, White reported, that there be no further delays since his term as presiding judge would come to an end on October 31, and he was most anxious to try the case himself. White was convinced by this time that Murphy was "one of the finest spirited men I have met." He had written Murphy after their first meeting, perhaps for tactical reasons but also because White believed it, that it had been "a most pleasant surprise to find one with such lofty ideals. It is so seldom that those of us who are trying to secure even-handed justice for Negro citizens encounter one like yourself you may well imagine our joy when that experience does come."[22]

On October 30 the NAACP launched a campaign to raise a $50,000 defense fund to defray the costs of the Sweet trial and two other cases that the Association was then pursuing through the courts. In good measure because of interest in the Sweet case, the NAACP raised about $75,000 for its new Legal Defense Fund by the middle of March, 1926. The total cost of the first Sweet trial was just under $22,000, toward which the national office contributed almost $12,600, the remainder being raised by the Detroit branch ($6,669) and a Detroit City-Wide Defense Committee ($2,650).[23]

The creation of the Legal Defense Fund, triggered by the Sweet case, was of considerable importance for the future of the NAACP because, as W. E. B. DuBois noted, it marked "the definite beginning" among blacks "of the habit of giving and of giving systematically for definite objects"; it was the first step in the establishment of what is today the Legal Defense and Education Fund. Appreciating the transcendent importance of the Sweet trial, the NAACP "whipped up every energy and [drew] upon every resource" in fighting the case. The United States Supreme Court had decided in Buchanan v. Worley (1917) that state laws and local ordinances requiring residential segregation were unconstitutional, and the NAACP was also seeking at the time of the Sweet case to persuade the Supreme Court to rule against the judicial enforcement of restrictive covenants. Victory in the Sweet case, the NAACP hoped, would put a halt to efforts to enforce residential segregation by mob action when the same result could no longer be accomplished by state and local legislation. The

Sweet case was thus for the NAACP "the dramatic high point" in a three-pronged attack on residential segregation.[24]

The first Sweet trial occurred at a time when racial and religious feelings in Detroit were already running high because of the bitter mayoralty contest between the Catholic John Smith and the Klan-supported Charles Bowles. In an open letter to the city's police commissioner on September 12, Smith blamed the recent racial disturbances in Detroit on the "criminal propaganda" of the Klan and accused the organization of attempting "secretly to set race against race, creed against creed, and group against group." Smith asserted that the police must protect the life and property of anyone moving into a new neighborhood but, graphically revealing the limits of his conception of racial equality, went on to "deprecate the moving of colored persons into neighborhoods in which their presence would cause disturbances. I believe," the mayor declared, "that any colored person who endangers life and property simply to gratify his personal pride, is an enemy of his race as well as an incitant of riot and murder." Smith followed up his statement by appointing an interracial committee, which Reinhold Niebuhr eventually headed, to ameliorate "the very unfortunate condition which has arisen recently."[25]

Smith's rhetoric and action further stimulated the Klan's effort to unseat him, and Kleagle Ira W. Stout soon appeared in Detroit to direct the Klan campaign. Klan-approved Council candidates fared well in the primary of October 6, two days before the NAACP requested Darrow to take the Sweet case. The election campaign was at its height when the process of selecting the jury for the Sweet trial was initiated, and the taking of testimony began two days after the November 3 election, in which Bowles lost by twenty-nine thousand votes.[26]

The selection of the jury, which began on October 30, 1925, was completed on November 4 after 108 veniremen had been examined. There were no blacks on the jury—the sole black man in the panel had been unacceptable to the prosecution—and no women. William Pickens, the NAACP's field secretary, thought that Darrow had "poor material . . . from which to sift a jury." Hays, however, recalled that the defense attorneys "were satisfied, or rather not dissatisfied, with the jury" since it was "about as good as we could get." "The case is won or lost now," Darrow remarked after the jury had been picked. "The rest is window dressing."[27]

One untoward incident occurred during the jury selection

process. When a prospective juror admitted racial prejudice, a few of the blacks who crowded the courtroom made some unpleasant remarks about the venireman. This led Murphy, who maintained a close relationship with White throughout the trial, to warn the NAACP representative that the defense would be "seriously damaged" if any more incidents of this sort took place. White passed this word along and also arranged for a half dozen "level headed people" to mingle with the crowd and to "keep down trouble." Murphy provided passes to the trial for the individuals in question.[28]

The trial, described by the Detroit *News* as "one of the most dramatic and bitterly fought cases ever witnessed in the local courts," played to an overflow audience from beginning to end. When Darrow complained to Murphy that court attendants gave preference to white spectators, Murphy apparently ordered that a certain proportion of the seats be reserved for blacks. As the trial continued, more blacks and fewer whites appeared for the daily court sessions.[29]

Murphy's view of the case, the attention that it was receiving, and his own role in the proceedings were nicely revealed in a letter that he wrote his sister as the trial was getting underway. "The Sweet trial," he declared with his customary appreciation of the dramatic, "is more or less of a big show." He noted that a dozen or more reporters representing newspapers in various parts of the country were present, and he was obviously pleased that a New York paper had wired for his picture. "Throughout it all," he asserted, "the question of how to secure a fair trial for the eleven colored defendants is constantly in my mind. Above all things I want them to know that they are in a court where the true ideal of justice is constantly sought. A white judge, white lawyers and 12 white jurymen are sitting in judgment on 11 who are colored black. This alone is enough to make us fervent in our effort to do justice. I want the defendants to know that true justice does not recognize color."[30]

The prosecution was conducted by Robert M. Toms, a "tall, pleasant . . . affable man," and his handsome, able, and sometimes arrogant assistant, Lester S. Moll. Hays was the legal tactician for the defense, and Darrow the expert in dealing with people in the courtroom.[31]

In response to a defense motion that it submit a bill of particulars specifying the nature of the charges against each of the defendants, Toms relied on "the prosecutor's delight," the law of conspiracy.

The theory of the people in this case [the bill of particulars stated] is that the defendants premeditatedly, and with malice aforethought, banded themselves together and armed themselves with a common understanding and agreement that one or more would shoot to kill in the event, first, of threatened or actual trespass on the property wherein they were assembled; or, second, of the infliction of any damage, real or threatened, however slight, to the persons or property of them or any of them. Further, that the deceased came to his death by a bullet fired by one of the defendants aided and abetted by all of the others, in pursuance of their common understanding as above set forth. Further, that such understanding and agreement was to commit an unlawful act, to wit, to shoot to kill without legal justification or excuse.[32]

Since the prosecution did not know who had fired the shot that killed Breiner and could not identify the gun from which the fatal bullet had been fired—the bullet was not found after the shooting[33]—it really had no alternative but to rely on a conspiracy theory as the basis of its case. It would have to prove that the shooting was unprovoked and had occurred with malice aforethought.

As in the preliminary examination, the police witnesses put on the stand by the prosecution testified that there had been only a small number of persons outside the Sweet house, that those present had been orderly, and that police protection had been available. One policeman who had examined the house after the shooting claimed that he had found no broken windows. Other prosecution witnesses corroborated the police testimony that all had been serene outside the Sweet home. In his cross-examination of the witnesses, Darrow exposed contradictions in their testimony that were "so glaring as to be unmistakable," and he elicited from one witness the admission that he had been coached by the police and from others that they had heard glass breaking before the shooting. David Lilienthal, who observed the trial, was correct in his judgment that the prosecution witnesses made "sorry spectacles under Darrow's pitiless cross-questioning and biting sarcasm," and Toms later conceded that the "big handicap" from the prosecution point of view was that "the colored people involved were so far superior to the white people [witnesses] involved."[34]

Murphy made several significant rulings during the eight days that the prosecution was developing its case. On November 9 Mrs. Breiner fainted within ten feet of the jury, but Murphy denied a defense motion for a mistrial since no jury member knew who she was. In his cross-examination of members of the Waterworks

Improvement Association, Darrow sought to establish that the purpose of the organization was to keep blacks out of the neighborhood. The state objected that this was "immaterial," "too remote," and of "no probative value," but Murphy overruled the objections.[35]

Murphy made two especially important rulings on November 13 that weakened the prosecution's line of argument. In what White described as "the most fiery tilt of the trial," the state began presenting as exhibits the guns, bullets, and empty shells found in the Sweet house, and Toms started a line of questioning designed to show that several of the guns had been fired. Darrow and Hays, however, contended that it was prejudicial to leave the impression that since the guns had been fired, this meant that they had been fired on September 9. Murphy sustained the defense objection and then excluded the jury so that he might listen to further argument on the point. The prosecution failed to alter Murphy's view of the matter, and he ruled that the state could show only that the guns had been fired some time since their manufacture. The defendants, he stated, were "charged with murder," and he was "not going to let anything in, any evidence, that may be vague or speculative." When the jury returned, the detective who had been testifying conceded that he did not know when the guns had been fired and could only say that this had occurred since their manufacture. "Thus," White concluded, "a strong link in the prosecution's chain has popped."[36]

"The second great victory" for the defense on November 13 came after Inspector McPherson had testified regarding his entry into the Sweet house on September 8 to advise the occupants that they had police protection. Darrow asked the court to instruct the jury that McPherson's remarks were relevant only as to those defendants whom he could identify as actually having heard what he had said. Moll jumped to his feet and contended that, since the charge was conspiracy, Murphy should rule that a statement made to any one of the eleven applied to all of them. Murphy then, in White's judgment, "hit the prosecution the hardest blow of the trial" by stating that he did not believe that the state had established proof of a conspiracy and he would therefore instruct the jury that the conversation was relevant only with regard to those defendants actually present when it took place. "The outlook," White now reported, "*is* encouraging."[37]

The prosecution rested on November 14, and the defense moved for a directed verdict on the grounds that the state had failed to prove either the existence of a conspiracy or who had fired the fatal shot. Before the motion was filed, the defense and prosecution engaged in a lengthy debate on the merits of the conspiracy charge. Murphy indicated doubts about the validity of the charge, but Toms noted the "concerted and simultaneous shooting," the presence in the house of a weapon for each defendant and sufficient ammunition to supply each weapon for several rounds, the assignment of the defendants to various stations, the empty shells of five different calibers, the admission of one defendant that he had fired, and the fact that the Sweet house was "not equipped for social entertainment, comfort, or a show of hospitality." A directed verdict, he concluded, would mean that "one racial group will know that it can literally get away with murder."[38]

In the end, Murphy denied the motion for a directed verdict, which was a bitter disappointment to the defense. White, who had expected such a verdict, nevertheless saw a "great advantage" to the NAACP in having the defense put in its testimony since this would complete "the job of education that gives the trial its greatest ultimate value." Walter Nelson had stated before the trial that some members of the Detroit bar thought that the case would never go to a jury, "their only doubt" being whether Murphy would have "the grit to stand boldly and face the issue." It was later alleged that a politically ambitious Murphy had been afraid to offend his white constituents by taking the case away from the jury,[39] but it is difficult to agree with this judgment. Murphy, to be sure, was politically ambitious, and he appeared to be dubious about the validity of the conspiracy charge, but since a man had been killed, since the need for self-defense had not yet been established, and since the right of self-defense did not necessarily mean that firearms had to be used in its exercise, he could hardly have been expected to do otherwise than to let the case go to the jury, and it is hard to think of a judge at the time who would have done otherwise.

The nub of the defense argument was that the accused had shot in self-defense because of "reasonable apprehension of danger from a mob"—in Michigan, a mob or "riotous assemblage" was defined as twelve or more men who were armed or thirty men who were unarmed. To demonstrate that the defendants had reason to be apprehensive, the defense contended that the September 9 affray had to be seen in the context of "a Negro besieged in his own home with [the] history of his race behind him."[40]

The most effective witness for the defense in its effort to demonstrate that the crowd outside the Sweet house was much larger than the prosecution witnesses had indicated was Philip A. Adler, a Detroit *News* reporter who had observed the scene at Garland and Charlevoix on September 9. Adler testified that there had been a "considerable mob"—between 500 and 650 persons—across the street from the Sweet house. Some of the persons present, he thought, were "of the residential type," but others were "more like people preparing for something," and he had heard one of them say," 'A Negro family has moved in here and we're going to get them out.' " The testimony of the black occupants of the car that had been stoned near the Sweet house was also put into the record, and one of the men in the car described the crowd as "a mob of howling Indians."[41]

If the defense were to prove that the accused had acted in self-defense, it was essential that it be permitted to introduce testimony relative to the black experience in America and Dr. Sweet's knowledge of previous racial disturbances in Detroit. The state objected to this line of argument, but Murphy, in his most critical ruling in the entire trial, decided that it was relevant since it had a bearing on the state of mind of the accused.[42]

Darrow put Dr. Sweet on the stand, and Lilienthal described what followed as "one of the most remarkable direct examinations to be found in all the records of criminal cases: a vivid picture of the fear-ridden mind of a black man, terrified by a hostile crowd of whites outside his home." Ossian denied any "common understanding" with the others in the house to shoot to kill if any one trespassed on his property. He told of racial troubles in Orlando, Florida, where he had grown up, of black homes that had been burned and of a black who had been lynched. He recounted his knowledge of the race riots of the World War I era, the blacks driven from their homes in Detroit, and the threats directed at himself. "When I opened the door [to admit Otis and Davis to the house] and saw that mob," he stated, "I realized in a way that I was facing that same mob that had hounded my people through its entire history. I realized my back was against the wall and I was filled with a peculiar type of fear—the fear of one who knows the history of my race." Moll later said that Dr. Sweet's testimony was the turning point in the trial.[43]

The arguments to the jury began on November 24. Moll led off for the state. Because Dr. Sweet was black, Moll stated, he claimed "a certain latitude" that others could not claim, but the shooting of Breiner was "a cowardly act," and the claim of self-defense was "a lot of poppycock." Each of the defendants, Moll contended, "took a hand in the killing of Breiner in cold blood," and each had "aided and abetted" the others. Hays asserted that the eleven persons had been in the house for a lawful purpose and that no evidence had been presented of an agreement to shoot or kill trespassers. The defendants, he declared, had fired in self-defense, and that was no crime.[44]

In making his argument, Darrow spoke to a courtroom that was crowded to the limit of its capacity. His voice was "tense with emotion," and he "held his audience spellbound," bringing tears to the eyes of some of his listeners. His clients, he began, were "charged with murder, but they are really here because they are black," and the jurors, consequently, were deciding not only the fate of the defendants but were "to a certain extent . . . determining the problems of two races." All of the state's witnesses, Darrow continued, had lied—"there is not an honest person in the whole bunch"—and the police had not only perjured themselves but had been "utterly ineffective" in protecting the Sweet house. The crowd outside the house was a mob, "a criminal organization," and was there "to awe and intimidate" the Sweets—there were "no innocent men in that bunch." As for the shooting, "You must imagine yourselves," he told the jurors, "in the position of those eleven . . . , with their skins, with the hatred, with the infinite wrongs they have suffered on account of their skin, with the hazards they take every day they live, with the insults that are heaped around them, with the crowd outside, with the knowledge of what that crowd meant, and then ask the question of whether they waited too long or stopped too quick."

Darrow's peroration was powerful and moving:

I speak not only for these eleven people, but for a race that in spite of what you may do will go on and on to heights that it has never known before. I speak to you not only in behalf of them, but in behalf of the millions of black faces who look to these twelve white faces for confidence and trust and hope in the institutions of our land, and in the guarantees that the laws have made to them, those blacks who live all up and down the length and breadth of our land, and whose ancestors we brought here in chains. I speak to you for those black people of Detroit who have come to work in your factories and your mills by the invitation of your men of business, and who must live or they cannot work. I speak to you in behalf of those faces that have haunted this court room from the beginning of this case, and whose lives and whose hearts and whose hopes and whose fears are centered upon these 12 men before you. . . . I ask you in the name of the future to do justice in this case.

Murphy seemed overcome by Darrow's appeal. Attorney Mahoney later stated that he had heard "about lawyers making a judge cry but Darrow was the first man I actually saw do it."[45]

Toms, obviously, had a hard act to follow, but Rowlette thought that the prosecutor made "one of the most moving appeals" that Rowlette had ever heard. Toms asserted that it was improper to convert the proceedings into "a sociological clinic" and that it was not the jury's responsibility to solve the race problem. He conceded the right of a person to live where he pleased, but Breiner's "right to live," Toms urged, was a more important right than "the right to live where you please, in a certain house on a certain street." The only issue in the case, Toms argued, was who had killed Leon Breiner, and the only mob involved was the one composed of the defendants, "lying in ambush, fully armed." "Back of all your sophistry and transparent political philosophy, gentlemen of the defense," Toms concluded, "back of all your prating of civil rights, back of your psychology and theory of race hatred, lies the stark dead body of Leon Breiner with a bullet hole in his back."[46]

After once again refusing a defense motion for a directed verdict, Murphy delivered his charge to the jury. "Seldom in any court," Walter White wrote, "has a more impartial, learned or complete charge to a jury been heard." Murphy instructed the jurors that if any of the accused had shot Breiner and the shot was fired "under an honest and reasonable belief, based on the circumstances as they appeared to him or them at the time, that he or they were in danger of losing their lives, or suffering great bodily harm, or were resisting a forcible and violent felony in the only effective manner that it could be resisted, the shooting would be justifiable and the defendants would not be guilty." In effect accepting the argument of the defense regarding the defendants' state of mind, Murphy instructed the jury, "Their [the defendants] situation, race and color, the actions and attitude of those who were outside the Sweet home, all have a bearing on whether or not the sum total of the surrounding circumstances as they appeared to them at the time were such as to induce in a reasonable man the honest belief of danger."

Under the law, Murphy advised the jury, anyone aiding or abetting a defendant who might have shot and killed Breiner was "equally guilty," but, after defining "aiding and abetting," Murphy made it clear to the jurors that "you can not surmise or guess or speculate about one aiding or abetting"; it was necessary to prove this by evidence. To find any one of the defendants guilty, the jurors, Murphy instructed, "must be satisfied beyond a reasonable doubt that without legal justification or excuse, he shot to death Leon Breiner, or aided and abetted the person who did shoot to death Leon Breiner, such person not having any legal justification or excuse . . . ."

Dr. Sweet, Murphy informed the jury, had the same right to buy and occupy a home on Garland as any other man. "Under the law," Murphy stated in words that were to be long remembered in black Detroit but which simply echoed Lord Coke's famous strictures in Semayne's Case, "a man's home is his castle. It is his castle whether he is white or black, and no man has the right to assail or invade it." In conclusion, Murphy "especially" cautioned the jury against "prejudice or intolerance."[47]

Although one can well understand why Darrow thought that Murphy's "clear and forcible" instructions to the jurors "scarcely left a chance for them to do anything but acquit," they advised Murphy after deliberating for a total of forty-six hours that they could not reach a verdict. White learned that five jurors had favored complete acquittal and seven favored the acquittal of eight defendants and a second-degree sentence for the three others. He thought this a victory, "after a fashion," since everyone had told him when he first came to Detroit that conviction was certain. Some of the jurors, no doubt, were influenced by the fact that no one in the crowd had used firearms or had even set foot on the Sweet property, and they may have wondered whether the defendants had exhausted all other remedies before they opened fire.[48]

Murphy's conduct of the Sweet trial brought him a good deal of favorable attention in liberal and black circles. Lilienthal reported in the *Nation* that the trial, presided over by an "extraordinary young judge," was "probably the fairest ever accorded a Negro in this country," and he wrote Murphy's clerk, "If I'm ever run in, in Detroit, I shall insist on being tried in that [Murphy's] court; it would almost be a pleasure." Throughout the trial, Walter White wrote in the NAACP's *Crisis,* Murphy exerted every effort to assure a "completely fair trial," a judgment in which the black press concurred.[49]

Murphy himself later remarked, "What attracted attention was that I *wasn't* prejudiced. I merely saw to it that the defendants were accorded rights equal to those of anyone in my court." The defense, however, did not misunderstand where Murphy's sympathies lay and the assistance that, in effect, he had given them. It was "the first time in all my career," Darrow later wrote Murphy, "where a judge really tried to help, and displayed a sympathetic interest in saving poor devils from the extreme forces of law, rather than otherwise." A black attorney who had observed the trial advised the NAACP, "by all means," to arrange to have Murphy try the second Sweet case. "I have found in the trial of cases," the attorney wrote, "there is that indefinable something called 'atmosphere' in a court room that is worth considerable. If the Judge is sympathetic, if in his rulings, he does it with courtesy, smiles and talks in a sympathetic manner, it helps mightily."[50] That Murphy had helped to provide the right kind of "atmosphere" in the courtroom for the defendants is quite apparent.

Immediately after the jury agreed to disagree, Darrow petitioned to have the defendants released on bail. Murphy set bail on the murder charge at $5,000 for eight of the defendants but at $10,000 for Ossian and Henry Sweet and Leonard Morse, who had been found with a shotgun in his hand in the house and had implicated himself by his statement at the police station. Murphy also reduced the bail on the assault charge from $5,000 to $500 for all the defendants.[51]

Toms stated after the jury had been discharged that the public interest in the case was so great that he would retry it ten times if that were necessary. Darrow indicated that separate trials would now be requested for the defendants. He had probably come to this conclusion after consulting with Thomas F. Chawke, reported by Murphy's clerk to have been "the most able and successful criminal lawyer in Michigan," and learning of Chawke's concern about the possibility of a compromise verdict in a case with so many defendants. Darrow also thought it unlikely that there would be more than one or two additional trials, regardless of the outcome. If the state lost at the outset, it would become "discouraged," and if it won, it would feel that this was "enough of a victory."[52]

The state decided to try Henry Sweet first since he was the only defendant who had admitted firing a weapon on September 9. Chawke agreed to enter the case, "as a business matter," for a fee of $7,500, which was more than Darrow was to receive. Darrow thought that he could get by without Hays if Chawke were in the case, and since Darrow believed that there had been too many defense attorneys in the first trial, the black lawyers were told that only one of them could serve; Dr. Sweet preferred Perry, and so he continued in the case. The cost of the second trial was just under $16,000, which was met by the national office of the NAACP.[53]

Although its tone was occasionally strident, the second Sweet trial was a more subdued affair than the first one. The Klan had ebbed in influence since the first trial, there was no mayoralty contest this time to heat up the pretrial political atmosphere, and race relations in Detroit appeared to be less tense.[54]

The examination of jurors for the second trial began on April 20, 1926, after Murphy had granted Darrow's motion for separate trials for the defendants. This time it required five days and the resort to three separate jury panels totaling 197 talesmen before the defense and the prosecution could agree on twelve jurors, all white males, to decide Henry Sweet's fate.[55]

The courtroom was crowded every day, with more blacks than whites present this time. The celebrities occasionally appearing among the spectators included Ann Harding, who was given a front seat so that she could see her favorite judge in action, Jeanne Eagles, who was performing in Detroit in *Rain,* Anita Loos, who was in the city for *Gentlemen Prefer Blondes,* and the veteran reformer Charles Edward Russell.[56]

The prosecution argued that Henry Sweet, without justifiable provocation, either fired the fatal shot or aided and abetted the person who did. The defense responded that if Henry had fired the fatal shot, and this was not known, he was innocent because he believed his action necessary to defend his family and his brother's home. The testimony for both the prosecution and the defense was largely a replay of the testimony in the first trial, and Murphy once again permitted the defense to develop the racial background of the case.[57]

After Murphy denied a defense motion for a directed verdict, the prosecution and the defense proceeded to make their closing arguments. Little was said by the attorneys that they had not said in the first trial. When Moll called Dr. Sweet "evasive and only quasi-intelligent," Murphy sustained a defense objection. During Toms's argument, Chawke, thinking that the prosecutor was making an indirect reference to the fact that Henry Sweet had not taken the stand in his own defense, demanded a mistrial. Murphy excused the jury and then told the attorneys the subject was a "dangerous" one but that he believed the matter could "properly be cured" by instructions, and so he denied the motion.[58]

Darrow's argument again took as its theme that "there is nothing but prejudice in this case." "Take the hatred away," he said, "and you have nothing left." Darrow's appeal had a profound effect on many who heard it. Murphy told a friend when he came off the bench that listening to Darrow's argument was "'the greatest experience of my life.'" James Weldon Johnson, who replaced White as the NAACP's observer at the trial, thought it was "the most wonderful flow of words I ever heard from a man's lips." After congratulating Darrow, Johnson "broke down and wept."[59]

In his charge to the jury Murphy traversed the same ground that he had covered in the first trial. "The charge," Johnson wrote, "contemplated the law involved from every point and yet it was not the dry dust of the law books. It was eloquent and moving." This time the jury took only three hours and thirty-five minutes to decide, and its verdict was "not guilty." Since Murphy had warned the spectators against any kind of demonstration, the vocal reaction in the courtroom was only "one loud 'Ah' and a clap of the hand." According to one observer of the trial, however, "few eyes were dry. Even that cool, unemotional man, Mr. Chawke, was unable for a moment to speak. Tears rolled down the cheeks of Clarence Darrow and of Henry Sweet." Toms was "plainly surprised and almost stunned" by the verdict, and Mrs. Breiner commented bitterly, "My husband was murdered and the murderers go free." Murphy stated that the trial was "a great compliment to law and order in Detroit," and he told Henry and the others, according to one reporter, "'I believe it is a just and reasonable verdict, and may God bless you.'"[60]

The NAACP thought that Henry Sweet's acquittal was "one of the most important steps ever taken in the struggle for justice to the Negro in the United States," and even the ultraconservative Detroit *Saturday Night* observed that the trial had performed "a public service in bringing before the people the many angles of a serious situation confronting not only Detroit, but most great industrial cities of the country." Racial bigots, however, were discomfited by the verdict and castigated the jurors as "nigger lovers." One juror received a postcard signed "100% White Man" that read: "Nigger Districts for Niggers. White Districts for White People. White trash and niggers love each other. We know you are a nigger lover. May your sister or daughter marry a nigger."[61]

For Frank Murphy, the consequences of the Sweet trials were enormous. As Charles Mahoney asserted, Murphy "certainly got a lot of publicity" as the result of the trials. "Everybody knew him when he got through." Murphy's role in the trials also gained him the friendship, admiration, and support of such NAACP and American Civil Liberties Union luminaries as White, Darrow, and Hays. "You have made to me a rare gift," White wrote Murphy after the second trial. "That gift is the experience of seeing a man preside over a trial who was not only completely free from the slightest suggestion of prejudice but whose high moral character, ability and learning surpasses[*sic*] that of any man I have ever known. Frankly, I had no idea such a man existed." Darrow wrote the judge, "You were so kindly and human that it made a troublesome case easy to try." Before long Murphy was advising Darrow regarding his stock-market investments. In his published account of the first trial, Hays commented that "a fair and impartial judiciary has never been better represented than by Judge Frank Murphy."[62]

Of greatest importance for Murphy's career, the Sweet trials made him the hero of black Detroit. "Our people are not ungrateful," Leonard Morse said of Detroit blacks in a letter to Murphy. Another Detroit black, to whom "it seemed a miracle in this city of prejudice, that twelve white men would agree that a Negro has a right to defend his home and family," wrote Murphy that his "stand for justice" would always be "a comforting memory" to her. She knew no way to "prove" her gratitude to him "except to be the best citizen that I know how to be, and by giving you my most loyal support whether it be for judge, mayor or president of these United States." Future election returns indicated that the letter's authoress spoke for the preponderant majority of Detroit's black voters.[63]

After the second Sweet trial Murphy worked closely with the NAACP in its efforts to secure the dismissal of the suits against the remaining ten defendants. Toms, however, was reluctant to go along because, according to Murphy, he feared the possible political consequences. When Toms told Murphy that the prosecutor's office was preparing to go to trial again, Murphy's rejoinder was, " 'Surely you are not in earnest,' " and he asked Toms how he could expect to win if another trial were held after the state had lost in "its strongest case." Finally, in July, 1927, Toms moved to have the cases nol-prossed, and Murphy then dismissed all the defendants. The NAACP expressed its gratitude to Murphy for "the best news we have had in some time." Justice had triumphed, Hays wrote Murphy, but "I am not so sure it would have . . . had there not been such a just judge on the bench."[64]

Toward the end of 1930, by which time Murphy was mayor of Detroit, Breiner's widow revived a $150,000 damage suit against the defendants that she had originally filed shortly after her husband's death. The NAACP was reluctant to finance the defense this time both because it believed that Dr. Sweet could afford to do so himself and because he was thought to be hostile to the organization. Murphy, who was "hurt" and angered because Sweet, almost alone among prominent blacks in Detroit, had not supported Murphy in the 1930 mayoralty election, shared the NAACP's antagonism toward the doctor.[65]

Only Darrow, more forgiving than the others, thought that the NAACP could not "afford to leave the Dr." If Sweet lost the civil suit and went to jail because he could not afford to pay the damages, Darrow advised, it would "discount" the results of the earlier trials. "A hostile verdict," moreover, would be "a hard blow to the Negro and a great triumph for the bigot." That Sweet was a difficult person, Darrow thought, was "hardly a good excuse" for leaving him "in the lurch." If he had been an agreeable person, the criminal lawyer observed, he would not have defended his home as he had. Ill and aging, Darrow doubted that he could "live through" another Sweet trial, but if no one else could be found to defend Ossian, Darrow was willing to serve again. Whatever his real feelings, Murphy was disinclined to argue with Darrow about Sweet and to give the appearance of petulance. You are "right," he wrote Darrow, and he wished Darrow to know that the mayor stood with him even though Detroit's blacks were hostile to Sweet.[66]

When White and Darrow came to Detroit to discuss the damage suit, Murphy stated that he would be willing to help defray the cost of a new trial. White, Darrow, and others visited Sweet, and White concluded that the doctor was suffering from "a delusion of grandeur and of self-importance, as well as from a persecution complex." The NAACP, White recommended, should "wipe its hands clean of all association with Dr. Sweet." Even Darrow was shaken by the conference and was no longer so sure that he wanted to be involved in the case. In the end, the damage suit was denied, and the legal matters raised by the events of September 9, 1925, were thus brought to a close.[67]

Victorious in the courts, the Sweets were nevertheless defeated in life. Dr. Sweet's daughter died of tuberculosis in 1926 at the age of two, and Gladys succumbed to the same disease not long thereafter. In January, 1940, Henry Sweet became the third Sweet to fall victim to tuberculosis. Ossian Sweet was not the same man after 1926 that he had been before that date; his confinement and the tensions induced by the two trials "left their marks upon his body, while the disturbance to his . . . nervous mechanism . . . left its effects upon his personality."

Ossian remarried after Gladys's death, but the marriage ended in divorce, and still a third marriage came to the same end. He ran for office four times in the 1930s and 1950s, twice as a Republican, twice as a Democrat, but all the races ended in defeat. In the 1930s he was arrested and fined two dollars for selling cigarets without a license in the pharmacy that he owned, and in the 1950s he was in court again as the defendant in a paternity suit. He moved back to the house on Garland and Charlevoix in 1930 after having rented it out until that time, and he lived there until 1951, when he moved to Chene Street to live above his pharmacy. Suffering from arthritis, the man who had not fired a shot on September 9, 1925, took his own life on March 19, 1960, by shooting himself behind the right ear with a 32-caliber revolver. The dwelling at 2509 Garland was occupied at the time by a black who had once done odd jobs around the house for Dr. Sweet.[68]

In the short run, at least, the Sweet trials were a boon to the NAACP, both in Detroit and nationally, and it seemed for a time that race relations in Detroit had taken a turn for the better as the result of the case. Moses Walker thus noted some months after Henry's acquittal that there had not been a single attack on blacks moving into white neighborhoods since the trials and that even the "ordinary brutalities" that the police perpetrated on black citizens were lessening. When Toms moved to nol-pross the remaining Sweet cases, he observed that "a noticeably improved spirit of tolerance and forbearance has arisen between the colored and white groups in this city." Toms later expressed the opinion that the case had taught "the fringe of white people" that the law would not support them if they sought to block blacks by force from living where they wished and that among the blacks "it leveled off the bitterness which undoubtedly would have arisen, had these people [the defendants] been sent to prison."[69]

The Mayor's Inter-racial Committee submitted the results of its survey of blacks in Detroit toward the end of 1926, and, although the study was far from exhaustive, it provided a "more adequate picture of race conditions" in the city than had been available previously. The recommendations that the committee submitted were largely ignored, however, perhaps because of the optimism that surrounded the whole problem of race relations in Detroit at that time. The optimism was, unfortunately, entirely misplaced, and two major race riots, in 1943 and 1967, brought that fact forcibly and tragically to the attention of the entire nation. The only member of the Sweet family still alive at the time of the 1967 riot was Otis Sweet, and the ill fortune that had dogged the Sweets since the trials of 1925-26 now caught up with him, the most carefree of the three Sweet brothers: his dental office fell victim to the rage that swept the black ghetto in what was the worst of the nation's race riots in the unhappy summer of 1967.[70]

II

Murphy drew praise not only for his conduct of the Sweet trials but also for his day-to-day performance on the bench. Although Raymond Moley and the *Literary Digest* thought that municipal court judges in the 1920s were a sorry lot, they quite properly excepted Frank Murphy from this generalization. Their favorable view of Judge Murphy was shared by many people in Detroit. The head of the Progressive Civic League thus "eulogized" Murphy for his "fairness and mercifulness in trying all cases," and another Detroiter saw in him a judge who devoted his "time and intellect to lifting other's burdens." Fred Butzel, one of Detroit's most respected attorneys, concluded in 1929 that Murphy was not only "the soul of honor and a man of very high ideals" but was also "the strongest member" of the Recorder's Court and had "a better grasp of the problems involved than any of the judges." Murphy, Butzel noted, had even "helped a great deal in solving the problems of criminal courts in other cities. . . ."

After Dr. C. Burton Stevens visited Murphy's court, he wrote the judge, ". . . you dignify and glorify our judicial system as do few men whom I have ever known." Murphy, Stevens thought, was "performing a sacred ministry." Since Murphy saw public service as a "sacred ministry," no words about his performance on the Recorder's Court could have pleased him more.[71] It was altogether fitting that when the city of Detroit constructed a new Recorder's Court building in 1969, it named the structure the Frank Murphy Hall of Justice.

VIII

"The Great Jury of the People"

I

The attention that Frank Murphy received as a Recorder's Court judge was the result not only of his performance on the bench but also of the extrajudicial assignments that he undertook. Of these activities none was more important than his one-man grand jury probe into corruption in Detroit's municipal government.

The Detroit Bureau of Governmental Research had been complaining for some time of "crass inefficiency, if not downright graft," in various city departments, especially in the Department of Public Works.[1] The Bureau's suspicions about the department, regarded by the research group as the city's "most important department," began to be confirmed late in 1924 when Budget Director William J. Curran discovered substantial discrepancies between the payments for cinders by the department's Street and Alley Cleaning Division to William P. Garner's Wayne County Moving and Storage Company and the amount of cinders actually delivered. Several results flowed from this discovery: the commissioner of the Department of Public Works, John W. Reid, suspended John J. Knight, the superintendent of the Street and Alley Cleaning Division; Mayor John Smith ordered Curran to expand his probe into other departments; and Prosecuting Attorney Paul Voorhies petitioned the Recorder's Court on November 25 to appoint a one-man grand jury to look into the possibility of "misfeasance, malfeasance and willful neglect of duty" on the part of "certain public officials." Presiding Judge Charles L. Bartlett gave the assignment to Frank Murphy because of his experience as a federal attorney.[2]

Murphy held hearings from November 28, 1924, to March 14, 1925, during which time 107 witnesses appeared before him and thirty-five hundred pages of testimony were accumulated. The proceedings were secret, as the law required, but certain public actions during the period of the hearings provided clues as to what was going on behind closed doors: Commissioner Reid asked for the resignation of George H. Garner, the superintendent of the Sidewalks Division of the Department of Public Works and the brother of William; two weeks later Louis J. Hoffman and Bart H. Manning were arraigned for allegedly perjuring themselves before the grand jury with regard to the sale of a morgue site to Wayne County; Mayor Smith ousted Werner Helmboldt, the superintendent of the Motor Transportation Department; and Reid announced an impending reorganization of his department.[3]

The grand-jury inquiry was not without its political overtones. The alleged misdeeds that Murphy was scrutinizing had mostly occurred while Joseph A. Martin had been commissioner of public works (1920–1923) and then acting mayor (January 8–August 2, 1924); and since Martin was a "clean-government, business" type who enjoyed the support of upper-income and "good-government" groups in the city, the Detroit *News* and the Detroit Citizens League saw the probe as, in part at least, an effort by Mayor Smith and the Detroit *Times,* which supported the mayor, to discredit Martin and his allies. Murphy was not unaware of the "political crosscurrents" that swirled about his one-man grand jury, but he hoped "to steer clear" of them because he was anxious that there be no doubts among the people of Detroit concerning "the sincerity and honesty of the inquiry."[4]

As the writing of his report entered its final stages, the task on which he was engaged seemed almost to obsess Murphy. He agonized about the charges that he would make, wondered how the public would receive the report, and worried about making a misstep that might jeopardize his career. "Day and night, hour after hour I labored," he informed his sister a few days after the report had been submitted. "Food meant nothing or sleep either." He found it necessary to reassure himself that he had placed "politics[,] fear[,] . . . [and] favor" in the background. He had resolved all doubtful cases, he indicated, in favor of the accused so as to ensure that he had not been unjust to anyone. If some people, despite this, would be "displeased," he regretted that, but, he noted, "I don't want to be ashamed of myself in future years and I know I would be if I had done the usual thing."

Murphy expected his report to "make a great impression" on Detroit and to be "pleasing to the great mass of laboring people. This will be one grand jury," he wrote, "that will hit the big men of power and influence and not the little ones." In addition to attempting "to do something big for the people of my city," he had tried, he said, to sound an idealistic note in the report—"in a community where there is so little idealism I wanted mine displayed in this work."[5]

When Murphy submitted his grand-jury report to Mayor Smith on April 25, 1925, the judge "stunned" the city, according to the Detroit *Times,* since he recommended the criminal prosecution of nineteen officials and "in a scorching 10,000-word presentment laid bare corruption, incompetence and waste in six departments of the city and county governments." The investigation, Murphy noted, had turned up "nauseating instances of department heads and members of boards exploiting their public trust" and had revealed that the taxpayers' dollars were being dissipated because proper records were not kept, required inspections not made, contracts let illegally and without open and fair competition, and improper claims allowed. What was required, Murphy concluded in his covering letter to the mayor, was "something more than the punishment of a few betrayers of public trust." There was need for "a new spirit, strong and courageous, deep down in the political life of this city, a spirit sensitive to idealism in public duty and sturdy in defiance of venality and evil practices."[6]

Specifically, Murphy called for the issuance of warrants against nineteen individuals for such offenses as malfeasance in office, extortion, embezzlement, larceny, and conspiracy of one sort or another. He charged that the city had been bilked of hundreds of thousands of dollars for asphalt paving since 1914 because of the monopolistic power, "secured by unscrupulous practices," of the Detroit Asphalt Paving Company, which did about 70 percent of the city's paving. Murphy recommended that the city institute proceedings to dissolve the company, and, accepting the "yardstick" principle, he lauded the city's decision to build its own asphalt plant. "Constant bidding by the city," he observed, "will operate as a threat to other bidders and will have a tendency to keep the yardage price down."

Property owners, Murphy charged, had been mulcted out of thousands of dollars because of the "indifference, inefficiency and graft" attending the construction of sidewalks. Few sidewalks during the preceding four years, he stated, had been built according to specifications, and required inspections had not been made because department officials "worked hand in hand with the contractors for their benefit." The city since 1923 had paid for

about eighty thousand cubic yards of cinders but had receipts
for the delivery of only about twenty-six thousand cubic yards,
and the contracts for the cinders had been let without competitive
bidding and at an unduly high price. The Board of Education,
he discovered, had awarded the ubiquitous William Garner the
contract to haul coal to the city's schools without resorting to
competitive bidding and at too high a price. Murphy thought
it noteworthy that Garner, Joseph Martin, and the business manager
of the Board of Education were all associated in a business venture,
the Muscle Shoals Land Company.

Murphy attacked the administration of the Motor Transportation
Department as "base and sordid" and found it difficult to
understand how "the glaring corruption and waste" in the department had "gone unnoticed for so long a time." The department
spent about $1 million a year, and Murphy alleged that Superin-
tendent Helmboldt had "made a steady practice of endeavoring
to profit for himself in every transaction possible." The Water
Board, too, Murphy thought, presented a dismal picture of "political
considerations, favoritism in the award of contracts, and domination
. . . by influential contracting concerns," and he alleged that
various members of the board had "exploited" the opportunities
available to them because of their association with the board's
"large business enterprises." The misbehavior that Murphy pointed
to in the Department of Parks and Boulevards and the Department
of Street Railways involved modest sums, but derelictions of duty
and conflicts of interest nevertheless. Finally, Murphy charged
that two county officials had profited personally as the result
of the county's purchase of a site for a new morgue.[7]

Except for the Detroit *News* and the Detroit Citizens League,
Murphy's report was very favorably received. "It is doubtful
whether, in the whole history of American civic affairs," the
Detroit *Times* remarked, "there has been such a conscientious,
thorough and fair inquiry. . . ." Even the Detroit *Free Press* and
the Detroit *Saturday Night,* normally not among Murphy's admirers, gave the report high grades. Organized labor in Detroit
reacted to the document precisely as Murphy had hoped that
it would. "This time," the Detroit *Labor News* commented, "the
trail led to high places," but Murphy "had the courage to hew
[to] the line and let the chips fall where they pleased."

Murphy's report also attracted a good deal of attention outside
of Detroit—it made the front page of the New York *Times,* for
example—and when Murphy visited New York shortly after the

document had been released, he found himself "more or less famous." "We believe it is safe to assert," the *Journal of the American Judicature Society* commented, "that no community in this country has ever had such a penetrating and thorough survey of irregularities in office."[8]

Murphy's grand-jury report was clearly embarrassing to the Detroit *News* and the Detroit Citizens League. They had lauded the Martin administration as a prototype of the businessman's administration, but Murphy had revealed not only that there could be "crookery" in "a silk-hat administration" but that it would escape the criticism that newspapers like the *News* were so ready to level at the "bosses" and the "boodlers." Murphy's critics waited a few days to react to his report and then took the position that "most of the cases" that he had cited were of "a chicken-feed character" and that the report was "really a certificate of civic health for Detroit" since only a handful of the city's twenty-seven thousand employees had been accused of wrongdoing. Murphy's critics overlooked the fact that the report had stressed that the public should not "lose confidence in their officials because of the corruption of a few," and if some of Murphy's revelations involved graft of a petty sort, this hardly characterized the allegations as a whole.[9]

The *News* and the Citizens League accused Murphy of "tuning" his report "in the key of a political document" and, in effect, of serving the "political needs" of Mayor Smith by portraying him as "cleaning out the grafters."[10] It was not wrong for the *News* and the Citizens League to see some politics in the grand-jury report, but what they did not seem to realize was that Murphy was seeking to advance his own career, not that of John Smith.

As after the 1923 election, the anxiety and strain that Murphy experienced while conducting his one-man grand jury took their physical toll, and he feared that he would suffer "serious illness," perhaps "a complete breakdown," unless he found "new surroundings at once." He left for Europe three days after presenting the report, but even there, he wrote home, whenever he thought of the grand jury, "I seem weak and a strange feeling comes over me." He took a longer vacation from the court than was due him, but "I can't help it," he informed Marguerite, "my health must come first." Striking the martyr pose he was apt to assume in moments of crisis in his life, Frank complained that "in an effort to do the city a service I have put myself in bad condition."[11]

Murphy was understandably concerned about the legal action

that the city would take against those whom he had accused of wrongdoing. As he left for Europe, he urged the city's corporation counsel to "remember that hard fights bring the best results," and he designated George Murphy to look after brother Frank's interests in the case in his absence. Frank was especially concerned that the "powerful men" who had acted improperly should not be permitted "to smooth things over."[12]

The news that Frank received while abroad concerning the court action to which his report had led was far from pleasing to him. The nineteen persons whom he had named were suspended from their jobs and warrants were issued for their arrest, and, as Murphy had recommended, the city initiated a civil suit to dissolve the Detroit Asphalt Paving Company. The results of all this, however, were meager indeed. Witnesses who had testified before the grand jury suffered lapses of memory when they appeared in court, and case after case had to be dismissed for want of evidence. In the end, as the Detroit *News* gleefully pointed out, of the nineteen persons for whom Murphy had asked warrants, one was convicted of accepting a ten dollar bribe, and a second pleaded guilty to embezzling twenty-eight dollars. William P. Lovett of the Citizens League advised one of his correspondents that Murphy's report was coming to be seen as "a joke" in Detroit, that Murphy was said to be "politically dead," and that there was even talk of his impeachment.[13]

Murphy took such satisfaction as he could from the very modest results stemming from his inquiry. When the aforementioned bribe taker was convicted, Frank wrote Hester that he now felt "on the up about my grand jury," and he thought that the conviction would "have a big effect on the public." When after a first mistrial a second trial of the four principal figures in the Detroit Asphalt Paving Company ended in a hung jury, with nine of the jurors, however, having favored a guilty verdict, Murphy thought this "the best thing that has happened in a long time." "I have been completely vindicated," he wrote Marguerite, "and the great jury of the people know who the guilty ones are and also why their taxes have been so high."[14]

The results of the Murphy grand jury, if less impressive than Murphy liked to believe, were more substantial than the mere record of convictions indicates. Officials like George Garner had been removed from office while the inquiry was underway, and other office holders whose sense of public responsibility left something to be desired lost their jobs as the result of the probe even if the charges against them did not, in the end, stand up in court. Murphy's attack on the Detroit Asphalt Paving Company helped to reduce paving costs in Detroit, and the Common Council, in what Murphy regarded as a "final triumph" for his report, voted additional funds to expand the city's own efforts in the paving business.[15] All of this, however, was probably less important to Frank Murphy than the fact that "the great jury of the people," to whom the report was really addressed, had applauded his attack on graft and corruption. His political prospects now looked brighter than ever.

II

The efficiency and economy note that Murphy struck in his grand-jury report reflected one of the dominant themes of the 1920s. Murphy, in this and other respects, sometimes gave expression to popular conceptions and prejudices of the age, but he also began to expound ideas that were less typical of the era and that more accurately forecast the direction that his political career would take.

The blend of old and new in Murphy's thought in the 1920s was especially evident in his assessment of the role that government should play in American society. In speaking to the graduating class of the Michigan Law School in 1928 Murphy denounced the "pestilence of law making" that produced hordes of bureaucrats and "tax eaters" and advised that the lawyer, "instead of giving his talents to the rank fallacy that every social ill can be cured by some new legislation . . . , should give battle for the simple wisdom of Jeffersonian philosophy that 'that government is best which governs least.'" At the same time, however, Murphy urged the United States government not to forget charity and love and the needs of the afflicted as it pursued material ends. He similarly advised leadership elements in Detroit to pay heed to the distress of the workers of the city, who were struggling to subsist. What the city needed, he proclaimed, was "a mass movement of liberal and progressive thought that will unfurl its banners in behalf of downtrodden peoples . . . ."[16]

Murphy brought religion to his support in his plea for a government concerned about social justice and human frailties. Christianity, he contended, was not simply a creed to be professed on Sunday but a faith that had to be translated into action in a Christian's everyday life. "One of the greatest hours in Christian history will be struck," he asserted, "when all those who profess it will courageously go forth to apply it to our social, industrial and

international order." Speaking of Catholics, specifically, he remarked that "the very genius" of their faith required that they
have a "thirst . . . for social justice," and he liked to remind his
listeners of St. Paul's admonition that " 'the strong' " must " 'bear
with the infirmities of the weak.' "[17]

We know, of course, that the decade of the 1920s was not, despite
the popular mythology, a time when government followed a policy
of laissez faire, but, in stressing the social-justice role of government,
Murphy was parting company with those who saw government
primarily as the handmaiden of the business community, serving
its purposes and meeting its needs. To some degree, he was simply
reiterating the rhetoric of the progressive movement, but in his
advocacy of a government that was solicitous of the needs of the
workingman and of the distressed, Murphy was indicating what
reform would become rather than returning to what it had been.

III

As has already been suggested, the successful candidate for public
office in a nonpartisan system must develop a personal following
among the voters and must be mindful of the value of publicity.
In practicing "the politics of nonpartisanship" as a Recorder's Court
judge, Murphy started with a base of support in the veterans'
organizations and among Catholic voters of the city, and this support
did not diminish while he was on the bench. What was distinctive
about his political behavior in the 1920s, however, was the extent
to which he identified with the aspirations of the "relatively
discontented" and the strong ties that he developed with white
ethnic groups, blacks, and organized labor.

As a federal attorney, Murphy, it will be recalled, had expressed
his profound sympathy for "down-trodden people and people of
the lower classes" and his support of "their struggles for social
and industrial uplift." In the 1920s, as during the remainder of
his life, he demonstrated that these sentiments were keenly felt,
and, to be sure, they satisfied a need that was deep within him.
"Instead of children which I have been denied," he wrote at the
twilight of his career, "I have . . . a distressed minority group
or an unhappy friend awaiting me. All of it sums up happiness
to me. I love to help . . . ."[18]

Murphy was a vocal opponent of the restrictive immigration
legislation of the 1920s, and at a time when the ideological thrust
was in the direction of cultural homogeneity he was inclined to
defend the opposing ideology of cultural pluralism. He advised

the immigrant to become a citizen because "the Heterogeneous units, for their own good and the common good, must be identified with the homogeneous whole," but if ethnic groups wished to observe their own customs, Murphy asked, "who shall say them 'Nay'?" He condemned as "fatuous" the "superiority complex" manifested toward newcomers in America by the 100 percenters and attacked "the blatant intolerance" of a "militant minority" that was "preaching a general social regimentation" and trying to standardize social behavior.

Because he believed that "the handicaps of the newcomer whittle down his defensive powers," Murphy was concerned about the treatment the foreign born received in the courts—anyone who did not speak English, he thought, faced "an uphill fight in any court of justice"—and he was firmly opposed to contemplated legislation that placed aliens under surveillance and facilitated their deportation. When a Detroit Council for Protection of Foreign Born Workers was organized in 1928, Murphy was included among those on its advisory board.[19] Murphy had easily established a rapport with the Armenians of Delray when he taught at the Macmillan School in 1914–15, and in the 1920s the Poles, Hungarians, Italians, and Jews in Detroit came to respect and admire the young judge who appeared to understand them and to empathize with them and who welcomed them into the body politic.[20]

Murphy was as concerned about "the handicaps" under which blacks labored as about the handicaps of the unassimilated foreigner. "The equal citizenship of the colored man," he stated, "even though politicians throw him sops in the form of 'civil rights' statutes, is as much a myth today as in the days of slavery." The plight of the unfortunate always stirred Murphy's sympathies, and this was conspicuously true of the blacks. "I like them," he wrote Hester, "because they are so out of luck and get the worst of every deal."

Although there was a strong element of paternalism in Murphy's view of black-white relationships, he was nevertheless freer of racial prejudice than most white Americans of his time. "To me," he wrote Walter White, ". . . there is but the human family. Class and caste and race and creed I struggle to eliminate." Once when Hester returned from the South with a well-developed tan, Murphy, in a letter that revealed his "struggle to eliminate" racial prejudice but also his paternalistic views, observed that "all you fair Nordics who winter South come back looking more neutral at least," and, he concluded, "that is all there is to the race question anyway. . . . like religion humans were given a skin as well as a faith because of geographical considerations." The advantages, however, as Murphy saw it, lay with the whites, and this imposed some definite obligations on them. "Because of our color and our stirring Faith," Murphy thought, "we should long to be kindly and helpful to any who may suffer for that which is beyond their control. . . ."[21]

The Sweet trials solidified Murphy's position among Detroit's blacks, and his friendship with the NAACP leadership, locally and nationally, did nothing to weaken that position. "I am something of a guy of importance— at Negro meetings," Murphy noted shortly after the second Sweet trial. ". . . when I start speaking the Amen! Amens! will start in unison. . . . They are a good people and there is a great tomorrow before them."[22]

Organized labor in Detroit was as impressed with Murphy's behavior off the bench as with his performance on the bench. It was not usual for public officials in the 1920s to identify with organized labor, but Murphy, following in the footsteps of urban new-stock lawmakers of the progressive era, was a conspicuous exception. His pro-labor stance was a product both of altruism and self-interest: he had talked of devoting himself to the cause of the workingman as far back as his college days, and earlier than most he saw that organized labor, despite its limited strength in the 1920s, would eventually develop into a major political force.[23]

Two arbitration awards that Murphy made while he was a Recorder's Court judge were especially pleasing to organized labor. The first involved Benedict Robin, a Detroit Street Railways (DSR) platform man who had been discharged on the basis of evidence supplied by five unidentified "inspectors" of the department's intelligence division that he had been derelict in his dutes. Robin was subsequently reemployed by the DSR, but Division 26 of the Amalgamated Association of Street and Electric Railway Employees of America charged that he had been dismissed because of his union membership and his support of John Smith in the 1924 campaign and demanded that he receive back pay for the period of his enforced idleness. The matter was submitted to arbitration at the end of July, 1925. The DSR and the union each selected one member of the arbitration panel, and the two of them selected Murphy as the third member and to serve as chairman.

The arbitration board ruled in favor of Robin by a vote of

two to one, Murphy siding with the union representative. Murphy stated in the panel's opinion that the basis for its decision was that Robin had not received "a fair trial," that his trial, indeed, had not been "a trial at all." He had not been notified of the specific charges against him prior to his appearance before the trial board, no witnesses had come forward to testify against him, and he had been given no opportunity to confront his accusers. Unwilling to reveal the identity of its "spotters," the DSR had submitted only unsworn and unsigned complaints to controvert Robin's sworn testimony, and complaints of that sort, Murphy stated, "have no probative force in a proceeding of this kind." Delighted with the decision and with its implied criticism of the DSR's "spy system," the Amalgamated congratulated Murphy on "the wonderful service you rendered mankind." The union was further impressed when Murphy refused to accept the fee that the DSR and the Amalgamated were jointly to have paid him for his services.[24]

The arbitration decision that Murphy handed down in 1926 in the case of Detroit Stereotypers' Union No. 9 v. Detroit *Free Press* and Detroit *Times* was of even greater importance than his DSR award in helping to solidify support for himself in the ranks of organized labor in Detroit. The issue between the management and the workers that Murphy had to resolve concerned wages: the union was demanding $9.00 for an eight-hour day (or seven hours of night work), whereas the companies had offered $7.75. The publishers had argued that their financial condition should not be considered by the arbitrator, but Murphy, uninfluenced by the fact that one of the concerns involved was his principal journalistic supporter, concluded that this factor "should be a primary basis of decision" since it was "unfair and unsound" to deny the wage earner "the opportunity of sharing in the results of the increased production and prosperity he helped bring about."

The worker, Murphy contended, was entitled to receive a living wage, which he defined as a wage that would permit the recipient "through frugality" to "earn sufficient to develop within reasonable limits his physical, spiritual, moral, and intellectual faculties, and in addition be able to set aside a reserve to provide for accident, old age, idleness, and misfortune." Murphy also made it clear that by living wage he meant "a family living wage." Taking into account the prosperity that the employers were enjoying, the "trivial" increase in real wages for stereotypers in Detroit since 1914, the cost of living, and budget studies that provided some basis for applying "the living wage principle," Murphy set the minimum wage for stereotypers at $8.60 for an eight-hour day.[25]

It is probably more than a coincidence that Murphy's wage decision applied guidelines set forth by the Executive Council of the American Federation of Labor only a few months before. The DFL was understandably delighted, and Stereotypers Union No. 9 presented the arbitrator with a gold wristwatch.[26]

When the DFL or its affiliates needed a speaker for a union function after 1923, they often turned to Judge Murphy. Murphy was thus one of the featured speakers when the Federation staged a protest meeting in May, 1927, as part of the nationwide campaign to save the lives of Sacco and Vanzetti. He denounced the decision to execute the two anarchists as "judicial savagery," but he privately thought that the "net result" of the execution would be "good for the laboring classes for it has excited them more than anything since the war and will tend to create solidarity amongst them." Early in the next year Murphy agreed to address a DFL mass meeting in behalf of Pennsylvania coal miners who were on strike. Illness prevented him from appearing, but he did contribute to a miners' relief fund. The Federation also did not fail to notice that Murphy's clerk toward the end of his service on the court was John Taylor, a former DFL president.[27]

In his labor speeches, Murphy, in the purple prose that he often employed, stressed that it was not the auto magnates who had made Detroit a great city but rather labor, "with its unceasing toil, bleeding fingers, bent back, aching bones and its continuous energy," that was responsible. And how labor audiences loved to hear that kind of talk. Describing the labor movement as "inevitable," Murphy urged workingmen to join the ranks of the organized.

One of Murphy's principal themes before labor audiences was that organized labor must serve larger ends than simply the needs of its own members. Organized labor, he asserted, must be "the backbone of liberalism" and must "quicken the public conscience." It must provide relief for the needy, aid the unorganized who have "no strength to help themselves against the system," and contribute to the solution of the problems of the "industrial frontier."[28]

Murphy told the DFL that it should seek as political leaders men who had themselves earned their daily bread by the sweat of their brow and who set an example for the people by "humane and just dealings." The DFL and its long-time president Frank X. Martel thought that Murphy was just such a man—and so, obviously, did Murphy—and they consequently tried to induce him to become a candidate for mayor in both 1927 and 1929.[29]

As a candidate for a Recorder's Court judgeship in 1923, Murphy stated that "seeking the limelight is a most unfortunate craving of a judicial official. It evidences unjudicial qualities." Despite these remarks, Judge Murphy constantly sought to publicize his views and activities. Since the Detroit *News* and Detroit *Free Press* were consistently hostile to him, Murphy depended on the Detroit *Times* to project a favorable image. He worked closely with the staff of the *Times*, which covered his every move and consistently presented him to its readers in the most flattering terms.[30]

The ambitious Murphy was anxious to gain attention for himself outside of Detroit as well as in the city. He was responsive to the needs of the out-of-town reporters who covered the Sweet trials, sought to have the NAACP publish his charge to the jury in the second trial, and arranged to have information about his sentencing plan sent to influential persons. Murphy also gained some visibility as the result of several major speeches that he delivered away from Detroit. He spoke at the communion breakfast of the New York Fire Department's Holy Name Society in April, 1927, before an audience that included Governor Alfred E. Smith and Mayor James J. Walker. When, at William Randolph Hearst's instigation, the American Crime Study Commission was formed shortly thereafter, Murphy was among the organizers, and he delivered an address at the opening conference in Chicago on May 30, 1927. The next year Murphy, wondering how his "philosophy" would "go with my brethren the Kluxers," journeyed to Memphis to speak to the National Association of Probation Officers.[31]

The first major test after 1923 of Murphy's skill as a practitioner of the art of nonpartisan politics was the Recorder's Court election of 1929. Since only eighteen candidates were contesting for the ten judgeships, there was no primary election this time, and the campaign lacked the drama and intense controversy that surrounded the 1923 election. As an incumbent, Murphy defended the Recorder's Court and the procedures that it was following, but he also set forth his ideas for judicial reform.[32]

Murphy delivered a substantial proportion of his campaign speeches before labor, black, and ethnic groups,[33] and he made a direct appeal for their votes. He thus wrote the editor of the *Hungarian News* that since his (Murphy's) interest in the social and economic problems of the community had established "an intimacy" between himself and "the minority groups" and had "in some measure . . . alienated the more conservative groups" in the city, "it is upon my friends in the minority who have had their peculiar problems that I must lean in the main." In similar vein, he told the editor of the *Tribuno Italiana,* "My candidacy rests largely on the minority groups of the community."[34]

Appealing for black support, Murphy wrote Walter White that since "a little group" was organizing against his candidacy because its members believed that he had "not been the best kind of a white man," he wondered whether White or James Weldon Johnson would be willing to write in behalf of the Murphy candidacy to the two black papers in Detroit. White was only too happy to oblige. He wrote the editors of both the *Owl* and the Detroit *Independent* that Murphy had demonstrated on the bench that "justice knows no color line," and blacks could now show that they were "not forgetful or ungrateful."[35]

Murphy's appeals to organized labor and the minority groups in Detroit did not go unheeded. Frank Martel and the DFL left no doubt where they stood in the election. The ethnic press—Polish, Italian, German, Jugoslav—rallied to Murphy's support, and various ethnic groups endorsed his candidacy. Appealing "to the Colored Voters of the City of Detroit" not to forget "our friends whom it is our duty to support," a group of black leaders put the matter succinctly: "We needed Frank Murphy *then* [Sweet trials]. *He* needs *us now.*"[36]

As in 1923, the veterans once again gave Murphy their support. Several prominent Protestant clergymen also endorsed him, and since his commitment to social reform was joined with a belief in efficiency and economy in government and a demonstrated opposition to corruption and "boodling," he enjoyed a certain amount of WASP and business support. This time, also, the Detroit Citizens League awarded Murphy the accolade of "Preferred" candidate, having privately concluded that he was one of the "three best judges" on the court.[37]

In the April 1 Recorder's Court election all the incumbents except Judge Bartlett were reelected. Murphy came in second in the balloting, his 80,756 votes being exceeded only by the 81,146 votes cast for Judge John V. Brennan.[38] As in 1923, Murphy ran best in the wards with a high percentage of black residents and a low percentage of native-born whites of native parentage. In terms of the percentage of the vote cast for all candidates that he received, Murphy thus made his best showing in Wards 3, 5, and 7, in which more than half the residents were black (as compared to 7.6 percent for the city as a whole) and the percentage of native-born whites of native parentage was 11.26, 6.40, and 7.81 respectively (as compared to 34.28 percent for the city as a whole), and Ward 11, where 18.3 percent of the residents were black, 29.65 percent were foreign born (as compared to 25.45 percent for the city as a whole), and only 13.33 percent were native-born whites of native parentage. In the solidly black precincts Murphy consistently ran ahead of all other white candidates and was outpolled only by Cecil Rowlette, one of the black attorneys in the first Sweet trial. Murphy ran first in Precinct 2 of Ward 18, a district inhabited by persons of Hungarian descent, and he generally ran just behind Jeffries and Stein, but ahead of all the other candidates, in the Polish precincts of the city.

Murphy made his worst showing, relatively, in Ward 4, where 51.21 percent of the residents were native-born whites of native parents, which was far above the city-wide average, only 22.9 percent were foreign born, and a miniscule 0.573 percent were black. Wards 2 and 22, where Murphy ran sixth, were very similar demographically to Ward 4; but the other two wards in which he ran sixth (18 and 20), although almost lily white in population, had a smaller percentage of native-born whites of native parentage (25.10 and 25.82 respectively) than the city as a whole did. In another deviation from the general pattern of his vote, Murphy ran first in Ward 19, only 1.64 percent of whose residents were black and where the percentage of native-born whites of native parentage (36.12) approximated the city-wide average. The results in this ward and the fact that he ran no worse than seventh in any ward indicate that Murphy had a good deal of voting support outside the black and ethnic communities.[39] He had once again provided evidence both of his seemingly strong support among the blocs of voters who were to give the Democratic party its great majorities in the big cities of the nation and of his appeal to the Detroit electorate at large.

In the 1920s Murphy indulged not only in the politics of nonpartisanship but, to a lesser degree, in the politics of partisanship as well. George Murphy was an alternate delegate from Michigan's Seventh Congressional District to the celebrated New

York convention of the Democratic party in 1924, and in the absence of one of the two regular delegates was prepared to cast a vote for the minority platform plank that attacked the Ku Klux Klan by name. The chairman of the Michigan delegation and a major power in Michigan's puny Democratic party, William A. Comstock, ruled, however, that George was an alternate for the district delegate who was present rather than the one who was absent and therefore could not vote, a distinction that Comstock had not previously made. When the minority plank was narrowly defeated, Frank Murphy thought that the Democrats had "lost an opportunity of a life time. . . ."[40] The fight over the Klan plank was probably the modest beginning of a Murphy-Comstock feud that had large consequences for Michigan's Democratic party.

In the prolonged struggle for the Democratic nomination between the Catholic Alfred E. Smith and William McAdoo, the Michigan delegation split fifteen-fifteen, with George voting for Smith through thirty-seven ballots even though the delegate whose place he was taking was a McAdoo man. When Comstock, a McAdoo supporter, failed to persuade George to alter his vote, the delegation chairman telegraphed the absent delegate to return to New York. Frank was troubled about the bitter contest for the nomination, partly because he thought that if Smith had been "anything but a Catholic" he would have won "in a walk." Frank's choice as a compromise candidate when the convention deadlocked was Brand Whitlock, but he accepted the nomination of John W. Davis as "the best" selection that could have been made under the circumstances, even though Davis, in Frank's view, was "not as progressive as I would have the leader of a great party these days."[41]

In 1928 Frank attended the Democratic national convention in Houston as part of a Michigan delegation pledged by the unit rule to Al Smith. The delegation was split on the prohibition issue, with the Old Guard, led by men like Comstock, prepared to compromise on the issue and "a younger, more liberal and more progressive element," among whom Murphy was very prominent, urging the party not to adopt "an evasive and side-stepping platform." "On this and other issues," Murphy stated, "it is highly important that there be a progressive liberal platform that will adjust the fundamental Jeffersonian principles of Democracy to the complex social and economic order of this industrial age."

As in 1924, the small liberal element in the Michigan delegation lost out to the Old Guard at the Democratic convention. "Dismayed" at the convention's "evasion" on the liquor question, Murphy was also unhappy that the party's labor plank fell considerably short of what organized labor desired.[42] Murphy, however, was pleased with the party's candidate, believing that Smith's nomination was "a triumph for liberal and humanitarian forces after a decade of struggle." Frank went abroad in September, but he returned at the end of the month because "I feel duty-bound to do all in my power for Smith." Murphy thought it worthy of note that the captain, chief of staff, and chief engineer of the American ship on which he sailed were all Catholics. "Some bigots," he wrote his brother Harold, "say a Catholic is not safe for the head of our country; yet thousands blindly trust these good men to carry them safely across the ocean."[43]

The Democratic party requested Murphy to speak in Smith's behalf in some of the big cities outside Michigan, but Frank decided that he could do most for Smith's candidacy by confining his campaign activities to his home state. In his major campaign address, he hailed Smith's nomination as a victory for "the real spirit of America—the spirit of civil and religious liberty," and he contended that Hoover, by contrast, must be held responsible for the bigots in his camp. Although Murphy's candidate lost the election, a contribution that Frank made through James Roosevelt to the new National Foundation for Infantile Paralysis shortly after the election suggested that Murphy would be on the side of the winner in 1932.[44]

Murphy found little that pleased him in the behavior of politicians at the state level in Michigan in the 1920s. Politics in Michigan, he wrote in 1924, displayed "an inordinate amount of lack of character," and the office seekers, he thought, appeared to be "little attached to principle or political conviction." Liberal and progressive elements both inside and outside the Democratic party began to see Murphy as the man who could revitalize and modernize Michigan's somnolent and conservative Democratic party and "take Michigan out of the backwoods of reaction," and there was talk as early as 1926 of Murphy as a Democratic candidate for governor or United States senator. Two years later he resisted efforts by Michigan Democrats to enter him in the state's gubernatorial contest or in the race for the United States Senate. Although he was ambitious for higher office, he probably had concluded that a Democrat simply could not win in Michigan in 1928.[45]

Because of his judicial position Murphy was generally disinclined to become involved in Detroit's mayoralty politics. When John Smith, however, defeated Bowles and the Klan in 1925, the Catholic Murphy publicly applauded the decision of the electorate as a victory for "decency and fairness." In 1929 a coalition of forces that included organized labor, some former law students, school teachers, and civic reformers urged Murphy to run for mayor as the candidate "peculiarly fitted to lead the crusade against the old order of things." Murphy was not altogether unresponsive to the appeals that he become a candidate, but in the end he decided against the race, telling his supporters, in effect, as the Detroit *Saturday Night* gleefully put it, "I can't give you anything but love." Bowles won the mayoralty contest in November, just in time to preside over the city as it felt the first impact of what became known as the Great Depression.[46]

Few public officials anywhere in the United States and none in Detroit responded to the depression with greater compassion for its victims or with a greater understanding that the traditional ways of dealing with unemployment and relief were obsolete than Frank Murphy did. When Frank, in June, 1930, wrote that "the poor and helpless hold all my thoughts these days," he was not dissimulating.[47]

The depression quickly led Murphy to become active in the campaign to secure the adoption of old-age pension and unemployment-insurance legislation in Michigan and also to begin laying plans for a comprehensive attack on the problem of unemployment. As of the end of 1928 old-age pension laws were in effect in only six states, and a mere 1,221 persons were actually receiving benefits. None of the state statutes made the granting of pensions compulsory, and all provided for local rather than state financing. As Irving Bernstein has pointed out, the legislative experience with regard to unemployment insurance had been "even more discouraging": no state as of the beginning of the depression had adopted an unemployment-insurance program, and Wisconsin was the only state in which the subject had even been "seriously debated."[48]

In addressing the DFL in April, 1929, Murphy characterized the problem of old-age security as "a supreme challenge" to the nation. "Life," he asserted, "is made . . . unbearable . . . to thousands of families working on a meager wage, unable to save, terrorized with the specter of middle age and old age, fearful that they will be scrapped[,] with the park bench and over the hill to the poorhouse perhaps ahead of them." Early in November Murphy stressed that government would have to deal with the problems of the aged, the needy, and the ill, "those whose very vitality has been sapped by the consequences of great industrial and social processes over which they have no control." When the Michigan Old Age Pension League was formed in April, 1930, Murphy was elected to its board of directors, and attorney Harry Riseman and he were assigned the task of drafting an old-age pension bill for the state.

Working closely with Abraham Epstein, the founder of the American Association for Old Age Security, and Professor Joseph P. Chamberlain of Columbia University's Legislative Drafting Service, Murphy and Riseman prepared a bill that was approved by the Pension League for submission to the January, 1931, session of the Michigan legislature. The measure, more liberal than the statutes then in effect, provided pensions of up to forty dollars a month for citizens aged sixty-five and over who had incomes of less than one dollar a day, one-half the sum to be paid by the state, one-half by the county. Murphy pointed out that there already were five thousand old folks in the Wayne County Infirmary, others were going from door to door seeking alms since they did not wish to die in the county home, and two of five persons sixty-five years of age and over in Detroit were in a dependency status. "No self-respecting community," he declared, "can see this go on. . . ."[49] The state of Michigan, however, was prepared to "see this go on" for quite a while longer.

One of "a group of advanced students" who had helped to persuade Senator James Couzens to have the Senate Committee on Education and Labor investigate the causes of unemployment in 1928, Murphy was as concerned about the plight of the unemployed as about the plight of the aged. He complained about the silence of public officials regarding the extent of unemployment in Detroit and stated categorically that the United States was the most barbaric nation in the world, save possibly China, when it came to providing for the poor and infirm. Regarding unemployment insurance as one means of dealing with the problem, Murphy became a member of the advisory committee of the Unemployment Insurance League in June, 1930, and lent his support to a petition drive for a state-wide referendum on a compulsory unemployment-insurance bill. The measure, which failed of adoption, would have provided the insured worker with up to 40 percent of his wages for a maximum of twelve weeks. It was based on the principles of the pooled fund and merit rating, and the financing of the plan would have been by employer contributions alone.[50]

The problem presented by the depression, as Murphy clearly saw, was less one of establishing an insurance plan for employed workers than of providing relief for the mounting number of the unemployed. In April, 1930, he began laying plans to cope with the unemployment crisis in conversations with Professor William Haber, a Rumanian-born economist teaching at Michigan State College whose brief report on unemployment statistics had come to Murphy's attention and who became one of the nations' first academic experts on the subject of unemployment. Haber prepared a plan for Murphy that called for the creation of a "group" of representative citizens who would function through several subcommittees. One subcommittee would compile statistics on the number of unemployed in Detroit, a subject about which there was considerable mystery; another would concern itself with public employment bureaus; a third would seek to encourage the stabilization of employment, a serious problem in Detroit because of the seasonal ups and downs of automobile production; a fourth would attempt to find temporary employment for the unemployed; and a fifth would encourage the long-range planning of public works.

Invitations to join the "group" were sent out in June, but the effort does not appear to have gone beyond this stage, partly because Haber left Michigan to teach in the summer session at the University of Wisconsin. It was, nevertheless, the "only observable sign of organized concern" for the problem of unemployment in Detroit before August, 1930, when Frank Murphy, as a candidate for mayor, made the unemployment crisis his biggest issue.[51] Once elected, Murphy put the Haber plan into effect by creating the celebrated Mayor's Unemployment Committee.

While engaged in planning to deal with unemployment, Murphy converted his court chambers into "a sort of unofficial employment agency" and tried to help find jobs for the needy who sought his assistance. No better evidence could be provided of the fact that Murphy's court had become, in effect, a "people's court" and that many of the hard-pressed citizens of Detroit had come to look upon Murphy as their champion. "You are my last hope.

I am desperate," one of the city's unemployed wrote Murphy early in August, 1930.[52]

IV

Murphy's service on the Recorder's Court was critical in many ways for his subsequent career. During these years he shed the conservatism that had manifested itself from time to time in the past and began to espouse a liberal philosophy that soon would have considerable appeal. He also cast his political lot with organized labor, the white ethnic groups, and the blacks, forging the voting coalition that helped to elect him mayor of Detroit and governor of Michigan. He probably concluded at the same time that ideology, ties to particular voting blocs, and the personality of the candidate were more important than party organization in attaining political success, and he almost certainly formed a rather poor opinion of the leadership and character of the Democratic party in Michigan.

While a Recorder's Court judge, Murphy learned a good deal about welfare and social work from the professional staff of the probation department, and this knowledge stood him in good stead as mayor and as governor. As governor-general of the Philippines and attorney general of the United States, similarly, he drew on the knowledge of probation and parole that he had acquired on the Detroit bench. His experience as a criminal-court judge was of even greater consequence for his subsequent service on the United States Supreme Court. He added to the knowledge about the methods of prosecutors and the police that he had begun to acquire as a federal attorney, and it was because of this knowledge that he placed such great stress as a Supreme Court justice on the protection of the procedural rights of persons accused of crime. By its very nature, moreover, his Recorder's Court experience inclined Murphy to approach legal matters in practical rather than legalistic terms and to view the law from the perspective of the least fortunate members of society. He became convinced that law-enforcement officials abused their authority in dealing with blacks, the poor, and the inarticulate, and he did what he could on the nation's highest court to curb behavior of this sort.[53]

Murphy's last act as a Recorder's Court judge before he resigned to run for mayor was to place on probation a defendant found guilty in his court. "I'm glad my last sentence can be one of mercy," he remarked. He had said at the beginning of his service on the court that when he fell into error as a judge, he hoped that it would be "on the side of mercy," and so it was gratifying to him that his judgeship had ended as it did.[54]

V

Murphy suffered two hard blows while on the Recorder's Court, the death of his mother on October 11, 1924, and of his father on April 7, 1926, both as the result of heart attacks. When Mary Murphy took a turn for the worse in her final illness, "terror . . . reigned" in the Murphy household. Frank, at his mother's side until the end, saw himself, somehow, as directing the effort to save her life—"If *I* ever get her through this illness," he wrote Hester—but it was all to no avail. After his father's death, Frank himself became ill in Harbor Beach.[55]

The death of Murphy's parents added to the strain imposed upon him by his judgeship, his many activities off the bench, and his law-school teaching. Inclined to hypochondria, he often complained during these years about overwork, nervousness, physical exhaustion, and worry. "Sometimes, often in fact," he wrote Hester, "I want to bolt it all, run away to some quiet place and begin over again." A lucrative job offer tempted Murphy for a moment, but his commitment to a career in the public service, despite his complaints, was far too strong for him to change the style of his life and to become a private citizen.[56]

Early in January, 1930, while returning from the New York wedding of Bernice Chrysler, Murphy was stricken with acute appendicitis and had to be removed from the train in Albany for an emergency operation. After leaving the hospital, he went first to Florida and then to Nassau to recuperate, remaining away from the court for seven weeks. Complaining about "all the mischief I have done to myself in the rush of the last few years in Detroit" and "the tramp life" that he led as a bachelor, Murphy looked upon his extended period of convalescence as "a supreme struggle to recapture the health and peace of mind I once knew." He was soon feeling better, and in one of those abrupt turnabouts that was characteristic of him described himself as "something of a circus strong man."[57]

As was his habit, Murphy turned to exercise to stay in condition and to overcome "depression and nervousness." He played golf, swam a good deal, and took boxing lessons. Horseback riding became his favorite form of exercise toward the end of this period, and it remained so for the rest of his life.[58]

The horse shows and polo matches that Murphy came to love were among the diversions of the Grosse Pointe society whose "dogey [*sic*] affairs" and elegant style of life continued to fascinate him. Attracted, as always, to the very rich and the powerful, Murphy formed friendships during these years with such leading figures in the booming automobile industry as Lawrence Fisher and Walter Chrysler. Frank traveled in Europe with the Chryslers on one of his three trips abroad while he was a judge, and he enjoyed the hospitality of the Chryslers and the Foys when he happened to be in the New York area.[59]

Murphy derived important tangible benefits from his association with Walter Chrysler. Murphy was anxious "to . . . make some money," and the Chrysler connection provided him with the opportunity to do so. Early in 1924 Frank, Byron Foy, Thelma Chrysler (she became Mrs. Foy in December), and Walter Chrysler began placing money in an investment account that Chrysler managed. By the end of April, 1925, Murphy had made a profit of $17,000, and he was very optimistic about his prospects. "There is no mistake about this," he wrote Marguerite. ". . . one of the wealthiest men in the country is handling it [the account], he knows just what to do and I know he wants to befriend Byron and me. . . ." In August Chrysler decided to dissolve the "syndicate," and Murphy's share of the account was transferred to the Detroit branch of J. S. Bache and Company. The scale of Murphy's market dealings by this time is indicated by the fact that between August 28 and September 12, 1925, he purchased almost $160,000 worth of securities.[60]

The end of the "syndicate" did not mean that Murphy no longer profited from "inside" information about the market. Foy, a Chrysler executive, advised Murphy when to buy Chrysler stock— "I know some secrets," Frank wrote Hester in July, 1928, with regard to the market—and Walter Chrysler himself invested money for Murphy in Chrysler securities. On one occasion in 1928, Chrysler, in a matter of days, made a profit of $6,200 for Murphy on a $30,000 investment in Chrysler common stock.[61]

In 1928 Chrysler apparently offered Murphy the opportunity to join the Chrysler Corporation as legal counsel at a very substantial salary.[62] Although Murphy resisted the temptation, he arranged with Chrysler Corporation at the end of the year or the beginning of 1929 to receive a sizeable "retainer fee" for his services. When the firm's treasurer sent Murphy a check for $5,000 for "services rendered" during the first six months of 1929, he wrote the judge that the corporation was "well pleased . . . with the results obtained" and felt that there were "various matters coming up from time to time upon which we would value your advice to the extent of making the present arrangement very attractive to us." It appears that Murphy continued his association with Chrysler Corporation as long as he remained on the Recorder's Court.[63]

Since a Michigan statute forbade a Recorder's Court judge to "engage in private practice" or to "be in any way connected with any attorney or firm of attorneys engaged in such practice,"[64] Murphy was clearly violating the law in accepting a retainer from the Chrysler firm. It seems inexplicable at first glance that a public servant as incorruptible as Murphy and with so high a set of standards for the behavior of public officials could have allowed himself to become involved in such an unethical and illegal arrangement, but it may be that this very confidence in his own incorruptibility explains Murphy's behavior, although it obviously does not justify it: since he knew that the retainer would not influence his behavior on the court, he did not believe that the public interest would suffer from his acceptance of the fee. This puzzling and shabby episode reveals one of the less attractive facets of Murphy's character, his belief that something was due him because of the sacrifice in terms of income that he had made to enter the public service. This same factor probably explains Murphy's casualness about paying his bills, a dereliction for which he became notorious (the surgeon who operated on Murphy in January, 1930, had to go to court in April, 1933, to collect the remainder of the fee still due him).[65] Partly, this stemmed from the sheer lack of order in the Murphy household—Frank sometimes entrusted the payment of his bills to Marguerite, who was one of the world's least disciplined persons—but it also was the result of Murphy's conviction that something was due him ("es kommt mir") for his manifold services to his fellowman.[66]

When it came to spending money, Murphy could be very "close"—"all Frankie ever spends is his time," a hostile newsman once wrote. "His arms are so short he can never reach a dinner check"—but he also could be very generous. He was unfailingly generous with his family, he was sometimes a soft touch for persons in need, and he was hardly circumspect when it came to endorsing the notes of friends and acquaintances.[67] All in all, though, it is fortunate that an appraisal of Murphy's career need not rest on the manner in which he tended to his personal finances.

Not all of Murphy's friends were among the affluent or the socially prominent; he also formed friendships with persons at the bottom of the social order—small-time prize fighters, fight handlers, gamblers, and down-and-outers. The most publicized of these relationships was Murphy's friendship with Patsy O'Toole, née Samuel Ozadowsky, a former newsboy, prize fighter, whisky salesman, and ticket hawker who was reportedly able to make more noise at a Detroit Tigers baseball game than any other spectator in the ball park. Patsy attached himself to Murphy in the middle 1920s, ran errands for the judge, cheered him up after a wearying day, fed his ego, and generally played the role of court jester in Murphy's entourage. Relationships of this sort were essentially feudal, as Murphy's sister-in-law later pointed out; they were obviously not relationships among equals, and Murphy found this, up to a point, relaxing and comforting.[68]

Murphy clearly preferred the company of people at the top or the bottom to socializing with the usual sort of middle-class American businessman. While vacationing at Spring Lake Beach in 1926, he wrote Hester that the resort was "infest[ed]" by "the typical American Bourgoies [sic] gang" and that he "would prefer an interesting labor group or some real highbrows putting on the dog to the limit."[69]

While a Recorder's Court judge, as throughout his adult life, Murphy spent a good deal of his free time with persons of the opposite sex. This was the period when Hester Everard and Ann Harding appeared to be his favorite girl friends, but there were also Annette, Sue, Merle, Jane, Doris, Adele, Kathleen, Rae, Fran, Peggy, and Viola, to name at least some of the women who were attracted to Judge Murphy. As one of his girl friends wrote Frank, probably not fully appreciating the meaning of her words, he had a greater capacity than she did for "friendly love in diverse directions."[70]

Two of the women who were conspicuously drawn into the Murphy orbit toward the end of the 1920s were Peggy Ainsworth, "one of the prominent horsewomen of Detroit," and Viola Hammond, another of the wellborn young ladies to whom Murphy was so often attracted. When Murphy was recovering from his appendicitis operation in an Albany hospital, Viola and Hester appeared on the scene simultaneously to comfort their stricken boyfriend.

Peggy thought that this was "awfully funny," but it was not very funny for Hester and Viola. Hester, believing that her place under the circumstances was at Frank's side, was hurt and jealous because she feared that Frank preferred her rival, and Viola became aware that it was not only Frank's girl friends with whom she was competing. She was dismayed to discover that she was not included in Frank's inner circle and that it was his family that he most wanted and needed at his side.[71] Other women subsequently made the same discovery.

VI

The Murphy of later times is, as Murphy himself suggested, much the same Murphy whom we encounter in judicial robes in the 1920s. He was a man with an extraordinary amount of personal magnetism, a charismatic personality who induced in his supporters "an admiration that was close upon idolatry." Few could resist him when he made up his mind to win them over, and he had a remarkable ability to convince others of the nobility of his purposes.[72]

Murphy remarked at one point in the 1920s that he believed "a man gets the most out of his life by building a creed and sticking to it, by clinging stubbornly to his ideals." Murphy's idealism was manifested most conspicuously in his sympathy for the downtrodden and his struggles in their behalf. "Nowhere," he later asserted, "does government show its sound idealism more than in its concern for the afflicted and those unable to help themselves."[73]

Murphy possessed "a never-relaxing ambition." "I have more than my quota of the stuff they call ambition," he once wrote brother George, "and if conditions are right I'm restless unless forging ahead." Murphy had an abiding faith that a person could reach his goals if he dedicated himself to their attainment. "My whole philosophy of life," he observed, "might be summed up in the simple statement that I firmly believe that if a person wants a thing hard enough he will get it. This means setting a certain definite objective and letting nothing on heaven and earth interfere. It means continual sacrifices because it involves foregoing pleasures and side excursions up the by-ways that are off the main trail." Murphy clearly practiced what he preached— "You arranged your life and prepared yourself for the honors that have been bestowed on you," Marguerite wrote him when he was appointed to the last of the high offices that he held.[74]

As the letters to his mother make abundantly clear, Murphy was convinced that "destiny" was on his side as he pursued his goals. When he learned many years later that he would be appointed to the United States Supreme Court, he privately noted, presumably for the benefit of posterity: ". . . I mean it when I write that some good guardian angel so often called destiny guides and leads me. . . . While industry and some virtues I possess in a modest way have played their part as I advance to each rung in life's ladder[,] fate and the breaks[,] which I like to believe is my angel's way of doing her work[,] clears [*sic*] the path for me." Although regarding himself as destined to do great things, Murphy nevertheless believed in helping "destiny" as much as he could. "I am something of a fatalist," he wrote a friend, "but I still believe that the Lord helps those who help themselves."[75]

"Overindulgence and admiration in the family circle," Harold Laswell has written, tend to encourage "narcissistic types," and the generalization applies, at least to some degree, to Frank Murphy, who was so much admired by his family. Murphy was an immensely self-centered person whose favorite subject of conversation was Frank Murphy and his great achievements and who was inclined to view the tasks upon which he was engaged at any particular moment as being at the very epicenter of the universe. "I seldom read novels," he reportedly said at a later time, "because no novel could be as exciting as my life." Absorbed in himself, Murphy needed and craved the adulation of his associates, and he was easily wounded by criticism.

The pride that Murphy took in his own accomplishments was combined with a feeling of martyrdom. "Every one of Irish extraction," Murphy asserted, "likes to be—craves to be a martyr." He was so much inclined to portray himself as alone and suffering because of the sacrifices that he had made to serve the public that one of his girl friends thought that he really took "great pleasure in sacrificing."[76]

In presenting himself to the public, Murphy was ofttimes guilty of dissimulation. He liked to make it appear that he was "girl shy," shunned the world of the rich, the powerful, and the glamorous, was poor in worldly goods, was unimpressed with the trappings of public office, and accepted only part of the salary due him, none of which was true. An avid seeker of publicity, he was nevertheless able to convince one reporter that he could not be "coerced" into talking about himself, and he told another reporter that "from the first day I was in public life, I have always shuddered at the sight of my name in headlines." He attempted to hide his egotism behind a mask of humility, posing as a hard-working public servant of modest gifts and modest accomplishments. Felix Frankfurter was not incorrect in telling Murphy that "pretended modesty is the worst form of vanity."[77]

A "very lion of virtue," as Arthur Krock described him, Murphy was apt to speak in a pious and sanctimonious way about his abstemious personal habits, his "passion for purity," his refusal to join clubs, and the disinterested character of his public service. This was galling to some, and even brother George reproved Frank on one occasion for being "so virtuous" in letting it be known that a lifelong habit prevented him from accepting a glass of wine.[78]

It was common among those who knew Frank Murphy to say that he was "not a single personality," that he was "many men rolled into one," that he could "ride with the hunters or run with the hounds and do both equally well." As Philip Slater has reminded us, however, "traits and their opposites always coexist [in a person] if the traits are of any intensity," and this was certainly true of Frank Murphy, in whom contradictions abounded. There was the gentle, soft, compassionate, and sentimental Murphy, but there was also the Murphy who gloried in the strenuous life and was eager for combat. There was the parsimonious Murphy who was reluctant to pay his bills and the Murphy who endorsed a sizable note for a policeman on duty in his court. There was the Murphy who was at home in Grosse Pointe and Bloomfield Hills and the Murphy who was equally at home in Delray and in the black ghetto. There was the Murphy who loved the pomp and ceremony of high office, the vacations at Palm Beach, the yachts of the well-to-do, and the best that life had to offer but also the Murphy who was content to live as simply as the average workingman.[79]

In manner, Frank Murphy was dignified and aloof, and there was a reserve about him that few penetrated. "He guarded the inner man," one of his acquaintances recalled. Outwardly calm, Murphy was inwardly tense, and the mildness of his manner masked a resolute and sometimes intransigent will. He enjoyed social affairs, but he had little capacity for small talk, and as one reporter noted, he "had a certain air about him that didn't lend itself to a jovial informality." Although he had many acquaintances, he had few really close male friends, and he was essentially a very lonely man.

He was not without humor, as was sometimes alleged, but his humor was not of the spontaneous, unrestrained sort sometimes associated with the Irish. He spoke in a soft, hushed voice that both soothed and commanded—"the perfect voice for the confessional," according to *Fortune*—but its "deliberate soft purr" sometimes irritated newsmen.[80]

Murphy's overweening interest was his work. "I cannot remember the time," he wrote, "when work did not come first," and he self-consciously but truthfully asserted on another occasion that he always found the work on the problems before him "far more exciting and enjoyable . . . than anything else I could do."[81]

His Catholic religion was important to Murphy, but he did not believe that the church should encroach upon the sphere of the state or instruct officeholders regarding their secular responsibilities. " 'Love God and do as you please,' " a statement that he attributed, tongue-in-cheek, to St. Augustine, summed up Murphy's view of the role of the Catholic in public office.[82]

When Murphy was described on one occasion as being a " 'Midwest Catholic,' " his brother-in-law, never having encountered the phrase before, wrote Frank, "You always had a religion of your own." Murphy was actually a devout Catholic even if he did not observe all the practices of his church. He loved his religion dearly, believed in the efficacy of prayer and in a life after death, and had need of the "spiritual sustenance" derived from attending church. "I always feel better after communion," he wrote his mother on one occasion. Religion for him had to manifest itself in good works, and he thus wrote Hester in 1922 that although he was getting "very little cheer" out of his religion at that point, he would again derive "comfort and solace" from his faith when he became "strong enough to translate my good intentions into action."[83]

There was never anything narrow or parochial about Murphy's faith. Attributing religious intolerance to "lack of education," he believed that there was "much good" in practically all religions. He formed close friendships with several Protestant clergymen and Jewish rabbis in Detroit, declaring once that he admired the Reverend Lynn Harold Hough of the Central Methodist Episcopal Church "more than any other man in Michigan." When the Salvation Army appeared in Harbor Beach in 1922, Murphy informed Hester, "I love the Salvation Army people. . . . Bringing others to the sawdust trail is no sour task to them. I'm for 'em."

In 1932 Murphy gave evidence of his ecumenical approach to religion by becoming an honorary vice-president of the Detroit chapter of the interdenominational Fellowship of Faiths, founded to build understanding among "All Races, Religions, Cultures, Classes, Conditions, and Convictions." "This Roman Catholic," the Episcopal bishop of the Philippines would declare of Murphy, "has all the passion of the Christian religion that the most vociferous Evangelical Protestant could have," and so it must have appeared to many Detroiters as well.[84]

IX

Dew and Sunshine

I

Since automobile production and employment tended to decline during the last quarter of the year even in the best of times, there was little awareness in Detroit in the closing months of 1929 that the city was experiencing the early stages of the Great Depression. To be sure, new construction declined in Detroit in 1929, as it had been since 1926, business inventories accumulated throughout the year, new car sales lagged, and the average number of persons (163,431) employed in factories in the Detroit area in the final three months of the year was 21.5 percent below the average number (208,197) employed during the same months in 1928, but these danger signals did not persuade Detroit's business seers that the boom years had come to an end.[1]

There is, unfortunately, no entirely accurate measure of the number of the unemployed in Detroit during the first eight months of 1930. According to the Bureau of the Census, 76,018 Detroiters (13.3 percent of the labor force) were unemployed in April, 1930, and an additional 15,479 workers were experiencing layoffs without pay, which meant that Detroit had the highest rate of unemployment among the big cities of the nation. Factory employment in the Detroit area, according to figures compiled by the Employers' Association of Detroit and the Detroit Board of Commerce, dropped 37 percent from January to August, and employment in the latter month was almost 52 percent below the figure for the same month in 1929.[2]

The evidence of distress among the population was surely there for those who wished to see. Helen Hall, director of Philadelphia's University Settlement, reported that she had "never confronted such misery as on the zero day" in January, 1930, when she arrived in Detroit. In March 6,541 families who had never before sought relief applied to the Department of Public Welfare (DPW) for assistance. "All day long every week day," a reporter noted in May with regard to the employment exchanges maintained by the welfare department, "one can see sullen and despondent knots of men gathered about the doorways or congregated in the streets."[3]

As the signs of distress multiplied, business leaders and public officials, an astute observer of the Detroit scene later noted, "practiced Christian Science on the creeping economic blight, placed a taboo on the word 'depression,' and started like mad to advertise business back to prosperity." Some businessmen were willing to admit that there had been an economic downturn, but they treated this as an evanescent phenomenon, and there were authoritative predictions that 1931 and 1932 would be "the most prosperous years Detroit has ever seen."

Reflecting the views of the business community, the press, especially the Detroit *News* and Detroit *Free Press,* stressed the good economic news and played down the bad. Although some business-oriented Detroiters, such as William P. Lovett, thought that the employers of the city should "do something" to cope with unemployment if they wished "to avoid the unionizing, communizing, or even Russianizing of American industry," Detroit's business leaders, like business leaders elsewhere, found it difficult to believe or to admit that the economy was in a state of collapse and that remedial action was needed. Perhaps, as Robert and Helen Lynd have suggested in their study of Middletown, there was a reluctance to accept the idea of depression in a culture so geared to the concept of " 'the future.' "[4]

"Detroit's first line of defense against poverty" was its Department of Public Welfare. Detroit was one of the very few cities of the nation that had steadily adhered to the principle of public relief and family welfare service. The French and British traditions of public relief became "firmly imbedded" in pioneer Detroit, and the private charity movement of the nineteenth century, as a consequence, had relatively little impact on the city.[5]

Detroit's 1918 charter replaced the existing Board of Poor Commissioners with the Public Welfare Commission, consisting of four unpaid commissioners appointed by the mayor for four-year terms. The commission, the governing authority of the newly created Department of Public Welfare, was placed in charge of all public relief in Detroit. It was to maintain a bureau of welfare work or social service to care for and to rehabilitate needy, neglected, and deserted families; employ physicians, establish municipal hospitals, and contract with private hospitals for the care of the indigent; and supervise the public markets of the city. During the recession of 1920–21, when the number of the unemployed in Detroit may have reached 160,000, the DPW provided relief to a family case load that rose to more than ten thousand, established a public employment bureau, and maintained a lodging house and restaurant for needy single men.[6]

Between 1922 and 1928 the monthly case load of the DPW ranged from a low of 757 in 1923 to a high of 3,977 in 1927, a year of substantial unemployment in Detroit because of the Ford Motor Company's shift from the Model T to the Model A. As of the beginning of the depression in 1929, the department, which saw itself as standing "beside Detroit families when trouble . . . [overtook] them anywhere from the cradle to the grave," operated through a main office and seven district offices. One of the most efficient institutions of its kind in the nation, it was also indisputably one of the most progressive. The standard for relief, which was given "ungrudgingly" when needed and without unnecessary embarrassment to the recipient, was the "minimum" upon which families could be "safely maintained" and placed on the path to rehabilitation. The specific amounts granted for each individual in the family were based on budgets devised by the Visiting Housekeeper Association, an organization founded in 1912 to mitigate dependency by providing the needy with instruction in purchasing and budget planning.[7]

The impact of unemployment in Detroit during the early months of the depression was reflected in the case load of the DPW, which rose from 3,380 in October, 1929, to 21,759 in April, 1930. Although sickness, desertion, old age, and insufficient income had been the traditional reasons for the granting of relief, unemployment now accounted for more than 80 percent of the relief cases—the "new poor" had begun to make their disheartening appearance on the American scene.[8]

Relief in Detroit, as compared to other cities in the nation, was characterized by its overwhelmingly public character and its generosity. In 1929, 94.9 percent of the relief granted in Detroit came from public funds, as compared to 53.6 percent in seventy-four other cities; the comparable percentages the next year were 97.7 and 56.4, respectively. As these figures indicate, public expenditures for relief in the nation had come to exceed private expenditures, although hardly to the same degree as in Detroit, but private charity nevertheless overshadowed public relief in the popular consciousness.[9]

The $762,228 spent for public relief in Detroit in March, 1930, was the "largest amount" ever spent in a single month for outdoor relief by any city in the history of the nation up to that time. The average monthly amount spent per relief case during the period January–May, 1930, ranged from $31.48 to $40.90 in Detroit as compared to a range of $19.58 to $21.87 in forty-six other cities; and Detroit's per capita expenditure for public relief was the highest among 117 urban areas in the nation.[10]

The DPW sought to cope with the mounting demand for aid by increasing the number of its district offices from seven to ten and by enlarging its staff from the normal number of 125 to 200. Despite this, the burden placed on the case workers was "unreasonable and inhuman." In October, 1929, the ratio between supervisory personnel and visitors and active cases was 1 to 76, which was regarded as too high, and yet by May 1, 1930, the ratio was 1 to 209, which an expert on the subject described as "absurd." The same individual thought that the department, by July, was "floundering in a slough of applications for relief."[11]

Whereas material relief in Detroit was supplied by the DPW, the city's numerous private social agencies, eighty of which were linked together in the Detroit Community Union, provided services of a "specialized or supplemental character" that the city government was not prepared to offer. Funds for the private agencies were raised by the Detroit Community Fund, which had developed out of the Detroit Patriotic Fund of World War I and had an interlocking relationship with the Community Union. The advent of the depression confronted Detroit's private social agencies with what the *Community Fund News* described in March, 1930, as "the most serious problem in their history." Between June, 1929, and June, 1930, the Community Fund agencies aided 289,364 families and individuals, and the Fund by October, 1930, faced a deficit of $125,000.[12]

Like public authorities elsewhere during the first year of the depression, the mayor and the members of the Common Council in Detroit reacted to the spreading unemployment only fitfully and without much comprehension of either the nature or the extent of the economic crisis. In his last month of office, in December, 1929, Mayor John Lodge appointed a Mayor's Labor Committee to study the unemployment problem in Detroit and to suggest measures for its amelioration. The committee issued a report in January that urged the automobile companies to regularize employment and advised employers to give preference in hiring to Detroit citizens and to discourage persons from coming to Detroit in search of employment. The committee then disbanded, and its report was soon forgotten.[13]

On February 25, 1930, responding to complaints of the Detroit Federation of Labor (DFL) that thousands of Canadians were crossing the border daily to work in Detroit, the Common Council adopted a resolution calling for the discharge of all municipal employees who were not American citizens but providing, at the same time, for their reemployment if "extenuating circumstances" warranted such action. The Common Council revoked the anti-alien resolution at the end of March without its having had any appreciable effect on city government employment, but, in the meantime, the Detroit Board of Education and some private employers had begun to dismiss their alien employees.[14]

On March 6, 1930, Communists staged demonstrations around the world to protest unemployment and to demand relief. In Detroit, perhaps five thousand persons participated in the demonstration. The newly organized Detroit branch of the American Civil Liberties Union had urged the mayor and the police to use restraint in dealing with the crowd, but the police clubbed and rode down some of the demonstrators and made thirty-one arrests.[15]

Appalled by the increase in welfare expenditures, Mayor Bowles requested the Detroit Bureau of Governmental Research on June 18, 1930, to survey the DPW with a view to making recommendations that would permit the placing of "some reasonable limitations on its spending." The Bureau engaged Charles C. Stillman, professor of social administration at Ohio State University, to conduct the study. Stillman reported in July that the department, primarily because of insufficient personnel, was "in a pathological condition" and "reflected and re-enacted the hysteria of its clients." He directed his principal criticism at the inadequate investigation of cases by the department and what he thought was the almost total lack of individualized treatment of welfare clients. Stillman, reflecting the "contempt, or at least suspicion" with which most professional social workers viewed public outdoor relief, was assuming that traditional casework methods should be applied to the new poor, but the new poor needed jobs and relief until they found employment, not casework.[16]

Although public officials in Detroit tended to subscribe to the thesis that the acceleration of public works was a proper way for government to respond to unemployment, the action that resulted from this belief was rather meager. The financial plight of the city and political differences between the Bowles administration and the Council proved to be almost insuperable barriers to the development of a comprehensive public-works program in Detroit in the first year of the depression.[17]

The twin nightmares of the cities in the Great Depression were the increasing burden of unemployment and the threat of financial bankruptcy, and the shape of things to come was as evident with regard to the latter in Detroit during the first year of the depression as it was with regard to the former. In December, 1929, Ralph Stone, former secretary to Mayor and Governor Hazen Pingree and chairman of the board of the Detroit and Security Trust Company, declared in an address to the Detroit Real Estate Board that the city would have to reduce its taxes, decide which of its functions were of the greatest importance, and expend its funds accordingly. As a means of achieving these objectives, Stone suggested the formation of a citizens' committee to engage in financial planning for Detroit. The next day the Common Council invited Stone to form such a committee and to aid the city government in planning the next year's budget. Stone responded by putting together a Committee on City Finances that in addition to himself as chairman consisted of representatives of the Michigan Manufacturers' Association, the Detroit Real Estate Board, the Detroit Board of Commerce, the Business Property Association, the Detroit Automobile Club, the Woodward Avenue Improvement Association, the Detroit Citizens League, and the Detroit Bureau of Governmental Research.[18] As Mayor Bowles's successor learned, the Committee on City Finances quickly became a force to be reckoned with in depression-ridden Detroit.

II

In the normal course of events there would not have been a mayoralty election in Detroit in 1930, but the unprecedented decision of the city's voters to recall Mayor Charles Bowles in July, 1930, necessitated a special election in September. Several factors accounted for the decision to recall Bowles: the allegedly lax and selective enforcement of the vice laws in Detroit, the character of the mayor's appointments, his actions regarding the Detroit Street Railways (DSR), his relations with the press, and his dismissal of Police Commissioner Harold H. Emmons.

As a mayoralty candidate, Bowles had pledged himself to rid Detroit of vice, but, as it turned out, it was the manner in which the vice laws were enforced in Detroit during the Bowles administration that led to some of the harshest criticism of the mayor. On March 11, 1930, Bowles announced a major shake-up of the police department: seven veteran officers were retired, and, despite the opposition of Emmons and experienced officials of the department, enforcement of the vice laws was taken out of the hands of individual precinct commanders and vested in a central vice squad with city-wide jurisdiction. The press soon pointed out that there had been more blatant violation of the gambling and liquor laws after March 11 than before that date; and since the police apparently chose to enforce the law against some violators but not others, there were allegations that it was ties between the mayor and the underworld that influenced the character of law enforcement in the city, allegations that Emmons himself later insisted were accurate.[19]

An inefficient executive at best, Bowles made several appointments that reflected adversely on his judgment, to put the matter most charitably. As employment manager of the DSR, the only important area of city government not subject to civil-service requirements, Bowles appointed Wesley Stephens, a member of the Odd Fellows, who let it be known immediately that he would try to find jobs for fellow lodge members. The mayor had to relieve Stephens of his position after two days in office. Frank Dohany, a member of a law firm that handled a large number of claims against the DSR, was appointed to the three-man Street Railway Commission, and Joseph Wolff, a builder involved in a lawsuit against the city relating to the municipal building code, was appointed commissioner of buildings and safety engineering. Bowles placed one of his campaign workers at the head of the city's Civil Service Commission and rewarded other campaign lieutenants with similarly important positions.[20]

The most controversial and most criticized of the mayor's appointees was John Gillespie, a veteran Detroit politician whom Bowles selected to be commissioner of public works. Not only was Gillespie subjected to attack for actions by his department that seemed to be related to his private business interests, but he also came to be seen as the éminence grise of the Bowles administration—the " 'commissioner of the works' "—who was methodically building a corrupt, city-wide political organization to ensure Bowles's reelection and to serve as "a branch Republican machine" in nonpartisan Detroit.[21]

Bowles came in for a good deal of criticism in depression-ridden

Detroit when he agreed in March, 1930, to support a split decision of the Street Railway Commission to raise streetcar fares from six cents to eight cents. A public outcry persuaded the mayor to reverse himself before the new fare could go into effect. The next month the Street Railway Commission placed all DSR insurance with a single firm, Gorman and Thomas, although the practice had been to divide the insurance among several agencies and despite the fact that another agency had offered to carry the policy for a smaller sum than Gorman and Thomas were to receive. When Frank Couzens, the son of Senator James Couzens and the one commissioner who had opposed the fare increase, protested the insurance decision of his fellow commissioners, Bowles promptly asked for his resignation.[22]

In contrast to the Detroit *Times,* which pursued a policy of "'benevolent neutrality'" toward the Bowles administration, the Detroit *Free Press* and the Detroit *News* regularly pointed to the alleged shortcomings of the mayor and his associates. Bowles retaliated by virtually breaking off relations with City Hall reporters, denying them access to relevant records and refusing to respond to their questions. This, not surprisingly, led to press attacks on the secretiveness of the city administration.[23]

The immediate cause for the effort to recall Mayor Bowles was his dismissal of Harold Emmons. While Bowles and Gillespie were away from Detroit at the Kentucky Derby, Emmons, with newspapermen leading the way, raided several gambling establishments and brothels in the city. As soon as Bowles returned from Louisville, he requested Emmons to resign, and when the police commissioner refused to do so, the mayor dismissed him. The very next day, May 21, a "Citizens' Committee" for the recall of Mayor Bowles was formed, and it began circulating petitions for a recall election.[24]

The petition drive lagged until it was taken over by Walter B. Carey, the president of one of the firms that had carried a portion of the DSR's insurance before it had been assigned exclusively to Gorman and Thomas. Carey hired workers to gather signatures, and he was soon able to turn over to the city clerk petitions bearing signatures in excess of the number required (25 percent of the votes cast in the preceding gubernatorial election in Michigan).[25]

The Detroit *News,* the Detroit *Free Press,* the Detroit *Saturday Night,* and the Detroit Citizens League all supported the recall of Bowles, whereas the Detroit *Times* took no stand on the question.

The Klan charged that Catholics were responsible for the recall movement, and Bowles and his friends pointed the finger at the *News* and *Free Press,* alleging that they wanted the mayor removed because he had ended "a dynasty of newspaper control."[26]

The recall campaign, "notable for its vituperative violence," took place against a backdrop of gangland murders in Detroit—ten of them in a fourteen-day span beginning on July 4—that served to dramatize the issue of crime and law enforcement. The vote on July 22, which may have been influenced by the mounting unemployment in Detroit, went against Bowles, with 57 percent (120,863) of the voters favoring his recall.[27] This was the first time in the history of the United States that the mayor of a big city had been successfully recalled, but the election results were almost overshadowed in Detroit by the startling news that Gerald M. (Jerry) Buckley, the city's most popular radio newscaster, had been murdered in the early hours of July 23.

Buckley, an outspoken foe of the mayor and an advocate of the recall, had broadcast the election results from City Hall and had then returned to the La Salle Hotel, where he resided. He was sitting in the lobby when three gunmen walked into the hotel and fired eleven shots into his body. The assailants were never apprehended,[28] and there would be unanswered questions about Buckley's death just as there were unanswered questions about his life. A member of an old Detroit family, Buckley had enjoyed a varied career as a lawyer, investigator, realtor, and composer before turning to radio in 1928 and .a nightly program over station WMBC. In his broadcasts, Buckley vigorously attacked vice and gambling in Detroit, sometimes naming names, but he also campaigned for old-age pensions and other humanitarian causes. Once the depression began to affect employment, Buckley, playing the radio role that was eventually taken over by Father Charles E. Coughlin, pleaded for action to deal with unemployment, and he found jobs for hundreds of Detroiters during the winter of 1929–30.

His espousal of liberal causes and his concern for the victims of depression won Buckley a "tremendous following" among the ordinary people of Detroit, a devoted army of supporters who collectively became known as "the common herd." Some alleged, however, that Buckley was a Jekyll and Hyde character who, although concerned about the plight of the unfortunate, was at the same time linked to racketeers and used his broadcasts for blackmail purposes. Those who saw Buckley as a crusading opponent of Bowles were convinced that the broadcaster had been slain by "gun men employed by the vice ring" that had opposed the recall, whereas those who stressed the Mr. Hyde in Buckley maintained that his alleged associations with the underworld had led to his undoing.[29]

Although the immediate reaction in Detroit was to regard the Buckley murder as a horrible by-product of the recall, the Detroit *Times* chose to view the killing in quite another light. In the early hours of the morning of July 23 Carl Muller of the *Times* was writing up the story of the election results when he received the news of Buckley's murder. About the same time Henry Montgomery, the managing editor of the paper, appeared in the newsroom—"he wasn't himself," Muller recalled—and insisted on the depiction of Buckley as a blackmailer in the account of his death. The *Times* story discounted the theory that Buckley had been killed because of the part that he had played in the recall and contended that he had been named in a kidnapper's confession as having been involved in a kidnap ring that "preyed" on wealthy Detroiters, was "an associate of underworld racketeers," and had been accused of using his broadcasts for blackmail purposes. The story also noted that Bowles had charged that Buckley had indirectly offered to stop his criticism of the mayor if the price were right. An editorial in the same issue stated that the police believed Buckley to be "one of their enemies IN the racket rather than OUTSIDE of it."

As Muller recalled, using an interesting choice of words, when the *Times* hit the streets on July 23, "it was murder." Complaining telephone calls lit up the *Times* switchboard, circulation quickly fell by about twelve thousand, and advertisers found reasons to cancel their contracts with the paper. "The *Times* was in a terribly bad way and had to do something to redeem itself."[30]

Three days after the recall election, on July 25, George Engel, who had served the city under six different mayors, announced that he would run for mayor to succeed Bowles. It quickly became evident that Engel was the hand-picked candidate of the establishment in Detroit—one after another of the "civic influences" rallied to his support—and of such major proponents of the recall as the *News* and *Free Press*. Since Bowles, despite his recall, was to continue to serve as mayor until the special election of September 9 and was permitted to be a candidate in the election, Engel's backers urged that no other candidate enter the race lest a divided opposition permit Bowles "to creep back into City Hall" by a minority vote and make Detroit the laughing stock of the nation.

Engel, his supporters argued, was the right man for mayor because he had the ability, experience, and business talent required for the position.[31]

The Detroit *Times* was not inclined to join the united front against Bowles. In 1923 it had successfully exploited the Recorder's Court candidacy of Frank Murphy to boom its meager circulation, and now it saw in a "noisy, roaring campaign" to elect Murphy mayor the means of salvaging its "prestige, circulation and declining profits" and repairing the damage that it had inflicted upon itself by its neutrality in the recall campaign and its ill-advised treatment of Buckley's murder. The day after the announcement of Engel's candidacy the *Times* reported that Murphy was being beseiged with requests to enter the race for mayor; and it left no doubt from that point forward that it considered him the man best qualified to rescue Detroit in its hour of need. From the point of view of the *Times,* Murphy was close to being the perfect candidate: he was immensely popular in the city; as a Recorder's Court judge he had remained aloof from the bitter and divisive recall fight; he had had a friendly association with Buckley, who had often sought Murphy's advice and, according to one source, had told Murphy that he was "the logical candidate for mayor" should Bowles be recalled; and he was identified with some of the same causes— old-age pensions and aid to the unemployed in particular—that had gained Buckley such a large following.[32] Although the publisher of the *Times* wrote a close friend that Murphy was "not in the slightest sense the *Times'* candidate," the evidence indicates that the publisher himself pleaded with Murphy to enter the race.[33]

Although its own interests were at stake, the *Times* was by no means inaccurate in reporting that Murphy was being importuned from a variety of directions to become a candidate for mayor. The DFL, veterans groups, black leaders, representatives of various white ethnic groups, the aged, unemployed citizens, some attorneys, and members of "the common herd" all urged Murphy to enter the mayoralty race.[34]

When he spoke at the memorial service for Buckley on August 1, Murphy unmistakably identified himself with the "great group whose name Gerald Buckley gave new lustre [*sic*]—'the common herd.'" That the followers of Buckley saw Murphy as Buckley's heir was altogether evident. "You stand among the people about on same standing as Jerry Butley [*sic*]," one of them wrote Murphy. "You known as a man of the People and By the People and For the People." "I as one of the common Herd," another Buckley follower wrote Murphy, "am Calling on you to come out and Run for Mayor and We the Common Herd will put you over."[35]

Murphy also received some advice not to run. Some of his correspondents feared that his candidacy would divide the anti-Bowles vote and ensure the mayor's victory, a consequence, they thought, that might irreparably damage Murphy's career. Several Catholics, including the Reverend John P. McNichols, the president of the University of Detroit, also feared that Murphy's presence in the race would give Bowles the opportunity to exploit the religious issue once again. "It is his big card," Father McNichols wrote, and he was afraid that there was "enough small minded Protestantism in Detroit to make it count."[36]

Although Murphy convinced even some insiders that he was reluctant to leave the Recorder's Court to run for mayor, this is true only in the sense that he was not inclined to enter the race unless he was reasonably sure of victory, an understandable caution considering what his contribution to a Bowles victory would probably have done to his career. Vera Brown, a Detroit *Times* reporter who was close to Murphy, revealed in 1935 that Murphy had told her, "I am stagnating here [Recorder's Court]. . . . A man can not stand still. He must either go ahead or go backward. If I remained on here I would go backward. . . . It is time I got out."[37]

Within a few days of the recall election, Murphy made it clear that he did not subscribe to the argument that the friends of good government must unite behind Engel. "The people," he said, "do not recognize the right of any little group—however good their intentions—to get together in a back room and select the Mayor of this city. . . . This is not popular government; it is rather a high-toned form of 'gang rule.'" Murphy promised that if he became a candidate he would "not accept one cent of contributions for my campaign." The mayor must go into office "free and unshackled"; he must not be "mortgaged by campaign cash" nor "tied, bound, [and] captured to gain the support of political workers."[38]

Murphy also began to provide hints of the kind of mayor he would be. He stated that the mayor, above all, had to be "a man whose sympathies lie with the weary people, the people whose jobs are gone or whose wage does not meet the requirements of a decent living." Sympathizing with the jobless and sensing before other mayoralty contenders did the question on which the election would turn, Murphy proclaimed unemployment to be "the first issue, municipal, state or national" and attacked what he regarded as the "conspiracy of silence" surrounding the problem. "They say nothing can be done about it, but," Murphy announced to the electorate, "something can be done."[39]

While quietly taking private soundings about his probable support should he enter the race, Murphy, undoubtedly to contrast the manner in which he was proceeding with the behind-doors selection of Engel, shrewdly announced on August 11 that he would become a candidate only if a petition drive indicated that there was "a very substantial and general public demand" for him "to lead this fight for good government." The call for volunteers to gather signatures on Murphy-for-mayor petitions brought a crowd of fifteen hundred persons to the Fort Wayne Hotel on August 12. Murphy had left neither the size nor the composition of the crowd to chance. As his personal papers reveal, he had arranged every detail in advance and had made provision for his friends in organized labor, the minority and ethnic groups, and the servicemen's organizations to bring large numbers of "volunteers" to the meeting. He had also, for tactical reasons, decided to "put ex-servicemen to the fore" in the petition drive. The committee of five placed in charge of the petition campaign was headed by Robert G. Brand, the commander of the Wayne County Council of the American Legion, and included four other veterans. Although the committee was later enlarged, former servicemen remained its most conspicuous members.[40]

While signatures were being gathered on Murphy petitions, jockeying was going on among the candidates and prospective candidates to reduce the number who would finally take the field. Although it is difficult to ascertain the truth regarding these negotiations, Murphy was apparently led to believe that if he became a candidate, Bowles would withdraw from the race. It also appears that after John Smith began circulating petitions for his candidacy, there were discussions between Murphy and Smith backers to secure the withdrawal of one or the other of the two men since it was assumed that they appealed to the same black and ethnic constituencies. Just what went on between the Murphy and Smith camps is unclear. One story making the rounds was that Murphy supporters had offered Smith the police commissionership in a Murphy administration if he remained out of the race but that Smith had spurned the offer. Smith, on the other hand, later claimed that Murphy, protesting that he was being pressured to run by the *Times,* proposed that the two meet with a group of citizens who had supported both of them in the past to decide who should make the race. As Smith told the story, these individuals preferred Smith, which led Murphy to remark, according to the former mayor, "That will help me avoid a very embarrassing situation."

There is no corroboration of Smith's tale, but it is known that Smith backers did make a determined effort to get Murphy out of the race. Their trump card, they thought, was Ossian Sweet, of all people. Sweet, almost alone among prominent blacks in Detroit, preferred Smith to Murphy, allegedly because Sweet believed Smith to be the more "experienced and capable" of the two men and because of all that Smith, as mayor, had done for blacks. Murphy was summoned to a hotel room to confer with Smith supporters, including Sweet, and was told that since Sweet allegedly controlled thirty thousand black votes that were certain to go to Smith, Murphy should withdraw from the race. Murphy remained in the race, however, as did Smith.[41]

At a meeting of Murphy supporters at the Fort Wayne Hotel on August 19 Brand's committee presented Murphy with petitions bearing seventy-three thousand signatures. Murphy now, for the first time, proclaimed himself a candidate. In his speech, he adumbrated the themes that he stressed throughout his campaign. Detroit, he declared, was "in ashes, a political ruin, burned to the ground, by hate, by discord, by selfishness, by government put to corrupt and selfish ends." Because the city was "dead broke," economy would have to be the watchword until Detroit was once again on its feet. The DSR was running at a loss not just because of the business slump but because it had been made "a political instrument for certain people." He would put friends of public ownership, not its enemies, on the Street Railway Commission and would run the DSR along business rather than political lines.

Murphy deplored the fact that the police department had lost the confidence of the people of Detroit and that the morale of the department had been destroyed. He attributed all this to "political interference" and to the influence of vice leaders. "Vice," he asserted, "just doesn't exist in Detroit. . . . vice is supreme. . . . It does the dictating." He also complained that the forty thousand municipal employees had been made insecure about their jobs because of efforts "to whip them into a political machine," and he declared that deserving employees would be secure in their positions should he become mayor.

Murphy promised that he would not permit anyone to deflect him from his "conception of social and progressive justice." He would take care of the sick, see to it that the aged were pensioned, and, "with all the Master has given us," tackle the desperate problem of unemployment. "We will help solve that problem. Don't let them tell you it cannot be done. They are afraid of treading on toes and we are not. . . . They walk into their clubs, into their security, into their isolation of influence and affluence. But, we will not miss them [the unemployed]. We will see them. We will give them a helping hand, every one of them."

Noting that the people of Detroit had lost confidence in their government and their leaders, Murphy pledged himself to a "new deal" in the city's political life. "Detroit's past," he said in words that resounded throughout the remainder of his career, "should belong to [the] dead yesterday. . . . We want something new. We want the dew, the sunshine of a new morning." The campaign now became the "dew-and-sunshine campaign" and Murphy the "dew-and-sunshine candidate." As reporter Blair Moody later observed, Murphy had delivered "the pivotal speech of his career," and "if it was bunk," Moody commented, "it was magic bunk."[42]

When Murphy declared that he would be a candidate, men and women in the crowd stood on their chairs and cheered. There was a rush of well-wishers toward Murphy when he finished his speech, and when he left the hotel the throng outside lifted him to their shoulders and passed him hand-over-hand to his car. The "common herd" was delighted with the address, one of the group writing Murphy that she had not heard "anything so much worth while since 'Jerry' went away."[43]

The race for mayor was, in the end, confined to Murphy, Bowles, Engel, Smith, and Phil Raymond, who ran with Communist party support. Murphy resigned his Recorder's Court post on August 26—the law did not require that he do so to become a candidate—officially filed as a candidate on the same date, and opened his campaign with a radio address that evening. By that time the leadership of the rather disorganized volunteer group that had conducted the Murphy petition drive had been entrusted by Murphy to Harry Mead, a Detroit lawyer whom Murphy had first met when they were both Sigma Chi members at the University of Michigan. A salty character with an earthy sense of humor and an eye to the main chance, Mead practiced the old politics of patronage and organization while Murphy concentrated on ideology and programs; the two men would make an effective

political team for a long time to come. Mead gave some semblance
of organization to Murphy's campaign, but a campaign insider
nevertheless remembered the effort as "the most helter-skelter,
unorganized, ill-financed, weird campaign that you ever heard
of."[44]

Murphy, who gained a good deal of favorable publicity from
his reiterated statement that he would not accept any campaign
contributions excepting sums not to exceed $1 to defray the costs
of his petition drive, did not abide by this resolve. The total
cost of the campaign was only $3,845.55, partly because the Detroit
Times provided so much free publicity; but a mere $326.75 of
the $2,157.25 officially reported to have been collected by election
time derived from contributions of $1 or less, and Mead acidly
recalled that the members of the volunteer organization who
concentrated on this phase of the campaign consumed a greater
sum of money in the form of ham sandwiches and coffee than
they raised in contributions. In contrast to the small total raised
by one dollar contributions, $1,500 was collected in amounts
of $50 to $200, and the remainder in sums of $5 or more. Mead
raised some of the money by "hitting a few of the boys Murphy
didn't know," including some blind-pig operators; and Murphy's
former political mentor, William F. Connolly, was "the Santa
Claus," as Mead recalled it, for the campaign deficit.[45]

Murphy campaigned at a feverish pace in what the Detroit
News characterized as "the shortest and most important mayoralty
contest" in Detroit's history. His life became a succession of
meetings, twenty-seven of them on September 7 alone, if the
Times is to be believed. Murphy concentrated much of his effort
on the black and ethnic voters of the city. Thus, of the eleven
groups that he addressed on the night of September 5, six were
black, one Polish, one Hungarian, and one Serbian.

Clubwomen, servicemen, the DFL and its affiliates, the Buckley
family, ethnic groups, and the black leadership rallied to Murphy's
support. The defection from the black ranks of Dr. Sweet and
Clarence Diggs, a black undertaker of some influence in the
black community, caused Murphy a good deal of concern, and
he turned to Clarence Darrow for help. Darrow liked Smith but
wrote Murphy, "there is no comparison between you and him
or between you and anybody else I know of." He enlisted the
aid of Walter White, who arranged for Oscar DePriest, the only
black member of Congress, to come to Detroit to speak in Murphy's
behalf. Murphy himself reminded blacks of the Sweet trials and

how he had "preserved" their rights. "I have done you no favor," he told them, while pointing out that they were "unused to [the] application of our fundamental laws to all, instead of one group and not another." Referring to the reaction of a black audience to a Murphy speech, Harry Mead recalled, "You would have thought it was the second coming of Lincoln or second coming of Christ." In the end, the blacks of Detroit, 47,586 of whom were registered, worked as hard for Murphy's success as any single voting bloc in the city.[46]

A consummate orator in an era when "hot" oratory was still the vogue, Murphy was especially effective on the hustings and was able to adjust his "mood, tempo and approach" to the particular audience he was addressing. "To Legionnaires and veterans' societies," one writer later summarized, "he is the tough butt-and-bayonet doughboy. To Poles and Slovaks and hunky mill hands he is the descendant of humble immigrants. To ladies' societies he is the blushing, self-deprecating sacrifice to public duty." Through the "idealistic ring" of his oratory and its "inspirational quality," Murphy, as the *Nation* observed, was able to convert a campaign for public office into "a huge crusade to recapture Detroit."[47]

Carl Muller, who covered the Murphy campaign for the Detroit *Times,* sought to capture for his readers the nature of the Murphy campaign by presenting his impressions of a day on the campaign trail with the candidate. At 11:30 A.M. Murphy appeared at the Fisher Body plant. The factory windows were lined with workers, and there were people in the street. "Resounding cheers. Factory audiences usually silent and glum. Something unusual here. . . . Funny thing about this factory group. Their faces are not the dead, immobile faces of men who have despaired of a better day. How they cheer." At 4:00 P.M. Murphy appeared at the Hostess Cake Kitchen, where a group of fifty Gold Star mothers had gathered. He was introduced by seventy-six-year-old Mrs. Margaret Byrne, who said that Murphy was like a son to her. "No hectic cheering here." Affecting the boyish charm that older women found irresistible, Murphy seemed "nonplussed" as to what to say. "No politics here," Muller erroneously concluded. At 7:40 P.M. Murphy spoke over the radio. One hour later he addressed an audience of one thousand at the Holy Name Church. "The crowd has gone wild. . . . Never saw such an ovation." Murphy was then off to the East Side and the Dom Polski hall. "Look at the crowd." Not every one could get into the hall, which was packed with "cheering, shouting, gesticulating men and women. . . . Never saw anything like it, anything approaching it until this campaign. What in the world. has happened to Detroit? All over town—'Murphy, Murphy, Murphy.' " Then the candidate went to the Deutsches Haus and a businessmen's group. "Again an audience rising, cheering lustily, shouting. They say there [*sic*] a stolid people. They don't know these people." Finally, Murphy appeared before the Veterans' Political Association and just smiled for a few minutes until the applause subsided. "What's happening in Detroit? Something's happening. Never saw the people so stirred. Never saw such enthusiasm."[48]

Murphy, who was critical of "the disorder, unrest and chaos that affected the city government like a pestilence" in the Bowles regime, had relatively little to say about the financial side of government, but he spoke a good deal about the "human" side. "I am for a humanized government," he asserted, "a government that will touch the citizens in all their activities, in all their distress." Undoubtedly affected by the tales of agony that his correspondents related to him, Murphy placed his greatest emphasis on the issue of unemployment. If elected, he said, he would see to it that no one starved even if the city had to open soup kitchens, and he would provide municipal lodging houses for the homeless, establish municipal employment agencies, and launch construction projects that were consistent with "sound public finance." Although Murphy was careful to point out that unemployment was a "national problem" and could not "be attacked by a single remedy," he conveyed to the voters of Detroit the impression that he was the candidate most concerned about this issue and the one most likely to do something about it if elected. ". . . you seem to have the Engel supporters in the air about this unemployment situations [*sic*] and that it can be remedied," one of Murphy's correspondents correctly advised the candidate.[49]

There was an unmistakable class appeal in Murphy's campaign oratory and a touch of the same kind of demagoguery that Franklin D. Roosevelt was later accused of employing in his attack on the "economic royalists" in the 1936 presidential campaign. "A little group of rich people downtown," Murphy asserted, was trying to control the city, and unless these "royalists of Detroit" paid more attention to the needs of the common people and stopped opposing social and economic reforms, "off will go their heads." Murphy hastened to add that he meant this only in a political sense. Those in authority, he remarked in one campaign speech, looked for inspiration to big business, the newspapers, and the money changers, but they were looking in the wrong places. They should look rather, he advised, to "the common people" since governments were designed to serve them, not "those occupying places of economic security." He portrayed himself as "the people's candidate," whose special concern was "the lowly, . . . the man and woman who is broke and hard pressed, and hasn't a chance. . . ."[50]

In his campaign addresses, Bowles, naturally enough, defended his record as mayor and insisted that the recall campaign alone had prevented him from introducing a public-works program that would have mitigated the effects of the depression. At the close of the campaign the Reverend Billy Sunday appeared in Detroit, seeking votes for Bowles as a dedicated dry. Engel, described by one reporter as "a polished gentleman who wore a high hat and promised to make Detroit as highly moral as a wax works exhibition of saints," stressed crime as the most important issue facing the city. Relegating unemployment to second place, he declared that Detroit needed "a sound, level-headed and strong business administration." In an obvious swipe at Murphy, he maintained that it was a poor time for "fooling and experimenting" and trying out "idealistic theories." Engel's views of what the city required were echoed by the Detroit Citizens League, the *News*, the *Free Press*, and the Detroit *Saturday Night*, all of which stressed Murphy's alleged lack of qualifications; but, as one observer noted, Engel "engaged himself to save Detroit's soul" and, unlike Murphy, did not pay adequate attention to its "empty belly."[51]

It was charged at the time that Johnnie Smith, at the behest of Engel's newspaper supporters, entered the mayoralty race with the specific purpose of splitting the vote that otherwise would have gone to Murphy alone. Whatever the validity of this allegation, Smith largely ignored Engel in the campaign and centered his attack on Murphy and, to a lesser extent, Bowles. When Murphy espoused lodging houses and soup kitchens as means of coping with distress, Smith countered, "This is what you might expect from a visionary who knows nothing about the office of mayor." When Murphy stated that the underworld had sought to bribe him, an allegation that Mead later dismissed as "largely crap," Smith charged that Murphy was himself linked to the underworld through some of his campaign supporters.[52]

The candidates campaigned until the early hours of the morning on election day, and all of them delivered final appeals to the voters over the radio. More than 300,000 voters went to the polls on September 9, and a plurality of them selected Frank Murphy to be the next mayor of Detroit. Murphy received 106,637 votes; Bowles, 93,985; Engel, 85,650; Smith, 21,735; and Raymond, 3,508. Not only did the voters disprove the hypothesis that Bowles would be reelected if the opposition were divided, but the black and ethnic constituencies that were supposed to divide their vote between Murphy and Smith cast their ballots overwhelmingly for Murphy.[53]

Murphy received more than 65 percent of the vote (as compared to 31 percent for the city as a whole) in Wards 3 (65.89), 5 (69.06), and 7 (66.30), in each of which more than half the residents were black. In the black precincts throughout the city Murphy compiled majorities that ran as high as 80 percent. Smith generally ran second to Murphy in these precincts, but it was always a distant second. "Your people," Murphy informed Walter White, "stood by me almost to a man."[54]

In addition to Wards 3, 5, and 7, Murphy received at least 50 percent of the total vote cast in Wards 9 (57.60), 11 (60.28), and 13 (52.75). What these three wards had most in common, demographically speaking, was their low percentage of native-born white residents of native-born parents (16.29, 13.33, and 17.08, respectively) as compared to the city as a whole (34.28), which suggests that Murphy probably appealed strongly to the foreign-born voters of the city and their children. The very heavy vote that Murphy received in the largely "Polish" precincts in these and other wards—and persons of Polish birth and ancestry made up the largest European ethnic community in Detroit—bears out this supposition. "The Polish people," Murphy wrote one of his Polish acquaintances, "did me more than justice," and he could have made the same comment about the Hungarians and most other ethnic voters in the city.[55]

Murphy fared worst of all in Ward 22, where he received only 18.66 percent of the total vote. This was a ward in which there were virtually no blacks and where more than half the residents were native-born whites of native white parentage. He also received less than 30 percent of the vote in Wards 2, 4, 12, and 21, all wards in which the percentage of native-born whites of native-born parents exceeded the city-wide average (53.38, 51.21, 36.89, and 44.27 respectively).

Engel ran best in the "silk-stocking" districts of the city, receiving, for example, 495 of 689 votes in the exclusive Indian Village-Whittier Hotel section of Ward 17 (as compared to Murphy's 78 votes) and 816 of 1,309 votes in the Palmer Woods section of Ward 2 (as compared to Murphy's 160). Bowles ran best in the native-American areas, especially in Wards 18, 20, 21, and 22, in all of which he ran first.[56] The "old" Detroit voted for Engel and Bowles, but the "new" Detroit that William Lovett had seen emerging in the results of the 1923 Recorder's Court election and that had contributed substantially to Murphy's 1929 electoral totals provided Murphy with his margin of victory.

Even had 1930 been a year of prosperity in Detroit, Murphy undoubtedly would have run well in the black and white ethnic areas of the city because of his record on the bench and his general identification with the members of these communities. Since, however, the heavy unemployment in the city—factory employment in August, 1930, was a whopping 51.71 percent below that of August, 1929—particularly affected blacks and the foreign born, Murphy, as the only candidate whose "voice . . . carried any real hope to a troubled citizenry," considerably enhanced his appeal to voters from these groups. Because of the nature of their "elites," nonpartisan cities tend to elect conservative mayors, but a candidate who is able to capitalize on voter grievances can defeat the forces of the establishment, and this is precisely what Murphy did in 1930.[57]

There was almost no open discussion of religion in the 1930 campaign, but it may be that Murphy's religion was also an electoral asset. Although he undoubtedly lost some votes because he was a Catholic, his religion could hardly have been a handicap in a city in which 50 to 60 percent of the church members were Roman Catholics.[58] We can be certain as a matter of fact that Murphy's heavy vote in white ethnic areas in some measure reflected the Catholicism of so many of the voters in these districts. Smith, of course, was also a Catholic, but his political star was falling while Murphy's was rising.

"Detroit," the *Times* reported on September 10 in describing the city's reaction to the election results, "went mad last night and early this morning. Shrieking sirens, beating drums, tooting horns, snow storms of paper—it rivaled Armistice Day as thousands of men and women swept over the sidewalks and over the pavements shouting the name of Frank Murphy." There was parading for hours on Woodward Avenue, Washington Boulevard, and near City Hall, and jubilant Detroiters danced on the sidewalks.[59]

Murphy had portrayed himself as "the people's candidate," and there certainly was exhilaration among those who saw themselves as "the people." "In your brilliant success," one citizen wrote Murphy, "we, the plain people of the city, feel that we have scored a great victory, that our voice has been heard and that we have now a true spokesman for our cause." It was the first good night's sleep that she had enjoyed since Jerry Buckley's murder, a "poor uneducated working woman" wrote Murphy with regard to the election results. "You surely have been sent from Heaven."[60]

Not only the downtrodden, blacks, and white ethnic groups saw "a new deal for our city" in Murphy's victory. Catholics ("We Catholics of Detroit are especially proud"), a few residents of fashionable Grosse Pointe, the president of the Detroit Women's Republican Club, many attorneys, the director of the Detroit Bureau of Governmental Research, some very prominent Detroit businessmen and auto executives (K. T. Keller closed up his home on election day so that his servants could vote for Murphy), clergymen, and social workers took satisfaction in Murphy's success. Although it was a nonpartisan election, Democrats in the state and nation were impressed by Murphy's triumph, and liberals rejoiced that Detroit had elected a "liberal" mayor. "No recent event," Oswald Garrison Villard wrote Murphy, "has given me so much hope and cheer as the success of your remarkable campaign." William Randolph Hearst, not surprisingly in view of the part that the Detroit *Times* had played, was "delighted" at the election's outcome, and the New York *Daily Mirror,* which observed that a reputedly materialistic city had "gone lock, stock and barrel for idealism," predicted that Murphy would "make municipal history."[61]

The charismatic effect of Murphy's personality and the appeal of his idealism have no better illustration than the reaction to Murphy's election of newspaper reporter Carl Muller. He had taken up newspaper work eleven years previously, Muller wrote Murphy, because he thought it provided an opportunity for "service to mankind," but he had found it "to be anything but what" he had expected, and he had become "unutterably weary of earning a livelihood as nothing more than a panderer to the basest appetites of man." If he never again did "a worth-while thing," however, he would "always feel that in helping to make Frank Murphy mayor I was indirectly of service to my fellow-man in the kind of way I dreamed of. . . . I think, probably," Muller wrote, "there are many like me, who feel you are the personification of all they would like to be. We weaker vessels like to think that your achievements are our compensation. Whatever the future may hold,

I shall always feel that in the year 1930, Carl Muller was able to find justification for being. That's why I'm so damned grateful."[62]

After hearing the news of his victory, Murphy went to the offices of the Detroit *Times* to make a statement. "The people of Detroit," he proclaimed, "have recaptured their government. Without a 'machine,' without a campaign 'slush fund,' with only the unselfish labors of volunteer workers, but with unfaltering faith in the people, this fight has been fought and won." He pledged himself to be "mayor of, and for, all the people. In no other way may I hope to justify the people's faith in me as expressed at the polls."

After his brief remarks, Murphy walked through swarms of well-wishers to a nearby building to speak to his campaign workers. His clothes, by then, were torn, his hat smashed, and his hair awry. He said a few words to the faithful and then went to a downtown hotel to retire for the night. The task before him, he remarked a few days later, was one of "restoration, cleansing, and reconstruction."[63] Detroit's "new deal" was about to begin.

X

"A New Era in the Tabernacle"

I

Four thousand persons gathered inside and outside Detroit's City Hall on the morning of September 15, 1930, to witness the expected installation of Frank Murphy as mayor, but Charles Bowles blocked the event at almost the last moment by petitioning the City Election Commission for a recount of the mayoral vote on the ground that there had been "frauds" and "irregularities" in the balloting and the compilation of the results. The recount revealed only minor discrepancies in the official count, and so Bowles surrendered his office to Murphy, who was sworn in on September 23. Once again a large crowd was on hand for the event, and they heard Murphy proclaim that his inauguration signified that "a new and freshened spirit" had "entered" the city's affairs. "I want the people . . . to understand," he said shortly thereafter, that "there is a new era in the Tabernacle."[1]

The Detroit city charter gave the mayor a good deal of power. The city clerk, the city treasurer, and members of the Board of Education were elected by the voters, but the mayor, without requiring the assent of the Common Council, could otherwise appoint and remove department heads and the members of those boards and commissions that exercised supervisory authority over departments that were not run by a single commissioner. He proposed the annual budget to the Common Council, could recommend appropriate legislation to the Council, and could veto, in whole or in part, the measures that it approved.[2]

Since they tended to look upon the administration of city government as primarily a matter of business management, the Detroit Citizens League and its allies preferred the city-manager plan to the strong mayor form of municipal government, which, as they saw it, gave the mayor a political as well as an administrative role. The Citizens League complained after a few months of the Murphy administration that the mayor's emphasis on what

224

he regarded as the "'human' qualities" and his efforts to become "the hero of all the unfortunates" made him "more political than administrative," and the League thought that this not only led Murphy into error on such matters as finances and taxes but also that he might be laying the foundations for a "political machine of [the] Tammany type." Knowing that they were unlikely to secure the adoption of the city-manager plan, the Citizens League and the Detroit Bureau of Governmental Research began pushing in 1930–31 for a charter amendment that would authorize the mayor to appoint an administrative assistant, selected in accordance with civil-service procedures, to manage the city's affairs in a businesslike, nonpolitical manner. Murphy, not mistaking the thrust of the proposal, resisted the "goo-goo" effort to diminish the responsibilities vested in the mayor. He pronounced the city-manager plan a failure—it had not, to be sure, improved the quality of municipal government—and insisted that the appointment of either a city manager or an assistant mayor would remove the city's government from the control of the people.[3]

Murphy, actually, was fully and sincerely committed to the principle that the "business aspects" of government should be "handled in a business-like way," and he subscribed to the middle-class ideals of efficiency, economy, civil service, and nonpartisanship; but he realized, as the Citizens League did not, that city government was not just a business—"God pity the day," he remarked, "when we consider government as only a business"—that the chief executive of a municipal corporation had to be more than a business manager, and that business efficiency was not the sole criterion of "good government." City government, as he understood it, not only had its business aspects but was also "a social organization for the education of the youth, the peace, health and safety of the people, and for the care of the poor and sick." Because of the nature of the times, moreover, Murphy believed that the "social aspects" of government must "loom up above all others."

The provision of "non-partisan, non-political, business-like municipal administration," Murphy asserted in a remarkable address in 1931, was "only the great beginning and continuing task—not the end and the completed solution" for city government. There was "an urgent need in Detroit for administrative ability backed by expert experience to solve the business problem," but, he observed, "over and beyond the necessity for executive ability and experience, we cannot lose [sight of] the other great necessity of striving to administer social justice. If enterprise in government succeeds and social justice in the community fails or remains unsolved, the great task of municipal government is still incomplete." The mayor of the city, Murphy declared, "must have ears sensitive to the pleading and protests of all who hunger for the social justice the day demands." Murphy was actually describing the kind of mayor he himself was, a mayor who was responsive to both the "middle class" and the "immigrant" conceptions of the public interest. As William V. Shannon has shrewdly observed, Murphy was "the only politician of those days who could act like a social worker with one hand and a banker with the other, while all the time maintaining intact the gentle otherwordly air of a modern St. Francis."[4]

Although it was altogether characteristic of Murphy to attach a cosmic importance to the task upon which he was engaged, he was not very wide of the mark in seeing the depression-scarred big cities of the Hoover years as the "battleground of and for social justice" in the nation. "Washington, and even Lansing," he accurately observed, "are too far off, or too helpless, or too indifferent to answer the demand for action which arises from every factory, every social group, and almost every home. . . ." The cities, by contrast, had to grapple with "the great social problems" of the day and were in the best position to understand the needs of the people and to solve the problems that affected their lives and well-being. It was this understanding, and his readiness to act on it, that made Murphy a New Dealer before there was a New Deal and led the historian Hans Kohn to conclude that Murphy, as mayor of Detroit, was " 'the founder of the whole New Deal idea.' "[5]

Irish in descent, appearance, and manner, in his mystical bent, his gift for words, his "sense of the histrionic," and his tolerant view of man's transgressions, Murphy nevertheless departed considerably from the stereotype of the Irish politician in America. His career had been aided along the way by Irish-American politicians of the traditional sort, but where the archetypical Irish politician was interested in power for its own sake, Murphy was interested in political power as a means for effecting social change; where the Irish politician was concerned with the individual person and his needs, Murphy was interested in the welfare of the mass of the people; where the Irish politician was distinguished by his loyalty to the organization, Murphy was inclined to minimize the importance of organization and to rely on his own charisma to attain electoral success; and where the Irish politician shunned the "visible signs of upward mobility," such as participation in the "social world of celebrities and socialites," Murphy sought the company of the rich, the wellborn, and the famous. The Irish-American political personality was the product of working-class origins, a separatist, parochial school education, and limited structural assimilation, but Murphy was the son of middle-class parents, he had been educated in public schools, and he was highly assimilated. Shannon is altogether wrong in his conclusion that whereas the Irish politicians of Murphy's time were "shaped by the interplay between the Irish heritage and American life, Murphy was someone Ireland could have produced unaided. . . ."[6] The reverse, indeed, would be closer to the truth, although it would not be the whole truth.

Quite apart from other considerations, the fact that Murphy began his career in public office in nonpartisan Detroit helps to explain his distinctive political style and his deviation from the norm of the Irish political leader. The Detroit charter had brought an end to the old style of politics in Detroit, and no one was more aware of this than Murphy. Soon after he took office he let it be known that it was his duty as mayor "to defend the neutrality specified in the charter against efforts to link up the mayor or the city government with party elections or party candidates." Restructuring the past to make it more consistent with the present, he inaccurately insisted that he had "always been an independent" and had "never played a part in party organization." Murphy shrewdly realized that "the smartest politics in the long run is to impress the public with the fact that things are being done honestly and on a basis of efficiency, regardless of partisanship." He acted on the principle that " 'the best politics is no politics,' " and he believed that "if a man is zealous enough and sincere enough in the cause of good government for all the people, the people will be sufficiently appreciative to make political machines, spoils and the usual concomitants of politics unnecessary."[7]

In selecting the men to run the city's departments, Murphy had an opportunity to demonstrate to Detroit's voters the extent of his commitment to the principle of nonpartisanship embodied in the city's charter. Murphy declared that he would pick the ablest men available, "an aristocracy of intelligence," and would not appoint any professional politicians. It was "an age of experts and specialists," he remarked, and these were not the kind of persons who belonged to party machines. Murphy did not always live up to the lofty standard for appointments that he had set for himself, but it became his hallmark as an administrator that he surrounded himself with men of ability and then backed them to the limit, permitting his appointees, on the whole, to run their agencies with little interference from on high. ". . . if you make good appointments . . . ," Murphy reportedly said, "the city will run itself."[8]

The major Murphy appointments that attracted the most favorable attention in Detroit were those of Clarence E. Wilcox as corporation counsel, Joseph E. Mills as commissioner of public works, James K. Watkins as commissioner of police, and G. Hall Roosevelt as controller. Wilcox, one of the ablest lawyers in Detroit, had served as corporation counsel under Mayors Couzens, Lodge, and Bowles; Murphy reappointed him despite the fact that he was a Bowles supporter and a Republican. Harry Mead, who coveted the job of corporation counsel, recalled that on election night Murphy, indignant at Wilcox's endorsement of Bowles, had said that Wilcox would be the first "that walks the plank" in the new administration, but Senator Couzens, whose attorney Wilcox was, wanted Wilcox kept in his post, and Murphy was anxious to please the powerful and influential senator.[9]

". . . whatever I have achieved in this world," Mills wrote, "has been due to the harshest kind of work." He had been "badly crippled" as a boy and had known hunger after coming to Detroit in 1912 from Greenville, Michigan. He became Detroit's commissioner of purchases and supplies in 1926 after having worked for the Interborough Rapid Transit Company in New York and the Packard Motor Car Company in St. Louis and Detroit. Like Wilcox, he had been a Bowles supporter, but Murphy recognized his extraordinary business and managerial abilities by appointing him commissioner of public works and then, on January 16, 1932, general manager of the DSR. Murphy later described Mills as "the best executive I have ever known and the most perfect public servant I have ever met."[10]

When he announced on January 11, 1931, that James K. Watkins would become the city's police commissioner, Murphy stated that the purpose of the appointment was "to get politics out of the Police Department." Watkins, who had never before held public office, had played football at the University of Michigan when Murphy was a freshman there and had then gone on to earn a law degree at the Detroit College of Law and to study at

Oxford as a Rhodes scholar. He attended the first training camp at Fort Sheridan, as Murphy had, and after the war became one of Detroit's most respected attorneys. A quiet but very determined person, Watkins, like some of Murphy's other appointees, was "a hard boiled Republican." In selecting Watkins, the mayor rejected the advice of William F. Connolly, the influential Michigan Democrat and a major contributor to the Murphy campaign, and the Ford Motor Company to give the job to Joseph A. Palma, a Ford agent who "talked the language of politicians."[11]

The appointment of G. Hall Roosevelt to the position of controller in January, 1931, after he had already served as head of the Mayor's Unemployment Committee, has been characterized as "the most important of Murphy's political career." Hall, the brother of Eleanor Roosevelt and the husband of a Detroit girl with whom Murphy had been acquainted before her marriage, received a master of engineering degree from Harvard in 1914 and then worked for the Canadian Klondike Mining Company and General Electric before coming to Detroit in 1928 to join the Eastern Michigan Railways Company. He became a vice-president of the American State Bank the next year and had interests in several other concerns as well. A Democrat, he was anxious to do what he could to secure the 1932 Democratic presidential nomination for his brother-in-law Franklin. The selection of Hall, a highly intelligent person with a delightful sense of humor, drew praise in Detroit, but it was widely assumed that the politically ambitious Murphy had not been unconcerned with Hall's family connections in making the appointment.[12]

Murphy made several other appointments of men whose skills were primarily technical and managerial and who were not identified with partisan or, at least, Democratic politics: Douglas Dow, the son of Detroit Edison's president, Alex Dow, as commissioner of purchases and supplies to succeed Mills; L. G. Lenhardt, the assistant chief engineer of the Water Board, to replace Mills when he went to the DSR; and Frank Couzens and Sidney D. Waldon, the president of the Rapid Transit Commission, as members of the Street Railway Commission. Appointments of this sort caused the defenders of "good government" and nonpartisanship to praise Murphy even though they remained critical of his social programs. Even the Detroit Citizens League conceded that the mayor had surrounded himself with some of "the best official and citizen advisers to be found in America."[13]

To criticism from liberals and organized labor that his conception of government by experts had led him to seek out businessmen and bankers and to pay insufficient heed to persons who brought other talents to public service, Murphy responded that he was interested in "good executives, not maudlin sentimentalists" and that he would not hesitate to appoint conservatives whom he could "guide" if they were persons who could produce results. At the same time, Murphy did not entirely ignore the liberals in making his appointments. He placed Caroline Parker, the former chairman of the executive board of the Detroit branch of the American Civil Liberties Union (ACLU), on the House of Correction Commission, and, of greater importance, he selected Josephine Gomon as his assistant secretary. Mrs. Gomon, a former teacher who had first met Murphy when they were both students at the University of Michigan, was one of the liberal-minded women who had helped to influence Murphy's thinking in the 1920s, and she had written speeches for him in the 1930 mayoralty campaign. As Murphy's assistant secretary and as recording secretary of the Mayor's Unemployment Committee, Mrs. Gomon was the chief force for liberalism within the Murphy administration, and she familiarized the mayor with left-of-center thought concerning the depression and the problem of unemployment.[14]

Despite protestations to the contrary, Murphy did not entirely ignore political considerations in staffing his administration. His most obvious political appointment was the choice of Harry Mead as one of the three civil-service commissioners, a selection that raised some eyebrows in Detroit since it was not customary for mayors to place professional politicians on the agency. Murphy also gave due recognition to the servicemen, labor, and ethnic constituencies that had contributed so importantly to his election and that formed the core of his personal political organization. He recognized his Legion supporters by appointing Raymond J. Kelly, the commander of the Department of Michigan, to serve as the DSR claims attorney and Robert Brand to serve as secretary of the Department of Parks and Boulevards. As his secretary, Murphy selected John T. Taylor, the former president of the Detroit Federation of Labor (DFL), who had served as Murphy's clerk on the Recorder's Court. A DFL vice-president was appointed by the mayor to the Public Lighting Commission; the national representative of the Bricklayers' International Union was appointed to the Water Board; and George Krogstad, a member of the Pattern Makers' Association and a state deputy labor commissioner, was selected by Murphy to serve on the Street Railway Commission because, the mayor announced, the laboring man, as a streetcar rider and DSR employee, was entitled to representation on the commission. Krogstad would have been the first representative of organized labor to serve on the commission, but he was unable, in the end, to accept the appointment. Murphy also placed Frank Martel and three other DFL leaders on the executive committee of the Mayor's Unemployment Committee. "I want to balance the government," Murphy explained with regard to his labor appointments, and "labor must have its share in a well-balanced government." Mayor Murphy, the Detroit *Labor News* happily observed, was the first mayor in many years to have provided organized labor with "direct representation" in the city's government.[15]

The most prestigious appointment received by a black was Murphy's selection of John C. Dancy, the executive secretary of the Detroit Urban League, as a member of the House of Correction Commission, only the second black to serve on a city commission since the adoption of the 1918 charter. "It is rewards like this," one black wrote Murphy, "that serve to keep kindled in the Negro breast the sparks of hope. The Negro Race will not despair if there can be developed a few others of your courage. . . ." In addition to making the showcase appointment of Dancy toward the end of his administration, Murphy was responsive to the patronage requests of black leaders like State Senator Charles A. Roxborough, the Reverend R. L. Bradby, Dancy, and Beulah Young, the publisher of the Detroit *People's News*.[16]

Detroit's Poles were better represented in the Murphy administration than in any previous city administration. Murphy retained Joseph P. Wolff as his commissioner of building and safety engineering, returned William T. Skrzycki, whom Bowles had dismissed, to the Water Board, and appointed Dr. J. Stanley Leszynski to the City Planning Commission. There were three prominent Poles on the Mayor's Unemployment Committee, two Polish doctors were appointed to the Receiving Hospital staff, and several young Poles secured executive positions in the DSR. Like the blacks and the Poles, the Jewish, Hungarian, and German communities of Detroit also received recognition from the mayor in the form of appointments.[17]

Murphy's great talent as an administrator was his ability to inspire persons of different backgrounds, temperaments, and social philosophies to work together under his leadership and to contribute the best that was in them to the public service. Not only did he succeed in winning the "unswerving and sometimes almost fanatical loyalty" of most of his appointees, but he was able to inspire them with his own conception of the public service. When Clarence Wilcox, far to the right of Murphy, decided that he must give up his position as corporation counsel after having served four mayors, he wrote Murphy: "I believe you have brought a fuller vision of the duty of public officials than has ever been brought to the public and I can personally testify that your insistence on protecting the rights of the forgotten man, despite wide misunderstanding of the problem generally by the more favored persons, has given me a fuller sense of the privilege of public service than I ever before experienced." In similar fashion, Joseph Mills wrote of Murphy, "No one could have given me a greater inspiration to do that which was necessary in the interests of the entire city." [18]

Although the mayor of Detroit had almost unlimited discretion in the selection of his "cabinet" and the members of the various boards and commissions, his patronage power with regard to the approximately forty thousand municipal jobs was severely limited by the city's civil-service requirements, which were "probably . . . stronger and more effectively administered than in any other large city in America." [19] When he took office, Murphy sought to assure the city's employees, an especially influential voting bloc in a nonpartisan government, that efficiency rather than politics would determine whether they retained their positions. "I am going to wipe out the spoils system," he categorically declared. The acid test of a Detroit mayor's commitment to the merit system was his appointment policy with regard to the DSR, the principal area of the city government to which civil-service requirements did not apply. Characterizing the street railway as "the greatest political plum tree in the history of the City government," Murphy, upon assuming office, reiterated his campaign pledge to "root politics out of the department." He made good on his promise, but civil service came to the DSR only gradually since Murphy did not wish to restrict the dismissal of excess employees, particularly those appointed by Bowles. The first group of DSR employees was brought within the civil-service system in October, 1931, and the process continued, step by step, until by the beginning of 1933 all but the platform men, whose employment was governed by a union contract, and laborers were covered by civil-service procedures. [20]

Before civil service came to the DSR, the Murphy administration had an opportunity to replace the approximately seven thousand incumbents on the payroll with its own men, and the administration took some advantage of the opportunity. With total employment on the street railway falling because of the depression, the DSR took on 46 new employees between October 1, 1930, and the end of the year while discharging 59 persons; and in 1931 it hired 77 employees and terminated 435. Most of those let go were Bowles appointees, and one may assume that the new employees were largely Murphy administration adherents. The Bowles administration, by comparison, had taken on 194 new employees in the first eight months of 1930, and between 1924 and 1929, years of DSR expansion, the average number of new employees per annum had been 232.[21]

Laborer jobs in the Department of Public Works were also outside the civil service, and some of these positions were also distributed on a political basis by Harry Mead and others. This occurred particularly during the early months of the new administration, and it is possible that Murphy, who preferred to be unaware of the crasser side of politics, did not know precisely what was taking place. Once Mills took control of the department, he flatly refused requests from politicians to put men on his payroll; and Murphy, who thought that politics "ought to be way in the background" in a department like Public Works, stood behind his commissioner. When Mills was offered the job of commissioner, he told Murphy that this might not be "the proper thing" for the mayor to do from a political standpoint, but Murphy had replied, "I am not asking for a single thing," and he was true to his word.

Harry Mead, who believed that the "victor is entitled to a few ladles of gravy," complained in November, 1931, that he was experiencing difficulty in finding jobs for persons in the Murphy administration because there was no "disposition on the part of certain officials to help out in this situation." It is not unusual for politicos addicted to the politics of organization and patronage, as Mead certainly was, to complain about restraints on their efforts to find jobs for the faithful, but Murphy, less inclined to play the conventional political game than most, certainly made Mead's task considerably more difficult. "There wasn't one God damned Democrat that ever got even a half-assed appointment in the whole regime," Mead bitterly recalled many years later.[22]

In filling the lowlier jobs in his administration as in making his major appointments, Murphy was mindful of the ethnic basis of his political following. He was thus not only very much concerned about working conditions in the garbage division of the Department of Public Works, a black enclave, but he also rejected suggestions that he lay off black workers in the division to make room for unemployed whites. When a delegation of persons of Italian descent complained to him that workers of Italian origin had been discriminated against in a reduction of force by the Department of Water Supply, the mayor wrote the secretary of the department that although the public good and considerations of efficiency came first in determining who should work, "there is a practical problem here that must be confronted. The Polish, Irish, Italian and other groups have had representation so far as possible within the Department, and certainly as readjustment is made, it ought not to be done at the expense of any one group; it ought to be generally done." The mayor wanted "these good citizens" who were being laid off to know that they were being dealt with fairly. The secretary did not miss Murphy's point; he soon informed the mayor that layoffs in the department accorded with his prescription.[23]

Pursuing the politics of nonpartisanship, Murphy also endeared himself to veterans, organized labor, and the city's ethnic groups by means other than patronage. Legionnaires could not help but take favorable notice of a khaki-clad mayor who led the Armistice Day parade astride a brown charger and who urged his department heads to aid in the Legion's membership drive. Murphy brought the annual Legion convention to Detroit in 1931, told the delegates "'you can do no wrong,'" and defended them against attacks by the drys. It is not surprising that Murphy was hailed as the "'Legionnaire Mayor.'"[24]

Detroit's Jews, about 10 percent of the city's population, were impressed when Murphy attacked British efforts to halt Jewish immigration to Palestine as "a manifestation of intolerance," provided a fulsome welcome for the president of the Jewish National Fund when he visited Detroit, recommended to the Legion that it postpone the opening of its convention, scheduled for Yom Kippur, and appeared at a meeting protesting the Nazi persecution of German Jews. Murphy regularly praised Jewish contributions to the "intellectual, business, artistic and spiritual life" of Detroit, the nation, and civilization itself, applauded the "great humanitarianism and social sense of responsibility" of the Jews and their stress on "the communal good," declared that "my kind of government is their kind of government," contended that Jews were better Americans because of their Judaism, and stated, "I wish we had more of them in our community."

When a rabbi protested the scheduled showing of a motion picture of the Freiburg Passion Play to raise funds for the Mayor's Unemployment Committee, Murphy withdrew the committee's sponsorship. "Detroit," he wrote in a revealing letter to the exhibitor of the film, "is made up of people of all Faiths, Nationalities, and Races. We have lived together in a remarkably harmonious manner, and everything must be done to preserve that harmony. Our Jewish people have made a great contribution to this Community, and we must not be unappreciative of what they have done when an objection of this kind arises, *even though we may not fully comprehend their point of view.*"[25]

Reflecting his belief in cultural pluralism and his awareness of the importance of Detroit's large Polish community, Murphy stated on the first radio broadcast of the *Polish Daily Record* Radio Hour that the Poles, "while good and loyal Americans, . . . are not forgetful of their birthright and their beginnings and they have built up in our midst a great community in their own right and strengthened us by so doing." When requested to appear at a mass meeting protesting anti-Semitism in Poland, Murphy, caught in a conflict between two groups of his supporters, deferred to the force with the larger battalions. He wrote the editor of the *Polish Daily Record* that the mayor would not attend the meeting if the editor thought it "inadvisable" or if it would offend the Polish people of the community, but, if the editor wished to prepare a paper presenting the "salient facts" regarding the behavior of the Polish government, Murphy would be glad to read the document to the audience. Ignoring the obvious facts, Murphy later stated that he knew of no Polish persecution of the Jews, and he charged that the effort to promote this view was nothing but "a subtle bit of propaganda by an extremist group."[26]

Blacks appreciated Murphy's liberal welfare policies, and middle-class blacks, more concerned about matters of status than lower-class blacks, were also impressed with other actions of the mayor that indicated his sympathy for their aspirations and feelings. Murphy, one black leader recalled, was the first mayor to be seen publicly in friendly association with members of the black community. When the National Association for the Advancement of Colored People (NAACP) launched a membership drive in the fall of 1930, Murphy was the principal speaker at the initial meeting. Although reiterating that he belonged to no organizations, he nevertheless became a member of the NAACP. The next year, at a time when many other white officials would have shunned the assignment, Murphy became a member of the NAACP board of directors. When Walter White warned Murphy that it might be "politically or otherwise disadvantageous" for the mayor to accept the position, Murphy replied that he would be delighted to serve if he could make a contribution.[27]

When the NAACP and other groups protested the showing by a Detroit theater of *The Birth of a Nation*, Murphy requested the theater not to run the film "in the interest of the public safety and welfare of a large number of our citizenry," and police censors, backed by the mayor's office, ordered the film withdrawn. Although the Detroit branch of the ACLU protested this act of censorship, Murphy once again opted to please a large group of his followers at the cost of displeasing a much smaller number of civil libertarians whose causes he normally championed.[28]

A black Detroit newspaper publisher wrote Murphy after he had been in office only a few months that all of black Detroit was "happy" as the result of his policies, and "our votes are sealed." When his service as mayor came to an end, a committee of prominent blacks arranged a tea in his honor and presented him with a plaque describing him as "A Champion whose Vision is not dimmed by the shafts of the prejudiced[,] whose mind is open to the Entreaties of the Oppressed[,] a Gallant [in] defending and lending Cheer to those in Distress."[29]

In thanking the DFL for its support in the 1930 election, Murphy asserted that the laboring people of Detroit could "be assured that in office or out of office, I shall always have their interests and problems at heart. . . ." Soon after he became mayor, the DFL arranged a banquet in his honor at which Murphy criticized the "smug" people of Detroit who did not want organized labor to participate in city affairs despite the excellence of the men in its ranks and its commitment to the public interest.[30]

In 1931 Murphy invited American Federation of Labor vice-president Matthew Woll to help Detroit celebrate Labor Day. When Woll arrived in Detroit, he stated that this was the first time to his knowledge that any city had invited the Federation to share in its observance of Labor Day. The next year Murphy administered the oath of office to the newly elected officers of the DFL and in the process criticized the critics of the organization. "We need the labor movement now more than ever . . . ," Murphy stated. When the mayor of a city as large as Detroit assisted in installing the officers of a central labor union, a trade-union journal commented, that was " 'news,' " and when he lauded the labor movement and criticized wage cutters, that was also " 'news,' " and Murphy had done both on the same night. It was also "news" in Detroit when the city's mayor "demonstrated his respect for the rights of the workers" by refusing to cross a picket line in front of a Cleveland hotel where he had planned to stay.[31]

Throughout his mayoralty Murphy took the position that government must "set the pace for business as a model of justice and fair play" in the establishment and maintenance of labor standards. Early in his administration he told a representative group of contractors, architects, and labor leaders that there must be no reduction in wages, no unnecessary overtime, and no advertising for labor outside the city by contractors engaged on municipal construction projects. If it could be done legally, he indicated, he wanted a stipulated wage scale and the expected average working hours per day written into the specifications for city construction work before bids were submitted.

Acting on the mayor's suggestion, the Board of Education agreed to require contractors bidding on construction jobs to specify the scale of wages that they would pay and to indicate if they required Sunday work or overtime. The board also instructed its business manager to tell contractors that the board frowned on low wages, overtime, and Sunday work. Soon thereafter the board rejected the lowest bid submitted for plumbing and ventilating work in a school building because the contractor proposed to pay a lower hourly wage than the contractor whose slightly higher bid was accepted. In the submission of bids for the relatively little public construction undertaken while Murphy was mayor, contractors were required to provide the same kind of information regarding their labor standards as the Board of Education had specified.[32]

When the Street Railway Commission proposed as an economy move in April, 1931, to abolish the one-week vacation with pay enjoyed by the DSR's unionized platform men, Murphy declared that he was "unalterably" opposed to the idea. It might be "sound from the business standpoint," he remarked, but his "sympathies," nevertheless, were "with the men," and he was clearly concerned about the "tumult" among them should the plan be adopted. Murphy's opposition dissuaded the commission from enforcing its proposal until 1932, when the union itself agreed to the move on a temporary basis.[33]

The Murphy administration adopted a tolerant attitude toward the unionization of public employees in Detroit. The only employee organization in the Department of Public Works when Murphy became mayor was the Garbage Workers' Union, but Frank Martel, in January, 1931, successfully organized about four hundred workers in the Street and Alley Cleaning Division as well. John Taylor appeared at an organizational meeting of the group and stressed "the value of organization," and when reporters pressed Murphy for an explanation of his secretary's behavior, the mayor stated that he saw no difference between an alley cleaners' union and a garbage workers' union.

When the new Street and Alley Cleaners' Union complained that men in its division were being laid off without regard to seniority, Murphy arranged a conference between union representatives and Mills, and the commissioner assured the union that a seniority list would be prepared. "We must have fair play for these men," the mayor declared. Mills then announced that unclassified employees in the entire department would be retained and laid off according to seniority, a move hailed by the Detroit *Labor News,* which gave Murphy "no small part of the credit," as "a clear-cut victory" for the new union and as "the first constructive thing that has been done in the D.P.W. in many generations." When Martel, however, sought to form a union of truck owners who worked for the city, Murphy advised the DFL president that there was no need for such an organization in his administration since there would be no discrimination in the hiring of the vehicles as there had been in the past. Martel thereupon abandoned his efforts to organize the truck owners.[34]

Only the platform men of the DSR were organized when Murphy became mayor, but Division 26 of the Amalgamated Association of Street and Electric Railway Employees of America, which represented the men, began to spread its organization to shop workers also in May and June, 1931. Although denying "confidential reports" that he had urged the shop workers to join the Amalgamated, Murphy did not see the development as harmful in any way. Detroit businessmen, however, were patently disturbed by what was going on. The organ of the Detroit Board of Commerce complained that Murphy was "sympathetic with the aims and ideals of the Closed Shop," and a spokesman for the Board lamented that the effort to organize the DSR "seems to fit in with the scheme of things under the present city administration to acquiesce with the organization plans of the Federation of Labor."[35]

As mayor, Murphy continued his labor-supported efforts to secure the enactment of unemployment-insurance and old-age pension legislation. He characterized unemployment insurance as "far superior to any emergency relief work or to general philanthropy," and he criticized employers for opposing the reform. Murphy, who served on the Advisory Council of the American Association for Old Age Security, favored a federal old-age pension law as a means of relieving the burden that the depression imposed on industrial cities like Detroit. If he could not obtain a federal law, however, he wanted a state law, and he appeared with Martel before a committee of the Michigan House of Representatives in March, 1931, in a vain effort to secure an effective statute.[36]

"Mayor Murphy," the Detroit *Saturday Night* unhappily observed, "is a labor union mayor in open shop Detroit." What displeased the Detroit weekly was most pleasing to organized labor, and it was not ungrateful. When an Italian group requested the city to provide it with free music in the form of the policemen's or firemen's band, the president of the Detroit Federation of Musicians wrote John Taylor that this was against the union's policy, but, he stated, "if this will be an aid to the Mayor in more closely cementing the Italian brethren to his political machine, we will very gladly . . . withdraw any objections whatsoever and you can go as far as you please with the bands in question, and you will hear nothing more about it from us."[37]

Just before Murphy left Detroit for the Philippines, the DFL held a farewell banquet in his honor and made him an honorary president of the Federation for life. "There are times," Murphy said, "when a man in public office cannot do everything he would like to do. I have not done all the things for Labor that I should have or that I would like to have done."[38]

As mayor in nonpartisan Detroit Murphy continued his zealous pursuit of a good press. Before he had been in office very long, the Detroit *Saturday Night,* an inveterate opponent of the mayor, reported that newsmen thought that Murphy was seeking publicity for himself more avidly than any other municipal official in the recent history of Detroit. Murphy had been complaining that he worked too hard, and he had been warned of a breakdown by his physician, but the *Saturday Night* judged that the mayor's real trouble was that he spoke too often, posed for the cameras too frequently—he would "walk a mile for a snapshot"—and "act[ed]" too much. Murphy was the only mayor in Detroit's history who thought it necessary to appoint a military aide, and whereas other mayors had been content to have one bodyguard,

Murphy was protected by two men in uniform and two plain-clothesmen. This augmented bodyguard was supplemented by a retinue of Murphy retainers that included Patsy O'Toole and Alex Rivers, a black who had once been a batboy and handyman for Ty Cobb and who now served as a messenger for the mayor.[39]

The *Times,* its publisher later wrote, gave Murphy "the finest and most consistent support I have ever seen in a metropolitan newspaper," and Murphy expected no less. He regarded the *Free Press* as beyond hope, but he thought that it might be possible to persuade the Detroit *News,* the city's most influential newspaper, to appraise his public performance in a friendlier manner than in the past. He was able to establish a close and friendly relationship with reporters Blair Moody and Frank E. W. Bright, who covered the mayor's activities for the *News,* and Carl Muller of the *Times* recalled that Murphy cultivated the *News* by supplying it with "exclusives."[40]

When a new daily, the Detroit *Mirror,* began publishing in Detroit in 1931, Murphy quickly won the admiration of its managing editor, Frank Carson, who concluded that he had never before encountered a public official who was "so much on the square." The *Mirror* became an enthusiastic supporter of the Murphy administration, and the mayor reciprocated by seeking to have the contract for the publication of the city's official advertising transferred to the *Mirror* from the *Free Press.*[41]

Murphy was not only concerned about his relations with Detroit's daily newspapers; he also cultivated the publishers and editors of the city's ethnic newspapers. He established an unusually close relationship with Beulah Young, the publisher of the Detroit *People's News* and the second vice-president of the National Negro Press Association. If he would "lean" on her, Mrs. Young wrote the mayor, she would "not only keep all the coloured peoples votes in Detroit sewed up," but she would also organize the state for him, and when he ran for president, she would "throw every worthwhile newspaper in the U.S. for you." The *Abendpost* had opposed Engel even though he was of German descent and had "always been for the Mayor," and Murphy rewarded the journal by appointing its business manager to the Water Board, the first political recognition that the German-language newspaper had received since the progressive era. Murphy also found a position in the city health department for Franz Prattinger, the editor of the *Hungarian News.*[42]

Murphy's concern about press relations was further indicated when he appointed Norman H. Hill to replace Taylor as the mayor's secretary as of October 1, 1932. Hill, whom Murphy had met at the University of Michigan, where Hill had been captain of the baseball team, had edited Chase S. Osborn's Sault Ste. Marie *News* and worked for several Hearst publications, including the Detroit *Times,* and he was the *Times's* candidate for the secretaryship. Unlike Taylor, who had been ineffective in the realm of press relations, had been guilty of bad judgment, and had embarrassed the mayor on more than one occasion, Hill was very good at his job. He became the principal intermediary between Murphy and the working press and the source of much of the copy concerning Murphy's activities.[43]

Murphy initiated his administration at a furious pace, pushing himself to the limit of his physical endurance. Partly this was because he had to take office immediately upon his election, whereas there was normally a two-month interval between the election of a mayor and his accession to office, a time when the mayor-elect could formulate his plans and decide upon his major appointments. It was also due, however, to the extraordinary number of people to whom the mayor was willing to give an audience. Murphy himself was soon complaining about the waste of his time that this kind of a policy entailed. Mayor James J. Walker of New York, Murphy noted, spent a good deal of time talking to people, but New York's playboy mayor, Murphy thought, did not do any "real work," whereas Detroit's chief executive expected to be "a working Mayor."[44]

Murphy, although "a working Mayor," was not a disciplined person, with regular work habits, and he was never able to devise a sensible office routine and to budget his time effectively. Apt to work on the city's business at any time of the day or night, he was just as likely to drop everything to go horseback riding or to see some lady friend. It was not unusual for the mayor to spend an evening in the company of one of his glamorous female companions, tend to some city business at his apartment in the wee hours of the morning, retire at 2:00 or 3:00 A.M., and then appear at the office at 10:00 or 11:00 A.M. Also, Murphy had too small a staff considering the duties of the mayor, the nature of the city's problems, and the activist role that he played: his entire office staff consisted of a secretary, an assistant secretary, two secretary-stenographers, and a telephone operator. Yet, when the Common Council authorized Murphy to employ an additional stenographer for three months, Councilman John S. Hall complained that the mayor's staff was already too large and that Murphy was "spending money like a drunken sailor."[45]

Murphy made himself accessible to his constituents because he wished to contrast his own open-door policy with the closed-door policy of his predecessor, because he wanted to restore the confidence of the people in their municipal government at a time when that confidence had been badly eroded as the result of the record of the Bowles administration and the bitter recall campaign, and because this was consistent with his desire to "humanize" the city's government and to involve the public in civic affairs to a greater degree than had been common in Detroit. Capturing the atmosphere of City Hall while Murphy was mayor, Mrs. Gomon described the mayor's office as "a kind of court of last resort for those who are in need, in trouble or in doubt. Rich men who want to give money to the poor," she wrote, "poor men who are unable to take care of their families, business men who want to sell something to the City, imaginative people who have new ideas, or old ones untried . . . they all find their way sooner or later to the Mayor's Office. . . . There are no two days alike and no two cases alike. The world as lived in Detroit passes in and out of the doors of City Hall."[46]

Not only was Murphy untidy in his administrative habits and haphazard in budgeting his time, but he could be quite indecisive when difficult decisions had to be made. This quality stemmed from his naïve hope that he could operate by consensus and could please the various and often conflicting groups with whom he had to deal. Murphy was "too fearful of offending anyone," the fearless Senator Couzens thought. "Mr. Mayor," Couzens bluntly advised Murphy, "this cannot be done, and if you fail, this will be the cause of your failure." Similarly, one of Couzens's associates in Detroit, William J. Norton, thought that although Murphy's purposes were "sound," he had to learn "the essential lesson that any executive has to learn, namely, that decisions have to be made, and when they have to be made, it is just too bad if somebody is standing in the way."[47] Murphy did learn this lesson, and it must be said in his defense that if he sometimes procrastinated and was annoyingly evasive, the general thrust of his policy and the nature of his goals were clear enough.

Although administration in the conventional, bureaucratic sense was not his forte, Murphy introduced some sensible administrative practices during his mayoralty. He initiated a series of monthly meetings with his department heads in an effort to secure closer cooperation among them and to keep them informed of his policies, a practice that the Detroit Citizens League commended. These meetings provided Murphy, who seems to have done most of the talking, with the opportunity to expound his ideas on government and government service and to articulate the goals of his administration. ". . . you have made us see the governmental problems in their larger sense," the secretary of the Arts Commission wrote the mayor after the first of these meetings. In similar fashion, at Murphy's suggestion, Norman Hill later organized a bimonthly meeting of department secretaries to discuss common problems and the improvement of departmental procedures. In an effort to convince the public of the integrity of his administration, Murphy forbade city employees to accept gifts or services from anyone doing business with the city, directed his department heads to "stamp out all forms of petty graft" in their units—"There will be no graft, large, small or medium, under my administration," the mayor stated in his customary categorical manner—and ordered them on pain of dismissal neither to accept gifts from their employees nor to collect money from them for one purpose or another.[48]

Murphy, who brought a dynamism, vitality, and enthusiasm to City Hall that had been sadly lacking, succeeded not only in restoring popular confidence in the city's government but also in making it a focus of public interest. Soon after he took office, one of his constituents addressed a poem to "Our New Leader":

> Mayor Murphy you are a blessing
> In this City of depression;
> The unemployed gain new courage and hope through you
> You seem to know exactly what to do.

"I think," one of the mayor's devoted followers wrote him, "you have a very great ability to bring out the best in all of us and your leadership has made us all more brave. I want to thank you for a sense of spiritual quickening." "You have certainly made municipal government a living, breathing thing to me," another of Murphy's constituents informed him when his service as mayor was drawing to a close.

Murphy not only cared about the suffering people of his city but was one of those rare persons who is able to communicate the concern that he has for others. "The rank and file," the president of the Detroit Carburetor Company wrote Murphy, "should be for you strong, for you have a sympathetic heart and an understanding feeling for them." A member of the "rank and file" wrote the mayor, "you Certainly are doing everything With in your power for your city and for your fellow Man and for the Sake of humanity." "I think you are Just wonderful," another of Detroit's citizens wrote Murphy, "& i hope we will never have anothor mayor in city hall unless you be come President."[49]

Despite his administrative innovations, it is unlikely that Murphy would receive very high marks from students of administrative practice who stress orderliness, regularity, chain of command, clear lines of authority, and so forth. These, however, are matters of detail and are of much less importance from the point of view of leadership, service, and the purposes of government than Murphy's ability to select men of talent for administrative positions, to inspire them to give the best that was in them to the public service, and to persuade the citizenry that their government was concerned about them and anxious to serve them. Murphy raised the tone of government in Detroit and provided the people of the city with an appealing model of both rectitude and compassion.

To implement his programs, Murphy had to gain the approval of a majority of the city's nine-man Common Council. Detroit's councilmen met five times a week as a committee of the whole to conduct public hearings, receive communications, and discuss the city's business, and they convened at least once a week to take such formal action as they saw fit. The Council member who had received the largest number of votes in the preceding biennial election served as president of the Council and as mayor when the office was vacant or the mayor was unable to perform his duties. Since councilmen, like the mayor, were elected on a nonpartisan basis, the city's chief executive could not appeal to party loyalty in seeking Council support.[50]

The Council with which Murphy had to deal when he became mayor had been elected in 1929 before the depression had affected the city in any substantial way. Like most municipal legislative bodies elected on an at-large and nonpartisan basis, it tended to be more responsive to middle-class concerns than to the aspirations of the lower-class, ethnic, and labor elements that had contributed so importantly to Murphy's election. Five members of the Council were realtors, one (Hall) was a dentist, and the president, John Nagel, was on the payroll of the Detroit Edison

Company as a tax expert. Robert Ewald, a bricklayer by trade, was the only Council member who had a trade-union background, and John Kronk, who was of Polish descent, was the sole councilman with ties to one of the city's ethnic communities. Six members (Arthur E. Dingeman, George A. Walters, Phillip A. Callahan, Fred W. Castator, Ewald, and Kronk) were Republicans, and three (William P. Bradley, Nagel, and Hall) were Democrats, but Democrats cast in the Grover Cleveland rather than the Frank Murphy mold. Although the Council did not normally divide along party lines, five councilmen (Walters, Callahan, Kronk, Ewald, and Dingeman) were allegedly allies of John Gillespie and the Gillespie faction of the Republican party.[51]

Murphy was reelected in 1931 to serve a two-year term, but "widespread popular dissatisfaction" with the Council was reflected in the defeat of the entire Gillespie bloc, which had consistently opposed Murphy. The nine winners in the order of their vote were Frank Couzens, John Smith, John C. Lodge, Richard Lindsay, Hall, Edward J. Jeffries, Jr., Castator, and Eugene I. Van Antwerp. The Council was now controlled by an independent group, for which Murphy people had quietly campaigned, that included two former mayors (Smith and Lodge) and three future mayors (Couzens, Jeffries, and Van Antwerp). The Detroit *News* thought that the newly elected aldermen constituted "the strongest group, from the standpoint of qualification and experience, ever named to the . . . Council," a judgment in which William P. Lovett concurred. Despite the change in membership, however, the Council remained a middle-class body, and its partisan alignment of five Republicans, three Democrats, and one independent was not materially different from the party division of the old Council.[52]

Since they sold their product in a national market, the Detroit area's most important industrial concerns, the big automobile manufacturing companies, were normally less interested in exercising influence in municipal affairs on a continuing basis than major retail merchants, such as the J. L. Hudson Company, were. The years 1930–33 were not normal years, however, and the city's grave problems caused the Ford Motor Company, General Motors, and Chrysler to involve themselves more conspicuously in city affairs than they had in the past. Detroit's business interests sought to make their influence felt in the city government chiefly through the Detroit Citizens League and the Governmental Committee, which had been organized in 1923 by the Detroit Board of

Commerce and the Detroit Bureau of Governmental Research and was the organization through which the Board of Commerce carried on its political activities. The main concern of the Governmental Committee was to prepare an annual analysis of the city's budget in cooperation with the Detroit Bureau of Governmental Research and then to work through the Common Council to have its recommendations adopted. By 1930 the Detroit Citizens League had also become primarily interested in taxation and budget problems, and its opinions on these subjects did not differ from those of the Governmental Committee.[53]

The civic associations commanded substantial sums of money, and their views were generally echoed in the *News* and the *Free Press*. It was not, however, the upper and middle-class elements of the community for which the civic associations and the "'downtown government'" spoke that had elected Murphy, and he was in no way beholden to them. Although he worked with the "economic notables" when it suited his interests, he could always appeal against them to the larger electorate, which was the real source of his power. "I want to arouse the people," he declared soon after taking office, "to keep them alert and out from the insidious drugging influence of some of our so-called 'best people,' who by unofficial commissions seek to delegate the powers of government to themselves or a small, smug group. We need the judgment and help of everybody."[54]

II

The dominating event of the Murphy administration as of the Hoover administration was the Great Depression. Peculiarly sensitive to the ups and downs of the business cycle because the purchase of an automobile is in most instances postponable, Detroit was the hardest hit big city in the nation during the Hoover years. "The enormous organism of Detroit . . . ," Edmund Wilson wrote in 1931, "is now seen, for all its Middle-Western vigor, to have become atrophied. It is clogged with dead tissue now and its life is bleeding away. . . ."[55]

The decline in employment in Detroit during the years that Murphy was mayor was of staggering proportions. The index of industrial employment for the Detroit metropolitan area, which stood at 74.8 (1923-25 = 100) the month that Murphy became mayor and averaged 86.9 for 1930, fell to 66 in 1931 and 56 in 1932, and ranged from 28.8 to 50 during the first four months of 1933. An estimated 123,200 of the city's 689,566 gainful workers were unemployed in October, 1930; 178,000 in December, 1930; and 223,489 in January, 1931 (including 48,959 workers who had been laid off), which was about 32.4 percent of the city's labor force. The director of casework for the Department of Public Welfare (DPW) estimated in November, 1932, that 350,000 potential wage earners in Detroit, or more than 50 percent of the total, were without regular work and that many others were working only part-time. What was happening at the great Rouge plant of the Ford Motor Company, just outside Detroit, provides some indication of the magnitude of Detroit's unemployment problem: the average number of hourly workers at the plant fell from 98,337 in 1929 to 28,915 in 1933.[56]

The evidence of economic decline was apparent in every aspect of life in Detroit. The number of plants in the Detroit industrial area dropped from 2,794 in 1929 to 2,005 in 1933, and the wages paid in the district fell almost 60 percent (from $511,474,257 to $218,715,100). More than 19,000 new buildings were erected in the city in 1929, but the number was a mere 1,484 in 1933. Construction expenditures during the same years fell from over $100 million to less than $4 million. As of April, 1933, there were 55,500 vacant pieces of property in Detroit, including 384 vacant factories. Between 1929 and 1933 the number of DSR riders decreased by almost 50 percent (525,565,780 to 251,302,722), the number of telephones by more than 100,000 (351,597 to 238,818), the number of electric meters by forty thousand (570,832 to 530,036), and the number of gas meters by about the same number (394,561 to 353,983). In 1929 there were 114,464 new cars registered in the city; the figure for 1932 was 32,084.

If Jane Addams is to be believed, fifty thousand homeowners in the Detroit area lost the equity in their property during a sixty-day period in 1931. In one Detroit factory about 40 percent of the 230 or so employees who had been homeowners had lost their homes by May, 1932. There were no "reds" in the plant, one of the men wrote Murphy, but he thought that if the depression continued much longer, it was likely "to make bad men out of good Americain [*sic*] people." Not including those small businesses that disappeared from the scene without leaving a trace, there were 518 business failures in the city in 1930, 502 in 1931, and 552 (with assets of more than $14 million) in 1932. "After glancing over these figures," the secretary of the city's Board of Assessors wryly remarked, "we might wonder how long Government would last if it were directed by some business men who are always shouting for business administrations."[57]

The demographic facts of life, like the economic facts, reflected the extreme seriousness of the economic decline. The city's population decreased by more than 137,000 (from 1,568,662 to 1,431,000) between 1930 and 1932, and the birthrate per 1,000 fell from 23.5 in 1929 to 15.7 in 1933. In Wayne County, the number of marriages declined from 17,946 in 1929 to 12,418 in 1932; the number of divorces, a reflection to some extent of ability to pay, decreased from 6,129 to 3,707 between 1929 and 1933; and the number of the insane in the county increased by approximately 70 percent from 1930 to 1932. There were 19.7 (300) suicides per 100,000 population in Detroit in 1931, a 30 percent increase over the five-year average. Of the suicides for which the cause was known, almost half were directly attributable to unemployment.[58]

Only the statistics regarding public health seemed, in the main, to run counter to the demographic trends. The death rate per 1,000, "not the most precise measure of health," fell from 11.6 in the year ending June 30, 1929, to 9.3 in 1930; 8.8 in 1931; 8.7 in 1932; and 8.4 in 1933. The Detroit death rate in 1930 and 1931 was the lowest among the ten largest cities of the nation. The infant mortality rate per 1,000 births, a crucial index of the well-being of a society, fell every year between 1929 and 1933, ranging from 63.3 in the year ending June 30, 1929, to 51.3 in the year ending June 30, 1933. Tuberculosis is a disease associated with poverty, and the 3,885 cases reported in Detroit in 1931 were the highest number of cases in any year to that date, but the tuberculosis death rate, which averaged 91.1 per 100,000 between 1925 and 1930, was 73.8 in 1931 and 70.3 in 1932. The Department of Health hailed the years 1930, 1931, and 1932 as "the healthiest in the City's history." The head of the department, Dr. Henry F. Vaughan, thought that this was primarily because the depression had forced Detroiters to abandon "luxurious methods of living" and improper eating habits, but this explanation probably tells us more about Dr. Vaughan and others like him than it does about the relationship of the depression to the public health. It is more likely that the Detroit experience was the result of long-term trends affecting the nation as a whole that continued without important interruption even during the depression years.[59]

It may be, as the Lynds pointed out in their study of Middletown, that the health costs of the depression were simply not apparent on the surface and that the "slowly cumulating [health] debits" resulting from unemployment—malnutrition, disorders of the digestive system, and infections of the respiratory tract—are simply not recorded in most of the available statistics. A field investigator for the federal government thus noted in November, 1931, that doctors in Detroit had reported "a marked increase" in heart and stomach trouble resulting from "mental distress" and improper diets. Whereas 5.9 percent of the Detroit school children were found to be underweight in the 1928-29 school year, 6.4 percent were underweight in 1929-30, and 8.5 percent in 1931-32. The city did not conduct the usual school health examinations in the 1932-33 school year, but a survey of six thousand school children by volunteer doctors in the fall of 1932 revealed that 18 percent were underweight, a "sudden and alarming increase" that boded ill for the future. What was especially interesting about the 1932 survey was that in the congested parts of the city, where there were high rates of dependency and unembarrassed resort to welfare services, the weights of the children examined were about the same as they had been in 1929, but in the outlying home-owning districts, more than 20 percent of the children were underweight. This suggested that many families that were "making a last struggle with pride" to live in "independent obscurity" were "going through unknown and untold depredations" and their children were falling "far below" the minimum standards of health required for their own safety and that of the community.[60]

What the aggregate statistics of unemployment and reduced income meant for particular Detroiters was graphically revealed when the Mayor's Unemployment Committee decided in the summer of 1932 to study the effects of the depression by surveying a district selected by the DPW as the most representative of Detroit as a whole. Of the 1,286 family heads studied, only 34 percent were actually on payrolls when the survey was taken, and 74 percent were looking for work. Among the 880 heads of families providing information, 353 (40 percent) had not worked at all in the preceding week, and an additional 209 (23.75 percent) had worked three days or less. The median weekly earnings of the family heads in the week preceding the survey had dropped 67 percent (from $33.05 to $10.82) as compared to the typical week in 1929, and the average hourly earnings had declined 32 percent (from 67.45 cents to 44.2 cents).

Of the 145 families whose homes were mortgaged, 14 had seen their mortgages foreclosed, 63 were in arrears in mortgage payments, and 98 were delinquent in tax payments. Of the 828 who did not own homes, 269 were in arrears in rent payments, and 28 had been evicted for nonpayment of rent. Twenty-two percent of the families had savings accounts at the time of the survey as compared to 56 percent in 1929. Of the families purchasing goods on the installment plan, 10 percent had lost what they had bought through repossession. Two hundred and sixty of the families had had to surrender their life insurance; and of the 30 percent who owned automobiles, 17 percent had not yet purchased their 1932 license plates. Forty-eight families had felt it necessary to remove their children from school, and 25 percent of the families had been unable to provide fresh milk for their children during the two days preceding the visit by the interviewer. One-quarter of the families had received some form of financial assistance during the year, and 34 percent had availed themselves of the city's free clinic, as compared to 17 percent in 1929. The survey, its authors concluded, revealed "the dismal signs of a process of pauperizing, that is rapidly reducing the proud American citizen to a level of insecurity and want, and destroying what had once been known as the American standard of living."[61]

Most of Detroit's black inhabitants, relegated, as John Dancy observed, to "the fringe of the city's industrial life," had never enjoyed what was thought of as "the American standard of living," and the depression brought a further deterioration in their economic condition. Because they were the first fired and the last hired and because so many were unskilled, their unemployment rate was double that of whites; and although they constituted only 7.6 percent of the population, they made up 30-35 percent of those on the relief rolls while Murphy was mayor. At the beginning of 1933 Dancy reported that in employment, housing, health, recreation, and "family disorganization," the situation of blacks in Detroit presented "a very dismal picture." Many black children were going to school without having eaten properly, and the city clinics were crowded with impoverished blacks who could not afford private medical care. Dancy reported a few months later that information gathered concerning fifty black families on welfare revealed that husbands and wives had separated in six of the families, ten had doubled up with relatives, seven had taken in roomers—a child of nine had been raped by one of these roomers—and seven had removed their children from school on the verge of their graduation.

The health of Detroit's blacks during the depression years was substantially inferior to that of whites. In 1930, for example, the death rate of blacks was almost double that of whites, the tuberculosis rate was seven times higher, and the venereal disease rate was eight times higher. There was, on the other hand, improvement in the infant mortality rate of blacks, largely because welfare workers persuaded welfare mothers to take their babies to the city's clinics for medical treatment.[62]

The statistics of unemployment and distress in Detroit while Murphy was mayor do not, in themselves, portray for us the men, women, and children, some with burlap wrapped around their feet, rummaging for food in garbage cans in the city's alleys, the petty thievery in grocery stores and small retail establishments, the theft of dog biscuits from the city dog pound, the death of the child in the unheated flat, the homeless "dug into the ground," and the strain that unemployment produced in the relationship of husbands and wives and between fathers and children.[63] The anguish of the distressed, the agony of the depression, were, however, poignantly captured in the numerous letters that victims of the economic crisis sent to their mayor and to other city officials. One woman wrote that her husband had been out of work for five months and that although the welfare department provided the family with groceries, their gas and electricity had been shut off, they were losing their furniture, they had received a notice to move, and two of the family's three children could not attend school because they lacked suitable clothing. "Now we are American citizens . . . ," the writer concluded, "and surely we must be given a chance to live." Conditions were "unbearable," another of the impoverished wrote the mayor, and "we feel ourselves sinking." One woman wrote that her family, having "lost everything" and facing eviction, had "no place to go, no family to turn to," and no friends "to help."[64]

Several of Murphy's correspondents described themselves as on the verge of starvation. One female correspondent informed the mayor, "I havn't [sic] a slice of bread in the house," and "the children are crying for food." A widowed mother of a twelve-year old child reported that there had not been a crust of bread in her house for several days—"I am destitute[,] almost starving to death." A woman who had been removed from the welfare rolls and had a husband and son in prison and two children at home, advised Murphy that she had been begging for food from door to door without success. "I eat out of the garbage can and stail [sic] meat," she wrote. "Please Mayor Murphy give me some food."[65]

There was a note of absolute desperation and a threat of suicide in many letters that Murphy received. A husband and wife who had thirteen children wrote the mayor, "I don't mind telling you that were [*sic*] just at that desperate stage and I am afraid something terrible is going to happen." The wife of a fireman whose husband had been out of work for ten months informed a member of the Fire Commission, "I know of just one way out of this hellish life."[66]

Many letters of distress to Murphy revealed the strain that unemployment placed on the family and particularly on the head of the family no longer able to play his accustomed role of breadwinner. One woman described her husband as "losing his mind" and as "wasting away" as the result of brooding over a prolonged period of unemployment. A sixteen-year-old girl whose father had been unemployed for eighteen months wrote that it broke her heart to see her parents "day and night crying and worrying."[67]

Quite a few of the unemployed who wrote the mayor blamed themselves for their predicament and revealed how difficult it was for those brought up on the American creed to apply for welfare even when they were destitute. "It seems to me," an unemployed white-collar worker who spurned welfare aid wrote Murphy, "I have lost all my ability as a responsible man. It seems to me I have some short comings some where." One man informed the mayor that his children "would die with the hunger before they would Eat Welfare Bread." Obviously regarding himself as a failure, he noted that his own father had managed to provide for eight children. A fifty-eight-year-old man wrote Murphy, "I have lived in the hope that by my own effort I would be able to procure employment with remuneration sufficient to keep myself and wife," but he had not worked for eight months, had exhausted his savings, and was being told that he was too old for a job. He could no longer say, "I will stand alone! That I will not ask for help!," but, he insisted, "*I do not want a dole* (I hate that word!). . . . I just cant [*sic*] ask for relief."[68]

"I am literally sick at heart at the hardships and privations being suffered by hundreds and thousands of our very finest people today," Murphy wrote one of his constituents, and there is no doubt that the "pathetically worded letters that sen[t] out a mute plea for help" had their effect on the compassionate Murphy and strengthened his resolve to use whatever resources were available to the city to deal with the crisis. He did not shrink from the responsibility imposed by the problems he faced, nor did he bemoan the fate that had placed him in the mayor's chair in so troubled a time. Rexford Guy Tugwell, in an apt characterization, has observed that for Herbert Hoover the depression was "a cross to be borne" whereas for Franklin D. Roosevelt it was "a challenge to action." Murphy, it is clear, reacted to the depression much as Roosevelt did. It was, Murphy asserted, "a blessed privilege" to serve in a public capacity during this great crisis, "a wonderful time to be a public servant." For the public official who viewed his office as "a kind of ministry," here was an unparalleled opportunity to erase from the public mind its stereotyped opinions concerning the nature of government and to demonstrate that "unusual times can be met with unusual measures."[69] In Detroit while Murphy was mayor, the "unusual times" were, indeed, "met with unusual measures."

III

The distinguishing feature of Murphy's thought and public expression while he was mayor was the emphasis that he placed on positive government and the welfare state. Whatever lingering doubts Murphy may have had about the need for the interventionist state—and he had few by 1930—were removed by the depression, the appalling human misery that he saw all about him, and the failure of private enterprise to create jobs for the jobless and of private philanthropy to provide succor for the distressed. As mayor, Murphy became a leading spokesman for that body of reformist thought that was to distinguish the 1930s in general and the New Deal in particular.

"We have been in an era of extreme individualism," Murphy observed in his final year as mayor. "It has been best expressed in the industrial order, where it was believed that every man should look out for himself. But this individualism is ruthless and un-Christian, because every man does not have a chance to look out for himself. We shall have to substitute a socialistic sense for this individualistic sense. We have got to realize that no one is secure until all are secure; that injustice to anyone is injustice to everyone." To be a liberal, Murphy contended, meant to place human rights above property rights—his whole philosophy, he said, was based on this point—and to place government at the service of the helpless and the needy. To those who pointed to the immutable laws of economics as the controlling force in the market place, Murphy responded that "the Lord still helps those who help themselves and the economic forces can operate with greater ease if directed by enlightened human intelligence."[70]

Despite the almost intractable nature of the problems he faced as mayor, Murphy, like the New Dealers, never lost faith in the ability of a democratic society to cope with adversity. "No problem arising out of the carelessness of man is insoluble," he asserted in his annual message of 1933, "no condition in the body politic is incurable." The cure, he believed, lay in "the keen diagnosis of our economic diseases" and in their "orderly treatment," but because the nation was a democracy reliance would also have to be placed on "the mass judgment of the people." In Bryanesque fashion, Murphy proclaimed that "the battle will be nine-tenths won when the facts are confided to the people." From "the sentiment, the emotions and the feelings and the experience of a people," he optimistically maintained, there will "always come good."[71]

Although Catholicism has tended to stress communal responsibility more than individual morality, Catholic social thought in the United States did not come of age until the 1930s, and relatively few American Catholics were associated with reform activity before that decade. In embracing a variety of reforms in the 1920s, Murphy had thus departed from the Catholic norm, but it was not until he became mayor that he began to find sanction for his welfare-state ideas in papal encyclicals. In his efforts to solve Detroit's vast problems, the mayor asserted, he was simply applying "Catholic principles of justice and charity" and the relevant precepts of papal encyclicals. In an address entitled "A Mayor's Interpretation of the Encyclical of Leo XIII, Forty Years After," that he delivered to the National Catholic Alumni Federation, Murphy stated that he had been guided as a public official by the "moral sign-posts" erected by the Church and, especially, by the *Rerum Novarum*'s instruction that rulers should "anxiously safeguard the community and all its members." The encyclical, he stated, had helped him to see that he must "put government at the service of humanity" and must place "the welfare of our fellowmen above the balancing of fiscal budgets." It was a call to "fight for social justice through social action," to put the idle to work, to remove the causes of poverty, to care for the "destitute aged," to protect working women and children, and to redistribute purchasing power.[72]

The increasing reference to papal encyclicals in Murphy's

speeches as mayor may have been the result of the very close friendship that had developed between Murphy and Father Charles E. Coughlin. Born in Hamilton, Ontario, in 1891, Coughlin was formally incardinated into the diocese of Detroit in 1923. He was assigned to Royal Oak, Michigan, in 1926, and he began his radio broadcasts on a Detroit station that same year. By the time Murphy became mayor the remarkably eloquent Coughlin was expounding a Catholic brand of social justice and reform, and he soon became a bitter but immensely popular critic of Herbert Hoover and the Hoover depression policies. Murphy and Coughlin met shortly after Coughlin's arrival in Detroit, and the priest became a family friend while Murphy was on the Recorder's Court.

As Detroit's two most influential advocates of positive governmental programs to deal with unemployment, as critics of those in high places who seemed indifferent to the plight of the jobless, and as supporters of Franklin D. Roosevelt for the presidency in 1932, Murphy and Coughlin were "constantly together" during the bleak depression years in Detroit, and the mayor assisted the priest in the writing of some of his speeches. Pleased that he had been enrolled in Coughlin's League of the Little Flower, Murphy wrote the priest in October, 1930, that he could "be assured that I am always a booster of you and your works." Some time later Coughlin wrote in a similar vein to the mayor, "You know that you have my entire and absolute support both in word and deed. A mere suggestion from you as to whatsoever you expect from me will always be honored and fulfilled."[73]

In discussing the role of the contemporary big-city mayor, James Q. Wilson has distinguished between the mayor's local constituency and the "audience" outside the city whose "favorable attitude and responses" he may seek to win support for his programs and, possibly, his later career. In his words and deeds as mayor, Murphy was clearly addressing himself not only to the city's inhabitants but, in some degree, to men of influence and an anxious citizenry elsewhere in the nation as well. "Talking the language of the audience," Wilson observes, "is an important way for a mayor to win esteem and to become a state or even national figure."[74]

IV

As mayor of a city that did not provide an official residence for its chief executive, Murphy, for a time, shared a modest apartment with brother George and Ed Kemp, and then after Marguerite married William Teahan on June 2, 1931, he lived with the Teahans in the fashionable Indian Village district.[75] Although his real passion, as always, was his work, he still found time for his favorite sports, the theater, some reading, and the now familiar covey of female companions, several of whom undoubtedly envisioned themselves, prospectively, as Detroit's first lady. Hester Everard, at long last, wisely decided that Murphy was a lost cause and married another man. Ann Harding, whose first marriage ended in divorce in 1932, continued to see Murphy as quite superior to other men, but she was shrewd enough to sense that all that he wanted from the opposite sex was "surfaces—pleasant ones" and that he was unlikely ever to commit himself fully to a mere woman.[76]

Murphy himself became one of the victims of the economic collapse whose consequences he had to deal with as mayor when the stock-market crash and the sharp decline in the price of Chrysler stock wiped out the " 'Murphy fortune.' " "Like everyone else," Murphy wrote a relative early in 1933, "my possessions of four years ago have slipped away." On his way to the Philippines he sanctimoniously and inaccurately informed the press that once he had decided on a public career, it became his "goal" to divest himself of his wealth, and he had now attained his goal.[77] When Murphy reached the Philippines, he set about repairing his personal fortune.

When Murphy appeared in Washington for a conference a few months after he became mayor, a wire-service reporter was impressed with the youthfulness of the man from Detroit. The "fearful strain" of being mayor from 1930 to 1933 took its physical toll of Murphy, however, and the columnist Mark Hellinger, who had not seen Murphy for a year, was "shocked" at his "tired and worn" appearance when Hellinger visited him as he was about to leave for the Philippines.[78] The depression, we can be sure, had left its mark on Murphy, but the manner in which he responded to it had helped to make him a figure of national importance and had served to advance his career in a very significant way.

XI

"An Important Drop"

When Frank Murphy took office as mayor, he assumed that the city faced only a "temporary emergency" and that prosperity would return before he began his second year in office.[1] It did not take Murphy long to realize that these assumptions, though common, were false and that prosperity was not just around the corner. Detroit, as it turned out, remained a city in distress throughout his mayoralty, and no public official in the country was more insistent than Detroit's mayor that relief for the victims of depression was government's most important business.

There was a widespread belief in the United States before 1929 that a person who wished to work could find employment and that the able-bodied poor had only themselves to blame for their condition. Insofar as relief was provided to the jobless, it was extended grudgingly and in a manner designed to encourage the recipient to seek employment. In many jurisdictions, those on relief were still required to take a pauper's oath, in some states they were not permitted to vote, and in a few places single relief recipients were forbidden to marry. It was also widely believed that although the state should provide assistance to persons with mental and physical defects, the aged, and mothers with dependent children, unemployment relief should be dispensed by private charitable agencies.[2]

To Murphy's everlasting credit, he challenged the conventional wisdom concerning the depression and unemployment at every turn. "The worst thing . . . that is taking place in this nation today, next to the gaunt tragedy of unemployment," he stated soon after taking office, "is the callous attitude of public officials toward it, the participation in the conspiracy of silence, their contribution to keep the facts from the people." He made it abundantly clear that it was "the duty of the state" to provide relief "not as a matter of charity, and not paternally, but as a matter of right." The government that failed to accept this responsibility, that lacked the compassion or the good sense to see the poor through their travail, was, in reality, "no government at all."[3]

The depression, Murphy recognized, was a national, indeed an international, phenomenon requiring remedies such as the stabilization of employee income, the restoration of purchasing power, and "limitations upon exorbitant wealth to maintain the security of the revived prosperity" that were beyond the power of Detroit to provide. What the citizens of Detroit had a right to expect from their government, however, was that it would "do everything humanly possible" to relieve distress among the city's afflicted inhabitants. "No one in this great city of plenty," Murphy announced as his credo, "must be allowed to go hungry, or cold, or unhoused, or unclothed." Detroit, he asserted, should proclaim to the nation its pride in having assumed "complete responsibility for the proper care and shelter of those helpless ones at life's extremities."[4]

In meeting the crisis that faced Detroit and the nation, public authorities, Murphy believed, should not be restrained by the traditional inhibitions on governmental action or even by the usual "processes of law." In view of the circumstances, he boldly stated, he was "more disposed to hear the present cry for elemental social justice even above the loud demand for the traditional sanctity of contract."[5]

Murphy lost no opportunity to explain to his constituents that the idle and the homeless, the people on welfare and those seeking relief, were not "abnormal individuals" or "bums" but "good people" who were unemployed and destitute through no fault of their own. He was critical of the comfortable persons who seemed indifferent to suffering and want, looked disdainfully at the unemployed, and maligned the relief efforts of the city. He thought that they were obsessively concerned about the small number of grafters and malingerers who received welfare and that they failed to recognize how inadequate was the relief extended and how many of the unemployed—the vast majority indeed—suffered privation courageously rather than seek public aid. "If we are going to worry," Murphy declared, "let us worry over the forgotten and neglected ones and not consume ourselves in a fret over the few unfortunate misfits who cheat." It was Murphy's contention, furthermore, that unless relief were extended to the "great city of destitute folks, living within a city," the peace and well-being of Detroit would be endangered, class hatred aroused, and the very foundations of the social order undermined.

"Detroit," he asserted in 1931, "would have been on fire without relief."[6]

The mayor's wish was that Detroit should not only provide adequate relief but should do so "in a friendly and kindly way." "Please," Murphy told the social workers of the Department of Public Welfare (DPW), "by touch, by attitude, by sympathy, by such material aid as you can give, exert yourselves just a little more in helping the unfortunate over the rough places they are encountering." Murphy, who wanted to make City Hall "the real capitol of our jobless and broken friends," was the first Detroit mayor to place a welfare worker in the mayor's office to assist the needy who came to City Hall seeking aid. Straitened financial circumstances placed severe limitations on the assistance that Detroit could provide, but the "jobless and broken" had little reason to doubt that their mayor understood and sympathized with their plight and that welfare work had become the city's "major activity."[7]

In contending that relief should be dispensed by public authorities, Murphy was conforming to tradition in Detroit. The applicant for relief presented himself for an interview at one of the DPW's district offices, received an emergency grocery order if this seemed indicated, and was advised to wait for a visit by a caseworker or to visit the district office in a stipulated number of days if he had not received a home visit in the meantime. If the department determined that the applicant family qualified for aid, it dispensed the relief, as most cities did, not in cash but in kind. In Detroit this took the form of grocery orders, issued for a two-week period and usable at any grocery store in the city. In addition, the department generally paid the rent and utility bills of its clients and provided for certain incidentals such as insurance premiums. If an indigent person required hospitalization, the department assigned him to the Receiving Hospital, which was operated by the DPW and cared for about one-half of those hospitalized at the city's expense, or to one of several private hospitals, which were compensated at a flat rate of $3.50 per day for the care of city patients. The department also included a City Physicians division that provided medical care in their homes or in a city clinic for welfare patients. To provide care for preschool age children of working mothers, the DPW, in June, 1929, established the Minnie E. Jeffries Nursery School, intended, apparently, to have been the first of several such units.[8]

Although the DPW was subject to the direction of the city administration, the department was traditionally operated in a nonpolitical manner. Murphy, however, could hardly have been satisfied either with the composition of the Public Welfare Commission or with the efficiency of the executive staff of the department. None of the four commissioners spoke for the liberal or labor elements in the city, and it is doubtful if any of the four fully subscribed to the mayor's views on welfare. Dr. W. J. Seymour was primarily concerned about the medical portion of the department's work and was ill-informed about other phases of its operation. Mrs. Paul W. Tara and Dr. A. W. Blain failed to grasp either the nature or the magnitude of the welfare problem that confronted Detroit, and their views on the subject of relief were antediluvian. Blain, in particular, assumed that welfare had become something of "a racket" for the ne'er-do-well, and he was intensely suspicious of most of those receiving aid. "Let's not worry so much about a few Hastings street pickaninnies," the Detroit *Free Press* quoted him as saying, "and start worrying more about the white tax payers." Although Blain denied having made this remark, it was characteristic of his approach to the welfare problem. Harry E. Andrews was described by the Detroit *Times* as the "best qualified member" of the commission but as being "so upset by the trying conditions" that he had lost his poise.[9]

The general superintendent, Thomas Dolan, was directly responsible to the Public Welfare Commission for the operation of the DPW. Dolan had been associated with public welfare in Detroit since 1891 and had served as general superintendent of the DPW from its inception in 1918. "A man of great sensitivity and compassion," he was better suited to run the department when its case load had been three or four thousand than to direct the tremendous expansion of the agency that the depression induced. He had only "a very hazy impression of the procedures and problems of the Districts," and he was reluctant to seek the advice of his district supervisors. He suffered "a complete nervous collapse" early in 1930 and had to remain away from his job for almost two months. The director of social service, Harry Zahrn, ran the department while Dolan was ill, but the two men were "at loggerheads most of the time" after Dolan's return, and the general superintendent hardly ever spoke to Zahrn "except in anger." The department, in the meantime, expanded in an unplanned and haphazard fashion. It increased its case load, engaged more investigators and added new districts, and went to the Common Council each month for an appropriation to cover the deficit of the preceding month, but otherwise it simply muddled along.[10]

Murphy, who should have addressed himself forthwith to the trouble brewing in the DPW, initially was content to leave matters to the Public Welfare Commission and the department's executive staff while he struck out along new paths, outside the established bureaucracy, in a wide-ranging effort to confront the city's greatest problem. While still a Recorder's Court judge, Murphy, it will be recalled, had begun laying plans for the formation of a citizens' committee that would address itself to the unemployment crisis. The implementation of the scheme had been aborted, but now the idea originally proposed by William Haber emerged in expanded form as the Mayor's Unemployment Committee (MUC).

In creating the MUC rather than simply relying on existing agencies to deal with unemployment, Murphy had several objectives in mind. He hoped, above all, to arouse the entire community to the magnitude and importance of the unemployment issue and to convince the despairing that the problem could be ameliorated. Murphy, furthermore, was aware that the social workers of the public and private agencies were attuned to dealing with the "old poor," the unemployables, and he thought that a volunteer group drawn from the community as a whole was more likely than the professionals to confront the plight of the new poor with sympathy and understanding.

A new committee, Murphy also believed, could attack unemployment "from every possible angle," whereas the DPW had the much narrower responsibility of simply dispensing relief to the needy. The department, moreover, was limited by law, regulations, and custom even in the kind of relief that it did provide; it did not, for example, give relief to single persons, and it did not normally supply clothing to its clients. The MUC, on the other hand, could "meet the desperate need lying in certain twilight areas wholly outside the field of operations" of the DPW and the private agencies. The bureaucracy of the DPW, furthermore, moved slowly, according to prescribed routines, but a new agency "divorce[d] from red tape or any kind of formalism" could follow "a mobile policy of quick and pertinent action in any new situation that demanded its help." It could serve as a stimulus and a "guide" to the public and private welfare agencies and could coordinate the entire relief function in the city.[11]

If his unemployment committee were to wage a "social crusade," Murphy believed that it would have to reflect "every social tendency and . . . every phase of opinion." There were approximately one hundred persons on the committee at the outset, and among them were spokesmen for business groups, organized labor, Detroit's white ethnic communities, blacks, social-service organizations, and the churches. It was, as one observer noted, "a medley of conflicting interests," ranging from "pink radicals" to "stiff-shirt conservatives." This coalition approach to the unemployment problem was altogether consistent with Murphy's predilection for the politics of consensus, and if it was not the sort of arrangement that augured well for the long run, it had something to recommend it in the context of the depression in Detroit in the fall of 1930.[12]

Murphy scheduled the first meeting of his unemployment group for September 15, intending it to be the first official act of his new administration, but Bowles's reluctance to surrender his office imparted an unofficial character to the initial session. The MUC, as Beulah Amidon noted in *Survey,* was nevertheless launched "with loud beating of drums and fanfare of trumpets." G. Hall Roosevelt was selected by the mayor as the chairman of the committee. This was almost certainly a political appointment since Hall, despite the part that he had played in the unemployment relief effort in New York in 1921, was, in the words of one active committee member, "wholly untrained, wholly uninformed, wholly inexperienced. He had . . . no knowledge at all [about unemployment]." Dr. Frank D. Adams, the pastor of the First Universalist Church, was designated the vice-chairman of the MUC; E. E. Kramp, the secretary of the Industrial Committee of the Board of Commerce, became the executive secretary; Eugene W. Lewis, president of the Industrial Morris Plan Bank, agreed to serve as treasurer; and Josephine Gomon, the mayor's personal representative on the committee, was designated the recording secretary.

The officers, the chairmen of the various subcommittees through which the MUC proposed to conduct its activities, and four representatives of organized labor constituted the Executive Committee of the group. The Executive Committee was supposed to react to reports by the subcommittees and to make recommendations to the General Committee, the name given to the membership as a whole. When this structure proved to be unwieldy, the Executive Committee was transformed into the Advisory Committee, but how the change in name, which was primarily what seemed to be involved, was to improve matters is not clear—administrative organization, as we have seen, was not an area in which Murphy excelled. The concerns of blacks, the group hardest hit by the depression, were channeled to the MUC through a Colored Advisory Committee, of which John Dancy served as chairman.

Initially, seven subcommittees were created by the MUC to deal with research, relief, employment agencies, regularization of employment, legal aid, public works, and publicity. The housing and feeding of homeless men and women were at first made the responsibility of the relief committee, but a separate subcommittee on homeless men was created in November. Two new subcommittees, one to deal with creative employment, the other with investigations and emergencies, had been created by then, and the work of legal aid had been transferred to the relief subcommittee.[13]

Funding was a major and troublesome problem for the MUC from its inception to its demise. Despite some concern that the new committee would simply duplicate DPW activities, the Common Council, in response to a request by the mayor in his inaugural address, appropriated $35,000 for the MUC, but the aldermen did so, it seems, on the understanding that the money would be used solely for administrative expenses. Although most MUC work was performed by volunteer labor, the committee did have to engage a small salaried staff, and it had an irreducible minimum of overhead expenses. The money received from the Council was budgeted to meet these administrative costs, but all of it had been expended by April 1, 1931.

Money to finance the various MUC programs had to be privately raised, and the committee resorted to a variety of methods to secure the funds. There were benefit shows, dances, athletic events, a skating carnival, a moonlight cruise, tag days, concerts by the Detroit Symphony and the Vienna Boys Choir, and even a Symposium on Faith in which the agnostic Clarence Darrow debated spokesmen for the nation's three major religions. In the final months of its existence the MUC placed thousands of coin boxes in private homes and restaurants, including some "respectable blind pigs." The three major sources of income for the committee were its share ($36,637) of the receipts of a football game between the University of Michigan and the University of Chicago, contributions from city employees that netted about $30,000, and proceeds of about $34,000 from a tag day in November, 1931.[14]

In all, the MUC raised about $250,000, much of it before

December, 1931. This sum was hardly sufficient to enable the committee to mount an ambitious relief program of its own, but it did serve as seed money that fertilized many important projects. The MUC, after all, was not the only relief agency in the community, and it could turn to the Community Fund and the DPW to come to its rescue temporarily or to take over one or another of its projects entirely.[15]

The first task of the MUC was to conduct a registration of the unemployed in Detroit. The degree of unemployment in the city, as Murphy indicated, was "in a state of fog and mist," and the mayor thought it was important on this as on other subjects to expose the facts. The census was conducted by the research subcommittee, which invited the unemployed who had lived in the city for at least twelve months to register and to supply certain basic information about themselves. Not more than one person per family was supposed to register. Registration was scheduled to begin on September 15 at 4:00 P.M., but since persons were already in line just after dawn, the signing-up at the twenty-seven registration stations was initiated before noon. One man fainted in line the first day; others indicated that they had no homes and were sleeping in the parks. Some who had walked long distances to register were given streetcar tickets for their return journey. A reporter who observed some of the registrants thought that they were neither "stolid" nor "hysterical." "Hope, belief in themselves and their future and their city," he thought, "was still strong."[16]

A total of 75,471 men and 3,565 women had registered by the time the census was completed on October 5. Since each registrant was believed to represent 1.4 unemployed persons, on the basis of the census the total number of unemployed persons who had lived in Detroit for at least one year was slightly more than 110,000. Of the 79,036 registrants, 63,762 (80 percent) indicated that they had no income whatsoever; 21,964 (27 percent) of those who registered were black, 16,576 were single, and 7,348 had at least five dependents. Although 32 percent of the registrants were unskilled, nearly all occupations were represented, and some registrants were professional people. The census was undoubtedly quite inaccurate, but, as one observer noted, "it brought home the fact of unemployment" in Detroit; and that, after all, was one of the mayor's principal purposes in creating the MUC.[17]

The research subcommittee resumed registration of the unemployed on October 10 in an effort to identify persons who had missed the first registration or had since become unemployed. More than 118,000 registration cards had been filled out by July 1, 1931, but this total includes persons who had found permanent or temporary jobs after having registered, and so it does not reveal the precise number of unemployed even though city officials used current registration figures in indicating the number who were unemployed at any particular moment.[18]

Registrants were asked to state whether they required immediate assistance, and it was the responsibility of the relief subcommittee to respond to such requests. Investigators from the social-service agencies and volunteer workers visited those asking for help, supplied them with emergency food orders if that seemed warranted, and checked to see if they were already receiving aid from some source. About one-third of the 13,551 families indicating need received emergency relief in the form of food and clothing, single men and women were referred to private agencies for lodging and food, a small number were provided with legal aid, and more than eleven hundred were referred to the City Physicians or the Receiving Hospital for medical care. About 75 percent of the cases were referred to the DPW, with an almost catastrophic effect on its operations.[19]

Although it was initially assumed that the MUC's direct relief function would quickly come to an end, the evidence provided by the registration that the needs of many Detroiters were not being met by the established agencies argued for the continued existence of an organization that could act with more dispatch than the regular welfare agencies and could "augment" their facilities "whenever and wherever necessary." This was precisely the sort of role that Murphy had in mind for the MUC, and so a small relief unit consisting of two social workers and ten clerks was maintained by the committee after its major relief activity had come to an end. Beginning in August, 1931, the MUC set up an emergency food division that distributed baskets of food containing rations for one week to needy persons who were not receiving welfare aid. By July 1, 1933, the division had distributed almost forty-two thousand food baskets. The emergency division also distributed 12,520 food baskets to unemployed persons who had formerly worked for the Michigan Central Railroad. This food, paid for by the company, helped to keep some families off the welfare rolls.[20]

In addition to family relief, the relief subcommittee was concerned with the assembling and distribution of clothing to those in need. It discharged this function through the Clothing Bureau, which performed a considerable service for the city at a very low cost. Although the MUC contributed some of its meager funds for the purchase of apparel in short supply, most of the clothing that it distributed was donated by individuals and stores and collected by volunteer workers as part of several clothing drives that the Bureau conducted—"we will ransack every attic, basement and clothes closet," the head of one of the drives declared. At the central office of the bureau, cobblers repaired shoes that had been donated, and seamstresses repaired and refitted clothing and made quilts from scraps. The clothing was distributed largely to persons not on welfare, to families, as Murphy described them, of "the great, silent, suffering public" who were trying to get by without becoming clients of the welfare department. The chief beneficiaries were school children, many of whom could not have attended school without the shoes, coats, and underwear made available to them. The Clothing Bureau was transferred to the DPW in December, 1931, by which time it had helped to outfit more than 265,000 persons.[21]

Legal aid was another function of the relief subcommittee. Headed by Louis C. Miriani, a future mayor of Detroit, the legal-aid unit was concerned with the various legal problems that the poor encountered, especially the eviction of homeowners and renters who could not meet their financial obligations. Mayor Murphy, as opposed to the eviction of persons from their residence as he later was to the forcible eviction of sit-down strikers, stated categorically, "No family must be thrown into the street . . . . I certainly don't want it said that in this great wealthy city a single family is made homeless."

The legal-aid group sought to convince landlords to lower rents and not to evict tenants, and it urged holders of mortgages to reduce interest rates and to delay foreclosure actions. Small payments were sometimes made to mortgagors on the condition that they suspend foreclosures temporarily. By the end of 1930 the legal-aid unit had forestalled eight hundred evictions and hundreds of foreclosures. Its work was taken over in 1931 by the city's Legal Aid Bureau, with which the MUC group had cooperated from the start.[22] Despite Murphy's rhetoric, however, legal-aid officials were unable to stem the tide of evictions as the depression worsened.

Finding jobs for the unemployed was a major concern of the MUC from the start. The subcommittee on public works favored the acceleration of public works by the city to spur employment, a policy to which Murphy fully subscribed. In his inaugural address, the mayor urged that all construction programs for which money had been appropriated should be put into effect at once and that planned construction for the succeeding fiscal year be anticipated so that the jobless could be put to work over the winter. In November, 1930, on the basis of recommendations from department heads, the city administration submitted a $24.6 million construction program to the Common Council that it anticipated would give employment to 6,580 men for an average of seven months. The Council, however, authorized only $5.6 million of this sum, and it appears that even this amount was not fully expended because of the city's financial condition. In the spring of 1931 the city administration decided to hold up all public improvements already approved but on which work had not yet been initiated, and the public-works holiday thus inaugurated continued as long as Murphy remained in office.[23]

The subcommittee on public works urged that contractors hire only Detroit labor, which fitted in with Murphy's "buy Detroit" policy, a harbinger of the "Buy America" policy of the early New Deal. "Detroit should be for Detroit business men and Detroit workmen first," Murphy announced soon after becoming mayor. He stipulated that persons working for the city would henceforth have to live in the city, and he indicated that he favored the award of construction contracts to Detroit firms even if they were not the lowest bidders and the purchase of police and nurses' uniforms in Detroit even though they could be obtained more cheaply elsewhere. "To do otherwise," the mayor declared, "would be to encourage outside, cheap, cut-throat labor at a time when we are doing our best to provide all the labor possible in Detroit."[24]

It was easier to announce such a policy, however, than to implement it, and pressures on the city government to economize soon became stronger than the desire to buy in Detroit. When the Board of Education awarded a contract for mill work on a new school to a Detroit firm rather than an out-of-town company despite the fact that the bid of the latter was 40 percent below the bid of the former, Murphy vetoed the action as not being "a sound exercise of discretion" and as probably illegal. Similarly, the city announced toward the end of 1930 that the police would buy their uniforms in 1931 in Philadelphia, not in Detroit, to effect a saving of $10,000 to $15,000.[25]

The subcommittee on regularization sought to persuade employers to increase jobs by shortening hours and spreading the work and to regularize employment by a careful planning of production schedules, a matter of no little importance in Detroit because of the astronomically high labor turnover rates in the automobile industry. The regularization group, in addition, seems to have persuaded many employers to give workers preference in employment on the basis of the number of their dependents. Although the subcommittee expected to continue its activities on a long-term basis, little was heard of the group after the end of 1930, and its accomplishments seem to have been rather meager.[26]

When the MUC established its creative employment subcommittee, there were hopes that the mayor's group had initiated its most important venture, but the new subcommittee, despite a good deal of effort, never succeeded in "creating" very much new employment in Detroit, which is not surprising considering the state of the city's economy. When the New York *Times* concluded in December, 1930, that it was "problematical" that the subcommittee could solve the employment problem in Detroit, it was being excessively cautious in its choice of language.[27]

The activities sponsored by the creative employment subcommittee included, at one time or another, the performance of odd jobs for homeowners, the cutting of wood for Michigan farmers, the sale of sand to householders for use on their sidewalks, aid in spring housecleaning, the distribution of peat for lawns and gardens, the construction of sandboxes, the changing of license plates, the conduct of tours through the old House of Correction building and the maintenance of an educational museum there, the establishment of work shops in the Old Water Board building, and, most important, the sale of apples.

Most projects of the creative employment group produced temporary jobs for no more than six to thirty men. Thus, the effort of the Detroit Federation of Women's Clubs to create as many as five thousand full-time jobs by persuading sixty thousand women to engage unemployed persons to perform odd jobs around their homes for four hours per week produced a grand total of twenty-seven jobs after six weeks of effort and a thorough canvassing of the city in which school children assisted. Because of the meager results obtained from this and other ventures, the MUC, as part of a reorganization of the committee in February, 1932, dissolved the creative employment subcommittee although continuing the apple-vendors project as a separate enterprise.[28]

The apple vendor on the street corner has become a major symbol of the Great Depression, although Herbert Hoover chose to believe, incredibly, that "many persons left their jobs for the more profitable one of selling apples." The apple vendor made his appearance in Detroit in the fall of 1930. Having learned that New York City was permitting its unemployed to earn money by selling apples, Murphy called the idea to the attention of the MUC. The creative employment group then worked out a plan in connection with the Detroit Produce Terminal Company whereby unemployed men would sell apples that cost two cents apiece at a price of five cents—"Remember that you are business men not beggars," the secretary of the subcommittee told the vendors. The slogan of the project was "An apple a day chases unemployment away." By the end of the year 650 men were supporting themselves and their families by the sale of apples, and for the remainder of Murphy's mayoralty an average of 250 families remained off the welfare rolls by this means. Many vendors were physically handicapped persons who would have found it difficult to secure any other kind of employment.[29]

The major activity of the subcommittee on employment agencies was the establishment and maintenance of a Free Employment Bureau. Such an agency was urgently required since most of the numerous fee-charging agencies in Detroit were corrupt and unscrupulous, the employment bureau maintained in the city by the state of Michigan and the DPW's own employment bureau were ineffective, and the employment office of the United States Employment Service, like the agency as a whole, was useless.[30]

The Free Employment Bureau began operating at the end of September, 1930, in a building donated by the Detroit *Times*. Murphy instructed the city departments to hire workers through the Bureau whenever possible, and the cooperation of Detroit employers was solicited and received. The MUC maintained the Bureau until August, 1931, when the DPW took over its operation because the MUC was short of funds. Itself hard pressed, the welfare department divested itself of the responsibility as of July 1, 1932, and the MUC, once again, had to finance the Bureau as best it could.[31]

The two principal policy issues concerning the operation of the Employment Bureau were the rate of pay that skilled workers supplied by the Bureau should receive and the possible merger of the city agency with its state and federal counterparts in Detroit. Employer representatives on the MUC contended that it was not for the MUC to instruct employers regarding the wages they should pay nor to tell the unemployed that they could not accept a job unless they received a particular rate per hour. DFL representatives on the committee, by contrast, thought that the city's own standard of wages should be the criterion for employers availing themselves of the Bureau's services, and Murphy and the majority of the General Committee sided with the labor members. This was softened somewhat by an ambiguous decision of the Advisory Committee that the Bureau should do nothing to undermine wage standards in Detroit or to prevent the unemployed from securing jobs.[32]

The issue of the merger of city, state, and federal employment offices in Detroit was debated throughout the early part of 1931, but no merger was effected. Quite apart from differences of opinion among the various parties regarding the financing and control of a merged agency, it seems clear that Murphy was a major obstacle to any scheme of unification since he insisted that the city's unit must maintain its identity as "an independent, non-partisan, impersonal organization." Pride and politics were undoubtedly involved in the mayor's stand, but he was correct in condemning the federal and state agencies for having done nothing to cope with the unemployment problem in Detroit and for failing to ascertain that the problem even existed. Although willing to agree to cooperation among the various public agencies, Murphy would not sanction a merger that swallowed the city's Free Employment Bureau.[33]

During the entire period of its operation the Bureau offices, like the MUC offices, were "crowded with victims of the depression." If word was out that jobs were available, the unemployed began lining up outside the Bureau's building the night before in the hopes of gaining preference when the agency opened its doors the next morning. Of 210,000 persons who had registered by the end of February, 1933, the Bureau, which gave preference in job assignments to the unemployed with the largest number of dependents, found steady work (one month or more) for 19,867, odd jobs lasting anywhere from one hour to one week for 20,519, and city employment—temporary work, generally, of one or two weeks in the Department of Public Works—for 14,520, a grand total of 54,906 jobs. By the time the Bureau closed its doors on July 1, 1933, it had placed an additional forty-six hundred persons on temporary and permanent jobs. "Never before," Josephine Gomon wrote in the middle of 1932, "has a free employment agency been so important to the unemployed." Although this was probably an exaggeration, there is no doubt that the Bureau had performed admirably under the most difficult of circumstances.[34]

To check up on Bureau registrants about whom there were questions, the MUC created an investigation and emergency committee that was financed by the Red Cross and private employers. This committee functioned until February 15, 1931, by which time it had made almost five thousand investigations of persons referred for employment by the Bureau. It also performed a variety of tasks for the MUC, such as transporting persons to their jobs, investigating questionable employment practices, and directing people who were seeking help to the city office that could best serve their needs.[35]

Of the various aspects of the relief problem, none aroused such strong emotions among policy makers in the city as the treatment to be accorded homeless men. As the center of the automobile industry, Detroit had become a Mecca for single men seeking employment; and as the registration of the unemployed by the MUC revealed, they were a conspicuous element among those without work in the city.

The haven for homeless men in Detroit before 1929 had been the McGregor Institute, founded by Thomas McGregor, who had come to the city in 1890 to establish a mission for homeless men similar to the institution that he had launched in Toledo. Managed from 1915 by Thomas's son Murray, the McGregor Institute expanded its facilities at the beginning of the depression, and both the DPW and, briefly, the Community Fund aided it in defraying the cost of the meals that it served. Since it could accommodate only about seven hundred men per night, the Institute dispatched the overflow to one or another of the numerous private lodging houses and hotels that were springing up in Detroit, and they charged the city fifteen cents per night for each man whom they lodged. Almost eighteen hundred homeless men were being housed in the fall of 1930, and more than four thousand free meals were served daily to the homeless.[36]

In his inaugural address, Murphy requested funds to rent a municipal lodging house to accommodate homeless men. The problem, Murphy was aware, was no longer that of the "shiftless, migratory, unemployable men" of the 1920s but rather of "self-respecting, sensitive men, willing to do some kind of work but unable to find it," and new methods, he thought, were required to deal with this "entirely new type of man." The MUC, although concerned about homeless men from the outset, did not at first accept Murphy's proposal for a centralized approach to the problem.

The MUC created a special subcommittee to deal with homeless men and after a few weeks brought in John Ballenger to head its Homeless Men's Bureau, which by then had become "pretty badly mixed up." After having served as assistant chief of training of the Veterans' Bureau in Washington, Ballenger came to Detroit in 1922 to take charge of the Detroit office of the Bureau. He soon joined the staff of the Community Fund and in 1928 became executive secretary of the Detroit chapter of the American Red Cross, which continued to pay his salary when he became the head of the Homeless Men's Bureau. A tough, efficient administrator and, to use Josephine Gomon's phrasing, "a happy combination of social worker and practical human," Ballenger provided the Bureau with firm direction and readied it for the large task that it soon had to assume.[37]

The MUC was initially content to have the McGregor Institute process the homeless men who had come to the committee's attention as the result of its census of unemployment, but it decided toward the end of October, 1930, to conduct the registration of the homeless itself and to supervise the commercial lodging houses to which it sent men who could not be accommodated at the McGregor Institute. The MUC began the task of registration on December 1 under the aegis of the DPW, which assumed the full cost of the program. The men whom the Homeless Men's Bureau processed were generally given two fifteen-cent tickets that they could use at one of the private lodging houses and two twenty-cent tickets with which they could purchase breakfast and dinner for two days at a licensed restaurant. Only persons who had been resident in Detroit for one year were eligible for aid, and they had to support their claim with a letter from a "respectable" citizen, preferably a taxpayer. By the end of December forty-six hundred men whom the Bureau had registered were receiving lodgings and meals, and an additional thirty-four hundred were receiving meals only.[38]

In the meantime a "stormy" debate was taking place within the MUC as to whether the committee should abandon the decentralized housing of the homeless in favor of a centralized approach and whether the use of private facilities should be entirely discontinued. Employers on the committee and the representatives of private charities opposed a "liberal" policy for the homeless lest it attract derelicts to Detroit. They believed that all applicants for lodgings or food should be thoroughly investigated and that a work test should be used to discourage malingerers.

They also preferred that the decentralized system be continued and that private enterprise play a part in lodging and feeding the homeless.

Liberal MUC members, who enjoyed the mayor's support, opposed investigatory techniques and work tests that humiliated the homeless and, instead, favored a simplified procedure that would "keep a roof over their heads and some victuals in their stomachs." The liberals were able to marshal evidence that discredited the decentralized system then in effect. Some of the lodging houses, it was revealed in an investigation by a subcommittee of the committee on homeless men, were "unfit for habitation." Also, the ticket system had led to many abuses. Some of the homeless sold their tickets and used the money for liquor—more than one hundred were sentenced for drunkenness in a ten-day period—and then sought a free meal from the Salvation Army or a similar organization. Finally, the liberals contended that a centralized, publicly operated system was a considerably more economical method of meeting the problem than the existing procedures were.[39]

The dispute within the MUC over homeless men was resolved when the Fisher Body Division of General Motors, in December, 1930, offered the city its plant on West Fort and Twenty-third Street as a lodging house. The company agreed to maintain the facility at no cost to the city provided that relief agencies would equip it and the Salvation Army would be entrusted with the "operation and general supervision" of the building. The Advisory Committee voted unanimously to authorize the use of $13,000 to equip the plant as a municipal lodging house, to be known as the Detroit Emergency Lodge. In January the Studebaker Company advised the mayor that the city could use its Plant 10, at Piquette and Beaubien, as a municipal lodging house on the same terms as prescribed by Fisher Body. The city also decided to establish feeding stations for homeless men for whom it did not provide lodgings. The first of these opened in January in the headquarters of the Homeless Men's Bureau, another began to operate soon thereafter in the black ghetto, and by March, 1931, the city, in addition to the 5,784 persons to whom it was supplying lodgings and food, provided two meals a day, prepared by such organizations as the Volunteers of America and the Industrial Lunch Company, to almost eight thousand men at five different feeding stations at a daily cost of eighteen to twenty cents per man.[40]

The men applying for places in the two lodges were processed at the headquarters of the Homeless Men's Bureau. There they received a medical examination, a bath, a meal, and a night's lodging—the building could accommodate 250 men—and their clothes were fumigated. If Detroit residents, they were then transferred to one of the two municipal lodges, where they remained until they found employment. Altogether, 17,190 men were registered by the Bureau from December 1, 1930, to May 9, 1931, and the information that they supplied provides us with some data about the "detached" men who attracted so much attention in Detroit during the depression. Forty-four percent of the men were native-born whites, 30 percent were foreign born (compared to 25.45 percent for the city as a whole), and 26 percent were black (compared to 7.6 percent for the city as a whole). About 56 percent of the registrants were under forty years of age; 8.6 percent were married but lived apart from their families. Although only 8.9 percent of the men had been born in Detroit, they were not, as they were commonly pictured, "just Wanderers, here today and gone tomorrow, new ones drifting in and old ones leaving": 44.6 percent of them had lived in Detroit at least ten years, another 46 percent had lived there from three to ten years, and only 9.4 percent had resided in the city less than three years.[41]

The Fisher Lodge opened on December 31, the Studebaker Lodge on January 20, and Murphy appeared at the dedication ceremonies subsequently held at both places. The Detroit *News* described the Fisher dedication as "a motley affair." The one thousand homeless men in the lodge were the hosts, and entertainment was provided by the Salvation Army Citadel Band and the Detroit Police Quintet. Some of the " 'best people' " had said that he should not attend such affairs, the mayor declared, but, he told his appreciative audience, "I have no patience with this talk about the 'best people.' You are as good as any people on the face of the earth." At the Studebaker Lodge ceremonies, where the Boys' Recreation Band and a Detroit singer provided the music, Murphy repeated that those seeking shelter in the municipal lodges were "not bums, but normal, healthy and wholesome people" who were unemployed through no fault of their own.[42]

The Fisher Lodge, as the larger of the two municipal facilities, received far more publicity than the Studebaker Lodge. A Detroit *News* reporter who visited the Fisher Lodge soon after it opened commented on "the weariness of some, the pathetic, ragged, thin clothing; . . . the shame that seems to lie heavily on some shoulders that charity must be accepted; the lonesome look, the longing look that comes when some pause to think of the yesterdays." He was impressed by the "oddly mixed groups" that had formed—young and old, white and black, literate and unlettered. A student of the municipal lodging houses of the period—there were similar establishments that winter in sixteen cities, including New York, Chicago, Cleveland, St. Louis, and Buffalo—thought that the Detroit homeless were of "a definitely higher class than the usual type" of homeless men. Although most of them were blue-collar workers, there were also among them a large number of white-collar workers and "a vice-president or two."

To some, the Fisher Lodge looked like an army barracks. The men slept on army cots equipped with mattresses and woolen blankets but lacking sheets. The sleeping quarters were racially segregated—to the "material satisfaction" of both races, according to the New York *Times.* Each man received a towel and a nightgown, and showers, laundry facilities, and barbers were available. The former factory hospital served as a clinic. A city physician called daily and, when necessary, arranged for the removal of the sick to Receiving Hospital. Entertainment was provided by a radio, a piano, various games that had been donated, visiting entertainers, and the men themselves. At the outset, there were complaints that the Salvation Army provided the men with too much "salvation" and too little recreation and that the music emanating from the lodgers' orchestra was "drowned in the roar of trumpets and the roll of drums of the Salvation Army Band, urging the unemployed to confess their sins," but this state of affairs was quickly corrected.

The men had breakfast at 6:00 A.M., spent the day out on the streets, ate dinner at 6:00 P.M., and retired at 9:00 P.M. The food, prepared by the Salvation Army at the Fisher Lodge and the Industrial Lunch Company at the Studebaker Lodge at a daily cost of twenty cents per man, was ample and of "good quality." "It isn't a rich man's club by any manner of means," a reporter concluded with regard to the Fisher Lodge, "but it's heaven to a man who thought he might have to sleep in a hallway in company with an empty stomach." Some lodge inhabitants wrote the mayor that, although "little resembling a center of culture," the Fisher Lodge produced "a psychological effect" that was "benificial [*sic*] rather than detremental [*sic*] to the social and moral behaviour [*sic*]" of the lodgers.[43]

In the spring of 1931 the need for economy in a city finding it increasingly difficult to balance its budget caused the Homeless Men's Bureau to take steps to reduce the number of men it was supporting. Some of the able-bodied were persuaded or induced to leave the lodges; others, the winter over, left of their own volition. By the middle of June the number of homeless being housed or fed by the city had dropped to 3,362, as compared to 10,331 in April. Toward the end of March, also, the Bureau began asking the men in the lodges to volunteer for work in the lodges or for the city in return for their support. Most of the men were willing to work—2,559 of them worked 107,481 hours during April—but a small number refused. The Unemployed Councils, established by the Communists in Detroit and elsewhere in 1930 to organize the jobless, had been seeking from the start to infiltrate the lodges, and they now seized on the effort to put the lodgers to work to protest to Murphy about the city's alleged use of forced labor.[44]

Detroit derived tangible social and economic benefits from the housing of the homeless in the Fisher and Studebaker Lodges. Despite mounting unemployment, panhandling and disorderly conduct in the streets were "markedly reduced" during the winter of 1930–31. The lodges also removed from the streets persons who could have become a menace to the public health and who in the preceding winter had "cluttered" the offices of the City Physicians. "Too much credit cannot be given this enterprise," declared Dr. J. Frank Kilroy, the supervisor of the City Physicians.[45]

The homeless men not only received better treatment in the municipal lodges than in the private lodging houses, but they were also cared for at less expense to the city: the total cost per man per day was 20.25 cents at the Fisher Lodge and 22.5 cents at the Studebaker Lodge as compared to an average cost of 35 cents per day at the private flop houses. This was of no small consequence to the DPW, which financed the lodges once the MUC had put them into operation. "We have managed to solve the problem of homeless men in Detroit," Ballenger announced in January, 1931, and when the secretary of agriculture visited the city in February, he remarked that Detroit was ahead of all other cities in its treatment of the homeless. Murphy's promise that the homeless men in Detroit would "be taken care of decently and economically" was apparently being realized.[46]

Despite the benefits the city derived from the municipal lodges, there was formidable opposition to their continued operation. The owners of private flop houses considered it an "outrage" for the city to engage in the "hotel business" in competition with private enterprise. Comfortable persons who continued to cherish the illusion that anyone who was willing to work could find employment insisted that most of the men in the lodges were loafers who preferred the dole to remunerative employment and who preferred to play craps than to work for the city. Despite evidence to the contrary, opponents contended that the lodgers were mostly "foreigners" or recent arrivals to Detroit, and it was also claimed that the lodges had become "hot beds" of Communist activity.[47]

Increasingly, there was talk that the indigent homeless should be sent to the Wayne County Infirmary at Eloise, about fifteen miles west of Detroit. The infirmary had originally served as the county's poorhouse—it was known by that name until 1908—but by 1931 Eloise had become an institution primarily for the aged and infirm, the physically handicapped, and the feeble-minded and insane. It seemed to be just the right place—this institution with its cheerless atmosphere—to send the homeless if one believed them to be a species of subhumans, and the completion of a new building in February, 1931, provided the necessary spaces. Ideology rather than economics clearly motivated those who proposed sending the homeless to Eloise since the cost of forty-four to seventy-seven cents per day to keep a man at Eloise, largely borne by Detroit taxpayers, substantially exceeded the maintenance cost at the lodges. It may be, however, that the advocates of Eloise were cynical enough to know that most of the homeless would refuse to go to the county infirmary and that the closing of the lodges would therefore serve both the interests of the taxpayer and the imperatives of principle.[48]

Responding to the lobbying of the flop-house owners and echoing the litany of charges against the homeless men, the Common Council voted 6-3 on June 16 to close the lodges as of June 30. In a strong veto message of June 23, Murphy pointed out that homeless men were doubly handicapped in that employers gave preference to married men and the welfare department was concerned almost exclusively with family relief. The Council had stated that the men could go to Eloise or to the private flop houses, but Murphy noted that this would increase the city's costs. To ask the men to go to Eloise, moreover, was to send them to an institution that they regarded as a poorhouse, and men who were being denied their "inalienable right" to work, the mayor remonstrated, should not be required to bear that "stigma" nor should they be placed in an environment where their inability even to look for work would reduce them to despair and shatter their morale. The MUC agreed with Murphy, but the Public Welfare Commission, a far more conservative body, tabled Ballenger's proposal that it request the Common Council to maintain at least one of the lodges.[49]

In an action hailed by the Detroit *Free Press* on the grounds that the homeless men "deserve[d] neither pity nor pittance," the Common Council on July 2 unanimously overrode the mayor's veto. Ballenger had already closed down the Studebaker Lodge, and the feeding stations, except for the one maintained by the DFL, which enjoyed a charmed life, were also soon closed, but Ballenger delayed the closing of the Fisher Lodge in the hope that some way could yet be found to keep it in operation.[50]

Bitter at the charges directed against them, the "army of hopeless men" at the Fisher Lodge sent a delegation to the mayor that included John Schmies and William Reynolds, two prominent Detroit area Communists who were not residents of the lodge, to protest the Council's action. Murphy chided the delegation for including men who were not "true" representatives of the lodgers, whereupon Reynolds responded, "Listen mayor, we'll get you out of our way. You've always been in our way." Although Reynolds's remarks were nothing more than inflated rhetoric and are almost certainly to be interpreted in a political context, the federal government, for a time, reportedly assigned two Secret Service men to Murphy, and the Detroit police detailed a detective to protect the mayor.[51]

On the night of July 6, before "a roaring, cheering, booing throng" of fifteen hundred that included the mayor, many lodgers, and some Communist leaders, the Council, heeding Murphy's plea, voted to keep the Fisher Lodge open for two more nights. Following the Council action, "a floundering and divided City government" confronted the issue of the Fisher Lodge in an utterly confused manner. Murphy told Ballenger one thing, and G. Hall Roosevelt, by then not only the head of the MUC but also the city's controller, told him another. The Public Welfare Commission voted unanimously on July 7 to close the lodge and to send the men to Eloise, then reversed itself the next day and decided to keep the lodge open until July 15. In the meantime, the Common Council, irritated by the attempt of eight hundred lodgers, led by Communists, to storm City Hall, let it be known that it simply would not authorize the money required to keep the lodge open any longer.

Angered by Murphy's obvious failure to have his administration speak with a single voice and by the almost daily policy changes regarding the lodge, Ballenger, at a conference in the mayor's office on July 9, lost his temper and, shaking his finger at Murphy, shouted, "This is a serious proposition. . . . You have simply got to make up your mind about these things. I refuse to be put in the middle any longer." If Murphy, however, had failed to exercise firm leadership on the lodge issue, the Public Welfare Commission and the Common Council had been irresponsible, and Ballenger was in no mood to let them escape his wrath. "You don't know what you're doing," he said to the aldermen at the meeting, "any more than the Public Welfare Commission knows what it's doing."[52]

The Fisher Lodge closed its doors on July 10 after the men had eaten their evening meal. About three hundred men went to Eloise within the next few days, but a far larger number slept in the flop houses, the parks, boxcars, and church pews or simply "roamed the streets." The men who went to Eloise received three meals a day, and facilities were better than at the lodges; but at the infirmary, its grounds surrounded by an iron gate, the homeless were "inmates," and they were deprived of whatever dignity they might still have retained when they entered the institution. They were permitted to go to Detroit only a few days each month, at most, and the amount of "liberty" they were given depended on their conduct and the number of hours they worked at the infirmary. To the homeless, Eloise was a poorhouse, and as one of them said, "I'm a working man out of a job. I'm not a pauper." It is no wonder that the Wayne County Infirmary failed to attract the homeless and that those who did go there found the conditions "unendurable."[53]

Believing that the closing of the lodges had been "a grave mistake and a grave injustice to the homeless men," the mayor and the MUC were determined to reopen at least one of the buildings. Since the cost of operation for sleeping purposes only was minimal, the MUC, in an action that infuriated the Common Council, reopened the Fisher Lodge as a dormitory on September 10. The men did not receive any meals until the night of November 2, when six hundred of the twelve hundred lodgers, led once again by Unemployed Council representatives, demonstrated at City Hall and persuaded Ballenger to arrange with the Community Fund, on a temporary basis, to pay the cost of two meals a day for the men. Although Ballenger indicated that he might have made "a mistake," Murphy thought that the city should "find a way" to feed the homeless men, and the Public Welfare Commission, perhaps in reaction to the mayor's decisive reelection victory in November, was soon paying the food bill for the lodgers.[54]

Rejecting the advice of the superintendent of public welfare, the Public Welfare Commission voted on May 31, 1932, to close down the Fisher Lodge once again and to dispatch the lodgers to Eloise. The specious economy argument was advanced as the reason, but one may surmise that Commissioner Blain's view that the lodge was "a breeding place for bad citizenship" was the real cause for the decision. Getting word of what was about to occur, four hundred lodgers marched to City Hall and fought with the police in a tumultuous effort to present their case to the Council. "They are sending us to the crazy house," the spokesman for the lodgers declared. "It is a matter of life and death and we won't stand [for] it." Unmoved, the Council voted down a resolution to keep the lodge open, and the protests of the MUC, the plea of the homeless men that they at least be permitted to sleep at the lodge, and the attempt of the "better element" among the lodgers to dissociate themselves from "the small but loud minority of communists whose efforts we believe to be more detremental [sic] than helpful" were all unavailing.[55]

The Fisher Lodge closed a second time on June 15, and once again relatively few of the peak number of 1,607 men who had lived in the facility transferred to Eloise. Soon after the lodge closed, John Dos Passos found the homeless men "everywhere, all over the vast unfinished city, the more thrifty living in shacks and shelters along the waterfront, in the back rooms of unoccupied houses, the others just sleeping any place." It was, he reported, "a sluggish, drowsy, grimy life, of which Grand Circus Park is the social center and the One Cent Restaurant operated by some anonymous philanthropist on Woodward Avenue is the Delmonico's."[56]

By fall thirteen hundred to seventeen hundred men were sleeping out of doors, and this had its effect on the social pathology of the community. Not only was there an increase in panhandling, for which the homeless were partly responsible, but the commissioner of police also reported that the crimes of petty larceny and breaking and entering had increased more than 35 percent in the past year, and he attributed this, in some measure, to the homeless men. They were committing "nuisances" in the streets and alleys and on vacant premises, he stated, and they had become "something of a menace" to citizens walking the streets. Both the "wise" as well as the "humane" thing to do, he advised, was to get the men off the streets. The commissioner of health reported that the homeless men sleeping outdoors were a threat to public health, and he feared an increase in colds, influenza, and pneumonia if the men were not properly housed before winter.[57]

Despite Murphy's pleas, the Public Welfare Commission re-mained unwilling to assume the financial burden of maintaining a municipal lodging house—a frustrated Murphy removed Mrs. Tara from the commission over this issue—but after the Recon-struction Finance Corporation (RFC) included funds for the homeless in a relief loan to the city, the commission reluctantly bowed to the wishes of the mayor and Ballenger. At what has been described as "one of the most caustic meetings" in its history, the commission agreed on November 29 to reopen the Fisher Lodge solely as a dormitory, to limit the occupants to men who had resided in Detroit for at least two years and were no more than thirty-two years of age (so that the residents would not have to associate with the "regular homeless indigent type"), to require the lodgers to work for their maintenance, and to forbid the homeless at Eloise to transfer to the lodge.[58]

The Fisher Lodge reopened on December 9, 1932, and it was "homecoming" day for the homeless, 80 percent of whom were former residents. The MUC accepted responsibility for the opera-tion of the lodge, but it was able to carry the burden for only one month; and then, at Murphy's request, the Public Welfare Commission agreed to finance the institution provided that the cost for the fifteen hundred residents did not exceed fifteen cents per man per day. At the same time, the age limit for residents, which Murphy had opposed from the start, was removed.[59] Little more was heard of the lodge or its residents during the remainder of Murphy's mayoralty.

The Fisher Lodge was kept open after Murphy left Detroit until Fisher Body decided to demolish the building in August, 1933. The nine hundred men who still occupied the Fort Street structure, the surviving remnant of that large army of single, detached men who had so troubled Detroit during the Hoover years, were then transferred to another building at Piquette and St. Antoine provided by Fisher Body. The new facility continued to serve as a lodge for homeless men until wartime production absorbed most of the residents who were employable. The building was maintained as a refuge for families of defense workers until the welfare commission closed it down once and for all on September 10, 1942.[60]

Few episodes of the depression years more graphically reveal prevailing attitudes regarding unemployment and poverty than the reaction of much of official Detroit to the homeless men of the city. The Common Council, the Public Welfare Commission, business leaders, the *Free Press,* and other elements of the establishment viewed the homeless men with a mixture of contempt and fear and found it difficult if not impossible to empathize with them. Almost alone among leadership groups in the city, Mayor Murphy and members of his unemployment committee understood that most of the homeless men, caught up in a vast economic cataclysm and buffeted about by forces over which they had no control, had a claim upon the resources and the compassion of the community. Although the leadership that Murphy provided on the issue was sometimes wavering, the mayor did not control the appropriation of funds in Detroit, and we can be certain that without his presence on the scene the lot of homeless men in Detroit would have been even more desperate than in actuality it was.

Unlike the problem of homeless men, the plight of homeless women in Detroit never became a subject of public controversy, mainly because as many as fifteen religious and secular agencies quietly concerned themselves with the problem. One of the units of the relief subcommittee of the MUC devoted its attention to the matter, and Murphy, reflecting his experience on the bench, expressed the fear that the problem was more serious than social workers realized. Largely at the mayor's behest, the MUC initiated the centralized registration of homeless women in December, 1930, but after two weeks the Women's Registration Bureau reported that only thirty women had bothered to register, which ended speculation that the city would establish a lodging house for women. The MUC did, however, arrange food and lodgings and sought to find employment for perhaps one hundred homeless women during the winter of 1930–31. The Public Welfare Commission then assumed the burden and agreed to finance the care of the small number of the approximately eight thousand homeless women in Detroit who were not being looked after by private agencies. The commission, however, eventually decided, just as it did with regard to homeless men, that the Wayne County Infirmary was the proper agency to care for homeless women who required public assistance.[61]

Still another area of relief in which the MUC made a pioneering contribution was the school-lunch program for indigent school children, which was launched in the Detroit schools in the fall of 1930. Where there were school cafeterias, the needy children received a plate lunch; elsewhere, they were supplied a half pint of milk and eight graham crackers. Initially, the costs were met by the MUC and by contributions from teachers and the income derived from lunches purchased by children who could afford to do so. The MUC, which helped to finance the school lunches until some time in 1932, spent over $100,000 on the program, part of which was distributed to the city's parochial schools.[62]

Increasingly, the major contributor to the school-lunch program came to be the Children's Fund of Michigan, a self-liquidating foundation that James Couzens had established in August, 1929, to "'promote the health, welfare, happiness, and development of the children of the State of Michigan primarily, and elsewhere in the world.'" The secretary of the fund and a man who was to play an important part in the welfare efforts of the Murphy administration was William J. Norton. Norton, born in Maine and a Bowdoin graduate, was one of the principal figures in the development of the community-chest idea in the United States. He organized the first general financial federation in Cleveland in 1913, performed a similar service in Cincinnati, and was then invited to Detroit in 1917 to help set up the Detroit Patriotic Fund, which eventually became the Detroit Community Fund. "A hard-headed yet progressive and liberal-minded social worker," Norton served as Couzens's man in Detroit.[63]

Having made its first contribution to the school-lunch program in January, 1931, the Children's Fund agreed at the end of November to meet the cost of the lunches insofar as funds could not otherwise be obtained. This decision was made after Murphy had claimed that eighteen thousand school children were still going hungry at lunch time and the supervisor of one school district had declared, "Starvation among our school children is not a rhetorical phrase but an actual fact." The school-lunch program was already benefiting about nine thousand school children by the middle of December, 1930, and during the next two-and-a-half years an average of about twenty thousand children received a hot lunch or milk and crackers on the days that school was in session. In the summer of 1932 a daily average of 6,889 children took their lunches at the forty school lunchrooms that were kept open for their benefit. Initially, the program accommodated primarily the children of families not on the welfare rolls, but as welfare allowances were reduced, an increasing number of welfare children also began to receive their lunches through the schools. In March, 1933, at a time when half the children receiving free school lunches were from welfare families, the Public Welfare Commission agreed to assume the cost of lunches for all welfare children being fed at the schools, including children attending parochial schools. There is no indication that the decision to use public funds for parochial school children aroused any opposition.[64]

The outstanding popular success of the MUC and, in the opinion of the mayor, "perhaps" its "most important undertaking," was the Detroit thrift-garden program. The suggestion that the MUC undertake this activity came from Murphy himself, who had been reading George Catlin's *The Story of Detroit* and had been impressed with the account of Hazen Pingree's famous "potato patch plan" and the manner in which a substantial number of welfare families in Detroit during the depression years 1894-96 had grown a portion of their food on vacant lots donated to the city for that purpose. The MUC decided in March, 1931, to undertake a similar program of "vacant lot gardening."[65]

Murphy and the MUC saw the Detroit thrift gardens as serving twin objectives: the gardens, of course, would provide food for some of the needy; but the plan's sponsors, fearful, as Murphy expressed it, that "the psychological effect of idleness of large groups of our people" was "dangerous to the safety and morale of the country," also hoped that the project would help to preserve the "work habits" of the unemployed. The supervisor of one garden plot stated bluntly that the principal virtue of the gardens was that they served to "keep funny ideas out of the minds of our unemployed" and helped them to maintain their "self-respect." When the depression was over, he said, the gardeners would consequently be "the same industrious law-abiding citizens they were before."[66]

The MUC allotted $10,000 to the thrift-garden program in 1931. The remaining funds for the project were derived from the profits ($8,000) of a Spring Festival held to stress Detroit's cultural diversity. Murphy astutely linked the festival with the thrift gardens and the "potato patch plan" by naming Mrs. Hazel Pingree Depew, the former mayor's daughter, the honorary chairman of the affair.[67]

The gardeners were drawn from two groups, welfare clients and the unemployed or partially employed who were "near the verge of dependency" but were not on the welfare rolls. The land was obtained through the efforts of the Detroit Real Estate Board; the Department of Parks and Boulevards decided which land was suitable for the gardens and provided the equipment to prepare three hundred acres of soil; and the Department of Public Works staked out the individual garden plots (one hundred feet by forty feet) in the twenty-seven fields that were utilized. An experienced gardener, engaged for each group of gardens, planted a model garden that the thrift gardeners could copy, assigned the individual plots at the direction of the Detroit Thrift Gardens Committee, which ran the project, distributed seeds, insecticides, and the necessary gardening instructions, and maintained order in his field. The gardeners, working in shifts, protected the fields at night, and three buses leased by the Thrift Gardens Committee provided free transportation to and from the fields.

The 2,785 field gardeners each received the same amount and types of vegetable seeds for their gardens, but they could plant whatever they pleased in a fifteen-by-forty foot portion of their plots. In addition to the field gardens, the Detroit Thrift Gardens Committee furnished seeds and instructions for 1,604 "home gardens" grown in the gardeners' back yards or on lots that they themselves spaded and prepared. A nutrition expert from the Extension Division of Michigan State College instructed the field gardeners in the canning of their surplus vegetables, and Detroiters were asked to contribute mason jars for this purpose.[68]

The first year of operation of the thrift gardens proved "an unqualified success." At a cost of about $18,000, the 4,369 field and home gardeners produced a crop valued at $218,450 (about $50 per gardener) and thereby benefited about twenty thousand people. The results justified the continuation of the project for another year. Most of the funds for the 1932 gardens were privately raised by William Norton, but the MUC also made a contribution. This time 6,200 gardeners (3,184 field and 3,016 home), at a cost of a little over $17,000, raised a crop valued at $310,000 and contributed to the support of an estimated thirty-one thousand persons.[69]

In 1933 the welfare department, once again picking up a project that the MUC had pioneered, decided to bear the cost of gardens tended by welfare clients but to reimburse itself by deducting up to $5 from the grocery allowance of field gardeners and up to $1 from home gardeners. The Thrift Gardens Committee assumed the financial responsibility of aiding needy gardeners not on the welfare rolls, but it would have had to abandon its share of the project had not James Couzens come to the rescue. Of the 5,921 field and home gardens cultivated in 1933, 4,211 were tended by welfare clients and 1,710 by needy persons not on welfare. The estimated value of the crop was $177,630 ($30 per garden), the cost was under $13,000, and the number benefited was 29,615.

The project was continued in Detroit for an additional three years.[70]

Not only did the thrift gardens supply 16,490 gardeners during the years 1931–33 with a grand total of more than $700,000 worth of vegetables of every conceivable variety, but they also seem to have had the effect on the morale of the gardeners that Murphy and the MUC had anticipated. "The work on the garden," one gardener noted, "was a great relief from walking the streets. It gave my mind a rest and made me physically fit for a job when I got one." The gardeners in one field wrote Murphy that the value of the project should be reckoned less in monetary terms than in "the physical, mental, and spiritual well being of the individual as well as the Community as a whole. What [else] would we men and women have done to pass away the long summer days and months?"[71]

The field meetings that gardeners held to solve their common problems sometimes helped to develop a sense of community among them, a not unimportant consideration in view of the fact that gardeners of different nationalities sometimes cultivated plots in the same field—a reporter described the Delray field, for example, as "a Babel of tongues." The gardeners formed clubs, arranged picnics and barbecues, and exhibited their products at the Michigan State Fair. The Thrift Gardens Committee thought that the project had "created among the gardeners the feeling that they were one big family."[72]

Insofar as the thrift gardens had political consequences, their beneficiary was Frank Murphy. One gardener who had been unemployed for seventeen months wrote to thank the mayor for "the magnitude of your gift" and "for the things which I and my family have received from you, by means of the Garden." The family, the gardener assured Murphy, would be "not ungrateful on election day."[73]

There were "assisted gardening" projects in five or six states in 1931, but because it was a form of relief that could be easily organized and did not involve a large expenditure of funds, there was a large increase in garden projects in 1932. The Detroit project, however, was the most important in the nation. When the Department of Commerce issued a publication on subsistence gardening in 1932, it devoted more attention to the Detroit plan than to any other.[74]

Unlike other MUC committees, the Colored Advisory Committee did not initiate programs of relief but rather sought to monitor ongoing programs to ensure that they operated without discrimination. Murphy stated categorically that Detroit distributed relief without regard to "race, creed or color," and John Dancy, the head of the Colored Advisory Committee, corroborated this evaluation. Detroit, he informed his correspondents, had taken "very good care" of its indigent citizens, black and white, and there were "no barriers of participation" in the relief programs. Thanks to the MUC, Dancy reported, blacks had also received "a very fair break" in securing city employment as common laborers. He might also have noted that protests to the mayor regarding the attitude of welfare workers toward blacks did not go unheeded. When two black leaders complained to Murphy about the "discourteous treatment" accorded some black welfare clients, he promptly wrote the superintendent of public welfare to "insist that there be no prejudice against the people of Color." The superintendent took prompt corrective action and assured the mayor that the department would not tolerate discourtesy toward its clients.[75]

The high proportion of blacks on the welfare rolls convinced some Detroit whites that the mayor was simply seeking to build a political machine among black voters. How else, they thought, could one explain the city's welfare policies? There was also some concern among whites that blacks preferred the dole to jobs. A committee of industrialists that examined welfare procedures in 1932 concluded that "because of the peculiar characteristics and temperments [sic] of the colored people there are at least a noticeable proportion of those now receiving welfare who because of this are definitely settling back and looking upon this as a very satisfactory solution to the problem of a happy existence." A prominent Detroit businessman thought it a "mistake" to provide black and white welfare recipients with the same kind of food. The blacks on welfare, he suggested, should be "segregated" and placed on "the 'hog and hominy diet'" of Southern blacks. This would not only be adequate for them but might even induce "many of the colored gentry" to leave Detroit. He had interviewed dozens of blacks who were not on the welfare rolls, and they had told him, he reported, that Murphy "'took such good care of the colored people'" that they found living on the dole in Detroit preferable to returning to the South. If, as some whites foolishly suspected, the mayor was seeking by his welfare policies to build a political machine among Detroit's blacks, he was obviously running a very considerable risk of antagonizing the more numerous whites in the process.[76]

The relief programs initiated by the MUC were carried forward against a backdrop of discord, disarray, and confusion within the committee itself. Murphy, naïvely, had hoped that the members of the committee would be able to submerge their differences in the common cause, but the consensus that was briefly achieved at the outset was fractured before the year was out, and from that point forward only the determination of the mayor kept the committee alive. As its last chairman indicated, the MUC was, "in a certain sense," Murphy's "child,"[77] and the mayor had no desire to commit infanticide.

At the outset, three major groups were represented on the committee: a conservative employer faction, for whom John L. Lovett, general manager of the Michigan Manufacturers' Association, Chester Culver, general secretary of the Employers' Association of Detroit, and Harvey Campbell, vice-president and secretary of the Detroit Board of Commerce, were the spokesmen; organized labor, whose chief voice was Frank Martel; and a middle-class, reformist group, one of whose prominent members was Frank D. Adams. The first major split in the committee's ranks occurred in November, 1930, when Martel sought to persuade the group to adopt resolutions calling for a five-day week in Detroit and barring Canadian residents from working in the city. It seemed at first that the committee would sidetrack his proposals, which prompted Martel to charge that "reactionaries" were "in control" of the MUC. When the advantage shifted to the labor-liberal group, Lovett stated that the MUC had already "done all the good it can do" and urged that its functions be transferred to the DPW. With Martel saying that he would not "recede one inch" and Lovett declaring that he had no desire "to fool around with a committee" whose members spent their time "arguing among themselves," the conservative press, which regularly wrote premature obituaries of the MUC as it got itself into and out of trouble, portrayed the committee as on the verge of collapse.[78]

Murphy, however, had other ideas. "If the people who are on the committee persist in open disagreement and can't manage to stop jeopardizing the work," he declared, "I can put people on who are capable of finishing the job." The storm was weathered when, at "two turbulent meetings" on December 1 that the mayor attended, both the Advisory Committee and the General Committee, by split votes, officially approved Martel's five-day week proposal.[79] Temporarily bolting the committee, Culver fumed that the MUC's chief purpose was "pulling Frank Martel's chestnuts out of the fire," and Campbell, who also took a walk, protested that the usefulness of the committee was at an end if the employers were to be ignored to please Martel. Murphy remarked that disagreement among the committee's members was inevitable since they had been selected to represent a "true cross-section" of public opinion in Detroit, but he thought that once a decision was reached, all should cooperate in its implementation. Soon thereafter the mayor added five prominent industrial and business leaders to the Advisory Committee, an action that some saw as intended to overcome the labor-liberal majority on the committee, although it is more likely that Murphy was signaling to the Lovetts, Culvers, and Campbells that they did not speak for the entire business community in their attacks on the MUC.[80]

Although the Detroit *News* thought that Murphy had emerged the victor in this first great crisis in the life of the MUC, the committee had clearly been weakened as a community-wide enterprise, and it never again enjoyed very much conservative support. The *Michigan Manufacturer and Financial Record* now condemned the appointment of "unofficial and irresponsible bodies to cope with important public problems which must be dealt with by persons with experience and authority," and the *Free Press* complained that the MUC had been "deliberately prostituted to political and class purposes." The *Civic Searchlight* thought that "a radical element" had subverted the committee and that in supporting the radicals—Murphy had said that "Martel won because Martel was right"—the mayor had failed to make "a proper analysis" of the unemployment problem. The New York *Times,* which had reported in October that "no city in the country" had initiated "a more systematic or sensible effort . . . to ameliorate the economic condition" than Detroit, now decided that Murphy was not a "political genius" after all; and it asserted that "thoughtful citizens" had concluded that the work the MUC had undertaken should be left to the established welfare agencies. This was very much the view of the Common Council, which indicated that the MUC could not look forward to any additional financial support from the city's legislature.[81]

Again and again in the next two years lack of funds brought the MUC to the brink of dissolution, only to have Murphy rescue the committee before it plunged into the abyss. In January, 1931, the Advisory Committee made a tentative decision to disband the MUC on April 1 since the Council's appropriation would run out by then, but Murphy would not hear of this. The committee, he declared, would endure as long as the emergency lasted. "I think that some influences in Detroit would rather see it dead than alive," he observed. "They are bound to be disappointed"— and they were. The MUC did undergo a change, however, once it became apparent that the Council, despite Murphy's protestations, would provide the committee with no additional money. Lacking a dependable source of funds and on the verge of bankruptcy, the MUC began to place greater stress on its research and fact-finding functions, and it looked to others to finance the relief projects that it had successfully launched.

The MUC, however, was not able to divest itself entirely of its relief responsibilities, partly because the DPW, the Community Fund, or some other agency could not or would not agree to support a particular MUC activity, partly because there always appeared to be needs that the established agencies were not meeting. The MUC thus continued at different times to accept responsibility in whole or in part for the Free Employment Bureau, the Fisher Lodge, the school-lunch program, the Detroit thrift gardens, and the material relief of the needy not on the welfare rolls.[82]

In April, 1931, just after the *News* had concluded that the committee was in the grip of "apathy," the MUC leadership appointed five new subcommittees, and soon the unemployment group was again "seething with activity." The new committees, however, were indicative of the direction in which the MUC was now tending. One was concerned with old-age pensions, another with the adequacy of welfare food budgets, a third with working conditions in Detroit, a fourth with infant and prenatal care, and a fifth with the price and quantity of milk allotted to welfare families. Of these committees, only the milk committee, in whose work Murphy took a special interest, had any important effect—the studies that it initiated led within the next few months to a reduction not only in the special price of milk for welfare families, which saved the DPW an estimated $160,000 a year, but also in the retail price of milk, Murphy's objective from the start. In subsequent months the MUC became an advocate of federal and state aid for relief, state legislation to protect the consumer, a moratorium on municipal debt payments for the duration of the financial emergency, and ratification of the child-labor amendment.[83]

In July, 1931, Frank Adams succeeded Roosevelt as MUC chairman. The liberal and labor members on the committee had become increasingly antagonistic toward Roosevelt, in some degree because they regarded him as too conservative—Martel, in his harsh way, charged that Roosevelt was "completely devoid of a social sense"—but also because they believed that his duties as controller and the consequent pressures upon him to economize conflicted with his role as MUC chairman. Adams's accession to the chairmanship was more a victory for the liberal than for the labor bloc on the committee. Martel, who thought Adams an improvement over Roosevelt, nevertheless complained that the clergyman was a "dogmatic parliamentarian" and lacked "practical experience." Adams held the post until the end of 1932 when, his congregation no longer able to pay him a salary that had been reduced by 50 percent in three years, he left Detroit for a new pulpit. He was, as he wrote Murphy, "one of the casualties" of the "war" against the depression that the MUC and the mayor had been waging. Father Edward J. Hickey, a professor at the Sacred Heart Seminary, succeeded Adams.[84]

After Adams became the MUC chairman, the membership of the Advisory Committee was altered to reflect the fact that business members of the committee no longer evinced any interest in its affairs. Although now a committee made up almost exclusively of liberal and labor members, the MUC was still by no means a harmonious group. When its labor subcommittee, headed by Rabbi Leon Fram, reported in August, 1931, that its investigations indicated that, although smaller Detroit firms had cut wages 10 to 20 percent, the larger employers had not reduced the pay of their workers, Martel, who had been critical of the subcommittee, succeeded in having the unit dissolved. At Murphy's suggestion, the dissolved committee was quickly replaced by a new labor and legal problems committee, free from Martel's "bludgeoning." As a matter of fact, organized labor began to show less and less interest in the affairs of the MUC, and it became the preserve, increasingly, of "a handful of idealists" and middle-class liberals. Father Hickey, with some exaggeration, complained at the end of Murphy's mayoralty that the only persons who had been attending committee meetings regularly were those who had "a hobby, a pet theory of reform, or who championed a radical socialistic policy."[85]

By early 1933 even dedicated members of the MUC were beginning to wonder whether it was worth preserving the committee in view of the seeming failure of its fund-raising efforts and the dwindling interest of the membership. As usual, it was Murphy who insisted that the committee must be continued, even though limited funds forced a further reduction in its staff. When Murphy resigned in May to take up his new post in the Philippines, the committee, whose name was now changed to the Detroit Relief Committee since Mayor Frank Couzens wished to dissociate himself from a group so conspicuously identified with his predecessor, was left with a debt of about $7,000, mainly owed to the small staff that operated the Free Employment Bureau. The city was unwilling to assume this debt, and a portion of the obligation, much to Murphy's annoyance, remained unpaid as late as September.[86]

In the winter of 1930–31 "citizens' emergency committees" were established in numerous American cities in response to the rising tide of unemployment. Some of these committees were designed to raise emergency funds for relief purposes, others have been characterized as "long-term fact finding and stabilization bodies," but none developed as varied a program as the MUC, and only the Philadelphia Committee for Unemployment Relief,[87] which coordinated the entire relief program in a city that granted no public outdoor assistance, received as much national attention. Although even Murphy would have agreed by the time he left office that the Detroit committee had not, after all, had "a perfect plan" for dealing with unemployment, as he had once boasted, the MUC, nevertheless, had a record of accomplishment of which he could justly be proud. As he had hoped, it had succeeded in focusing the attention of Detroit on the enormity of the unemployment problem and had "broken down the barriers of indifference and bewilderment" that surrounded the question. Always sensitive to the plight of the unemployed and the needy both on and off the welfare rolls, it had been the progenitor of numerous worthwhile relief programs, it had acted when the DPW had been unable to act, and it had indicated how novel problems could be met in novel ways. In some ways, it had played the same sort of role that the Office of Economic Opportunity later played in the effort to combat poverty in the nation. As Frank Adams noted, the money expended by the MUC was "only a drop in the bucket" compared to the city's welfare expenditures as a whole, but it was "an important drop."[88]

In addition to the MUC, a variety of voluntary and private organizations and groups supplemented the efforts of the DPW in distributing relief. Although welfare remained overwhelmingly a public function throughout Murphy's mayoralty, the problem of unemployment was so great, and the money available to the city government for relief so limited that there was always a substantial gap between the needs of the distressed and the public funds available to meet those needs. Private agencies, consequently, sought by one means or another to fill this gap, and, although they succeeded in doing so to only a limited degree, their efforts helped to make it possible for Detroit to survive until more abundant aid for relief became available from outside the city. The principal effort to raise private funds for unemployment relief in Detroit was the Emergency Relief Fund campaign of 1931-32, about which we shall have more to say later, but there were many less well publicized relief activities that also helped to tide the city over its time of troubles. It is altogether proper to stress the ever-increasing importance of public as compared to private relief during the depression—in this sense, the rest of the nation simply caught up with Detroit—but we shall be missing an essential aspect of the depression story if we ignore the myriad ways in which voluntary agencies—some old and some new—supplemented the admittedly more important relief efforts of public authorities.[89]

In Detroit, as William Norton pointed out, there was at the beginning of the depression "a rather complicated system of interrelations" between the DPW and the numerous private agencies affiliated with the Detroit Community Union (it became the Council of Social Agencies of Metropolitan Detroit in February, 1932). The charitable agencies did not normally concern themselves with the problem of material relief, but the depression forced them to take on some "fragments of the job" even though the failure of the Community Fund to reach its money-raising goals led to reductions in the size of their budgets.

In November, 1931, the welfare agencies of Detroit formed the Advisory Relief Committee of the Detroit Community Union to coordinate activities of the numerous organizations seeking to aid indigents who were not on the welfare rolls and to determine how the private agencies could "supplement, encourage, and assist" the public agencies that dispensed relief. During the next year several private agencies picked up some of the slack occasioned by the sharp reduction in the DPW's budget. The Associated Charities, which normally had a case load of about one thousand, cared for about thirty-five hundred families in 1932. The Jewish Social Service Bureau, which customarily looked after Jewish families requiring casework, now also sought to provide relief to families suffering from unemployment; it was caring for fourteen hundred families in October, 1932. The Salvation Army not only aided transient women, but in October, 1932, it was assisting twenty-three hundred families pending their acceptance by other agencies. In that same month the Servicemen's Bureau, which catered to needy veterans, was looking after sixty-three hundred families, the five children's relief agencies were providing food, clothing, and shelter for forty-one hundred children, and the Polish Aid Society was looking after five hundred cases.[90]

In addition to the feeding stations maintained by the DPW, a variety of private groups also supplied food to the needy. The Hungarian Free Kitchen, which opened in the fall of 1931, had served 100,000 meals by the end of 1932, and the Jewish Emergency Relief Fund provided free meals to needy Jews who wished to eat kosher food. The Capuchin monks, with Mayor Murphy aiding their efforts, supplied 200,000 free meals in 1931 and 1932. Assisted by the Department of Public Works, which provided it with space, transportation, and some manpower, the Burgess Relief Association, founded by two Detroiters at the beginning of 1930, fed five hundred persons two meals a day and also cared for from fifty to sixty families in their homes. The Madonna Guild not only furnished layettes for the babies of impoverished families but supplied a free hot lunch daily to about six hundred women and children in city space made available by the mayor. The McGregor Institute, throughout the depression, provided food and lodgings to thousands of homeless men, and the League of Catholic Women, the YWCA, and the Jewish Social Service Bureau performed a similar function for homeless women.[91]

Until salary reductions made it difficult for them to continue doing so, city employees, in effect, taxed themselves to provide relief for the indigent. By May 1, 1931, the Detroit City Employees Relief Committee had raised $45,000 from voluntary contributions of 1 percent of the salaries of the employees of most city departments. The bulk of this money was assigned to the public schools to help provide free lunches and items of apparel for needy school children, supplementing the sums contributed for the same purpose by the school teachers, the MUC, and the Children's Fund. By the end of 1932 the public schools had provided needy children with more than three million free lunches. They had also repaired 200,000 pairs of shoes, distributed shoes and clothing to thousands of children, supplied or repaired eye glasses for 883 students, and provided textbooks for about 27,000 children.[92]

City firemen, each of whom contributed twenty-five cents a day, fed the hungry at fifty-eight fire stations beginning in November, 1931, and provided food and fuel to twenty thousand persons during the next year. The police department set up the Police Quick Relief Association to supply food, fuel, and clothing to indigent persons whom policemen discovered while walking their beats. More than $50,000 was distributed by the department for material relief in 1931.[93]

When budgetary restraints forced the Department of Health at the beginning of 1932 to discontinue the dental service that it maintained for school children, the Detroit District Dental Relief Committee came to the rescue. Hundreds of dentists volunteered their services to examine children in the school clinics and to provide the indigent among them with free dental care; the children of semi-indigent parents were sent to dentists who had volunteered to treat them at reduced fees. The Dental Relief Committee and the Northwestern Dental Club also operated free dental clinics for indigent adults. The Medical Relief Committee of the Wayne County Medical Society, anxious to serve those whose self-respect made them reluctant to avail themselves of the services of the City Physicians, worked out an arrangement with the Public Welfare Commission at the end of 1931 whereby volunteer doctors provided free medical care for indigent patients on and off the welfare rolls who wished to use the service. Obviously not wanting to disturb existing patient-doctor relationships any more than was necessary, the Medical Society stipulated that the volunteer doctors were to send indigent patients to their family doctors whenever this was possible, and it was careful to describe the program as "an emergency measure" rather than as "free medical service." More than 650 patients were being treated by the volunteer doctors soon after the program went into effect.[94]

The board of trustees of the Children's Fund of Michigan instructed its secretary in December, 1930, to investigate relief conditions in Detroit to ascertain if the fund could in any way relieve the "material needs" of the city's children. On the basis of Norton's subsequent report, the Children's Fund began contributing to the material relief of Detroit school children, and it seems to have spent more than $200,000 for this purpose by the end of the 1932–33 school year. It also helped to support the relief efforts of Detroit's dentists and, to a much lesser extent, Detroit's doctors insofar as they provided for the care of indigent children.[95]

Murphy hoped that the major employers in the Detroit area would themselves look after the needs of at least some of their employees for whom they could no longer provide jobs. It was "only just," he thought, that those who had acquired "vast fortunes" as the result of the labor of Detroit workingmen should accept the responsibility of looking after these workers when they lost their jobs. He met with the principal employers in the district to discuss the unemployment crisis within a few days of his taking office, but it does not appear that the meeting produced anything more than an exchange of views. Although Murphy later became involved in an acrimonious debate with the Ford Motor Company regarding the degree to which it provided for its former employees—and there is no doubt that Ford grossly misrepresented the extent of its welfare activities—many of the large firms, including Ford, did make an effort to aid at least some of their laid-off workers.

Some Detroit employers took vigorous exception to the thesis that industrial firms had a responsibility to care for workers to whom they could no longer give employment. An obligation of this sort, the *Michigan Manufacturer and Financial Record* declared, would encourage businessmen to locate their plants somewhere other than in Detroit. The journal suggested that, instead of making heretical suggestions of this sort, the mayor should save some of the money being "frittered away in doles" by cutting off relief to "aliens" and "an unacclimated population of southern negroes" and inducing them to return to the lands and regions whence they had come.[96]

Since never more than a minority of the unemployed in Detroit were on the welfare rolls, the relief provided by the MUC and the voluntary agencies to those unable to qualify for public aid or unwilling to seek it was a much needed supplement to the assistance extended by the city government itself. The major share of the relief burden was, however, carried by the DPW, and it was the budgetary requirements of this department that decisively affected the formulation of public policy in Detroit while Frank Murphy was its mayor.

XII

"Capitol" of the "Jobless"

I

In April, 1931, the acting deputy superintendent of Detroit's Department of Public Welfare (DPW) stated publicly that the city administration would have to realize that it could not establish "a record" both for "generosity" and for "economy."[1] In making this remark, the welfare official was pointing to the almost insuperable obstacle Murphy faced in seeking to implement a generous public-welfare program at a time when the financial resources available to the city were steadily declining. It was one thing for the mayor to state that no one in Detroit would go hungry; it was another thing for him to find the funds to make good that pledge.

The fiscal problems of Detroit between 1930 and 1933 were of truly formidable proportions, and there was little that the political leadership of the city could do to alleviate them. The city's "most crucial" budgetary problem was its debt structure. The principal evidence of this was the constantly decreasing proportion of the annual tax levy that was available for purposes other than debt service as the fixed charges in the budget mounted to meet the costs of the vast bonded debt that the city had incurred during the era of expansion in the 1920s. Whereas debt service absorbed 21.6 percent of the tax levy in the fiscal year 1929-30, the proportion rose to 24.2 percent in 1930-31, 25.9 percent in 1931-32, and a staggering 42.5 percent in 1932-33. Excluding education, the city's borrowing power as of November, 1930, was limited by charter provisions and state law to 9 percent of Detroit's assessed property values (only half of this sum could be devoted to general public improvements; the remainder was allocated to water, light, and other utilities).[2] Detroit had only a modest bonding leeway for public improvements when Murphy became mayor—about $22 million as of November 5—and as its assessed property valuation declined in the next two years, this margin vanished. Also, the municipal bond market virtually disappeared during the depression years so that it was difficult for Detroit to arrange conventional long-term funding even to the extent authorized.[3]

Detroit's debt problems were compounded by the slipshod budgetary procedures and the "tradition of carelessness" that had developed with regard to the short-term borrowing to which the city regularly resorted in anticipation of tax collections and bond sales and to meet welfare and other departmental expenditures that could not be precisely calculated at the time the budget was put together. Given the Detroit practice that had been followed since about 1920 of allotting only a nominal sum (usually $200,000) for welfare in the annual budget and then financing current welfare charges by monthly deficit appropriations, the substantial welfare costs incurred in the depression years added to the "floating debt," as did the frequent failure of the Common Council to take prompt action in spreading the cost of public improvements among the benefited property owners. Murphy's initial problems regarding the floating debt were aggravated by the fact that Bowles, in an unprecedented move, had failed to make provision in the 1930–31 budget, which Murphy inherited, for $6.9 million of the cash deficit that had been incurred in the previous fiscal year. This action, growing deficits in the next two fiscal years, and state legislation of 1931 that placed new restraints on the city's ability to finance its needs by short-term borrowing against current and delinquent taxes and to refinance special improvements[4] made it increasingly difficult for Detroit to secure new short-term loans or to refund old ones. About one-third of the floating debt of $60 million was retired in December, 1930, but the deficit incurred during the remainder of the fiscal year raised the short-term indebtedness to about $62 million as of July 1, 1931.[5]

Intensifying the debt problem and forcing the Murphy administration to resort to ever greater economies was the increasing difficulty the city encountered in collecting its taxes. Tax delinquency in the depression years has been described as "the creeping paralysis" that was "destroying local government." Bad as the experience of other cities was in this regard, however, the Detroit experience was worse. Whereas in 145 cities of over fifty thousand population, the tax delinquency rate was 10.8 percent in 1930, 13.3 percent in 1931, 20.1 percent in 1932, and 25.2 percent in 1933, tax delinquency in Detroit amounted to 14.89 percent of the tax levy in the fiscal year 1930-31, 24.89 percent in 1931-32, and an astronomical 34.61 percent in 1932-33. In prosperous times the city had sold most of its delinquent taxes to tax-title buyers, who could look forward to making a profit on their transactions when the owners eventually reclaimed their property and had to pay the interest and penalty charges that had accumulated; but in the depression years 1931 and 1932 tax-title buyers simply did not appear to purchase the delinquent taxes offered for sale, and the city itself had to "buy in" virtually all the titles, which was simply a bookkeeping transaction. Many of the city's taxpayers were no more able to pay the special assessments levied against them than they were able to pay their taxes, and this added to Detroit's budgetary problems.[6]

Forced to turn to bankers for funds as their tax revenues declined and their debt charges became more onerous, city governments sometimes discovered that they could procure necessary loans only if they agreed to place certain restrictions on their expenditures. "Financial dictators" in this way began to acquire some of the power normally exercised by elected officials in these municipalities. In Detroit, the Committee on City Finances—the Stone Committee—was already advising the city government on fiscal matters when Murphy became mayor; and, consistent with Stone's view that it was necessary to organize "the otherwise inarticulate and ineffectual citizenship" so that it could "outweigh the influence of office-holders and public employees," the committee eventually assumed the role of "financial dictator." Concerned primarily with the economical and efficient operation of the city government and the balancing of the city's budget without any appreciable increase in taxes, the Stone Committee advocated a sharp reduction in welfare expenditures and a cutback in city operations in general. This brought the committee into conflict with Mayor Murphy, who was necessarily concerned not only with economy and the demands of bondholders but also with the provision of needed services.

Murphy, to be sure, had rather conventional ideas about balanced budgets and government spending, but, unlike the bankers, he did not think of government as a business whose well-being was to be measured only in terms of its financial balance sheet. Although it was necessary, he observed, to balance the budget, this was "only an objective. It isn't a god, a sacred thing that is to be accomplished at all costs. It is not right to shatter living conditions and bring human being[s] to want and misery to achieve such an objective. . . . To sacrifice everything to balance the budget is fanaticism."[7]

The shift in power from the political leadership in some municipalities to bankers and business leaders who were not responsible to the electorate had implications not only for the provision of government services but for democracy itself. Since Murphy was quite sensitive to the meaning of banker control—his staff referred to Stone as "the tenth councilman"—it was predictable that he would react adversely to the role that the Stone Committee was coming to play in Detroit's affairs. The fact that Stone was quite lacking in "political finesse" simply added to the strain of what would have been a troubled relationship in any event.[8]

As it became evident by the end of 1930 that the $6.9 million deficit in the Bowles budget for 1930-31 would grow to perhaps $23 million by the end of the fiscal year, primarily because of welfare expenditures, Murphy began stressing the need for "drastic" economies in the nonwelfare portion of the budget. "There can be no restriction on those things which are necessary for health, safety and life," the mayor told the Bankers Club of Detroit in December, "but in every other way the City will have to practice retrenchment."[9]

In a series of executive orders beginning in January, 1931, Murphy, making good on his promise to economize, instructed the departments to reduce overtime work to the absolute minimum; make only such expenditures for maintenance and supplies as were essential for the peace, health, and safety of the city; obtain the prior consent of the controller to fill vacancies, effect transfers between funds within their budgets, encumber balances of capital-cost items in their budgets, and request the Council for advances against the 1931-32 budget; and appoint three-man departmental efficiency and economy committees. At the end of January the mayor also requested the departments to take steps to reduce their budgets by 12-1/2 percent.[10]

In an effort to coordinate and provide direction for the efforts of departmental efficiency and economy committees, Murphy, in May, 1931, created a central Committee on Efficiency and Economy, chaired by Clarence Wilcox. "The most valuable suggestion we can now make," the committee tautologically advised the mayor soon after its formation, "is that in order to *stop* expenditures, our various departments must *stop spending*." This is precisely what the departments were attempting to do, and their reports to the Wilcox committee indicated their concern to pare even the smallest items of expense. Instructions were thus issued to departmental personnel to eliminate telephone extensions, curtail private phone calls, replace long-distance calls with letters, and reduce the use of electric lights.[11]

In making recommendations for the city's 1931–32 budget, the Stone Committee initially proposed that the anticipated deficit of more than $20 million be absorbed by a slight increase in the tax rate and by drastic economies effected over a two-year period. Murphy, however, let it be known that the Stone Committee's ideas about the budget did not "square up exactly" with his own. He advised the Council in his annual message in January that he was opposed to a tax increase, that only about one-third of the deficit could be liquidated in the 1931–32 budget, and that the remainder should be absorbed over a two- or three-year period. In what can only be construed as a slap at the Committee on City Finances, Murphy appointed another advisory group of six bankers—they were, he said, mostly young bankers with "life, energy and judgment"—to aid him in drawing up the new budget; then, a few weeks later he appointed an additional "bankers committee" to advise Controller Roosevelt on day-to-day fiscal matters.[12]

Murphy exercised far greater control over the preparation and presentation of the city's 1931–32 budget than had been customary for Detroit's chief executives. Departmental budget requests to be covered by taxes totaled more than $106 million, but Murphy pared this figure to $76 million, which left the tax levy virtually unchanged as compared to 1930–31. Since the budget absorbed $7.8 million of the preceding year's deficit and provided for an increase of more than $2 million in the sum allotted to meet debt charges, Murphy, in effect, had slashed the city's operating budget as compared to 1930–31 by almost $10 million. Unfortunately, however, a 10 percent reduction (from $3,774,861,000 to $3,358,431,390) in the real-property assessment that was subsequently ordered by the Board of Tax Review and reluctantly accepted by Murphy raised the tax rate correspondingly (from $20.15 per $1,000 of assessed value to $22.64).[13]

Murphy's budget was applauded in Detroit, and the *Times* editorialized that the mayor had turned out to be "a pretty good business man—for the taxpayers. . . . And he appears to have considerable dew and sunshine left in his soul, too." Much as it was praised, however, the Murphy budget had two basic weaknesses: it provided only the usual $200,000 for welfare, and, like the budgets of most other cities, it made no allowance for delinquent taxes. [14]

Murphy presented his budget to the Council on March 10. It had been customary for department heads to appear before the Council to seek higher appropriations for their units than the mayor had provided in his budget, but Murphy, in an action believed to have been "unprecedented" in Detroit's recent past, summoned the city's commission members and department heads to a meeting on March 9 and impressed upon them the need to abide by his recommendations and to "practice an economy which is altogether new." The budget hearings, as a consequence, turned out to be "a panorama unique in the City's fiscal history" as department heads simply accepted the mayor's recommendations; and the Council, in the end, approved the budget almost exactly as submitted by Murphy. Even the mayor's political foes were impressed. The *Civic Searchlight* described what had occurred as "an outstanding event in the municipal history of Detroit" and commended Murphy for devising a budget "which comes near to performing a miracle of city financing. . . ." [15]

In May the city was able to dispose of a $19.3 million bond issue at an interest rate of 4.16 percent, below the rate Detroit had paid when it last borrowed. In arranging for the loan, however, Detroit had to pledge that it would not again enter the long-term bond market before the end of the fiscal year 1931–32 and that it would reduce its floating debt as rapidly as was possible and reasonable. [16]

In June a cash shortage resulting largely from tax delinquency and unpaid special assessments produced the first of the major cash crises that beset Detroit while Murphy was mayor. As the end of the month neared, the city was running about $6–7 million short in the cash required to meet obligations that would be incurred before July 15, when tax collections began, and it was unable to negotiate a short-term loan in New York on anything but the most onerous terms. At virtually the last moment, however, the city was rescued by a $1.3 million purchase of delinquent 1930 taxes by a tax-title buyer, the last such action of any significance while Murphy was mayor, and a $5 million short-term loan from the Ford Motor Company at a modest interest rate of 3.5 percent. Since Ford was then feuding with the Murphy administration over welfare matters, it undoubtedly startled a good many people to learn that the company had come to the city's assistance in its hour of need. Murphy's explanation, according to Josephine Gomon, was that " 'Ford hates the New York bankers worse than he hates us,' " but the more likely reason is that the company, which was getting the worst of it in the welfare altercation with Murphy, was seeking to repair its somewhat tarnished image in Detroit.[17]

When Murphy met with department heads on March 9 to forge a solid front in support of his proposed 1931–32 budget, he stressed that "there must be no cessation in welfare relief." In February the welfare department had expended more than $1.78 million for relief and had cared for 50,858 families and a grand total of about 229,000 persons, assuming that the average family case represented 4.5 persons.[18] The family case load for August, 1930, had been about fifteen thousand, but the emphasis placed on unemployment in the Murphy mayoralty campaign, the registration of the unemployed that followed the election and dramatized the whole problem of unemployment and relief, and Murphy's instructions to the welfare department that "everything possible should be done to give relief" led to substantially increased applications for welfare assistance and a mounting departmental case load. Total expenditures of the DPW for city relief during the period September, 1930–February, 1931, were about $8 million, the highest for any six-month period in the history of Detroit to that time.[19]

The enormous increase in its case load put the welfare department to "the most severe test" in its history. The department added six new districts in November and December, bringing the total number to sixteen, and its Social Service Division increased its staff from 93 in September to 257 in March, but the case load expanded more rapidly than the staff, and the number of workers was simply not adequate, "either numerically or in maturity," to cope with the flood of applicants. The initial investigation to determine if applicants were entitled to relief was being conducted in a cursory manner, the necessary follow-up work was very much in arrears, and, as in other cities, the quality of the casework, where this was required, declined. "Confusion" had "seized the internal machinery of record-keeping and accounting" in the DPW by the beginning of 1931, and there is no doubt that some of those on the rolls did not belong there.[20]

Preoccupied with the organization of his new administration, Murphy, at first, paid almost no heed to what was happening in the welfare department. The general disarray in the DPW and the increasing criticism of its procedures, however, caused a "disturbed" Murphy in January, 1931, to appoint a committee chaired by Dr. Edward H. Pence, pastor of the Fort Street Presbyterian Church, "to find out where and how our welfare funds are being spent, and whether they are being spent wisely."

The Pence Committee discovered that the DPW had "completely broken down" under the load it was carrying. Privately having concluded that neither Dolan, who was "a sick man," nor any of his assistants had the ability to "bring order out of chaos," the committee recommended that the position of deputy superintendent of welfare be created and that the person appointed to the job be placed in charge of all of the department's relief work. It also recommended that the DPW appoint sixty new investigators, enlist several hundred volunteer workers, and temporarily engage an office efficiency expert to reorganize its system of record keeping.[21]

Upon receiving the report of the Pence Committee, Murphy announced that its recommendations would be put into effect forthwith. Stuart A. Queen, a casework expert, was loaned to the DPW by the Community Fund to serve as acting deputy superintendent, and after a few weeks the position was given to an altogether reluctant John Ballenger; Norman H. Hill was assigned the task of reorganizing office procedures; and the Common Council provided funds for sixty new investigators. Thanks to the city's social-service agencies, a corps of volunteers that soon numbered 350 began to aid the department in its investigatory work, and in May the Public Welfare Commission placed a nonsalaried business executive in charge of the business operations of each of the welfare districts. Two weeks after the Pence Committee report had been submitted, Dolan announced that the department, owing to its larger staff, was now uncovering four to five fraud cases per day. "We have turned the corner," he optimistically proclaimed, "and are very much encouraged."[22]

In view of prevailing attitudes toward relief and the pressures for economy in Detroit, it was inevitable that the unprecedented expenditures for welfare in the winter of 1930–31 would lead to criticism of the city's relief effort. The Detroit *Labor News* and the Detroit *Times* stood by the mayor and a generous welfare program, but much of the business community, the Committee on City Finances, the Detroit Citizens League, the Common Council, the Detroit *Free Press*, the Detroit *News*, and the Detroit *Saturday Night* initiated an attack upon public relief that did not cease as long as Murphy remained mayor. At a meeting of the Stone Committee on March 9 Harvey Campbell complained that Detroit had become "the sap city of America" because of its generous welfare policy. This was also the theme of a radio address by C. C. McGill, spokesman for the Detroit Board of Commerce, who asserted that "the open-handed, come one-come all welfare policy of Detroit" had "attracted . . . derelicts from all parts of America" who were being taught to live "without effort." "This is a glorious time for a lot of people who have never worked in their lives and never will work," Councilman John S. Hall declared.

Ralph Stone admonished the Murphy administration to display as much sympathy for the taxpayers as it did for those in distress, and the Detroit Citizens League recommended that welfare expenditures be cut "progressively" every month. Even such staunch advocates of a public relief policy as William J. Norton and Senator Couzens, who were critical .of the "stand-pat and reactionary crowd that disapproves of all of our welfare work," thought that the welfare program required more effective administration and that Murphy's reluctance to face up to the issue had contributed to the "growing clamor" about the city's relief policies.[23]

Murphy did not let the attack upon Detroit's welfare program go unanswered. "What do the men on the Stone committee know about the practical problem of human welfare?," he asked. He noted that the same men who were calling loudly for economy had been responsible for the city's extravagant expenditures in the 1920s and that it was the "mess these spendthrifts" had created that was the real cause of the city's financial troubles. He criticized the "loose and inaccurate talk" about " 'parasites' " and " 'derelicts' " on the welfare rolls, and he wondered if McGill, for example, would be willing to repeat remarks of this sort to welfare families living on a few dollars a week.[24]

Detroit's severe financial problems, however, had their effect upon welfare as upon other activities of the city government. During the last several months of the 1930–31 fiscal year the DPW, in line with the overall policy of the Murphy administration, made a determined effort to reduce the cost of its operations. In February the department quietly began to reduce the weekly food allowance of welfare families, and by April a family of five was receiving a maximum of $7 ($4 per married couple and $1 for each child) and sometimes as little as $6, as compared to $11.24 in November. The Visiting Housekeeper Association, which thought that the reduced cost of living since November justified a $10 allowance, remonstrated that the department had passed the "danger point" in its food-budget reductions.

When he became aware of what had been taking place, Murphy protested that the DPW had apparently been overzealous in implementing his economy orders. What he had intended, he declared, was that the department should eliminate the undeserving from its rolls, not that it should arbitrarily reduce allowances. Murphy ordered an investigation of the adequacy of the existing food allowance—"we can not go below a certain line," he remarked—a task that was undertaken by a subcommittee of the MUC. The subcommittee concluded that a family could get by on a food allowance about at the level the DPW was providing, although the group regarded a food budget of this amount as "an irreducible minimum" rather than "a desirable standard." [25]

The most obvious way for the DPW to economize was to reduce the number of families to whom it provided aid, and welfare officials devoted a good deal of effort to this end. The department's augmented staff of investigators, the volunteers who aided them, and 250 city employees who normally worked for other departments relentlessly investigated those seeking relief or already on the rolls. Home calls were made twice a month, and these were supplemented by "collateral" calls, that is visits to "others" to check on the bona fides of welfare recipients, and by weekly visits of welfare clients to the welfare offices. Investigators checked factory payrolls to ensure that welfare applicants were actually unemployed or were receiving insufficient wages to support their families, and Detroit banks were asked to set up a clearing house that would make it possible to ascertain if welfare clients or applicants had bank accounts. Two detectives and an assistant prosecutor were assigned to the DPW to assist it in apprehending cheaters, and there was talk of conducting searches of the homes of those applying for relief.

Although the DPW had a deserved reputation as one of the most progressive welfare departments in the United States, the investigatory procedures that it adopted in 1931 smacked more of the police than of a relief operation. There were some malingerers on the welfare rolls—292 cases of fraud were detected during the first six months of 1931—but it must have seemed to the honest and dishonest alike that they were viewed by their fellow citizens and by welfare officials as well more as criminals or potential criminals than as persons who, for the most part, required assistance through no fault of their own. Criticism of welfare and the pressures for economy in Detroit and elsewhere in the nation were transforming the role of the social worker from one of "inquiry and interpretation" to "investigation and detective work," and the procedures adopted, as Stuart Queen pointed out, played "havoc" with the "personality" of relief recipients.[26]

Aided by slightly improving economic conditions beginning in February,[27] the DPW was able to cut its case load from the February peak of 50,858 to 32,114 in June, and monthly expenditures during these months fell even further, relatively, from $1,709,045 to $928,591. For the fiscal year 1930-31 as a whole, relief expenditures ran to more than $14 million, $12.7 million of that sum having been expended after August. The cost of relief per family during the first six months of 1931 decreased by 12 percent, but during the period January–September, 1931, the expenditure for family relief on a per capita of population basis in the Detroit metropolitan area ($5.81) was exceeded only by the expenditure in the Boston metropolitan area ($6.57) among the fifteen largest metropolitan regions in the nation (the average for the fifteen was $2.98), and the total Detroit expenditures for family relief were topped only by New York. For the calendar year 1931 Detroit's per capita expenditure for all forms of public and private relief ($7.97) was exceeded among 117 cities only by Rochester ($12.00) and Boston ($10.34).

Whereas in 120 urban areas of the nation, 66 percent of the funds for general relief were derived from public sources in 1930 and 64 percent in 1931, in Detroit, which was making a greater public effort to cope with unemployment than any other city, 98.7 percent of the relief was provided by the city in the last six months of 1930 and 95.5 percent in the first six months of 1931. Detroit, alone, accounted for more than 25 percent of *all* the public general relief dispensed in the United States in 1930 and more than 13 percent in 1931, and its case load for the fiscal year 1930-31 constituted about 27 percent of the total case load of the public agencies in seventy principal urban areas. The major new emphasis in relief programs across the country during the winter of 1930-31 was the collection of relief funds by semiofficial agencies and their distribution to private charitable agencies or, as in Cleveland, the setting aside of a portion of the Community Fund contributions for relief, but in Detroit it was the DPW, supported by public funds, that dispensed almost all the family relief. As Murphy had hoped, City Hall had become the "capitol" of the "jobless."[28]

In June, 1931, the DPW was "rocked . . . to its foundations" first by a major scandal and then by a bruising battle with the Ford Motor Company. Before the department had fully recovered from the consequences of these events, it was dealt an even more paralyzing blow by the decision of the Common Council to limit the deficit for family relief in 1931–32 to $7 million. "The most colossal swindle in the history of the City government" is how the Detroit *News* characterized the news that Alex F. Lewis, a counter clerk in the DPW who had served two sentences in Leavenworth and one in the House of Correction, had embezzled $207,000 in welfare funds. What Lewis had done was to steal a large number of canceled grocery orders for which grocers had already been reimbursed, remove the original grocer's name from the order form, substitute the name "E. W. Rentz and Co.," a nonexistent firm, sign the required affidavit that the company had supplied the items indicated on the form, and then turn in the order for payment. The fraud was discovered when the bank where Lewis deposited the welfare checks became suspicious of the rapid increase in his account.[29]

Detroit critics of the Murphy administration seized upon the Lewis scandal to assail the city's relief program in particular and the Murphy regime in general. "It is the dole-takers against the taxpayers in Detroit politics," the *Saturday Night* observed. The *News* thought that the Lewis scandal proved that the chief executive of the city should be a "highly-trained business executive," which Murphy was not; and the *Free Press* commented that, although Murphy's heart was "in the right place," his constituents had "been wondering . . . where his head has been, while people inside and outside the welfare department were making a $20,000,000 charity fund a grab-bag."[30]

Despite the criticism leveled at Murphy as the result of the Lewis embezzlement, it is doubtful that the affair impaired the mayor's standing with the lower-income groups in the city. "Jest a few Lines to Let you No we are Still with you . . . ," one of the inarticulate poor wrote Murphy a few days after the Lewis peculation had been exposed. ". . . we no you are a man that try to Help the Poor[.] that is the Reason the Big So Call good People is fighting you So Hard." William Lovett of the Detroit Citizens League bitterly complained that "nothing else matters" for "the masses of unemployed and their sympathizers . . . so long as they are sure Mr. Murphy is fighting their battle. . . . Even the question of honesty, economy and efficiency in administering public welfare is made secondary to the assumption that employers of labor and other 'rich folks' simply are on the wrong side of the question."[31]

Seeking to blunt criticism of his administration, Murphy issued orders stipulating that welfare employees who did not already have that status should be placed on civil service,[32] requiring the bonding of welfare clerks for the full amount of public money that they handled, calling for a twenty-four hour audit of the DPW by the controller or some other agency, and requesting an investigation of all welfare department personnel. At the same time the mayor, in an effort to bolster the morale of the DPW, told a meeting of department employees that criticism of the welfare program should be directed at him rather than at them, that much of the criticism of the department was "political," and that he wanted to express his "deep, deep gratitude" for their efforts.[33]

Within twenty-four hours of the discovery of the Lewis embezzlement four separate investigations of the affair were underway, the most important being that conducted by Harry S. Toy, the Wayne County prosecutor, who selected the New York firm of Touche, Niven and Company to conduct an audit of the department. After first recommending some changes in the DPW's business operations that the city promptly adopted, the auditors issued a preliminary report that scored "the utter lack of internal check and the inadequacy of the so-called public auditing" of the department. The firm's final report, issued in September, led to a necessary reorganization of the DPW's auditing and accounting system, which Ballenger conceded was "the weakest link in our organization." The city, by that time, had recovered most of the money that Lewis had stolen, and Lewis was serving a ten-year term in the House of Correction.[34]

Welfare commissioner Blain thought that the Ford Motor Company's attack upon Detroit's welfare program was even "more damaging" to the DPW than the Lewis scandal. The acidulous controversy between Murphy and Ford originated in the pressures on the welfare department to reduce its expenses and Murphy's concern that although a substantial proportion of those on the relief rolls were former Ford employees who lived in Detroit, the Ford Motor Company paid no Detroit taxes since the giant Rouge plant was located outside the city. In April, 1931, the

DPW released a report indicating that of the thirty-two thousand family heads on the welfare rolls who had enjoyed regular employment for at least six months before being laid off some time after August, 1930, 6,965 (21.5 percent) worked outside Detroit, and 5,061 (15.6 percent) were former Ford workers. In the light of this information Murphy suggested that the large industrial concerns outside the city should set up their own welfare departments to relieve the city of its heavy relief burden.[35]

The Ford Motor Company bided its time in replying to the mayor until the Lewis scandal provided the company with the opportunity to take the offensive against the city administration. In a wildly inaccurate statement that was all too typical of the Ford Motor Company of that era, Harry Bennett categorically asserted, "There is not a former employe of the company in destitute circumstances that we are responsible for whom we have not tried in some way to relieve." Of a list of welfare clients who indicated Ford as their last employer, the company alleged that 329 were drawing welfare checks although actually employed by Ford at that moment, and it claimed that others on the list had never worked for the company or had been discharged for cause or temporarily laid off. Noting that the city had been "heavily defrauded" and that its relief program entailed the "enormous waste" of the taxpayers' money "month after month," Bennett called for "a wholesale reorganization of the entire welfare machinery."[36]

Murphy responded that the Ford charges were "far more in the nature of political propaganda than accurate criticism," but he nevertheless called for an investigation of the 329 welfare clients allegedly on the Ford payroll, and he shrewdly appointed a blue-ribbon committee headed by Norton to look into the Ford charges. Also, since Ford claimed that it cared for former employees who were in need, Murphy approved a DPW letter to the company inquiring to whom in Ford the department could refer the numerous welfare clients who had worked for the company.

This ploy provoked an angry, unbalanced reply from Bennett. Murphy and the DPW, Bennett loftily asserted, were "the defendants in this matter, the Ford Motor Co. is not." It was "folly," he said, to expect Murphy to "clean up the mess" in the welfare department, and Ford was not about to permit the mayor "to substitute the usual political stunts for service in this instance." The way to uncover the fraud in the DPW, the Ford spokesman suggested, was through a grand-jury investigation, not by "a privately packed committee." When the five-man Norton committee asked Ford to name five representatives to join the group, the company refused on the grounds that to accept would make it appear that the issue was between Ford and Murphy whereas the real question was what had happened to most of the funds spent in "so-called welfare work."[37]

Seeking to avoid controversy, the Norton committee did not submit a report on the alleged cases of fraud pointed to by Ford although it did make some procedural recommendations designed to improve the efficiency of the DPW. The Ford Motor Company had some of its auditors examine the DPW's records, but their investigation apparently failed to substantiate the Ford allegations since the company remained silent about the results. The Detroit *News* also conducted an investigation of some of the Ford "cases" and found little evidence to support the charge of wholesale fraud. The most complete examination of the charge that persons allegedly employed by Ford were fraudulently drawing welfare checks, which was the central issue in the controversy, was made by the DPW itself. In the end, Ford supplied the department with 226 not 329 names of persons in this category—the numbers kept changing throughout the dispute—and of this number the DPW found a total of 31 cases of fraud. The DPW, moreover, pointed out that if the Ford Motor Company had complied with department requests for the work records of relief applicants, as other firms had done, the fraud could have been avoided.[38]

Murphy received some criticism as the result of the Ford controversy, including a warning note from "Ten Men" that if he did not "lay off" Ford and other business concerns, "we will get you just as we did Buckley. You Irish son of a bitch"; but, in standing firm against Ford, Murphy probably endeared himself further to the unemployed and the poverty-stricken in Detroit. When Coughlin's associate Louis B. Ward advised Murphy that "the most promising thing that can happen to you politically is the active open antagonism to the Ford organization," Murphy immediately replied, "The idea is well set in my mind, and I appreciate its possibilities before the public."[39] Murphy also "appreciated" that there was little logic in a welfare system that required Detroit to shoulder unaided a relief burden imposed upon it, to some degree, by concerns that were not subject to its taxing power, and this was one of the factors that impelled him to seek county, state, and federal aid for the hard-pressed city.

Whatever the local repercussions of the Lewis scandal and the Ford imbroglio, the Murphy administration, which had initially been hailed in the nation for its ambitious efforts to cope with the depression,[40] received a bad press outside Detroit as the result of the June "Duel over Doles." Those who opposed large-scale public relief seized upon the Detroit experience as evidence of the danger of adopting such a policy. In so doing, they revealed a good deal about middle-class attitudes on the subject of relief rather than any particular understanding of what was going on in Detroit. In an editorial entitled "Detroit's Dole Spree," the Washington *Post* asked, "Of what advantage is an era of 'dew and sunshine' if it brings in its wake a disastrous storm of debts, higher taxes, deficits, and a shattered morale on the part of thousands of people who have been recklessly converted into public charges?" Describing Murphy as an official "whose poetic genius seems to surpass his knowledge of economics," the Springfield (Missouri) *Leader* expressed the view that the Detroit mayor's "grandiose" statement that no one would go hungry in the city had attracted "all the bums in Christendom" to Detroit. "The mayor's enterprise," the Chicago *Tribune* remarked, "is glorious in sympathy and irresponsibility. Mr. Murphy radiates kindness and buns, short order steaks and ice cream cones and may soon have all the taxpayers and property owners in Detroit reduced to the line with tin cups waiting their turns at the handouts."[41]

II

Detroit's financial health took a decided turn for the worse in the fiscal year that began in July, 1931. Although, as Murphy pointed out, Detroit's financial plight was "only in small part" the result of the city's welfare policies, critics of public relief were prone to identify the city's fiscal troubles with its relief program. Murphy, who believed that "every government, no matter its humanitarian and social ideals, must be sound in its fiscal phase," was determined to do whatever was required to have Detroit live within its income and to maintain its credit; but he hoped, at the same time, to "give an intelligent application to the principle that government has a responsibility toward its people in time of a famine, something which," he bitterly contended, "is not recognized by many of the Municipal and State Governments, and has been almost completely ignored by the Federal Government."[42] Whatever the mayor's wishes, however, the remorseless pressure to reduce municipal spending had its effect upon welfare as it did upon all other city services.

In analyzing the city's financial position and its cash requirements for the 1931–32 fiscal year, the Stone Committee expressed "grave apprehension for the future" and the need for "drastic action" by the mayor and the Common Council. The city's floating debt of $62.4 million as of July 1, 1931, was scheduled to mature during the next few months and was likely to increase by another $22.6 million during the year. Although the committee believed that it would be necessary to fund part of this debt in short-term bonds, it urged the preparation of "a definite plan" to provide for the liquidation of the floating debt and the city's return to a cash basis. The committee recommended a sharp reduction in expenditures for welfare and other city services, the spreading of special assessments as expeditiously as possible after the completion of improvements, discontinuance of local improvements in districts substantially delinquent in taxes and assessments, an end to capital expenditures for several years, a quarterly analysis of departmental revenues and an appropriate reduction in departmental budgets if receipts proved to be below estimates, an intensified effort to collect delinquent taxes, and "rigid economy" in the preparation of Wayne County's budget, largely financed by Detroit's taxpayers.

The Common Council, which had already decided to limit family relief expenditures in 1931–32 to approximately $7 million, adopted all of the Stone Committee's recommendations. Murphy then issued an executive order specifying that whenever the quarterly budget analysis revealed that revenues had not matched expenditures, there was to be a commensurate reduction in spending in the next quarter. The city government, which had adopted budget procedures probably "not surpassed by any large city in the nation," was now committed to living within its income, whatever that income might be, an objective that the Murphy administration struggled with increasing difficulty to meet as the rising tax delinquency steadily eroded the city's revenue.[43]

Detroit was able to retire $30 million in short-term notes in August by converting $22 million of the sum into five-year refunding bonds, an action made possible by recently enacted state legislation, and $8 million into three-year emergency bonds, authorized by the "calamity clauses" in the city charter. The Council's approval of the Stone Committee's recommendations and Murphy's assurances to the New York bankers that his administration was embarked on a "drastic campaign to improve the credit of the city, reduce taxes and relieve the home owners" facilitated the transaction. In November, in an effort to help meet Detroit's cash requirements for the remainder of the fiscal year, the city refinanced an additional $40 million in short-term paper maturing in that month and in December. Half of this sum was taken up by Detroit banks and some of the area's larger nonbanking concerns, and the remaining $20 million was supplied in the form of a line of credit by New York bankers on the pledge that Detroit would live within its actual income during the remainder of the fiscal year. Of the latter sum, $11.4 million was provided immediately, and the remainder was to be made available as required, provided that the city lived up to its agreement to eschew deficit financing.

In pursuance of Detroit's understanding with the New York banks, an arrangement was quietly worked out whereby Stone and Henry Hart, the vice-president of the First Detroit Company, were to certify to the out-of-town bankers when Detroit applied for funds that the money was actually needed and that the city's budget was in balance. The two Detroit bankers, in turn, delegated to C. E. Rightor, the chief accountant of the Detroit Bureau of Governmental Research, the responsibility for confirming the city government's allegations of need. This important step in the direction of banker control of Detroit affairs led William Lovett to write that Rightor and Lent Upson of the Bureau of Governmental Research "actually, but secretly, are the chief dependence of our Mayor, City Controller, et al, in steering the financial ship through the present troubled seas. . . . but of course the public cannot be informed of these facts. . . ." Three months later, in "a brass-tacks statement, strictly confidential" that he asked the addressee to "destroy as soon as you have read it," Lovett reported that Roosevelt and Budget Director William Curran were "in daily long conferences" with Upson and Rightor and that Detroit's financial affairs were being handled by Stone, with the aid of Rightor, Upson, and Divie B. Duffield, president of the Detroit Citizens League. It was Rightor whom Murphy appointed as the city's controller when Roosevelt resigned at the end of November, 1932, and it is safe to assume that the bankers insisted on the appointment.[44] It is not surprising that Mayor Murphy chafed under the extrapolitical restrictions that had been imposed on the city's operations.

When Detroit negotiated its $20 million line of credit, a New York banker was quoted as saying, "I think Detroit is doing a better job of living within its income than any other city in the country." Because of a tax delinquency of about 25 percent, "living within its income" meant, for Detroit, living on much less than had been appropriated: for the fiscal year 1931–32 the city government actually spent not the $76 million that had been appropriated but rather $57 million. Before the fiscal year was more than a few days old the city administration was already seeking to pare $5 million from the budget, and the quarterly budget reviews and the periodic shortages of cash in the city's coffers forced still greater economies, each more painful than the preceding one, as the months passed.[45]

From the start, Murphy had hoped that the budget cuts would not have to include the salaries of city employees, partly because he feared that this would set a "bad example" for private employers and partly, no doubt, because he was conscious of the political power wielded by the city workers. Since salaries, however, constituted the single heaviest charge on the budget, it was difficult for the city to effect substantial economies without including the payroll. As a result, in December, 1931, as part of an effort to reduce the budget by $6 million that drew "some blood with the water," Murphy not only agreed to a further reduction in the number of city workers but reluctantly sponsored an ordinance, which the Council passed in January, 1932, calling for a 10 percent reduction in city salaries and an additional 10 percent cut on salaries above $4,000. Roosevelt hailed the economies effected as "the most drastic reduction any American city ever has made in its salary and payroll," and Murphy drew praise from the city's conservatives; but the mayor was blistered by his former associate on the Recorder's Court, Edward J. Jeffries, who charged in a demagogic address that Murphy had "climbed over the backs of the people who elected him . . . to the heights of the moneyed interests," who were "tempting" him with the prospects of still higher office.[46]

In the latter part of March, 1932, as the city was finding it difficult to implement the $6 million economy program to the full, Stone let it be known that, unless the city agreed to payless paydays or other economies, he could not certify that Detroit was living within its income. This meant that $3.6 million of the $20 million line of credit would not be forthcoming to meet the city's payroll of March 24, 1931. Murphy wrote Stone that the deficit would be made up by the suspension of salary payments or increased tax collections, but, reluctant to take the lead on so painful a matter, the mayor sought to have the Council go on record in advance as authorizing the imposition of payless paydays if this proved to be necessary. The Council rightly saw this as an effort on Murphy's part to shift to it the responsibility for the salary suspension that seemed to be looming. John Smith, now a Council member, fulminated that a vacillating mayor, who had been "sliding to the right and to the left, backward and forward," was attempting to "lay in the Council's lap the responsibility for a situation that the Administration has brought upon itself by poor financing and wasteful extravagance." In the end, though, the Council, having learned of Murphy's letter to Stone, passed the necessary resolution, Stone was satisfied, and the funds for Detroit were released by the bankers.[47]

In an effort to avoid continued wrangling between the aldermen and the mayor over the city's budget, Murphy created a Joint Finance Committee, chaired by Wilcox and including the mayor, Roosevelt, four councilmen, the president of the Board of Education, and the superintendent of schools, and assigned it the task of finding a solution for the city's financial woes, the immediate problem being the need to reduce the budget by an additional $4 million before the end of the fiscal year. To accomplish this result, the committee proposed at the end of March that city employees receive only two months pay for the remaining three months of the fiscal year, a recommendation that initiated an acerbic controversy involving the mayor, the Common Council, and Ralph Stone that continued until the end of April.[48]

Wilcox prepared an ordinance embodying the Joint Finance Committee's salary-reduction proposal, but the Council refused to pass the measure. Much to the annoyance of Councilman John Lodge, who as a member of the joint committee had introduced the ordinance, Murphy now repudiated the salary-reduction plan that he had reluctantly agreed to accept and sought to place the onus for Detroit's problems on the bankers. Some months earlier Murphy had expressed appreciation for the "intelligent and sympathetic helpfulness" of the Detroit bankers, but he had come to resent the fact that, no matter how much the city cut its budget, it could not obtain funding from outside unless Stone indicated that Detroit was living within its income. Murphy's resentment had, on the whole, been temperately expressed before the great salary crisis of the spring of 1932. Then, apparently urged on by "repeated long distance messages" from Senator Couzens, who, according to one Detroit source, was revealing his "ancient prejudice against banking interests," a frustrated mayor lashed out at the city's "financial dictators."

The bankers, Murphy fumed, were "without a semblance of

social responsibility" and were telling the city, even though it had curtailed expenditures more than any other municipal government in the history of the nation, that it could not obtain needed funds unless it agreed to "shatter" the personal budgets of city employees, reduce police and fire protection, and "practically starve" welfare families. The bankers, he charged, had encouraged the reckless expansion of Detroit and other cities in the 1920s, but now when people were suffering and in need, these same bankers took a "cold-blooded statistical" approach to the problem and demanded "unreasoning economy." Murphy warned the bankers that during the next fiscal year the city might be compelled to use its tax money to care for the destitute, provide needed services, and pay city employees rather than meet its debts to the bankers. "I am not for repudiation," he asserted. "I am simply not for permitting the City and the government to be wrecked and ruined, if we can stop it."[49]

Stone was stung to the quick by Murphy's remarks, which the banker characterized as a " 'red herring' " designed to divert attention from the city's need to economize. He contended that the contemplated salary reduction, coupled with the earlier 10 percent reduction, constituted a pay cut that was exceeded by the decline in the cost of living and was less than the reduction in wages and salaries in the private sector of the economy. "Property owners," Stone declared, "cannot look with favor upon an administration which uses their money to further . . . [its] own political fortunes by paying salaries in excess of the scale which they themselves receive. . . ." He charged that the Murphy administration was destroying the city's credit by attacking banks and threatening to repudiate its pledge to keep the budget in balance, and he characterized the mayor, metaphorically, as "the political Nero" who was "fiddling while the city burns." Even worse than the evils resulting from default, Stone remonstrated in language of the sort that became all too familiar in the New Deal era, was "the damage to our social structure, to our form of government, and ultimately the safety of the people, which must result from the appeals which our principal city officials are making to passion and prejudice, and the arraying of class against class among our people." Stone had a single and peremptory solution for the immediate problem: the Council must pass the salary ordinance without further delay.[50]

Although some of "the fellows who pay the bills" agreed with Stone's assessment that the city administration was playing politics at the taxpayers' expense—"I wish to Heaven you were King," one of them wrote the banker—the Council refused to heed his advice, and some of its members joined Murphy in attacking the bankers. Councilman Edward J. Jeffries, Jr., the judge's son, suggested that the aldermen might consider telling the bankers "to go jump in the lake for their money." As the financial crisis mounted, Murphy instructed Roosevelt to pay welfare expenses first and to use whatever funds remained for salaries; the Detroit Board of Commerce called for "a Moses to lead . . . [Detroit] out of a wilderness of hooey, balderdash and political bunkum"; and Stone privately complained to an auto executive, "It seems difficult to get the Mayor and the Common Council to understand the business principles upon which budgets should be fixed and the city's finances regulated." The city passed its April 15 payroll, the first time anything of this sort had happened in Detroit but something already experienced by Chicago, Philadelphia, and Atlanta, among other cities; and Murphy suggested, menacingly, that it might require some type of "'coercion'" or "'duress'" to bring the bankers into line. The Murphy administration now sponsored a compromise ordinance that provided city employees with two-thirds of their pay and made payment of the remaining one-third contingent on 1931–32 taxes collected after June 30, but the bankers insisted that such taxes would have to be used to retire the floating debt.[51]

On April 21 the Common Council, by a 5–4 vote, finally passed the Lodge ordinance, but the mayor then stunned the city and infuriated some councilmen by vetoing the measure and suggesting that the Council override the veto. Although Murphy's action seemed bizarre and altogether political, it was not lacking in logic. As passed, the ordinance could not have gone into effect until May 23, and this would have saved the city only $1.75 million, the budget still would have remained in deficit, and the city would have been unable to borrow the funds that it needed to meet its payroll. If, however, the Council overrode the veto and used the six votes required for this action to give the ordinance immediate effect, the city's financial problems would be temporarily solved.

The Council could not muster the votes to override the mayor's veto or to adopt the alternative proposal that the administration had put forward. While the aldermen dawdled, welfare recipients were reduced to a ration of bread, flour, and milk; there were increasing signs of unrest among city employees and those on relief; and the city announced that it had enough oil in its water pumps for only twenty-four more hours of service. Pressed to the wall, the Council on April 30, by the necessary 6–3 vote, approved the Lodge ordinance, which had been modified because of the one-month delay to provide for a 50 percent reduction in pay for May and June. The $400,000 remaining from the $20 million line of credit of November, 1931, was now made available to Detroit, and the bankers, appeased at last, supported the city in the refinancing of $4 million of short-term paper. The Murphy administration was able to stagger through to the end of the fiscal year, although it had to use 1932–33 taxes, collected in advance, to meet the June 15 payroll.[52]

There is no doubt that Murphy, as his critics charged, had tried "to work both sides of the street" in dealing with the city's great salary crisis of April 1932, and he had provided unmistakable evidence of the indecisiveness that sometimes afflicted him when painful decisions had to be made. One may surmise that his strategy had called for the Council to approve the Lodge ordinance at the beginning of April, for him to veto the ordinance, and then for the Council to override the veto and for the salary reduction to go into effect. When the Council failed to oblige him, however, he was reluctant to take command of the situation. In his frustration, he lashed out at the bankers; but since Roosevelt convinced him that the city could not afford to break with the bankers, he confined his opposition to rhetoric, and, in the end, he met the Stone Committee's terms. The experience was a bitter one for Murphy, and he did not forget it in the months and years to come. Stone was also bitter about what had occurred, and he complained privately about having to deal with "an unpleasant type of politician, who blames everything on the bankers, calls them bloodsuckers, Shylock, tells them to go to the hot place in public speeches and the next day asks them to loan the city millions of dollars."[53]

The economies implemented by the Murphy administration in the fiscal year 1931–32 affected every phase of municipal government. Several thousand employees were laid off, working hours were reduced, maintenance costs were trimmed, restraints were placed on the use of city-owned cars, and the lighting in city offices and buildings was reduced. Even the newspaper clipping service to which the mayor had subscribed was discontinued so that the city could save $500 a year.[54]

What the depression meant for the functioning of city government was evidenced by the steps the various city departments were compelled to take to curtail their spending. The most drastic economies, as in 1930–31, were effected by the Department of Public Works, "the first municipal operation" to be deflated in Detroit and elsewhere as the result of the depression. The total expenditures of the department declined from $25,501,492 in the calendar year 1930 to $9,389,973 in 1931 and $4,854,305 in 1932, dramatic evidence for the contention of the department's commissioner that its "wings" had been "clipped quite strenuously." By the end of the fiscal year 1931–32 the Department of Public Works had laid off eighty-two hundred employees, abolished two of its divisions, and drastically cut street and alley maintenance costs. Murphy praised public works as "the outstanding department" of the city government. "The shame of the city," the mayor pointed out, was associated with graft-ridden and politically minded departments of public works, and he was proud that the scandal-free, efficient Detroit department, ably led by Joseph Mills and then by L. G. Lenhardt and conforming to the Murphy view that the business side of government should be conducted in a business-like way, was an exception. A price had to be paid, however, for so severe a reduction in expenditures. The streets became "pretty dirty," pavements showed the signs of inadequate maintenance, garbage collections were made less frequently, and by the end of 1932 Lenhardt was complaining to the mayor about the "extremely poor physical condition of the equipment and plant" of the city. [55]

The DSR, in a largely successful effort to wipe out its large deficit, cut the salaries of its executives, discontinued vacations with pay, and laid off personnel. The Public Lighting Commission agreed in December, 1931, to reduce street-lighting voltage by 10 percent and also not to use one-half of the lights on a score of business streets; and in May, 1932, it reduced the number of street lamps in use by one-seventh. The result of these economies was a 20 percent increase in fatal traffic accidents at night during the first ten months of 1932 as compared to the same period in 1931. This led to a partial restoration of service in November, 1932. [56]

The Department of Recreation was "hounded" by the Budget Bureau to reduce its expenditures and was periodically threatened with extinction. Although unemployment led to a substantial increase in the use of free recreational facilities, the department's budget and staff were cut back again and again, and the unit survived only because Murphy believed that its playgrounds and community centers were a bulwark against "crime, unsocial conduct and poisonous ideas." The Department of Parks and Boulevards, in what its commissioner described as "an economic triumph," survived on a budget that was comparable to what the unit had received ten years earlier although the park area of the city had tripled in the meantime and the population of Detroit had doubled. Murphy had ambitious plans for the much needed development of Detroit's river front and for river and harbor improvement to enhance the city's status as a port, but the ban on capital improvements thwarted his efforts. His desire to make Detroit the aviation capital of the world was similarly frustrated by the pressures for economy.[57]

The educational and cultural institutions of the city were especially hard hit by the administration's program of economy. In the public schools, new teachers were not hired, teaching vacancies remained unfilled, married women teachers with employed husbands were invited to take a year's leave of absence, the size of classes was increased, the school term was shortened by one month, the summer school program was curtailed, and night school and city college fees were increased. Because of cuts in its budget the Detroit Public Library had to reduce its hours of service and close five of its twenty-three branches and all of its thirty-two subbranches and deposit collections in industrial centers, settlements, and the like. The library's book fund was slashed from $175,000 in 1929–30 to $72,000 in 1931–32 and $39,600 in 1932–33. In June, 1932, the library decided to replenish its book fund by charging adult users of the library a twenty-five cent registration fee, but the results were disappointing. Only a veto by Murphy, who believed that the "enforced leisure" of thousands of Detroiters made the public library more valuable than ever, forestalled a Common Council budget decision that would have compelled the library to close half its branches.

The budget of the Detroit Institute of Arts, one of the few municipally owned art museums in the nation, was reduced to such an extent that the museum would have had to close in 1932 had not Murphy, in what the secretary of the Arts Commission characterized as a "courageous and resolute stand" in behalf of Detroit's cultural life, overruled the Committee on Efficiency and Economy and the Common Council and provided enough funds for the museum to operate and to safeguard the city's investment in a $4 million building and a $15 million collection. It required private contributions, however, for the museum to retain its curatorial and educational staff.[58]

The shrinking city budget forced the Department of Health in January, 1932, to eliminate the dental and medical service that it provided for school children. The budget adjustments of that month led to the discharge of one hundred nurses, part-time doctors, and others, and the commissioner of health warned the mayor that further reductions would result in "disaster involving the health and the wellbeing of our people at all ages, especially children, and in the spread of epidemic diseases with resultant increases in mortality." "We have reached the bottom," the commissioner concluded.[59]

Of the agencies of the city government, the police and fire departments were most resistant to the demands for economy, and the mayor, because of the relationship of the two to the public safety and perhaps because he respected their political muscle, was disinclined to force the issue with them. In January, 1932, budget officials requested the police department to drop 500 patrolmen, 20 detectives, and some civilian personnel, but Commissioner Watkins succeeded in limiting the layoff of patrolmen to the equivalent of 200. The department decided to effect the reduction by having each of its patrolmen donate eleven days of work to the city during the remainder of the fiscal year, but this plan, whose implementation Murphy sought to avoid, was abandoned at the end of January, and the men were reimbursed for the one day that they had actually contributed. The police department, however, could not escape the budget axe, and by the end of the fiscal year the department was short 236 patrolmen, a reduction partly achieved by not filling vacancies, and it had also laid off at least 53 of its 313 civilian employees. The department's division of weights and measures seems to have been eliminated entirely, but the slight budget saving thus achieved probably cost the consumer more in the form of dishonest weights than it saved him in taxes. The reduction in their pay, furthermore, caused the police to abandon the relief activities they had initiated in 1930.[60] The economies in the police department, as elsewhere, were not without their ramifying effects on the life of the city, as a saving at one point generally produced a cost at another.

The fire department, which in a 1930 survey by the National Board of Fire Underwriters had received "the highest rating ever received by any [fire] Department in the United States," was requested during the city's economy drive in January, 1932, to reduce its force by 196 men. Department officials, however, persuaded the mayor that this was too large a number for the safety of the city and might even lead to an increase in Detroit's fire insurance rates. In the end, the department apparently laid off only 120 firemen and 23 other employees, but this still made Detroit one of the few large cities to reduce its fire department personnel during the depression years.[61]

Concurrently with his efforts to reduce spending in 1931–32, Murphy was engaged in putting together the city's budget for the fiscal year 1932–33. The most troublesome problem that faced him was, to use his own words, "this Frankenstein of debt service." As he pointed out in his annual message to the Common Council in January, 1932, since sinking fund and interest charges for 1932–33 totaled $31.8 million as compared to $20.4 million in 1931–32, there would be still fewer dollars available to run the city in the new budget year than there had been in the old unless some means could be found to ease the debt burden or some form of external aid could be obtained.[62]

The budget Murphy submitted to the Council in March called for $76 million in taxes, as in the fiscal year 1931–32. Of this total, $3 million was assigned to family relief, the first time since the adoption of the charter that anything more than a nominal sum had been included for welfare in a Detroit mayor's budget. Although a tax delinquency of $18 or $19 million was anticipated for the fiscal year, Murphy allowed for only $1 million of this sum, which meant that a budget that was technically in balance was really quite unbalanced, and there was, in addition, a "hidden deficit" of at least $5 million in the form of deterioration of the city's physical plant because of lack of maintenance. Although the Council reduced the proposed tax budget to about $72 million, this did not satisfy Stone, who pointed out that the probable tax income would sustain the city government for only eight months in view of the anticipated tax delinquency. Stone wanted Murphy to use his item veto to bring the budget into balance, but a budget reduction of the magnitude that Stone desired would have left the city only $23–24 million on which to operate after debt charges were deducted. Rejecting Stone's advice and asserting that "a city's budget cannot be balanced by a banker's yard-stick alone," Murphy made only minor changes in the budget as approved by the Council. He realized, however, that some sort of financial plan was required to carry Detroit through the fiscal year 1932–33 without default and without a catastrophic decline in the city's services, and efforts to work out such a plan were well underway as the old fiscal year drew to a close. [63]

The tax levy, after work on the 1932–33 budget had been completed, was set at $72,632,991, a sum below the 1931–32 levy, but since the property assessment for the fiscal year was reduced by 23.1 percent, the tax rate per $1,000 of assessed valuation rose to $27.426. [64] Taxes were much too high from the point of view of many of Detroit's hard-pressed property owners, and the makings of a Poujadist uprising against taxes, to use the terminology of a later time, were very much in evidence before the new tax levy went into effect.

Since the city's efforts to collect delinquent property taxes had been unproductive, the Common Council, desperately seeking operating funds, decided at the end of January, 1932, to authorize the sale of tax titles that the city had bid in when tax-title buyers failed to purchase them. The proposed sale involved ninety thousand parcels of property worth $500 million on which taxes had not been paid in 1930 or in earlier years and which now threatened to pass from the hands of their delinquent owners. At tumultuous Council hearings at which the sale was considered, angry property owners, represented by such organizations as Howard A. Starrett's Committee of 51 and Frederick A. Wayne's Taxpayers' Protective Association, branded the sale as "Communistic" and threatened the recall of councilmen who approved the sale and a "split" with Murphy if he did not take a stand against it. The sale was held in June despite all the threats, but it was an utter fiasco as an income-producing device. [65]

Taxpayers not only directed their wrath at the sale of tax titles but also at existing tax rates. At a Council hearing in March, Wayne was "wildly cheered" by a large audience when he called for a 25 percent reduction in taxes in the 1932–33 budget. He suggested that the city adopt both a sales tax and a $5 poll tax and, giving vent to the sentiments of at least some middle-class property owners, observed that a poll tax would "eliminate a lot of these group votes." Wayne threatened city officials with a tax strike if property taxes were not substantially reduced. Murphy, whose own embarrassing failure to pay personal property taxes due the city for the years 1921–25 had not been corrected until December, 1931, [66] had to stave off this threat while at the same time trying to meet the welfare needs of a city descending ever deeper into the pit of depression. Welfare and economy, as from the beginning of

Murphy's mayoralty, continued to be the city government's major preoccupations.

III

In deciding in July, 1931, to limit the deficit for family relief in 1931-32 to $7 million,[67] about half of the expenditure for this purpose in the previous fiscal year, the Council was responding not only to the strong pressures for economy, Ballenger's opinion that "sharp cuts" could be made in the welfare rolls, and Roosevelt's judgment that reduced prices and increasing efficiency justified considerably reduced welfare appropriations but also to the aldermen's conviction, as one of them put it, that "the Welfare Department has been going wild, absolutely wild." Although the Detroit *Times* castigated the $7 million decision as "legislative hysteria" and Murphy, deploring "the unwillingness of so many to face the real facts," did not believe that the DPW could live within the sum stipulated, the mayor did not resist the Council's action, probably because he assumed that additional funds could be raised privately to supplement the $7 million. Whatever Murphy's view of the matter may have been, however, the Council's decision was interpreted as a defeat for the mayor and for his welfare policy. *Time* thought that what had happened indicated that "most of the dew, dawn and sunshine had vanished from Detroit" and that the city's voters would soon consign the mayor himself to the ranks of the jobless for whom he had shown such tender solicitude[68]

The limitations imposed by the Council on the welfare deficit for 1931-32 compelled the DPW to reduce its rolls substantially and to seek means to dispense the relief that it did grant in a more economical manner. The stark alternative that the department immediately faced was whether to cut its rolls in half, from about thirty-two thousand cases (the June figure) to sixteen thousand cases, or to reduce by 50 percent the amount of relief that it granted its clients. As the issue was later succinctly phrased, the question was whether to "feed half the people or half-feed the people." Since, however, the Social Service Division of the DPW believed that the relief allowance had already been cut "to a point below which nourishment can be had," the Public Welfare Commission decided on July 8 to reduce the rolls by fifteen thousand within ten days but to maintain existing standards for relief for the time being. As one district supervisor put it to the commission shortly thereafter, "we are down to minimum allowances now. Do you want these families slowly to starve to death?"[69]

Using methods that William Norton described as "drastic and brutal," the DPW sought to achieve the reduction in the case load that the welfare commission had prescribed. As long as they were able-bodied, the very few single adults on the rolls, adult families of two or more members, childless couples and then couples with fewer than three children, families that had any income at all, families that could be supported by relatives (whether or not the relatives were legally obligated to do so), families that had resided in Detroit for less than two years, families with bank accounts, families that engaged in "anti-social practices (gambling, bootlegging, prostitution), and legally resident families that refused to accept transportation to other communities willing to provide them relief were all cut off from support. They were dropped from the rolls even though, the district supervisors reported, a large proportion of them were "genuinely destitute, they had no resources, no plans."[70]

At a special meeting of the welfare commission on July 17, by which time the welfare staff had complied with the directive to reduce the rolls by 25 percent, Irene Murphy, a district supervisor and the mayor's sister-in-law, reported that although the supervisors had performed their task "quickly and quietly," they had acted "against our own better judgment, against our natural feelings of justice and sympathy." They had now reached "absolute bed rock as far as reducing families with intelligence, justice, or consideration" was concerned, and they could not accept the responsibility for the consequences of further reductions. ". . . we are walking," she warned, "into the hazards of Death, Disease, Crime and Violence on the part of Radical Groups." Commissioner Blain responded, "We can't afford to let sentiment enter here," and Commissioner Andrews, although expressing sympathy for the families pared from the rolls, asked, "What is sympathy going to do when the city has no money?" Ballenger thought that if the DPW were not careful in its efforts to achieve economy, it would "undermine . . . the whole social structure, the things held nearest and dearest," but despite his and Mrs. Murphy's warnings the order of the commission was to drop eleven thousand additional families.[71]

On July 24, by which time the case load had been reduced to about eighteen thousand, the welfare commission ordered a reinvestigation of all those remaining on the rolls in the hope that this would permit the withdrawal of support from several thousand additional families. The burden of proof was placed on welfare recipients, and their need for assistance had to be verified by taxpayers, former employers, and disinterested citizens. The average city case load for August was only a little more than sixteen thousand, a drop of about 50 percent since June, but since expenditures had not declined in anywhere near the same proportion—the larger families had remained on the rolls—it became necessary in half the districts to require welfare families, on at least two occasions, to subsist for two weeks on grocery orders designed for a single week. "Last year," Irene Murphy declared in December, "we attempted to help applicants to maintain a certain standard of living. This year we are interested only in sheer survival."[72]

Not only did the DPW eliminate a substantial proportion of those already receiving aid, but budgetary constraints also compelled it to turn aside a large percentage of those newly seeking assistance. Of forty-five hundred applicants for welfare in August, for example, only five hundred "extreme cases" were granted relief.[73]

Since more than 100,000 persons in Detroit were unemployed in July and August, 1931, heads of families cut off from public assistance could hardly look forward to finding jobs. Their initial reaction to their fate was "very orderly—and silent," but the district supervisors thought that it was "the silence of brooding and despair." This was followed by a stage that the secretary to the supervisors described as one of "quickened irritability" as "afflicted members" of welfare families went to the DPW's adjustment bureau, other social agencies, City Hall, and the newspaper offices, wherever "an orderly person would seek redress." By the third week in August the supervisors thought that the reaction of those cut from the rolls was becoming "militant. We hear threats daily of violence—we are hearing of suicidal attempts. . . ." There was even one instance of infanticide as a former welfare mother killed her five-year-old son for fear that he would otherwise starve to death. When the case was tried in Recorder's Court, Judge John A. Boyne ordered a verdict of not guilty and denounced the Common Council for taking the budgetary action that he believed had induced the crime![74]

"There is actual starvation in Detroit," Murphy publicly stated at the end of July, and he indicated that ever since the welfare rolls had been slashed, "half-starved families" had been coming to City Hall seeking food. Two days later the welfare department also revealed that a preliminary survey of the results of the paring of the rolls had turned up cases of "starvation" among the affected families.[75] The issue of starvation in Detroit attracted national attention in October, 1931, when the *New Republic*, basing its account on a story that had appeared in the *Labor News*, reported that medical authorities in Detroit estimated that one person died of starvation in the city every seven hours and fifteen minutes, quoted a Receiving Hospital physician as saying that four persons a day were brought to the hospital "too far gone from starvation for their lives to be saved," and stated that three persons had died of starvation in Grand Circus Park in a single day.

The *New Republic* story, which was picked up by *Pravda* and became the source for testimony before the Senate Committee on Manufactures by Father John A. Ryan, was denied by the Public Welfare Commission, the Detroit Board of Commerce, and, despite his previous remarks, Mayor Murphy; they submitted affidavits by the county coroner and the head of the Receiving Hospital as proof that there had been no deaths from starvation in Detroit. The reporter who was responsible for the original story had based his account on information supplied by a Receiving Hospital doctor, but the reporter now found it difficult to secure direct testimony to corroborate the story, and his informant turned out to be "a mighty timid animal" who would not permit his name to be used. The reporter learned, however, that in filling out death certificates doctors were instructed not to report "symptoms" as the final cause of death, and thus if a starving person contracted pneumonia and then died, pneumonia was officially listed as the cause of death. It seems likely from what the mayor, welfare workers, and others had to say that starvation was at least a contributing cause of death in Detroit during the early depression years even if death certificates cannot be cited to demonstrate this.[76]

An increasing number of evictions was another consequence of the precipitate reduction of relief rolls in the summer of 1931. The police reported at the end of July that persons were wandering all over the city without shelter and that some were seeking overnight quarters in police precinct stations. An eviction riot on August 13, quelled by a force of seventy policemen, resulted in five injuries and ten arrests.[77]

In October, 1931, the DPW decided to investigate 1,200 families, randomly selected, that had been dropped from the rolls in July. Of 897 families that could be located, 222 (25 percent) were found to be living on their earned income, but the social workers who interviewed these families judged that this income was insufficient in 148 cases; 544 of the families were being supported by friends, neighbors, or relatives—"The poor are caring for the poor," Murphy declared—and the sources of income of the others were given as credit (196 cases), other social agencies (25 cases), sale of furniture and dishes, pawning, churches, insurance, mortgages, bonuses, and aid from landlords. Forty families had begged for food from one source or another.

Among the 876 families supplying information on the subject, 525 were in arrears in their rent payments, 151 were being housed by friends or relatives, 22 had been evicted, 33 had moved because they could no longer pay their rent, 11 had moved to cheaper dwellings, 2 had had their mortgages foreclosed, and 11 were anticipating a similar fate. The social workers found "changes in the mental, physical, or domestic situations" in about one-third of the families. They discovered that parents were "depressed, nervous, morbid, discouraged, neurotic, and hysterical." One man had attempted suicide and had threatened to kill the members of his family. In four families the parents were reportedly ill because of lack of food. The children in seventeen families looked undernourished, and one child had fainted in school because of malnutrition. Although "domestic contention" accounted for a few of the fifty-eight family separations that had occurred, the immediate cause for most of the separations was economic conditions, as husbands, wives, and children went off to live with different relatives.

Of 740 families about whom data could be obtained, the social workers concluded that 404, whose average weekly income was $2.05 per person, no longer needed relief and that 336, whose average income was $1.01 per person, below a minimum budget for food alone, should be granted relief as soon as funds were available. The DPW study, the most reliable information that we have on the families removed from the Detroit welfare rolls in the summer of 1931, reveals the two contrasting faces of the depression: the toughness and resilience of the human spirit when confronted by adversity and the agony, despair, and hardship that were the lot of so many in those difficult years.[78]

Quite apart from the reduction in the number of its clients, the DPW sought to dispense the aid that it did provide in as efficient and economical a manner as possible. Although Ballenger did not officially succeed Dolan as superintendent until February

15, 1932, he effectively ran the department from almost the beginning of the fiscal year, and the DPW was "radically reorganized" under his direction. The department was divided into eight divisions along functional lines, its budgetary procedures were improved, an independent auditing system was established, its detective service was expanded, and five of the sixteen business executives who had been assisting the department were named to an advisory committee to cooperate with the central office staff. Using devices of this sort, the DPW, by May, 1932, had effected savings of $125,000 in its overhead costs for the fiscal year. Some business leaders continued to complain, stereotypically, that the department's point of view reflected "a sociological rather than a business or economic atmosphere" and that this "automatically" led to inefficient administration; but the prevailing view was that Ballenger had brought "order" out of "chaos" in a very short time and that the department was being run "efficiently and honestly." William Lovett lamented that "heart throbs, dew and sunshine, etc." had been "the curse of Detroit," and he claimed that the city could have saved "millions" had Murphy let Ballenger run the department from the start.[79]

In its effort to economize, the DPW discontinued some services that had contributed to its high reputation in social-work circles before the depression. It no longer provided supplementary relief in mother's pension cases, it stopped paying for the boarding care of needy children, and it withdrew support from the Minnie E. Jeffries Nursing School, a progressive but high-cost operation. To the undoubted satisfaction of Dr. Blain, who thought that "being a city patient" had "gotten to be a racket," the department decided in July to limit its monthly expenditures for welfare patients in private hospitals to $15,000 as compared to $100,000–$160,000 in 1930–31. Whereas there had been 3,200 such patients in May, 1931, the number was steadily reduced to a mere 373 in May, 1932. Some patients were transferred to the Receiving Hospital or Eloise, but others, such as expectant mothers, were treated at home by city or private physicians or simply left to fend for themselves. The DPW also cut the budget of the Receiving Hospital by reducing its out-patient service and instructing the hospital to transfer some of its psychiatric cases to Eloise.[80]

The DPW thought that it could achieve substantial economies by boarding some of its clients on Michigan farms, an idea that appealed to Murphy, who favored the redistribution of population from the city to rural areas. The department set up a Farm Bureau in October, 1931, to supervise the project, but it turned out that welfare families did not wish to leave the city for the countryside and that farmers were equally unwilling to accept Detroit reliefers. The scheme was abandoned after one futile month of effort during which a grand total of two families were placed, one of which returned to the city after two weeks. Despite this fiasco, the idea lingered on throughout Murphy's mayoralty, testimony to the power of the agrarian myth.[81]

The DPW also sought to economize in the provision of shelter, clothing, and food to welfare recipients. Sharply reducing the proportion of its expenditures allocated to pay the rent of its clients, the department sometimes assigned two welfare families to a single rental unit, and in December, 1931, it began to withhold rent checks from fifteen hundred landlords who were delinquent in their tax payments, crediting the rent to their taxes. The Department of Purchases and Supplies, which began to do all the purchasing for the DPW, saved $60,000 for the welfare department in 1931–32 by letting contracts to seventeen shoe stores that had submitted the lowest bids to supply eight different types of shoes to welfare clients, who now received orders for a particular type of shoe. Similar arrangements were worked out with clothing stores to supply twenty-seven articles of apparel below the retail price, and substantial savings were also realized by substituting coal for coke and by using a system of bids in purchasing the fuel. The next year the department switched to soft coal to achieve additional savings.[82]

Since the expenditure for food constituted the single largest item in the DPW budget, it is not surprising that the hard-pressed department explored the possibility of reduced spending in this phase of its operation. It had begun in April, 1931, to feed one thousand childless couples in four central dining halls instead of providing them with the usual grocery orders and had discovered that it could supply a couple two meals a day of twenty-five hundred calories for about $2.50 a week as compared to a normal grocery order cost of $3.50. Since not all those assigned to feeding stations appeared for every meal and some did not appear at all, additional savings were incurred. The low cost, the elimination of the allegedly undeserving ("The biggest job is to get rid of customers," observed the ineffable Dr. Blain), and the fact that the kitchen plan made possible the provision of a balanced diet were believed to be the principal advantages of this method of distributing food. The welfare lunchrooms, on the other hand, were thought to disrupt home life; as variants of the odious bread line and soup kitchen, they were thoroughly disliked by participants; they could be effectively employed only in congested parts of the city; they did not allow for special diets; and in cold weather they presented problems for families that had to walk any distance to reach them. The feeding station, an authority on the subject observed, was actually "a thoroughly discredited and positively harmful means of extending relief," and although the method was widely used in the nation to feed homeless men, Detroit was almost alone among American cities in utilizing this "inhumane" means to feed families.[83]

Despite the disadvantages of the feeding stations, the Public Welfare Commission decided in July, 1931, to increase the number of lunchrooms and to use them to feed families with children above five years of age. By the beginning of August, 1932, about eleven thousand adults and children had been assigned to ten emergency kitchens, operated for the city by the Volunteers of America. The cost of feeding was steadily reduced, from about twenty cents per day in July, 1931, for the two meals served—the children, in addition, received a free lunch donated by the Volunteers—to about fifteen cents in June, 1932. The large number of "no shows"—an average of at least 20 percent for each meal—further reduced the daily cost by the latter date to about eleven cents, which compared with a daily grocery-order cost per person at that time of about sixteen cents.

Although economical to operate, the emergency kitchens were regarded with disfavor by Ballenger and the welfare workers and even by business leaders—"it is a good deal like refugee feeding during the World War," the supervisor of casework for the DPW declared. The welfare department, consequently, investigated alternative methods of reducing its food costs and talked of closing the kitchens, but some continued to operate until September, 1933.[84]

Toledo, Pontiac, and Milwaukee, among other cities, used a commissary system to distribute food to reliefers, and this scheme was favored for Detroit by Roosevelt and the city's Budget Bureau, but two separate committees established by the Public Welfare Commission to investigate methods of food distribution concluded that the plan could not be effectively employed in a city as large as Detroit. It would have been necessary to supplement such a system with grocery orders for meat, fresh fruits, and vegetables; and, in any event, it was not believed that a commissary plan would save the city any money since the grocery chains in Detroit that supplied food for many department clients realized a net profit of only 1.2 percent, a fact that also argued against the introduction of a competitive bidding plan for the purchase of welfare food.[85]

Following the advice of one of its committees, the welfare commission, in March, 1932, adopted as a supplement to the continued use of the emergency kitchens a modification of the existing grocery-order system known as the "Minimum Price, Suggested Ration Plan." The plan was designed "to keep the Welfare order to the lowest amount on which a family can maintain itself without malnutrition, and to show the family just how the money must be spent to accomplish this task when buying at existing retail stores at [the] lowest existing retail prices." A "maintenance ration" for welfare families was devised under this plan based on the maintenance diet recommended by the Bureau of Home Economics of the Department of Agriculture. Each welfare order was accompanied by a list of specific foods, the amount of each food that constituted the ration, and the current retail price for each item. The orders were scaled up and down as prices changed. The welfare clients were not obliged to buy the foods listed or to pay the prices indicated, but they deviated from the recommendations only at their peril. The ration plan reduced the cost of the average grocery order for a family of five from about $6.50 per week to about $5.40, more than 18 percent, and by July, 1932, the average allowance had been further reduced to $5.09. This was well below the $7.65–$10.25 estimate for a "minimum adequate sustenance" diet set by the United States Children's Bureau for a family of five and was designed, at most, to maintain a family without health problems in "fairly good health" for a short period of time.[86]

Even before the DPW reduced the amount and cost of the average grocery order, there was concern in Detroit about the adequacy of the department's "survival food allowance." The Department of Health therefore decided at the end of 1931 to conduct physical examinations twice a month for three months of four hundred children and four hundred adults on the welfare rolls. The initial examinations revealed that 68 percent were in "good" nutritional condition, 25 percent in "fair" condition, and 7 percent in "poor" condition. In July, however, a study of the case reports of about two hundred welfare families indicated that there was illness among about one-half of them. The presence of the children of welfare families in bread lines outside the fire stations and at private relief centers also raised questions about the adequacy of the welfare food allowance. When the Children's Fund investigated the circumstances of 442 children in bread lines on January 11, 1932, it discovered that 199 were in families receiving relief from some source.[87]

The DPW decided in the late summer of 1931 to increase the number of its clients who worked for their relief allowance and to convert its work-relief plan into a wage-work program. Since, as Gary Wills has put it, some Americans have "always suffered moral disorientation at the mere thought of anyone's 'getting something for nothing' " and since relief granted to the able-bodied was widely believed to be "demoralizing" to the recipient, it is not surprising that Detroit, like some two hundred other communities, initiated a work-relief program in the winter of 1930–31. Beginning in December, 1930,[88] the DPW required able-bodied heads of families on welfare, insofar as their services could be utilized, to earn their relief by working for departments of the city government, particularly the Department of Public Works. By the end of January more than eighteen thousand welfare clients were working for their relief. At first the men worked three days a week, later about forty-eight hours per month. They received no wages, which was at variance with the practice in many communities, but the hours that they worked were credited at a rate of fifty-five cents per hour against their relief allowance. The value of their labor on this basis was estimated by the DPW at more than $1.5 million for the period from December, 1930, to the end of the fiscal year.[89]

The principal change effected by the wage-work plan, devised by a committee headed by Joseph E. Mills, was to permit the heads of families to earn the equivalent of their welfare allowance in cash by paying them at a rate of forty cents per hour for the labor they performed. The advantages of the plan, a forerunner of the work-relief program of the New Deal, were that it enabled the wage-worker to maintain "the pride of himself and family" since he was now working for what he received, it allowed the participants to spend the money they earned as they saw fit, it helped the wage-workers to maintain their work habits and not to "deteriorate mentally and physically," it benefited the city by providing some departments with a regular work force in contrast to the haphazard and irregular allocation of labor under the old work-relief system, it provided the taxpayer with some "return" for the money spent by the city for welfare, and it helped the DPW to achieve administrative economies by reducing the number of families that it served.[90]

The wage-work plan, characterized by Murphy as "the most satisfactory means of handling relief for the unemployed," went into effect on September 10, 1931, and continued in operation until the end of May, 1932, when it had to be abandoned because the city could no longer meet the wage-work payroll. The work force was gradually built up, reaching about eleven thousand in the final month of the plan's operation, which was approximately one-half of the DPW case load at that time. Although some men were placed in white-collar jobs, most of them worked for the Department of Public Works, and they contributed more than $2.25 million to the city by their labor. They earned an average of $8.39 a week, which was designed to cover not only their food costs but also their rent, carfare, and other expenses. The plan was adjudged a "tremendous success" by the participants—"We're earning real money again. It makes a man feel more like a man," one wage-worker remarked—the departments for which they worked, and the political leadership of the city. About the only objection came from certain businessmen, who, continuing to think of those on welfare as a lesser breed of humans, preferred that the reliefers be paid in kind rather than cash lest they misuse their wages.[91]

One feature of the care of the needy in American cities during the year 1931-32 was increased coordination between public and private assistance, and Detroit was no exception. Since it was obvious that the DPW would be unable to support all families needing aid during the winter of 1931-32, Senator Couzens, on August 21, 1931, offered the city $1 million for relief contingent upon the contribution of an additional $9 million by other Detroiters. Murphy turned to "the leaders of wealth and industry" in Detroit to match the Couzens offer, but the four meetings that he held with a small group of the very rich simply "fell flat." The well-to-do to whom Murphy appealed regarded the sums that were discussed as "utterly impossible," and they also were suspicious of the mayor's motives, incorrectly viewing the entire affair as "a political move" on Murphy's part to aid his reelection in November.[92]

Once it became evident that the original Couzens offer would not be taken up, Murphy, Norton, and Couzens worked out an alternative plan that called for the creation of an Emergency Relief Committee, to be headed by Norton, that would solicit and receive private contributions to be disbursed through the DPW for the benefit of the unemployed but not for the "ordinarily dependent" or single men. Couzens agreed to contribute $200,000 to the fund, and procedures for the expenditure of the money were devised to assure contributors that the money would be honestly spent and that there would be "no political considerations involved in any way."[93]

Murphy bided his time until after his reelection and the conclusion of the annual Community Fund drive and then, on November 7, announced the formation of the new committee. But now an unanticipated difficulty developed. A few days earlier, Murphy had established another committee, headed by Detroit businessman Lloyd Grinnell, to solicit weekly contributions from various groups to support the MUC. Although it appeared unwise for two major fund-raising drives to take place simultaneously, the mayor, once again betraying indecisiveness, was reluctant to choose between the two committees. Adams and his associates threatened to dissolve the MUC if it were not permitted to go ahead with its fund-raising plans, whereas Norton, who apparently shared the professional caseworker's distrust of the freewheeling MUC, wanted the committee to "drop out of the relief field," if it were to continue at all.

Murphy would not agree to the dissolution of the MUC—this "would be printed in every paper in the United States," a MUC official had warned the mayor. At the same time, he wanted the support of the Norton group of "big business men" and believed that the city could not do without the funds that, it appeared, only they could raise. Confusion reigned for several days while the mayor, who, Norton thought, "did not quite know what he was talking about," issued a series of contradictory statements regarding the roles to be assigned each group. In the end, it was decided that the Emergency Relief Committee would be the major fund-raising organization but that the MUC could sponsor a tag day to raise money for school lunches and could continue to look after homeless men and support the thrift-garden program.[94]

The Emergency Relief Fund campaign, directed mainly at the well-to-do, was officially launched on November 18. It was not, as Norton put it, "a formalized campaign along the lines usually run" but rather "a continuous reminder that employed citizens must lend a helping hand to their jobless neighbors." Although it was originally hoped that the Emergency Relief Committee would be able to raise $3.5 million over a five-month period, the committee reduced its goal first to $2.25 million and then to $1 million, and in the end it raised only $645,000. Various explanations for this meager result were offered, but the real reason was the inability or unwillingness of the rich, whom Norton characterized as "just plain scared," to match Couzens's generosity. Norton was "not very proud" of what had happened, and he looked back upon the affair as "one of the very unhappy experiences" of his long career. Murphy stated publicly that there was no city in which the rich had contributed so little to aid their fellow citizens, and it was perfectly clear to him, as it should have been to any Detroiter willing to face the facts, that there was no longer any alternative for Detroit but to seek state and federal aid for relief.[95]

Although the Emergency Relief Fund drive fell far short of its original goal, it did enable the DPW by the middle of April, 1932, when the fund-raising effort came to an end, to add almost 9,000 families to the relief rolls, mostly from the categories that had been excluded during the previous summer. The department's case load rose to 28,247 in April, falling to a little over 22,000 in July, as the weather improved. Among the heads of families on relief as of July 22, 36.6 percent had previously been employed in automobile plants, 8.5 percent in other manufacturing establishments, 13.1 percent in the building trades, at least 18.5 percent in various white-collar occupations, and 94 reliefers were professional people. "The highest grade of people now are applying to us for aid," Ballenger had said in March, and Murphy had revealed that the relief rolls included not only forty-five ministers and three doctors but also a descendant of the first French family that had settled in Detroit and members of two families after whom Detroit streets had been named.

An estimated 6.4 percent of the city's population was drawing relief in July, 1932, but whereas only 3.8 percent of the native-born whites were on the relief rolls, 10.2 percent of the foreign born, and 17 percent of the black population were receiving public assistance, a reflection primarily of the depression's differential impact on the city's diverse population but also, perhaps, an indication of differing attitudes toward relief among the basic components of the city's people. Among the relief recipients, 10.7 percent had been on the rolls for more than two years, 61 percent for between six months and two years, and 28.3 percent for less than six months.[96]

The modest sum deriving from the Emergency Relief Fund campaign plunged the DPW into a severe cash crisis that lasted from April, 1932, until federal aid was authorized in August. Since it was evident that funds would be insufficient to carry the DPW through to the end of the fiscal year, the welfare commission instructed the department on May 10 to cease paying the rent of welfare families as of May 15 and to stop the distribution of clothing to its clients. Having cut its aid drastically and believing that it could "retreat" no further, the commission also sought to obtain an additional $792,000 from the Council to tide the department over until the end of the fiscal year. The Council approved the sale of $1 million in welfare bonds, an action made possible by recent state legislation, but Roosevelt, who was having difficulty marketing the welfare bonds previously authorized, was unable to sell the securities as the crisis deepened. The DPW ran out of money altogether on May 24, and it remained able to feed its clients, the sole aid that it continued to provide, only because some grocery chains were willing to extend credit on grocery orders and to supply the welfare kitchens, although it became necessary to reduce the rations at the latter. It is not surprising that Ballenger suffered a "nervous breakdown" in the midst of the crisis, just as Dolan had experienced a nervous collapse during the great welfare crisis of 1930-31.[97]

While Ballenger was recuperating—he returned to the department on August 1—the Public Welfare Commission began to formulate its policies for the forthcoming fiscal year, and the prospects were grim indeed. It appeared that two-thirds of the $3 million allocated for family relief in the 1932-33 budget would have to be used to pay off debts the department was accumulating, and what remained was certain to be diminished by the inevitable tax delinquency. Conceding that its action could lead to "chaos and violence," the commission decided toward the end of June to drop the 17,800 families on its rolls who were drawing relief because of unemployment and to continue giving aid only to the 5,900 families in the category of the "old poor." In what some commission members viewed as a "'grand stand play,'" Murphy rushed to Detroit from the Democratic party's national convention in Chicago to countermand the commission's order and to express the hope that federal funds would become available to assist these "solid citizens" who faced "starvation" if aid were denied them. In July, however, the DPW began to reduce its case load by once again eliminating most childless couples and also families headed by able-bodied unemployed persons who had been on the rolls for two years or more. By the middle of August 2,300 families had been cut off from support, and only one new family was being added to the rolls for every three that were removed.[98]

Since the DPW no longer paid the rent of its clients, many welfare families were evicted from their dwellings in the summer of 1932, the number reaching about 150 per day by the end of July. Three to four welfare families were being placed in quarters designed for a single family, and toward the end of July eighteen families were housed in tents in Clark Park, the Communists predicting that this would be "the first of a series of Murphyvilles." On August 1 the grocers, staggering under the burden of unpaid DPW debts, cut off credit to the city, and for a few days, as in the great salary-reduction crisis of April, 1931, welfare clients had to subsist on a diet of bread, milk, and flour. One observer thought that "genuine rebellion" was "smoldering" in Detroit. The elimination of families from the relief rolls and the numerous evictions led to minor riots and some property damage, and it was alleged that there were "angry expressions of dissent" in working-class districts. Petty thievery increased—grocery stores were the chief victims—and children snatched the food bundles of unwary shoppers. Like Philadelphia, which was altogether without funds for welfare for ten weeks in the summer of 1932, and like some of the other great cities that could by then provide relief only on "a disaster basis," Detroit had come to the end of its resources by the beginning of August. The city required assistance from outside if it were to avert the disaster that seemed to be impending.[99]

XIII

"The 'Revolt of the Cities'"

I

From an early date, the Murphy administration sought to persuade Wayne County and the state of Michigan to assist Detroit in meeting its critical welfare and fiscal problems. The failure of county and state governments to lend the city a helping hand left Murphy with no real alternative but to address his pleas for help to Washington, and in the end the federal government came to Detroit's aid.

When Murphy became mayor, relief in Michigan was provided entirely by local units of government. As the system operated, the six cities and eighteen townships of Wayne County dispensed relief to indigents who had resided in the particular locality for at least one year, and the county government provided for the needy who did not have a legal residence in a city or township. In Detroit, where about 3 percent of the welfare case load consisted of county cases, county, as distinguished from city relief, was distributed by the Department of Public Welfare (DPW), but the cost was borne by the county.

In April, 1931, the Murphy administration, because of the location of the Rouge and other automobile plants, suggested that relief in Michigan should be considered "a metropolitan rather than a city problem," and the mayor had Detroit's corporation counsel submit a bill to the state legislature authorizing county boards of supervisors to contribute funds for the relief of indigents in cities and townships of the counties. As the budget problems of the city became more severe, there was talk in Detroit of vesting exclusive responsibility in the county government for relief in Wayne County. The county had more bonding leeway than Detroit did, and since centralization in a single county agency would presumably reduce the overhead cost of distributing relief, the city fathers assumed that an all-county relief program would benefit Detroit taxpayers even though Detroit paid about 80 percent of the county's taxes. It required a two-thirds vote of the county Board of Supervisors to effect this change, however, and this proved an insuperable obstacle since the communities outside Detroit, which had more than enough votes to defeat the plan, feared that centralization would result in an increase in their taxes. Indeed, the Wayne County Board of Auditors complained in February, 1932, that the county was being charged too much by Detroit—an excess of $150,000 in 1931—for the expenses it incurred in administering county relief, and this became a contentious issue between city and county.[1]

"Michigan has not shown up well during this depression," William J. Norton correctly observed at the beginning of the New Deal with regard to the state government's performance in aiding Detroit and other units of local government. This was partly the result of rural domination of the legislature, but it also reflected the antediluvian ideas concerning public relief of Wilber M. Brucker, who became governor of Michigan in January, 1931. Although Brucker believed that local communities should be responsible for relief, he was highly critical of the Detroit welfare system, which he characterized as "'not a good thing.'" Detroit, he declared in an interview, had "suffered mostly through its own generosity in establishing the dole." Brucker warned that "Communist agents find in the dole system one of their chief allies."[2]

Murphy suggested in March, 1931, that the state government assist Detroit in carrying its relief burden, but the regular session of the Michigan legislature that adjourned in May failed to provide any financial aid for local relief. Unlike many other states, at that time Michigan had not yet established a state committee to assist local governments in the organization of their relief efforts. In August, 1931, however, Brucker responded to Washington's prodding and finally appointed a State Unemployment Commission to coordinate relief work in Michigan. The commission, which had no funds to disburse, served mainly as a clearing house for information concerning unemployment and welfare. Its commitment to rhetoric rather than action was captured by its chairman, a Niles manufacturer, when he wrote a newspaper editor, "The war was won by enthusiasm, initiative and work. The depression will succumb to the same aggressive offensive."[3]

Four states made unemployment relief funds available to local units in 1931, and ten states provided some assistance of this sort in 1932, but Michigan, although the sixth wealthiest state in terms of assessed real-estate valuation, did not choose to follow this path. Michigan insisted that it was contributing to the alleviation of unemployment by initiating in the last few months of 1931 the $10 million road-building program and the $2 million road-maintenance program scheduled for 1932. This construction did result in the part-time employment of thirteen hundred Detroiters taken from the welfare rolls, but all that was involved was the early disbursement of funds already appropriated, and even a State Unemployment Commission official characterized the program as only a " 'gesture.' "[4]

Dissatisfied with Michigan's performance, Senator Couzens sought to persuade the governor in September, 1931, to call a special session of the legislature to secure a $10 million appropriation to meet Detroit's welfare needs. Brucker, however, chose to believe that Detroit's problems stemmed not from a lack of funds but from its " 'hopelessly inefficient and wasteful organization of relief work,' " and when he convened a special session at the end of March, 1932, its purpose was to provide financial relief for counties that held covert road bonds, not to provide direct unemployment relief for Michigan's hard-pressed cities.

Seeking to ease the crushing burden that fixed debt charges would impose on Detroit's 1932–33 budget and in that way to free funds for other purposes, such as relief, the Murphy administration proposed that Brucker request the special session to authorize the return of "a substantial proportion" of the state weight and gas taxes to local communities to be used for schools and other purposes, authorize Detroit to refund over a ten-year period the $30 million in three- to five-year serial bonds it had issued in 1931, defer payment for a few years on an additional $30 million in two-year notes, and authorize the issuance of emergency welfare bonds up to one-half of 1 percent rather than one-fourth of 1 percent of assessed valuation. Wayne County, which contributed $16.5 million of the $41.5 million in weight and gasoline taxes paid to the state, received only $3.5 million of this sum for local road purposes, the rest being retained by the state Highway Department—this was true of the entire gas tax and one-half the weight tax—or distributed to less populous counties. If Wayne County, however, were to receive all or most of the sum that it contributed and Detroit could use its share for purposes other than roads, the city's budget problems would be accordingly eased. "We need no new roads," Councilman John Smith declared. "What we need is money with which to care for the sick and feed the children and carry on the necessary business of government."[5]

Although Governor Brucker responded to Detroit's pleas by asking the legislature to deal with the refunding and emergency bond issues raised by the city, he recommended that the legislators provide for the return of only the weight tax to the counties and that the money be used exclusively for road purposes. The legislature enacted legislation authorizing the cities to issue emergency bonds up to three-eighths of 1 percent of assessed valuation (rather than one-half of 1 percent, as Detroit had requested), and it partially met the city's demands with regard to refunding. Bowing to the powerful highway lobby, however, the legislature refused to adopt Detroit's proposal with respect to gas and weight taxes and followed the governor's recommendations instead. Murphy took to the air to attack the highway lobby—"Are we to allow the selfish interests of this group to defeat the very purpose for which American society was organized?," he asked—but he had no more success in contending with the road contractors and cement manufacturers than he later had as Michigan's governor.[6] The hope that the special session would markedly ease Detroit's budget and relief problems was thus not realized.

In June, 1932, Murphy advised Governor Brucker that the state government could help the city stave off starvation by purchasing emergency welfare bonds for which Detroit could not find a market. Controller Roosevelt made the mayor's plea specific the next month by requesting that $1.8 million in Detroit emergency welfare bonds be purchased by the state's Sinking Fund, but the State Bond Purchasing Commission refused to buy the bonds at par value, and the Detroit charter forbade the city to issue the bonds at a price below par or to offer them as collateral for a state loan at less than their face value.[7]

At the end of its resources and largely frustrated in its efforts to enlist the aid of private philanthropy and the state and county governments, Detroit, of necessity, looked to Washington for assistance in coping with the city's welfare problems. It was not a plot hatched by New Dealers but desperate necessity and the lack of reasonable alternatives that led Detroit and other big cities to push for a new relationship between themselves and the federal government. The "alternative," as one student of the question put it, had come to be "Federal aid or chaos."[8]

When he became mayor, Murphy assumed that local governments

had the primary responsibility for coping with the consequences of unemployment, although he also spoke vaguely of federal aid. President Hoover, who feared that federal relief would undermine the " 'spirit of responsibility' " of state and local governments and charitable organizations and would impair the "character" of the recipients, created the President's Emergency Committee for Employment (PECE) in October, 1930, but it had no money to distribute to state and local governments and served primarily as "a huge correspondence mill" and "an organ of exhortation for the American way." Its efforts to encourage state and local construction and to persuade employers not to reduce their labor force were almost entirely futile and were so viewed by the Murphy administration. In contrast to the PECE approach, by the early months of 1931 Murphy was calling for federal unemployment insurance and old-age pensions as means by which Washington could aid the cities in dealing with their relief problems, and he also favored a large-scale program of federal public works.[9]

When Senator George W. Norris convoked a National Progressive Conference in Washington in March, 1931, to propose programs for the nation's major problems, he invited Murphy to address the group because of his "outstanding" record in dealing with joblessness in Detroit. In his address Murphy stressed "the necessity and the justice and the equity of Federal help" in dealing with unemployment and justified such assistance for Detroit in particular on the grounds that firms like the Ford Motor Company paid federal taxes but not Detroit city taxes. He complained that the federal government had been "brutally callous" in its reaction to the unemployment crisis and that the state of Michigan had similarly done "nothing" about the matter. The chief form of federal aid for which he called was unemployment insurance.[10]

When the Mayor's Unemployment Committee (MUC), in March, 1931, began to consider whether it should petition President Hoover to call a special session of Congress to provide federal relief, Murphy indicated his strong support. The letter finally sent to the president in July pointed out that the apportionment of relief costs on an "equitable basis" required the intervention of a unit of government larger than the city and called upon Washington to "assume leadership" in the unemployment crisis and to provide Detroit and other communities with financial assistance. Murphy endorsed a similar request for a special session issued a few months later by the People's Lobby.[11]

President Hoover ignored the requests of the MUC and the

People's Lobby that he call Congress into special session. He replaced the PECE with the President's Organization on Unemployment Relief (POUR), but this represented no real change in the administration's policy regarding federal aid for relief. The MUC regarded POUR as "merely a 'Gesture' on the part of the President to fool the people," and the committee was undoubtedly confirmed in its opinion when the head of POUR advised a Senate subcommittee early in 1932 that federal aid would be " 'a disservice to the unemployed.' " [12]

Although the Hoover administration was unpersuaded by the appeals for federal aid, individual members of Congress began to recognize that the efforts of state and local governments to cope with unemployment would have to be supplemented by federal assistance. In December, 1931, Senators Robert M. La Follette, Jr., and Edward P. Costigan introduced similar bills providing for federal grants to the states of $375 million for relief. The hearings on these bills conducted by a subcommittee of the Senate Committee on Manufactures have been characterized as providing "the first comprehensive and detailed study of unemployment during the Great Depression." One of the key witnesses before the committee was the mayor of Detroit. Although Detroit, Murphy informed the committee, had wanted to provide relief on the basis of the facts and "the social justice involved," lack of funds had compelled the city to reduce its assistance to the "survival" level. The lamentable consequences of this policy had begun to manifest themselves, Murphy declared, but Detroit could do no more for the victims of depression unless it received state and federal assistance. "Instead of one government saying it is the responsibility of the other," Murphy asserted, "I think each government should be vieing [*sic*] with the other for the privilege of playing its part in this situation." Murphy's views, however, were not those of the majority of the Senate. On February 15, 1932, the Senate defeated a Democratic substitute for the La Follette-Costigan bill, and the next day the La Follette-Costigan measure suffered a similar fate. [13]

Opposed to direct federal relief for the unemployed, Hoover, in January, 1932, approved legislation establishing the Reconstruction Finance Corporation (RFC) and authorizing it to provide loans to banks and other financial institutions, railroads, and farm-mortgage associations. While the RFC measure was before the Senate, Senator Royal S. Copeland of New York introduced an amendment authorizing the agency to make its credit available to cities. Although this provided the kind of aid for cities about which Murphy had been speaking, he nevertheless sent a wire to Senator Couzens expressing opposition to legislation that relieved municipalities of the need to economize to balance their budgets. He did add, however, that federal aid was justified when a city had resorted to "uncompromising economy." The Copeland amendment was defeated after Couzens read Murphy's message on the floor "at an opportune time." Murphy's ill-advised action is difficult to comprehend but is probably explained by the mayor's desire to accommodate the influential Senator Couzens, who solicited the wire. Murphy soon had cause to regret his telegram to Couzens; a few weeks later he stated, "If the Federal Government can assist industry financially, it should also with good grace help local governments," which is precisely what he should have said when the Copeland amendment was before the Senate. [14]

Although it was a modest beginning, the Hoover administration embarked upon a program of federal aid for relief when the president, on March 7, 1932, approved a joint resolution of Congress directing the Federal Farm Board to transfer forty million bushels of wheat to the American Red Cross for distribution to the needy. Another joint resolution, approved in July 1932, added forty-five million more bushels of wheat and also made 500,000 bales of cotton available for relief. Detroit was a conspicuous beneficiary of this program. The 200,000 barrels of flour that the city's quota of wheat yielded by April, 1933, substantially reduced the welfare department's expenses for food, and during the trying days of late April and early August, 1932, only the federal government's wheat enabled the DPW to continue feeding the families on its rolls. The surplus cotton distributed to Wayne County made it possible for Detroit to supply its relief clients with 800,000 yards of clothing. [15]

In the middle of May, 1932, the MUC agreed to Josephine Gomon's proposal that it convoke a meeting of Michigan mayors and city managers to consider federal relief for the unemployed. Murphy had suggested a conference of mayors to deal with unemployment as early as November, 1930. In July, 1931, Benjamin Marsh, the executive secretary of the People's Lobby, wrote Murphy that he could "take the leadership" on the unemployment issue by inviting the nation's mayors to serve notice on Hoover that they refused "to be made the goats of the present economic system through being held responsible chiefly for relief of . . . unemployment." Speaking in Detroit shortly thereafter, Marsh publicly called on Murphy to convene a conference of big-city mayors to deal with unemployment. Marsh indicated that he had turned to Murphy because he was "the first among the chief executives of our largest communities who has given expression to the idea that in the last analysis it is the duty of government to take care of the people in time of distress."

Murphy responded that it was "logical and practical" for the federal government to aid the cities, but he thought that the proposal for a mayor's conference was "too important . . . to allow an immediate decision." As it turned out, Murphy did not act on Marsh's suggestion until Detroit's desperate financial plight in May, 1932, persuaded the mayor that the time had come to "take the leadership" in urging federal assistance for the stricken cities of the land. Inviting the chief executives of Michigan's cities to a meeting in Detroit on May 18, Murphy stated that the purposes of the gathering were to discuss how Congress might aid the cities in relieving unemployment and in meeting their financial difficulties and "to crystallize the sentiment" of the state in favor of such a program. Murphy noted that the specific plans to be considered by the mayors—ideas then being advanced in Washington—were federal aid for relief, assistance to the cities by the RFC, and William Randolph Hearst's proposal for a $5 billion "prosperity loan" to provide employment on public works for several million unemployed. [16]

Seventeen Michigan mayors and city managers joined Murphy in Detroit for the first conference of its kind in the history of the state. Murphy chaired the meeting and was its principal speaker. Like the other cities of the state, Detroit, he declared, had done all that it could to meet the unemployment crisis, but thousands of people in the city had nevertheless been "reduced to a state of wretchedness and misery." Now that the special session of the Michigan legislature had ended, it was clear that the state government would not provide the cities with aid, and so, he said, they had to turn to the federal government. The principle of federal relief had been recognized in the creation of the RFC, Murphy observed, but the RFC had "not been extended down directly on the human side"; it provided aid for business but not for municipal corporations even though they antedated the banks and the railroads and were entitled in an emergency to receive "that fair, just and intelligent assistance" due any community.

Echoing Murphy's criticism of the state government and agreeing with him regarding the need for federal assistance, the mayors and city managers unanimously called upon the federal government to adopt a program for "the direct relief of the unemployed," urged amendment of the RFC statute to permit the agency to invest in municipal obligations for public welfare, refunding, and to cover delinquent taxes, and endorsed the proposal for a $5 billion prosperity loan. In conveying these resolutions to President Hoover, Murphy explained that the cities' debt charges, "alarming tax delinquencies," and expenditures for relief had exhausted their resources, that "social unrest" was increasing and there was a threat of "complete collapse," and that the federal government was "the one remaining source" to which the cities could turn. [17]

The conference of Michigan mayors produced less of an immediate reaction in Washington than it did in Detroit, where Ralph Stone protested that the mayors had placed Detroit in the "humiliating position" of seeking funds in Washington for operating expenses whereas the proper course for the city to pursue was to reduce its expenditures. Federal purchase of refunding bonds, he said, would simply increase Detroit's interest costs and impair the independence and weaken the fiber of the city government.

Nettled by Stone's remarks and his seeming refusal to concede that the city had already reduced its expenditures to "the bare fundamentals," Murphy responded to the banker in unusually sharp terms. According to Stone, the indignant mayor declared, "it is sound and prudent to give Federal aid to the banks, but there is no wisdom in extending it to humanity." The mayor charged that although the bankers were themselves unwilling to purchase Detroit's bonds, Stone nevertheless objected to the RFC's doing so because he feared that this would reduce the amount of RFC funds that could be loaned to financial institutions—"He wants all the money available for the banks." Murphy contended that the bankers also feared that RFC aid for the city would "break" their "grip" on Detroit, deprive them of "monopolistic control" of the market for city securities, and lower the interest rate on municipal obligations. "The indifference and unconcern of the bankers," he declared, "is not only inhuman and brutal; it is not even sound fiscal policy. They are advocating the building up of hidden deficits, the most costly kind, which the City and the nation will have to reckon with in the future." Stone had appealed to the Common Council against the mayor, but the aldermen, painfully aware of the city's plight, authorized the refunding of almost $6.5 million in refunding bonds should Congress respond to the plea of the Michigan mayors.[18]

Responding to suggestions by Murphy and the Grand Rapids city manager, George Welsh, the conferees at the May 18 meeting resolved that Murphy should communicate with the nation's mayors with a view to convening a national conference of municipal chief executives to impress upon Washington the seriousness of the problems that faced the cities. Mayor Daniel W. Hoan of Milwaukee had earlier explored the advisability of holding such a conference and had found a good deal of support for the idea, but the Milwaukee mayor had not followed through on the matter.[19]

Although federal agencies such as the Bureau of Standards provided a variety of services to the cities, it had been presumed before 1932 that the cities, in the main, should look out for themselves and should deal with the federal government when that became necessary only through their state governments. The American Municipal Association, established in 1924 as a national federation of the various state leagues of cities, was thus primarily "a city-state lobby." Mayors were attached to the organization only through their state leagues of cities, rather than directly, and insufficient weight was given to the big cities in the Association. The Association, moreover, had been ineffective and did not even have a permanent central office or an executive secretary until the beginning of 1932. The kind of national conference of mayors that Murphy set about to organize was thus without significant precedent in the history of city government and in the evolution of the federal system in the United States.[20]

After some preliminary consultation with Mayors James J. Walker of New York and Anton Cermak of Chicago, Murphy invited the mayors of cities with populations of more than 100,000 to attend a conference in Detroit on June 1 to "unite in an appeal to Washington for direct Federal aid for unemployment relief." Providing eloquent testimony as to the need for the conference, the mayor of Erie, Pennsylvania, responded that neither his city nor he could afford the expense of his attendance, but only the mayors of Baltimore and Atlanta objected to the purpose of the conference.[21]

Forty-eight mayors attended the Detroit conference, including Massillon's venerable Jacob S. Coxey, still expounding the virtues of his non-interest-bearing bond bill. "Everybody had a good time," the Detroit *News* reported, and for some this included a trip across the Detroit River from dry Detroit to wet Windsor to take advantage of the hospitality offered by the Canadian city's chief executive. Murphy, who served as both the temporary and permanent chairman of the conference, explained that the straitened circumstances in which the cities found themselves stemmed from four factors: debt charges incurred during an era of expansion that had to be met in a time of deflation; tax delinquency; unemployment; and legal limitations on their borrowing power. Mayor after mayor rose to describe the depressed condition of his city, to state that private charity in his jurisdiction had reached the end of its resources, and to testify that state aid had been exhausted or had not been made available. In the opinon of Boston's James M. Curley, unless the federal government acted promptly, the continued existence of the nation was "problematical."

Murphy and his aides had arranged the conference so that discussion would center on the three main proposals for federal aid endorsed by the Michigan mayors. There was little real debate on the resolutions approved by the conference since the mayors, with only two or three exceptions, agreed on the need for federal assistance and were not inclined to quibble about the form that it should take. "It is a crisis, imminent and terrifying," the preamble to the resolutions declared, and "the very foundations of our social order are imperiled." The problem was national, the city officials asserted, and the federal government was "the one remaining source" to which they could turn for help. They advocated the $5 billion prosperity loan, extension of RFC credit to the cities to provide for the "conservation" of the American people, and use of RFC money to refund the maturing obligations of municipal governments. Agreeing on the need for a permanent organization of mayors, the conferees assigned Murphy the task of appointing a committee to undertake the necessary planning.[22]

Although the Detroit *Times* thought that the mayors had correctly diagnosed the ills of the cities and had prescribed the correct "remedy," Murphy's critics in Detroit, ignoring the conditions that had led to the conference, saw only politics in the affair. Men like Murphy, Curley, and Walker, it was said, were Democrats who were trying to embarrass the Republican Hoover and to advance their own political careers. "We here who have watched this ardent Democrat, and an active Roman Catholic besides," a Republican informant in Detroit advised Hoover regarding Murphy, "can see principally politics in it for him." Greatly exaggerating the importance of what may possibly have been a minor motive for the meeting, some of Murphy's foes also chose to believe that the real purpose of the conference, attended by mayors from so many cities with Hearst newspapers, was to promote Hearst's prosperity-loan proposal and to advance the fortunes of its author.[23]

"The important thing to do now," Murphy wrote just after the conference, "is to arouse public opinion so that Congress cannot adjourn without effecting some sort of plan for Federal relief." A committee consisting of Murphy, Curley, Hoan, Welsh, William A. Anderson of Minneapolis, T. Semmes Walmsley of New Orleans, and Ray T. Miller of Cleveland sought support for the mayors' resolutions in Washington. They arrived in the capital as Congress was considering a variety of measures providing for federal relief, the expansion of federal public works, and RFC loans to the states for self-liquidating public works. The debate in Congress was given a good deal of urgency because of the desperate relief crisis in Chicago, partly caused by the exhaustion of state funds that had been appropriated for relief. The Murphy group presented the mayors' resolutions to John Nance Garner, the speaker of the House of Representatives, and the majority and minority leaders of the lower chamber. The New York *Times* reported that the mayors had attracted "considerable attention" on Capitol Hill, and they were given credit in some quarters for the passage on June 8 of the Garner relief bill.[24]

When the mayors visited President Hoover on June 8, Murphy and Curley made a forceful presentation of the gravity of the urban situation. Although Hoover indicated his opposition to the prosperity-loan proposal, he expressed support for some form of RFC assistance to local government. Hoover later vetoed the Wagner-Garner relief bill, but the president gave his approval on July 21 to the Emergency Relief and Construction Act, a revised version of the Wagner-Garner measure. The statute, the "first . . . to place municipalities in intimate contact with the Federal Government," was influenced by decisions taken at the June 1 conference and may be regarded as something of a victory for the lobbying efforts of Murphy and his mayoral colleagues.[25]

In its most important section, the Emergency Relief and Construction Act provided for RFC loans to the states for relief of $300 million at 3 percent interest. The loans could be applied for by state governors, who had to certify that state resources were inadequate to meet the unemployment problem, either under Title

I, Section 1, subsections (b) and (c), which required repayment beginning in fiscal 1935 in the form of annual deductions from the federal grants to the states for highway construction, or subsection (e), which required a city to put up its own collateral for the loan. The statute also provided somewhat more than $322 million for federal public works and $1.5 billion in RFC loans to the states for self-liquidating public works and to private corporations for low-income housing and slum clearance. "Self-liquidating," however, was so restrictively defined in the statute that very few municipal projects, including the two that Detroit first considered, could qualify. The result was that this section of the law proved "a complete and dismal failure."[26]

By making it possible for relief loans to be granted under subsection (e), the Emergency Relief and Construction Act created a serious problem for Detroit since it had to gain approval for its loan requests from a governor who believed that cities should finance their relief costs without state aid. Whereas Chicago, the first city to be awarded an RFC relief loan, received its money under subsections (b) and (c), Governor Brucker required Detroit to apply for its initial loan under subsection (e). Legally permitted to issue only $1.8 million in emergency welfare bonds at that time, Detroit applied to the governor for a loan of that amount for the months of August and September. Since Detroit estimated that its welfare costs for the fiscal year 1932–33 would average about $900,000 per month, it was apparent that the loan request of late July would not be the city's last.[27]

Although the RFC expressed concern that the state of Michigan had not done enough to meet its relief needs, the agency, on August 4, granted Detroit the $1.8 million it had requested. In return, the RFC stipulated that the city was to deposit with the RFC an equivalent sum in welfare bonds. The RFC also specified that before Michigan applied for another loan the governor would have to consider methods of providing relief funds from within the state. The RFC loan could be used to pay grocery and other bills due in August but could not be utilized to pay bills that should have been liquidated before August 1. Tax funds, however, could now be diverted to meet these obligations.

"The black clouds of uncertainty that have hung over Detroit's relief activities lifted today for the first time in three months," the Detroit *News* observed after learning that the city's RFC loan had been approved. Officials now began to use tax money to pay off the city's welfare debts, and the grocers, as a result, agreed to extend credit to the DPW once again. When funds for the relief loan—the first, appropriately enough, that the RFC made directly to a city—actually became available for use on September 23, Detroit received its first dividend from what the Detroit *Times* had described as "the 'Revolt of the Cities.' "[28]

Although the $7,886,259 in city funds expended by the DPW in 1931-32 slightly exceeded the $7,575,000 originally authorized by the Common Council[29] and was augmented by contributions from the Emergency Relief Fund, Detroit by the time it began receiving federal aid could no longer legitimately claim that it was preeminent among the nation's cities in the generosity of its welfare program. Among the fifteen largest metropolitan areas in the country, only Detroit (including Hamtramck and Highland Park) and Los Angeles reduced the amount of relief per capita of population that they distributed in the months January–September, 1932, as compared to January–September, 1931; and the Detroit expenditure of $4.05 per capita of population in the first nine months of 1932 was topped by seven metropolitan areas. For the calendar year 1932 Detroit's per capita expenditure for all forms of public relief ($6.10) was exceeded by 31 of 117 urban areas, partly because of state aid to some of these cities.[30] The decrease in Detroit's spending for relief did not stem from any change in the attitude of the Murphy administration regarding welfare but was rather the result of the city's severe financial problems. Despite federal aid, these problems became even more severe in the fiscal year 1932-33.

II

As Murphy and his aides surveyed Detroit's fiscal prospects in June, 1932, it was painfully obvious to them that "drastic measures" would be required if the city were to provide its citizens with essential services during the next fiscal year without defaulting on its obligations. Detroit was certain to begin the new fiscal year with a deficit of about $6.3 million; the administration anticipated an additional deficit of $23.7 million by June 30, 1933, largely because of tax delinquency; the city was about $3.5 million short of the cash needed for July and August; all but $4,903,000 of the floating debt of $53,396,000 was to mature by August 5; and the likelihood that the city could refund that portion of the long-term debt maturing in 1932-33, even to the extent permitted by state law, was virtually nil in view of the condition of the bond market. Given this set of foreboding circumstances, the mayor thought it prudent to counsel with the city's leading industrialists and bankers and its largest taxpayers in an effort to devise a plan that would enable Detroit to preserve its financial integrity and meet the needs of its inhabitants during the forthcoming year. The "informal discussion" that followed resulted in the preparation of a "big new financial plan" for Detroit and in the formation of an Industrialists and Bankers' Committee on City Affairs, headed by B. E. Hutchinson, a Chrysler Corporation vice-president, to assist the city government in its implementation.[31]

Murphy made a very effective presentation of the new plan at a July 5 meeting of city officials and Detroit's economic elite—Councilman John Lodge described Murphy's talk as "one of the finest and most constructive speeches I have ever heard"—and the mayor then formally submitted the scheme to the Common Council. The plan called for the city to effect additional economies of $7 million, which was the unfunded amount borrowed against 1932-33 taxes in the preceding fiscal year and was the price Murphy had to pay to receive big-business support for the plan. The budget reduction was to be accomplished by the enactment of an ordinance reducing the work week of city employees to five days and forty hours, which was the equivalent of a pay cut of 14-1/2 percent and was expected to produce a saving of $5.4 million, and additional economies of $1,693,795, mainly at the expense of the police, the firemen, and the schools. Economies beyond this, the mayor stated, would not permit "organized government to continue."

Contingent on achievement of the proposed economies, some of Detroit's larger taxpayers agreed to pay a sufficient portion of their December tax installment in advance to enable the city to meet its cash requirements for July and August; holders of most of the city's short-term debt committed themselves to renew the notes; state legislation was to be sought permitting Detroit to issue $20 million in five-year faith-and-credit bonds, one-fifth of which would be accepted by the city annually in payment of taxes; and a group of "influential citizens" agreed under these circumstances to arrange for the sale of the bonds. The $20 million in bonds, the $7 million in economies, and an estimated income of about $3 million from the sale of delinquent taxes were expected to wipe out the predicted deficit of $30 million and to permit "an orderly handling of the City's business and the restoration of the City's credit."[32]

"I know of no better plan," Ralph Stone told the Common Council shortly after the mayor had unveiled the new scheme, and a business spokesman declared that the program had the approval of "practically all competent students of municipal and financial affairs." Business leaders were delighted that the mayor had enlisted the aid of "the best business experience of the community," but a writer in the liberal journal the *Nation* commented glumly that Detroit was now "at the mercy of the bankers," which was not far from the truth. Although Murphy stated that he was "glad to sponsor and take full responsibility" for the plan,[33] he was obviously making a virtue of what could only have appeared to him to be dire necessity.

The implementation of the city's new fiscal program and, in a very real sense, the life of the city government itself were immediately threatened by a rival proposal advanced by several property-owning groups that had leagued together to form the Associations for Tax Reduction (ATR). The ATR called for an amendment to the city charter that would limit the property tax for 1932–33 to $61 million and would reduce it by an additional $1 million each year until 1937–38, when the tax levy would be $56 million. When the ATR had gathered the requisite number of signatures to compel the city government to hold a special election on the tax-cutting plan, it placed the petitions in a truck drawn by seven horses and staged a parade through downtown Detroit. The Council scheduled the balloting for August 9, 1932, after the Wayne County Circuit Court dismissed a city petition for a declaratory judgment to block the proposed election as illegal.[34]

The ATR was really a front group for the Detroit Real Estate Board. The proposal for the $61 million tax limitation, a proposal to legislate "a limited tax strike," had been advanced by the president of the Board; the "manager" of the group was the executive secretary of the Board; and the ATR president was a former Board president. When the Council reluctantly accepted the resolution for the special election, it did so "amidst a storm of denunciation of the Real Estate Board." The leaders of the tax-reduction drive, the Murphy administration charged, were men who in the post-World War I era had speculated in land later annexed by the city, had then sold lots at inflated prices to purchasers who had been forced to surrender the land when they could not fulfill their contracts, and who were now delinquent in tax payments on the still vacant property. Their objective, according to the administration, was to have the Detroit tax question "tied up" in the "legal tangle" that was sure to develop if their proposal was approved and thereby to secure a "moratorium" of several years on their tax payments and to "get out from under."

Although the tax delinquency rate on vacant land was considerably higher than on improved land, the Murphy administration, in arguing as it did, may have created the impression that Detroit's tax delinquency problem was attributable to the holders of vacant land. Such land, however, actually accounted for only 6 percent of the city's property tax income. The city government was not in error, however, in charging that large subdividers and real-estate promoters of yesteryear who were delinquent in their taxes were supporting the tax-reduction drive: the president of the ATR was himself a prominent subdivider who owed the city $150,000 in back taxes.[35]

To the argument that the $61 million tax limitation would force a sharp reduction in government services, the plan's proponents replied in conventional laissez-faire terms that the city needed "less" rather than more government. Opponents of the tax-cutting proposal said that it would lead to "chaos and disaster," but the manager of the ATR declared, "The only 'chaos and disaster' that will result will be the 'chaos and disaster' that befalls a few non-essential and over-paid hangers-on who should have been eliminated long ago." What was involved, the tax cutters' statistician argued, was "a struggle between the taxpayer and the tax spender."[36]

Some ATR literature was specifically directed at Mayor Murphy. "The issue is Murphy and his Political Future vs. the Citizens and Lower Taxes," an ATR handbill declared. "It is a campaign of Dew and Sunshine vs. Bread and Butter!" Murphy was advised by a doctor supporting the tax cut that it was "the little home-owner, your former most faithful worker," who was "most bitter" against him. When a Detroit radio station attacked the plan, its president received a good deal of hate mail, including a letter berating him for his support of the "present HOODLUM administration."[37]

The Murphy administration did not underestimate the threat posed by a proposal with such obvious appeal to property owners, many of whom had suffered catastrophic declines in income. "We must furnish leadership for the people in this fight and we must furnish them with the facts," the mayor told a meeting of his department heads. The city departments mobilized their staffs to carry out the mayor's orders. There was no politics in this, Commissioner L. G. Lenhardt declared, since the issue to be decided by the voters was "whether the government is going to keep going or whether it is not." The Department of Recreation posted literature at all playgrounds and community centers explaining the implications of the tax plan, employees sent out personal letters about the proposal to friends of the department, and the department hired a sound truck to urge votes against the plan at baseball games and other recreational events on the Sunday before the election.[38]

The efforts of the Murphy administration were aided by most of Detroit's civic leadership, which recognized the threat to orderly government posed by the proposal to impose "a financial straight-jacket" on city operations. The Detroit Citizens League, the Bureau of Governmental Research, the Board of Commerce, the Stone Committee, the American Legion, the Detroit Federation of Labor (DFL), the *News*, the *Times,* the head of the property owners' division of the Detroit Real Estate Board, Senator Couzens, and Arthur Lacy, the president of the National Taxpayers' Association and a recognized tax expert, all urged voters to reject the tax amendment.[39]

Opponents of the $61 million scheme pointed out the implications for the city of what on the surface appeared to be an alluring proposal. Unlike the plan devised by the mayor and the Industrialists and Bankers' Committee, the $61 million budget, opponents noted, made no provision for the cash needed for July and August. If it were adopted, they alleged, the holders of short-term notes falling due early in the fiscal year would not agree to their renewal, and thus upwards of $40 million would have to be added to the tax budget; and the $20 million in faith-and-credit bonds that alone would stave off a massive deficit could not be sold. The result would be a huge tax increase or, more likely, default, a rush of the city's creditors to the courts to enforce their claims through a court-ordered tax lien, and probably state-government intervention and the imposition of a financial dictatorship.

Critics of the $61 million plan stressed that it would result in a catastrophic decline in city services. A $61 million tax budget was certain to be reduced to about $45 million because of the anticipated tax delinquency of 25 percent, and more than $31 million of the latter sum would be required to meet fixed debt obligations. Of the approximately $14 million remaining,

$10,296,000 had to be spent for schools and the public-library system if state funds for education were to be forthcoming. This left a grand total of $3,668,610 to operate the rest of the government, which was only 13 percent of the amount for the same purposes provided by the revised Murphy budget. In an extremely effective series of articles, Detroit *News* columnist Blair Moody pointed out just what an 87 percent decline in services would mean for the citizens of Detroit.

Quite apart from the plan's other shortcomings, Corporation Counsel Wilcox, a respected conservative and a lawyer's lawyer, argued that the $61 million budget illegally included charges for certain city services and provided for unlawful transfers of funds, and Controller Roosevelt exposed some of the "hidden tricks" in the budget that made it appear to provide more services than actually was the fact. Citing figures supplied by the city assessor, the Detroit *News* noted that insofar as the proposed budget would yield savings to the taxpayer, they would go mainly to the few large taxpayers rather than to the average homeowner since the holders of the 480 largest pieces of property paid about the same percentage of the city's property tax as did the 198,000 taxpayers who owned homes or stores assessed at less than $10,000.[40]

The star actor in the campaign against the $61 million amendment was the mayor himself. Murphy gave his greatest performance before an audience of 780 persons that gathered at the Statler Hotel on July 19 for the official presentation of the $61 million budget. After the ATR statistician explained the proposed budget, Murphy, who had been invited to the meeting, rose to respond. The hostile crowd tried in vain to shout him down. "We are going to meet you with facts and figures on every corner," the mayor remarked. "And the people of Detroit are not going to accept your boos, catcalls and hisses as arguments." There were cries of "Throw him out," more boos and hisses, and shouts that Murphy was delinquent in the payment of his own taxes. The mayor, his jacket off, his sleeves at the elbow, calmly continued. "You ought to listen to the facts whether you like them or not," he told his audience, "and you won't like them." Loosening his collar and tie, Murphy proceeded to demonstrate the ways in which the $61 million budget was both "impractical" and "illegal." The booing continued to the end, and the mayor, in complete command of himself throughout, left the platform in the midst of an uproar.[41]

News of the Statler meeting quickly made the rounds in Detroit, and there was no doubt as to who had won the "debate." "I want to add my cheer to the chorus of approving shouts which are going up all around town," B. E. Hutchinson wrote Murphy; and from men like Ralph Stone, Packard's Alvan Macauley, and Rabbi Leo Franklin there was praise for the "masterly" way that Murphy had "handled a difficult situation."[42]

When Murphy learned that blacks were being advised by landlords that their rents would be reduced if the $61 million budget were adopted, he drafted a letter for the city's black preachers to read to their congregations. He charged in the letter that his opponents, having failed to defeat him for reelection in 1931, were now "trying to get their results in a different way, that is, by wrecking our government." Murphy urged blacks to repulse "this bald [*sic*]-faced attempt to defraud you of your rights," and his numerous friends among the black clergy saw to it that the mayor's message reached their parishioners.[43]

In his final appeal to the electorate, Murphy characterized the election as "a rare test of democratic government." The next day Detroit's voters passed that test as they overwhelmingly rejected the $61 million amendment by a vote of 126,578 to 40,050. In only one of Detroit's 895 precincts did a majority of voters approve the ATR amendment. "The election," Murphy asserted, "was one of the most extraordinary political events which I can recall where a people on a technical question of taxation wisely showed sound discrimination, repudiating a proposal which on its face assured tax reduction." There was a good deal of truth in what Murphy said, but the voters were not simply making a choice between two budgets, whose intricacies, one may presume, most of them did not fully comprehend. They were also rendering a judgment on the Murphy administration and its management of city affairs. In a year in which there was no mayoralty election, the ATR proposal compelled the Murphy administration to ask the electorate for a vote of confidence, and the voters responded in unmistakable terms. The election, the Detroit *Labor News* accurately observed, was "a victory for good government and for Mayor Murphy."[44]

While the campaign for the $61 million plan was underway, the Murphy administration and the Industrialists and Bankers' Committee were engaged in implementing the fiscal plan they had devised for the city. On July 19 the Common Council reluctantly approved the five-day week ordinance, and, as Murphy had anticipated, there was considerable opposition to the measure by the police and fire departments because of the reduction in personnel that the implementation of the shorter work week entailed. The Council permitted the police to return to the six-day week in February, 1933, the Fire Department was allowed to effect the required 14-1/2 percent saving without going on the five-day week, and there was less than perfect compliance in other units, but, despite this, the savings in salaries contemplated by the shorter work week were largely realized by one means or another.[45]

Since the salary measure did not go into effect until July 22 and thus fell short of achieving the anticipated $5.4 million in reduced spending, the Stone Committee insisted that, besides putting into effect the additional $1.6 million in budget cuts that the new fiscal plan required, the city government should also economize in other areas to make up the difference. Committed as ever to a balanced budget, Murphy pressed his subordinates to "cut to the very fundamentals," and that is precisely what most of them attempted to do. In early 1933 Murphy pointed out that since becoming mayor he had reduced the city's operating costs by more than 35 percent (from $76 million to $49.2 million), laid off 10,500 of the city's 42,000 employees, and cut salaries 25 percent. ". . . the outstanding thing in my administration . . . ," Murphy later said, "was the economy program." Among the nation's ten largest cities, Detroit was eighth in the per capita cost of its government in 1933, and even the president of the Detroit Citizens League conceded that the city's budget had been cut so drastically that further reductions could be achieved only by eliminating "vital services."[46]

The large taxpayers who had agreed to pay a portion of their December taxes in advance so that the city could meet its July and August cash requirements were true to their word, but since the rate of tax delinquency mounted to 36 percent rather than the planned-for 25 percent, it looked as though the city would realize about $8 million less in taxes during the fiscal year than it had anticipated. This led Murphy to appoint a Mayor's Tax Committee and also to consider means other than the property tax to raise revenue for the city. The tax committee seems to have concerned itself almost entirely with the tax-delinquency problem, but its proposals, most of which required amendment of the city charter, were not adopted before Murphy left Detroit and did little if anything to increase tax collections in fiscal 1933. As of February, 1933, 195,000 of the 480,000 tax parcels in the city were delinquent (as compared to 125,000 parcels at the same time in 1932), and at the end of the fiscal year the city had collected only 65.39 percent of the taxes due that year.[47]

To facilitate the renewal of the city's troublesome short-term debt, which was part of the July 5 fiscal plan, the Council at the beginning of August empowered Controller Roosevelt to set aside a sufficient portion of the initial tax payments to meet interest and sinking-fund obligations for the first half of the fiscal year. This decision annoyed the president of the Council, Frank Couzens, who, like his father, did not believe that the city should give preference to bond and note holders in paying its bills. Couzens secured a reconsideration of the debt resolution and the adoption of a new resolution simply authorizing the payment of any debt obligations accruing before September 1, 1932. It was now Ralph Stone's turn to become annoyed, and in another of his tactless letters he bluntly informed the Council that its action jeopardized the success of the July 5 plan. If the aldermen failed to readopt their original resolution, he warned, he would not ask the large taxpayers to advance any more of their tax payments, and the holders of $25 million in short-term notes who had agreed to extend them would not make any further extensions.[48]

Chafing under banker control, as the mayor was, the Council reacted angrily and vocally to Stone's minatory letter. Couzens charged that the bankers were trying to "whip the City into line to further their own selfish interests," and Councilman Hall, after the aldermen had discovered that Stone's remarks about the renewal of the short-term debt were ill-founded, accused the financial-industrial group for whom Stone was speaking of "building specters to scare the people." In the next few days holders of the short-term notes agreed to renew them until the first of the year, and a spokesman for the Hutchinson committee stated, "I am confident Detroit is getting out of the woods."[49]

Success of the July 5 plan hinged to a considerable extent on the floating of $20 million in five-year tax-anticipation bonds. The Murphy administration had assumed that the city could safely wait until the regular January session of the state legislature to secure the necessary legislative authorization for the issuance of these bonds, but the cash shortage resulting from the greater-than-expected tax delinquency and the consequent likelihood of default on January 15 persuaded Murphy early in December to request Governor Brucker to call a special session of the legislature before the year was out. By that time a lame-duck governor and at sword's point with Detroit's mayor, Brucker chided the city for waiting until the last moment to request a special session and demanded documentary proof both that the session was required and that the tax-anticipation bonds would be purchased in sufficient quantity to protect Detroit against default. In the end, however, Brucker called the special session for December 27 to consider the Detroit proposal.[50]

In a testy, politically tinged message to the legislature Brucker grudgingly recommended the enactment of a bill embodying the Detroit proposal, but he could not resist criticizing the Murphy administration for "the unconscionable accumulation" of Detroit's bonded debt and its "lavish spending" of public funds. At a public hearing in the House chamber, Murphy was "eloquent," to quote the Detroit *News*, in responding to these charges, and Hutchinson and the mayor demolished the governor's allegations of extravagance in the management of Detroit's public business.

After the inevitable remarks had been made about "dew and sunshine" and Murphy's allegedly excessive "sympathy for the down-trodden," the legislature, on December 29, authorized Detroit to issue five-year tax-anticipation bonds against both delinquent and current taxes up to four-fifths of 1 percent of the city's assessed valuation (somewhat in excess of $20 million). A maximum of 20 percent of these bonds could be used in any one year to pay taxes, and Detroit was required to place $4 million in its budget each year for five years beginning in 1933–34 to retire the securities. The industrialists associated with the Hutchinson committee announced that they would take up $7.5 million of the bonds from the New York syndicate that seemed likely to purchase the entire issue, and C. E. Rightor, the new controller, stated, "I see no reason, unless something unforeseen develops, why we should not be able to meet all payrolls and all other obligations during the remainder of the 1932–1933 fiscal year."[51]

Although Detroit's immediate fiscal problems thus seemed on the way to solution as the calendar year 1932 came to an end, Murphy was wondering where the city would find the more than $43 million apparently required during the 1933–34 fiscal year to service the municipal debt. If the tax budget remained at $72.6 million, about sixty-six cents of every tax dollar would have to be devoted to debt service, and if tax delinquency continued at the 1932–33 rate, only the ridiculously inadequate sum of about $4 million would actually be available to finance all city activities. It was pointless in the midst of the depression and the massive deflation to seek a tax increase to help the city service its debt, and the obvious alternative of refunding a substantial portion of the debt by arrangement with private banks also seemed out of the question because there was simply no market for Detroit's bonds, excluding, perhaps, the type of tax-anticipation bonds recently sanctioned by the legislature. As the "smartest bond man" on Wall Street told Blair Moody, even though the Murphy administration's record for economy had "not even been approached elsewhere," the city, for a variety of reasons, had a very poor credit rating. In the judgment of investors, Detroit suffered because it was a one-industry town that had been unusually hard hit by the depression and because its credit had been "ruined by a flood of misleading publicity." National attention had focused on the city as the result of Murphy's well-publicized welfare program, and there had been a good deal of nonsense in the press about a prodigal relief policy that was driving Detroit to bankruptcy. The sometimes acrimonious controversy between the city administration and the bankers and the undiplomatic manner in which the bankers had insisted on reduced spending had also strengthened the impression of a city that was a poor credit risk.[52]

With other possibilities closed off, Murphy not surprisingly concluded that the way to loosen the choking grip of debt service on the Detroit budget was to have the RFC purchase the city's refunding bonds and also the securities of revenue-producing utilities like the DSR and the Department of Water Supply that were finding it difficult to meet their operating expenses. Only in this way could Detroit taxes be kept at a reasonable level in 1933–34 and the DSR and the Water Board spared the painful necessity of raising rates in the midst of depression. Since other cities were experiencing the same kind of financial difficulties, Murphy and Paul V. Betters, the executive secretary of the American Municipal Association, who for some months had been exchanging views about another meeting of mayors, decided to convene a second conference of mayors to petition Congress to amend the RFC statute so as to permit the corporation to purchase municipal refunding bonds and the securities of municipal public utilities.[53]

On February 11, 1933, three days before the already alarming Detroit financial situation became actually desperate, Murphy invited the mayors of ninety-five cities with populations over 100,000 to a conference in Washington to seek the liberalization of the RFC statute so that the corporation could be of greater service to the cities. Twenty-two mayors gathered at the Mayflower

Hotel in Washington on February 17 in response to Murphy's invitation. Murphy, who was chosen to preside at the conference, remarked that although the problem of the cities had not been so "distressing" in all of American history, the solution for the problem was at hand in the form of federal credit. If the RFC could extend credit to private corporations, he noted, it should, with more reason, be empowered to purchase the refunding and utility bonds of the cities since the taxing power and the faith and credit of municipal corporations that stood behind municipal credit instruments provided the federal government with greater security than private corporations could offer.

The mayors and city officials present echoed Murphy's remarks in depicting the financial plight of their cities. ". . . out my way," Mayor William Mahoney of St. Paul declared, "they use ropes on anybody that tries to foreclose mortgages. We have a revolution right now in our midst. Does Congress know that?" Mayor Curley asserted that at their previous conference the mayors had appealed to Congress to save the people from starvation. Now, he said, they were asking the nation's lawmakers to preserve "the integrity of the units that go to make up the United States of America."

In effect accepting the relief proposal for Detroit worked out by the Murphy administration, the mayors, in their principal resolution, urged that the RFC be authorized to extend loans to municipalities or their publicly owned utilities and also to purchase their tax-anticipation warrants. In deciding whether to extend a loan to a municipality, the RFC, the resolution stated, could consider not only the soundness of the investment but also whether the affairs of the unit had been conducted efficiently and economically. In addition, the corporation could suggest additional economies as a condition of the loan. The mayors also resolved that the federal government should assume a greater degree of financial responsibility for unemployment relief and that Congress should authorize the grant of additional relief funds directly to the cities.

The mayors once again took up the "great need for a permanent organization of the mayors," a matter that Murphy had failed to pursue despite the resolution on the subject adopted at the June, 1932, conference. They resolved that the mayors of the larger cities, preferably those with over fifty thousand population, should form "a permanent organization to establish closer cooperation, make a careful study of municipal problems and keep before the government and the people of the nation the vital interests of municipal government." They adopted a constitution for the new organization, to be known as the United States Conference of Mayors, and unanimously elected Murphy its first president. Murphy, Mayor Walmsley asserted, was "the man that has impressed it [the need for organization] most upon us all, and has had the courage to lead us. . . ." Curley was selected vice-president, and Mayors Hoan of Milwaukee, Anderson of Minneapolis, and Anton Cermak of Chicago, then at death's door as the result of an assassin's bullet, were named trustees. An urban "bloc," of which Murphy was the acknowledged leader, had been formed to save the cities from collapse, and "the collective interests of the people of the cities" that had "gone unprotected so long" now had an effective organizational spokesman.[54]

The officers of the United States Conference of Mayors asked the American Municipal Association to serve as the Conference's secretariat, and Betters was designated the organization's secretary. It was Betters who converted the decision to form the Conference into an organizational reality. Within ten days of the February meeting he was advising the mayors eligible to join the new organization that it would provide members with information on federal legislation that affected the cities, maintain a municipal information service to which members could turn for data on municipal problems, and publish reports and bulletins. The secretariat was soon providing a variety of services to member mayors, and by arrangement with the American Public Welfare Association it began to offer a consulting service on all welfare problems.[55] No one had more reason to take pride in what had been accomplished than the mayor of Detroit, whose initiative had been decisive in the formation of the new organization.

The first official act of the United States Conference of Mayors was the appearance of Murphy and several other mayors before the Senate Banking and Currency Committee on February 18 to urge increased RFC aid to the cities. In response to questioning, Murphy indicated that, if the refunding measure were approved, Detroit would need $35-37 million in federal refunding loans.[56] For Detroit, Murphy stated, it was "either R.F.C. aid or default." Although the senators were sympathetic to the needs of the cities, Senator Robert F. Wagner informed Murphy that there was too little time remaining in the session for the Senate to act on a measure for whose passage the upper house was "not quite ready."[57] This was an accurate appraisal of the situation, and Murphy himself within a very few days was compelled by conditions in Detroit to seek a more drastic federal solution for the city's fiscal problems.

Although the February 17 conference also called for increased federal aid for relief, it was the need to refund Detroit's debt that had persuaded Murphy to call the nation's mayors together once again. This did not signify any lessening concern about the welfare problem on the part of the Murphy administration or, indeed, that the relief burden in Detroit was easing but only that with the passage of the Emergency Relief and Construction Act the means were available to finance Detroit's relief costs without imposing any real strain upon the taxpayer.

At the end of August, 1932, the Public Welfare Commission estimated that more than $10.3 million would be required to finance the welfare department's operations until June 30, 1933, and it seemed altogether unlikely that any substantial portion of this sum could be supplied locally. Of the $3 million included in the budget for family relief, some money was used to pay debts incurred in the preceding fiscal year, and tax delinquency eroded a substantial part of the remainder. In the end, only $400,658 of the city's own money was expended for family-relief purposes during the entire fiscal year 1932–33—all of it before January 1, 1933. The federal government, by contrast, provided Detroit with $11,050,289 in RFC welfare loans, more than 95 percent of the sum spent for city relief during the fiscal year. It was federal funds and federal funds almost alone that enabled Detroit during Murphy's last year as mayor to finance its welfare operations and to increase its case load from 22,076 in July to 41,427 in December and 55,043 in April, an all-time peak to that date.[58]

Historians have been inclined to minimize the relief activities of the RFC, to stress its "exasperating slowness" and the "grudging" manner in which it dispensed relief funds, and to criticize it for extending relief loans as though it were conducting "a banking rather than a welfare program."[59] Much of this criticism is justified, but it was primarily RFC aid that permitted Detroit to feed its hungry during the single worst year of the Great Depression and made it possible for the city to dispense at least some relief to a substantial minority of its population until Federal Emergency Relief Administration (FERA) funds became available. What was true of Detroit was true of Chicago and other cities as well; the mayors assembled in Washington on February 17, 1933, understood perfectly when Murphy told them that RFC relief loans to the cities had been "the only means by which some of them have survived to the present time." The mayors themselves were, of course, partly responsible for what the RFC had accomplished, and they could also take some credit for the

FERA, which greatly expanded the relief role of the federal government.[60]

After its initial $1.8 million loan, Detroit would have preferred to obtain a single RFC loan of $9,874,330 to carry it through to the end of the fiscal year. The RFC, however, applying a policy of "hand to mouth advances" that hampered systematic relief planning, viewed its loans as serving only a short-run, emergency purpose, and so it doled out funds to Detroit, two or three months at a time, requiring a separate justification for each loan. In the end, Detroit received five separate loans, totaling $9,250,289, to meet welfare costs for the period October 1, 1932–May 19, 1933. The RFC allowed the city funds for food, clothing, fuel, rent, sundries, administrative expenses, care of homeless men, work relief, and administrative costs, but it refused to include any funds in its loans for the hospital care of welfare patients, fearing that it would be swamped by similar requests. As a condition for its March, 1933, loan, the RFC required the DPW to increase its supervisory and investigatory staff and to carry out "more intensive home investigation," indicating the federal corporation's support for the increasing stress on the detective aspects of welfare work.[61]

In seeking to qualify for federal relief loans Detroit was less troubled by the restrictive policies of the RFC than it was by the uncooperative attitude of the state government. The specific point at issue between Detroit and Lansing was the terms under which RFC aid should be sought, but the controversy really stemmed from the quite different attitudes toward public relief of Mayor Murphy and Governors Brucker and William Comstock, Brucker's Democratic successor. Although Detroit had received its first RFC loan under subsection (e) of the Emergency Relief and Construction Act, it was determined to rely on subsections (b) and (c) in seeking additional RFC aid. Not only was the amount of collateral for loans under subsection (e) that Detroit could legally provide far below the sum required to meet the city's welfare needs for the year, but, of greater importance, subsection (e) loans added to Detroit's debt, whereas subsection (b) and (c) loans were to be repaid from the state's share of federal highway funds. When Detroit, however, sought its second RFC loan under subsections (b) and (c), Governor Brucker specified that the city apply once again under subsection (e) because of his unshakable conviction that each community in the state must pay "every cent" of its own relief costs. "There will be no jack-pot created into which communities may dip without restriction," the governor declared.[62]

Rebuffed in Lansing, Murphy attacked the governor as " 'indifferent' " to Detroit's relief needs, whereupon Brucker, in the midst of a tough reelection campaign in which his relief policy was under fire, came rushing to Detroit to defend his position before the Common Council. "It is the old Army game of something for nothing," he said of subsection (b) and (c) loans, "an attempt to lift a present from a Christmas tree." When Murphy, who to Brucker's surprise was present at the session, protested that the governor simply did not understand Detroit's relief needs and the limitations on its borrowing power, Brucker replied that he would not be "stampeded by any political grand standing." Philosophically opposed to public relief, Brucker was always suspicious of the motives of men like Murphy who insisted that the unemployed were entitled to public assistance. For Brucker, this was all politics, the "use [of] tax money for political bribery," the modern version of "bread and circuses."[63]

Pressured by Murphy, the Common Council, and the MUC and perhaps persuaded by the fact that $30 million of the first $35 million loaned for relief by the RFC had been granted under subsections (b) and (c), Brucker, in the end, requested funds for Detroit for the remainder of the calendar year under the sections Detroit preferred. He did so, however, only on the condition that the city pledge as security all money that it would receive from the state for street-widening purposes or as Detroit's share of the state's weight tax. In switching to subsections (b) and (c), Brucker thus did not depart from his views concerning local responsibility for relief, and he imposed a requirement on Detroit that no other state government had imposed on its local subdivisions.[64]

Like Murphy, the RFC was "unfavorably impressed" with Michigan's performance regarding relief, and when the corporation granted the state a loan for the period October–December, 1932, it advised Lansing that it would have to provide greater assistance to the distressed with its own funds if it were to receive additional federal aid. This was the message that the RFC, Murphy, and William Norton conveyed to Governor-elect Comstock in December, and he responded by telling the legislature early in January that it was its "plain duty" to cooperate with the federal government and the cities of the state in providing relief even to the extent of a "direct appropriation, if necessary." The RFC now loaned the state funds for January and February, and Murphy looked forward to a new era in state-city relations.[65]

Deeds, however, did not follow words in Lansing. An RFC field representative thought that the state could immediately appropriate $5-6 million for relief and could raise additional funds by an increase in the gas tax, but Comstock, a Grover Cleveland style Democrat who complained that federal relief was ruining the "morale" of those who received aid, insisted that nothing could be done until the new fiscal year began on July 1. Dissatisfied with the governor's explanations, the RFC advised him that Michigan would not receive any relief loans after March 31 unless the state government itself first appropriated funds for welfare purposes.

Indignant that Detroit had been unable to "pry some funds" out of Lansing and aware now that Comstock's views on relief were really not too different from Brucker's, Murphy publicly criticized the governor. Recalling Brucker's charges that the mayor's relief efforts were politically motivated, Murphy stated, "We have worked under two state administrations. Let the public now decide whether we are motivated by politics or by considerations of the welfare of our community." He announced that a delegation of welfare and city officials from throughout Michigan would visit Lansing on March 28 to "get action from the State." This information nettled Comstock, and in what one prominent Wayne County Democrat regarded as "a dirty 'rap'" at Murphy, the governor angrily declared, "If Mayor Murphy wants to run the State, perhaps I'd better resign. Now Frank Murphy is a good friend of mine, but in all kindness, I can advise him to keep his nose out of State affairs." Murphy was not to be deterred, however. The governor, the mayor responded, thinks that "my schnozzle is too long. Well, I intend to push my schnozzle into any affairs that have to do with obtaining relief for our destitute families," and Murphy indicated that he would go to Lansing, if necessary, even if Comstock did think of him as "a Cyrano de Bergerac." The split between the Comstock and Murphy wings of the Democratic party that had such a profound effect on Democratic politics in Michigan during the New Deal era was nakedly exposed in the struggle over relief at the outset of the Comstock administration.[66]

The "organized pressure" exerted in Lansing on March 28 by an "excited gathering" of city officials and township relief administrators induced a reluctant Comstock to back Detroit-sponsored legislation authorizing the diversion of a portion of the weight-tax money for relief purposes. The RFC released additional funds for Michigan only after it had obtained written support for this legislation from nearly all the members of the two finance committees of the state legislature and had "exacted" a pledge from the governor to include $12 million for relief in the next state budget, which met another demand of the local officials who had gathered in Lansing.[67] It is no wonder that, after an experience of this sort, mayors like Murphy increasingly looked to Washington rather than their state capitals for help in meeting municipal problems.

The availability of federal loans for relief did not mean that Detroit was able to provide adequate clothing, shelter, and food to its welfare clients. Four thousand children did not attend school in October because they lacked proper clothing, a condition that led to "disturbances" at several welfare clothing stations as parents demanded apparel for their children. The welfare department was able to resume rent payments for its clients in August because of the imminent RFC aid, but it reduced the amount of the monthly rent checks by 50 percent in most instances. Detroit, on the other hand, was altogether unusual among American cities in its assumption that rent was a legitimate item to include in the welfare allowance.[68]

During the period of RFC aid Detroit continued to allow its welfare clients only about fourteen to sixteen cents per day for food, "a pittance," Murphy remarked, "that is not likely to cultivate a beggaring class many are worrying about." To one of his constitutents who was "worrying about" allegedly unworthy recipients of public relief, Murphy wrote that Detroit's welfare problem was not to be measured by the number who were receiving relief but by "the many more who are neglected and receive nothing. Our limitations do not permit us to do the job . . . as it should be done."

A few days before he wrote the above words, Murphy lunched at a downtown hotel with a large group of Detroit's industrial and financial leaders who had been brought together by the Hutchinson committee—"There was hardly a figure of distinction missing"—to consider the city's troubled financial condition. The discussion turned to a highly critical report on the DPW prepared for the group by a task force of prominent businessmen, most of whom had only the dimmest understanding of welfare work and the city's welfare problems. When some of those present used the report as the basis for an attack on the alleged extravagance of the mayor's welfare program, Murphy lost his temper. As he recalled the event a few years later, he angrily said to the group, "How dare you spend more money for each luncheon in this room than I need to feed a hungry child for a week! . . . The cold fact of the matter is that I'm saving the city of Detroit for you people!" Two or three of the businessmen present rose to defend Murphy, and the effort to have the report officially adopted came to naught. Because he believed it important for the city and for himself to retain the support of the group whom Hutchinson had assembled, Murphy quickly regretted the "one or two intemperate things" that he had said. Attempting to explain his behavior to Hutchinson, Murphy observed, "while I am able to make plain the progress in matters of honesty in government, efficiency and in whatever you can show clearly in ink, it is almost impossible to make myself understood about the intangibles and the social aspect of government."[69] What the mayor said, unfortunately, was only too true.

If some were concerned that Detroit's welfare policy was still too generous, others, aware that Detroit was spending one-fourth to one-third less per family than New York, Chicago, Boston, and Milwaukee, were worried that relief was "too limited to cover the actual needs of those receiving help." In December, 1932, the city's health department initiated a study of 371 adults and children on the welfare rolls whom it had examined at the end of the previous year when the welfare food allowance had been about 25 percent greater. On the basis of these tests, which revealed a slight improvement in the health of welfare clients since the earlier survey, the commissioner of health concluded that the average person could maintain a "narrow margin of health" on the welfare food allowance if he used good judgment in the selection of foods for his diet. Among the groups tested, school-age children were in the best health, which was attributed to the supplementary food they received through the school-lunch program. On the other hand, only 64 percent of the preschool age children (as compared to 79 percent of the school children) were deemed to be in good health. This was among the symptoms of distress that Irene Murphy feared were "just the beginning of a pathology which . . . may arise in a large city and thereby threaten the very security, safety, and health of all who reside there."[70]

Murphy replaced three of the four members of the Public Welfare

Commission between November 11, 1932, and the end of his term as mayor, and he at last had a commission that largely shared his view of the welfare problem. In a move perhaps designed to blunt some of the mindless business criticism of the department's efficiency, Clarence E. Weiss, the employment manager of the Packard Motor Car Company, who had been working part-time for the DPW and had been a member of the business task force that had found so much fault with the department, was brought into the DPW on a full-time basis to assume most of Ballenger's purely administrative responsibilities. Weiss was responsible for the introduction of new personnel standards in the department and also for a zoning system that permitted the department to provide service to its families with a minimum of staff and equipment. Actually, the reforms introduced by Weiss were of a minor sort, but they gave the DPW, at long last, "the glamor of efficiency usually halo-ing only Big Business." Weiss's appointment and his service in the DPW were, more than anything else, a triumph in "public relations."[71]

Shortly after the beginning of the 1932–33 fiscal year the DPW reintroduced the work-requirement program that it had utilized at the outset of Murphy's mayoralty. Once again, able-bodied welfare recipients were assigned on a part-time basis to perform city work without receiving wages for their labor. Some of the men, instead of being asked to work for the city, were assigned, incredibly, to perform specific jobs in their own homes, such as repairing a fence or the roof. Welfare recipients bitterly resented the forced-labor character of the program, and many simply refused to perform the tasks assigned to them—of almost twelve thousand men assigned to various jobs as of the end of the calendar year 1932, about five thousand had refused to work. The welfare commission announced in November that it would prosecute "dole strikers" for nonsupport of their families, and in at least one instance the commission actually did so. This, however, had a negative effect on the willingness of welfare clients to work, and Ballenger conceded at the end of the year that the program had been a failure.[72]

The failure of the work-requirement plan and the availability of RFC money led the welfare department in January, 1933, to reinstitute the wage-work plan. In an effort to encourage labor efficiency and as "a measure of discipline" the welfare commission set the hourly rate for the worker who performed satisfactorily at thirty cents and the rate for "dilatory people" at twenty-five

Campaigning for mayor of Detroit, September, 1930.

Mayor Murphy and Senator Couzens, 1930. (Photo by the Detroit *News*)

Murphy at a meeting of the Mayor's Unemployment Committee, 1931.
Left of the pillar, G. Hall Roosevelt.

Mayor Murphy confronts Common Council, 1931.

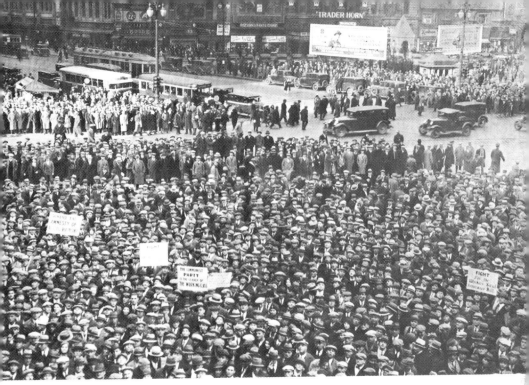

Demonstration in front of Detroit City Hall, February, 1931.

Murphy meets with the Emergency Relief Committee, 1931.
Fourth from the left, William J. Norton.

Murphy and Father Coug[...]
June, 1931.
(Photo by the Detroit Ne[...]

*Front seat, Mayor Murphy[...]
back seat, left to right,* Pre[...]
dent Hoover and Govern[...]
Brucker, at the American
Legion Convention, Detro[...]
September, 1931.

Murphy, Governor Frankl[...]
D. Roosevelt, and G. Hall
Roosevelt, Hyde Park,
June, 1931.

Mayor for a second term, January 12, 1932. Richard W. Reading administers the oath. (Photo by the Detroit *News*)

Mayor Murphy at the Fisher Lodge, December, 1931. (Photo by the Detroit *News*)

Murphy and Henry Ford.

Addressing the Conference of United States Mayors, June 1, 1932.
Second from the left, Mayor James J. Walker; *third from the left,* Mayor
James M. Curley. (Photo by the Detroit *News)*

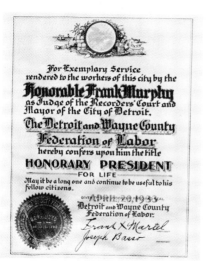

Honorary president of the
Detroit Federation of
Labor, 1933.

At the 1932 Democratic
National Convention.

Murphy takes oath as governor-general of the Philippines, May 10, 1933. *Extreme left,* Frank Couzens. (Photo by the Detroit *News*)

With Governor Comstock, May, 1933.

cents. Initiating a controversy that foreshadowed the conflict in the New Deal era concerning the wage rates of relief labor, the MUC and the DFL protested the rates set by the welfare commission as "contributing to the destruction of wage standards" in private employment and urged that wage-workers performing common labor be paid the prevailing hourly wage rate of fifty to fifty-five cents. The DFL also complained that wage-workers were replacing city employees and thus causing unemployment.

The DFL carried its protest to the mayor, who stated that wage-workers would not be permitted to replace city employees and that the city government would not take any action that impaired existing labor standards. "My Government has gone too far in the other direction," the mayor declared, "to now permit itself to be used as an instrument to destroy [the] standards of any group of workers." It is not clear whether Murphy's support for the DFL went beyond rhetoric, and it may be that Ballenger convinced the mayor that wage-workers were, in effect, earning the standard rate when the free fuel, clothing, and medical attention that they received were taken into account. The wage-work program, in any event, continued for the remainder of Murphy's mayoralty; when Murphy left Detroit about fourteen thousand heads of families were employed as wage-workers.[73]

III

On February 10, 1933, Henry Hart, executive vice-president of the First Detroit Company, went to New York to "iron out certain minor differences" with New York bankers concerning the disposition of the $20 million in tax-anticipation bonds that had been authorized by the Michigan legislature. Hart was having breakfast in a New York restaurant on February 14 when he read in a front-page story in the New York *Times* that all the banks in Michigan had just been closed by order of Governor Comstock. Hart rushed from the restaurant, hoping to find someone who would cash his check on the First National Bank of Detroit so that he could purchase a ticket to return to Detroit.[74] The city of Detroit, which probably had the highest rate of unemployment of any large city in the United States, now had to contend with a bank holiday as well.

"In no other large city," Jesse H. Jones recalled, "was the drama of the banking crisis so prolonged or so tense as in Detroit." In the end, the Detroit bank crisis "proved to be the time bomb that temporarily toppled the whole American banking structure."

Detroit's two major banking groups, the Guardian Detroit Union Group, whose principal bank was the Guardian National Bank of Commerce, and the Detroit Bankers Group, whose kingpin was the First National, the city's largest bank, were both in a dangerously illiquid condition by the beginning of 1933, and both were careening toward default and dissolution. The immediate crisis was precipitated by the request of the Guardian group for an RFC loan of $65 million, later reduced to $50 million, that was in part designed to shore up the collapsing Union Guardian Trust Company, the most vulnerable bank of the Guardian empire. The Guardian group, however, did not possess enough sound collateral to cover the proposed loan, and efforts by the RFC and the Hoover administration to make up the deficiency by persuading the great motor companies and Senator Couzens to contribute new money to the group while simultaneously subordinating their existing deposits came to naught. Since the Union Guardian was in no condition to survive further withdrawals and since its closing was almost certain to topple the First National, federal officials and local and outside banking interests decided that there was no alternative to the temporary closing of the state's banks. Governor Comstock was summoned to Detroit, the parlous situation was explained to him, and in the early hours of the morning of February 14 he proclaimed an eight-day "banking holiday" for the state, a holiday, later extended, that eventually merged with the national banking holiday proclaimed by President Franklin D. Roosevelt on March 5.[75]

News of the banking holiday came "like 'a bolt out of the blue'" to Murphy, who had not been consulted about the decision. Murphy said that he had known that the great Detroit banks were in trouble and that he had done "all I could to iron them out," although he did not specify what his precise role had been. He had "refused," he asserted, "to make any commitments unless all the cards were on the table," and he thought that "the bankers' refusal to put their cards on the table"—an investigation by the Senate Banking and Currency Committee soon revealed what those "cards" were—was the basic "cause" of the trouble. The Chicago *Tribune*, ignoring the depression, the deflation, and the bucaneering practices of some of the Detroit banks, had a different explanation of the Michigan banking holiday and its spread to the nation as a whole: it was "the program of crazy financiering" that Murphy had inaugurated "in the vain effort to support the idle" that was the catalytic agent in the crisis.[76]

Just as we know relatively little about Murphy's role in the events preceding the Michigan banking holiday, so there is scant documentation on the part he played in the decision of the federal government to replace the Guardian National Bank of Commerce and the First National Bank with the new National Bank of Detroit. It appears that James K. Watkins, Murphy's police commissioner and the principal spokesman for the two old banks, asked the mayor to intercede with President Roosevelt to save the two banks and that Murphy refused to do so. The chief antagonist of the old banks was Murphy's good friend Father Charles E. Coughlin, and it is evident that Coughlin consulted with the mayor about the city's banking problems. Murphy's sympathies were with the radio priest, so much so that Coughlin erroneously concluded that the mayor would dismiss Watkins because of his role in the crisis. It also seems that Murphy vainly attempted to persuade Coughlin to moderate his public attacks on Detroit banks and bankers.[77]

Murphy must have derived some secret satisfaction from the fate of the Detroit bankers, who had so often lectured him on the basic principles of money and banking. On March 14, in a somewhat petulant gesture, he fired former banker Walter G. Toepel, the president of the House of Correction Commission, after Toepel had refused to resign. " 'I propose to have no bankers in my administration,' " Toepel reported Murphy as saying. " 'The banking business used to be an honorable profession, but it has now become the curse of the country. I do not propose to allow bankers to sink my ship.' " There were five other bankers serving on various city commissions, but Murphy, having made his point, did not carry out his threat.[78]

The proclamation of the banking holiday stunned the unsuspecting people of Detroit. Seeking to reassure his constituents, Murphy urged the populace to be "calm" and pledged that the city government would do all that it could to care for the needs of the community. "The Government is going to keep its head," the mayor stated, "and we are sure that the people will, also." Depositors were allowed to withdraw 5 percent of their deposits on February 16, and an additional 5 percent was released on March 13 to depositors who could demonstrate that the funds were needed for specific purposes, but the money famine did not really come to an end in Detroit until April 24, when the First National Bank and the National Bank of Commerce began to pay out 30 percent of the unencumbered deposits of their 800,000 depositors.[79]

The group in Detroit least affected by the banking holiday

was the Unemployed Citizens' League of Michigan (UCL), which had been launched in August, 1932, to implement the principles of "mutual cooperation and self support." The Detroit equivalent of similar self-help organizations spawned by the depression in other states, particularly Washington and California, the UCL operated on the barter principle, exchanging the labor of its members for food, clothing, and shelter. Having already separated themselves from the money economy, the approximately four thousand members of the League were able to view the banking holiday with a certain amount of detachment, and the organization's self-help approach began to attract a good deal of attention. In March the Detroit Council of Churches, the social-service agencies, the welfare commission, the MUC, and the mayor lent their support to the formation of the Michigan Labor and Commodity Exchange, an association designed to facilitate barter arrangements on a city-wide basis, and the executive secretary of the UCL was selected to serve as chairman of the new group's planning committee. The Exchange died aborning, however. Soon the UCL itself became wracked with dissension, and its membership dwindled.[80]

The lack of cash created a major crisis for most Detroiters and added significantly to the economic woes of the city. "Where is my money—and who is going to keep my family?," one Detroiter inquired of Murphy, and another, whose last $500 were in the First National Bank, informed the mayor that her family no longer had "any way of living and we would be ashamed to ask for welfare." The index of industrial employment in the Detroit metropolitan area, which stood at 49.2 in February, 1933 (1923-25 = 100), as compared to 68.6 in February, 1932, and 135 in February, 1929, fell to 41.8 in March, when unemployment in the city may have exceeded 350,000. "Out here," the secretary of the Detroit Urban League wrote as the cash famine continued, "conditions are terrible."[81]

Some Detroiters, having no other alternative, followed the example of the UCL by turning to barter arrangements. Professional people thus began trading their services for needed commodities—a dentist, for example, might agree to extract a grocer's tooth in exchange for a stipulated amount of food—and one shoe store traded shoes for commodities of equal value. Some "more or less well-to-do citizens," embarrassed by their lack of cash, sought aid, unsuccessfully, at the district offices of the DPW. Most people simply sought to purchase food and sundries on credit, and the mayor threatened "official action" against dealers who allowed their customers to suffer by insisting on cash. When reports reached Murphy of food profiteering, he let it be known that he was contemplating the appointment of a "food dictator." Invoking the specter of red revolution, he warned that the Communists were trying to create "serious disorder," but he stated that he would not tolerate "food mobs" even if the municipal government had to take "complete control of everything in the city." Leading merchants promised the mayor their cooperation, and most of them apparently extended credit to their customers and did not engage in profiteering.

The big auto firms solved the cash problem for their employees by trucking currency into Detroit from outside the city. Agents for some smaller firms went to Chicago and New York with empty suitcases that were then stuffed with greenbacks for the return trip. The twenty-six thousand city employees were less fortunate and were among the chief victims of the Detroit banking holiday. They received their February 15 checks as usual, and the city was able to cash many of these checks on a first-come first-served basis with the 5 percent that it was able to withdraw from Detroit banks and $350,000 in cash on deposit in New York that it now transferred to Detroit. The city government, however, passed its March 1 payday, and city employees received no further remuneration for their services until April 25.[82]

Hundreds of city employees in the Department of Public Works alone were reported in "extreme need" by early March, and at least two of them collapsed because of lack of food. The MUC began supplying food baskets to needy city employees, but the committee's funds were limited; and so beginning on March 8 the DPW issued food and fuel orders, on a loan basis, to city workers who requested assistance. On March 19, by which time the DPW had issued 10,500 orders to 6,500 employees, a newly organized City Employees' Relief Committee, established to remove the taint of being welfare clients from city employees, assumed the responsibility of looking after needy municipal workers. The food allowances that the committee provided as an advance against salary were 20 percent greater than the welfare food allowance and were obtained by the employees from local merchants on the credit of the city. The city government had provided its employees with about $600,000 worth of relief by the time it resumed salary payments.[83]

Some city departments were especially hard hit by the bank holiday. The DSR suffered a 25.6 percent drop in revenue in

February, and for a time it seemed that it would have to default on its obligations. The Department of Health depended on county funds to operate the William H. Maybury Sanitarium and the Herman Kiefer Hospital, and with Wayne County unable to transfer any money to the city, Commissioner Henry F. Vaughan threatened to "close up shop" and send home two thousand patients with communicable diseases. Murphy wired Comstock for assistance, and the governor responded with alacrity.[84]

The private welfare agencies in Detroit were devastated by the effects of the bank holiday. The Community Fund was able to withdraw only $20,000 of the $544,000 it had in the bank, and the quarterly pledge payments that it normally would have received on March 1 were imperiled. As soon as it began to appear that the banking holiday would continue for some time, the Community Fund and the Council of Social Agencies gave "dictatorial power" to a newly created Emergency Committee to adjust, combine, or discontinue the eighty agencies that the Fund helped to support. The committee gave preference to agencies looking after dependent children and helpless sick and aged persons, discontinued agencies whose main source of revenue was not the Community Fund, "skeletonized" others, and placed still others "in suspense." Emergency aid from the RFC for March and April and the handsome response of its donors to an appeal that they pay their unpaid pledges improved the financial condition of the Fund. It was also able to work out an arrangement with the welfare commission whereby the city assumed the cost of 543 family relief cases that previously had been the responsibility of Fund agencies, and in return the Fund agencies provided the casework for these families and for a thousand additional city welfare families requiring individualized treatment. As the result of these developments, it appeared by early April that about 60 percent of the private social work in Detroit could be continued for the remainder of the year.[85]

When Governor Comstock proclaimed the bank holiday, the DPW was caring for 42,800 families and 7,300 single men and women, a total of 208,460 persons. No immediate crisis confronted the department since it had clothes and fuel on hand for its clients and its grocery orders were not immediately redeemable in cash. Also, the RFC on February 23 released $400,000 to the DPW, the final installment of the government loan for January and February, which, ironically in view of the record, temporarily placed the welfare department in a more favorable cash position than other city agencies. The department, however, had about

$2.5 million in RFC money on deposit in the Union Guardian Trust, and as its cash dwindled and the number of applicants for relief increased, the inability of the DPW to secure the release of its deposit caused a good deal of apprehension among welfare officials. By March 26 the welfare case load had risen to 48,360, the DPW had accumulated $1.3 million in debts, and there were allegations that thousands of Detroiters were "suffering from lack of food." New RFC money, however, was released to Detroit on March 10 after Governor Comstock gave Washington the necessary assurances about state aid, and this ended the last of the many welfare crises of the Murphy mayoralty.[86]

Detroit's fiscal stability and its budgetary planning for 1933–34 were dealt a paralyzing blow by the bank holiday. The city government, which had sacrificed so much to avoid default, was unable to make the interest payments on the municipal debt on February 15, the day after Comstock closed Detroit's banks, and the prolonged bank holiday and its deleterious impact on city finances caused Detroit to default on its public debt for the remainder of Murphy's term in office. The holiday also ended the Hutchinson committee's efforts to sell the $20 million in tax-anticipation bonds that were to have provided the city government with enough cash to carry it through to the end of the fiscal year. The only advice that the committee had to offer the city government to avoid the huge deficit that impended was to limit government activity to the "absolutely essential services necessary for the protection of life and property and the education of children."[87] Murphy now faced the necessity of providing Detroit with a circulating medium that would end "the complete paralysis of trade" and permit the city government to resume salary payments to city employees and also of making some arrangement to reduce the city's debt obligations for 1933–34 so that Detroit could provide its people with adequate services while keeping taxes at a reasonable level.

Scrip was the obvious solution to the cash famine in Detroit. The Detroit Clearing House Association developed a plan to issue a clearing-house scrip only to abandon the scheme as too complicated. A committee of business and civic leaders weighed the possibility of issuing private scrip, but major concerns like the J. L. Hudson Company that spent only a portion of their income within the city were unwilling to commit themselves to absorb substantial amounts of a currency that would have only local value. This left municipal scrip as "the last rabbit in the bag," and Murphy appointed a Mayor's Scrip Committee, headed by Frank N. Isbey, the president of the Detroit Union Produce Terminal, to work out the details.

The Isbey plan, announced on March 10, called on employers to purchase scrip equivalent to 10 percent of their payroll, which they could then use to meet the equivalent portion of their wages bill, the remainder to be paid in cash. The scrip would be acceptable for taxes and rent, and taxpayers were urged to buy their share of the new currency. It was assumed that the city government, like private employers, would pay 10 percent of the wages of city employees in scrip and the remainder in cash, using the proceeds from the sale of the scrip for the cash portion of the wages. The hope was that the general use of the scrip for which the plan provided would discourage the discounting of the municipal currency.[88]

The Common Council authorized the issuance of $5 million in scrip—it eventually authorized $18 million, which Wilcox ruled was the legally permissible limit—and made it redeemable in six months at 5 percent interest; but the permission of the state legislature was also required, and this was not forthcoming until April 6. The scrip committee now ran into considerable difficulty in its efforts to sell the new currency despite the mayor's plea for acceptance of the Isbey plan. Major industrialists, miffed because they had not been consulted before the plan was unveiled and apparently persuaded by leading bankers that the city should first have eliminated "unessential services," declined to cooperate unless a strict limit was placed on the amount of scrip issued, even if this would make it difficult for the city government to pay its employees in full. By April 26 the committee had collected only $130,000 in cash, which was below the sum needed for even a single city payday. As a result, the original Isbey plan had to be abandoned, and city employees began receiving their back pay on April 25 entirely in scrip. They continued to be paid in scrip as long as Murphy was mayor.[89]

To enhance the acceptability of the scrip, the Common Council provided early in May that all scrip not used for taxes would be redeemed ahead of schedule on August 16, the day after fall tax payments were due. By that time the larger firms and the privately owned utilities were refusing to accept scrip, and the currency was circulating at a small discount. The city government issued an additional $23.9 million in scrip during the fiscal year 1933–34, but by the beginning of July, 1937, all but $5,000 of the municipal currency had been redeemed.[90]

The problem of debt charges in the Detroit budget for 1933–34, it will be recalled, had concerned Murphy well before the bank holiday and had prompted him to call the nation's mayors together for a second time. The bank holiday and the technical default on the Detroit debt that it occasioned understandably increased Murphy's anxiety about Detroit's ability to continue meeting her debt charges. The result was that at the mayors' conference, on the train back to Detroit from Washington, and in conferences with Detroit business leaders and city officials after the conference, Murphy began to give consideration to a more drastic solution for Detroit's debt problem than the conference-endorsed RFC purchase of Detroit credit instruments—a moratorium for a period of years on the city's debt payments.

By the end of February Murphy had become committed to the moratorium approach to the problems of Detroit and the more than six hundred cities then in default on their public debt. Detroit, the mayor stated, could not pay her debt charges in 1933–34 and also provide adequate public services. If the banks could declare a holiday when they ran into trouble, why should the cities not do the same if this were required to avoid "chaos or sky-high taxes"? Again and again in the next few weeks Murphy, quite accurately, portrayed the municipal-debt issue as involving a naked conflict between the needs of the people and the interests of city creditors, and he insisted that in such circumstances the public interest must be "supreme." "The City," the mayor emphatically declared, "cannot be permitted to dissolve."[91]

In the closing days of the Seventy-second Congress and during the early months of the Seventy-third Congress, Congress was asked to consider two quite different methods of dealing with the urban debt problem, one embodied in the McLeod bill, the other taking the form of first the Fletcher and then the Wilcox bill. The McLeod bill, energetically sponsored by Murphy, was originally limited to cities with a population of fifty thousand or more and with a bonded indebtedness of at least $1 million. If such a city were in default, the bill authorized it to petition for relief in a federal district court, which could halt payment of both the interest on the city's debt and the principal and set a date for a hearing on the petition for a final decree, at which the creditors could present their side of the case. In its final decree, the court could order the postponement of all debt payments for up to two years, and it could extend this moratorium for additional two-year periods up to a maximum of ten years. At any time during the moratorium period the court, on the petition of the creditors, could order the city to set aside for debt service any revenue not required for "the reasonably necessary and economical operating expenses" of the city and for welfare purposes. [92]

The Fletcher and Wilcox bills authorized federal district courts to impose a plan of debt adjustment on a municipality only after receiving a petition stating that creditors of the taxing district holding more than 50 percent of its debt had agreed to the plan for the adjustment and composition of their claims; the plan could not go into effect unless subsequently confirmed by creditors holding 75 percent of the debt. This procedure prevented a small minority of bondholders from thwarting the will of the majority, but, unlike the McLeod bill, it did not permit a city to gain relief from its indebtedness until the holders of 75 percent of its debt agreed to a plan of adjustment. This meant delay while numerous bondholders scattered across the globe were consulted, and a delay of this sort might mean default. As Murphy saw it, the Fletcher-Wilcox approach placed the interests of the bondholders ahead of the interests of the city and, under certain circumstances, would effectively turn the reins of city government over to the bondholders. For him, it was the old issue of banker control all over again, and Murphy did not look kindly upon a mechanism that might "interfere with duly elected officials in carrying out the essential functions" of city government. "We'll not stand for it in Detroit," he belligerently stated. "I would resort to physical resistance, if necessary to prevent it." The federal government, he asserted in the Populist rhetoric that came rather easily to him during this last great struggle of his mayoralty, "has a choice . . . between the people and Wall Street." [93]

Although the Murphy stand-still plan did not involve any scaling down of municipal debts and although there was some banker and insurance-company support for the forced refunding of the debts of individual cities like Detroit, the idea of a "general moratorium" was anathema to "the financial forces of the country." A Prudential Life Insurance Company executive thus privately informed Henry Hart that the big insurance companies would "rather lose every penny invested in Detroit" than consent to the "radical legislation" Murphy was proposing. As important investors in municipal bonds, fraternal organizations and labor unions also threw their weight against the McLeod bill, and opponents of the idea were further reinforced by those who feared that the enactment of a stand-still measure would make it impossible even for solvent communities to find a market for their bonds. The lobby against the Murphy plan was powerful indeed, so powerful, the mayor declared, that it "reached right into Detroit."[94]

Murphy hoped to secure the enactment of the McLeod bill before Congress adjourned on March 3. When the House Committee on the Judiciary assembled on March 1, its members had not even seen the recently introduced McLeod bill; but Murphy, in two appearances before the committee, was persuasive in arguing the case for the moratorium, and after considering the bill for less than three hours, the committee reported it favorably to the House. Speaker Garner, however, let it be known that he would not bring up any new bills in the House in the final days of the session unless they had previously received Senate approval.

Although prospects for the McLeod measure in the Senate did not look bright because of the lateness of the hour, Murphy made a very impressive argument for the bill before the Senate Committee on the Judiciary on March 2. What he was proposing, the mayor declared, was not "repudiation" but "an orderly process by which we may be given the opportunity to reorganize." He described all that Detroit had done in response to the depression but noted that "after three years of struggle," the people had "reached bottom in every way." Since the United States government, he asserted, had always offered private business the opportunity to "reorganize," he did not think that it would now say that preserving the well-being of the people of the cities was less important than preserving banks, railroads, and other businesses.

A majority of the Senate committee favored the McLeod bill, but it required unanimous consent for the measure to be brought up in the Senate, and this could not be obtained. Although the bill, therefore, had to be abandoned, the Detroit *News* thought that Murphy had performed "a remarkable legislative feat" in gaining so much favorable attention for his moratorium proposal in so short a time, testimony, probably, to the crisis atmosphere that had come to grip the nation's capital.[95]

The McLeod bill was reintroduced soon after Congress reassembled on March 9, 1933, and Murphy, by his "untiring and well nigh ceaseless efforts," helped to keep the measure before the legislators for several weeks. He appealed for support to the Michigan congressional delegation, the nation's mayors, Hearst, and, above all, the Roosevelt administration; and he tried, in vain, to win over the big banks and the Organization of Life Insurance Executives for a program that, he contended, would "take the place of the present drifting and the chaotic conditions attending default everywhere." To broaden the bill's appeal, the Murphy forces consented toward the end of March to reduce the maximum time that the moratorium could be in effect from ten to four years and to have the legislation apply to cities with as few as five thousand inhabitants.[96]

Murphy appeared before the House Judiciary Committee once again on April 4 and largely repeated the testimony that he had given the Senate on March 2. The business interests of Detroit, viewing the moratorium as "the logical solution" for the city's problems, made evident to the committee both their support of Murphy's proposal and the gravity of the situation in Detroit, and Congressman John Lesinski of Detroit warned, "you must help and help quickly or you will have revolution in Detroit. I know that the city of Detroit is standing on gunpowder, and all you need to do is to strike a match and light it and up it will go."[97]

Despite repeated attempts, Murphy was unable to secure President Roosevelt's endorsement of the McLeod bill even though the president expressed sympathy for the general purposes of the measure and promised the Murphy forces "all the help possible." In the end, Attorney General Homer Cummings, in what became a characteristic of legislative draftsmanship in the Roosevelt administration, began to work on a bill that combined the moratorium idea with some of the creditor proposals incorporated in the Wilcox bill.

The McLeod bill was all but dead by early May when the coup de grace was delivered, to Murphy's surprise and chagrin, by spokesmen for the United States Conference of Mayors. Murphy, who had just resigned his presidency of the Conference because of his appointment as governor-general of the Philippines, made it clear from the start that he was not speaking for the mayors in pushing the moratorium plan; but now, Mayor Curley, appearing before the House Judiciary Committee to argue for federal loans to the cities and annoyed that Murphy was ignoring this issue in his quest for a moratorium, stated that the executive committee of the Conference believed that the moratorium measure would "destroy the credit of all cities and would not help Detroit." Murphy continued to press for appropriate municipal debt legislation until the end of his stay in Detroit, but the Municipal Debt

Readjustment Act, which was designed to provide some relief for debt-burdened cities, was not approved until May, 1934.[98]

There remained two other means of dealing with Detroit's debt problem, action by the state government and the negotiation of a refunding agreement by the city and its creditors. The idea of some sort of state receivership for Detroit was favored by certain business circles in the city as "a second line of defense" and as a means "to save the situation when and if the lid blows off." The measure being considered by proponents of a state receivership permitted the governor, on the application of ten taxpayers and three bondholders of a city in default, to appoint a three-man commission to run the city government. Murphy, who had almost certainly been inaccurately informed that the receivership idea had originated with "the cold-blooded New York representative of [the] bondholders," charged that the plan would "place the whip in the hands of the New York financial interests" and left no doubt that the scheme was totally unacceptable to him. "Powerful interests" were reported to be pushing the bill, but their efforts were unavailing.[99]

After a Council-sponsored amendment providing for the creation of a Board of Refunding Debt Commissioners to prepare plans to refund all or part of the city's debt had been defeated by the voters on April 3, Murphy, who was probably beginning to doubt that the McLeod bill would be passed, appointed a committee to negotiate a "voluntary moratorium" with the city's creditors. The New York syndicate that handled Detroit's debt was prepared to agree to a two-year moratorium on the payment of principal, a substantial reduction in the interest due in 1933–34 and refunding of the remainder, refunding of the troublesome short-term debt into long-term bonds at a lower rate of interest, and refunding of the remainder of the debt into bonds that would mature by 1940. In return for these concessions, the syndicate demanded an $8.5 million reduction in the city's budget, which would have meant a 20 percent salary cut, and cancellation of the city's scrip plan, which would have meant that city employees could not have been paid until June 30.

Unwilling to accept the conditions stipulated by the bankers, Murphy told the bondholders that, although he had always insisted that the city must meet its financial obligations, he also had to insist that the "people be provided a government first." The bondholders quickly withdrew most of the conditions to which Murphy had objected, and a tentative agreement was reached by the two parties on April 18. The plan, however, had to be abandoned ten days later when it turned out that the proposed schedule of bond maturities would produce a debt charge two years after the moratorium ended not of $23 million, as had originally been thought, but of more than $33 million, which meant that the city, in a short time, would be facing the same kind of debt problem as was then causing it so much trouble. There was also a question as to whether an agreement involving creditors who held only about one-third of the city's debt could bind the other creditors and prevent them from going into court to secure writs directing the city to levy taxes so that the debt to them could be paid.[100] It is no wonder that Murphy, from the start, found the plan for a voluntary moratorium much less desirable than a moratorium provided by act of Congress.

In June, 1933, Murphy's successor, following the principles worked out by Murphy's refunding committee, concluded an elaborate agreement that provided for the refunding of almost the entire Detroit debt and converted tax-supported bonds maturing during the next ten years into "callable sinking fund bonds" that matured in 1962-63. It was "the largest refunding operation that . . . [had] ever been tackled outside the field of national government securities."[101]

Since he had been unable to make any arrangements for the refunding of the city's debt when he submitted his 1933-34 budget to the Council on March 14, Murphy had to include a debt item of $30.7 million in his $68.1 million tax budget, a reduction of more than $4 million as compared to the 1932-33 tax budget. The budget made no provision for tax delinquency lest this add to the tax burden and further discourage tax payments, and it included only a little more than $1.8 million for welfare on the assumption that the federal government would continue to pay most of the city's welfare bills.

The Common Council, complaining about "the rapidly-growing dictatorship of Wall Street over the representative municipal governments of America," eliminated the $18,569,000 included in Murphy's budget for interest on the debt. When an assistant corporation counsel pointed out that this action was illegal under the charter, the aldermen's response was to restore the interest item but to eliminate the $15 million that had been budgeted to pay for maturing bonds, which was also illegal.

The Council chamber, according to the Detroit *News*, had "probably never before been the scene of a more far-reaching or bitter row than the one which preceded the vote on the debt item." Councilmen dared the bondholders to "'try to force the taxpayers to pay,'" Councilman Edward J. Jeffries, Jr., said that he was willing to go to jail if the budget was illegal, and Councilman Lodge struck Councilman Castator. Murphy had no choice but to veto the illegal budget, and the Council then sustained the veto by a divided vote. The desired tax reduction was, however, achieved since the refunding agreement of June, 1933, which temporarily reduced debt charges, cut the budget to $55,655,238 and thus lowered the effective tax rate from $27.43 per $1,000 to $24.09 per $1,000 even though the real-property assessment by that time had been slashed another 12.7 percent. [102]

Grappling to the end with the twin problems of welfare and city finance, Murphy had failed to secure either the compulsory or the voluntary moratorium on debt charges that would have enabled Detroit to provide its inhabitants with adequate services at a reasonable tax rate. He had, however, initiated efforts that resulted eventually in the enactment of municipal debt readjustment legislation at the federal level and the negotiation of a comprehensive refunding plan at the local level. He had enjoyed greater immediate success in dealing with the welfare problem largely because he had been able to secure federal aid when Detroit was no longer able to continue its own impressive effort to cope with unemployment. At the end of his mayoralty, Murphy could legitimately write that "welfare, under fire from a dozen different angles, with every enemy and critic of my administration watching keenly for the vulnerable points of attack, has emerged with credit and honor." Detroit, as William Norton pointed out, had done its part "awkwardly enough but not too awkwardly" to keep "a republic afloat through an economic convulsion." [103]

XIV

"Such Wonderful Things"

I

Although welfare and finance were at the center of his concerns as mayor, police administration, Murphy declared in 1931, was "not the least vexatious and perplexing problem" that he faced. Looking back on his term of office, Murphy concluded that the manner in which a police department operated in a municipality was "something of a key to good government."[1]

As James Q. Wilson has pointed out, "the prevailing police style" in any community "is not explicitly determined by community decisions," and police departments are peculiarly resistant to change. Although the police may not always be "governed" by their political environment, they are, nevertheless, "sensitive" to it, and the "political culture," at the very least, provides "a source of cues and signals" regarding expected police behavior. Since the principal means by which the political culture conveys its expectations to a police department is through the choice of its chief officer, no more important decision regarding the police is made by the political leader of a city than the type of commissioner whom he appoints.[2] Murphy, who, because of his previous experience as a federal attorney and a Recorder's Court judge, brought a considerable knowledge of the police function to his job as mayor, selected a quality person to serve as his police commissioner. He also provided the police force with appropriate "cues and signals" as to what was right and what was wrong police behavior on the beat, in the station house, at radical demonstrations, and in dealing with picket lines.

For approximately the first three months of his mayoralty Murphy retained Thomas C. Wilcox as the city's police commissioner. No stranger to police work, Wilcox had been associated with the Racine, Wisconsin, police department, had served in an investigative capacity for the federal government in the World War I era—he helped to gather the information that enabled

Murphy to secure the conviction of Grant Hugh Browne—and had headed the FBI bureaus in Philadelphia and Detroit. Wilcox cracked down on blind pigs and gambling establishments after replacing Harold Emmons as police commissioner and then intensified his war on vice and crime after Jerry Buckley's murder. This endeared him to the Anti-Saloon League and to vocal advocates of law and order, but he was a man with a rather unsavory reputation who sometimes enforced the law in a lawless manner and was believed to have "made a mess" of the Buckley case. Although it "greatly disappointed" some of the mayor's friends that he retained such a man, Murphy, who was probably impressed with the strong support for Wilcox, let it be known that he would not make a final decision about the police commissionership until the grand jury looking into the Buckley murder had reported.[3]

The grand jury did not complete its work until September, 1931, but Murphy, thoroughly displeased with Wilcox's management of the police department, decided in January to replace the commissioner with a far different sort of person, the former Rhodes scholar James K. Watkins. In appointing a well-educated "civilian" rather than a professional to run the department, Murphy explained that because police officers had to be carefully selected and carefully trained, the head of the department should be someone with "the highest educational qualifications." The mayor also stated that because of the "mental unrest" that the depression had created, the position required a man familiar with the American tradition of civil liberties. Watkins actually knew nothing about police work, but, as the *Journal of the American Judicature Society* indicated, he brought "character, courage, and good judgment" to his task. After a long interview with the new commissioner, Caroline Parker, the executive secretary of the Detroit branch of the American Civil Liberties Union (ACLU), reported to Roger Baldwin, the director of the ACLU, that Watkins was not "a cunning sleuth" but an "intelligent" man and "a man of integrity," and she consequently looked forward to "a better conduct of police affairs."[4]

Murphy let it be known from the start of his administration that City Hall would not interfere with the operation of the police department and that police promotions would be on the basis of merit alone. He was true to his word, and when he left office he proudly declared that he had not once ordered or requested a promotion or a transfer in the department. Watkins, in turn, was "always able to do his work knowing that he had the Mayor in back of him."[5]

Although Murphy depoliticized the police department, this did not mean that the mayor's office ignored citizen complaints about police actions or that Murphy did not attempt to influence police behavior. On one occasion, the mayor's assistant secretary became annoyed because the police department always seemed to defend officers against whom complaints had been lodged rather than considering "the point at issue." Making it clear that she wished the department to respond to the substance of the complaints forwarded by the mayor's office, Josephine Gomon reminded the acting police commissioner, "There is possibly no department in the city which touches so vitally the public and so largely involves their attitude toward their government."[6]

Recalling that as a judge he had encountered police officers who were unfit for their responsibilities, Murphy believed that, because of the great power vested in them, police officers must be selected with unusual care and carefully trained. Agreeing with Murphy that too much emphasis had been placed upon brawn and too little on brains and character in the selection of police in the past, Watkins created a personnel committee consisting of a psychiatrist, an educator, an expert in testing, and a person familiar with municipal affairs to assist the department in selecting members of the force.

Although the Detroit department already had a training school emphasizing technical matters, Watkins shared Murphy's view that it was also important to give student officers "a sense of civic responsibility." In April, 1931, the police commissioner appointed a committee of citizens to formulate plans for the establishment of a police college similar to New York City's Police Academy. When the reorganized Detroit Police College began its fall term that year, its curriculum included not only the usual police matters but subjects like civics and government, the historical and political background of police work, American police systems, criminal law, and social problems and agencies. Its faculty now included civilians like Lent Upson, and instruction was provided not only for probationary officers, as before, but also for regular force members. The Detroit branch of the ACLU thought that the curriculum should include instruction in the constitutional rights of citizens, and Watkins "most emphatically" agreed with this idea. Before the end of the Murphy administration an outline prepared by Caroline Parker was being used as the basis for a lecture on constitutional rights, and the head of the college had agreed to make instruction in the subject a regular part of the curriculum.[7]

During Murphy's mayoralty the size of Detroit's police force, like that of most other cities in the depression, declined. The number of policemen on daily duty dropped from 2,780 at the beginning of the Murphy administration to 2,160 by early 1933, but the reassignment of personnel from inside to outside work and the use of automobiles and radios, in which the Detroit department pioneered, enabled the force to meet the bulk of its responsibilities without any decline in effectiveness. Actually, because of improved selection and training of personnel, the undoing of some of the organizational damage inflicted on the department in the Bowles era, the operation of the department on the merit principle, and his own capable leadership, Watkins developed what the *Journal of the American Judicature Society* described as a police force "unequaled in any other large city."[8]

Murphy wanted a police force that not only was carefully selected and trained but that operated within the law, that was, indeed, a "model of justice." He thought that there could be "no more perilous and prolific source of lawlessness in a city than a lawless police department."[9] Murphy's police commissioner was in complete agreement with the mayor, but it was easier for the two men to state a policy than to have it uniformly observed in the day-to-day activities of individual policemen.

A field investigator for the National Commission on Law Observance and Enforcement concluded that the use of the third degree by the Detroit police was "limited" as of 1930, and he discovered no instances of "the more extreme type of cases." What this seemed to mean was that suspects were not compelled to stand while being questioned and no weapons were used by interrogators, but there was some slapping, hitting, and arm-twisting. Murphy saw the third degree as part of "the system" and believed that it would continue until "the system" was altered so that prisoners were questioned in the presence of a magistrate immediately after their arrest and after being informed of their constitutional rights. The police department advised Murphy in September, 1931, that the "unlawful use of force" on prisoners was "practically at an end," but a few weeks later it was revealed that an eighteen-year-old boy had been beaten with a rubber hose by police at the Canfield station, held for three days, and then flogged again in an effort to extract a confession. Watkins took severe disciplinary action against seventeen officers attached to the station and announced that this was "the first move to end this practice."[10]

At this point, Watkins apparently learned for the first time that Caroline Parker of the ACLU and Murphy were attempting to monitor police behavior by having the superintendent of the Receiving Hospital send the mayor reports on patients treated at the hospital because they had received police beatings. The mayor then transmitted these reports to Parker. The practice had been initiated in the spring of 1931, and by the time of the Canfield station affair, Miss Parker had received reports on fourteen cases. She now presented the reports to Watkins, who was understandably "a bit ruffled" that he had been kept in ignorance of the procedure. After discussion among the parties, it was agreed that the hospital reports would henceforth go directly from the mayor's office to Watkins, with a copy to Parker. Only one case was reported in the next five months, possibly because Watkins made it clear to his officers after another young prisoner had been beaten that he simply would not "stand" for "all this rough stuff." As a matter of fact, Watkins improved upon the procedure that Murphy and Parker had devised by ordering that all prisoners who confessed be taken at once to Receiving Hospital for a physical examination. This "independent audit," the *Journal of the American Judicature Society* declared, "goes a very long way to clear up the third-degree problem." The third degree probably continued to be used despite the efforts of Watkins, the mayor, and the ACLU, and the police sometimes used excessive force, including deadly force, in dealing with crime in the streets or with prisoners under their control, but there had been at least some improvement in an area of police work that is difficult for public officials to control.[11]

As a Recorder's Court judge Murphy had been concerned about the overnight or weekend jailing of alleged but uncharged misdemeanants, some of whom, he knew, had been illegally arrested and were being harassed by the police. Because he believed that "what is a matter of right should not be made a matter of favor," he had also been disturbed by the release of such prisoners when a judge or some other influential person interceded in their behalf. Murphy thought that alleged misdemeanants were entitled to immediate bail, whether or not the courts were in session, and when he became mayor he was determined to establish procedures to deal with this problem. One possible means was for the police to establish their own bail-bond bureau as an adjunct to the Recorder's Court. The Murphy administration attempted in 1931 to secure legislative authorization for this procedure, but the bill that it supported failed of enactment in Lansing.

In June, 1932, Watkins and Murphy devised a set of procedures to meet the problem that were satisfactory to all concerned, including the judges of the Recorder's Court. Henceforth, when the courts were not in session, prisoners arrested for a misdemeanor, a gambling offense, a traffic or ordinance violation, or as police witnesses were to be released if the precinct inspector or the night police superintendent was "reasonably sure" that the suspect would appear in court when his case was called. If the commanding officer thought that a statement should be taken from someone arrested for a gambling or a prohibition offense, he was required to hold the prisoner until an assistant prosecutor had been summoned; the release could then be effected at the discretion of the officer or on the recommendation of the assistant prosecutor. Probation violators were to be released only to a probation officer, and disorderly women were to be released at once if the precinct inspector or the night superintendent decided that there was no case against them. Felony suspects were not to be released without the approval of the arresting officer or his superior. The ACLU was delighted with the new procedures. "It is an admirable code," Roger Baldwin asserted. He advised Murphy that the ACLU was sending copies of the rules to its local committees in the hope that other police departments might follow the Detroit example. [12]

After the Detroit branch of the ACLU complained to him about what it regarded as the "Star Chamber" methods employed at police trials, Murphy, asserting that misbehavior by the police was the public's business, ordered that sessions of the Police Trial Board should henceforth be held "with open doors." Although police officials, who were opposed to the policy, may have prevented the full implementation of this order, Watkins did devise a procedure whereby the complainant, his attorney, his witnesses, and anyone else whom he designated could attend a police trial resulting from the alleged violation of a citizen's rights. Watkins also sensibly ordered that police officers found guilty of minor infractions by the Police Trial Board were to attend a "disciplinary school," where they would receive instruction appropriate to their offense, rather than being required to perform extra duties or being deprived of days of leave, as had been the practice. [13]

Murphy's insistence that the police must operate within the law in enforcing the law was put to a severe test in the most troublesome area of police work during that era, the enforcement of prohibition. The issue presented itself to Murphy when he became mayor because the police were making abundant use of the so-called "tip-over" raid, a tactic first employed in Detroit in 1924 and sporadically resorted to thereafter whereby the police, without benefit of search warrant, burst into a blind pig or what was suspected to be a blind pig and applied the axe to everything in sight. "The raiding squad," an authority on police behavior noted, was "judge, jury, and executioner." [14]

Given his views on law enforcement and civil liberties, it is not surprising that in November, 1930, Murphy instructed the police not to enter private dwellings assumed to be blind pigs unless they were armed with a search warrant; then, although they could seize the evidence, they were not to destroy anything in the establishment. "The sanctity of the home, as protected by the law on searches and seizures, and the fact that law enforcing agencies themselves should be required to live up to the law, are fundamental principles of our Government," the mayor declared. "I expect the police to live up to them. . . ."

The new order resulted in a drastic drop in prohibition raids. In the week before the anti-tip-over order went into effect, the police had conducted 230 tip-over raids and three legal raids; in the week following the order the number of illegal raids dropped to six. and there were five legal raids. The anti-tip-over order remained in effect throughout Murphy's mayoralty, but there was less than perfect compliance with its ban on "trial by axe and sledgehammer." Watkins was in sympathy with the order, but he nevertheless sanctioned deviations from it when the police were unable to gain the evidence required for a search warrant by legal means, which, of course, was something of a problem. Although the press reported that the ban on tip-overs had "opened" up Detroit, there was little hard evidence to support this conclusion since no one really knew how many blind pigs were actually operating in the city. [15]

Watkins, who personally favored repeal, believed that the prohibition laws should be enforced in the same manner as other laws were enforced—"that and no more," he said. He realized, however, that it was difficult to enforce the prohibition statutes in a legal manner, and he discovered that most Detroiters did not really want these laws fully enforced. He tried, nevertheless, to close blind pigs operating near schools, always resented by the public and even by " 'good blind pig operators,' " and also to persuade the owners of buildings housing illegal drinking establishments to close them down voluntarily or face the possibility of having their property padlocked. In February, 1932, the police began to "picket" some of the "swankier" night clubs that appeared to be violating the liquor laws, a tactic that induced most of them to close their doors. Watkins also sensibly changed the personnel of the liquor squad at least once a month to discourage the kinds of relationships between the police and the lawless that have bedeviled the enforcement of the laws against vice and crime. On the whole, the Watkins police force did about as good a job as could have been expected in enforcing a law that commanded so little respect in the community. "There will be no hysteria, no sporadic outbursts of rigid enforcement," Watkins had promised, and police performance was largely consonant with the commissioner's prescription.[16]

The teetotaling Murphy, who had advocated repeal of the prohibition amendment long before 1930, did not alter his stand after he became mayor. When the American Legion convened in Detroit in September, 1931, Murphy urged the Legionnaires to come out for repeal because prohibition had "poisoned and rottened the standards of public life and the standards of public service," trespassed upon "personal liberty," and led to "a cheap and vicious exploitation of . . . poor people." When a huge beer parade was staged in Detroit in May, 1932, the mayor himself was the marshal, and when the Master Brewers Association of America met in the city in September, 1932, Murphy informed them that they were " 'in the house of friends.' "

Attacking "the straddling and evasion" of public officials on the issue, Murphy favored the incorporation of a repeal plank in the 1932 Democratic platform and the repeal of the state prohibition law as well. He did not regard repeal as an issue of the same importance as "the recapture of economic independence and the attainment of social justice," but prohibition, he contended, was so "interwoven" with these questions and was "such a distraction" from them that he believed the time had come to dispose of the matter. When Michigan repealed its prohibition law in November, 1932, Murphy stated that he would not direct the police to prosecute offenders under the federal law, which was still in effect.[17]

Unyielding with regard to commercial gambling in Detroit, Murphy instructed the police to close down the gambling houses in the city. When slot machines, which had been driven from Detroit after the Buckley murder, began to reappear in the city, Murphy ordered the police into action against the devices. Initially, he barred tip-over raids against gaming establishments, but, deferring to

Watkins, the mayor eventually stated that he would not hamper the police if the commissioner felt obliged to use the tactic in the war on gambling. The police found this sufficient sanction for crashing into "'closed blind pigs'" believed to harbor slot machines.[18] The mayor failed to explain why tip-over raids were permissible in police enforcement of gambling laws but illegal in the enforcement of prohibition.

Insofar as police statistics are a guide—statistics in this area are notoriously unreliable—Detroit's experience largely confirms the generalization that in hard times crimes against persons tend to decrease but crimes against property are likely to increase. There was a sharp decline in Detroit between 1929 and 1932 in such crimes as murder (158 in 1929 and 96 in 1932) and manslaughter (68 in 1929 and 41 in 1932), a smaller decrease in the number of aggravated assaults (670 in 1929 and 612 in 1932), and almost no change in the number of rapes (227 in 1929 and 222 in 1932). On the other hand, in these years the number of burglaries (breaking and entering) rose from 1,581 to 3,771 and larcenies from 10,789 to 20,326. Within the larceny category, larcenies of $50 or more decreased from 1,182 to 740, but larcenies of $50 or less increased sharply, from 9,607 in 1929 to 19,586 in 1932, which reflects the pressures that the depression imposed on some of its victims. The police department and its friends, not surprisingly, took some of the credit for the decline in major crime, and they blamed the depression, the increase in the number of vacant dwellings and stores in the city, and the decrease in the size of the police force for the increase in crimes against property.[19]

II

One week after becoming mayor, Murphy met with Police Commissioner Wilcox, Caroline Parker, the city's corporation counsel, and Dr. Malik of the India Independence Central Committee, which the Bowles administration had refused a permit to hold a parade. Murphy instructed Wilcox to issue the permit, stating that he wished his administration to become "notable" for its protection of freedom of speech and freedom of assembly. No large city was more "notable" in that respect while Murphy was Detroit's mayor.[20]

"I think," the mayor told a journalist, "free speech is healthy and wholesome and more important than any political personality or even any government." To abridge it in any form, he observed, would imperil "not only our democratic form of government, but the peace and safety of society." Murphy thought that free speech took on "added significance" in times of distress. The depression had made the people "impatient, miserable and unhappy," he wrote a businessman who had complained about the exercise of free speech in a Detroit park, and it was "only good sense to let them fully and completely express themselves." He had discovered in his studies of "movements, revolutions, and the like," he wrote another correspondent, that violence occurred when the authorities tried to suppress "a suffering population," not when the people were permitted to assemble and express their grievances. Murphy accordingly criticized the use of force by the federal government to drive the Bonus Expeditionary Force out of Washington at the end of July, 1932, as an "example of recklessness" at a time when "patience and broad understanding" were required. He declared that every city in the United States would have "almost open warfare" if it behaved toward its unemployed in similar fashion. It was "wrong and unjust and actually dangerous," Murphy asserted, for society to deny people employment and then to say that they could not assemble to protest their condition.

To those who professed a belief in free speech and freedom of assembly but wished to deny these rights to Communists, Murphy replied, "You cannot apply the rule to one group and deny it to another." To use strong-arm tactics against the Communists simply created sympathy for them—"They glory," the mayor observed, "in that sort of self-advertised martyrdom." The Communists, he felt, fed on discontent, and so he believed that the proper way for public authorities to deal with Communism was to address themselves to the causes of that discontent. "Fight them," Murphy advised, "by giving better service to the people." As a matter of fact, he thought, government was less likely to suffer from the clamor of "radical extremists" than it was from "the real underminers of our institutions and our present order of things," those people who were "indifferent to the suffering of others."[21]

To implement his free-speech views, Murphy urged soon after he became mayor that the entire city—the parks, the streets, City Hall—be dedicated to the discussion of public problems. Murphy soon concluded, however, that it was important for the city to set aside "an established space" as a free-speech forum, and he recommended this course of action to the Council in his annual message of January, 1931. After discussing the issue at an open meeting late in March, the Council decided on East Grand Circus Park, in the heart of downtown Detroit, as the site for the forum.

Although the police feared that any sizable meeting in this very small park would interfere with the heavy traffic in the area and the commissioner of parks and boulevards was concerned that the park would be ruined, the civil-liberties forces, who wanted "a central, public, sufficiently frequented location," prevailed.

Merchants whose stores ringed the park and landowners in the area vociferously protested the Council's action, and so the aldermen, sensitive to business opinion, rescinded their decision after "a hot fight" and officially set aside the steps of City Hall for "general forensic purposes." Some alleged friends of free speech preferred an "obscure out-of-the-way place," but Murphy insisted on a conspicuous location, and the Council obliged him by picking a site just below his office from where he could hear himself denounced by forum orators. The board of directors of the ACLU adopted a resolution expressing their "warm appreciation" for Murphy's leadership in the free-speech fight, and Baldwin wrote the mayor that Detroit's action was "the kind of demonstration of genuine regard for the free-speech principle which we wish every American city would recognize."[22]

The battle for a free-speech forum, however, was not yet over. The city's corporation counsel ruled on April 13 that city ordinances forbade the use of City Hall and its environs as a free-speech forum and required a police permit for speeches or parades "within the one mile circle from City Hall," which included Grand Circus Park. The Detroit ACLU branch, fearful lest free speech be "muzzled and annihilated," asked Murphy to press once again for Grand Circus Park as a free-speech site, but the mayor, embroiled at the time in controversy concerning public welfare and the city's budget, was reluctant to fight on still a third front. The Council rescinded its City Hall decision, but despite the absence of an officially designated forum, "public open air free speech," Miss Parker reported to Baldwin, was "*established and going strong*" in Detroit, especially in front of City Hall and in Grand Circus Park.[23]

Late in August, the city government, although permitting the jobless and homeless to sit on the City Hall steps, as they regularly did, decided to enforce the ban on meetings at the City Hall site, but talk went on in Grand Circus Park. Although there were no restrictions on "small impromptu meetings," a police permit was required for advertised meetings and demonstrations, ostensibly to avoid conflict between "hostile groups" wishing to hold meetings at the same time in the limited space available, to prevent interference with traffic, and to protect the rights of other users of the park. Murphy knew that civil libertarians were not satisfied with this, but he was prodded to accept "some supervision" of free speech and freedom of assembly by his police commissioner, who complained that "under the guise of exercising constitutional rights, people have interfered very noticeably with the rights of other people in the use of public spaces." The mayor was also constantly importuned by businessmen in the Grand Circus Park area to "do something to prevent the unsightly and dangerous gatherings" in the park that the merchants claimed interfered with business, led to thefts and damage to business property, and caused "a great deal of annoyance" in general. Although the Common Council sided with the protesting merchants, Murphy specifically instructed the police to permit the continued exercise of free speech in the park.[24]

The acid test of the Detroit free-speech policy was the manner in which it was applied to organizations probably less interested in the right of free speech than in seeking a confrontation with the city in the hope of advancing the cause to which the protesters were committed. In Detroit during the depression years this meant the Communist party and the Unemployed Councils. There were probably no more than two thousand Communist party members in Detroit in 1930, but no one could be certain how many Communist sympathizers there were in affiliated groups like the Unemployed Councils, which the Communists created as a front organization in the hope of attracting recruits to the party and of gaining support for issues of importance to it. There were twelve to fifteen Unemployed Councils in the Detroit area, and as in other cities they staged frequent demonstrations, demanded more generous relief and a variety of free services for the unemployed, protested and sometimes forcibly resisted evictions of tenants, and advocated such reforms as national unemployment insurance.[25]

Murphy handled his first confrontation with the Unemployed Councils with exemplary skill, thus revealing what a difficult target he would be for the Communists and their front groups. The Unemployed Councils had called for a demonstration in Grand Circus Park on October 24 to "Smash the Murphy Ford Starvation Conspiracy," and in contrast to Bowles's reaction to the Communist unemployment demonstration of March 6, 1930, Murphy instructed the police to issue a permit for the meeting—the department had initially refused to do so—and not to "harass" the demonstrators in any way. The demonstration proceeded without incident, and two thousand protesters then marched down Woodward Avenue to City Hall, where the mayor received a committee of twelve and patiently conferred with them for two hours.

Caroline Parker, invited by the mayor to the session as an observer, reported to ACLU headquarters that Murphy could not have been more courteous to the Unemployed Councils committee had it been a delegation from the Detroit Board of Commerce. Murphy told the demonstration leaders that he was delighted that they had come to visit him and that, although some of their demands were unreasonable, others were just, and he would see what could be done about implementing them. He chided committee members for being unfamiliar with the city's unemployment relief policies—"There is no place on earth," he could not resist saying, "where greater measures have been taken for public relief than in Detroit, and that includes Moscow"—and he invited them to find this out for themselves by naming two representatives to serve on the Mayor's Unemployment Committee, which the demonstrators refused to do. When committee members complained that the police had interfered with their demonstration, Murphy turned to Miss Parker, who had witnessed the meeting in the park, and she contradicted the committee. Murphy closed by criticizing the demonstration leaders for not making it known that the Unemployed Councils were not sincere in their "demand for work and relief" but constituted rather "a general recruiting movement, national in scope, intended to bring the distressed and the dissatisfied into your [Communist] ranks."

Murphy's response to the October 24 demonstration delighted Miss Parker, who like so many well-to-do, reform-minded women was simply fascinated by Frank Murphy. The whole affair, she wrote Roger Baldwin, was as different from the events of March 6 as "daylight from darkness." The ACLU in New York was also impressed with Detroit's new mayor. "It sounds as if Mayor Murphy is almost too good to last," an ACLU executive replied to Miss Parker.[26]

For the next several months large demonstrations of the Communists and the unemployed were held in Detroit "without interference and without disorder." The police routinely granted the permits requested for the larger meetings, and on several occasions the mayor met with delegations to discuss their demands. Murphy, the ACLU announced in the annual report it issued in June,

1931, had "reversed completely the policy of police repression" in Detroit. Communist demonstrations in Detroit, an Associated Press reporter observed, were "about as exciting as an Epworth league convention."[27]

When a major confrontation between Communist demonstrators and the police finally occurred in the latter part of November, 1931, there can be little doubt that the clash was deliberately provoked by Communist leaders of the Unemployed Councils. A committee from the Unemployed Councils requested permits to stage a hunger demonstration in Grand Circus Park on November 25 at 1:00 P.M. and another demonstration by women and children in the same place at 10:00 A.M. on November 28. Since Watkins felt that large meetings in Grand Circus Park at those hours would seriously interfere with downtown business and traffic and that the organizers of the demonstrations had deliberately selected the times with that in mind, he denied the permits and suggested that the meetings be held at different hours or at a park away from the downtown area. When the demonstration leaders announced that they would meet in Grand Circus Park with or without a permit, Murphy stated that the city would not be dictated to by the Communists.

The expected happened on November 25. The police charged the five hundred demonstrators who had gathered in Grand Circus Park and drove them from the area. Seeking a confrontation with the mayor, the crowd then proceeded to City Hall, where the police used clubs and tear gas to chase them away from the building. One patrolman and two demonstrators were injured, and thirty persons were jailed. All were quickly released on the mayor's orders, but at least four of those arrested, including John Schmies, the Communist candidate for mayor of Detroit in 1931, were later convicted. There was a repeat performance in Grand Circus Park on November 28. This time two thousand demonstrators assembled, and the police, claiming that a department undercover agent had forewarned them that the Communists had ordered their people to mobilize in the park and to be prepared to rush the police, broke up the demonstration and made eight arrests.[28]

The Communists and the Unemployed Councils, their objective achieved, charged that Murphy had now revealed himself as "the agent of the bosses, who is determined to use police clubs, tear gas and jails to stop the workers' demand for bread." The Detroit ACLU branch, unwilling to strike at the throne, blamed the police for what had occurred and deplored the city procedure that permitted the police to act as "censors over public meetings on grounds of presumed interference with traffic or speculation as to possible disorders." Forced to make a choice between the ACLU conception of free speech and the Watkins view of the matter, Murphy, although regretting what had occurred, sided with the police. "I think they [the police] handled it with good judgment and due regard to the rights of all," he declared. "Our Communist visitors [?] will learn that the laws are not to be flouted and the rights of the majority are not to be trampled upon. . . ." The mayor, however, hastened to inform liberal acquaintances across the land that he remained "anxious . . . to have this city [Detroit] loom up above the others" as a protector of civil liberties. Although he believed it necessary to regulate the exercise of free speech and freedom of assembly under certain circumstances, he stated that he would still "guard jealously all the freedoms in every phase of our municipal government."[29]

The disturbances of November 25 and 28 persuaded the city government that the prevailing informal arrangements governing the exercise of free speech in Detroit would have to be replaced by precise regulations. The police department and the mayor's office collaborated in the formulation of a set of free-speech rules that was announced on December 4, 1931. They provided that "small impromptu meetings" as well as individual speech could take place anywhere in the city without a permit provided there was no interference with traffic or "unlawful interference" with the rights of others. "Advertised" meetings and demonstrations could be held in public parks and places after "reasonable notice" had been given to the police, except that advertised meetings in East Grand Circus Park also required a police permit. Police permits were similarly required for parades through the city's streets. The rule that only a notice had to be given for other than advertised meetings in East Grand Circus Park was a victory for the Detroit ACLU, which had pressed the point on Murphy over the objections of the police.

Although the December 4 regulations did not fully meet the ACLU's desire for an official "free speech center," Baldwin nevertheless later described himself as "in entire agreement" with Detroit's policy regarding demonstrations and parades. This is entirely understandable since, with the possible exception of the provisions for the use of East Grand Circus Park, whose location admittedly presented certain problems, the rules do not appear to have been unreasonable. The requirement of notice was hardly a burden on the exercise of free speech, and the right to parade through the streets of a big city must necessarily be subject to some kind of regulation. Despite the continued complaints of Grand Circus Park merchants and the objections of some to street-corner meetings, the December 4 regulations remained unchanged to the end of Murphy's mayoralty.[30]

For several months following the disturbances of late November, 1931, demonstrations were conducted in Detroit without incident. "Policemen," Murphy later wrote, "have been schooled to amiably supervise and regulate rather than interfere; policemen's clubs are never exposed, and they are indifferent to taunts and offensive remarks."[31] The free-speech issue in Detroit had virtually faded from public attention when a bloody confrontation took place on March 7, 1932, between marchers from Detroit and a combination of Dearborn police and Ford Motor Company guards that raised questions about the possible involvement of the Detroit police.

The final plans for the Ford Hunger March, as history came to know the event, were spelled out by the Communists at a secret meeting on March 3 and then at a large public meeting on March 6 addressed by William Z. Foster, the secretary of the Trade Union Unity League. The report of the secret meeting supplied to the Detroit Citizens League by its "investigation system" reveals clearly that the organizers of the march anticipated trouble and probably arrests. The destination of the march was the Ford Motor Company's employment office at the great Rouge plant, where the marchers planned to present a set of demands calling on Ford to improve working conditions in the Rouge and to provide relief for the thousands of laid-off Ford workers.[32]

The marchers[33] had not applied for a permit to parade through Detroit to their assembly point near the Detroit-Dearborn line, but the Detroit police, ignoring this fact, provided the marchers with a large escort, and there was no disorder whatsoever. Some demonstrators proceeded to the meeting point at the edge of Detroit by streetcar and, by prearrangement, refused to pay their fares. This brought the Detroit police into action, but just what occurred then has been lost in a maze of conflicting accounts. In any event, there were no later complaints by the marchers of mistreatment by the police—the official Communist line was that "the militant crowd" had prevented the police from clubbing the freeloaders.

Approximately three thousand persons gathered for the march into Dearborn. There were Communists among them, and their leadership was undeniably Communist, but the bulk of the marchers were former Ford workers and, above all, members of the great army of the unemployed. "Whatever malevolent motive from far in the background may have inspired the march," the Detroit *News* editorialized, "nobody could look at the marchers themselves and accuse them of any destructive purpose." When the marchers reached the city limits of Dearborn, they were met by forty Dearborn policemen, who sought to block the demonstrators' advance into the city since they did not have the required permit to parade in Dearborn. When asked whether they possessed a permit, a marcher shouted, "We don't need one," and the battle was on. The Dearborn police used tear gas in an effort to disperse the marchers, and the marchers responded by hurling a variety of missiles at the officers. The police soon exhausted their supply of tear gas, and the marchers forced them into a retreat of about one-half mile to the No. 1 gate of the Rouge Plant.

At the No. 1 gate two Dearborn fire companies sought to connect their hose lines to a hydrant, but the marchers swarmed over the firemen and drove them to the No. 3 gate, where they finally succeeded in turning a hose on the demonstrators. The Dearborn police, joined by Ford's private police, reassembled at the gate, and then shots rang out that fatally wounded two of the marchers. At this juncture Harry Bennett suddenly drove onto the battlefield, only to be felled either by a rock or chunks of slag. By this time the demonstrators had been told by one of their leaders to retreat, but as they milled about in confusion, the police fired into the crowd—"Get your gats out and let them have it," a newspaper photographer overheard a policeman say—and two more marchers were killed. In all, four marchers were killed, nineteen were wounded by gunshot, nine were otherwise wounded, and twenty-five Dearborn police were injured by assorted missiles. "Dearborn pavements," the New York *Times* reported, "were stained with blood, streets were littered with broken glass and the wreckage of bullet-riddled automobiles and nearly every window in the Ford plant's employment building had been broken." That night police and deputy sheriffs in the Detroit metropolitan area raided the headquarters of Communist and Communist-front groups and also seized several dozen radicals. The injured demonstrators were all placed under technical arrest, some were held in hospital rooms under police guard, and there was a nationwide search, later abandoned, for Foster and four local Communist leaders who had vanished from the scene.

One of the "hotly disputed" questions that quickly arose after the Ford riot was the extent to which the Detroit police had been involved in the fighting within the city of Dearborn and what role, if any, they had played in the raids on the offices of Communist organizations and in the arrest and jailing of some of the marchers. Confused news accounts of the riot agreed that about 120 Detroit police and detectives had arrived at the riot scene at some point during the day to reinforce the Dearborn police; Detective Hugh Quinn of the Detroit police provided what appeared to be an eyewitness account of the Bennett affair; and District Inspector William Black, who led the Detroit reinforcements to the Ford plant, was quoted by the Detroit *Free Press* as saying that when the rioters did not heed a warning to disperse after his car had been stoned, "our officers charged with their night sticks. You know the rest." The Detroit *News* and other sources reported that Detroit police had participated in the post-march raids, and the *News* listed ten persons who had been arrested by the Detroit police and then turned over to Dearborn authorities.[34]

Communist sources and sources friendly to the Communists embellished the accounts in the press that seemed to implicate the Detroit police and city government in the Ford riot. Detroit police, the Communists and their allies charged, were present at the scene of the trouble before, during, and after the shooting and had shot at and tear-gassed the marchers. Mayor Murphy's "uniformed butchers," they alleged, had participated in the "wave of terror" that followed the riot, raiding offices and even private homes without search warrants, arresting and torturing unemployed workers, and holding them as prisoners even after writs of habeas corpus had been issued for their release. Seizing on the issue as a means of discrediting liberal reformers and other "social fascists," the Communists alleged that Detroit's role in the Ford affair proved that Mayor Murphy, the darling of the liberals and the socialists, was really Ford's "puppet," Henry and Edsel's "assistant murderer." To repay the Ford Motor Company for its $5 million loan to the city in June, 1931, Murphy had slashed relief payments and had joined in the "murder conspiracy" to drive workers to their deaths by starvation, wage cuts, and the speed-up.[35]

The Communists mobilized their entire front apparatus to protest the "Ford massacre" and the part that the Murphy regime had allegedly played in it. To dramatize the issue, the Communists staged a mass funeral in Detroit on March 12 for the four marchers who had been killed outside the Rouge plant. The scarlet banner held aloft at the head of the vast funeral procession of perhaps ten thousand persons carried the words, "Smash the Ford-Murphy Police Terror," and some of the funeral marchers declaimed, "We wanted bread; Ford and Murphy gave us bullets." As a crowd of about fifteen thousand looked on, the marchers proceeded to Grand Circus Park, where some remained for a memorial service and speeches, while others went on to Woodmere Cemetery, in the sight of the Rouge plant, where the bodies were lowered into a common grave. Hundreds of Detroit police, their night sticks concealed under their uniform coats and under orders to ignore everything but actual violence, stood guard during the funeral march, and motorcycle police led the way to the cemetery. The mayor, who had received "threats and pressures" not to permit the Communists to stage a public funeral, viewed the march from a downtown hotel, pleased that "no difficulty of any kind occurred." [36]

Their dead buried, the Communists staged their own workers' trial on March 25 "To Brand As Murderers Those Responsible For [The] Ford Massacre." A "workers' jury" of twenty-five listened to two hours of testimony and then included Murphy among those "guilty" of murder because of the role that his police had allegedly played in the affair. A quite different "verdict" was rendered by a grand jury that probed the riot under the direction of Wayne County Prosecuting Attorney Harry Toy. After conducting what one of its members, a prominent Murphy supporter, characterized as "the most biased, prejudiced and ignorant proceeding imaginable," the grand jury concluded that the riot had been instigated by "a few agitators who go about the nation taking advantage of times of industrial depression or other misfortune for the purpose of influencing those who are unable to find employment to care for themselves and family." The jurors found that although the conduct of the Dearborn police might have been "more discreet and better considered" when they first encountered the demonstrators, which grandly understated the matter, the resort to gunfire had been justified "at the moment of its use," a judgment that is surely at variance with the facts. The grand jurors mistakenly reported that no Ford Motor Company personnel had taken part in quelling the riot, and they made no reference to any participation by the Detroit police once the marchers had crossed into Dearborn. [37]

The ACLU also sought to ascertain who was responsible for

"the tragedy at [the] Detroit city limits" on March 7. When Roger Baldwin initially queried Murphy about the part the Detroit police might have played, he replied that "the entire conflict was between the Dearborn police, the Ford police and the demonstrators." Detroit police seen at the Ford plant, the mayor noted, had been sent there at the request of Dearborn authorities; they had arrived after the violence had occurred and had had "nothing to do" with it.

Murphy's remarks about the Detroit police were actually a rather free translation of what Watkins had reported to him about their participation. The police commissioner had advised the mayor that when the superintendent of police received word of the trouble in Dearborn, he had sent Black to investigate and, upon learning from Black that a riot was taking place, had dispatched a police contingent to the scene of the disturbance. The trouble was "pretty much over" when the Detroit police arrived, Watkins reported, "and they merely *assisted in maintaining the peace.*" Watkins did not define what that meant, but added, "*So far as I can ascertain,* our men took no part in quelling the disturbance. I am sure they did no shooting and, *I think,* had no occasion to use any force whatsoever."[38] Watkins did not explain why he could not be more precise, and if he had checked out the account of the affair attributed to Black, however inaccurate it may have been, he did not say so.

At the request of the Detroit branch of the ACLU and the International Labor Defense, the legal arm of the Communist party, Baldwin journeyed to Detroit to conduct an on-the-spot investigation of what he described as "the first oppressive massacre in the United States." He conferred with Murphy, among others, and then Baldwin and Walter Nelson, the chairman of the Detroit ACLU, issued a "statement of fact, of law, and of public policy" that criticized the action of the Dearborn and Ford police as "wholly out of keeping with sane methods of dealing with such demonstrations" and noted that there was a dispute as to whether Detroit police had arrived on the scene before or after the shooting. On the strength of Murphy's assurances, however, Baldwin had indicated the day before that he was satisfied that the Detroit police had not participated in the riot.[39]

Wondering after a while whether he had been a bit hasty in his judgment, Baldwin pressed Murphy for further information about Detroit's participation in the Ford riot. Murphy again turned to Watkins, who now defined the Detroit police role as merely one of assistance in "restoring order, directing traffic and the like." He explained that Detective Quinn, who had been ignored in Watkins's first report to the mayor, had been at the Detroit-Dearborn line with the marchers and had simply followed along as an observer when trouble developed. Watkins, incredibly, reported that he knew nothing about arrests by Detroit police following the riot, but he was nevertheless satisfied that nothing more than "merely routine police duty" had been involved. Although Watkins's reply was incomplete and insubstantial, Murphy accepted it at its face value, and Baldwin thought that it provided "just the information we need."[40]

As additional information about the Ford riot, partly supplied by "our Communist friends," became available to the ACLU, some of the organization's members regretted that the ACLU had "completely whitewashed" the Murphy administration. Not wishing to have it appear that the ACLU was concealing something because Detroit had "a liberal mayor" and anxious to include all those responsible in civil suits for damages on behalf of the killed and the wounded,[41] Baldwin turned to Maurice Sugar, the International Labor Defense attorney in the Ford case and a sometime ACLU attorney as well, to ascertain what he knew about the matter. Sugar, who would dearly have loved to implicate the Murphy regime, contended that the evidence pointed "convincingly" to Detroit police participation, but he was unable to provide the data to support that conclusion. Baldwin also continued to press Murphy for information. The raids on Communist headquarters and the arrest of persons without warrants were "indefensible," he wrote the mayor, and he characterized the reported chaining of wounded prisoners as "revolting."[42]

Murphy assured Baldwin in reply, "There will be no lawless policy on the part of the Detroit police that *I can control*," which, of course, was the crux of the problem. Conceding that he had failed to investigate the police raids that had followed the hunger march, Murphy told the ACLU head that the Detroit mayor was just as much opposed to an illegal search of Communist headquarters as to any "lawless" search. He had not previously heard about the alleged chaining of wounded prisoners, but when he looked into the charge, he discovered that one of the five riot prisoners held in the prisoner's ward of the Receiving Hospital had indeed been chained to his bed because of his allegedly "unfriendly attitude." He also learned that it was the practice of the police department, which was solely responsible for guarding prisoners in the hospital, to chain all prisoner patients charged with felonies. Horrified, Murphy wrote the head of the hospital that "the chaining of patient prisoners to beds is a brutal practice that should find no encouragement in an enlightened hospital," but it is not clear that the mayor ordered the practice halted. Although Watkins categorically assured Murphy that the Detroit police had not participated in any post-riot raids or taken any part in rounding up radicals wanted by the Dearborn police, this was simply inaccurate. The Detroit police had even arrested and turned over to the Dearborn police three women whose only "offense" had been to transport two of the wounded marchers to the Receiving Hospital.[43]

Although the Detroit police were more involved in the Ford riot of March 7, 1932, and its aftermath than Murphy originally indicated, convincing evidence is altogether lacking to link them with the killing or wounding of any of the hunger marchers, and their part in the affair seems to have been essentially peripheral. What is equally evident is that no adequate effort was made to ascertain how the Detroit police had behaved, and for this Mayor Murphy is largely to blame. In seeking the facts, he relied entirely on Commissioner Watkins, and Watkins, although a superior police commissioner, failed to investigate the matter with the thoroughness its importance deserved. Not particularly fond of radicals and inclined, as heads of organizations tend to be, to defend his department against outside criticism, he sent the mayor evasive and insubstantial replies to his inquiries, but Murphy accepted these unsatisfactory reports without complaint or challenge. Considering the gravity of the issues that had been raised, the mayor probably should have arranged for some agency outside the department to conduct a full-scale probe of the affair. This, however, might have led the much-admired Watkins to resign, and Murphy was unwilling to accept the political risks involved. Less explicable is Murphy's failure to address himself to the crucial issue of the mayor's control over his police department by accepting Baldwin's sensible suggestion that the final decision regarding support of a neighboring community by the Detroit police should rest with the mayor rather than with the police department.[44]

On June 6, 1932, two months after the Ford Hunger March, the Unemployed Councils and the Communist-dominated Auto Workers Union staged a hunger march in Detroit itself, and once again the police—"Detroit police," Maurice Sugar could not resist saying—clashed with the demonstrators. The target of the march, for which a police permit had been obtained, was the employment office of the Briggs Manufacturing Company. When the approximately two thousand marchers reached the Briggs plant, the police ordered them to hold their meeting in a vacant lot across the street from the plant. A committee of the marchers crossed the street and approached the gates of the plant, where they were met by police and representatives of the company, who refused the committee's request for a conference with the plant management. The marchers began to follow the committee across the street toward the plant gates, and when the police, who were commanded by Norton Schuknecht, of Sweet trial fame, tried to stop them, one of the leaders of the demonstration hit Schuknecht in the mouth, dislodging two of his teeth. "A general melee" ensued in which, as Murphy conceded, the police, some mounted, some dismounted, were "somewhat indiscriminating [*sic*] in their resistance" as they threw tear gas at the demonstrators, rode them down, and engaged in "some very indiscriminate clubbing." "This happened," Sugar sarcastically reported to the ACLU, "several miles from Dearborn, and so far the blame has not been placed on the Dearborn police to the exclusion of others."[45]

Having learned his lesson from the Ford Hunger March, Murphy "carefully investigated" the Briggs confrontation, and, although he believed that the police had been provoked, he did not condone what he regarded as their excessive reaction. He thought it important for the ACLU to realize, however, that there had been "so much abuse" of the city's free-speech policy by the Communists that the Detroit public was "being educated up to a more conservative view" of free speech than had prevailed when he first became mayor. "The crystallized judgment of the dominant groups in the City," Murphy wrote Baldwin, "is now demanding vigorous police action. . . . In other words, our problem now is not one of educating the conservatives to the necessity for free speech and assemblage, demonstrations and the like, but to gain or compel, in some manner, the cooperation of small vocal minority groups who do not share our views on these questions."

Because Murphy recognized that it was difficult to learn exactly what had happened through "postmortem inquiries" into affairs like the Briggs riot, he suggested that it might be wise to place "a trustworthy group of witnesses" at the scene of demonstrations to observe what transpired. Baldwin thought this a good idea, and the Detroit ACLU branch informally decided to implement the suggestion. As for the Briggs affair, Murphy's high standing with the ACLU led Baldwin, who professed to know "what Communist tactics are on such occasions," to accept the mayor's description of what had occurred rather than the somewhat different account provided by Maurice Sugar.[46]

There continued to be clashes between the Communists and their front groups and the Detroit police after the Briggs Hunger March as the Unemployed Councils demonstrated outside and sometimes inside the welfare district offices or sought to prevent evictions by one means or another. The Communists complained about police brutality in these confrontations, while John Ballenger, speaking for the welfare department, praised the "calmness" of the police and "the splendid manner" in which they "handled these communist demonstrations." One writer in the *Nation* thought that the Watkins police were "destroying what . . . [was] left of . . . [Murphy's] reputation as a liberal" and that Communist propaganda was making "deep inroads" among the workers, but this was a gross misrepresentation of the actuality. Although sometimes violated by the police, the Murphy free-speech policy almost certainly helped to relieve "the tense feeling among the people" and denied the Communists, for the most part, the advertising, the sympathy, and the martyrs that a repressive policy might have produced. They seized upon events like the Ford Hunger March to belabor Murphy because he gave them so few legitimate opportunities to do so, and William Lovett of the Detroit Citizens League was correct in his judgment that the man in Detroit "most cordially hated" by the Communists was Frank Murphy.[47]

When he was a United States Supreme Court justice, Murphy was often accused of holding to a doctrinaire conception of free speech, but as chief executive of a big city who had to respond to a varied constituency and who had to govern, Murphy, without abandoning his essentially liberal view of the constitutional guarantees,[48] concluded that the exercise of free speech and freedom of assembly had to be subjected to a modest degree of supervision. Murphy's standing with professional civil libertarians remained high despite this, and they forgave him the occasional violations of high principle that occurred. When Murphy became mayor, the ACLU was enthralled with this fresh and exciting public figure who appeared to be so committed to the protection of civil liberties—"Such wonderful things are happening every day under the leadership of Mayor Murphy that I could write pages," Caroline Parker informed the New York office of the ACLU at the end of October, 1930—and the civil-liberties organization maintained close and affectionate ties with Murphy throughout his mayoralty and in the years thereafter as well.[49]

III

Because of the massive unemployment and the enfeebled state of the labor movement, strikes by the employed while Murphy was mayor were a far less common phenomenon in Detroit than demonstrations of the unemployed. Murphy discovered, however, that the police were as difficult to control in dealing with pickets at the scene of a labor disturbance as they were in dealing with radicals in Grand Circus Park. A strike against the Briggs Manufacturing Company, maker of automobile bodies for the Ford Motor Company and Chrysler Corporation, was the only major industrial dispute in Detroit during the Murphy mayoralty.[50] Occurring early in 1933, at the very nadir of the depression, and staged by unorganized workers, the Briggs strike "just burst like lightning" on the Detroit scene. Because of the interrelated processes of automobile manufacturing, the strike had a reverberating effect beyond the Briggs plants, which led the New York *Times* to characterize it as "the hardest single blow which has struck Detroit since the depression became acute."[51]

In a prelude to the main event, 450 employees of Briggs's small Vernor Highway (Waterloo) plant struck on January 11 to resist a 20 percent wage cut. The tiny Communist-dominated Auto Workers Union (AWU) took over organization of the strike, and it is probable that the Communists, who were planning a strike movement in the automobile industry, had instigated the walkout by capitalizing on the very real grievances of the workers in the plant. The company, caught unawares, rescinded the wage cut after three days, and the strikers returned to their jobs.[52]

A few days after the Waterloo settlement twelve hundred workers of the Motor Products Company, another auto parts firm, struck against a wage cut and succeeded after three days, again under AWU leadership, in persuading the company to rescind the cut and abolish piece work. The strike movement came to a head on January 23-24 when more than six thousand workers struck the Briggs plant in Highland Park and the three Briggs plants in Detroit, the large Mack Avenue plant and the much smaller Vernor Highway and Meldrum Avenue plants. The principal grievances of the Briggs workers were their exceedingly low wages—strikers were able to produce pay checks of less than twenty cents—the result, in part, of management's recent abandonment of a guaranteed hourly base rate and the substantial amount of dead time for which they received no compensation. The strikers also complained of a speed-up of production, unhealthful, unsanitary, and dangerous working conditions, irregular employment, extremely long hours of work on occasion, unexplained deductions from their wages, and the company practice of charging workers for tools that they damaged.

Although the strikers were guilty of some exaggeration in their complaints about the terms of their employment and overlooked the fact that their low wage rates were, to some degree, the result of work sharing and the difficulties that management had faced in getting "a new run of production underway," there is no doubt that working conditions at Briggs were among the worst in the city. As Robert M. Pilkington, the federal conciliator assigned to the dispute, concluded, the Briggs workers had "good and sufficient reasons to rebel against conditions imposed upon them." A Briggs worker who had earned a grand total of $10 in the preceding month explained in a poignant letter to Murphy that "no one would go on the strike this time thousands unemployed, we wanted to work, and must work but the rope had to break if you didn't want to die on the job you can't imagine, you can't explain, how bad it is unless you're working there sweat all day but no time to wipe off your brow." He had "seen many fall on the job, taken out, and forgotten work so hard, if you do work all day, you're crippled, paralyzed, broken when you get home. . . ." He thought that Briggs, which workers called the "'butcher shop'" or "the slaughterhouse," should be investigated by a grand jury for "cruelty" and manslaughter. "We have Humaine [*sic*] Society for animals," he observed, "why not have it for human beings." "If poison doesn't work," Detroit workers used to say, "try Briggs."[53]

Since the inexperienced strikers had great difficulty "in getting the strike organized," they accepted the leadership of the AWU and the Communists, who were only too happy to take advantage of the situation that presented itself. This led to charges that it was a Communist strike, but the consensus of neutral observers was that "the strike originated among the workers themselves," that "it . . . was not the result of communistic influences," and that Communists "assumed leadership" only after "the movement was underway." When the Communists later tried to turn the strike to their own ends by seeking recruits for the AWU, attempting to bring the Unemployed Councils into the battle, and stressing the agitational rather than the organizational aspects of the strike, the strikers became confused and factious. Following a few days of uncertainty they voted at a mass meeting of February 7 to dissociate themselves entirely from the AWU and the Communists and to make the strike an "all-Briggs" affair.[54]

After the strikers repudiated their Communist leadership, the General Strike Committee issued a remarkably candid public statement in which they explained why they had permitted Phil Raymond, secretary of the AWU and Communist candidate for mayor of Detroit in 1930, "to come among us" after the walkout— "it was the drowning man grasping for a straw"—and how they had decided that "Raymond and his associates and organization" should have "nothing more to do with the strike" once it became clear that the strikers' welfare was not the real concern of the Communists. "We dare any one," they said, "to accuse us to our faces of being other than true American working men with any other motives than that of seeking living wages and reasonable working conditions through this strike action."[55]

The strikers had to contend not only with the troublesome "Red" question but with "a stubborn and unsympathetic employer" as well. The Briggs management initially characterized the walkout as having been "inspired and planned by Communists" rather than being "a trade union strike," and the company's treasurer and spokesman, William F. Connolly, Murphy's quondam political mentor, declared, "I will not join in any meeting with Communists." The Communist presence among the strikers, however, was simply a convenient excuse for the company to offer in defense of a policy it would have pursued in any event; and when the strike committee shed its Communist advisers, Connolly made it evident that, although willing to confer with employees as individuals, the company "would meet with no group of workers of any make-up." When asked about his attitude toward collective bargaining, Walter O. Briggs, the president of the company, replied that "he had never heard of it."

The Briggs management professed to see the strike as "the initial attempt" to organize automobile workers generally by "attacking a strategic point in automobile manufacture." It thus pictured itself as defending the open-shop automobile industry as a whole, and it may well be, as Pilkington reported to Washington, that additional body orders for Briggs from the principal auto manufacturers were "contingent upon the . . . Company's successful resistance to any settlement that might involve union recognition in any form."[56]

The Briggs strike led to the shutdown of Murray Body, whose contracts with Ford interlocked with those of Briggs, and this idled four thousand additional workers. The Murray Body workers converted their shutdown into a strike, but the dispute was quickly composed. Far more serious for the Detroit economy was the shutdown of the Ford Motor Company on January 26, which affected more than forty thousand workers in the Detroit area. Finally, Communists "provoked" a strike of three thousand employees of the Hudson Motor Car Company body plant, and this idled about three thousand additional Hudson workers as well; but the company agreed to confer with a strike committee of its own employees, and the strikers after six days decided to return to their jobs on the condition that their grievances would be dealt with once work was resumed.[57]

On January 27, possibly under pressure from the Ford Motor Company, which had leased Briggs the old Ford Highland Park plant to produce bodies for the Ford V-8 and which tended to see the Briggs strike as "a part of sabotage by rivals to prevent them [Ford] from bringing out a new model," Briggs abolished dead time and instituted a guaranteed hourly rate of twenty-five to seventy-eight cents. Although "miserably low," to quote the Detroit *Labor News*, the new rate partially met one of the principal demands of the strikers. Determined to resume production, Briggs announced that it would give preference in rehiring to old employees until January 30.[58]

The resumption of production at Briggs began on January 28, and by February 7 the company had a full complement of employees at its Highland Park plant and about one-half the prestrike labor force at the Mack Avenue plant. At most half of those who returned to work were former Briggs employees. The return of workers to the Highland Park plant, which was outside the jurisdiction of Detroit, was menacingly protected by Highland Park police, sheriff's deputies, special deputies sworn in by the Wayne County sheriff and paid by Briggs, and state police sent in by Governor William Comstock. The presence of the law-enforcement officers made it almost impossible for the Highland Park strikers to maintain a picket line; an investigating committee appointed by several Democratic party organizations in the area found that the police units had "repeatedly clubbed and struck and otherwise used violence without excuse against the strikers."[59]

When a committee of three strikers met with Briggs officials on February 6 to ascertain if the company would be willing to confer with the strikers' negotiating committee, the three were unceremoniously "kicked out" of the plant. Although Briggs officials did meet with the negotiating committee on February 20, "nothing was accomplished," and the strike remained "in just the same shape" as before. The strike dragged on for several more weeks—it was never officially called off—but it was evident by February 20 that the strikers, their ranks dwindling and production on the upswing, would not prevail.[60]

Although the official posture of the Murphy administration was one of strict neutrality, the mayor and other city officials made a number of decisions with regard to the dispute that were, on the whole, less pleasing to management than to the strikers. The city's Free Employment Bureau and the Department of Public Welfare, consistent with Murphy's expressed wishes, rejected requests from the company to make welfare recipients and the Bureau-registered unemployed available to replace strikers. Despite demands by some employers, Murphy also refused to withhold relief from needy strikers. "Our welfare policy," the mayor announced, "is going to be to supply help on the basis of exact need of the individual, temporarily at least." Not only did strikers receive aid from the welfare department, but the Mayor's Unemployment Committee (MUC), secretly operating out of the boiler room in City Hall, also provided them with emergency relief. City physicians looked after impecunious strikers who suffered frostbite on the picket line during the bitterly cold days of early February.[61]

When Briggs resumed production with strikebreakers at the Mack Avenue plant, it requested the Street Railway Commission to order the Detroit Street Railways to make special stops in front of the plant so that employees could more easily be escorted to and from the streetcars without being harassed and possibly assaulted by the pickets. The Street Railway Commission rejected the request on the grounds that it must remain "absolutely neutral," and it similarly refused to make buses available to the company at charter rates lest this action "tend to make it [the commission] a partisan." On the other hand, when it was suggested that streetcars should not stop at their regularly scheduled stops near the Mack Avenue plant to avoid the possible stoning of passengers by pickets, Murphy demurred, arguing, "we should first exhaust every means of protecting the people in their rights without changing the car schedules. To abandon the regular schedule," he declared, "would be to encourage strikers to stone cars."[62]

Anxious to end a dispute so important to the city's well-being and equally desirous of avoiding the kind of controversy that had developed about the facts of the Ford Hunger March, Murphy, on January 27, appointed the Mayor's Non-Partisan Committee on Industrial Disputes to study the causes of the strike and then to report to the mayor. The Non-Partisan Committee—better known as the Fact-Finding Committee—was headed by the Reverend H. Ralph Higgins, senior curate of St. Paul's Episcopal Cathedral, and consisted of eight members, none of whom was connected with the disputants.[63]

At an early meeting of the Fact-Finding Committee, Murphy, although he sympathized with the strikers and thought that Briggs had "brought the . . . trouble largely upon itself," stressed that if the committee were to play a role in settling the dispute, it must take special care "not to offend either side." He wanted the committee to try to arrange a meeting between the strikers and the company and to suggest "some sort of mediation" to the management. If this was unacceptable to the company, the mayor thought that perhaps he could summon both sides to his office, or, if the company thought the suggestion politically motivated—company officials, as a matter of fact, viewed the very establishment of the committee as a "political move" that was likely "to do a great deal of good" for the Communist cause—the governor or someone else could extend the invitation.[64]

Members of the Fact-Finding Committee met three times with Briggs officials, but the company rejected the committee as a mediator, temporarily rejected the suggestion that it confer with the strikers, and indicated that it would not retreat from this position even if requested to do so by the mayor. The company's intransigent attitude was graphically illustrated in its first meeting with the committee when Walter Briggs "banged the desk with his fists and called attention to the fact that he had reduced his own pay to a mere eighteen hundred dollars per month," complained that he had been obliged to leave Florida because of the strike, and observed that butlers in fashionable Grosse Pointe who had once earned $150 per month were now earning only $75. A subcommittee of the Fact-Finding Committee met daily to hear witnesses, nearly all of them strikers. Although Briggs officials refused the committee's invitation to testify, the company made its records available to the committee, responded to a questionnaire, and permitted committee members to visit the company's plants to gain information.[65]

The Fact-Finding Committee presented its report to the mayor on February 21. The committee found that the strikers' complaints about low wages, lack of a guaranteed minimum rate, and the speed-up had been "in many respects well-founded." It was critical of the company's "lack of an effective way of taking cognizance of the workers' grievances," and it deplored the company's initial refusal to meet with the strikers. At the same time, the committee noted "the degree of orderliness" among the strikers, a judgment that deserved some qualification, and characterized as "unfortunate" the use of state police and company-paid deputies at the Highland Park plant. The committee recommended the organization of workers in every industry so that they could discuss their grievances with their employers, more frequent and thorough state inspection of factories, and the establishment in Detroit of "a permanent non-partisan commission on industrial relations" empowered to investigate labor disputes and to compel mediation and arbitration.[66] Only this last recommendation could have been implemented by the city government, but neither the mayor nor the Common Council took steps to do so.

The Fact-Finding Committee report provided a reasonably accurate picture of the Briggs strike, but it did not in any way affect the structure of power that determined its outcome. Although Murphy asserted that the "beneficial results" of the report had spread beyond the city since "the whole country has been looking at Detroit in this crisis,"[67] his high opinion of the Fact-Finding Committee and its report was not shared by the MUC. Critical of the Fact-Finding Committee for its "aloofness, secretiveness and unwillingness to acquaint the public with the facts pertaining to the strike," the MUC, at a meeting of February 8, before the Higgins group had reported, authorized its subcommittee on labor and legislation, headed by Larry S. Davidow, to conduct a rival investigation of the strike. The MUC criticism of the Higgins committee, if justified at all, was altogether misdirected since it was the mayor himself who had cautioned the group to maintain a low profile. When the committee had issued a brief interim report on February 3 that seemed to place it on the strikers' side, Murphy had criticized the action as a "tactical error" and had chided the group for making "a somewhat ex parte statement that was not quite becoming this committee." Murphy, who was present at the February 8 meeting, protested the decision for another investigation, but Davidow, who wished to have Briggs "pilloried by public opinion," countered that the mayor had repeatedly stated that he wished the MUC to serve as "a sounding board of public opinion." "If we cannot sound public opinion on this strike, which affects the welfare of our entire community," Davidow stated, "we may as well close up." Murphy should have overruled the MUC, but since a certain amount of administrative untidiness did not particularly bother him and since he did not wish to frustrate a volunteer group, he allowed the Davidow investigation to go forward.[68]

The report of the Davidow subcommittee, which was completed at the beginning of March, blamed the strike on "the attitude" of the company as "manifested in its maintenance of deplorable working conditions" and its "stubborn refusal" to engage in collective bargaining. Consistent with Davidow's purpose, the report expressed the hope that public opinion would cause Briggs to "realize that its methods and attitudes" were "in irreconcilable conflict with American ideals." Because the report was so strident in tone, MUC chairman Father Edward J. Hickey, who had been a member of the Fact-Finding Committee, refused to accept the document when it came before the MUC for approval. Father Hickey was supported by a bare majority of the committee, with the result that the Davidow report received scant public notice.[69]

Since Murphy neither requested nor desired state police assistance at the Mack Avenue plant, the responsibility for maintaining law and order there devolved on the Detroit police.[70] It was not an easy assignment because, as is usual in such circumstances, the company's efforts to remain in operation despite the strike created a good deal of discord outside the plant. The strikers harassed, assaulted, stoned, and even knifed those who were working, and the strikebreakers, in turn, threw missiles at the strikers from the plant. A police search of workers entering the plant one day in March yielded three bushel-loads of guns and blackjacks.[71]

The police sought to prevent stranger picketing; they did not permit cars to park near the plant lest strikers use the vehicles to follow and assault those who were working; they escorted Mack workers who had been hired at the Highland Park plant from the Highland Park line to the Mack Avenue plant; they convoyed workers to streetcars when they left the plant and diverted automobile traffic from Mack Avenue at these hours; and they kept pedestrians moving on the street across from the plant, removed "Communists" who were loitering there, and ordered stores on Mack Avenue closed when they became crowded with "sightseers and possibly with others who might be intent on mischief." The police battled with the strikers on one occasion when several hundred of them stoned the streetcars transporting workers from the plant, which led the passengers to barricade the windows of the cars with seats torn from their fastenings.

On February 7, in a fight between police and strikers that took place as workers left the plant, one man was shot by the police, and seven others were beaten or stabbed. On March 3 the pickets, claiming that workers were throwing bricks and stones at them from inside the plant, rushed the Warren Avenue gate and were teargassed and driven back by the police, who then forbade picketing at that gate. The police arrested fifty-eight strikers and held some of them incommunicado, and, on one occasion, they raided the strikers' headquarters. The strikers protested the "police terror," while the Briggs management complained of inadequate police protection.[72]

Murphy's instructions to the police were clear enough in principle but difficult to apply in practice: the police must not take sides, and they must protect both the "property rights" of the company and the "personal rights" of the strikers. The mayor could not legally compel Briggs to close his plant, and since the company kept its plant open, Murphy believed that those going to work were entitled to "a certain amount of protection." He condemned "intimidation" of workers by pickets and stated flatly that he "would undertake any measure necessary to have it stopped." At the same time, Murphy insisted that the police must not interfere in any way with peaceful picketing; he forbade them to use police cars to transport workers to or from the plant; he forbade them to accept meals from Briggs; and in response to striker complaints he issued orders that the police were to permit strikers to distribute leaflets at other factories in the city and sell dance tickets to raise funds. He informed the police that there must be "no illegal arrests," that all those arrested without cause must be released at once, and that no prisoner was to be held incommunicado. No one, he stated, was to be deprived of his rights simply because he was protesting industrial conditions or was on strike. "My whole interest in this matter," Murphy wrote regarding the strike, "is to see that order is preserved and that all are treated fairly."[73]

The Detroit police, for all their transgressions, were far less blatant in their antistrike activities than law-enforcement units at the Highland Park plant were. The Fact-Finding Committee praised "the level-headed and tolerant attitude" of the Detroit police, but Murphy, who asserted that he had made "every effort" to take preventive action, conceded that "now and then, the police go too far." As Roger Baldwin had warned him and as he learned from his experience as mayor, "the police . . . are, in matters relating to radicals, always difficult to control."[74] Murphy remembered this when as governor of Michigan he had to deal with the great General Motors sit-down strike, just as he harked back to the Briggs strike and created another fact-finding committee during a major strike in the Philippines while he was governor-general.

Despite a gap between rhetoric and performance in Murphy's dealings with the Detroit police, the mayor's "signals and cues" had their impact on police behavior, most notably in the area of free speech and freedom of assembly. Already sensitive to the matter of police conduct as the result of his service as a federal attorney and a criminal-court judge, Murphy enlarged his understanding of the subject while he was mayor. What he had learned was reflected in his subsequent career and particularly in the opinions that he rendered when he served on the nation's highest court.

XV

"The People's Fight"

"The people of Detroit, at last, have a real champion," the Detroit *Labor News* editorialized at the beginning of 1932, "and it is the duty of every citizen to back him to the limit."[1] The Detroit Federation of Labor (DFL) organ was referring to Mayor Murphy's efforts to eliminate the last vestige of private ownership from Detroit's municipal transportation system, but the DFL was equally supportive of Murphy's consumer-oriented campaign to secure a reduction in electric, gas, and telephone rates and to maintain Detroit's low water rates.

In Detroit in 1930 the street railways and waterworks were publicly owned, while private companies supplied the city with electricity, gas, and telephones. The battle for public ownership of Detroit's street railways had been initiated by Mayor Hazen Pingree in 1891 when he vetoed an ordinance extending the franchise of the Detroit City Railway Company, and for the next thirty years the question of municipal versus private ownership of the street railways was a staple of Detroit politics. The issue was finally resolved in favor of public ownership in 1922, when, under the driving leadership of Mayor James Couzens, the Detroit electorate, which had approved the establishment of a city-owned streetcar system two years earlier, overwhelmingly voted to buy out the Detroit United Railway Company for $19,850,000.[2]

The Detroit Street Railway (DSR) system, which covered 373 miles of track when it was inaugurated, was the nation's largest publicly owned surface transportation facility. By the time Murphy became mayor trackage had increased to 450 miles, there were 1,834 streetcars and 582 buses in operation as compared to 1,260 streetcars and no buses in 1922, and the valuation of the property had risen to $58,675,739 as compared to $36,659,913 in 1922. The DSR acquired an equity of $16 million in its property between 1922 and 1930, and during that period it also paid the city $7 million in taxes and paving charges. Its six-cent fare was among the lowest in the country.[3]

In his inaugural address, Murphy promised to provide the DSR with a "business administration, free from political control," and to defend the principle of municipal ownership. The DSR was clearly in need of a "business administration" because there had been an "almost complete breakdown" in its efficiency during the Bowles era and because the depression-induced decline in DSR revenue imperiled the six-cent fare and the ability of the system to meet its bonded indebtedness.[4]

In an effort to improve the DSR's internal administration, the Street Railway Commission, whose quality had been measurably improved by Murphy's appointment of Frank Couzens and Sidney D. Waldon, began to meet weekly with the system's executives, and Couzens located himself at DSR headquarters so that he could more readily keep in touch with DSR operations. Staff and payroll reductions resulted in the paring of the monthly deficit from $250,000 when Murphy became mayor to $60,000 by the beginning of May, 1931, but outgo continued to exceed income during the remainder of the calendar year. In January, 1932, in an effort to arrest the decline and to counteract continuing charges of politics in the DSR, Murphy appointed the best business executive in his administration, Joseph E. Mills, as general manager and gave him virtual dictatorial power over the system.

Mills performed brilliantly as DSR head. After twenty-seven consecutive months of deficits, the system operated in the black in February, 1932; by the end of October Mills had slashed the deficit by almost $1.65 million despite a decline in revenue for the preceding ten months of more than $1.5 million as compared to the first ten months of 1931. The DSR's performance during 1932 compared very favorably with that of any street-railway system in the nation. DSR operating expenses for the year were reduced by 22.24 percent as compared to 14.54 percent for 116 street-railway companies across the land, and whereas the operating revenue of the 116 companies declined 16.93 percent and their net revenue 25.17 percent, Detroit's operating revenue declined only 12.51 percent, and its net revenue actually increased 33.28 percent. The cities in which the 116 companies were located defaulted on $53.3 million in street-railway bonds maturing during the year, but the DSR met all its bonded indebtedness. Whereas the average street-railway fare in 1932 in cities with a population of more than twenty-five thousand was 8.17 cents, the Detroit fare remained approximately six cents.[5]

The DSR was thus in "excellent shape" when it received a " 'sock in the nose'" because of the Briggs strike and then sustained the "heaviest blow of all" as the result of the bank holiday. Its revenues dropped 20 percent in January, 25.6 percent in February, and 35 percent in March as compared to the same months in 1932, and there was fear that it would have to default on $186,000 in bonds maturing in May, 1933. In April, however, it successfully negotiated a refunding arrangement for the entire portion of its debt scheduled to fall due in 1933, and it once again was placed on a sound financial basis. When the refunding agreement had been consummated, Murphy proudly stated that the DSR was "by all odds the best managed public utility in the country," and this was not very much of an exaggeration.[6]

Charging that "big interests" in Detroit were "working secretly to strangle municipal ownership," Murphy appointed men to the Street Railway Commission who were committed to public ownership of the system. He was anxious to improve the financial condition of the system so as to shield municipal ownership from criticism, and he vainly supported a proposal to end the DSR's obligation to pay municipal taxes and paving charges since he viewed this as being in the "best interests" of municipal ownership. When the Common Council early in 1931 authorized the Detroit Downriver Transit Company, an apparent reincarnation of politically influential "jitney interests" that had been eliminated from the streets in 1926, to operate thirty buses between Detroit and various downriver communities, Murphy vetoed the measure on the grounds that only one transportation system should be permitted to operate on Detroit's streets. The Council overrode the veto, but Murphy, characteristically stating that he had received promises of "political support" if he would permit the bus line to operate, announced that he would not grant the company a license unless the Street Railway Commission first recommended such action. Since the city's corporation counsel ruled that only the mayor could grant the permit required for the company to operate, the Council rescinded its action.[7]

It remained for Frank Murphy to complete what Hazen Pingree and James Couzens had begun by removing from the streets of Detroit the sole remaining private competitor of the DSR: the Detroit Motorbus Company. The Detroit Motorbus Company, which was permitted to operate on a day-to-day basis, served a densely populated section of the Detroit area, whereas DSR buses traversed routes in outlying and more thinly settled districts. The 350 buses of the Motorbus Company, which the DFL complained was "milking the city system of the cream of the business," carried as many passengers as the almost six hundred buses of the DSR, and despite declining income the company still registered a small profit in 1930, although not on its Detroit runs. Since some Common Council members thought that the DSR might be able to resolve its financial problems without a fare hike if it took over the Motorbus Company, the Council instructed the Street Railway Commission in March, 1931, to report within thirty days on the wisdom of acquisition of the company; and Murphy announced that he favored the municipal takeover of the Motorbus firm. The commission reported in favor of termination of the right of the Motorbus Company to operate and urged the acquisition of such portions of its property and equipment as might be useful to the DSR if the items could be purchased at a fair price. The Council authorized the commission to negotiate with the Motorbus Company on this basis.[8]

Negotiations between the Street Railway Commission and the Motorbus Company during the summer and fall of 1931 failed to produce an agreement. Finally, on December 22, the Council ordered the Motorbus Company off the streets of Detroit at the end of the year. It was Murphy who apparently "turned the tide" in favor of ouster at the Council hearing that preceded the decision. He declared that "there had been enough delay" in resolving the issue and that the time had come to act. "If municipal ownership is to survive in Detroit," the mayor stated, "it must be municipal ownership only, one system over all our streets."[9]

Prompted by powerful business interests in the Detroit area, represented by John L. Lovett of the Michigan Manufacturers' Association, Harvey Campbell of the Detroit Board of Commerce, and Louis J. Colombo, a Ford Motor Company attorney, Councilman George A. Walters moved for reconsideration of the Council's decision. After "one of the most turbulent hearings in the history of the Council," the aldermen, however, rejected Walters's motion by a 6-2 vote. Opponents of ouster claimed that since the DSR was not prepared to take over the Motorbus routes immediately, ouster would have an adverse effect on business and industry and would lead to "a great deal of confusion, public wrath and possible misery." Whatever the merits of this argument, it is evident that men like Campbell were speaking for major stockholders of the Motorbus concern who saw their investments threatened with extinction. "There is a surprising amount of pressure brought to bear against every measure advanced to help the municipally owned system," Councilman Fred Castator was constrained to observe.

Murphy, who led the ouster forces at the Council hearing, stated that he would not grant the Motorbus Company a permit even if the Council rescinded its resolution. He asserted that there was "no legal or moral argument in favor of this delay," and he charged that Motorbus stockholders had "gone out and shaken the bushes and brought in the right ones to protect their interests." He noted with regard to Colombo's presence that the first vice-president of Motorbus also happened to be Ford's chief engineer. This led Colombo to pound the table and to respond amidst considerable booing from the gallery that Ford was speaking for "all the people" whereas Murphy represented only "Frank Martel and the labor unions." Mayor Murphy, the Detroit *Labor News* exulted after the motion to reconsider had been defeated, "gave the finest demonstration of constructive leadership the City of Detroit has had within memory of man."[10]

On January 1, 1932, the DSR, using its own idle equipment and some buses rented from the Motorbus Company, began operating on Motorbus routes within Detroit, while the company continued its interurban service. The changeover from private to public service was effected without conspicuous difficulty. Detroit, for the first time, now enjoyed the "unified control" of its streets for which Murphy had campaigned.[11]

Just as Murphy was "unalterably opposed" to a DSR fare increase, so he was determined that the Department of Water Supply, despite a mounting deficit, should preserve its low rate structure. The department's budget difficulties stemmed from its inability to collect $900,000 in special assessments for the laying of pipe in new subdivisions, the decline in its receipts after June 30, 1931, and an increase in the proportion of its revenue that had to be devoted to debt service. Although the department slashed its payroll by almost 75 percent between 1930 and 1932, it still faced an estimated deficit of $2.3 million for the fiscal year 1932-33 as 1932 drew to a close. Since Detroit's water rates were about 50 percent lower than those in most American cities, the Department of Water Supply decided to reduce its deficit by substantially raising its rates. Murphy, however, apparently overruled the department, and water rates in Detroit remained unchanged.[12]

Like Pingree and Couzens, Murphy clashed with Detroit's privately owned utilities in an effort to secure reduced rates for the consumer. Pingree had persuaded Detroit to construct a municipal generating plant to provide electricity for street lamps and public buildings, though not for private consumers, and had threatened to establish a municipal gas plant as well. Murphy was similarly attracted to the idea of public ownership, at least in theory. When he first met Carl D. Thompson, the secretary of the Public Ownership League of America, in the spring of 1931, Murphy, an admirer of George W. Norris and his brand of progressivism, figuratively swept Thompson off his feet by telling him that he (Murphy) "wanted to get into this utility struggle, not only locally but nationally." "The public utility question," Murphy observed, "is inextricably interwoven with other basic economic and social questions in which the consistent progressive is interested, and I see nothing else ahead for the progressive and friends of good government but to join the movement." In the end, Murphy did not press for public ownership of Detroit's privately owned utilities, but even Thompson conceded that the demand for lower rates was probably a necessary first step in winning popular support for public ownership.[13]

There was much criticism of privately owned public utilities during the depression years because they generally failed to provide significant rate reductions even though their net income remained rather stable. Should utility rates in Detroit remain the same, Murphy asked, while "readjustments" were being required of Detroit's citizens "in every direction"? The interests of the consumer, the mayor declared, must be placed ahead of stockholder interests. "This," Murphy said, "is the people's fight."[14]

Taxed by political opponents for failing to act earlier, Murphy launched his campaign for lower telephone, electric, and gas rates in February, 1932. He sought and gained the backing of the Detroit *Times* in the struggle, and the DFL and the Taxpayers' Protective Association strongly supported his efforts. Murphy placed Corporation Counsel Clarence Wilcox in charge of the campaign, and Wilcox, in turn, assigned one of his assistants to each of the three companies involved—Michigan Bell Telephone, Detroit Edison, and Detroit City Gas—to prepare the legal data required. "I am in earnest about this," Murphy informed his department heads, but the city was handicapped because it lacked the funds to hire the real-estate appraisers and engineers required to develop its cases properly.[15]

The Michigan Public Utilities Commission had ordered a reduction in telephone rates some years before Murphy became mayor, but Michigan Bell had blocked implementation of the order by taking the case to the federal courts. Wilcox sought to speed up the appeal process, while Murphy urged Michigan Bell officials to reduce rates without awaiting the results of the court action. When the company refused, Murphy attacked its behavior as "unconscionable" and declared that he would seek lower rates by "legal action and by crystallizing public sentiment." The city filed another application for reduced rates before the Public Utilities Commission, which initiated a new appraisal of the company's property. This eventually led to a "substantial" rate reduction, but not until after Murphy had left Detroit.[16]

The Detroit Edison Company, which had lived "under the threatening shadow of municipal ownership" since its incorporation in 1903, generally had been regarded as a "good citizen" in Detroit, but the average cost of electricity to consumers in the city in 1931 was 2.46 cents per kilowatt hour as compared to 2.3 cents in Los Angeles, where the system was municipally owned. The head of Detroit Edison, Alex Dow, had run the municipal lighting plant under Pingree and had been a member of the city's Water Board since 1915. The Detroit *Labor News*, thinking it anomalous that so staunch an opponent of public ownership should be associated with a publicly owned utility, urged Murphy to dismiss Dow; and the mayor, annoyed by what he thought was Dow's uncooperative attitude with regard to the lowering of electric rates and apparently displeased with the performance of the Department of Water Supply, did not reappoint the Detroit Edison president when his term expired on March 1, 1932. Dow's son Douglas, claiming that he was being subjected to "vicious personal attacks" by some of Murphy's associates and that he was no longer confident that he enjoyed the mayor's support, resigned as commissioner of purchases and supplies a few days later. Murphy ungenerously applauded the decision on the grounds that privately owned utilities should be "entirely divorced" from the city government.[17]

Alex Dow regarded Murphy's campaign to lower electric rates as strictly politics, which was partly but not wholly correct. When Murphy and Wilcox sought to persuade Detroit Edison to reduce its rates voluntarily, Dow stated that he would not submit a new rate schedule to the Michigan Public Utilities Commission simply to "meet the political needs of the City Administration"; he also refused to open the corporation's books to city investigators. The city, consequently, filed a petition with the state commission in May, 1932, for a 25 percent reduction in Detroit Edison rates.

Although Wilcox's staff had hoped that the data presented to the commission would justify an immediate temporary rate reduction, the commission decided that Detroit had not made a prima facie case for a temporary rate adjustment, and it therefore initiated a full-scale investigation.

The commission's study of the Edison case continued until August 15, 1933, when it dismissed Detroit's petition as not supported by the evidence. It nevertheless ordered the company to reduce its annual revenue by $1.5 million, about 3.5 percent of its revenue for 1932, by cutting its rates to commercial customers. Detroit Edison secured a temporary injunction restraining the commission from enforcing its order, but the company then put the reduction into effect voluntarily, as it had indicated it would once proceedings before the commission had ended. Appeals of the commission's ruling by Detroit and the Michigan Manufacturers' Association were dismissed by the Ingham County Circuit Court, in August, 1935, which brought the case to an end.[18]

Murphy could have fought Detroit Edison by having the city itself enter the commercial lighting and power field, as the charter authorized. Because of the capital expenditure that would have been required, however, the times were hardly propitious for such a venture. Murphy did instruct the Public Lighting Commission to displace Detroit Edison as a supplier of electricity to the DSR and the Water Board to the extent that this was practicable, but nothing came of the mayor's order since it would have required the city to invest in new substations and transmission lines and would, in any event, have violated a contract between the city and Detroit Edison that ran until 1938.[19]

Largely frustrated, at least in the short run, in his efforts to induce Detroit Edison and Michigan Bell to reduce their rates, Murphy enjoyed better success in negotiating with the Detroit City Gas Company, which alone among the three firms was subject to municipal regulation. Despite the general deflation of prices resulting from the depression, the company, which had been operating without a franchise since 1923, continued to charge the rates set in 1924 by the arbitration panel of which Murphy had been a member. The gas rate issue was complicated by the fact that the introduction of natural gas into Detroit, the only important city east of the Mississippi without natural gas, would in itself have led to lower gas prices. Councilman John Smith insisted that the Michigan gas fields could meet Detroit's needs but that the "utility trust" was keeping this information from the people. The gas company and the Michigan Manufacturers' Association, on the other hand, contended that the available natural gas in Michigan was insufficient to supply Detroit's needs for any extended period, a judgment in which the state geologist concurred, and that gas from Texas would therefore have to be piped into the city from the Indiana-Illinois line. The gas company stated that, although it was prepared to construct the necessary pipe line as soon as a sufficient supply of gas was available, it could not finance the venture if its rates were simultaneously reduced by any substantial amount.[20]

The city's announced objective was to secure an annual gas rate reduction equivalent to $1.5 million, about 10 percent of the Detroit City Gas Company's yearly income. The company was willing to implement a more modest rate cut than this immediately and to commit itself to an additional reduction when natural gas became available in Detroit, but this arrangement was initially unacceptable to Murphy, who declared that the city would "stand for no delay" in securing the reduction it desired. In May, 1932, however, Murphy worked out an agreement with the company by which it reduced its maximum rate from seventy-nine cents per thousand cubic feet to seventy-seven cents, a saving to consumers of about $850,000 per year, and promised to cut its rate by an additional two cents when natural gas became available in Detroit and not later than January 1, 1933. The Detroit *Times* hailed the agreement as "one of the best jobs" of Murphy's career.[21]

Murphy submitted the gas agreement to the Common Council, which accepted the rate reduction and, in addition, imposed an annual license fee (later converted into a rental charge) of $1.5 million on the company for the use of the city's streets. Murphy signed the new ordinance into law, but the company, which had already put the two-cent rate reduction into effect, secured an injunction from the federal district court in Detroit that restrained the city from collecting the fee. The court eventually ruled that although the city could set the terms under which a public utility whose franchise had expired could use its streets, it could enforce such an ordinance only by ousting the company. The Council, in March, 1933, also imposed rental charges for the use of Detroit's streets on Detroit Edison and Michigan Bell, but it had no more success in collecting these fees than it did the charge imposed on the gas company.[22]

Regarding the June 14, 1932, ordinance as only a temporary

solution for the gas problem, Councilman John Smith persuaded his colleagues to submit a charter amendment to the voters that empowered the city to construct and operate a natural gas distribution system of its own. The proposal, which would have required the issuance of $2 million in public-utility bonds, was not based on a careful appraisal of either the engineering or financial factors involved and was strongly opposed by Controller Roosevelt and the Committee on City Finances. Murphy, content that he had achieved a reduction in gas rates and aware that there was little support for a public-ownership amendment, maintained a discreet silence on the matter, and the voters buried the proposal in November by a three-to-one margin.[23]

All in all, the Murphy campaign to reduce utility rates achieved only modest success, partly because of the laborious and time-consuming processes of the public-service regulatory system that were so much criticized during the depression era. Murphy, however, was more inclined to blame the utility magnates for the difficulties that he had encountered. "The attitude of the utilities during the distressing days in Detroit," he noted in 1935, "was an example of utter selfishness that I will not soon forget"; and that he had not forgotten became evident when he developed his reform program as governor of Michigan. Whatever the immediate results of the campaign, however, Murphy's efforts to secure lower utility rates for Detroit consumers strengthened his image as a "consistent progressive" and as a spokesman for the common people. It was this image that enhanced his appeal in both local and national politics.[24]

XVI

Frank and Franklin

As mayor of Detroit and a candidate for reelection in 1931 Frank Murphy was obliged to pursue the politics of nonpartisanship, but as a Democrat ambitious for success beyond Detroit he also found it necessary to involve himself in partisan politics at both the state and national levels. His skill in performing the separate but interrelated roles of nonpartisan and partisan politician necessarily determined the shape of his future career.

There was never any question that Murphy would seek reelection in 1931. Late in May a sixty-man committee whose composition reflected the ethnic and serviceman basis of Murphy's political support in Detroit began to circulate petitions for the mayor's nomination. In the next few months the committee gathered 138,000 signatures, which the Detroit *Times* reported was "far and away the greatest number of signatures ever filed by any aspirant for any public office in Michigan."[1]

Murphy's opponents in the October 6 primary were Mark R. Hanna, a paving contractor who had often done work for the city but against whose firm bankruptcy proceedings had just been initiated; Harold H. Emmons, Bowles's one-time police commissioner; John C. Nagel, a member of the Common Council since 1918 and its president since 1928; Howard A. Starrett, an industrial engineer and chairman of the tax-conscious Committee of 51; John Sosnowski, a former Republican congressman and former Water Board commissioner; Bowen R. Gover, a small businessman whose Business Men's Political League was apparently a nonexistent organization; and John Schmies, the candidate of the Communists.[2]

Other than Murphy, only Emmons and Nagel appeared to be serious candidates, and both of them, despite Detroit's nonpartisan character, were really partisan candidates. At least some members of the Wayne County Republican Committee were active in drumming up support for Emmons, he was the choice of the Detroit Republican Club, and he stated flatly that he was running as a Republican candidate. Nagel, a veteran politician, was the candidate of " 'old line' " Democrats like William F. Connolly. These Democrats were angry because Murphy had spurned their advice on appointments, they quite correctly did not regard the mayor as their kind of Democrat, and they feared that his ties with Governor Franklin D. Roosevelt of New York, the prime candidate for his party's presidential nomination in 1932, threatened their position in the Democratic party. Nagel maintained that Murphy neglected his mayoral duties while "chasing the will-o-the-wisp of national political honors," whereas Murphy charged that Nagel's candidacy was "nothing more than Tammany Hall invading Detroit" and was part of a national plot to block Roosevelt's nomination.[3]

The criticism of Murphy by his opponents centered on his welfare and fiscal policies. Schmies, whose campaign, of course, was atypical, maintained that public relief in Detroit was niggardly, but the other candidates complained that it was too generous, and Emmons charged that Detroit had become "a Mecca for non-resident derelicts, bums and indigents, who have taken welfare money by the millions from citizens of Detroit." All the candidates except Nagel also found fault with Murphy's management of Detroit's fiscal affairs. Sosnowski claimed that the city could be run on a much smaller budget; Emmons charged that Detroit was "just next door to being broke"; and Starrett made tax relief for the small homeowner the centerpiece of his campaign effort. Some of the mayor's opponents also accused him of coddling the Communists; Nagel declared that if he were elected he would not permit Detroit to become "the American capital of Communism," which Murphy, presumably, was threatening to make it.

The campaign rhetoric of Murphy's opponents was essentially negative, and they offered the voters little more than the promise that, if elected, they would manage the city's affairs in a more efficient and businesslike manner than Murphy had. This was not the kind of argument likely to attract voters in the midst of a severe depression. "These 'business men,' " Murphy declared of his opponents, "are drab, cold and frigid candidates who should take their sensibilities and business management back to the affairs of business and industry and try to open the factories."[4]

Although Legionnaires served as chairman and secretary of Murphy's campaign, it is likely that Harry Mead, who had managed Murphy's 1930 campaign, ran the 1931 campaign from behind the scenes. This occurred despite Murphy's protestation that it would be "all wrong" to permit a civil-service commissioner like Mead to play "any part" in the contest. Murphy's speeches, "with the tears and the sobs" that came so easily to him, were largely written by Josephine Gomon, but just how much part other city employees may have played in the campaign is difficult to say. Although the mayor instructed department heads not to participate in the campaign and issued orders to city employees not to engage in political activities, it is doubtful that these instructions were fully observed.

Murphy declared that he would not accept campaign contributions from city officials, city employees, or persons doing business with the city, but the records no longer exist to indicate whether the mayor's instructions were observed. Murphy later asserted that the cost of the campaign had not exceeded $8,000, and there is no doubt that his campaign expenses were quite modest. It is also evident, however, that the mayor was not kept fully informed of all the expenditures made in his behalf.[5]

As incumbents must, Murphy ran on his record. His administration, he stated, had restored the confidence of the people of Detroit in their government, put city finances in order, greatly improved the character of law enforcement, staunchly supported the principle of municipal ownership of the Detroit Street Railways, and protected the rights of free speech and freedom of assembly. Murphy pointed proudly to the character of his major appointments, his attack on the spoils system, and his scandal-free record ("No one can point to any dishonest act of Frank Murphy"). Above all, Murphy, better understanding the mood of the electorate than his opponents did, made no apologies for his welfare program and, instead, proudly claimed that Detroit was first among the cities of the nation in its efforts to alleviate want. It was not true that his government had done too much for the poor and the "downtrodden," he asserted. "I say enough hasn't been done for the poor." He conceded that his administration had made mistakes, but they were "mistakes . . . in the interests of the people, not mistakes for the power or privileged crowd," who opposed him because they favored "a government for the few and not for the masses." "And if mistakes are made in the future," he remarked, "and are made in the interests of the common people, I will be happy."[6]

Murphy's campaign was especially directed at veterans, blacks, white ethnic groups, and workingmen. The annual American Legion convention, held in Detroit in the midst of the campaign, enabled Murphy to dramatize his Legion ties. He received a "loud and noisy greeting" when he appeared in Legion regalia at the opening session, and his uncompromising defense of the Legionnaires against criticism of their behavior in the city did nothing to impair his already high standing among World War I veterans. Murphy spoke frequently to black, ethnic, and labor gatherings, and they responded enthusiastically to his appeals to "my people" and his "emotional style of oratory." "I'm your representative," Murphy asserted to a black audience. Their "group" had been "good" to him in the past, he told them, and he would "not forget" if they were "good" to him "in this fight." On another occasion, Murphy took a different tack and told a black gathering that he did not regard them as "a particular group, to which special favors are to be extended, but just as part of the citizenry, who ask only for their rights." Black leaders like Beulah Young worked assiduously to line up black support for the mayor, and the sanitary workers band appeared at several Murphy campaign rallies.[7]

Since Sosnowski had been injected into the campaign, most likely by Emmons supporters, to attract Polish votes that, it was believed, would otherwise go to Murphy, Murphy's campaign workers made a special effort to hold Polish voters in line. Polish leaders publicly criticized Sosnowski's "disgusting" role as a stalking horse for the mayor's opponents, and they reminded voters of Polish descent how well represented their "group" was in the city administration and how active Murphy had been in promoting the interests of minority groups in general. Mayor Anton J. Cermak of Chicago came to the support of his fellow mayor by urging Detroiters of Bohemian descent, like himself, to support Murphy, and his appeal did not go unheeded. Other ethnic groups in the city similarly pledged their support. Although the press thought it detected some coolness between the mayor and the leaders of the Detroit Federation of Labor (DFL) as the campaign got underway, Murphy received the solid backing of the DFL and its affiliates.[8]

There was not much doubt where most Catholics stood in the primary. In the weekly paper of St. Elizabeth's parish, distributed at all masses on the Sunday before the primary election, Father Schulte urged his parishioners as a "favor" to him to vote for Murphy "if all things are equal with you in regard to the one for whom you will cast your vote." Father Coughlin endorsed Murphy as a mayor who " 'fed the poor,' " and on the day of the primary the sisters, Magdalens, and children in the Convent of the Good Shepherd said prayers and kept candles burning in the hope that, "if it were God's holy will," Frank Murphy "might be the choice of the people of Detroit."[9]

Once again, Murphy received the all-out support of the Detroit *Times*. That Murphy was also backed by the Detroit *Mirror* reflected, to some degree, the interrelationship between Detroit politics and presidential politics. Joseph Patterson, the New York owner of the *Mirror*, was not as enchanted with Murphy as the managing editor of the paper was, but G. Hall Roosevelt thought that if his brother-in-law Franklin interceded in Murphy's behalf, the New York publisher might throw his support to the mayor. In urging this action, Hall led the Roosevelt forces to believe that Murphy's reelection was essential to the New York governor's winning the Michigan delegation in 1932. It may be that Governor Roosevelt responded to Hall's request since the *Mirror*, in the end, warmly supported Murphy's candidacy.[10]

Murphy won a smashing victory in the October 6 primary, gathering 55 percent (123,026) of the 222,531 votes cast, the largest number of votes in a purely municipal primary in Detroit's history up to that time. Although Murphy won a clear majority in the crowded election field, which the Detroit *News* correctly evaluated as "a remarkable expression of approval," the city charter required a final election between the top two vote-getters in the primary, which meant that Emmons, whose 36,967 votes placed him second, remained in the race. The weakness of the old-line Democrats in the city was reflected in Nagel's dismal showing, the veteran councilman netting only 15,901 votes and placing fourth.[11]

Although Murphy ran well throughout the city, winning at least a plurality of the vote in every one of the twenty-two wards, he fashioned his victory most conspicuously in the black and white ethnic districts of Detroit, among voters who had responded affirmatively to him ever since his first race for city-wide office in 1923 and who were now experiencing a higher rate of unemployment than the average for Detroit. Whereas Murphy received 55 percent of the vote in the city as a whole, he garnered more than 80 percent of the vote in Wards 3 (81 percent), 5 (86 percent), and 7 (83 percent), the only three wards that had black majorities; the mayor's electoral margins in the black precincts throughout the city generally ran above 90 percent. In contrast to previous elections, almost as high a percentage of blacks (41.7) as whites (42.2) was registered for the primary, a further testimonial to Murphy's appeal to the city's blacks. Detroit's blacks were overwhelmingly Republican, and their leading newspaper advised them not to vote for Murphy since he was a Democrat, but the black electorate appears to have ignored this advice and, as is generally true in nonpartisan elections, voted its interests rather than its party.

Other than in the three black wards Murphy made his best showing in Wards 9 (68 percent), 11 (72 percent), and 13 (59 percent), all of them wards in which the percentage of inhabitants who were native-born whites of native-born parents was less than half that for the city as a whole. Although Sosnowski ran ahead of Murphy in some Polish precincts and reduced the mayor's totals in such districts generally, Murphy nevertheless bested his opponent in most of the predominantly Polish precincts. Murphy also ran well in predominantly Hungarian, Italian, Jewish, and Greek districts.

As in his previous Detroit elections, Murphy made his poorest showing, relatively, in wards with the largest percentage of native-born whites of native-born parents and in the upper-income, "silk-stocking" districts of the city. He thus received only 39 percent of the vote in Ward 22, a former Bowles stronghold in which almost no blacks lived and more than half of whose inhabitants were native-born whites of native parentage, and 44 percent of the vote in Ward 2, which had the highest percentage of native-born whites of native-born parents of any ward in the city. Murphy netted only 24 of 141 votes in the very wealthy Precinct 15 of Ward 1, 301 of 864 votes in the Palmer Woods section, and 135 of 483 votes in the Indian Village–Whittier Hotel districts of Ward 17.[12] The profile of the Murphy and the anti-Murphy vote rather accurately forecast the division of the vote between Democrats and Republicans in Detroit in the New Deal era.

Murphy remarked that the results of the Detroit primary were "interesting" in view of the opinion of the "timid" that it was "perilous to champion causes in large industrial cities." Although a charismatic political figure like Murphy probably would have impressed himself favorably upon the electorate even in more normal times, the circumstances of the depression obviously enhanced the appeal of a candidate who identified so strongly with the stricken and the unfortunate. " 'Frank Murphy,' " an unhappy editor remarked some weeks before the election, " 'could be elected president or emperor of any great country in the world as the Great Humanitarian.' "[13]

Since the outcome of the November election was hardly in doubt, there was an "almost unprecedented lack of public interest" in the contest until the desperate Emmons forces, toward the end of October, injected the religious issue into the campaign in a pamphlet entitled *How and Why are You Voting on November 3rd.* The alleged purpose of the pamphlet was to reveal to Detroiters "an amazing political situation, showing how Catholic men and women, by exercising a plain political commonsense not displayed in the past by their Protestant brothers and sisters, have assumed control of our municipal government." The thesis was that Catholic voters always "concentrated" their votes on "selected Catholic candidates" whereas the Protestant voters scattered their votes or did not vote and thus allowed a Catholic minority to win elections in a city that was predominantly Protestant. On the assumption that Catholics voted only for Catholic candidates and Protestants for Protestant candidates, it was argued that in the 1930 election 127,811 Catholics had voted for Murphy (106,203 votes) or Smith (21,608 votes) and that Murphy had been elected despite a Protestant vote of 179,328 divided between Bowles (97,772 votes) and Engel (85,556 votes). Since Murphy's 123,026 votes in the October primary, it was asserted, approached the maximum Catholic vote, if the 179,328 Protestants who had voted in 1930 cast their votes for the Protestant Emmons in the final election, he could defeat the mayor.[14]

The pamphlet, which assumed its own conclusions and offered no empirical evidence to substantiate them, was allegedly put out by the "Citizens' Fact Finding Committee," a nonexistent organization. The real authors were probably Ku Klux Klan officials who arrived in Detroit about two weeks before the publication of the crude tract and whose appearance had led the Detroit *Saturday Night* to speculate that the religious issue would soon be raised in the campaign. Emmons denied any connection with the pamphlet, but his canvassers and he used its arguments and its figures from the moment that the document appeared until the end of the campaign. In the primary, Emmons declared in his final campaign address, Murphy had received all the votes of "those who think as he does, but those who think as we do are in the vast majority and can win easily if we all go to the polls."[15]

The *How and Why* pamphlet angered Catholics and Protestants alike and probably helped Murphy more than it hurt him. When efforts were made to circulate the pamphlet outside Protestant churches on the Sunday before the election, quite a few ministers denounced the document and drove the circulators away. One

Protestant clergyman who normally ignored politics but who resented "the vicious attempt to stir up strife and bitter prejudice" warned his congregants not to permit "cheap religious prejudices" to "warp" their judgment when they cast their ballots. A woman wrote Murphy that "any broadminded Protestant would rather associate with any broadminded Catholic . . . then [sic] with any narrowminded Protestant." Murphy wisely decided not to dignify the pamphlet by making a formal reply.[16]

Murphy devoted only two weeks to the campaign against Emmons, mainly reiterating the themes that he had developed in the primary. As in the October contest, he was endorsed by one ethnic group after another, by the Legion, and by the DFL. Radio station WJR broke precedent by endorsing him, and even the 22nd Ward Republican Club announced its support for the mayor.[17]

The 166,748 votes cast for Murphy on November 3 constituted 64 percent of the total vote and gave the mayor the greatest proportion of the vote that a mayoral candidate had received in Detroit since 1923. Murphy's vote was distributed in much the same fashion as it had been in the primary. He made his best showing once again in the three black wards and overwhelmed Emmons in black precincts by margins of up to thirty to one. Since Sosnowski had been eliminated from the race in the primary, Murphy ran even better in Polish districts than he had in October, gaining about 83 percent of the votes in these precincts, and he ran ahead of his city-wide average, predictably, in Italian, Greek, Hungarian, and Jewish precincts. As in October, Murphy fared worst in wards with a high percentage of native-born whites of native-born parents and in the upper-income precincts.[18]

Murphy's victory was widely regarded as a "crushing rebuke" to the "old time political intolerance and tactics" as well as "a resounding vindication" of his "policies of a new humanitarianism in the management of civic affairs." The beneficiaries of the "new humanitarianism" were understandably delighted with Murphy's triumph. "I am so happy today over your victory for we the poor folks needed you so," one of them informed the mayor. "You have been a 'Father to Detroit,'" another Murphy supporter wrote the mayor in congratulating him on his victory.

Murphy himself stressed the social justice implications of his victory. "I know what this vote means," the victorious mayor declared, "that the people are anxious for the new born social mindedness that has come to our city. . . . We must realize we all belong to one great brotherhood. In Detroit we will not pattern our government after that of any other city, but will govern along lines of humanity and charity." [19]

The Detroit *Mirror* thought that Murphy's victory "served to focus upon Detroit's still youthful chief executive with sharpened glare the spotlight of national recognition into which he has been steadily projecting himself because of his progressive social-mindedness." The results, indeed, were viewed with interest in Albany. "I am perfectly delighted to hear of your re-election," Governor Roosevelt advised the mayor. [20]

As chief executive of Detroit, Murphy proclaimed that it was his duty to defend the principle of nonpartisanship for which the city's charter provided. When William A. Comstock, the Democratic candidate for governor of Michigan in 1930, sought to create "a 'Me and Murphy' impression" by capitalizing on Murphy's popularity in industrial centers in the state, the mayor let it be known that he would "greatly resent" any attempt to involve him in "party politics," a reaction that state Democratic leaders were long to remember. In January, 1932, similarly, Murphy refused to serve on the finance committee of the Wayne County Democratic organization. [21]

Murphy had been conditioned by the nonpartisan offices that he had held since 1924 to stress his independence from the conventional politics of party and organization. Since the Democratic party in Michigan, moreover, was a miniscule, ineffective, and altogether conservative body, Murphy had little reason to identify with it. He stated early in 1931 that although he was affiliated with the Democratic party, he should be categorized as an "Independent Progressive" since he had had no direct contact with the state organization for eight years, had been interested in the La Follette movement of 1924, and was a supporter of the Republican but independent-minded Senator Couzens. Two months later Murphy asserted that he was "not much of a Democrat" although he "never would fall far enough to become a Republican."

Consistent with these views, Murphy evidenced some interest in the League for Independent Political Action, formed in September, 1929, by such men as John Dewey, Oswald Garrison Villard, and Paul Douglas to denote their disillusionment with the two major political parties. "There is no doubt," Murphy wrote the executive secretary of the League in January, 1931, "that the near future must see a redefinition of parties and new alignment of forces in the United States." When George Norris and some fellow insurgents convened a national conference of progressives in Washington in March, 1931, Murphy, as already noted, accepted an invitation to attend. Describing himself as "a political maverick," he lauded Norris as "the greatest man in the United States Senate" and declared that if the Nebraska senator were nominated to head a third-party ticket, "I'd be with him all the way." Murphy's presence at the convention angered the titular head of Michigan's Democratic party, William Comstock, who asserted that the Democrats of the state did not have to take instruction from "these so-called progressives."[22]

As the invitation to Murphy to attend the National Progressive Conference indicates, his performance as mayor of Detroit was attracting attention beyond the city's limits and was gaining him national visibility as a political figure who might be "On His Way Up." Detroit's welfare program, understandably, was widely noticed in a nation so beset with unemployment, and until the revelation of the Lewis embezzlement, the city's relief effort enjoyed a rather good press. The "entire nation conceeds [*sic*] that you have had more human sympathy and a more intelligent programme of help than any Mayor in our nation," one of Murphy's ministerial friends wrote him from Boston in April, 1931. "The impact of what you have done has hit the eastern slope with a bang."

Murphy was "cheered lustily" when he spoke at the National Progressive Conference. One reporter thought that the Detroit mayor "stole the show," and a United Press correspondent commented that "there were those present who wondered if a new figure had not made his political debut on a national platform." Nationally syndicated correspondent William Hard was simply dazzled by the mayor. Murphy, Hard wrote, had "personality plus, and then another plus." The "unanimous view," Hard reported, was that Washington had "seldom . . . seen a man more on his way or more likely to make that way go far."[23]

In the months following the conference Murphy continued to receive a good deal of attention in the nation's press. Mark Hellinger, for example, reported in his syndicated column in September, 1931, that Murphy was "the kind of chap that the country should have in Washington, D.C. But that's something," Hellinger guessed, "that could never happen. The politicians wouldn't go for Frank Murphy. He's a trifle too much of a square

shooter. . . ." In an article in *Collier's* of April 30, 1932, entitled
"City of Hope," John B. Kennedy praised Murphy as personifying
"the new . . . order in American municipal politics; the order
that calls for management, not manipulation." You have "fashioned
me as I would like to be," a grateful Murphy wrote Kennedy.
Edmund Wilson, Raymond Clapper, and Mauritz Hallgren also
had occasion to call attention to "Detroit's liberal mayor."[24]

Though he proclaimed his political independence, Murphy nevertheless realized that his vaulting ambition for high office could
be realized only through the Democratic party. Sensitive to the
political winds, Murphy increasingly linked his political aspirations
with the presidential candidacy of Franklin D. Roosevelt. Privately,
Murphy regarded Alfred E. Smith as "in many ways the most fit
man for President in the United States," but the Detroit mayor
was enough of a political realist to understand that the Catholic
Smith was not likely to receive the Democratic nomination a second
time. Murphy may also have reasoned that if Roosevelt, whose
principal support was in rural areas and the South, won the
nomination, he might seek to appease disgruntled Catholics by
selecting a Catholic running mate with an urban background.
Perhaps the way for a Catholic to gain the White House was first
to serve an apprenticeship as vice-president and, by so doing, to
lessen public concern about a Catholic as president.[25]

In February, 1931, Murphy proclaimed himself "a great admirer"
of Franklin D. Roosevelt, and a Murphy-for-vice-president boomlet
developed. The reaction of the state Democratic organization to
talk of Murphy for vice-president was "lukewarm," to say the
least. Alfred Debo, the chairman of the Democratic State Central
Committee, thought that the idea would not be "taken seriously"
since the 1932 convention would certainly name a Democrat,
and Murphy, after all, had let it be known that he was an
independent progressive. Horatio J. Abbott, the Democratic national committeeman, asserted that Michigan Democrats would support
party members "who are ready to stand up at all times and
be counted" rather than men like Murphy. The Detroit *Saturday
Night,* wont to mock Murphy's ambitions, wondered in a bit
of doggerel why Murphy seemed to covet the vice-presidential
post:

> Does he expect more speeches there
> And cameras to flick and flare,
> With armies of reporters to
> Relate what he intends to do?

Aye, sad indeed would be his lot—
Vice-presidents are soon forgot;
And sadder still, it is expected,
He would become, if not elected.

However, he might make the grade,
If Democrats would only aid,
Who now sit down and cross their fingers;
While dew awaits and sun malingers.[26]

Although stating that he was not seeking the vice-presidency and sometimes protesting that he did not desire the post, Murphy almost certainly found the idea attractive. It is doubtful, however, that the Roosevelt camp ever seriously considered Murphy for second place on the ticket, and Michigan Democrats continued to give the suggestion "a gentle razberry."[27]

Hall Roosevelt informed his brother-in-law Franklin just after Murphy defeated Bowles that the mayor-elect was "a friend of mine and outstanding" and that his victory reflected voter dissatisfaction with the "'old crowd.'" It was to Hall and the mayor that Franklin Roosevelt soon turned to look after his interests in Michigan. Murphy and his controller visited Hyde Park in June, 1931, and Hall advised Louis Howe in August that, if Murphy were reelected, he would be able "to control the State Convention and the National Committeemen." This was quite in contrast to the view of the Connolly forces that the Murphy wing of the Michigan Democratic party consisted only of Murphy and G. Hall Roosevelt. Presidential politics took a holiday in Detroit until after Murphy's reelection, and then Howe thought that the time had come for Hall and the mayor to act. "Now that you fellows have won," Howe wrote Hall, "isn't it time for us to get busy delegate collecting? We have done absolutely nothing in Michigan waiting for you people to say when to move!"[28]

Murphy's support was actually far less important to Franklin Roosevelt's winning of the Michigan delegation than Hall had led his brother-in-law and Louis Howe to believe and than some New Deal historians have since assumed.[29] However popular Murphy may have been with the masses, his influence within the Democratic organization in the state was negligible, as events were soon to demonstrate. At the Wayne County Democratic convention in March, 1932, "certain members of the old organization," led by Connolly, blocked efforts by the Roosevelt adherents, with whom Frank Murphy was allied, to instruct county delegates to the state convention to support the New York governor for the nomination.

At the Democratic state convention in Saginaw two weeks later, the regulars sought to humiliate Murphy by refusing to name him a delegate to the national convention, a designation that Murphy later conceded "meant everything to me." Stressing the issue of party regularity, a vengeful Comstock declared, "It is not a question of what Mr. Murphy will do, but of what he has done in the past." The choice of two delegates to the national convention from the First District of Michigan, Murphy's home district, was entrusted to the delegates from that district attending the Saginaw convention; and in "a riotous caucus session" the Old Guard, whose slogan was "Stop Murphy at any cost," came within a hair of implementing a prearranged scheme to name George G. Sadowski and A. J. Wilkowski as the district's delegates. After Harry Mead pleaded Murphy's case, however, Sadowski withdrew his name, and Wilkowski eventually moved the nomination of Murphy and Comstock, who otherwise would have been named a delegate at large. Sadowski, who was presiding, asked for the "ayes" and "nays" and, ignoring the chorus of "nays," declared the motion carried. Bedlam ensued. There were shouts of "'treachery,'" "'sell out,'" and "'double cross,'" women delegates wept, fists flew, and one overwrought delegate had to be restrained from shooting another delegate.

It was later alleged that Murphy gained his place in the delegation to the Democratic national convention only because he had promised city jobs to First District delegates to the Saginaw convention. Although Murphy denied this, it is evident that the mayor and some of his Polish friends had put a good deal of pressure on Wilkowski just before the state convention; and Harry Mead, who later remarked that he had experienced more difficulty in having Murphy named a delegate to the Chicago convention than in having him elected mayor, recalled that Murphy advocates succeeded in the district caucus because "we had packed in three or four extra voters there." [30]

Although Connolly and some other Smith supporters hoped to send an uninstructed Michigan delegation to the Chicago convention, the Saginaw convention voted to instruct the delegation to support Roosevelt in Chicago, under the unit rule, "as long as, in the best judgment of the delegation, party welfare so dictates." The opposition to Roosevelt among some of the regulars was partly based on the fear that Murphy, because of his association with the candidate, would receive credit for a decision to support the New York governor and would gain control of patronage in the state should Roosevelt be elected. The regulars, as Mead put it, "wanted to make sure that there would be no late-starting jockies coming in to split the spoils." Debo, however, dissipated this concern by reading a letter from James A. Farley, Roosevelt's campaign manager, promising that patronage would be channeled through the state organization in the event of a Roosevelt victory.

It was Farley's practice to work through the regulars wherever possible, but it may also be that when he visited Detroit on March 16 "to look the situation over," he discovered that Murphy's enthusiasm for Roosevelt did not really run very deep and that men like Abbott and Debo were not only more committed to Roosevelt than Murphy was but also enjoyed far greater support in the party. The president of the People's Democratic Club of Michigan informed Roosevelt just before the Saginaw convention, with considerable exaggeration, that Murphy had "in no way" contributed to the increasing sentiment for the New York governor in Wayne County and that the mayor was "nothing more nor less than a political climber, without principle and willing to sacrifice his nearest and dearest friends on the alter [sic] of his political ambitions." Although Farley wrote the mayor, "I know you will stay right on the job to make sure that nothing happens to upset the program [to commit the Michigan delegation to Roosevelt]," Murphy did not even attend the Saginaw convention until its closing session, and he took no part in its deliberations. It was organization Democrats like Abbot and Debo who, in the end, delivered the Michigan delegation to Roosevelt.[31]

After the Saginaw convention Roosevelt could hardly have entertained any illusions concerning Murphy's standing with the Democratic regulars. The New York governor knew, however, that the Democratic organization in Michigan needed the support of men like Murphy, who had considerable voter appeal, if the party were "to cut into the Republican vote in that rock-ribbed State." Acutely conscious of the party's narrow base in Michigan and the conservatism of its titular leaders, Murphy, for his part, was full of advice to Roosevelt both before and after the Saginaw convention as to what was required to achieve victory in the state in November. The Democratic party, the mayor said, would have to broaden its appeal to attract additional voters to its ranks, especially voters of "the young progressive type." Roosevelt would have to offer the state "a progressive, a liberal, and a strong leadership," and the state organization would have to be led by men of the same type, not identified with the "reactionary members of the party."

Roosevelt sentiment in Michigan was "entirely unorganized," Murphy reported, but it could be given cohesion by the formation of "Roosevelt for President Clubs." From these clubs would emerge "a crystallized sentiment and a new personnel" that could "take over" the party and "build up a complete organization" in the state. It would also be wise, Murphy thought, to set up a Detroit headquarters run by "a prominent progressive type Democrat who would appeal to the new voters and others besides the Democrats," a position that Murphy thought might be entrusted to his brother George. The campaign itself, Murphy advised, should be conducted "entirely on principles," and since the economic situation was "so extreme," it was essential that "humanitarian and economy considerations . . . stand before all else." Murphy also let Roosevelt know that the mayor's good friend Father Charles E. Coughlin, who had "the biggest following of any single person in the United States," would announce for the New York governor at the proper time.

Although Murphy's advice to Roosevelt was not unrelated to his own ambitions, he was correct in his perception that the Democratic party in Michigan had to be restructured along what later would be described as New Deal lines if Michigan were to cease to be a one-party Republican state. Farley rejected Murphy's advice to set up a Roosevelt headquarters in Michigan before the national convention, but the proposal to establish a Roosevelt-for-President club met with the New York governor's "complete approval."[32]

When Michigan Democrats gathered at the Chicago convention in July, the press reported that Comstock had adopted a conciliatory attitude toward Murphy and his alleged vice-presidential ambitions. Actually, Comstock, who had recently advised a Detroit friend that "the Mayor and I are not exactly buddies," made little effort to conceal his true feelings about Murphy. "The trouble with Frank Murphy," Comstock stated, was that he was a nonpartisan in "lean years" but a Democrat in a "fat year"; if he expected the party to be more "enthusiastic" when he wanted something, Comstock animadverted, he should "take some interest in us in our adversity." However, since it was reported that Murphy hoped to gain the vice-presidential nomination by delivering a speech to the convention at the proper moment, Comstock professed himself willing to give the Detroit mayor the chance "to spout." In the end, Murphy did not receive his opportunity "to spout," and the Detroit *News* was not incorrect in its judgment that he was "a complete washout" at the convention.[33]

Murphy hoped that the Democratic platform would urge "drastic federal action" to deal with unemployment, but he was not given the opportunity to press his views in person before the platform committee. He considered the plank on unemployment adopted by the convention[34] both "inadequate and unsatisfactory" although still preferable to what the Republicans had to offer. "The forgotten man," Murphy asserted, "is still forgotten. The Democratic party has let a great chance to do big things for the nation slip away." Murphy thought that the prohibition question had to be "courageously handled" in the platform, but it was Comstock, not Murphy, who led the fight among the Michigan delegates for a repeal plank, and it was Comstock rather than the Detroit mayor who was awarded the Michigan seat on the resolutions committee.[35]

When Farley asked the Michigan delegation to provide a speaker to second Roosevelt's nomination, Abbott and Debo made "peace overtures" to Murphy, asking him to deliver the address. Affronted when he learned that the Roosevelt organization had not specifically requested that he be the speaker, Murphy failed to agree until it had been decided that there should be no more seconding speeches. Connolly failed in his efforts to crack the Michigan delegation, which remained with Roosevelt until his nomination on the fourth ballot, but Murphy could take no special credit for this, and Burton K. Wheeler later claimed that Murphy had wilted under pressure at "a crucial point in the proceedings." After the convention made its decision, Murphy stated that Roosevelt was "the best selection that could have been made at this time," but he spoke more warmly about Smith than about the party's nominee. Murphy, of course, did not receive the vice-presidential nomination, nor did the post go to an urban Catholic. Murphy's only moment of glory at the convention came when he was invited by James and Anna Roosevelt to join members of the Roosevelt family and others in meeting the New York governor at the airport when he flew to Chicago to accept his party's nomination.[36]

Although Murphy had been unwilling to identify with the Democratic party during the 1930 elections, he campaigned vigorously for Roosevelt in 1932 because he now saw his political future as linked with the election of the New York governor. In 1930, similarly, Murphy was not favorably disposed toward the Democrats of Michigan, but in the summer of 1932 he was enthusiastic about the change that he saw taking place in the state party. He thought the party's revival in Detroit and Wayne County "a pretty significant thing, having in mind that this spot has been the most conservative Republican strong-hold in the Country during the past two or three decades." He believed that the "new vigorous movement of young progressive Democrats" would "freshen the whole situation" and that, with "militant, crusading leadership" and the advocacy of "progressive reforms," the Democrats might even do the unexpected and capture the state in November. Murphy accepted an invitation to join the Speakers Bureau of the National Progressive League, a bipartisan group organized by Norris and others to mobilize progressive support for Roosevelt, but it was as a Democrat that Murphy campaigned for the New York governor.[37]

The high points of the presidential campaign in Detroit were the appearances in the city of Franklin D. Roosevelt on October 2 and President Hoover on October 22. More than 100,000 people turned out to see Roosevelt, who, as the Detroit *Times* commented, "came, saw, was seen and conquered." Murphy boarded the Roosevelt train when it arrived in the city and later "brought the crowd to its feet, cheering and applauding," when he introduced the governor to a campaign audience in the Naval Reserve Armory. Speaking in the home area of Murphy and Coughlin, Roosevelt quoted approvingly from the *Quadragesimo Anno* of Pius XI, an action that one historian has described as "perhaps the most attractive thing" that Roosevelt did in the campaign from a Catholic point of view.[38]

The newsman Thomas E. Stokes has left us a graphic account of Hoover's campaign appearance in Detroit. When reporters left the Hoover train at the Michigan Central depot, they found "a howling mob" that was "shouting imprecations" at Hoover. The president emerged and entered a limousine provided by the Ford Motor Company. "Never can I forget that experience," Stokes wrote. "We drove to a hall [Olympia Stadium] where he was to make his speech through miles and miles of silent men and women gathered along the streets. They looked on glumly. Occasionally there would be a hoot and a jeer." At the Olympia, "the usual stalwart crowd of regular Republicans. . . . put on a good show," but when the president rose to speak his face was "ashen grey," and his hands were "shaking."[39]

Murphy spoke for Roosevelt and Comstock, the Democratic nominee for governor, throughout Michigan, almost always to large, appreciative audiences, and he also made a campaign address for Roosevelt in Cleveland. Murphy's speech in Flint was delivered to "the largest indoor political rally in the history of Genesee County," while the Iron Mountain meeting was reportedly "the largest ever held" in the Upper Peninsula. In his Bay City address, Murphy, according to his former boss John E. Kinnane, "held the immense crow[d] in his right hand more perfectly than I have ever seen an orator do," and the mayor's radio speech in Detroit, "The Procession of Forgotten Men," was described by a listener as "one of the greatest addresses in behalf of humanity that I have ever listened to."[40]

In his speeches, Murphy stressed unemployment as the "greatest problem" facing the United States. He attacked the Hoover record as one of "brutal, cold, un-American indifference to the welfare of our government and our people" and alleged that the relief measures sponsored by the president served banks, insurance companies, and industrial concerns "while he . . . turned a deaf ear toward the pleas of American humanity stretched out along the roadside." Governor Brucker, Murphy charged, was "the only important official in America" with a worse relief record than Hoover.

The "rebuilding" of the United States, Murphy contended in Republican Michigan, must be in the hands of "real progressives" from both parties, and he appealed to the voters to place the issues and the needs of the people ahead of the ties of party. Noting that he himself was "not that much of a party man," Murphy urged his listeners to "set aside bias, prejudice and foolish tradition, and vote for the party that is right, that is unanimously progressive—and that, today, is the Democratic party."[41]

Quite apart from his campaign speeches, Murphy sought to foster the Democratic cause by announcing on October 20 that he was forming a Non-Coercion League to protest the pressure certain employers were allegedly exerting on their workers to vote Republican. Murphy's action followed a radio address by Henry Ford in which he praised Hoover and Brucker and also the posting of notices in Ford plants that Hoover "must be re-elected" "to prevent times from getting worse and to help them get better." The League, whose membership included "the most distinguished clergymen, [and] partisan and non-partisan leaders" in Detroit, apparently redounded to the benefit of the Democrats in the election contest.[42]

Roosevelt carried Michigan in November by 130,000 votes, the first time a Democratic presidential candidate had won the state since 1852; the Democrats also captured the governorship and both houses of the state legislature. In Detroit, Roosevelt received 62.4 percent of the vote, as compared to a Democratic percentage of 53.1 in 1930. "Politically Michigan lay inert and cold," a Murphy associate wrote the mayor regarding the condition of the state before the election. "A huge warm spirit stirred her from her slumber. It was you." Murphy was "entirely responsible" for the Democratic victory in Michigan, one Michigander wrote Farley, an opinion that was echoed by others. Although it is impossible to calculate Murphy's precise effect on the Michigan vote, he surely deserves some credit for the 88 percent increase (from 19.5 percent in 1930 to 36.7 percent) in the Democratic vote among blacks in Detroit and the 51 percent increase (from 54.2 percent in 1930 to 72.1 percent) in the Democratic vote of foreign-born voters. "It has been our inning," Murphy commented, and he hoped that it would mean "something for all the poor . . . people in our country."[43]

It was widely assumed in Michigan that Murphy would receive a major federal appointment from the new Roosevelt administration. Murphy deserved serious consideration both because of his importance to the future of the Democratic party in Michigan and because of his status as a prominent Catholic layman. Although he was not "close" to the party organization in the state, he was nevertheless now believed by many to be "the biggest Democrat" in Michigan. "The new captain of the ship, so far as Democracy is concerned, is one Frank Murphy," Frank Martel observed, ". . . because without him there would be no revival of Democracy in Michigan."[44]

Roosevelt was anxious to provide suitable recognition of the substantial Catholic element in the Democratic party, and a major appointment for Frank Murphy nicely served this objective. On November 20, 1932, Murphy addressed the National Catholic Alumni Federation in New York on the subject, "A Mayor's Interpretation of the Encyclical of Pope Leo XIII, Forty Years After." As a New York *Daily News* reporter advised a prominent Catholic layman in Detroit, Murphy simply "wowed 'em. A lot of hard-boiled Tammany lawyers whose interest in government is anything but altruistic were openly crying before he got through. Afterwards, most of the 400 present milled around for an hour or more trying to meet Murphy. It was one of the most remarkable personal triumphs I have ever seen. Aside from the publicity, I think your Mayor did himself a lot of good politically. He made a dent in the democratic consciousness down here and established himself in the big league candidacy class."[45] A "big league" appointment followed some months later.

Murphy's appointment to a major post was urged on Franklin D. Roosevelt by brother-in-law Hall and by Father Coughlin. "Don't forget my friend *Frank Murphy—he's valuable to you,*" Hall wrote Franklin. Murphy had "tremendous Catholic influence," Hall said of the mayor, and, although a devout Catholic, did not permit his religion to "stand in the way." He was "an orator of the first water," had "excellent executive training," knew human nature "intimately," and was "honest, obedient and energetic." Hall did not deceive Franklin D. Roosevelt about Murphy's ambition. Murphy, Hall wrote, had undertaken politics as "a life's work" and "would not sacrifice himself for a cause if avoidable," which was too harsh a judgment. He "will do a million dollar job for you," Hall summarized, "as long as it blazes the trail 'Frank Murphy for president!' " Although it is more difficult to document Coughlin's role as an advocate of a Murphy appointment than it is Hall Roosevelt's, the Royal Oak priest, then at the height of his influence, apparently argued Murphy's case before Raymond Moley, Roosevelt's chief brain truster, and before Roosevelt himself. Coughlin later took the credit for the appointment that Murphy received.[46]

Murphy was rumored to have declined several offers of appointment, but the only position he is known to have refused was the chairmanship of the Federal Trade Commission. The position Murphy most desired was the attorney generalship, perhaps because he appreciated the political advantages that could be derived from a war on crime, and he was willing to accept the governor-generalship of the Philippines as a second choice. Murphy indicated his preferences to Moley in January, 1933, only to learn that Senator Thomas Walsh had already been offered the attorney generalship and Homer Cummings had been promised the Philippines post. When the Catholic Walsh died on March 2 en route to the inauguration, Murphy confidently expected to be offered the attorney generalship, but Roosevelt immediately named Cummings, not Murphy, to replace Walsh.[47]

President Roosevelt seems to have had second thoughts about the Cummings appointment, telling Henry L. Stimson more than three weeks after the appointment had been announced that he was undecided as to whether to retain Cummings as attorney general or to send him to the Philippines. A week later, however, possibly influenced by Hall's advice that Murphy had "his heart set on the Philippines," Roosevelt wrote Felix Frankfurter, "I seriously think of Frank Murphy . . . for the Philippines—young, red-headed, idealistic, but at the same time an interpreter of warring elements." On April 7, 1933, without having consulted Democratic leaders in Michigan—Comstock later sent the president "a very bitter telegram" expressing the hope that Murphy would be as " 'loyal' " to the president as he had always " 'been to Frank Murphy' "—Roosevelt announced that the new governor-general of the Philippines would be Frank Murphy. The Detroit *News* commented that the position was regarded as the most important at the president's disposal after the cabinet and the Supreme Court.[48]

Murphy did not take his oath of office as governor-general until May 10, 1933. Although he would have preferred not to leave his Detroit position until the city's debt problems had been resolved, in the end he delayed his resignation until after May 8 not because of the debt question but to save the city the expense of holding the special mayoralty election in 1933 that the Detroit charter would have required had he resigned any earlier.[49]

A round of farewell banquets marked the final weeks of Murphy's tenure as mayor. On April 18 the mayor was feted by the John Faust Post of the American Legion. The next night "the Forgotten Men remembered their benefactor" as Murphy attended a dinner in his honor at the Fisher Lodge. A spokesman for the lodgers expressed their pleasure that the mayor had received so important an appointment but also noted their unhappiness at being deprived of "one who has striven courageously in our behalf against stubborn opposition." As he had often said, Murphy told these much maligned victims of the depression, "What I have been able to do for you, I did willingly, glad of whatever contribution I could make to sweeten the lives of good men caught, through no fault of their own, in the economic vortex." On April 20 the DFL tendered Murphy a banquet in recognition of all that he had done for the labor movement as mayor, Recorder's Court judge, and private citizen. "We hate to lose you even for a short while," Martel said to the mayor on behalf of the DFL's members.[50]

The city's official tribute to its mayor took the form of a citizens' testimonial banquet at the Book-Cadillac Hotel, followed by a "City-wide demonstration" at Olympia Stadium. "The banquet," the Detroit *Times* reported, "was marked by glittering oratory and applause; the mass meeting, by blaring bands, cheers and shouts of a less articulate but equally enthusiastic audience." Several hundred people at the hotel heard Governor Comstock strain credulity by referring to Murphy as "my friend" and by expressing the hope that Murphy would return to Michigan "to further fame, glory and service." In his remarks, Murphy stated that the major problems facing Detroit officials were to keep the city government honest and clean, to maintain a government that would serve "humanity," and to "reconstruct" Detroit by aiding the victims of depression and reducing property taxes.

From the hotel Murphy went to Grand River and Fifteenth, where he joined three thousand Legionnaires in a march to Olympia. Here, before eighty-five hundred people, Rabbi Leo Franklin asserted that it had always been said that Detroit was "a city without a soul" but that, thanks to Murphy, this was no longer true. When it came his turn to speak, Murphy declared, "There is no use fixing our minds on a restoration of the old order, because the old order is gone and cannot be revived. It should not be revived because it was grotesque and unsound. . . ." He thought that the day of the "big man" had ended and that the world was now looking for "an honest man who walks humbly with the people."[51]

Like the president of the Twin-Flex Corporation, some well-to-do citizens of Detroit, who had "disliked and distrusted" Murphy almost from the start, heaved "a sigh of relief" that he was departing the city. Roy Chapin, the president of the Hudson Motor Car Company, was willing to concede that Murphy, "in many ways," had been "a good mayor," but Murphy's "idealism and his desire to help the man in hard luck," Chapin thought, had "led him astray" in the welfare area and had "almost" bankrupted the city. The organ of the Detroit Board of Commerce regarded it as a sufficient commentary on Murphy's performance that, as his tenure came to an end, 250,000 Detroiters were on the welfare rolls, the city was in default on its debt, a municipal debtors bill was being considered in Washington and a municipal receivership bill in

Lansing, city employees were being paid in scrip, taxpayers were threatening revolt, and Detroit's reputation had been "damaged throughout the world."[52]

Unlike some of the " 'best people,' " middle-class citizens committed to social reform and the protection of civil liberties thought that Murphy had been an almost ideal mayor. "Together with you," Rabbi Leon Fram wrote the mayor, "the liberal hearts and minds in this community have been enabled during the years of your mayoralty to make the city of Detroit a place presided over by a spirit of sympathy with the common man. In the most dangerous times in all the history of our city, we have been enabled through you to retain the American citizen's liberty of expression and of protest." "How dreadfully we shall all miss you," a member of this group and her son wrote the departing mayor.[53]

Probably no single expression of favorable opinion pleased Murphy more than that of Senator Couzens's man in Detroit, the gruff, tough-minded, and forthright William J. Norton. Describing himself as "one of the quiet supporters of your policies here in Detroit," Norton wrote Murphy that his departure was "a severe loss" for the city. "Your constant insistence that the distressed people of the community should be given a fair shake, your thorough understanding of the troubles that beset them, the even-handed fairness with which you administered public affairs, and your splendid accomplishments have endeared you to many humble people."[54]

And how right Norton was about the "humble people." More than one thousand Fisher lodgers signed a testimonial expressing regret at Murphy's departure, and 119 victims of the depression who had found jobs through the city's Free Employment Bureau thanked Murphy for having enabled them "to maintain our . . . self-respect." One woman whom the city had aided when she was in desperate need wrote Murphy that she had hoped he would always be mayor, but another of his followers thought that he had "outgrown" Detroit.[55]

Like organized labor and the leadership of the black community, Murphy's Catholic constituents, immensely proud of him as "a model Catholic layman, truly good and devout and thoroughly Catholic," evaluated the mayor in flattering terms. After Murphy had been mayor for a year, Michael Gallagher, the bishop of Detroit, told Father Coughlin that Murphy had been " 'a God send to Detroit . . . and to the Catholic Church during these troubled times,' " and this remained the bishop's judgment when Murphy's mayoralty came to an end.[56]

One Detroiter characterized Murphy as "the best mayor" Detroit had ever had.[57] There is, of course, no entirely objective way to evaluate such a judgment, but the proposition that he was one of Detroit's great mayors is easy enough to defend. He restored faith in the city's government at a time when civic morale was at low ebb, provided Detroit with honest, economical, and generally efficient government, made excellent appointments and extended the merit system, revitalized and improved the police force, protected the rights of free speech and freedom of assembly in a time of troubles, ousted the last remaining competitor of the city-owned transportation system, initiated the process leading to lower rates for utility services, and involved blacks, white ethnic groups, and organized labor in the affairs of the city to a greater extent than any of his predecessors had. Above all, he recognized the enormity of the depression and the need to provide the unemployed with public relief, and he was one of the first public officials in the nation to press for federal aid to the cities for welfare purposes. Although desperate financial conditions forced Detroit to yield its position of preeminence as a dispenser of public relief, those on welfare and those seeking relief never doubted that Murphy was a sympathetic advocate of their cause and that their plight would have been much worse had he not been the city's mayor.

Murphy's policies were strikingly similar in many respects to those of his two most illustrious predecessors, Hazen Pingree and James Couzens. All three mayors had to deal with depressed economic conditions, and all were conspicuous among public officials of their time in their strong advocacy of public relief. They all favored municipal ownership of Detroit's street-railway system, battled with the privately owned utilities operating in the city, and were sympathetic to organized labor, and Couzens and Murphy, at least, defended free speech against those who sought to abridge it. All three mayors were advocates of the merit system in municipal government, and all were inclined toward political independence despite their party affiliations.[58]

Murphy, to be sure, was not without his faults as mayor. His performance did not always match his rhetoric, he was a sometimes vacillating administrator who was reluctant to offend politically powerful groups in the city, and he was probably too much concerned about his political future. There was no mistaking the objectives of his administration, however. If, as Harry Mead thought, Murphy was really "a pretty cold blooded operator" who "played everything close to the vest," he nevertheless acted on the laudable principle that the way for a public official to advance his career was to provide the public with the best service of which he was capable. No mayor could have solved the fiscal and welfare problems that Murphy faced since they were largely determined by conditions beyond his power to control and because the state and federal governments were reluctant to provide Detroit with the assistance it required. He was the right mayor for the times, however, and despite the fearful strain of his duties, he "saw Detroit through its darkest night."[59]

Murphy took his oath of office as governor-general of the Phillippines on the Bible that Mary Murphy had given him when he left Harbor Beach to enter the University of Michigan. "Honesty and the care of the poor," he said in making a few brief remarks at the ceremony, "have been the high spots of my government and I trust will continue to be." Three nights later Murphy received an "immense" send-off at the Michigan Central terminal. Coming directly from a farewell party at a country club, Murphy, with girl friends on both arms, arrived at the station just after midnight to be greeted by a crowd of about five hundred well-wishers. One of Murphy's socialite lady friends thought that she had never seen "such a mob" and observed that she "felt like a country wench seeing royalty off." It was, actually, a "typical Murphy gathering" as "Grosse Pointe and Hastings Street [in the black ghetto] rubbed shoulders." As newspaperman Henry Montgomery recalled the scene a few months later, there were people there "from every station in life from the lowest to the highest in religion, politics, commerce, industry, art and Sex! It was the best picture of a man's vote-getting power I ever saw."

It may have been an even better "picture" of Murphy's already legendary prowess with the ladies. One of Murphy's girl friends wondered how he had had the time "to line up all your ladies for 'a last moment.'" Murphy spent a half hour in the terminal, shaking hands with the men and kissing the women, and then at 12:30 A.M., with half the crowd following him to the tracks, he boarded the train that would take him to Chicago on the first leg of his long journey to the Philippines.[60] His Detroit years had come to an end; his New Deal years lay ahead.

Abbreviations

ACLU Archives	American Civil Liberties Union Archives, Firestone Library, Princeton University, Princeton, New Jersey
ALHUA	Archives of Labor History and Urban Affairs, Wayne State University, Detroit, Michigan
BHC	Burton Historical Collection, Detroit Public Library, Detroit, Michigan
CF Papers	Children's Fund Papers, Michigan Historical Collections, Ann Arbor, Michigan
DBGR	Detroit Bureau of Governmental Research
DCL Papers	Detroit Citizens League Papers, Burton Historical Collection
DFP	Detroit *Free Press*
DJ	Detroit *Journal*
DLN	Detroit *Labor News*
DN	Detroit *News*
DNC Records	Democratic Party National Committee Records, Franklin D. Roosevelt Library, Hyde Park, New York
DSN	Detroit *Saturday Night*
DT	Detroit *Times*
DUL Papers	Detroit Urban League Papers, Michigan Historical Collections
EG	Eugene Gressman
EG Papers	Eugene Gressman Papers, Michigan Historical Collections
EGK	Edward G. Kemp
EGK-BHC	Edward G. Kemp Papers, Burton Historical Collection
EGK Papers	Edward G. Kemp Papers, Michigan Historical Collections
EMB	Eleanor M. Bumgardner
EMB Papers	Eleanor M. Bumgardner Papers, Michigan Historical Collections

FDRL	Franklin D. Roosevelt Library
FM	Frank Murphy
FM Papers	Frank Murphy Papers, Michigan Historical Collections
GM	George Murphy
GM Papers	George Murphy Papers, Michigan Historical Collections
HE	Hester Everard
HE Papers	Hester Everard Papers, Burton Historical Collection
HM	Harold Murphy
HM Papers	Harold Murphy Papers, Michigan Historical Collections
IM	Irene Murphy
IM Papers	Irene Murphy Papers, Michigan Historical Collections
JAJS	*Journal of the American Judicature Society*
JFM	John F. Murphy
JFM Papers	John F. Murphy Papers, Michigan Historical Collections
JG	Josephine Gomon
LC	Library of Congress, Washington, D.C.
MBM	Mary Brennan Murphy
MD	*Michigan Daily*
MHC	Michigan Historical Collections
MM	Marguerite Murphy
MM Papers	Marguerite Murphy Papers, Michigan Historical Collections
MOR	Mayor's Office Records, Burton Historical Collection
MSB	Frank Murphy Scrapbooks, Michigan Historical Collections
NAACP Papers	National Association for the Advancement of Colored People Papers, Library of Congress
NARS	National Archives and Records Service
POUR Records	Records of the President's Organization on Unemployment Relief, Record Group 73, National Archives and Records Service
PWC Proceedings	Proceedings of the Public Welfare Commission
RC	Detroit Recorder's Court

RFC Records	Records Relating to Emergency Relief to the States, Reconstruction Finance Corporation Records, Record Group 234, National Archives and Records Service
RG	Record Group
TSB	Arthur J. Tuttle Scrapbooks, Michigan Historical Collections

Notes

1. Carl Muller to FM, Apr. 4, 1939, FM Papers; Edyth Gabel to FM, Feb. 24, 1940, EMB Papers; typed copy of clipping from Guelph *Mercury,* Jan. 23, 1892, in ibid.; "Harbor Beach-1892," JFM Papers; [Springfield (Mass.) *Sunday Union,* Jan. 8, 1939], MSB; "The Labor Governors," *Fortune,* XV (June 1937), 81; *DN,* Jan. 4, 1940; copy of Murphy genealogy, in possession of Sharon Keyes.
2. Unidentified clipping [1896], MSB.
3. Ibid.; Charles Moore, *History of Michigan* (Chicago, 1915), II, 1116; FM to Arthur Cuddihy, Dec. 17, 1945, FM Papers; transcript of FM speech at Gristmill Club dinner, Mar. 20, 1949, pp. 4-5, ibid.; FM to EMB [Apr. 19, 1949], EMB Papers; EG notes on interview with GM, 1949, EG Papers.
4. The company subsequently became the Huron Milling Co. and is now part of the Hercules Powder Co. Chet Hey and Norman Eckstein, *Huron County Centennial History, 1859-1959* (n.p., 1959), p. 37.
5. The information on Sand Beach and Harbor Beach is drawn from the following: *Portrait and Biographical Album of Huron County* (Chicago, 1884), pp. 429-30, 455-60; Ladies Aid Society of the Presbyterian Church, *Souvenir of Sand Beach Michigan, 1898* [Sand Beach, 1898], pp. 1-19; Hey and Eckstein, *Centennial History,* p. 37; GM Memorandum to H. G. [Hilmer Gellein] [1941?], GM Papers; Albert Hyma, manuscript biography of FM (1955), p. 37, MHC; *Census of the State of Michigan, 1894, Population . . . ,* I (Lansing, 1896), 20, 245; *Census of the State of Michigan, 1904, Population,* I (Lansing, 1906), clviii; Bureau of the Census, *Thirteenth Census of the United States, 1910, Abstract of the Census . . . with Supplement for Michigan* (Washington, 1913), pp. 579, 606; Harbor Beach *Times,* July 13, 1917, in EG Papers; Interview with Nell D. Wilson, July 5, 1968, p. 16, MHC; FM to Joseph Hanlon, Sept. 5, 1946, FM Papers.
6. Moore, *History of Michigan,* II, 1116-17; FM to EMB [Apr. 19, 1949], EMB Papers; Harbor Beach tax receipt, Dec. 6, 1924, JFM Papers; [Port Huron *Times-Herald,* Apr. 8, 1926], MSB; "Notes on the Life of Frank Murphy," undated, FM Papers; EG notes on GM interview.
7. See, for example [Springfield (Mass.) *Sunday Union,* Jan. 18, 1939],

MSB. J. Woodford Howard talks of John Murphy's "endless" financial problems. *Mr. Justice Murphy* (Princeton, 1968), p. 3.

8. Moore, *History of Michigan*, II, 1117; certifications as circuit-court commissioner, Nov. 17, 1884, Dec. 6, 1886, JFM Papers; unidentified clippings, in ibid.; unidentified clipping [1888], in ibid.; unidentified clipping [1890], in ibid.; EG notes on Huron *Times*, Nov. 21, 1884, Nov. 12, 1886, Nov. 16, 1888, Nov. 7, 1890, Nov. 11, 1892, Nov. 9, 1894, Nov. 20, 1896, EG Papers; EG notes on Sand Beach *Times*, Nov. 11, 1898, ibid.; EG notes on Harbor Beach *Times*, Nov. 16, 1900, ibid.; EG notes on *Huron County Tribune*, Sept. 13, 1912, ibid.; [Port Huron *Times-Herald*, Apr. 8, 1926], MSB; JFM to GM, Nov. 6, 1912, GM Papers; FM to MBM [Feb. 20, 1917], JFM Papers; George M. Deadry to E. O. Wood, Jan. 25, 1914, F. W. Merrick to Wood, Jan. 26, 1914, HM Papers; *Michigan Manual, 1915*, p. 482. Howard errs in stating that John Murphy received a postmastership in 1914. The post went to Harold Murphy. *Mr. Justice Murphy*, p. 5.

9. Thomas W. Brown, *Irish-American Nationalism* (Philadelphia, 1966), pp. 45–46.

10. Interview with Frank Potts, Jan. 8, 1965, pp. 4–5, MHC; MM to FM, Apr. 7, 1919, FM Papers; FM to MBM [May 17, 1915], JFM Papers.

11. JFM to MBM, Mar. 7, 1883, JFM Papers; Bad Axe *Democrat* [Jan. 1885], clipping in ibid.; certified copy of Marriage Record of JFM and MBM, in my possession.

12. Harbor Beach *Times* [1916], clipping in possession of Sharon Keyes; Murphy genealogy, EMB Papers; MM to FM, Apr. 1940, ibid.; *Portrait of Huron County*, p. 385; "Notes on Life of FM," FM Papers. Mary Brennan's birth is given as both June 27, 1850, and June 26, 1862. When she married on January 14, 1885, she gave her age as 28. Certified copy of Murphy Marriage Record.

13. MM to Cecilia Yulo, Nov. 25, 1940, FM Papers; *DT*, Mar. 23, 1933; MM to Miss Thornton [1925], MM Papers; George W. Potter, *To the Golden Door* (Boston, 1960), p. 90; Andrew Greeley, *That Most Distressful Nation: The Taming of the American Irish* (Chicago, 1972), pp. 110, 251.

14. Unidentified clipping, in JFM Papers; undated account of FM's birth, GM Papers; copy of Certificate of Baptism of William Francis Murphy, FM Papers; Ann Arbor *News*, July 19, 1949, clipping in ibid.; Interview with Carl Muller, Oct. 6, 1964, pp. 2–3, MHC. Moore, *History of Michigan*, II, 1117, incorrectly lists the birth dates of the Murphy children. The dates of birth of Harold and Marguerite were supplied to me by the county clerk's office of Huron County. Mrs. George Murphy supplied the date of George's birth.

15. GM to Maxine B. Virtue, Feb. 1, 1952, GM Papers; *Philippines Herald*, July 18, 1933, clipping in FM Papers; HM to FM, Oct. 22, 1925, ibid.; HM to GM, Mar. 12, 1917, GM Papers; Wilson interview, pp. 2, 4, 14; Potts interview, p. 4; MM to FM, Apr. 1940, EMB Papers.

16. Joan Lowell to MM, Jan. 13, 1928, FM to MBM, Apr. 28, 1922, FM to Frankfurter, Dec. 28, 1944, FM to HM, Jan. 8, 1946, FM Papers; FM to MM, May 12, 1935, MM Papers.

17. FM to MBM, July 15, 1918, JFM Papers; FM to HM, Jan. 12, 1943, HM Papers; FM to Mrs. Fielding H. Yost, Dec. 30, 1943, MM to FM, Sept. 8, Dec. 31, 1918, [1918], June 14, 1942, undated, FM Papers; Interview with John V. Brennan, Dec. 9, 1963, p. 8, MHC.

18. Arensberg and Kimball, *Family and Community in Ireland* (Cambridge, Mass., 1948), pp. 57-61; William V. Shannon, *The American Irish* (New York, 1963), pp. 22-23; *DT*, Mar. 25, 1923; *Pipp's Weekly*, Nov. 12, 1921.

19. On this question, see John C. Messenger, "Sex and Repression in an Irish Folk Community," in Donald S. Marshall and Robert C. Suggs, eds., *Human Sexual Behavior* (New York, 1971), pp. 24-25; Calvin S. Hall, *A Primer of Freudian Psychology* (Mentor Book; New York, n.d.), pp. 109-11; Kenneth Keniston, *The Uncommitted* (Delta Book; New York, n.d.), pp. 305-6; and EG notes on interview with MM, 1949, EG Papers. Without citing his source, Howard states that a psychiatrist who had examined Frank Murphy declared that he had "as pronounced an Oedipus complex as any patient in his experience." *Mr. Justice Murphy*, p. 8.

20. FM to MBM [June 20, Dec. 14, 1917], Sept. 11, Nov. 28, 1918, [Mar. 25, 1920], JFM Papers.

21. FM to Ann Walker, Sept. 23, 1934, FM Papers; FM to MBM [June 12, 1918], July 17, Aug. 13, 30, 1918, JFM Papers.

22. FM to MBM, Oct. 10, 30, Dec. 13, 25, 1918, Feb. 10, 13, Apr. 22, June 29, 1919, JFM Papers.

23. FM to MBM, May 22, Sept. 2, 1919, [Dec.] 22, 1920, June 30, 1921, Sept. 26, 1922, Oct. 6, 1923, May 11, 1924, ibid.

24. FM to MBM, Aug. 28, Oct. 22, 1918, ibid.; FM to HE, July 13, 1923, HE Papers; FM to MBM, Apr. 14, 1924, FM Papers; FM to Sylvan J. Grosner, Jan. 26, 1939, GM Papers.

25. Potts interview, pp. 5-6; EG notes on interview with MM; MBM to FM, Apr. 9, 1919, FM Papers.

26. FM to MM, Oct. 23, 1934, MM Papers; FM to HM, Jan. 12, 1943, HM Papers; MM to Mary——[1924], JFM Papers; *DN*, Feb. 21, 1935.

27. Mrs. William Walker to JFM, Mar. 5, 1926, JFM Papers; [*Philippines Herald*, May 21, 1934], MSB; FM to A. Walker, July 30, 1934, FM to IM, May 17, 1944, FM Papers; FM to HM, Mar. 20, 1944, HM Papers; Interview with IM, July 30, 1964, p. 69, MHC.

28. FM to MBM, Dec. 25, 1918, JFM Papers; FM to IM, May 17, 1944, Ruby —— to FM [1920], FM Papers; FM to HE, Aug. 24, 1922, June 18, 1930, HE Papers; HE to FM, Sept. 1922, July 12, 1923, FM Papers; Hall, *Primer*, pp. 82-83.

29. FM to MBM [June 14, Sept. 10, Dec. 9, 1917], July 15, 1918, FM

to JFM, Apr. 28, 1925, JFM Papers; FM to MM [May 1914], [Jan. 26, 1917], May 1, 1925, MM Papers.

30. "Notes on Life of FM," FM Papers; FM to Walter Popek, Apr. 18, 1938, ibid.; FM to EMB [Apr. 19, 1949], MM to FM, Apr. 1940, EMB Papers; *DT*, Jan. 7, 1940, in *DN* morgue, Detroit; FM draft of autobiography [1945], EG Papers.

31. See the election returns in the *Michigan Manuals* for the period 1880-1910. Cf. James H. Lincoln, in *Michigan Democrat*, Aug. 1949.

32. See FM, "Politics and the Laborer" (MS [1911]), FM Papers.

33. [*Philippines Herald*, June 15, 1935], MSB; Joseph H. Creighton, "Frank Murphy—Off the Record," Part Two (MS [Aug. 1938]), p. 1, FM Papers; FM to Mrs. T. J. Wadsworth, Mar. 6, 1946, ibid.; Wilson interview, pp. 16-17; EG notes on MM interview.

34. JFM to FM, Jan. 29, 1919, MM to FM [Nov. 1925], FM Papers; HM to GM, Mar. 12, 1917, GM Papers.

35. Certified copy of Murphy Marriage Record; MM to FM, Apr. 1940, EMB Papers. Marguerite reported that the Brennans opposed the marriage and that it was consequently kept secret from them. The religious ceremony was performed only after the secret had been discovered.

36. EG notes on MM interview; IM interview, p. 8; Richard D. Lunt, "The High Ministry of Government: The Political Career of Frank Murphy" (Ph.D. thesis, University of New Mexico, 1962), p. 1; JFM to MM [Mar.?] 12 [1907], MM Papers.

37. *La Defensa*, July 22, 1933, Norman Hill Scrapbooks, MHC; FM to GM, Dec. 13, 1944, FM Papers; FM to HM, Mar. 20, 1944, HM Papers; William L. Stidger, "Frank Murphy," *The Human Side of Greatness* (New York, 1940), pp. 16-17; "Notes on Life of FM," FM Papers; FM draft of autobiography [1945], EG Papers.

38. FM to MBM, Mar. 6, 1917, [Oct. 7, 1917], JFM Papers; FM to Charles Henigan, Jan. 10, 1940, FM to John A. Reynolds, Feb. 2, 1940, FM to Sharon Murphy, May 29, 1944, FM Papers; *DN*, June 14, 1932; *Time*, XXXIII (June 5, 1939), 16.

39. Wilson interview, pp. 5, 7-8; E. Shepard Bramble to FM, Sept. 13, 1930, FM to Francis Talbot, Jan. 30, 1939, FM Papers; Stidger, "Murphy," p. 18.

40. Stidger, "Murphy," p. 17; FM to Herman Jacobs, July 8, 1939, FM Papers; FM to Frankfurter [Dec. 1945], Felix Frankfurter Papers, LC. See also FM draft of autobiography [1945], EG Papers.

41. Harold Laswell, *Power and Personality* (New York, 1948), p. 47; Viditch and Bensman, *Small Town in Mass Society* (Princeton, 1961), pp. 350-56; Bernard Berleson and Gary E. Steiner, *Human Behavior* (New York, 1964), pp. 80-81, 469; Philip E. Slater, *The Pursuit of Loneliness* (Boston, 1970), p. 89.

42. *DT*, Mar. 23, 1933; Lunt, "High Ministry," p. 5; "Labor Governors," p. 81; MM to FM [Jan. 1940], FM Papers; MBM to GM, Nov. 6,

1912, JFM to GM, Oct. 16, 1912, GM Papers.

43. FM to MBM, Feb. 21, 1919, JFM Papers; FM to Leo Butler, June 15, 1939, GM Papers; FM to Popek, Apr. 18, 1938, FM Papers; Stidger, "Murphy," p. 23; Laswell, *Power and Personality,* p. 48.

44. FM to MBM [Jan. 5, May 12, 1918], Dec. 1, 1918, JFM Papers; FM to HE, Mar. 30, 1922, HE Papers; MM to FM [June 1920], FM Papers; HM to Ruth [Treglown], Dec. 7, 1938, HM Papers.

45. FM to Ezra Cronk, July 14, 1923, MM to FM, Sept. 8, 1918, FM Papers; EMB to Lenabelle K. Lucas, May 1, 1948, EMB Papers; FM to GM, Dec. 7, 1943, FM Papers; Port Huron *Times-Herald* [Jan. 5, 1940], MSB; *DT,* Jan. 7, 1940; Stidger, "Murphy," p. 16.

46. Wilson interview, p. 17; FM to MBM, Jan. 29, 1919, JFM Papers; biographical notes on FM, Jan. 16-31, 1941 folder, GM Papers; Port Huron *Times-Herald* [Jan. 5, 1940], MSB; Stidger, "Murphy," p. 19; IM interview, p. 62; EG notes on Harbor Beach *Times,* May 18, 1906, EG Papers; Theodore P. Greene, *America's Heroes: The Changing Models of Success in American Magazines* (New York, 1970), pp. 234, 239, 251, 259-62, 272-74, 276.

47. *DT* [Aug. 1937], MSB; [(Lansing) *State Journal,* Aug. 3, 1937], MSB; Stidger, "Murphy," pp. 20-21; EG notes on interviews with GM and MM.

48. Wilson interview, pp. 3-4; *DT,* Apr. 19, 1933; *Announcements,* June [1908], FM Papers; EG notes on MM interview.

49. Transcript of high school record of Frank William Murphy, FM Papers.

50. FM to Eva G. Pinkston, May 27, 1938, Lincoln to FM, Apr. 8 [1923], Sept. 10, 1930, FM Papers; *DT,* July 21, 1949, clipping in ibid.; Lura Lincoln Cook, *The Book of Esther* (New York, 1962), pp. 3-4.

51. EG notes on Harbor Beach *Times,* Oct. 27, Nov. 3, 10, .1905, Feb. 9, Mar. 2, May 18, Nov. 2, 1906, Feb. 14, June 6, Nov. 8, 1907, Feb. 21, Mar. 13, June 12, 1908, EG Papers; unidentified clipping [1905], in FM Papers; Saginaw *News,* June 18, 1938, clipping in ibid.; JFM to MM, June 1, 1907, FM to MM, Feb. 10, 1907, MM Papers; FM to MBM, Mar. 12, 1912, JFM Papers; Wilson interview, pp. 2, 13.

52. Class Day was pretty much a Murphy family affair. In addition to Frank's oration, Marguerite was the vocal soloist, and cousin Mary Brennan was the class valedictorian. *Announcements,* June [1908], FM Papers.

53. "Character" (MS [1908]), ibid.

54. *DT,* Mar. 15, 1923.

55. On this point, see Norman Hill to Don Cochrane, Sept. 10, 1936, FM Papers.

56. FM to MBM, Sept. 24, 1918, JFM Papers; *Pipp's Weekly,* Nov. 12, 1921; FM to HE, Oct. 14, 1921, HE Papers; FM to MM, June 2, 1925, MM Papers; FM to GM, Dec. 13, 1944, FM Papers; FM to Joan Cuddihy [Mar. 20, 1947], Joan Cuddihy Papers, in Miss Cuddihy's possession; Potts interview, pp. 9-10.

57. FM to MBM, Jan. 10, 1919, JFM Papers; *Graphic,* June 29, 1933, MSB; Philadelphia *Inquirer,* Jan. 3, 1939, MSB; Interview with Jack Manning, Dec. 4, 1964, p. 13, MHC.

CHAPTER II

1. William L. Stidger, "Frank Murphy," *The Human Side of Greatness* (New York, 1940), pp. 22-23.
2. *Pipp's Weekly,* Nov. 12, 1921; FM to MBM [Mar. 24, 1914], GM to MBM [June 3, 1914], JFM Papers.
3. Peckham, *The Making of the University of Michigan, 1817-1967* (Ann Arbor, 1967), pp. 106, 111, 124. See also Kent Sagendorph, *Michigan. The Story of the University* (New York, 1948), pp. 231-32, 243.
4. *MD,* Oct. 10, 1908, May 13-15, 1910; FM to MM, May 16, 1910, MM Papers; Joseph H. Primeau, Jr., to FM, Apr. 3, 1923, FM Papers; typed item copied from Harbor Beach *Times,* Oct. 16, 1908, ibid.; EGK draft of "Frank Murphy as Government Administrator" (1951), EGK Papers. On the alienated college student of a later era, see Kenneth Keniston, *The Uncommitted* (Delta Book; New York, n.d.), pp. 90-91, 102, et passim.
5. *MD,* Dec. 5, 1909, Mar. 12, 14, 16, 17, 18, 1910.
6. *DT,* Sept. 14, 1930; St. Louis *Post-Dispatch,* Jan. 23, 1938, clipping in FM Papers; Ann Arbor *News,* July 19, 1949, ibid.; W. B. Ricks to Orville S. Brumbach, Apr. 25, 1914, Ricks to FM, May 7, 1914, Dec. 8, 1930, Thurlow E. Coon to FM, Feb. 16, 1927, FM to Chester W. Cleveland, Aug. 6, 1941, Apr. 8, 1946, FM to Chase S. Osborn, Apr. 5, 1946, ibid.; FM to MBM, Mar. 23 [1912], [Mar. 1912], JFM Papers; Manila *Bulletin,* Apr. 11, 1933, Norman H. Hill Scrapbooks, MHC.
7. *MD,* Mar. 19, 27, Apr. 3, 20, May 15, June 2-4, 12, Oct. 6, 1910; FM to MM, May 16, 1910, MM Papers; FM to JFM, Nov. 10, 1911, JFM Papers.
8. Peckham, *Making of the University,* pp. 109-10, 123; Shirley W. Smith, *Harry Burns Hutchins and the University of Michigan* (Ann Arbor, 1951), pp. 139-40; *MD,* Oct. 29, 1909, Nov. 14, 1911, Jan. 18, Mar. 26, Dec. 4, 1912, Mar. 20, 1913, Jan. 14, Mar. 27, 1914; Henry T. Heald to FM, Mar. 24, 1914, FM Papers; FM to MBM [Mar. 24, 1914], JFM Papers.
9. FM speech [Apr. 4, 1914], FM Papers.
10. *MD,* June 21, 25, 1911, Apr. 28, May 18, 22, 23, 1913; FM to HM, Dec. 8, 1908, FM Picture Collection, MHC; *DT,* Apr. 9, 1933, Jan. 7, 1940; *DSN,* Dec. 1, 1923; Interview with Martin S. Hayden, Oct. 16, 1964, pp. 14-15, MHC; FM to MBM, Nov. 20 [1909], JFM Papers; FM to MM, Nov. 24, 1911, MM Papers; FM to GM, Oct. 27 [1911], Nov. 13, 1911, GM Papers; FM to Yost, Apr. 29, 1938, Michigan Athletic Department Papers, MHC; FM to Chester W. Cleveland, Jan. 27, 1948, FM Papers; "The Labor Governors," *Fortune,* XV (June 1937), 81.

It was claimed in the Harbor Beach *Times,* Oct. 17, 1924, that Murphy had become a member of the varsity football team but had sustained three cracked ribs and had therefore never played. EG notes, EG Papers.

11. *MD,* Nov. 13, 15, 1913; FM to MBM [Fall 1913], JFM Papers.
12. *MD,* May 17, 19, 1910, June 1, 8, 1911; FM to MM, May 16, 1910, MM Papers; James G. Frey to FM, May 18, 1932, MOR.
13. Arthur Moehlman to FM, Sept. 12 [1930], EGK Papers.
14. *MD,* June 9, 1910; EG notes on Harbor Beach *Times,* Jan. 12, 1912, EG Papers; Scranton *Times,* Jan. 3, 1939, clipping in FM Papers; Ann Arbor *News,* July 19, 1949, ibid.; Interview with Brigid Murphy, July 20, 1963; JFM to GM, Oct. 16, Nov. 6, 1912, MBM to GM [Oct. 1912], HM to GM, Nov. 13, 1912, GM Papers; Leland S. Bisbee to FM, Apr. 26, 1937, FM Papers.
15. Hayden to Jesse Reeves, Feb. 9, 1934, Joseph R. Hayden Papers, MHC; Dexter K. Reinhart to FM, Apr. 8, 1933, Bisbee to FM, Dec. 20, 1938, Feb. 8, 1940, FM to Justin J. Miller, Apr. 21, 1941, FM Papers; unidentified clipping [Feb. 1937], in ibid.; Interview with Norman H. Hill, Aug. 21, 1963, p. 35, MHC; Interview with Harry Mead, Aug. 5, 1963, MHC; JG, in *DFP,* Mar. 12, 1972.
16. FM to MBM, July 27, 1924, JFM Papers; *Graphic,* Jan. 28, 1933, clipping in FM Papers; Boston *Sunday Globe,* Jan. 7, 1940, MSB; Georgia Taylor to FM, Feb. 8, 1913, Moehlman to FM, Dec. 5, 1946, FM to Luther B. Moore, Mar. 1, 1949, FM Papers; *MD,* May 17, 1911, Apr. 9, 1914; Stidger, "Murphy," pp. 23-24. It is possible that Murphy engaged in an anti-Semitic prank while at the University of Michigan. Thomas W. Lanigan, a fellow student, later sent Murphy a copy of a picture of several students, including the two of them, sitting on a wagon and on their way "to clean the Jews" as part of a St. Patrick's Day caper. The picture contains the words: "'Down with the Juse.'" Lanigan wrote Murphy that these words could be eliminated "if you desire to stay in politics." Murphy ignored the reference to the Jews in his reply. Lanigan to FM, Sept. 11, 1930, July 29, 1937, and enclosed photograph, FM to Lanigan, Aug. 6, 1937, FM Papers.
17. Elizabeth Gaspar Brown, *Legal Education at Michigan, 1859-1959* (Ann Arbor, 1959), pp. 208-9, 722; *Calendar of the University of Michigan of 1911-1912* (Ann Arbor, 1912), pp. 234-35; JG to Robert M. Warner, July 20, 1964, MHC; Hill interview, p. 4. There is a copy of Murphy's transcript as a literary department student in the FM Papers.
18. *MD,* May 5-7, 9, 1911; EGK notes on J. Woodford Howard MS, June 22, 1959, EGK Papers. Cf. Howard, *Mr. Justice Murphy* (Princeton, 1968), p. 10.
19. FM, "Politics and the Laborer" (MS [1911]), FM Papers.
20. Ibid. The handwriting of the grader is unmistakably that of Cooley, who had overall responsibility for the course. See University of

Michigan, Department of Literature, Science, and the Arts, *Annual Announcement of Undergraduate and Graduate Courses, 1910-1911* (Ann Arbor, 1910), p. 91.

21. Brown, *Legal Education,* pp. 277-83, 716, 728-29; *Calendar of the University of Michigan of 1911-1912,* pp. 331-32; Wilfred B. Shaw, ed., *The University of Michigan: An Encyclopedic Survey,* Part V (Ann Arbor, 1951), 1020; Bates to Edgar N. Durfee, May 15, 1911, Henry M. Bates Papers, MHC. See also Bates to Harry B. Hutchins, undated, submitting report of the Law School for 1914-15, Harry B. Hutchins Papers, MHC.

22. Brown, *Legal Education,* pp. 82, 109, 112-13, 208, 276; Bates to Durfee, May 11, 1911, Bates Papers.

23. Brown, *Legal Education,* pp. 207-8; Bates to John B. Waite, May 24, 1911, FM to Bates, Dec. 25, 1945, Bates Papers; Bates, "Address of the President," *Proceedings of the Thirteenth Annual Meeting of the Association of American Law Schools, 1913* (n.p., n.d.), pp. 29-30; Jerold S. Auerbach, "Enmity and Amity: Law Teachers and Practitioners, 1900-1922," *Perspectives in American History,* V (1971), 557-59.

24. FM to JFM, Nov. 10, 1911, FM to MBM [Mar. 1912], JFM Papers.

25. Copy of transcript of Murphy's Department of Law record, FM Papers; Department of Law, Faculty Records, 1910-20, pp. 473-74, 502, 523-24, 532, 580, 585, 598, University of Michigan Law School, Ann Arbor, Michigan; *MD,* May 27, 1913; FM to MBM, June 22, 1914, JFM Papers. The "conditionally passed" grade required a student to submit to a reexamination in order to receive credit for the particular course.

26. *DT,* June 18, 1939, clipping in FM Papers; Goddard to FM, Jan. 15, 1940, ibid.; Bates to Dean Acheson, Oct. 11, 1939, Bates Papers; Howard, *Mr. Justice Murphy,* p. 12. Murphy was selected to be the speaker at the class-day exercise of the 1928 Law School commencement, and he maintained a friendly relationship with Bates and his successor, E. Blythe Stason. See p. 27 for the Law School recommendation of an honorary degree for Murphy.

27. FM to MM [Dec. 1913], [May 1914], MM Papers.

28. *MD,* May 27, 30, 1914; FM to MM [May 1914], MM Papers; GM to MBM [June 3, 1914], JFM Papers; FM speech [May 29, 1914], FM Papers.

29. FM to MBM [Dec. 17, 1915], [May 7, 1916], Nov. 1916, [June 6, 1917], [Nov. 3, 1919], Nov. 13, 1921, JFM Papers; FM to HE, Oct. 14, 1921, HE Papers; FM to Ruthven, June 6, 1939, FM to Yost, July 11, 1939, FM to Arthur Cuddihy, June 10, 1947, FM Papers.

30. *MD,* May 30, Oct. 29, 1909, June 9, Oct. 6, 1910, Jan. 21, 25, Feb. 15, Mar. 29, 31, Oct. 17, 1911, May 19, 1912, Mar. 20, May 23, 1913; Watkins to FM, Apr. 18, 1911, FM to Robert M. Williams, Mar. 1, 1939, FM Papers; JG to Warner, July 20, 1964, MHC; *Michiganensian, 1914,* p. 424.

CHAPTER III

1. *DT,* Jan. 7, 1940; GM to Fred Rodell, Oct. 5, 1955, GM Papers; FM to JFM, Oct. 15, 1914, JFM Papers; Ferris for Governor Club stationery, HM Papers; FM to Dear Friend, Oct. 30, 1914, MM Papers.
2. Memorandum page in 1915 Diary, FM Papers; FM to George M. Clark, Jan. 20, 1936, FM Papers; FM to Peter Monaghan, Aug. 31, 1935, EMB Papers; FM to MBM [Mar. 30, 1917], JFM Papers.
3. FM to MBM, Jan. 16, 22, [Jan.], 1915, JFM Papers; Hilmer Gellein, "United States Supreme Court Justice Frank Murphy . . ." (MS, n.d.), p. 3, Hilmer Gellein Papers, MHC.
4. FM to MBM, Feb. 5 [1915], [Aug. 23, Sept. 3, 1915], [1916], [Jan. 10, 1917], Jan. 20, 1917, [Feb. 1917], June 28, 1918, JFM Papers; GM to EG, Sept. 1, 1950, GM Papers; FM to P. Monaghan, Aug. 31, 1935, EMB Papers; Robert Clancy to Commanding General, Central Division, Apr. 27, 1917, FM Papers; Officers' Qualification card, Jan. 14, 1918, FM Service Record, ibid.
5. FM to MBM [Aug. 23, 1915], Mar. 8, 1916, [Jan. 27, Mar. 30, May 8, 1917], [1917], two undated letters, JFM Papers.
6. FM to MBM, Mar. 3, 1915, [May 5, June 15, Dec. 5, 8, 1916], [Feb. 4, 1917], [1917], JFM Papers.
7. Cyrowski v. Polish-American Publishing Co., 196 Mich. 648 (1917); *DT,* Mar. 25, 1923; unidentified clipping, MSB.
8. FM to MBM [Jan. 10, 11, 12, 15, 1917], JFM Papers.
9. FM to MBM [Jan. 22, 26, 28, 29, Feb. 13, 1917], [Feb. 1917?], [Feb. or Mar. 1917], ibid.
10. FM to MBM [1916], JFM Papers; *DLN,* Apr. 21, 1916.
11. *DLN,* Apr. 21, 28, June 30, 1916; Carl Haessler, "Behind the Auto Strike," *New Masses,* XXII (Feb. 2, 1937), 3; Thornhill v. Alabama, 310 U.S. 88 (1940).
12. Allan Nevins and Frank Ernest Hill, *Ford: The Times, the Man, the Company* (New York, 1954), pp. 377–80, 513–17; *DLN,* Feb. 4, May 19, July 21, Aug. 18, 25, 1916, Jan. 19, 1917.
13. Murphy taught night school from November 23, 1914, to February 11, 1915. He later implied that he had taught for a year, and one account has him teaching nine years. Memorandum page in 1915 Diary, FM Papers; FM to JFM [Feb. 12, 1915], JFM Papers; *DT,* Mar. 25, 1923; Wichita *Beacon,* July 23 [1932], MSB.
14. Raymond E. Cole, "The Immigrant in Detroit" (MS, 1915), Americanization Committee of Detroit Papers, MHC; Erdman Doane Beynon, "The Hungarians of Michigan," *Michigan History Magazine,* XXI (Winter 1937), 98; FM to MBM [Nov. 1914], Jan. 14, 15, 1915, JFM Papers; HZ to FM, Dec. 16, 1914, John Nerision to FM, Dec. 14, 1914, Aran Gaboodyian to FM, Dec. 17, 1914, Dans Dergagarion to FM, Oct. 19, 1915, FM Papers; *DT,* Jan. 7, 1940.

15. *DT,* Mar. 25, 1923, Jan. 7, 1940; J. Weldon Jones to Sidney Fine, Jan. 29, 1966. Italics supplied.
16. FM to MBM [Sept. 13, 1915], [Mar. 18, 1916], [1916], [Mar. 21, 28, 1917], JFM Papers; "Detroit Citizens League," 1923, Candidate Files, Box 23, DCL Papers.
17. FM to JFM, June 25, 1915, [Mar. 24, 25, Apr. 15, 30, 1916], JFM Papers; Daniel C. Roper, *Fifty Years of Public Service* (Durham, 1941), p. 132. Harold served as postmaster until 1925. EG notes on Harbor Beach *Times,* Jan. 9, 1925, EG Papers.
18. FM to MBM [May 5, Dec. 5, 1916], [Jan. 3, 16, Feb. 21, Apr. 4, 15, 20, 1917], [1917], JFM Papers.
19. FM to MBM [Jan. 28, 1917], ibid.
20. On Roosevelt and the strenuous life, see Theodore P. Greene, *America's Heroes: The Changing Models of Success in American Magazines* (New York, 1970), p. 234; G. Edward White, *The Eastern Establishment and the National Experience: The West of Frederick Remington, Theodore Roosevelt and Owen Wister* (New Haven, 1968), p. 92; and John Higham, "The Reorientation of American Culture in the 1890's," in *Writing American History* (Bloomington, Ind., 1970), pp. 78-84. For Murphy and Roosevelt, see FM to MBM [May 9, 1916], Jan. 8, 29, 1919, JFM Papers; and Blair Moody, "High Commissioner to Manila," *Survey Graphic,* XXIV (Dec. 19, 1935), 611. For a characteristic Murphy appraisal of Lincoln, see FM to HE, Apr. 17, 1922, HE Papers.
21. On this point, see Kenneth Keniston, *The Uncommitted* (Delta Book; New York, n.d.), p. 307; and John C. Messenger, "Sex and Repression in an Irish Folk Community," in Donald S. Marshall and Robert C. Suggs, eds., *Human Sexual Behavior* (New York, 1971), p. 17.
22. FM to MBM, Mar. 1912, Mar. 3, [May 22], 1915, [June 15, 1916], Jan. 16, 21, 22, Mar. 13, [29], May 16, [June], 1917, MM to MBM [July 1916], JFM papers.
23. FM to MBM, Jan. 14, 31, [Apr. 11, May 17], May 19, [Aug. 23, Dec. 17, 1915], [Apr. 26, May 7, Nov., Dec. 1916], [Jan. 6, 7, Feb. 5, 21, Mar. 5, 6, Apr. 4, May 15, 1917], GM to MBM [June 3, 1916], [Feb. 21, 1917], JFM Papers; *MD,* June 3, Nov. 9, 10, 1916; FM speech [June 2, 1916], FM Papers.
24. John Higham, *Strangers in the Land* (New Brunswick, 1955), pp. 197-99; FM speech [June 2, 1916], FM Papers.
25. FM to MBM [1916], JFM Papers; [Marshall *News-Statesman,* Dec. 1, 1917], clipping in ibid.; *DN,* Apr. 7, May 23, Dec. 22, 1917; Cash Asher, "Stories Never Told" (MS, n.d.), FM Papers.
26. FM to MBM [Feb. 1917], JFM Papers.
27. FM to MBM [Feb. 3, 6, Mar. 10, 29, 30, 31, Apr. 1, 2, 1917], ibid.
28. FM to MBM [Apr. 15, 20, 21, 25, 26, May, 1917], May 9, 16, 1917, ibid.
29. FM to MBM [Apr. 21, May 9, 11, 16, 17, 1917], ibid.

30. FM to MBM [Apr. 21, May 15, 1917], May 19, 20, 1917, undated, JFM Papers; *DFP*, May 13, 1917.
31. FM to MBM, May 19, 21, [28], [June, June 6, 11, 29, July, July 13, 22, 25, 1917], JFM Papers; FM to GM [May 28, 1917], FM Papers.
32. FM to MBM [June 15, July 23, 1917], JFM Papers. When Murphy became attorney general of the United States, the officer, who had entered the Canadian army after his discharge and had become a war hero, sought to have the records of the Fort Sheridan case destroyed. Murphy was "wholly sympathetic" to the idea, but the action would have required an act of Congress. James H. Lincoln to Robert M. Warner, Mar. 11, 1969, MHC.
33. FM TO MBM, May 22, [July, Aug., Aug. 18, 30, Sept. 1, 13, 14, 27, Oct. 3, 8, 29, Nov. 6, 26, Dec., Dec. 7, 14, 1917], [1917], [1918], [Mar. 30, 1918], undated, JFM Papers; Citizens' Training Camp, Efficiency Report of Frank Murphy, FM Papers; Statement of the Military Service of Frank Murphy, undated, ibid.; FM Service Record, ibid. I have translated the numerical ratings into the categories indicated on the basis of War Department, Adjutant General's Office, "Instructions for Rating Commissioned Officers," undated, copy in my possession.
34. FM to MBM [Sept. 27, 30, Oct. 3, 4, 10, 15, 1917], [Jan., Jan. 3, Feb. 1, 2, 10, 16, 21, 1918], JFM Papers; *DFP*, Feb. 18, 1918; *DN*, Feb. 18, 1918.
35. FM to MBM [May 27, July, July 4, 21, Oct. 10, 13, 14, 22, Nov. 12, Dec. 1, 14, 1917], [Feb. 1, Apr. 13, 21, May 4, 12, June 2, Dec. 31, 1918], undated, JFM Papers.
36. FM to MBM [June 17, Oct. 21, 22, 27, Nov. 4, 11, 14, 15, 30, Dec. 1, 5, 1917], [1917], undated, JFM Papers; undated Lansing, Michigan, newspaper clipping, in ibid., *MD*, Nov. 15, 1917.
37. FM to MBM [Nov. 1917], two undated letters, JFM Papers; [Marshall *News-Statesman*, Dec. 1, 1917], clipping in ibid.
38. FM to MBM [Jan., Jan. 8, 26, Apr. 27, 1918], ibid.; unidentified clipping, MSB; *DFP*, Jan. 7, 1918.
39. FM to MBM, June 28, 29, 1918, JFM Papers; Kalamazoo *Gazette*, June 29, 1918.
40. FM to MBM [Oct. 21, Nov. 26, 1917], [Feb. 3, 5, 6, 11, Mar. 4, 1918], JFM Papers.
41. FM to MBM [Mar. 5, Apr. 1, 16, 1918], ibid.; *DT*, Mar. 20, 1923; Albon Man, Jr., "Mr. Justice Murphy and the Supreme Court," *Virginia Law Review*, XXXVI (Nov. 1950), 892.
42. For the Pillinger-Windhorst case, see FM to MBM [Apr. 4, 16, 19, 21, 29, May 1, 9, 10, 13, 14, 15, 16, 17, 19, 20, 21, 28, 1918], JFM Papers; *DN*, May 7–10, 1918; Battle Creek *Enquirer*, May 14–18, 20, 21, 1918; *Trench and Camp*, Mar. 21, 1918; and *DT*, Mar. 25, 1923.
43. FM to MBM [May 12, 19, 20, July, July 8, 1918], JFM Papers.

44. FM to MBM [Dec. 18, 1917], [July 12, 31, 1918], Aug. 5, 8, 1918, ibid.; FM Service Record, FM Papers; FM Diary, July 22–Aug. 8, 1918, ibid.; FM to Richard C. Thompson, Jan. 16, 1940, ibid.
45. FM to MBM, Aug. 8, 1918, JFM Papers.
46. FM to MBM, Aug. 9, 21, 1918, ibid.; [Harbor Beach *News,* July 26, 1918], MSB; [Harbor Beach *News,* Aug. 9, 1918], clipping in FM Papers.
47. FM to MBM, Aug. 9, 11, 12, 13, 14, 17, 25, 26, 1918, JFM Papers; FM to GM, Aug. 9, 1918, GM Papers.
48. FM to MBM, Aug. 28, 29, 30, Sept. 29, 1918, JFM Papers; FM to MM, Sept. 30, 1918, MM Papers.
49. FM to MBM, Sept. 7, 16, 24, 25, 29, JFM Papers.
50. FM to MBM, Sept. 6, 12, 1918, ibid.; FM to MM, Sept. 30, 1918, MM Papers.
51. FM to MBM, Oct. 3, 6, 11, 19, 20, 21, 1918, JFM Papers; FM Service Record, FM Papers; Claude S. Hyman to Chicago *Tribune* [Jan. 1939], with Hyman to FM, Feb. 24, 1939, ibid.; *DT,* Mar. 5, 20, 29, 1923.
52. D. L. Murlin to FM, Oct. 9, 1918, FM Papers. For inaccurate versions of the episode, see *DT,* Apr. 23, 1933, and Joseph Creighton, "Frank Murphy—Off the Record," Part Two (MS [Aug. 1938]), FM Papers.
53. FM to MBM, Oct. 9, 12, 15, 24, 1918, undated, JFM Papers.
54. FM to MBM [Sept. 3, 1917], Aug. 22, 25, Sept. 10, 12, 15, 16, 30, Oct. 3, 9, 28, Nov. 4, 8, 1918, ibid.; Hyman to Chicago *Tribune* [Jan. 1939], FM papers; *Falcon,* Jan. 9, 1942, ibid.
55. FM to MBM, Nov. 8, 9, 10, 11, 1918, JFM Papers.
56. FM to MBM, Sept. 2, Nov. 11, 12, Dec. 26, 1918, ibid.
57. FM to MBM, Nov. 14, 15, 17, 20, 21, 22, 24, 1918, ibid.; Christian A. Bach and Henry Noble Hall, *The Fourth Division. Its Services and Achievements in the World War* (n.p., 1920), pp. 215–18; FM to MM, Nov. 19, 1918, MM Papers.
58. FM to MBM, Nov. 22, 24, 28, 1918, JFM Papers; Bach and Hall, *Fourth Division,* pp. 218–19.
59. FM to MBM, Dec. 2, 3, 4, 5, 6, 8, 9, 10, 13, 15, 16, 20, 1918, JFM Papers; Bach and Hall, *Fourth Division,* pp. 219–24, 226–30. According to one account, the band played the University of Michigan fight song, "The Victors," as Murphy led his men into Germany. *DT,* Nov. 11, 1922.
60. FM to MBM, Dec. 4, 8, 14, 1918, JFM Papers.
61. FM to MBM, Dec. 16, 19, 20, 25, 28, 1918, ibid.; Bach and Hall, *Fourth Division,* pp. 233–34.
62. FM to MBM, Nov. 30, Dec. 4, 22, 1918, Jan. 5, 17, 31, Feb. 4, 1919, JFM Papers.
63. FM to MBM, Dec. 29, 30, 31, 1918, Apr. 30, 1919, JFM Papers. See, for example, FM to MBM, Jan. 7, 1919, ibid.
64. FM to MBM, Jan. 25, 30, Feb. 1, 1919, ibid.
65. FM to MBM, Feb. 21, 22, 23, 25, 27, 1919, ibid.

66. FM to MBM, Jan. 11, 12, 20, 1919, ibid.; Frank Doremus to Peyton C. March, Mar. 10, 1919, FM Service Record, FM Papers.

67. Historical Division, Department of the Army, *United States Army in the World War* (Washington, 1948), XIV, 308, XV, 450-52; FM to MBM, Jan. 28, Mar. 9, 12, 1919, JFM Papers; HQ, 4th Division, AEF, Special Orders No. 60, Mar. 2, 1919, FM Papers.

68. FM to MBM, Mar. 10, 11, 12, [May 3], 1919, JFM Papers.

69. FM to MBM, Mar. 11, 1919, ibid. On the third-generation Irish in America, see W. Lloyd Warner and Leo Srole, *The Social Systems of American Ethnic Groups* (New Haven, 1945), p. 155.

70. FM to MBM, Mar. 5, 11, 1919, JFM Papers.

71. FM to MBM, Mar. 21, 26, Apr. 1, 21, 23, 24, 25, May 10, June 20, 1919, ibid.

72. FM to MBM, Jan. 6, Apr. 3, 4, 5, 29, May 14, 17, 29, June 21, 1919, ibid.; FM to GM, Aug. 31, 1944, FM Papers.

73. FM to MBM, Mar. 19, Apr. 20, 24 [?], 26, May 1, 14, 23, 27, July 1, 1919, JFM Papers.

74. FM to MBM, Apr. 26, May 7, 10, 16, 19, 27, 1919, ibid.; *Pipp's Weekly,* Nov. 12, 1921; Brooklyn *Daily Eagle,* Apr. 11, 1937; Wichita *Beacon,* July 23, [1932], MSB; "The Labor Governors," *Fortune,* XV (June 1937), 138; John B. Kennedy, "City of Hope," *Collier's,* LXXXIX (Apr. 30, 1932), 49.

75. FM to MBM, May 4, 7, [27], Oct. 16, 1919, JFM Papers; Alan J. Ward, *Ireland and Anglo-American Relations, 1899-1921* (London, 1969), pp. 168-79; Charles Callan Tansill, *America and the Fight for Irish Freedom, 1866-1922* (New York, 1957), pp. 296-97, 312-14; Joseph P. O'Grady, "The Irish," in O'Grady, ed., *The Immigrants' Influence on Wilson's Peace Policies* (Lexington, Ky., 1967), pp. 65-66, 72; John B. Duff, "The Versailles Treaty and the Irish-Americans," *Journal of American History,* LV (Dec. 1968), 592; *NYT,* Mar. 5, 29, May 2, 5, 1919.

76. FM to MBM, May 7, 9, 1919, JFM Papers; *NYT,* May 7, 10, 11, 1919.

77. FM to MBM, May 12, 1919, JFM Papers; Ward, *Ireland,* pp. 179-85; Tansill, *America and Irish Freedom,* pp. 314-20; O'Grady, "Irish," p. 73; Duff, "Versailles Treaty," 592-93, 596; *NYT,* May 6, 10, 13, 1919.

78. FM to MBM [May 3], 11, 28, 1919, JFM Papers.

79. FM to MBM, Apr. 27, June 17, 18, 26, 29, 30, July 1, 1919, ibid.; FM to MM, July 2, 1919, MM to Aunt Maggie [1919], MM Papers; FM Service Record, FM Papers; Messenger, "Sex and Repression," pp. 22-23. For the details of the pilgrimage, see *Pilgrimage of Lough Derg . . .* [June 1919], JFM Papers.

80. FM to A. T. Smith, Jan. 28, 1936, FM to James A. Ryan, Jan. 20, 1939, FM Papers; [Manila *Tribune,* Nov. 12, 1933], Norman Hill Scrapbooks, MHC.

CHAPTER IV

1. Records of the Appointment Clerk, Records of the Department of Justice,
   RG 60; A. L. Hicks to M. G. Zimmerman, Dec. 19, 1921, Elmer D.
   Sherburne to Attorney General, Nov. 11, 1922, File 23E20, ibid.; *DFP*,
   Dec. 30, 1921, TSB; [Washington *Post*, Jan. 7, 1940], MSB.
2. Hicks to Zimmerman, Dec. 19, 1921, File 23E20, RG 60; *DN*, Feb.
   10, 1922, TSB; Roy A. Haynes, *Prohibition Inside Out* (Garden City,
   New York, 1923), pp. 87-91, 284; F. Clever Bald, *Michigan in Four
   Centuries* (New York, 1954), pp. 383-84; Ernest W. Mandeville, "Detroit
   Sets a Bad Example," *Outlook*, CXXXIX (Apr. 22, 1925), 612-14; Leo
   Donovan, "Detroit: City of Conflict," in Robert S. Allen, ed., *Our
   Fair City* (New York, 1947), pp. 156-57; George W. Stark, *City of
   Destiny: The Story of Detroit* (Detroit, 1943), pp. 464-66; Larry Daniel
   Engelmann, "O, Whisky: The History of Prohibition in Michigan"
   (Ph.D. thesis, University of Michigan, 1971), pp. 498-503.
3. *DN*, July 24, 1920, Feb. 10, 1922, TSB; Hicks to Zimmerman, Dec.
   19, 1921, File 23E20, RG 60.
4. Hicks to Zimmerman, Dec. 19, 1921, File 23E20, RG 60; GM to EG,
   Sept. 1, 1950, GM Papers.
5. *Pipp's Weekly*, Nov. 12, 1921.
6. FM to MBM, Aug. 25, 1919, Jan. 19, 1922, JFM Papers; FM to HE
   [July 1, 1921], HE Papers; J. Stanley Hurd to FM, Mar. 4, 1922,
   FM Papers; *DSN*, Dec. 1, 1923; Interview with Thomas F. Chawke,
   Mar. 1965, pp. 1-2, MHC.
7. Palmer to Kinnane, Aug. 6, 1919, Kinnane to Palmer, Aug. 9, 18, 26,
   Sept. 19, Oct. 15, Nov. 18, 1919, Kinnane to Howard Figg, June 10,
   1920, Kinnane to Harry Daugherty, Mar. 17, 1921, File 24-23, RG
   60; Kinnane to Palmer, Apr. 19, 21, May 20, 1920, Kinnane to Alex
   C. King, May 26, 1920, Frank K. Nebeker to Kinnane, Feb. 1, 1921,
   File 24-563, ibid.; Kinnane to Figg, Feb. 16, 1920, File 24-423, ibid.;
   Stanley Coben, *A. Mitchell Palmer* (New York, 1963), pp. 157-64,
   303n; FM to MBM, Aug. 12, 15, 16, 1919, JFM Papers; Hillsdale
   News, Sept. 6, 1919, TSB; *DJ*, Sept. 6, 1919, TSB.
8. FM to MBM, Aug. 12, 1919, JFM Papers.
9. For the details of the plot, see Kinnane to Claude R. Porter, June
   17, July 28, 1919, Porter to Kinnane, July 3, 1919, Palmer to Kinnane,
   July 30, 1919, File 202657, RG 60; Indictment . . . , June Term, 1919,
   ibid.; *DFP*, July 8, 26, 1919, TSB; *DN*, Dec. 3, 1919, Mar. 5, 1920;
   DT, June 9, Dec. 2, 3, 1919, TSB; *DJ*, Aug. 1, 1919, TSB; *NYT*, June
   8, Aug. 27, 1919.
10. Kinnane to R. P. Stewart, Dec. 3, 1919, File 202657, RG 60; FM
    to MBM, Aug. 12, Dec. 1, 1919, JFM Papers; *DT*, Dec. 2, 1919, TSB.
11. Kinnane to Stewart, Dec. 3, 11, 1919, Feb. 11, 1920, Kinnane to Palmer,
    Dec. 20, 1919, Jan. 3, 7, 1920, Kinnane to Assistant Attorney General,
    Feb. 6, 1920, File 202657, RG 60; FM to MBM, Dec. 2, 4, 5, 6,

[Dec.], 1919, JFM Papers; *DN*, Dec. 3, 11, 12, 1919, Jan. 3, 4, Feb. 26, 27, 29, Mar. 2-4, 1920; *DT*, Dec. 3, 17, 20, 30, 1919, Feb. 26-28, 1920, TSB; *DFP*, Dec. 6, 9, 12, 1919, Feb. 26, 1920, TSB. For Felder's conviction, see *NYT*, Jan. 31, 1925.

12. *DN*, Feb. 28, 29, 1920; *DT*, Feb. 27, 28, 1920, TSB; William L. Stidger, "Frank Murphy," *The Human Side of Greatness* (New York, 1940), pp. 13-14; FM to MBM, Feb. 28, 1920, JFM Papers; Felder to FM, June 11, 1920, FM Papers.

13. *DJ*, Mar. 5, 1920, TSB; *DN*, Feb. 26, 27, Mar. 5, 6, 1920; *DT*, Mar. 5, 1920, TSB; Kinnane to Palmer, Mar. 6, 1920, File 202657, RG 60; Browne v. U.S., Waterbury v. Same, 290 Fed 870 (1923).

14. Proceedings in Chambers [Mar. 6, 1920], File 202657, RG 60; *NYT*, Mar. 23, 1920.

15. *DN*, Mar. 5, 1920; *DT*, Mar. 25, 1923, Jan. 31, 1925; Kinnane to Palmer, Mar. 6, 1920, File 202657, RG 60.

16. *DT*, Jan. 31, 1925; *DN*, Mar. 2, 1920; FM to F. C. Bolles, Dec. 13, 1922, FM to GM, Apr. 21, 1949, FM Papers.

17. FM to MBM, Oct. 2, Nov. 14, 1919, JFM Papers.

18. Coben, *Palmer*, pp. 209-11, 219; Kate Holladay Claghorn, *The Immigrant's Day in Court* (New York, 1923), pp. 367-73.

19. For the November raids, see Coben, *Palmer*, pp. 219-21; Robert K. Murray, *Red Scare* (Minneapolis, 1955), pp. 196-200, 207; Fred Yonce, "The Big Red Scare in Detroit, 1919-1920" (MS, 1963), pp. 13, 34-36, in my possession; *DN*, Nov. 8-10, 1919; *DFP*, Nov. 9, 1919; *DSN*, Nov. 15, 1919; and *NYT*, Nov. 8, 9, 1919.

20. FM to MBM, Nov. 14, 15, 1919, JFM Papers; *DN*, Nov. 15, 1919.

21. Coben, *Palmer*, pp. 226-29; Murray, *Red Scare*, pp. 210-22.

22. *DN*, Jan. 3-7, 1920; Frederick R. Barkley, "Jailing Radicals in Detroit," *Nation*, CX (Jan. 31, 1920), 136; Subcommittee of the Senate Committee on the Judiciary, *Charges of Illegal Practices of the Department of Justice, Hearings . . . ,* 66 Cong., 3 Sess. (Washington, 1921), pp. 697-743 passim; J. Edgar Hoover to Anthony Caminetti, Jan. 7, 8, 9, 10, 13, 14, 15, 31, 1920, File 205492, RG 60; Yonce, "Red Scare," pp. 37-39; House Special Committee to Investigate Communist Activities in the United States, *Investigation of Communist Propaganda, Hearings . . . ,* 71 Cong., 2 Sess., Part IV, I (Washington, 1930), 120-21; Claghorn, *Immigrant's Day*, p. 439; Max Lowenthal, *The Federal Bureau of Investigation* (New York, 1950), p. 205.

23. Barkley, "Jailing Radicals," p. 137; Barkley, "Improving on the Czar," *Nation*, CX (Apr. 10, 1920), 458-59; Yonce, "Red Scare," pp. 39-42; *DN*, Jan 7, 1920; *DSN*, Jan. 20, 1920; Lowenthal, *FBI*, pp. 205-6; Harry Barnard, *Independent Man: The Life of Senator James Couzens* (New York, 1958), p. 124; Louis F. Post, *The Deportations Delirium of Nineteen-Twenty* (Chicago, 1923), pp. 140-44. For Palmer's defense of what happened in Detroit, see House Committee on Rules, *Attorney General A. Mitchell Palmer on Charges Made against Department of*

Justice . . . , 66 Cong., 2 Sess. (Washington, 1920), pp. 60-63.

24. *DLN*, May 13, 1927; FM to J. J. Hunt, Nov. 10, 1921, Moehlman to FM, Apr. 2, 1947, FM Papers; unidentified clipping [May 1920], Joseph A. Labadie Collection, Harlan Hatcher Graduate Library, University of Michigan, Ann Arbor, Michigan.

25. Hicks to Zimmerman, Dec. 19, 1921, "Chief" Memorandum for . . . Holland, Dec. 31, 1921, Mabel Walker Willebrandt to Earl J. Davis, Feb. 23, 1922, File 23E20, RG 60.

26. Hicks to Zimmerman, Dec. 19, 1921, ibid.; FM to MBM, June 23, 1920, JFM Papers.

27. *DN*, Feb. 5, 1921; *Pipp's Weekly*, Nov. 12, 1921; "Get Together Club" notes [1922], HE Papers; R. G. Haynes to FM, Feb. 17, 1922, FM Papers.

28. For the Margolies cases, see *DN*, Sept. 21, Oct. 3, 4, 1921, Oct. 2, 1931, Jan. 2, 1939; *DT*, Sept. 21, 30, Oct. 4, 1921; *DFP*, Sept. 30, 1921, TSB; *DJ*, Oct. 3, 1921, TSB; and Hicks to Zimmerman, Dec. 19, 1921, File 23E20, RG 60.

29. *DN*, Oct. 4, 1921, Nov. 19, 1922, TSB; *DN*, Oct. 19, Dec. 4, 1921.

30. Allan Nevins and Frank Ernest Hill, *Ford: Expansion and Challenge, 1915-1933* (New York, 1957), pp. 212-13, 644n; *DN*, Jan. 24, 27, 1921; *DFP*, Jan. 27, 1921, TSB; *DJ*, Jan. 27, 1921, TSB.

31. FM to MBM, Nov. 6, 1920, Jan. 10, 17, 23, 24 (two letters), 27, 1921, JFM Papers; *DN*, Jan. 24, 27, 1921; *DFP*, Jan. 27, 1921, TSB; *DT*, Jan. 27, 1921, TSB.

32. *DFP*, Jan. 27, 1921, TSB; U.S. v. River Rouge Improvement Co. et al., 285 Fed 111 (1922); U.S. v. River Rouge Improvement Co. et al., 269 U.S. 411 (1926); *NYT*, Jan. 5, 1926; Nevins and Hill, *Ford*, p. 644n.

33. FM to MBM, Aug. 25, Sept. 29, 1919, JFM Papers; FM to HE [July 1, 1921], HE Papers; *DT*, June 21, 30, July 1, Dec. 22, 24, 1921, Jan. 10, Feb. 16, 1922.

34. *DN*, Mar. 16-19, 23, 25, 1921; *DT*, Mar. 24, 1921, TSB; *DJ*, Mar. 30, 1921, TSB; FM to MBM [Mar.] 23, Mar. 24, 1921, JFM Papers.

35. *DT*, Jan. 6, 17-20, 22, 1922; *DJ*, Jan. 17, 1922, TSB; *DN*, Jan. 17-19, 21, 1922; *DFP*, Jan. 20, Feb. 4, 1922, TSB; FM to MBM, Jan. 19, 1922, JFM Papers.

36. FM to MBM, Aug. 27, 1919, Jan. 17, 20, Dec. 20, 1921, Jan. 8, 24, 31, 1922, JFM Papers. Harry Daugherty, in a self-serving letter, later claimed that he kept Murphy on because he was efficient and was not "an offensive Democrat." Daugherty to FM, Jan. 4, 1940, FM Papers.

37. FM to MBM, Feb. 21, 24, 25, 1922, JFM Papers.

38. FM to Attorney General, Feb. 27, 1922, Records of the Appointment Clerk, RG 60. J. Woodford Howard is under the impression that Murphy did not serve beyond 1920. *Mr. Justice Murphy* (Princeton, 1968), p. 20.

39. Tuttle to FM, Mar. 8, 1922, Arthur J. Tuttle Papers, MHC; *DT*, Mar. 19, 29, 30, 1923; *DSN*, Dec. 1, 1923; Memo re Frank Murphy, Mar. 12, 1929, Candidate Files, Box 23, DCL Papers.
40. Sheet headed "Edward G. Kemp," in EGK Papers; [Port Huron *Times-Herald*, July 5, 1939], clipping in ibid.; information submitted for *Who's Who* [Nov. 14, 1939], ibid.; Osborn to EGK, Jan. 3, 1936, Jan. 8, Feb. 14, 1940, ibid.; card announcing the partnership of Murphy and Kemp, ibid.; *Michigan Alumnus*, Nov. 7, 1942, in ibid.; Interview with Alexander Holtzoff, Oct. 20, 1964, p. 6, MHC; Interview with G. Mennen Williams, Dec. 1964, pp. 17-18, ibid.; Interview with IM, July 30, 1964, p. 38, ibid.
41. FM to HE, Mar. 26, 30, Apr. 13, 1922, HE Papers.
42. FM to HE, Mar. 30, Apr. 6, Aug. 12, 30, 1922, ibid.; FM to MBM, Jan. 20, July 14, Aug. 1, Oct. 6, 29, Dec. 10, 1923, JFM Papers; Edward L. Bryant to Harry Mead, Sept. 5, 1930, GM Papers; Asher L. Cornelius to FM, June 30, 1934, FM Papers.
43. FM to MBM, Oct. 16, 1918, Oct. 2, 1919, JFM Papers; FM to HE, Aug. 4, 28, 30, Sept. 13, 1922, HE Papers.
44. Daugherty to FM, Sept. 7, 1922, FM to Daugherty, Oct. 6, 1922, FM to Lucking . . . , Dec. 4, 1922, FM to Byron Foy, Dec. 5, 1922, FM Papers; "In Account with Lucking . . . ," Nov. 23, 1922, ibid.; FM to MBM, Nov. 22, 1922, JFM Papers; FM to HE, Oct. 4, 1922, HE Papers; *DT*, Oct. 13, 1922.
45. FM to HE, July 24, 1924, HE Papers; *In re* McGraw, 228 Mich. 1 (1924); *DN*, July 25, 1924.
46. Eugene Strobel, "Frank Murphy: Crusading Judge, 1923-1930" (MS, 1932), pp. 4-5, in my possession; People v. Lewen, 226 Mich. 273 (1924); *DT*, Mar. 6, 23, 1924; JG to FM [May 1938], EGK-BHC Papers; Interview with JG, Dec. 7, 1973.
47. FM to HE, Sept. 29, 1923, HE Papers; Bryant to Mead, Sept. 5, 1930, GM Papers; *DT*, Dec. 21-27, 1923, Feb. 1, 1924.
48. FM to HE, Apr. 12, 1922, HE Papers.
49. FM to HE, July 14, 1923, ibid.
50. FM to HE, Aug. 10, 1922, July 23, 1923, ibid.; FM to MBM, Oct. 29, 1923, JFM Papers.
51. FM to MBM, Dec. 3, 1923, JFM Papers.
52. Seward Livermore, *Woodrow Wilson and the War Congress, 1916-1918* (Seattle, 1968), p. 112; FM to MBM, Jan. 28, 1920, JFM Papers.
53. Coben, *Palmer*, pp. 246-48, 254-68; Wesley M. Bagby, *The Road to Normalcy: The Presidential Campaign and Election of 1920* (Baltimore, 1962), pp. 71-72; FM to MBM, Mar. 23, June 29, July 1, 1920, JFM Papers; *DN*, Mar. 21, Apr. 6, 7, 1920; *DT*, June 24, 25, 28, 30, July 2, 3, 6, 1920.
54. FM to MBM, July 31, 1920, JFM Papers; *DT*, Aug. 2, 1920.
55. *DT*, Aug. 2, 13, Sept. 3, 7, 14, 15, Nov. 1, 1920; *DN*, Sept. 14, Oct. 22, 28, 1920; *Legionnaire* [1920], MSB; [*Michigan Citizen*], clipping

in EMB Papers; Kenneth T. Jackson, *The Ku Klux Klan in the City, 1915-1930* (New York, 1967), p. 128.

56. *DT*, Oct. 5, 1920.

57. *DN*, Sept. 22, Oct. 15, 1920; *DT*, Nov. 1, 3, 1920; FM to MBM, Oct. 21, 1920, JFM Papers; Ferris to FM, Nov. 1, 1920, FM Papers. Harding received 179,650 votes in Wayne County and Cox, 41,000 votes. Alex J. Groesbeck, the Republican candidate for governor, bested Ferris in the county, 177,248 votes to 49,036 votes.

58. FM to Ferris, Sept. 21, 1922, FM Papers; John W. Lederle, "Political Party Organization in Detroit—1920 to 1934" (MS [1934]), pp. 37-38, Bureau of Government Library, University of Michigan; FM to MBM, Feb. 16, Nov. 9, 1921, Feb. 2, 1922, FM to JFM, Nov. 22, 1922, JFM Papers; FM to HE, July 3, Aug. 3, 16, 1923, HE Papers.

59. Alan J. Ward, *Ireland and Anglo-American Relations, 1899-1921* (London, 1969), pp. 214-35; FM to MBM, Oct. 16, 1919, JFM Papers; *DN*, Oct. 16, 17, 1919; *DT*, Oct. 17, 1919.

60. FM to HE [Feb. 28], Mar. 21, Apr. 12, Sept. 1, 1922, HE Papers; FM to Joseph Cary, Jan. 16, 1923, FM Papers.

61. Ward, *Ireland*, pp. 249-51; FM to MBM, Dec. 18, 1921, JFM Papers; FM to HE, Aug, 24, 1922, HE Papers.

62. FM to MBM, May 28, 1920, [Jan. 12], Nov. 3, 1921, JFM Papers; FM to Father McGovern, May 1, 1922, FM to William Krichbaum, May 6, 22, Oct. 2, 1922, Jan. 22, Sept. 21, 1923, FM Papers; Jerold S. Auerbach, "Enmity and Amity: Law Teachers and Practitioners, 1900-1922," *Perspectives in American History*, V (1971), 584-88. See the class lists in the FM Papers.

63. FM to Ernest P. Lajoie, Feb. 5, 1922, FM to Barkey, Feb. 9, Aug. 1, 1922, FM to John J. Hunt, Feb. 14, 1922, FM to George Janisse, Sept. 21, 1923, Charles Shea to FM, Feb. 1, 1922, Mary I. O'Donnell to FM, Mar. 31, 1922, FM to F. Seymour, Dec. 7, 1922, William Wachs to FM, Mar. 28, July 15, 1922, C. P. Jones to FM, Sept. 25, 1922, Dec. 26, 1923, FM to Michael J. Gallagher, Dec. 26, 1923, FM Papers; FM to HE, Apr. 17, Aug. 10, 1922, Sept. 21, 1923, HE Papers; *Michigan Catholic*, Mar. 9, 1922, MSB; *DT*, Mar. 29, 1922, Jan. 1, 1923.

64. *DT*, May 5, 1920, Dec. 14, 1921, Mar. 20, 31, Nov. 10, 12, 1922; FM to MBM, Dec. 2, 1921, JFM Papers; FM to HE, Oct. 30, 1921, Sept. 1, 1922, HE Papers; *Legionnaire*, III (Dec. 10, 1921), 5. On the Learned Post, see Yonce, "Red Scare," pp. 20-21, 29, and *DT*, Jan. 4, 1922.

65. FM to MBM, May 21, Oct. 19, Nov. 13, 1919, Nov. 13, 1920, Oct. 23, Nov. 13, 1921, Feb. 13, 1922, Jan. 15, 1923, JFM Papers; FM to HE [Oct. 14, 1921], Aug. 22, 1922, Aug. 6, 1923, HE Papers; undated FM notes, FM Papers; *MD*, Nov. 21, 22, 1919.

66. FM to HE, Aug. 15, 1922, Aug. 16, 17, 1923, HE Papers; FM to

MBM, Dec. 15, 1920, JFM Papers; Kinnane to FM, July 3, 1922, FM Papers; *DT*, Mar. 25, 1923, Sept. 14, 1930.

67. FM to MBM, Dec. 6, 1919, Dec. 2, 1920, Jan. 30, 1921, JFM Papers; FM to HE [Sept. 28, 1921], Aug. 30, 1922, HE Papers.

68. GM to Elsie Picon, Apr. 14, 1955, GM Papers; *DT*, Feb. 4, 1923.

69. Gordon Dean Memorandum for the Attorney General, Jan. 15, 1939, FM Papers; *NYT*, June 16, 1939; Stidger, "Murphy," p. 13.

70. FM to MBM [Dec. 22], 1920, Jan. 6, 1923, Sept. 24 [1924], JFM Papers; Foy to FM, Sept. 6, 1927, FM to Fred Woodworth, June 15, 1926, FM to Henry T. Ewald, Oct. 10, 1930, FM Papers.

71. Ann Harding to FM [1920s], FM Papers; EGK to EMB, Sept. 31, 1958, EMB Papers; Interview with Norman H. Hill, Aug. 21, 1963, p. 30, MHC; Interview with Jack Manning, Dec. 4, 1964, p. 12, MHC.

72. Ann Walker to FM, June 9 [1935], ——to FM, Aug. 1 [1932], [Oct. 1932],——to FM, Nov. 22, 1934, FM Papers; FM to HE, Apr. 12, 1922, June 18, 1930, HE Papers.

73. ——to FM [1933], Nov. 22, 1934, Doris—— to FM, Nov. 2 [1928], FM Papers; HE to FM [1930], HE Papers.

74. Interview with Harry Mead, Aug. 15, 1963, p. 6, MHC; *Club-Fellow and Washington Mirror*, Feb. 17, 1926.

75. Marcet Haldeman-Julius, "The Defendants in the Sweet Murder Case," in *Clarence Darrow's Two Great Trials* (Girard, Kansas, 1927), p. 53; [Washington *Times-Herald*, Dec. 17, 1939], MSB; Harding to FM [Jan. 1932], Mercedes Rosebery to FM, Sept. 15, 1942, —— to FM [Aug. 28, 1923], FM Papers.

76. Marion —— to FM, Apr. 19, 1919, Ruby —— to FM [1920s], HE to FM [Mar. 1928], Harding to FM [Jan. 1932], Walker to FM, Nov. 1, 1934, Rosebery to FM, Sept. 15, Nov. 21, 1942, —— to FM [May 1933], Mar. 22, 1934, Claire —— to FM [May 1933], FM Papers; JG in *DFP*, Mar. 12, 1972.

77. Interview with Mrs. Joseph R. Hayden, Feb. 15, 1965, p. 11, MHC; Interview with Lucille Malcolm, Dec. 8, 1964; New York *Post*, Sept 25, 1942, MSB; [Washington *Times-Herald*, Dec. 17, 1939], MSB; Harding to FM [Aug. 7, 1932], —— to FM [1933], FM Papers; Mead interview, p. 31.

78. ". . . a community that overwhelms children with love, support, and praise cannot expect its grownups to live happily without it." Kenneth Keniston, *The Uncommitted* (Delta Book, New York, n.d.), p. 358.

79. Mead interview, p. 32; Interview with Lee Kreiselman Jaffe, Nov. 13, 1964; Interview with Frank Potts, Jan. 8, 1965, pp. 13-14, MHC; Atlanta *Constitution* [Jan. 1936], MSB; FM to HE, Sept. 16, 1925, HE Papers. See also Andrew M. Greeley, *That Most Distressful Nation: The Taming of the American Irish* (Chicago, 1972), pp. 133-35.

80. IM and Sharon Keyes interview, pp. 23-24; *DT*, Dec. 7, 1928; *DN*, Dec. 14, 1931; FM to MBM, Apr. 13, 1918, JFM Papers.

81. The summary of the Everard-Murphy romance is based on Hester's numerous letters to Frank from March, 1922, to May, 1933, in the FM Papers, and Frank's letters to her from September, 1921, to June, 1933, in the HE Papers.
82. FM to HE, Sept. 30, 1922, July 13, 1923, HE Papers; HE to FM, May 25, 1923, FM Papers.
83. FM to HE, July 26, 1924, Aug. 31, Sept. 21, 1925, Feb. 6, 1926, ibid.; "To all the World," Jan. 19, 1926, ibid.
84. Orchestra Hall program, Oct. 4 [1926], ibid.; FM to HE, Sept. 21, 1927, ibid.
85. FM to HE, June 18, 1930, June 4, 1933, ibid.
86. Haldeman-Julius, "The Defendants," p. 52; Harding to FM, undated, Sept. 10, 1922, Jan. 13 [1923], June 10, Dec. 15, 1925, Jan. 23, 1926, Feb. 11, 1927, [1920s], Oct. 8, 1931, [Jan. 1932], Aug. 1 [1932], [Oct. 1932], [Nov. 30, 1932], [1933], Nov. 4 [1935], July 17, 1936, FM Papers; Honolulu *Star-Times*, Feb. 8, 1935, clipping in ibid.; Harding to GM, Aug. 31, 1933, GM Papers; Harding to FM, May 24, 1935, EMB Papers; Mead interview, p. 30; Moehlman to FM, Dec. 5, 1946, FM Papers.
87. FM to HE, Sept. 21, 1922, HE Papers.
88. Washington *Star*, Jan. 8, 1939, clipping in FM Papers; *NYT*, Jan 7, 1940; (Manila) *Sunday Tribune*, Sept. 24, 1933, Norman H. Hill Scrapbooks, MHC; unidentified radio speech, Oct. 31, 1931, MOR; FM to Robert A. Williams, Mar. 1, 1939, FM to G. Mennen Williams, Nov. 18, 1940, FM Papers; unidentified clipping [1926], MSB; Manila *Tribune*, Aug. 2, 1933, MSB; Brightmoor *Journal*, Jan. 22, 1931, MSB.
89. James, *The Moral Equivalent of War*, American Association for International Conciliation, *No. 27* (New York, 1910), pp. 4, 8, 15–18.
90. Max Farrand, ed., *Benjamin Franklin's Memoirs* (Berkeley, 1965), p. 238.

CHAPTER V

1. FM to MBM, Dec. 16, 1918, JFM Papers. See Chapter III.
2. Leo Donovan, "Detroit: City of Conflict," in Robert S. Allen, ed., *Our Fair City* (New York, 1947), p. 151; DBGR, *Accumulated Social and Economic Statistics for Detroit* (Detroit, 1937), p. 3.
3. Maurice Ramsey, "Some Aspects of Non-Partisan Government in Detroit, 1918–1940" (Ph.D. thesis, University of Michigan, 1944), pp. 16–17, 25–26; William P. Lovett, *Detroit Rules Itself* (Boston, 1930), pp. 21–23, 26–27, 31, 62–63; Donovan, "Detroit," pp. 151–52.
4. The original name of the organization was the Detroit Civic Uplift League.
5. On this subject, see Samuel P. Hays, "The Politics of Reform in Municipal Government in the Progressive Era," *Pacific Northwest*

Quarterly, LV (Oct. 1964), 157-69.

6. Lovett, *Detroit Rules Itself,* pp. 29-30, 60-63, 80, 93-94, 106, 113-20; William P. Lovett to William H. Phelps, Aug. 7, 1936, DCL Papers; Ramsey, "Non-Partisan Government," pp. 18-19, 31-53, 129-31; Freeman A. Flynn, "Detroit Voters—A Thirty Years View" (M.A. thesis, Wayne State University, 1948), pp. 4-9; Donovan, "Detroit," pp. 151-53; David Allan Levine, " 'Expecting the Barbarians': Race Relations and Social Control, Detroit, 1915-1925" (Ph.D. thesis, University of Chicago, 1970), pp. 223-28.

7. Raymond Moley, *Our Criminal Courts* (New York, 1930), pp. 75-76.

8. Civil cases in Detroit were handled by the Wayne County Circuit Court. For the origins of the Police Court and the Recorder's Court, see Michigan Historical Records Survey Project, *Inventory of the Municipal Archives of Michigan: Detroit Recorder's Court* (Detroit, 1942), pp. 1-2.

9. Herbert Harley, "Detroit's New Model Criminal Court," *Journal of the American Institute of Criminal Law and Criminology,* XI (Nov. 1920), 398-401; DBGR, *Report on the Operation of the Recorder's Court of Detroit for the First Year of Its Reorganization, Apr. 20, 1920-Apr. 20, 1921* (Detroit, 1921), p. 10; "Detroit Gets Real Criminal Court," *JAJS,* IV (June 1920), 16; Michigan Project, *Recorder's Court,* pp. 16-17.

10. Harley, "Detroit's New Criminal Court," pp. 401-2; *DN,* Mar. 27, 1923; Pliny W. Marsh, "Detroit Succeeds under a New Organization," *Journal of the American Institute of Criminal Law and Criminology,* XIV (May 1923), 11; "Detroit Wins New Court," *JAJS,* III (June 1919), 5-6; "Detroit Gets Real Criminal Court," ibid., IV (June 1920), 14-17; Michigan Project, *Recorder's Court,* pp. 2, 5-6, 10-12, 15, 17, 19, 31; "Act No. 369," *Public Acts of . . . Michigan . . . 1919* (Fort Wayne, 1919), pp. 646-51.

11. Harry B. Keidan, *First Annual Report of the Reorganized Recorder's Court of the City of Detroit* ([Detroit], 1921), pp. 4-6, 11; DBGR, *Report on First Year,* pp. 1-3, 10-12, 36-43, 49; DBGR, *An Appraisal of the Recorder's Court of Detroit during Its Second Year* (Detroit, 1922), pp. 4-10; Marsh, "Detroit Succeeds," pp. 14-21; "Cleaning up Detroit," *JAJS,* IV (Aug. 1920), 39-40, 41-42, 43-44; "Efficient Criminal Court Machinery," ibid., XIV (Apr. 1931), 181; Harley, "Detroit's New Criminal Court," pp. 402-5, 410; *DN,* Feb. 4, 1923.

12. Keidan, *First Annual Report,* pp. 3-4, 6, 7-11; DBGR, *Report on First Year,* pp. 13-29, 34; DBGR, *Appraisal of Second Year,* p. 4; Harley, "Detroit's New Criminal Court," pp. 403, 405-9; N. R. [Deardorff], "A Breakwater for Detroit's Crime Wave," *Survey,* XLIX (Dec. 15, 1922), 389; Marsh, "Detroit Succeeds," pp. 12-13; Arch Mandel, "Why Crime Decreased in Detroit," *American City,* XXVII (Aug. 1922), 150-51.

13. Mark W. Haller, "Urban Crime and Criminal Justice: The Chicago Case," *Journal of American History,* LVII (Dec. 1970), 626; Keidan, *First Annual Report,* pp. 21–22; DBGR, *Report on First Year,* pp. 31, 36–37; DBGR, *Appraisal of Second Year,* p. 5; Marsh, "Detroit Succeeds," pp. 13–14; "Cleaning up Detroit," p. 42; Harley, "Detroit's New Criminal Court," pp. 409–10; Mandel, "Why Crime Decreased in Detroit," pp. 149–51; "Detroit Reduces Crime Rate 58 Per Cent," *JAJS,* V (Apr. 1922), 167–71; "Crime Problem Solved . . . ," ibid., IV (Apr. 1921), 189.

14. "Efficient Criminal Court Machinery," p. 180; Herbert Harley to Lovett, June 12, 1929, DCL Papers; George E. Worthington, "Prostitution in Detroit" (MS, 1926), Chapter VI, Additional Papers, Box 14, DCL Papers.

15. Lent D. Upson to John Faust, Oct. 13, 1923, FM Papers; Moley, *Our Criminal Courts,* pp. xi–xiv, 84, 87–88; W. McKay Skillman, "A Recorder's Court Judge Reviews the Parade of Detroit . . . ," *Michigan State Bar Journal,* XXX (Oct. 1931), 10–12; *DT,* Mar. 21, June 23, 1923.

16. David Greenstone, "A Report on the Politics of Detroit" (MS, Cambridge, Mass., 1961), II, 2; Moley, *Our Criminal Courts,* pp. xx–xxi, 241–44; Ramsey, "Non-Partisan Government," p. 231; Lovett, *Detroit Rules Itself,* p. 141.

17. Ramsey, "Non-Partisan Government," pp. 115–19, 123–39, 179–81; Lovett, *Detroit Rules Itself,* pp. 143–44, 154–56, 158–60; Greenstone, "Report on Detroit," V, 56–57; Lovett to Reinhold Niebuhr, Oct. 13, 1927, DCL Papers.

18. Ramsey, "Non-Partisan Government," pp. 140–46; Clarence M. Burton and M. Agnes Burton, *History of Wayne County and the City of Detroit, Michigan,* 5 vols. (Chicago, 1930), I, 664–66; Lovett, *Detroit Rules Itself,* p. 142; Greenstone, "Report on Detroit," V, 10.

19. Ramsey, "Non-Partisan Government," pp. 133, 136; Greenstone, "Report on Detroit," II, 14; Charles R. Adrian, "Some General Characteristics of Nonpartisan Elections," *American Political Science Review,* XLVI (Sept. 1952), 774–75. Cf. Eugene C. Lee, *The Politics of Nonpartisanship: A Study of California City Elections* (Berkeley, 1960).

20. Sidney Glazer, *Detroit* (New York, 1965), pp. 91, 94–97, 108–9; DBGR, *Statistics,* pp. 3, 4, 7, 14; Donovan, "Detroit," pp. 154–55.

21. Bureau of the Census, *Fourteenth Census of the United States,* III, *Population, 1920* (Washington, 1922), 496–97; Bureau of the Census, *Fifteenth Census of the United States: 1930, Population,* III, Part 1 (Washington, 1932), 1183; Arthur Pound, *Detroit* (New York, 1940), p. 247; John C. Leggett, "Class Consciousness and Politics in Detroit: A Study in Change," *Michigan History,* XLVIII (Dec. 1964), 294.

22. Mayor's Inter-racial Committee, *The Negro in Detroit* ([Detroit], 1926), Section II, pp. 3–6, 10–16, Section III, pp. 4–5, 8, Section V, pp.

1-2, 10, 28, 61-62; typed paragraphs, Aug. 1, 1919, DUL Papers; Director's Report for Apr. 1923, ibid.; "Negro Housing" [Apr. 26, 1924], ibid.; "Facts Concerning Negroes in Detroit . . . ," Nov. 21, 1925, ibid.; John Dancy, "Detroit Negroes in Industry," Mar. 1, 1926, ibid.; Levine, "Race Relations," pp. 215-20; "Race Prejudice in the North," *Christian Century,* XLIV (May 12, 1927), 283-84; Bruno Lasker, "The Negro in Detroit," *Survey,* LVIII (Apr. 15, 1927), 73.

23. Typed sheet, Aug. 25, 1917, DUL Papers; Levine, "Race Relations," pp. 81-84, 239-46; T. J. Woofter, ed., *Negro Problems in Cities* (Garden City, New York, 1928), pp. 68, 72-73; Kenneth T. Jackson, *The Ku Klux Klan in the City, 1915-1930* (New York, 1967), pp. 128-29; Marcet Haldeman-Julius, "The Defendants in the Sweet Murder Case," in *Clarence Darrow's Two Great Trials* (Girard, Kansas, 1927), p. 38.

24. Jackson, *Klan,* pp. 129-42; Norman Frederic Weaver, "The Knights of the Ku Klux Klan in Wisconsin, Indiana, Ohio and Michigan" (Ph.D. thesis, University of Wisconsin, 1954), pp. 268-72, 285-86, 288; *NYT,* Nov. 3, 1925.

25. Mayor's Inter-racial Committee, *Negro in Detroit,* Section IX, pp. 18-22, 37-38; *Report of the Mayor's Committee on Race Relations* (Detroit, 1927), pp. 7-8; "Detroit Urban League," Aug. 3, 1926, DUL Papers; Niebuhr, *Leaves from the Notebook of a Tamed Cynic* (Chicago, 1929), pp. 143-44; Minutes of the Meeting of the Board of Directors, NAACP, File A-2, Mar. 14, 1927, NAACP Papers; Walter White to James Weldon Johnson, Sept. 16, 1925, File D-85, ibid.

26. Ramsey, "Non-Partisan Government," pp. 171-73; "Facts Concerning Negroes in Detroit . . . ," Nov. 21, 1925, DUL Papers.

27. *NYT,* Dec. 14, 1931; Ramsey, "Non-Partisan Government," pp. 153-54; Sidney Fine, *The Automobile under the Blue Eagle* (Ann Arbor, 1963), p. 14.

28. Robert L. Duffus, "Detroit: Utopia on Wheels," *Harper's,* CLXII (Dec. 1930), 55-56; Donovan, "Detroit," p. 151; Niebuhr, *Leaves,* pp. 112, 116-17.

29. Edwin H. Sutherland and C. E. Gehlke, "Crime and Punishment," in President's Research Committee on Social Trends, *Recent Social Trends in the United States,* 2 vols. (New York, 1933), II, 1121, 1135.

30. Detroit Recorder's Court, *Annual Report . . . , 1924* [Detroit, 1925], pp. 24-25; Detroit Recorder's Court, *Annual Report . . . , 1929* [Detroit, 1930], pp. 23-24.

31. Larry Daniel Englemann, "O, Whisky: The History of Prohibition in Michigan" (Ph.D. thesis, University of Michigan, 1971), pp. 299, 372, 531; "Bootlegging and Murder in Detroit," *Literary Digest,* LXXVIII (Sept. 29, 1923), 48, 52, 55; Ernest W. Mandeville, "Detroit Sets a Bad Example," *Outlook,* CXXXIX (Apr. 22, 1925), 612-14; *NYT,* May 3, 27, 1928; Walter W. Liggett, "Michigan—Soused and Serene," *Plain Talk,* VI (Mar. 1930), 267.

32. National Commission on Law Observance and Enforcement, *Official Records*, 71 Cong., 3 Sess., *Sen. Doc. No. 307* (Washington, 1931), IV, 580-81, V, 214; Detroit Recorder's Court, *Annual Report . . . 1925* [Detroit,1926], pp. 4-5, *1926* [Detroit, 1927], pp. 4-5, *1927* [Detroit, 1928], pp. 4-5, *1928* [Detroit, 1929], pp. 4-6, *1929*, pp. 4-6, *1930* [Detroit, 1931], pp. 4-6.

33. Liggett, "Michigan—Soused and Serene," pp. 263, 266, 267, 271-73; Donovan, "Detroit," pp. 157-58; Skillman, "Recorder's Court Judge," p. 10; Worthington, "Prostitution in Detroit," Chapter VI; Lovett to Harley, Feb. 5, 1926, DCL Papers; *DN*, July 7, 1926; *DT*, July 7, 1926.

34. "The Labor Governors," *Fortune*, XV (June 1937), 138; Eugene Strobel, "Frank Murphy: Crusading Judge, 1923-1930" (MS, 1962), p. 6, in my possession; "An Efficient Criminal Court," *JAJS*, VI (June 1922), 21; Lovett to Russell F. Griffen, Apr. 16, 1923, DCL Papers; *DT*, July 31, 1920, Feb. 4, 11, Mar. 2, 1923; *DFP*, Apr. 6, 1923; *DN*, Aug. 12, 1939; *Pipp's Weekly* [1923], Reading Room File, BHC.

35. Stidger, "Frank Murphy," *The Human Side of Greatness* (New York, 1940), p. 14; FM to Stidger, Apr. 5, 1937, FM Papers.

36. Interview with Thomas F. Chawke, Mar. 1965, p. 4, MHC.

37. Strobel, "Murphy," pp. 4-5.

38. "An Efficient Criminal Court," p. 21; Washington Post, Jan. 7, 1940, MSB; Interview with Hilmer Gellein, Aug. 21, 1963, p. 2; Strobel, "Murphy," pp. 7-9; FM to Harry Bitner, Oct. 29, 1934, FM Papers.

39. Charles Bolden to Raymond Clapper, July 4, 1939, Raymond Clapper Papers, LC; Interview with Carl Muller, Oct. 6, 1964, p. 26, MHC; Interview with Jack Manning, Dec. 4, 1964, pp. 1-2, MHC.

40. Moley, *Our Criminal Courts*, p. 232.

41. FM to Vera Brown, Dec. 30, 1943, FM Papers; FM to MBM, Mar. 5, 1918, JFM Papers; Manning interview, p. 2.

42. MM to —— [1933-34?], MM Papers; *DT*, Feb. 4, 1923; form in Candidate Files, Box 23, DCL Papers.

43. The office of recorder dates from 1824. The recorder originally served as mayor in the event of the latter's disability and later presided over the Mayor's Court. Once the Recorder's Court was created in 1857, his duties became primarily judicial. He did serve ex-officio, however, as a member of the City Election Commission. See *Manual, County of Wayne, Michigan, 1926* (n.p., n.d.), pp. 186-87, and *DT*, Apr. 24, 1929.

44. *DN*, Feb. 5, 1923; *DT*, Feb. 11, 1923.

45. *DT*, Feb. 24, 28, Mar. 3, 1923; *DN*, Feb. 24, 1923; *Civic Searchlight*, Feb. 23, 1923; *DSN*, Mar. 3, 1923.

46. *DN*, Feb. 24, 1923; Lovett to Church Pastors, Feb. 26, 1923, DCL Papers. See also *DSN*, Mar. 3, 1923.

47. Jeffries disputed the Big Four's claims that it had cleaned up the

court's docket and minimized the "new" features of the court. *DT*, Feb. 18, 27, 28, Mar. 6, 1923.

48. *DT*, Feb. 24-28, Mar. 1-6, 1923.

49. *DT*, Feb. 20, 24, 27, Mar. 1-6, 1923; *DN*, Feb. 20, 1923; *Army and Navy Bulletin*, Feb. 26, 1923; *DLN*, Feb. 16, 23, Mar. 2, 1923; *Civic Searchlight*, Feb. 23, 1923.

50. *DT*, Feb. 24, 25, Mar. 1, 2, 4-7, 1923.

51. Frank D. Eaman and Frank A. Nolan to Alfred Lucking, Mar. 6, 1923, FM Papers; *DT*, Mar. 11, 20, 1923. The Big Four raised $6,118.61 for the primary. *DT*, Mar. 20, 1923.

52. *DT*, Mar. 8, 11, 12, 1923; *DN*, Mar. 9, 1923. Jeffries received 55,177 votes, Heston 35,310 votes, and Murphy 34,550 votes.

53. *DT*, Mar. 13, 15, 20, 23-31, Apr. 2, 1923; *DN*, Mar. 23, 1923. See "Contributions to Campaign" [Apr. 6, 1923], and "Judge Frank Murphy's Account," Apr. 6, 1923, FM Papers.

54. *DT*, Mar. 13, 15, 22, Apr. 2, 1923; *DN*, Mar. 22, 23, 1923.

55. *DT*, Mar. 22, 23, 25, 1923; *DN*, Mar. 22, 23, 1923.

56. *DT*, Mar. 23, 25, 31, 1923.

57. *DT*, Mar. 18-Apr. 2, 1923; *DSN*, Mar. 31, 1923; Lovett to Harry Olson, Mar. 23, 1923, Lovett to Harvey J. Campbell, May 21, 1923, DCL Papers.

58. *DT*, Mar. 11-Apr. 2, 1923; *DSN*, Mar. 31, 1923; William J. Murphy to FM, Mar. 25, 1923, FM Papers; Strobel, "Murphy," p. 9.

59. *DT*, Mar. 9, 11, 13-15, 17, 19, 23, 25-27, 30, 31, Apr. 1, 1923; *DLN*, Mar. 23, 30, 1923; W. J. Murphy to FM, Mar. 25, 1923, Herbert Gee to FM, Mar. 17, 1923, Herman A. Rozanski to FM, Mar. 8, 1923, Charles E. Shea to FM, Mar. 9, 1923, Victor Kulaski to FM, Mar. 14, 1923, Ruby M. Zahn to FM, Mar. 31, 1923, FM Papers; *Legionnaire*, IV (Mar. 15, 1923), 1.

60. *DN*, Mar. 17, 20, 25-27, 1923; *DSN*, Mar. 24, 31, 1923. In the end, the *Free Press* decided that Murphy's qualifications entitled him to a seat on the court. *DFP*, Mar. 26, 1923.

61. *Civic Searchlight*, Mar. 23, 1923; Lovett to William Walker, Apr. 6, 1923, DCL Papers; *DT*, Mar. 28, 29, 1923.

62. *DN*, Mar. 15-17, 1923; *DFP*, Mar. 15, 16, 18, 20, 1923.

63. *DN*, Mar. 15-19, 21, 24, 25, 29, 1923; *DFP*, Mar. 16, 18, 25, 1923; *DT*, Mar. 21, 25, 1923.

64. *DN*, Mar. 15, 1923; *DT*, Mar. 17, 1923.

65. *DN*, Mar. 15, 16, 20, 23, 1923; *DFP*, Mar. 16, 23, 1923; *DT*, Mar. 17, 19, 1923; FM to George Miller, Mar. 15, 1923, FM Papers.

66. DCL to Dear Friend, Mar. 28, 1923, Rogers to Pastors, undated, DCL Papers; *DN*, Mar. 17, 19, 31, 1923.

67. *DN*, Apr. 2, 1923; *DT*, Mar. 3, 5, 30, Apr. 2, 1923.

68. *DT*, Mar. 18, 26, 28-30, 1923. Cf. *DN*, Mar. 30, 1923. The text of Murphy's address is in the FM Papers.

69. *DN,* Apr. 2, 3, 1923.
70. The precinct by precinct results are available in the FM Papers. For the demographic data, see Bureau of the Census, *Fourteenth Census of the United States,* III, *Population, 1920,* 496-97. Bartlett received 96,854 votes.
71. Banfield and Wilson, *City Politics* (Vintage Book; New York, 1966), pp. 46, 154; Lovett to Arch Mandel, Apr. 3, 1923, DCL Papers. Lovett was agreeing in his statement with the views expressed by the Protestant minister Dr. Lynn Harold Hough.
72. *DT,* Apr. 3, 4, 1923; Burton and Burton, *History of Wayne County,* I, 665; Lovett to Olson, Apr. 3, 1923, DCL Papers.
73. *DN,* Apr. 3, 4, 1923; *DFP,* Apr. 3, 4, 1923; *DSN,* Apr. 7, 1923; *Civic Searchlight,* Apr. 1923; Lovett to Mandel, Apr. 3, 1923, Lovett to Olson, Apr. 3, 1923, Lovett to Griffen, Apr. 5, 1923, Lovett to H. W. Dodds, Apr. 6, 1923, DCL Papers.
74. FM to MBM, Apr. 5, 6, 8, 9, 10, 1923, JFM Papers.
75. *DT,* Apr. 10, 14, 15, 26, 1923; *DN,* May 10, 1923; FM to HE, Apr. 10, 1923, HE Papers; GM to Byron Foy, May 9, 1923, HM to GM, May 11, 1923, FM Papers; Harper Hospital bill, May 22, 1923, ibid.; Gellein interview, p. 2.
76. *DT,* Apr. 5, 1923.
77. For the details of the gas arbitration and its aftermath, see Doremus to FM, Nov. 26, 1923, FM to Doremus, Nov. 28, 1923, FM Papers; Agreement between City of Detroit and Detroit City Gas Co., Nov. 14, 1923, ibid.; *DT,* Nov. 19, Dec. 12, 19, 27, 1923, Jan. 4, Mar. 1, 6, 23, Apr. 2, 13-16, 24, 26, 30, May 18, 22, 24, 28, June 4, 15, Aug. 1, Sept. 10, 13, 1924, Apr. 25, 1925; *DN,* Apr. 13, July 31, Oct. 27, 1924. For evidence that Murphy at least considered using the fee for charitable purposes, see Andrew J. Eldred to FM, May 16, 1924, FM Papers.
78. *DT,* Apr. 19, June 22, 1923. The state legislature at the end of May amended the statute governing the court to limit the term of the presiding judge to a maximum of three months and a minimum of one month, but this provision required the approval of the Detroit electorate, and the Common Council failed to submit the measure to the voters. "Act. No. 278," *Public Acts of the Legislature . . . Michigan . . . 1923* (Lansing, 1923), pp. 446-47.
79. Lovett to Miller, Sept. 7, Dec. 28, 1923, Lovett to Harley, Oct. 5, 1923, DCL Papers.

CHAPTER VI

1. Richard D. Lunt devotes only two pages, and J. Woodford Howard, nine pages, to Murphy's years on the Recorder's Court. Lunt, *The High Ministry of Government: The Political Career of Frank Murphy*

(Detroit, 1965), pp. 25-26; Howard, *Mr. Justice Murphy* (Princeton, 1968), pp. 22-30.

2. Eric Friedheim release, June 11, 1932, in FM Papers.
3. MM to Aunt Maggie [Jan. 1924], MM Papers; Marcet Haldeman-Julius, "Clarence Darrow's Defense of a Negro," in *Clarence Darrow's Two Great Trials* (Girard, Kansas, 1927), pp. 45-46; Addresses Made at the Opening of Court . . . , Jan. 2, 1924, FM Papers.
4. MM to Aunt Maggie [Jan. 1924], MM Papers; FM to MBM, Jan. 3, 1923 [1924], JFM Papers.
5. Raymond Moley, *Our Criminal Courts* (New York, 1930), pp. 3-4, 9, 13n. See also JG to FM, undated, FM Papers.
6. FM to GM, Dec. 18, 1934, draft of statement attached to FM to GM, Feb. 11, 1947, FM to Charles Tucker, Apr. 21, 1932, FM to Thomas Cotter, Sept. 11, 1934, FM Papers; FM to Vera Nolan, Dec. 6, 1945, EMB Papers; *DLN*, Sept. 16, 1927; Interview with Hilmer Gellein, Aug. 21, 1963, p. 9, MHC; Blair Moody, "High Commissioner to Manila," *Survey Graphic*, XXIV (Dec. 1935), 611; *DT*, Aug. 9, 1930.
7. William P. Lovett to Harry Olson [Sept. 8, 1924], Lovett to Herbert Harley, Feb. 5, Oct. 23, 1926, Lovett to Clinton Rogers Woodruff, May 27, 1926, Lovett to Mayo Fesler, Nov. 22, 1926, Aug. 27, 1937, Lovett to Fred Green, Jan. 7, Feb. 2, 1927, Lovett to H. B. Stitt, Jan. 26, 1927, Lovett to Worth N. Tippy, Feb. 8, 1927, DCL Papers; Lovett to Members of Executive Board, DCL, June 4, 1928, June 4, 1929, Additional Papers, Box 3, ibid. See also Moley, *Our Criminal Courts*, pp. 84, 87-88.
8. Moley, *Our Criminal Courts*, pp. 85-87; "Efficient Criminal Court Machinery," *JAJS*, XIV (Apr. 1931), 185; Percy L. Monteith to Judges, July 19, 1930, FM Papers. Based on the annual reports of the court, 16.54 percent of the felony cases were pending at the end of 1921; 28.64 percent at the end of 1924; 44.08 percent at the end of 1925; and 32.31 percent at the end of 1928. Cf. W. Abraham Goldberg, "Waiver of Jury in Felony Trials," *Michigan Law Review*, XXVIII (Dec. 1929), 167.
9. *DT*, Mar. 4, 1927; Lovett to George E. Worthington, June 10, 1927, DCL Papers. The figures after 1928 are not comparable. "Efficient Criminal Court Machinery," pp. 185-86.
10. "Efficient Criminal Court Machinery," p. 187; Fred R. Johnson, *Probation for Juveniles and Adults* (New York, 1928), pp. 77-78, 84-85.
11. *DT*, Jan. 3, Nov. 9, 1924, Mar. 25, 1929; Lovett to H. M. Nimmo, Jan. 5, 1924, DCL Papers; Eugene Strobel, "Frank Murphy: Crusading Judge, 1923-1930" (MS, 1962), p. 12, in my possession; Charles S. Casgrain to FM et al., Jan. 7, 1924, FM to A. L. Jacoby, Jan. 10, 1924, FM to Fred R. Johnson, Jan. 10, 1924, Jacoby to FM, Jan. 14, 1924, Johnson to FM, Jan. 14, 24, 1924, Committee to the Judges, Jan. 18, 1924, Charles L. Chute to FM, Feb. 8, 1924, Elizabeth A.

Lee to FM, Apr. 17, 1924, FM Papers; Gellein to Sidney Fine, Dec. 4, 1971.

12. *DT,* Jan. 3, Sept. 27, 1924, Feb. 9, 1927; Moley, *Our Criminal Courts,* p. 90; *Civic Searchlight,* Nov. 1925, May 1927, Feb. 1928; *DSN,* Apr. 30, 1927, Mar. 24, Apr. 7, 1928; Lovett to Harley, Oct. 23, 1926, Marsh to Lovett, Dec. 21, 1926, Lovett to Green, Mar. 16, Apr. 26, 1927, Lovett to Charles Boyd, Apr. 16, 1927, Lovett to Editor *DFP,* Aug. 24, 1927, Marsh to Nimmo, Apr. 3, 1928, DCL Papers.

13. Lovett to Green, Jan. 7, Feb. 2, Mar. 16, Apr. 14, 1927, Green to Lovett, Jan. 29, 1927, Lovett to Bascom Johnson, Mar. 14, 1927, Lovett to Marsh, Apr. 16, 1927, Lovett to Worthington, June 10, 1927, DCL Papers; *DFP,* Mar. 31, 1927.

14. *DT,* Aug. 20, 21, 1929, Sept. 3, 1930; Johnson to Lovett [Mar.] 7, 1929, Candidate Files, Box 23, DCL Papers; Lovett, "Frank Murphy," Mar. 8, 1929, ibid.; Memo re Frank Murphy, Mar. 12, 1929, ibid.; Monteith to Judges, July 1, 1930, FM Papers; "Efficient Criminal Court Machinery," p. 187; Michigan Historical Records Survey Project, *Inventory of the Municipal Archives of Michigan: Detroit Recorder's Court* (Detroit, 1942), pp. 39-40.

15. Addresses . . . , Jan. 2, 1924, FM Papers; Johnson to FM, Feb. 27, 1929, Lowrie to FM, Mar. 3 [1930], FM Papers; Lovett, "Frank Murphy," Candidate Files, Box 23, DCL Papers.

16. *DT,* Feb. 3, Dec. 17, 1926, May 6, 18, 1928; FM to Sanford Bates, June 27, 1929, FM Papers.

17. Memo, Apr. 29, 1930, Recorder's Court Judges, Candidate Files, Box 23, DCL Papers; *DT,* May 6, June 8, 1928, Apr. 26, 27, 1930; *Civic Searchlight,* May 1930; Johnson to FM, May 14, 1930, FM to William J. Hale, Aug. 25, 1933, Lowell S. Selling to FM, Jan. 3, 1939, FM Papers. When the respected head of the clinic, Dr. Theophile Raphael, resigned in 1930, Murphy sought in vain to prevent his replacement by a political appointee.

18. Moley, *Our Criminal Courts,* pp. 45-49, 58-59; *DN,* Oct. 10, 11, 1925; R. H. Ferris to FM, Sept. 28, 1925, and enclosed, "The Bond Situation in the Recorder's Court . . . ," FM Papers.

19. FM to Presiding Judge, Municipal Court, Cleveland, Sept. 11, 1924, Ferris to FM, Sept. 28, 1925, FM to Joseph Mulcahy, Apr. 6, 1926, FM Papers; FM, "A Bond Bureau for the Recorder's Court" [1926], ibid.; *DT,* Jan. 17, 18, 20, 1926; Detroit Recorder's Court, *Annual Report . . . 1930* [Detroit, 1931], p. 4; "Efficient Criminal Court Machinery," p. 187; "Detroit Court Solves Bail Problem," *JAJS* (Feb. 1933), 143-49.

20. Moley, *Our Criminal Courts,* p. 67; *DT,* Feb. 21, 1924, Mar. 3, 5, 7, 17, 1925; Alvan D. Hersch to FM, Dec. 29, 1924, FM Papers; *DLN,* Mar. 6, 1925; Edwin H. Sutherland and C. E. Gehlke, "Crime and Punishment," in President's Research Committee on Social Trends,

Recent Social Trends in the United States (New York, 1933), II, 1451.

21. *DN*, Sept. 1, 3, Dec. 1, 1929; *DT*, Sept. 1, 1929; draft of court reform plan [1924], FM Papers; "Efficient Criminal Court Machinery," pp. 187-88; Detroit Recorder's Court, *Annual Report . . . 1930*, p. 4. For other reforms favored by Murphy, see draft of court reform plan [1924], FM Papers; *DT*, Jan. 19, 1929; and Memo re Frank Murphy, Mar. 12, 1929, Candidate Files, Box 23, DCL Papers.

22. *DT*, Mar. 26, 1929; FM speech [Mar. 25, 1929], FM Papers.

23. *DT*, Mar. 19, 20, 26, 1924; Ernest Jerome Hopkins, *Our Lawless Police* (New York, 1931), pp. 128-33; National Commission on Law Observance and Enforcement, *Report on Lawlessness in Law Enforcement* (Washington, 1931), pp. 121-23.

24. Hopkins, *Our Lawless Police*, pp. 27, 133-36.

25. *DT*, Dec. 25, 28, 1924.

26. *DT*, Mar. 20, 31, Apr. 1, 3, 1925, June 8, 1928; *DN*, Apr. 2, 3, Sept. 12, 1925; *Civic Searchlight*, Mar., Apr. 1925; Lovett to Condon, Apr. 3, 1925, DCL Papers.

27. *DN*, Sept. 2, 6, 8, 10, 1925; *DT*, Sept. 2, 1925; *DSN*, Oct. 31, 1925.

28. *DN*, Sept. 8, 12, 16, 1925.

29. *DN*, Sept. 15, 21, 23, 1925; *DFP*, Nov. 2, 3, 1925; *DSN*, Oct. 31, 1925; Lovett to John Lodge, June 4, 1925, DCL Papers; *DT*, Sept. 2, 23-25, Oct. 21, 23, 26, 29, Nov. 2, 1925.

30. *DT*, Oct. 20, 21, 23-26, 30, Nov. 1, 2, Dec. 17, 1925, Jan. 10, 1926; *DN*, Oct. 25, 1925; FM to William Boyer, Apr. 5, 1926, FM Papers.

31. *DN*, Oct. 25, 29-31, 1925.

32. *DN*, Nov. 4, 1925; *DT*, Nov. 9, 22, 1925.

33. The state legislature in 1927 authorized the governor to assign other judges in the state to aid the Recorder's Court when this seemed necessary. *DT*, Mar. 22, Apr. 27, 1927.

34. *DT*, Dec. 9, 15, 1925.

35. Goldberg, "Waiver of Jury," pp. 163-78; Goldberg, "Optional Waiver of Jury in Felony Trials in . . . Detroit . . . ," *Journal of the American Institute of Criminal Law and Criminology*, XXI (May 1930), 41-121; *DN*, Jan. 1, Mar. 4, 1928. During the first year the option was in effect, 952 defendants accused of felonies waived their right to a jury trial and 634 did not. The conviction rate was about the same for those tried with or without a jury, but the sentences imposed in jury trials tended to be less severe than in nonjury trials. See Moley, *Our Criminal Courts*, pp. 126-27.

36. *DT*, July 25, 1926, Feb. 25, Mar. 24, 26, 27, 1927, Dec. 2, 1928, Aug. 1, 1929; FM to GM, Mar. 18, 1935, FM Papers.

37. *DT*, Mar. 30, Apr. 1, 1927, Jan. 1, 3, Dec. 2, 4, 1928; *DFP*, Mar. 31, 1927; ——— to FM [Apr. 1, 1927], FM Papers. See *DSN*, Oct. 22, 1927, for a specific instance of a crime later committed by a prisoner released by Murphy.

38. *DT,* Jan. 18, Sept. 6, Nov. 9, 1924, May 27, 28, June 2, 1926, Jan. 19, Apr. 4, 9, 10, May 24, 1929; *DN,* July 27, Nov. 7–8, 1924; *DFP,* June 3, 1926; *Civic Searchlight,* June 1926.

39. *DT,* May 24, Nov. 10, 1929, Jan. 2, 1930; Historical Project, *Detroit Recorder's Court,* pp. 3, 17; *Public Acts of the Legislature . . . of Michigan . . . 1929* (Lansing, 1929), pp. 684–86.

40. Moley, *Our Criminal Courts,* xi.

41. Gellein, "Frank Murphy, Justice, United States Supreme Court" (MS, undated), p. 4, in my possession; Gellein, "United States Supreme Court Justice Frank Murphy" (MS, undated), pp. 19, 22, Hilmer Gellein Papers, MHC; FM speech, undated, FM Papers; Joseph P. Urick to FM, Aug. 12, 1927, ibid. See JG to FM, undated, ibid.

42. Cash Asher, in *DFP,* Jan. 2, 1927; W. J. Northern to FM, Mar. 5, 1927, FM to GM, Mar. 18, 1935, Feb. 11, 1947 (and attached draft of statement), FM Papers; Interview with Jack Manning, Dec. 4, 1964, p. 2, MHC; FM to HE, July 25, 27, 1925, July 29, 1926, HE Papers.

43. FM, "The Necessity for a Court Statistician," in *The Prevention and Cure of Crime* (n.p., 1927), pp. 34–36, FM Papers; *DT,* May 3, 1926, May 6, 1928.

44. Ferris to FM, Apr. 22, 1926, FM Papers; FM, "Necessity for Court Statistician," p. 35, ibid.; FM, "The Citizen and Liberty" (MS [Mar. 30, 1929]), ibid.; FM speech [1930], ibid.; *DLN,* Mar. 4, 1927, Aug. 23, 1929; *DT,* Mar. 26, 31, 1929. For the inefficiency of the system of criminal justice as of 1970, see Norton E. Long, "The City as Reservation," *Public Interest,* No. 25 (Fall 1971), pp. 31–32.

45. *DT,* Dec. 29, 1927, Mar. 31, 1929; FM, "The Citizen and Liberty," FM Papers; FM speech [1930], ibid.

46. FM to Roy McCann, Mar. 9, 13, 1933, MOR; FM, "Only the Helpless Hang" (MS, Feb. 1, 1927), FM Papers; FM speech [Apr. 24, 1927], ibid.; FM, "Necessity of Court Statistician," p. 34, ibid.; *DT,* Apr. 25, 1927, May 6, 1928.

47. Addresses . . . , Jan. 2, 1924, FM Papers; FM, "Only the Helpless Hang," ibid.; FM speech [Apr. 24, 1927], ibid.; FM to GM, Mar. 18, 1935, ibid.; *DT,* May 6, 1928.

48. *DT,* Jan. 25, 26, Feb. 10, 1927; A Citizen to FM, Jan. 30, 1927, James Slocum to FM [Jan. 30, 1927], FM to Slocum, Feb. 2, 1927, FM Papers.

49. *DT,* Feb. 1, 3, 1927; *DFP,* Feb. 1, 1927; *DSN,* Feb. 5, 1927; FM, "Only the Helpless Hang," FM Papers.

50. *DT,* Feb. 3, 1927; Ruby M. Zahn to FM [Feb. 1, 1927], Walter Oxtoby to FM, Feb. 1, 1927, H. Keith Davis to FM, Feb. 4, 1927, Slocum to FM [Feb. 7, 1927], Dickinson to FM, Feb. 4, 1927, Asher to FM, Feb. 26, 1927, Vincent J. Toole to FM, Mar. 4, 1927, Gordon H. McNab to FM, Feb. 13, 1927, Walter White to FM, May 17, 1927, Arthur Garfield Hays to FM, July 19, 1927, Clarence Darrow to FM, July 29, 1927, FM Papers.

51. *DT*, Apr. 7, 1927; Goldberg, "Optional Waiver of Jury," p. 45.

52. *DT*, Dec. 13, 1926; FM, "Necessity for Court Statistician," pp. 34-36, FM Papers; Moley, *Our Criminal Courts*, pp. 173-74.

53. Moley to Fine, Dec. 28, 1966; FM to HE, undated, HE Papers; FM to MM, Feb. 2, 1926, MM Papers; Monroe *Evening News*, Sept. 27, 1930, MSB; FM to GM, Dec. 7, 1943, FM Papers; Interview with John V. Brennan, Dec. 9, 1963, p. 4, MHC.

54. Walter Karig, "How Long Will Frank Murphy Stay on the Supreme Court?," *Liberty*, Mar. 2, 1940, p. 26; *DLN*, July 30, 1926; draft of article on FM [1930], FM Papers.

55. FM to HE, July 12, 1924, Sept. 17, 1925, HE Papers; FM to GM, Apr. 28, 1925, GM Papers; *DT*, May 8, 1927, Nov. 21, 1928; Drew Pearson and Robert S. Allen, in (New York) *Daily Mirror*, Oct. 22, 1938, clipping in FM Papers.

56. Lovett, "Frank Murphy," Mar. 8, 1929, Candidate Files, Box 23, DCL Papers; Memo re Frank Murphy, Mar. 12, 1929, ibid.; Daniel Bell, *The End of Ideology* (Collier Book; New York, 1961), p. 113; Edward M. Levine, *The Irish and Irish Politicians* (South Bend, 1966), pp. 91-92; *DT*, May 13, 1926, June 16, 17, 1928.

57. Gellein interview, p. 4; FM to HE, July 16, 1924, HE Papers; *DT*, Oct. 21, 1925, Mar. 24, 1927; Strobel, "Murphy," pp. 13-14.

58. FM to HE, July 16, 1924, HE Papers; unidentified clipping, in ibid.; *DT*, Jan. 19, 1924; *DN*, June 9, 1924.

59. *DT*, Feb. 21, 1924, July 7, 12, 26, 1925, July 12, 13, 20, 1926; Lee Smits column, undated, MSB; FM to Carl Sandburg, Feb. 11, 1944, FM Papers.

60. Memo re Frank Murphy, Mar. 12, 1929, Candidate Files, Box 23, DCL Papers; *DT*, Mar. 27, 29, Apr. 2, 5, 6, 12, Aug. 2, 1924, June 12, 1925, July 4, 1926, Feb. 5, 1927; *DT*, July 21 [?], 1949, clipping in FM Papers.

61. There is a copy of the chart in the FM Papers.

62. *DT*, Apr. 6, 1930; Moley, *Our Criminal Courts*, pp. 175-76; J. A. Fellows [Josephine Gomon], "Detroit's Crime Clinic," *Nation*, CXXX (May 14, 1930), 568; Gellein interview, pp. 10-11; Strobel, "Murphy," pp. 20-21.

63. Fellows, "Detroit's Crime Clinic," p. 569; Mark Hellinger, in [Detroit *Mirror*, Sept. 9, 1931], clipping in FM Papers.

64. "Taking Ancestors to Court, Too," *Literary Digest*, CXXV (June 14, 1930), 23-24; *DT*, May 23, 1930 (for *Survey* quotation); FM to HE, June 18, 1930, HE Papers; FM to Henry M. Bates, May 13, 1930, University of Michigan Law School Papers, MHC; Green to FM, May 20, 1930, FM Papers.

CHAPTER VII

1. W. J. Northern to FM, Mar. 5, 1927, FM Papers.

2. Detroit and Wayne County Federation of Labor to Central Labor Union,

Jacksonville, Florida, Jan. 9, 1939, George P. Raub to FM, Mar. 31, 1929, FM Papers; *DLN,* Mar. 27, Apr. 10, 24, 1925; Eugene Strobel, "Frank Murphy: Crusading Judge, 1923–1930" (MS, 1962), p. 16, in my possession.

3. *DLN,* Dec. 6, 1929.
4. Mayor's Inter-racial Committee, *The Negro in Detroit* ([Detroit], 1926), Section IX, pp. 18–19. Murphy is not identified by name but was almost certainly the source of the information. See Delos S. Otis to FM, Aug. 7, 1926, FM Papers.
5. Marcet Haldeman-Julius, "The Defendants in the Sweet Murder Case," in *Clarence Darrow's Two Great Trials* (Girard, Kansas, 1927), pp. 38–39; *DT,* June 24, 25, July 8, 11, 1925; *DFP,* July 11, 12, 1925; David Allan Levine, "'Expecting the Barbarians': Race Relations and Social Control, Detroit, 1915–1925" (Ph.D. thesis, University of Chicago, 1970), pp. 239–46.
6. *DFP,* July 12, 1925.
7. Kenneth G. Weinberg, *A Man's Home, a Man's Castle* (New York, 1971), pp. 6–7; Haldeman-Julius, "The Defendants," pp. 28–31, 34–36; Irving Stone, *Clarence Darrow for the Defense* (Garden City, New York, 1943), p. 474; *DN,* Sept. 10, Nov. 18, 19, 1925; Paul E. Baker, *Negro-White Adjustment* (New York, 1934), p. 121; Alex Baskin interview with Robert M. Toms, Nov. 28, 1959, p. 13, MHC.
8. *DN,* Nov. 7, 8, 12, 13, 19, 1925, May 2, 1926; Walter White to James Weldon Johnson, Sept. 16, 1925, File D-85, NAACP Papers.
9. Sweet to Ruby Darrow [Jan. 26, 1931], Clarence Darrow Papers, LC; Haldeman-Julius, "The Defendants," pp. 31–32.
10. Baskin interview with William C. Osby, Jr., July 27, 1959, p. 2, MHC; Haldeman-Julius, "The Defendants," pp. 32–33; Weinberg, *A Man's Home,* pp. 22–26; *DN,* Sept. 10, Nov. 19, 1925; *DT,* Sept. 10, Nov. 14, 1925; Statement of Dr. O. H. Sweet . . . , Sept. 12 [1925], File D-85, NAACP Papers; Walter White, "Negro Segregation Comes North," *Nation,* CXXI (Oct. 21, 1925), 459; Examination testimony, Sept. 17 [?], 1925, p. 6, RC Case Files 60317–60318 (the Recorder's Court files of the two Sweet cases have been consolidated), Frank Murphy Hall of Justice, Detroit, Michigan.
11. My account of the events inside and outside the Sweet house on September 9 is based on the following: *DN,* Sept. 10, Nov. 5, 6, 16–19, 1925; *DT,* Sept. 10, Nov. 6, 7, 1925; Haldeman-Julius, "The Defendants," pp. 33–34, 40–41; Weinberg, *A Man's Home,* pp. 26–27, 34, 102; Sweet statement, Sept. 12 [1925], File D-85, NAACP Papers; Examination testimony, pp. 8–11, 17–22, 29, RC Case Files 60317–60318; Robert Toms statement, Nov. 5, 1925, pp. 4–17, Lester Moll argument, May 10, 1926, pp. 15, 18, 45–46, Toms argument, May 12, 1926, pp. 23, 29–30, The People vs. Ossian Sweet, Gladys Sweet, et al., Nov. 5, 1925–May 13, 1926, BHC (there are two sets of transcripts

with this same title, but their contents are different; one is on film and will be so identified when cited).

12. *DT*, Sept. 10, Nov. 21, 1925; Haldeman-Julius, "The Defendants," pp. 41-42; *DN*, Nov. 19-22, 1925; Levine, "Race Relations," p. 258; Homicide File #1074, Sept. 9-10, 1925, Police Headquarters, Detroit, Michigan; Baskin interview with Otis Sweet, Aug. 1, 1960, pp. 4-5, MHC; Weinberg, *A Man's Home*, pp. 34-35; Hays argument, Nov. 24, 1925, People vs. Sweet, pp. 10-11.

13. *DT*, Sept. 10, 1925; *DN*, Sept. 10-12, 1925; *DFP*, Sept. 10, 1925; RC Case Files 60317-60318; Haldeman-Julius, "The Defendants," p. 42.

14. Examination testimony, RC Case Files 60317-60318; *DT*, Sept. 17, 19, 1925; *DN*, Sept. 17-18, 1925; White to Johnson, Sept. 17, 1925, File D-85, NAACP Papers; White, "Negro Segregation," p. 459.

15. RC Case Files 60317-60318; Weinberg, *A Man's Home*, pp. 57-58; Memorandum (Oct. 8) of . . . Conversation between Moses L. Walker . . . and Walter White on Oct. 7, 1925, File D-86, NAACP Papers. There is a copy of the motion for dismissal in the Darrow Papers.

16. Stone, *Darrow*, p. 476; Weinberg, *A Man's Home*, p. 41; Walker to White, Oct. 27, 1925, File D-86, NAACP Papers. See also John C. Dancy, *Sands against the Wind: The Memoirs of John C. Dancy* (Detroit, 1966), p. 25.

17. Oscar W. Baker to White, Nov. 9, 1925, Darrow Papers; Minutes of the Meeting of the Board of Directors, Sept. 14, 1925, File A-2, NAACP Papers; White to L. M. Hussey, Sept. 14, 1925, File C-93, ibid.

18. White to Johnson, Sept. 16, 17, 1925, File D-85, NAACP Papers; undated note in Sept. 16, 1925, folder, ibid.; Memorandum of Walker-White Conversation, Oct. 7, 1925, File D-86, ibid.; White to Roscoe G. Bruce, Jan. 20, 1926, File C-93, ibid.; White to Arthur B. Spingarn, Sept. 29, 1925, enclosing Walker to White, undated, Arthur Barnett Spingarn Papers, LC; White, *A Man Called White: The Autobiography of Walter White* (New York, 1948), p. 75.

19. White to Spingarn, Sept. 29, 1925, enclosing Walker to White, undated, Spingarn Papers; William E. Davis et al. to W. Hayes McKinney, Sept. 29, 1925, File D-85, NAACP Papers; Otis Sweet interview, p. 14.

20. Minutes of Board of Directors, Oct. 13, 1925, File A-2, NAACP Papers; Johnson to Roger N. Baldwin, Dec. 17, 1925, File C-17, ibid.; NAACP, *Seventeenth Annual Report, 1926* (New York, 1927), p. 8; Clarence Darrow, *The Story of My Life* (New York, 1932), p. 302.

21. RC Case Files 60317-60318; Baskin interview with Charles Mahoney, Aug. 3, 1960, pp. 7-8, MHC; Levine, "Race Relations," p. 269; *DN*, Oct. 16, 1925; *DT*, Oct. 17, 1925.

22. *DN*, Oct. 16, 1925; White to Ira W. Jayne, Oct. 22, 1925, File D-86, NAACP Papers; White to FM, Oct. 14, 1925, FM Papers; Charlotte

Goodman, " 'Dear God! Must We Not Live?' " (MS, 1963), pp. 26–27, in my possession.

23. Minutes of Board of Directors, Nov. 9, Dec. 14, 1925, File A-2, NAACP Papers; White to Johnson, Nov. 13, 1925, File D-85, ibid.; Report of Walter White on Trip to Detroit, Mar. 21–24, 1926, File D-86, ibid.; Detroit *Independent,* Sept. 18, Oct. 2, 1925, clippings in File D-87, ibid.; Thomas J. Crawford to R. W. Bagnall, Nov. 21, 1925, File G-95, ibid.; William Pickens to Spingarn, Nov. 2, 1925, Spingarn Papers; City-Wide Committee to All Fraternal Organizations, Nov. 1, 1925, DUL Papers; NAACP, *Seventeenth Annual Report,* p. 8; Mary White Ovington, *The Walls Came Tumbling Down* (New York, 1947), pp. 204–5; James Weldon Johnson, *Along the Way* (New York, 1933), p. 384; Alex Goodwin, " 'Dear God . . .' " (MS, 1966), p. 59n, in my possession.

24. Du Bois, "The Defense Fund," *Crisis,* XXXI (Feb. 1926), 163; White, "The Sweet Trial," ibid. (Jan. 1926), 126; Johnson, "Detroit," ibid., XXXII (July 1926), 117; Loren Miller, *The Petitioners: The Story of the Supreme Court of the United States and the Negro* (New York, 1966), pp. 247–54; NAACP, *Argument of Clarence Darrow in the Case of Henry Sweet . . .* (New York, 1927), p. 4; Eugene Levy, *James Weldon Johnson* (Chicago, 1973), pp. 283–88. In Corrigan v. Buckley (1926), after the Sweet trials had been concluded, the Supreme Court, in effect, upheld the judicial enforcement of restrictive covenants, "a major disaster" for the blacks. Miller, *Silent Petitioners,* pp. 254–55.

25. *DT,* Sept. 13, 14, 16, 24, 1925; *DN,* Sept. 13, 14, 1925.

26. Goodman, " 'Must We Not Live?,' " pp. 16–22, 24, 27–29.

27. Weinberg, *A Man's Home,* pp. 75–79; *DT,* Oct. 30, 31, 1925; *DN,* Oct. 30–Nov. 5, 1925; Pickens to Spingarn, Nov. 2, 1925, Spingarn Papers; Hays, *Let Freedom Ring* (New York, 1937), p. 201; Stone, *Darrow,* p. 478.

28. White to Johnson [Oct. 31, 1925], File D-86, NAACP Papers.

29. *DN,* Nov. 26, 1925; Darrow, *Story of My Life,* p. 308; Weinberg, *A Man's Home,* p. 87.

30. FM to MM, Nov. 6, 7, 1925, MM Papers.

31. Marcet Haldeman-Julius, "Clarence Darrow's Defense of a Negro," *Haldeman-Julius Monthly,* IV (July 1926), p. 6; Toms interview, pp. 3–4; Mahoney interview, p. 4.

32. Hays, *Let Freedom Ring,* pp. 202–3; Weinberg, *A Man's Home,* pp. 82–83; People vs. Sweet, Nov. 5, 1925, p. 2; White to Johnson, Nov. 13, 15, 1925, File D-85, NAACP Papers; *DN,* Nov. 4, 5, 1925.

33. *DN,* Nov. 5, 1925.

34. *DN,* Nov. 5–13, 1925; *DT,* Nov. 6–13, 1925; Weinberg, *A Man's Home,* p. 98; White to Johnson, Nov. 13, 1925, File D-85, NAACP Papers; Lilienthal, "Has the Negro the Right of Self Defense?," *Nation,* CXXI (Dec. 23, 1925), 724; Toms interview, p. 11.

35. People vs. Sweet (film), pp. 91, 97, 378, 588, 602–3, 781–82; *DT*, Nov. 10, 11, 1925.

36. White to Johnson, Nov. 13, 1925, File D-85, NAACP Papers; People vs. Sweet (film), pp. 1345–68; *DN*, Nov. 14, 1925.

37. White to Johnson, Nov. 13, 1925, File D-85, NAACP Papers; *DN*, Nov. 14, 1925; *DT*, Nov. 14, 1925; People vs. Sweet (film), pp. 1248–53.

38. *DN*, Nov. 14–16, 1925; *DT*, Nov. 15, 1925.

39. *DN*, Nov. 16, 1925; Hays, *Let Freedom Ring*, p. 231; White to Johnson, Nov. 15, 1925, Walker to White, Oct. 27, 1925, File D-86, NAACP Papers; Detroit *Herald*, Oct. 17, 1936; Weinberg, *A Man's Home*, pp. 100–101.

40. White to Johnson, Sept. 16, 1925, File D-85, NAACP Papers; *DT*, Nov. 15, 1925; White, "Sweet Trial," p. 127.

41. *DN*, Nov. 17, 1925.

42. *DN*, Nov. 18, 1925.

43. Lilienthal, "Negro Self Defense," p. 725; *DN*, Nov. 19, 1925; notes on Moll interview [1959], Alex Baskin notebook on Sweet case, in my possession.

44. *DN*, Nov. 24, 1925; *DT*, Nov. 24, 1925; Hays argument, Nov. 24, 1925, People vs. Sweet, pp. 1–2, 7–23.

45. Lilienthal, "Negro Self Defense," p. 725; *DT*, Nov. 25, 1925; Darrow argument, Nov. 24–25, 1925, People vs. Sweet, pp. 1–109; Mahoney interview, p. 10.

46. Levine, "Race Relations," p. 286; *DN*, Nov. 25, 26, 1925; *DFP*, Nov. 25, 26, 1925.

47. White, "Sweet Trial," p. 125; *DN*, Nov. 26, 1925; Darrow, *Story of My Life*, p. 310.

48. *DN*, Nov. 26–28, 1925; *DT*, Nov. 26–28, 1925; White to Harry E. Davis, Nov. 30, 1925, File D-86, NAACP Papers; White to Russell W. Jelliff, Dec. 10, 1925, File C-93, ibid. For other versions of the division among the jurors, see Levine, "Race Relations," p. 287, and Weinberg, *A Man's Home*, p. 122.

49. Lilienthal, "Negro Self Defense," p. 725; Lilienthal to Frank Nolan, Nov. 30, 1925, FM Papers; White to FM, Dec. 4, 1925, File D-86, NAACP Papers; Cleveland *Call*, Nov. 21, 1925, clipping in File D-87, ibid.; White, "Sweet Trial," p. 125; White, *Man Called White*, p. 77; *Owl* [1926], MSB.

50. Joseph Creighton, "Frank Murphy—Off the Record," Part Two (MS [Aug. 1938]), p. 5, FM Papers; Darrow to FM, Oct. 9, 1935, ibid.; Toms interview, p. 18; Baker to White, Mar. 8, 1926, File D-86, NAACP Papers.

51. RC Case Files 60317–60318; *DT*, Nov. 28, 29, Dec. 4, 1925; *DN*, Nov. 28, 1925; *DFP*, Nov. 28, 1925; Walter Nelson to NAACP, Dec. 1, 2, 1925, File D-86, NAACP Papers; *NYT*, Jan. 4, 1926.

52. *DN,* Nov. 28, 1925; *DT,* Nov. 28, 1925; Minutes of Board of Directors, File A-2, NAACP Papers; White Report, Mar. 21–24, 1926, File D-86, ibid.; Baskin interview with Thomas F. Chawke, Aug. 4, 1960, pp. 1–3, MHC.

53. Haldeman-Julius, "The Defendants," p. 42; White to Jayne, Sept. 21, 1925, File D-85, NAACP Papers; White Report, Mar. 21–24, 1926, File D-86, ibid.; NAACP, *Seventeenth Annual Report,* p. 8.

54. Arthur Garfield Hays, *City Lawyer* (New York, 1942), pp. 209–10; Weinberg, *A Man's Home,* p. 117.

55. *DT,* Apr. 19–25, 1926; *DN,* Apr. 20–25, 1926.

56. Haldeman-Julius, "Clarence Darrow's Defense," pp. 7–10; Toms interview, p. 21.

57. *DN,* Apr. 26–May 10, 1926; *DT,* Apr. 26–May 10, 1926; Haldeman-Julius, "Clarence Darrow's Defense," pp. 14, 16, 19–20; Baskin interview with John C. Dancy, July 27, 1960, pp. 2–3, MHC.

58. All the arguments are in People vs. Sweet. See Moll argument, pp. 16–17, for the comment on Dr. Sweet and Toms's argument, pp. 84–85, for the mistrial request. See also *DN,* May 10–13, 1926, and *DT,* May 11–13, 1926.

59. NAACP, *Argument of Darrow,* pp. 5, 7; White to Darrow, Jan. 16, 1926, File D-87, NAACP Papers; Stone, *Darrow,* p. 484; Johnson, "Detroit," pp. 118–19.

60. Charge of the Court, May 13, 1926, FM Papers; Johnson, "Detroit," p. 119; *DT,* May 14, 1926; *DN,* May 14, 1926; Haldeman-Julius, "Clarence Darrow's Defense," p. 74; Toms interview, p. 23; Cash Asher, "Waiting for a Verdict with Clarence Darrow," *Crisis,* LXIV (June, July 1957), 329.

61. NAACP, *Argument of Darrow,* p. 4; *DSN,* May 22, 1926; ———— to Charles Phillips, undated, FM Papers.

62. Mahoney interview, p. 10; White to FM, May 21, 1926, Darrow to FM, May 27, 1926, Jan. 3 [1927], July 29, 1927, Aug. 12, 1928, FM Papers; Darrow, *Story of My Life,* pp. 306–7; Ruby Darrow to GM, Jan. 1941, GM Papers; Hays, *Let Freedom Ring,* p. 231.

63. *Owl* [1926], MSB; Morse to FM, Apr. 21, 1926, V. A. Byrd to FM, May 14, 1926, FM Papers; Thomas R. Solomon, "Participation of Negroes in Detroit Elections" (Ph.D. thesis, University of Michigan, 1939), p. 18.

64. White to FM, July 29, 1926, White to Darrow, Sept. 10, Dec. 16, 1926, FM to White, July 21, 1927, Johnson to FM, July 21, 1927, Hays to FM, July 21, 1927, FM Papers; Minutes of Board of Directors, Sept. 13, Dec. 13, 1926, Mar. 14, 1927, File A-2, NAACP Papers; Toms motion, July 12, 1927, RC Case Files 60317–60318; *DT,* July 21, 1927.

65. *DT,* Sept. 27, 1925; White Report, Mar. 21–24, 1926, File D-86, NAACP Papers; Walker to White, Nov. 10, 1930, Perry to White, Nov. 10,

1930, White to Perry, Nov. 12, 1930, White to Walker, Nov. 14, 1930, FM to White, Nov. 15, 1930, Jayne to White, Dec. 4, 1930, File G-96, NAACP Papers; Memorandum to White from Mr. Andrews, Nov. 14, 1930, ibid.; [White] Memorandum Re the Sweet Case, Dec. 10, 1930, ibid.; Memorandum Re: Account of Damage Suit against Dr. Ossian H. Sweet, et al., Dec. 12, 1930, ibid.

66. Darrow to White, Nov. 30, Dec. 3 [1930], File G-96, NAACP Papers; Darrow to FM, Dec. 4, 1930, FM to Darrow, Dec. 5, 1930, FM Papers.

67. Minutes of Board of Directors, Dec. 8, 1930, File A-2, NAACP Papers; [White] Memorandum Re Damage Suit, Dec. 12, 1930, File G-96, ibid.; White to Darrow, Dec. 12, 1930, Darrow to White, Dec. 18 [1930], ibid.; Baker, *Negro-White Adjustment*, p. 122. For Dr. Sweet's defense of his position, see Sweet to Pickens, Dec. 20, 1930, File G-96, NAACP Papers.

68. Minutes of Board of Directors, Sept. 13, 1926, File A-2, NAACP Papers; Goodwin, " 'Dear God,' " pp. 115-17; Baker, *Negro-White Adjustment*, p. 122; Baskin interview with Osby [1959], Baskin notebook; *Michigan Chronicle*, Mar. 26, 1960; *DN*, Mar. 20, 1960, Aug. 15, 1965; *DFP*, Oct. 17, 1971; Weinberg, *A Man's Home*, pp. 135-36.

69. White, "Sweet Trial," p. 125; R. L. Bradby to Robert Bagnall, Dec. 30, 1925, File G-95, NAACP Papers; Minutes of Board of Directors, Sept. 13, 1926, File A-2, ibid.; Walker to White, Sept. 29, 1926, File D-87, ibid.; White to Spingarn, May 14, 1926, Spingarn Papers; White, *Man Called White*, p. 79; Toms motion, July 12, 1927, RC Case Files 60317-60318; Toms interview, p. 20; Baker, *Negro-White Adjustment*, p. 131.

70. Mayor's Inter-racial Committee, *The Negro in Detroit*, 2 vols. ([Detroit], 1926); *Report of the Mayor's Committee on Race Relations* (Detroit, 1927); Haldeman-Julius, "The Defendants," p. 36; *DFP*, Oct. 17, 1971. There were three racial incidents in 1928 resulting from black attempts to move into white neighborhoods. Levine, "Race Relations," p. 308.

71. *Literary Digest*, XCI (Oct. 16, 1926), 64; Moley, *Our Criminal Courts* (New York, 1930), p. 232; Moley, "Murphy and Jackson," *News-Week*, XV (Jan. 15, 1940), 60; *DT*, Jan. 22, 1926, Aug. 30, 1928; Butzel to Lovett, Mar. 21, 1929, Candidate Files, Box 23, DCL Papers; Lovett, "Frank Murphy," Mar. 8, 1929, ibid.; Quinn to FM, Jan. 7, 1927, Stevens to FM, Nov. 14, 1925, FM to Stevens, Nov. 28, 1925, FM Papers.

CHAPTER VIII

1. *DT*, Dec. 26, 1924.
2. *DT*, Nov. 19, 20, 25-28, 1924, Mar. 5, 1925; *DN*, Nov. 25-26, 1924; Curran to Smith, Nov. 24, 1924, FM Papers.

3. *DT,* Nov. 28, Dec. 22, 1924, Jan. 5, 6, 20, 24, 26, Feb. 7, 9, Mar. 3, 15, 1925.
4. Unidentified clipping [Dec. 1924], MSB; *DSN,* Nov. 7, 1923; Kenneth T. Jackson, *The Ku Klux Klan in the City, 1915-1930* (New York, 1967), p. 135; (Detroit) *Courier,* Feb. 13, 1925, MSB; *DT,* Nov. 20, 1924, May 6, 1925; William P. Lovett to H. W. Dodds, May 7, June 16, 1925, DCL Papers; FM to MM, Jan. 22, 24, Feb. 6, Mar. 20, 1925, MM Papers; FM to Henry M. Bates, Jan. 31, 1925, FM Papers.
5. FM to MM, Apr. 20, 28, May 2, 1925, MM Papers; FM to GM, Apr. 28, 1925, GM Papers.
6. *DT,* Apr. 26, 1925; FM to Smith, Apr. 25, 1925, FM Papers.
7. There is a copy of the document requesting the warrants in the FM Papers. The complete text of the presentment is in *DT,* Apr. 26, 1925.
8. *DT,* Apr. 27, 1925, May 8, 1926; *DFP,* Apr. 27, May 6, 1925; *DSN,* May 2, 1925; *DLN,* May 1, 1925; "Corruption in Detroit," *Literary Digest,* LXXXV (May 16, 1925), 14-15; *NYT,* Apr. 26, 1925; FM to GM, Apr. 28, 1925, GM Papers; FM to MM, Apr. 28, 29, 1925, MM Papers; "Notable Success of Michigan's 'One Man Grand Jury' Act," *JAJS,* IX (June 1925), 12.
9. *DSN,* May 2, 1925; *DN,* Apr. 29, 30, May 4, 5, 1925; *Civic Searchlight,* May 1925; Lovett to Advisory Council, DCL, May 23, 1925, Additional Papers, Box 3, DCL Papers; Lovett to Dodds, May 1, 1925, DCL Papers.
10. *DN,* Apr. 29, 30, 1925; Lovett to Dodds, May 1, 7, 1925, DCL Papers.
11. FM to MM, Apr. 28, 29, May 1, 17, 31, June 1, 1925, MM Papers; FM to GM, Apr. 28, 1925, GM Papers; *DT,* May 5, 1925.
12. *DT,* May 3, 1925; FM to GM, Apr. 28, 1925, GM Papers; FM to MM, May 2, June 1, 2, 1925, MM Papers.
13. *DT,* Apr. 27, 28, 30, May 6, 7, 12, 23, 29, June 19, 23, 27, July 2, 21, 1925; *NYT,* Apr. 29, 1925; *DN,* Oct. 15, 1925; FM to MM, June 2, 1925, MM Papers; Lovett to Dodds, May 23, June 16, 1925, DCL Papers.
14. FM to HE, July 20, 1925, Feb. 4, 1926, HE Papers; FM to MM, Feb. 2, 1926, MM Papers; *DT,* Aug. 9, Dec. 4, 1925, Jan. 5, 13, 14, 29, May 7, 1926; *DLN,* Feb. 5, 1926.
15. *DT,* May 17, 1925, Feb. 1, 7, 9, 1926; FM to MM, Feb. 6, 1925, MM Papers; FM to HE, Feb. 4, 1926, HE Papers; *DSN,* July 11, 1925; [*DFP,* May 1, 1925], MSB; unidentified clippings [Apr. 29, Dec. 1925], MSB.
16. *DT,* June 16, 17, 1928, June 4, Nov. 2, 1929; FM, "Address before the Detroit Federation of Labor" [Apr. 1929], FM Papers.
17. Draft of FM speech [1920s], FM Papers; FM speech [Apr. 24, 1927], ibid.; *DLN,* Mar. 15, 1929; *DT,* Apr. 17, 1929.
18. Monroe *Evening News,* Sept. 27, 1930, MSB; "The Labor Governors," *Fortune,* XV (June 1937), 138; FM to MBM, Nov. 14, 1919, JFM Papers;

FM to EMB, June 27, 1944, EMB Papers.

19. *DT,* Mar. 15, 1924, Jan. 7, 1928; FM speech [1926?], FM Papers; *DLN,* May 13, 1927; *Industrial Intelligence Bulletin,* I (Apr. 2, 1928), in FM Papers; FM to Phelps Newberry, May 17, 1928, ibid.

20. See, for example, *Polish Daily Record,* Apr. 14, 1928, and Detroit *Daily,* Sept. 4, 1929, MSB.

21. FM speech [1926?], FM Papers; FM to Walter White, Mar. 8, 1929, File C-97, NAACP Papers; FM to HE, July 30, 1926, Apr. 2, 1928, HE Papers.

22. Minutes of the Meeting of the Board of Directors, Mar. 14, 1927, File A-2, NAACP Papers; FM to HE, July 30, 1926, HE Papers.

23. John D. Buenker, *Urban Liberalism and Progressive Reform* (New York, 1973), pp. 80-91; J. Weldon Jones to Sidney Fine, Jan. 29, 1966.

24. Carey D. Ferguson to FM, July 28, 1925, FM to Board of Street Railway Commissioners . . . , Aug. 31, 1925, Neill McLellan to FM, Nov. 13, 1925, FM to McLellan, Nov. 28, 1925, FM Papers; *DN,* Sept. 1, 1925; *DT,* Aug. 20, 21, 26, 27, Sept. 1, 1925; *DN,* Sept. 1, 1925.

25. *Arbitration Award by Judge Frank Murphy, August 16, 1926* (Detroit [1926]).

26. Philip Taft, *The A.F. of L. from the Death of Gompers to the Merger* (New York, 1959), pp. 6-7; *DLN,* Aug. 20, 1926, June 13, 1930.

27. *DLN,* Jan. 9, 30, Feb. 27, Mar. 6, 1925, Jan. 22, July 23, 1926, Mar. 4, Apr. 8, May 13, 1927, Feb. 3, May 18, June 15, 1928, Feb. 15, 22, Mar. 22, 29, Apr. 19, 26, 1929; *DT,* May 6, 1927, Jan. 27, 1928; FM to HE, Aug. 23, 1927, HE Papers; Murphy check, Aug. 24, 1928, FM Papers.

28. *DLN,* Nov. 2, 1923, Apr. 8, Sept. 16, 1927, Mar. 29, Apr. 19, 1929; FM, "Address before DFL" [Apr. 15, 1929], FM Papers.

29. *DLN,* Sept. 16, Apr. 19, 1927, Apr. 26, May 17, 1929.

30. *DT,* Mar. 4, 1923; Corpus Christi *Press,* July 28, 1949, clipping in Cash Asher Papers, MHC; FM to Richard Berlin, Apr. 16, 1947, Roger M. Andrews to FM, June 30, 1930, FM Papers; FM to GM, Apr. 28, 1925, GM Papers.

31. White to FM, Mar. 11, 1927, White to Darrow, undated, File D-87, NAACP Papers; FM to White, May 13, 1930, File C-98, ibid.; FM to HE, Aug. 16, 1925, [Apr. 1928], HE Papers; *The Prevention and Cure of Crime* (n.p., 1927), FM Papers; *DT,* Apr. 25, May 31, 1927, Apr. 30, May 6, 1928, Mar. 25, 1929; *NYT,* Apr. 25, 1927; William Randolph Hearst to FM, Aug. 17, 1927, FM Papers.

32. *DT,* Mar. 24, 26-31, Apr. 2, 1929; *DLN,* Mar. 15, 1929.

33. See, for example, *DT,* Mar. 27, 1929.

34. FM to Franz Prettinger [Prattinger], Mar. 7, 1929, FM to Vincent Guiliano, Mar. 7, 1929, FM Papers; *DLN,* Mar. 22, 29, 1929.

35. FM to White, Mar. 8, 1929, White to FM, Mar. 12, 1929, White to Editor, *Owl,* Mar. 12, 1929, White to Editor, Detroit *Independent,*

Mar. 12, 1929, File C-97, NAACP Papers.

36. Martel to FM, Mar. 14, 1929, Wayne County AFL-CIO Papers, ALHUA; FM to Martel, Apr. 10, 1929, Guiliano to FM, Feb. 20, 1929, Robert J. Peretto to FM, Feb. 21, 1929, FM to I. A. Marohnic, Mar. 2, 1929, Estelle Corbett to FM, Jan. 23, 1929, Joseph L. Kania to FM, Mar. 22, 1929, FM to Edward Z. Wroblewski, Mar. 28, 1929, FM to Louis Wojick, Apr. 10, 1929, FM to R. L. Bradby, Feb. 21, 1929, William T. Patrick to FM, Feb. 25, 1929, FM Papers; undated handbill indicating endorsement by Steuben Society, ibid.; unidentified black newspaper [Mar. 1929], MSB; Bulletin of Jewish Section–Political Action Committee, DFL, Mar. 1929, MSB.

37. FM to Dave Jones, Apr. 11, 1929, FM Papers; Chester B. Emerson to Lovett, Mar. 14, 1929, Edgar DeWitt Jones to Lovett, Mar. 12, 1929, Lovett to Members of Executive Board, DCL, June 4, 1929, Lovett, "Frank Murphy," Mar. 8, 1929, Candidate Files, Box 23, DCL Papers; B. E. Hutchinson to FM, Mar. 1, 1929, FM to Wendall Hall, Apr. 11, 1929, FM to Charles Winegar, Feb. 7, 1929, A. K. Burrows to FM, Mar. 26, 1929, Herbert B. Trix to FM [Mar. 1929], FM Papers; *Civic Searchlight,* Mar. 1929; *DT,* Mar. 28, 29, 1929.

38. *DT,* Mar. 30, 1929.

39. The precinct-by-precinct results of the 1929 election are in the FM Papers. The demographic data are taken from Bureau of the Census, *Fifteenth Census of the United States: 1930, Population,* III, Part I (Washington, 1932), 1183. The black precincts are identified in Thomas R. Solomon, "Participation of Negroes in Detroit Elections" (Ph.D. thesis, University of Michigan, 1939), p. 146, and the Polish and Hungarian precincts in *DN,* Oct. 7, 1931.

40. *DN,* June 30, 1924; FM to MBM, June 30, 1924, JFM Papers.

41. *DN,* July 3, 1924; FM to MBM [1924], July 2, 7 [?], 1924, JFM Papers; FM to HE, July 8, 1924, HE Papers.

42. *DT,* May 9, June 24–29, 1928; *DLN,* July 13, 1928.

43. *DT,* June 29, 1928; FM to HM [Sept. 30, 1928], HM Papers; FM to GM, Sept. 30, 1928, FM Papers.

44. *DT,* Sept. 9, 15, Oct. 7, Nov. 3, 4, 1928; FM speech [Nov. 3, 1928], FM Papers; Basil O'Connor to FM, Feb. 3, 1929, FM Papers.

45. FM to HE, July 18, 1924, HE Papers; HE to FM, June 30, 1926, FM Papers; *DT,* Apr. 4, May 3, 30, 1926, May 10, June 25, July 1, 6, 8, 29, 31, 1928; [*Michigan State Digest,* May 1, 1926], MSB; [(Lansing) *Industrial News*], July 20, 1928, MSB.

46. H. M. Bitner to FM, Oct. 28, 1924, FM to Smith, Sept. 16, 1927, Rowland M. Fixel to FM, Apr. 22, 1929, FM to William M. Walker, Apr. 26, 1929, FM to David M. Welling, May 7, 1929, FM to Peter Quinn, May 15, 1929, FM Papers; *DT,* Nov. 4, 1925, Aug. 11, Sept. 1, 8, Nov. 2, 3, 6, 1929; *DLN,* Apr. 26, May 17, 1929; *Appeal to the Young Judge Frank Murphy* [1929], FM Papers; *DSN,* Apr. 27, June 1, 8, 1929.

47. FM to HE, June 18, 1930, HE Papers.
48. Roy Lubove, *The Struggle for Social Security, 1900-1935* (Cambridge, Mass., 1968), p. 136; Bernstein, *The Lean Years: A History of the American Worker, 1920-1933* (Boston, 1960), pp. 237-39.
49. FM, "Address before DFL" [Apr. 15, 1929], FM Papers; Epstein to FM, Apr. 19, 26, May 8, 1930, Epstein to Riseman, June 26, 1930, ibid.; *DT*, Nov. 3, 1929, July 22, 28, Aug. 11, 1930; *DLN*, Apr. 11, 18, May 2, 9, 23, July 11, 18, 1930; Isadore Pastor, "Public Old Age Assistance in Michigan" (M.A. thesis, Wayne State University, 1937), pp. 27-29; Lubove, *Struggle for Social Security*, p. 30.
50. *DLN*, May 23, 1930; Harry Slavin to FM, June 7, 1930, FM Papers; Michigan Unemployment Compensation Commission, *Annual Report for . . . 1937* (Lansing, 1938), pp. 4-5; *DT*, July 4, 1930.
51. Haber to FM, Apr. 18, 26, July 5, 1930, John L. Lovett to FM, July 2, 1930, Frank D. Adams to FM, July 3, 1930, FM Papers; FM to HE, June 18, 1930, HE Papers; Interview with William Haber, Jan. 13, 1972; *DN*, July 3, 1936; *DSN*, May 2, 1931; Mayor's Unemployment Committee survey [Sept. 1932], MOR; Robert S. Wilson, *Community Planning for Homeless Men and Boys: The Experience of Sixteen Cities in the Winter of 1930-31* (New York, 1931), pp. 91-92.
52. *DT*, Aug. 18, 1930; Interview with Hilmer Gellein, Aug. 21, 1963, p. 11, MHC; Rosario LaCasse to FM, Aug. 7, 1930, FM Papers.
53. Elva M. Forncrook to FM, Sept. 20, 1930, FM to George T. Gaston, June 1, 1939, FM to William J. Hale, Aug. 25, 1933, FM Papers; EMB to GM, Jan. 20, 1942, GM Papers; Interview with William O. Douglas, Oct. 22, 1964, p. 2, MHC.
54. [*DT*, Aug. 27, 1930], MSB.
55. *DT*, Oct. 6, 11, 12, 15, 1924, Apr. 8, 10, 1926; FM to HE [Oct. 1924], HE Papers; FM to MM, Oct. 27, 1924, MM Papers. Italics supplied.
56. FM to Patrick R. Dunigan, Mar. 3, 1924, FM Papers; FM to HE, July 9, 23, Aug. 26, 1925, July 26, 29, 30, 1926, Apr. 2, June 20, 1928, HE Papers; FM to MM, Mar. 20, 1925, [May 25, 1926], MM Papers. Murphy taught at both the Detroit College of Law and the University of Detroit Law School through 1925 but only at the latter after that date. M. Le Febre to FM, Jan. 25, 1928, FM to Detroit College of Law, Feb. 26, 1926, FM Papers.
57. *DT*, Jan. 6, 9, 12, 16, 20, Feb. 7, 24, 1930; GM to Wade Morrow, Jan. 14, 1930, GM Papers; FM to Thomas Cotter, Jan 18, 1930, FM Papers; FM to HE, several letters [Jan.-Feb. 1930], HE Papers.
58. FM to HE, July 12, 23, 1925, Sept. 3, 1927, June 18, 1930, HE Papers; FM to HM, Sept. 26, 1927, HM Papers.
59. *DSN*, Aug. 16, 1930; FM to MBM, Jan. 3, June 17, 1924, JFM Papers; FM to MM, Apr. 28, Sept. 14, 1925, Feb. 2, 1926, [May 25, 1926], Sept. 21, 1927, GM to MM [Sept. 20, 1927], Oct. 23, 1927, MM Papers; FM to Foy, Nov. 5, 1925, FM Papers.
60. FM to MBM, Oct. 2, 1919, JFM Papers; FM to MM, Jan. 6, 1924,

Jan. 29, Feb. 4, Apr. 28, 1925, MM Papers; FM to HE, July 22, 1925, HE Papers, Foy to FM, Jan. 5, 1925, Chrysler to FM, Aug. 13, 1925, FM Papers. For Murphy's stock-market transactions in August–September, 1925, see the J. S. Bache statements in ibid.

61. FM to HE, June 20 [1928], July 20, 1928, [1928], HE Papers; Chrysler to FM, Aug. 23, 1928, FM Papers.

62. FM to HE, Apr. 2, 1928, HE Papers. See also Juan A. Cabildo, "The Kinship of Darrow and Murphy" [1933], FM Papers.

63. Hutchinson to FM, July 26, 1929, L. A. Moehring to FM, May 14, 1930, FM Papers.

64. *Public Acts of the Legislature of . . . Michigan . . . 1919* (Ft. Wayne, 1919), p. 647.

65. For the doctor's case, see Augustus C. Ledyard to FM, Apr. 13, 1933, EGK to Howell S. White, Apr. 22, 1933, EGK to Glenn Curtis, May 5, 1933, GM Papers; and *DN*, Apr. 28, 30, 1933. See Box 3 of the FM Papers for a series of past-due Murphy bills as of 1929 and 1930, including a hotel bill that had been incurred in 1922.

66. Interview with Norman H. Hill, Aug. 21, 1963, pp. 29–30, MHC; Interview with Nathaniel H. Goldstick, Dec. 9, 1963, p. 1, MHC; Interview with Harry Mead, Aug. 15, 1963, pp. 28–29, MHC; Interview with Jack Manning, Dec. 4, 1964, pp. 21–22, MHC; Jones to Fine, Jan. 29, 1966.

67. *DFP*, Sept. 4, 1936; Gellein, "Frank Murphy, Justice, United States Supreme Court" (MS, undated), pp. 2–3, in my possession. Murphy signed a $1,500 note for a policeman assigned to his court that Murphy, in the end, had to liquidate himself. It took ten years for him to do so, however. See GM to FM, Apr. 28, 1942, FM Papers.

68. Interview with Carl Muller, Oct. 6, 1964, p. 4, MHC; Vera Brown in [*DT*, Jan. 1, 1937], MSB; Detroit *Daily*, Dec. 3, 1930, MSB; Goldstick interview, p. 1; *DN*, Sept. 7, 1940; *DN* [Nov. 1940], clipping in FM Papers; FM to MM, May 4, 1925, [1925], MM Papers; Interview with IM, July 30, 1964, p. 29, MHC.

69. FM to HE, Aug. 27, 1926, HE Papers; *DFP*, Aug. 23, 1930.

70. Doris ——— to FM, Nov. 2 [1928], FM Papers. See the FM Papers, passim, for these years.

71. *DT*, July 29, Dec. 1, 1929, Ainsworth to FM, Jan. 16, 1930, HE to FM [1930], Hammond to FM, two letters [1930], FM Papers; HE to FM [June 1930] (possibly not sent), HE Papers.

72. Jones to Lovett, Mar. 12, 1929, Candidate Files, Box 23, DCL Papers; *DN*, Jan. 4, 1930; Channing Pollock to FM, Mar. 9, 1932, Joseph R. Hayden to FM, Nov. 27, 1935, IM to FM, Nov. 6, 1945, FM Papers; Cash Asher, "The Judge in the Sweet Trial," *Crisis*, LXXVI (Jan. 1969), 17; Interview with Martin S. Hayden, Oct. 6, 1964, p. 23, MHC; Interview with Frank Potts, Jan. 8, 1965, p. 21, MHC; IM interview, p. 7.

73. *DT*, Mar. 25, 1923, Sept. 14, 1930, Apr. 23, 1933; *DN*, Nov. 4, 1936;

[Calumet *Daily Evening Gazette,* Oct. 18, 1938], MSB; Interview with Alexander Holtzoff, Oct. 20, 1964, p. 19.

74. *DN,* Apr. 8, 1933; FM to GM, July 7, 1934, FM to Students of Northern Light School, Feb. 25, 1932, MM to FM [Jan. 1940], K. T. Keller to FM, Aug. 27, 1934, Leland S. Bisbee to FM, Feb. 8, 1940, FM Papers; FM to Wanda Ropele, Jan. 4, 1933, FM to Julius Kahn, May 5, 1933, MOR.

75. FM to MBM [Sept. 3, 1917], [Nov. 28], Dec. 23, 1918, JFM Papers; FM, Cabinet Meeting Notes, Nov. 16, 1939, EG Papers; Washington *Star,* Jan. 8, 1939, MSB; Charles G. Ross column, Mar. 17, 1939, MSB; Interview with Mrs. Joseph R. Hayden, Feb. 15, 1965, p. 11, MHC; Interview with G. Mennen Williams, Dec. 1964, p. 15, MHC; IM interview, pp. 32-33; FM to Dorothy Roosevelt, July 24, 1936, FM Papers; *DN,* Nov. 4, 1936.

76. Laswell, *Psychopathology and Politics,* new edition (New York, 1960), p. 125; Goldstick interview, p. 1; IM interview, p. 68; Walter Karig, "How Long Will Frank Murphy Stay on the Supreme Court?," *Liberty,* Mar. 2, 1940, p. 26; "Labor Governors," pp. 79-80; "Lay Bishop," *Time,* XXXIV (Aug. 28, 1939), 16; New Orleans *Item-Tribune,* Sept. 17, 1939, MSB; [Washington *Times-Herald,* Feb. 21, 1941], MSB; JG to Fine, Sept. 8, 1966; Ann Walker to FM [Oct. 2, 1935], FM Papers; FM to Robert H. Jackson, undated, in Enderson v. Abbott folder, Robert H. Jackson Papers, in possession of Philip Kurland; FM to Frank D. Adams, Dec. 5, 1932, MOR; EMB to Evalyn Walsh McLean, Feb. 7, 1946, EMB Papers; Interview with Lee Kreiselman Jaffe, Nov. 13, 1964; Manning interview, p. 15; Muller interview, p. 5; M. Hayden interview, p. 7; Interview with Lucille Malcolm, Dec. 8, 1964.

77. *DN,* Apr. 23, 1933; [Detroit *Mirror,* Apr. 7, 1931], MSB; (New York) *Daily Mirror,* May 20 [1933], clipping in FM Papers; *DSN,* Sept. 13, 1930; Wichita *Beacon,* July 23 [1932], MSB; [Springfield *Sunday Union,* June 8, 1939], MSB; San Francisco *Examiner,* May 20, 1933, MSB; [Milwaukee *Journal,* Oct. 26, 1938], MSB; Stanley High, *Roosevelt—And Then* (New York, 1937), p. 320; FM to Elise Sendelbeck, Feb. 21, 1933, MOR; FM to Jerome Barry, Aug. 7, 1935, FM to Thomas Brady, Dec. 26, 1936, FM to Sarah Hanson Salomon, July 12, 1939, FM Papers; Addresses Made at the Opening of Court . . . , Jan. 2, 1924, p. 6, ibid.; *Unveiling and Presentation of Portrait* . . . , Sept. 30, 1946, EMB Papers; Muller interview, pp. 4-5; JG to Fine, Sept. 8, 1966.

78. *NYT,* Jan. 3, 1939; Joseph H. Creighton, "Frank Murphy—Off the Record," Part Two (MS [Aug. 1938]), p. 32, FM Papers; *DT,* Sept. 14, 1930; New Orleans *Item-Tribune,* Sept. 17, 1939, MSB; Frank Kent column, Feb. 15, 1939, MSB; *Current Biography, 1940* (New York, 1940), p. 611; John P. Frank, "Frank Murphy," in Leon Friedman and Fred L. Israel, eds., *The Justices of the United States Supreme*

Court, 1789-1969, 4 vols. (New York, 1969), IV, 2493, 2498; "Labor Governors," pp. 79-80, 81.

79. *DT,* Sept. 14, 1930; *DT* [Jan. 12, 1939], MSB; *DN,* Nov. 4, 1936; Henry M. Bates, "The New Supreme Court Justice; An Appraisal," *Magazine of Sigma Chi,* Feb. 1940, pp. 107-8; Goldstick interview, p. 1; Interview with John V. Brennan, Dec. 9, 1963, p. 2, MHC; Interview with Will Muller, Oct. 6, 1964, p. 7, MHC; Potts interview, p. 11; Jones to Fine, Jan. 29, 1966.

80. John Wallace to FM, Sept. 11, 1930, FM Papers; Asher, "Judge in Sweet Trial," p. 17; Creighton, "Murphy," p. 29; Marvin J. Petroelje and Richard T. Ortquist interview with J. R. Creighton, undated, p. 18, MHC; Potts interview, pp. 11-13; Holtzoff interview, p. 17; Interview with James K. Pollock, July 12, 1966, p. 17, MHC; Hill interview, p. 37; Interview with Arthur Krock, May 22, 1969; IM interview, pp. 31-32, 33; Mrs. Hayden interview, p. 11; Edward Doherty, "Is It True What They Say about Murphy?," *Liberty,* Sept. 4, 1937, pp. 11-12; "Murphy of Michigan," ibid., Aug. 14, 1937, p. 7; [*DT,* Jan. 12, 1939], MSB; New Orleans *Item-Tribune,* Sept. 17, 1939, MSB; San Francisco *Chronicle,* Mar. 28, 1935, MSB; [Washington *Times-Herald,* Feb. 21, 1941], MSB; Washington *Star,* Jan. 8, 1939, Washington *Daily News,* July 19, 1949, clippings in FM Papers; *Current Biography, 1940,* p. 611; "Labor Governors," p. 79.

81. FM to John A. Ruskowski, Jr., Sept. 2, 1935, FM to Russell B. Porter, Feb. 26, 1939, FM Papers.

82. *DT,* Mar. 23, 1933; FM to Joan Cuddihy, undated, Joan Cuddihy Papers, in Miss Cuddihy's possession; JG to FM, Apr. 12, 1948, FM Papers.

83. Asher, "Judge in Sweet Trial," p. 17; High, *Roosevelt,* p. 320; FM to MBM, May 25, 1919, JFM Papers; FM to HE, Oct. 30, 1921, Apr. 17, 1922, Aug. 3, 1923, HE Papers; J. R. Hayden to Shirley Smith, Aug. 12, 1934, Shirley Smith Papers, MHC; William Teahan to FM, Nov. 17, 1939, FM to IM, May 17, 1944, Arthur B. Moehlman to FM, Dec. 5, 1946, FM Papers; biographical notes on FM, in Jan. 16-31, 1941, folder, GM Papers; IM interview, pp. 8-9.

84. Unidentified clipping, 1926, MSB; *DT,* May 26, 1928; Emerson to Lovett, Mar. 14, 1929, Jones to Lovett, Mar. 12, 1929, Candidate Files, Box 23, DCL Papers; FM to HE, July 5, 1922, HE Papers; FM to Francis J. McConnell, May 3, 1933, S. S. Marquis et al. to John Taylor, May 25, 1932, MOR; Gouverneur Frank Mosher to J. R. Hayden, Nov. 4, 1933, Joseph R. Hayden Papers, MHC.

CHAPTER IX

1. Sidney Fine, *The Automobile under the Blue Eagle* (Ann Arbor, 1963), pp. 5-6; DBGR, *Accumulated Social and Economic Statistics for Detroit*

(Detroit, 1937), p. 14; Carol A. Horne, "Detroit, The First Year of the Depression, 1929–1930" (MS [1966]), p. 7, in my possession; William Haber, "Fluctuations in Employment in Detroit Factories, 1921–31," *Journal of the American Statistical Association,* XXVII (June 1932), 144. The figures cited by Haber account for about two-thirds of the factory employment in Detroit, Hamtramck, Highland Park, and River Rouge. Ibid., pp. 141–42.

2. Haber, "Fluctuations in Employment," pp. 144, 148; Terry Hamburg, "The Depression in Detroit: The First Year, October, 1929 to September, 1930" (MS, 1968), pp. 7–12, in my possession; Lent D. Upson to Clark Branion, May 8, 1930, MOR.

3. Helen Hall, "When Detroit's Out of Gear," *Survey,* LXIV (Apr. 1, 1930), 10; *DSN,* May 3, 10, 1930.

4. William J. Norton, "The Relief Crisis in Detroit," *Social Service Review,* VII (Mar. 1933), 2–3; *DSN,* Dec. 7, 1929; *DN,* Mar. 7, Apr. 11, 1930; Hamburg, "Depression in Detroit," pp. 2–7; Horne, "Detroit," p. 11; Lovett to James Couzens, Dec. 24, 1929, Mar. 15, 1930, DCL Papers; Lynd and Lynd, *Middletown in Transition* (New York, 1937), p. 15. Detroit employers were not as optimistic privately as they were publicly. See Minutes of the Urban League Board, Mar. 20, 1930, DUL Papers.

5. *DSN,* May 3, 10, 1930; Norton, "Relief Crisis," pp. 1–2; Rachel Ganapol, "Public Welfare Relief Activities in Detroit, 1802–1930" (Detroit, 1946), pp. 1–11; Opal V. Matson, *Local Relief to Dependents* (n.p., 1933), pp. 8–13, 19.

6. Ganapol, "Welfare in Detroit," pp. 11–15; Gordon W. Davidson, "Industrial Detroit after World War I—1919–1921" (M.A. thesis, Wayne State University, 1953), pp. 134–40; Hamburg, "Depression in Detroit," p. 1; Horne, "Detroit," pp. 5–6.

7. Haber, "Fluctuations in Employment," p. 151; Fine, *Automobile under Blue Eagle,* p. 2; Detroit Department of Public Welfare, *Annual Report for the Calendar Year 1929* [Detroit, 1930], pp. 10–11, 12, 14; *DSN,* May 3, 10, 24, 1930; Ganapol, "Welfare in Detroit," pp. 15–17; DBGR, *Outdoor Relief as Administered by the Detroit Department of Public Welfare* (Detroit, 1930), pp. 6, 23; "Review of Mr. Stillman's Survey . . . ," in ibid.

8. DBGR, *Outdoor Relief,* pp. 20, 26; "Review of Stillman." Different case load figures are given in Haber, "Fluctuations in Employment," p. 151, and *Community Fund News,* Mar. 1930.

9. Glen Steele, "Cost of Family Relief in 100 Cities, 1929 and 1930," *Monthly Labor Review,* XXXII (Apr. 1931), 23; Howard W. Odum, "Public Welfare Activities," in President's Research Committee on Social Trends, *Recent Social Trends in the United States* (New York, 1933), II, 1250–51. Cf. Emma A. Winslow, *Trends in Different Types of Public and Private Relief in Urban Areas, 1929–35* (Washington, 1937), p. 9.

10. Anne E. Geddes, *Trends in Relief Expenditures, 1910-1935* (Works Progress Administration, Division of Social Research, *Research Monograph X*) (Washington, 1937), pp. 8-9; DBGR, *Outdoor Relief,* pp. 1, 4, 9; Winslow, *Trends in Relief,* pp. 72-85.

11. DBGR, *Outdoor Relief,* pp. 17-19, 27, 44-50; *Community Fund News,* Mar. 1930.

12. James H. Norton, "A History of the Detroit Community Fund and the Council of Social Agencies of Metropolitan Detroit, 1917-1938" (M.A. thesis, University of Michigan, 1940), pp. 25, 31, 49-50, 76; *Community Fund News,* Nov., Dec. 1929, Mar. 1930; *DSN,* Oct. 4, 1930.

13. *Journal of the Common Council, 1929,* II, 3662-65; *DN,* Dec. 4, 1929, Jan. 7, 1930; Hamburg, "Depression in Detroit," pp. 42-44.

14. R. J. Dean, "Detroit's Melting Pot Boils Over," *Survey,* LXIV (May 15, 1930), 187-88; Horne, "Detroit," pp. 33-35; Hamburg, "Depression in Detroit," pp. 55-61.

15. Daniel J. Leab, "'United We Eat': The Creation and Organization of the Unemployed Councils in 1930," *Labor History,* VIII (Fall 1967), 305-7; Caroline Parker to Editor, *Nation,* CXXX (Apr. 30, 1930), 518; American Civil Liberties Union (Detroit Branch), *Report of Activities for the Year 1930* (n.p., n.d.), p. 4, MOR; Hamburg, "Depression in Detroit," pp. 63-67.

16. Bowles to DBGR, June 18, 1930, MOR; DBGR, *Outdoor Relief,* pp. 23-24, 26, 33-37, 50, 72-76; "Review of Stillman"; Roy Lubove, *The Professional Altruist: The Emergence of Social Work as a Career* (Cambridge, Mass., 1965), pp. 52-54; Norton, "Relief Crisis," p. 3.

17. Horne, "Detroit," pp. 16, 33, 35-36; Hamburg, "Depression in Detroit," pp. 37-40.

18. Egbert S. Wengert, *Financial Problems of the City of Detroit in the Depression* (Detroit, 1939), pp. 3-4; John L. Lovett, "Public Interest in Taxes . . . ," *Nation's Business,* XVIII (Nov. 1930), 20-23, 70; Ralph Stone, "Detroit Practises Economy," *Review of Reviews,* LXXXV (June 1932), 26.

19. Lawrence Veenstra, "The Recall of Mayor Charles Bowles of Detroit" (MS, Aug. 1963), pp. 3-11, 32-34, in my possession; *DSN,* June 7, 1930; *Civic Searchlight,* July 1930; *DN,* Sept. 4, 8, 1930.

20. *Civic Searchlight,* July 1930; Veenstra, "Recall of Bowles," pp. 16-20; *DSN,* July 19, 1930; *DN,* Sept. 4, 10, 1930.

21. Veenstra, "Recall of Bowles," pp. 13-18; *DN,* July 28, Aug. 29, Sept. 10, 1930; *DSN,* June 7, 1930; Cyril Arthur Player, "Gangsters and Politicians in Detroit," *New Republic,* LXIII (Aug. 13, 1930), 362; *Nation,* CXXXI (Aug. 6, 1930), 138-39; William Comstock to F. W. Walker, June 13, 1930, William Comstock Papers, MHC; Confidential Memo by W. P. L. [Lovett], Apr. 25, 1930, Candidate Files, Box 3, DCL Papers.

22. Veenstra, "Recall of Bowles," pp. 20-23; *DN*, Sept. 10, 1930; Cash Asher, *Sacred Cows: A Story of the Recall of Mayor Bowles* (Detroit, 1931), pp. 98-109.

23. Veenstra, "Recall of Bowles," pp. 23-25.

24. Ibid., pp. 26-32.

25. Ibid., pp. 38-42. For allegations that the signatures had been fraudulently collected, see *DN*, Aug. 23, 1930; Asher, *Sacred Cows*, pp. 128-55; and Interview with Harry Mead, Aug. 5, 1963, pp. 1-2, MHC.

26. Veenstra, "Recall of Bowles," pp. 39-46; *Civic Searchlight*, July 1930; *DSN*, June 14, July 5, 1930; *DN*, Aug. 23, 1930; Asher, *Sacred Cows*, pp. 24, 35-39, 124, 207-10.

27. *Nation*, CXXX (Aug. 6, 1930), 139; Charles T. Haun, "Bloody July: The Buckley Case—1930," in Alvin C. Hamer, ed., *Detroit Murders* (New York, 1948), pp. 120-24; Player, "Gangsters and Politicians," p. 362; Veenstra, "Recall of Bowles," pp. 46-53; Haber, "Fluctuations in Employment," p. 144.

28. On this point, see Haun, "Bloody July," pp. 128-34.

29. For Buckley's career, see ibid., pp. 120-22; *DT*, July 23, 1930; *DN*, July 24, 1930; Player, "Gangsters and Politicians," pp. 362-63; Edmund Wilson, "The Despot of Dearborn," *Scribner's Magazine*, XL (July 1931), 25; Cash Asher, *The Real Buckley Tragedy* (Detroit, 1931), pp. 9, 13; and Lovett to H. W. Dodds, Aug. 4, 1930, DCL Papers.

30. Roger M. Andrews to Charles B. Van Dusen, Aug. 21, 1930, FM Papers; Interview with Carl Muller, Oct. 6, 1964, pp. 29-30, MHC; *DT*, July 23, 1930; *DN*, Sept. 6, 1930.

31. *DFP*, July 25, Aug. 1, 1930; *DN*, May 21, July 25, 26, 29, 31, Aug. 3, 5, 6, 12, 15, 28, 1930; *DT*, July 27, 1930; Asher, *Sacred Cows*, pp. 196-99, 207-10; Andrews to Van Dusen, Aug. 21, 1930, FM Papers; Lovett to Dodds, Aug. 4, 1930, DCL Papers.

32. *DT*, July 24, 26-28, Aug. 2, 5, 9, 1930, May 14, 1931; *DN*, Sept. 6, 8, 1930; *DSN*, Aug. 2, 16, 1930; Charles W. Casgrain to FM, Aug. 5, 1930, FM Papers; JG, in *DFP*, Mar. 12, 1972.

33. Andrews to Van Dusen, Aug. 21, 1930, FM to Richard E. Berlin, Apr. 16, 1947, Berlin to FM, Apr. 22, 1947, John P. McNichols to FM, July 31, 1930, FM Papers; Lovett to H. B. Stitt, Aug. 16, 1930, Lovett to Van Dusen, Aug. 20, 1930, DCL Papers; *DSN*, Aug. 16, 1930; *DN*, Sept. 6, 8, 1930; Blair Moody, "High Commissioner to Manila," *Survey Graphic*, XXIV (Dec. 1935), 631; "The Labor Governors," *Fortune*, XV (June 1937), 138; Muller interview, p. 30; Mead interview, p. 3.

34. *DT*, July 26, 29, Aug. 1, 2, 9, 13, 1930; *DN*, Aug. 8, 1930; *DLN*, Aug. 1, 8, 1930; Joseph Nowak to FM, Aug. 13, 1930, A. Robert Morrison to FM, Aug. 16, 1930, Edward M. Noone to FM, Aug. 11, 1930, Margaret Rose Fleiss to FM, Aug. 1, 1930, Mark De Vergilis to FM, Aug. 15, 1930, James Sharkey to FM, Aug. 3, 1930, George L. Berry to FM,

Jan. 6, 1939, FM Papers; Petition and Resolution of Lawyers Association of Detroit, undated, ibid.

35. *DT,* Aug. 2, 1930; J. C. Fogarty to FM, Aug. 17, 1930, James Ley to FM, July [Aug.] 4, 1930, Carl Reichmann to FM, Aug. 8, 1930, Arthur Walker to FM, July 28, 1930, J. D. Allan to FM, July 29, 1930, Lillian Street to FM, Aug. 5, 1930, Irving Janis to FM, July 31, 1930, Ed F. Dibble to FM, July 31, 1930, FM Papers.

36. Joel R. Moore to FM, Aug. 14, 1930, Edgar DeWitt Jones to FM [Aug. 1930], McNichols to FM, July 31, 1930, Thomas Emmet Cosgrove to FM, July 31, 1930, Joseph F. Mayes to FM, Aug. 1, 1930, Joseph Mulcahy to FM, July 30, 31, 1930, E. L. Osborne to FM, Aug. 18, 1930, FM Papers; *DSN,* Aug. 30, 1930.

37. *DN,* Aug. 13, 1930; Mead interview, p. 3; Muller interview, p. 31; *Philippines Herald,* Nov. 16, 1935, MSB; Myles M. Platt, "Frank Murphy: Detroit's Liberal Mayor (1930–1933)" (MS, 1954), p. 4, MHC.

38. *DT,* July 29, 30, Aug. 2, 1930; *DN,* Aug. 11, 1930; *DLN,* Aug. 1, 8, 1930.

39. *DT,* Aug. 2, 7, 9, 10, 1930.

40. Henry H. Weideman to FM, July 30, 1930, FM Papers; draft of instructions in FM's handwriting [Aug. 1930], ibid.; *DN,* Aug. 11, 21, 24, 1930; *DT,* Aug. 11, 13, 14, 18, 19, 1930; *DLN,* Aug. 15, 1930.

41. *DN,* Aug. 10, 11, 13, 20, 22, 24, Sept. 6, 8, 1930; *DFP,* Aug. 12, 13, 1930; *DLN,* Aug. 22, 1930; *DSN,* Aug. 2, 23, Sept. 13, 1930; *DT,* Aug. 13, 1930; [Walter White] Memorandum Re: Account of Damage Suit against Dr. Ossian H. Sweet, et al., Dec. 12, 1930, File G-96, NAACP Papers; Ossian Sweet to William Pickens, Dec. 20, 1930, ibid.

42. Transcript of Stenographic Notes of Address by Frank Murphy, Aug. 19, 1930, FM Papers; *DN,* Aug. 20, 1930; Moody, "High Commissioner," p. 631. The transcript of the speech gives the word as "dews"; it is "dew" in the *News* text.

43. *DT,* Aug. 20, 1930; Mrs. George A. B. Steinbrecher to FM, Aug. 21, 1930, Frances Breen to FM, Aug. 21, 1930, J. P ——— to FM, Aug. 22, 1930, "A born and bred Detroiter" to FM, Aug. 26, 1930, FM Papers.

44. Transcript of FM Address, Aug. 19, 1930, FM Papers; *DN,* Aug. 25, 1930, June 9, 1931, June 22, 1969; *DT,* Aug. 22, 23, 27, 1930; *DFP,* Sept. 15, 1931; Mead interview, p. 1; Muller interview, p. 31.

45. Committee Treasurer's . . . Statement of Nomination and Election Expenses for the Special Mayoralty Election of Sept. 9, 1930, FM Papers; *DN,* Aug. 16, 1931; Mead interview, pp. 5–7, 8.

46. *DN,* Aug. 28, 30, 31, Sept. 1, 3, 6, 8, 9, 1930; *DT,* Aug. 25, 28, 29, 31, Sept. 3–5, 7, 9, 1930; *DLN,* Aug. 29, Sept. 5, 1930; Darrow to FM, Aug. 25, 1930, Max M. Silverman to FM, Aug. 28, 1930, Annie High to FM, Sept. 1, 1930, White to FM, Sept. 2, 1930, J. Jackson to FM, Sept. 2, 1930, C. W. Clark to FM, Sept. 3, 1930, McKinley

Light to FM, Sept. 6, 1930, Jas. E. McCall to FM, Sept. 10, 1930, Moses L. Walker to FM, Sept. 10, 1930, G. G. Lopez to FM, Sept. 8, 1930, Julius Fodor to FM, Sept. 12, 1930, Franz Prattinger to FM, Sept. 13, 1930, D. W. Wade to FM, Sept. 22, 1930, FM to DePriest, Nov. 26, 1930, DePriest to FM, Sept. 13, 1930, FM Papers; Ruby Darrow to White, Aug. 26, 1930, File C-63, NAACP Papers; Thomas R. Solomon, "Participation of Negroes in Detroit Elections" (Ph.D. thesis, University of Michigan, 1939), p. 89; Mead interview, pp. 4, 8, 9-10.

47. *DN,* July 20, 1949; Walter Karig, "How Long Will Frank Murphy Stay on the Supreme Court?," *Liberty,* Mar. 2, 1940, p. 26; Moody, "High Commissioner," p. 631; William P. Lovett, "Detroit's Recall Election," *National Municipal Review,* XIX (Oct. 1930), 730-31; R. Rothman, "Detroit Elects a Liberal," *Nation,* CXXXI (Oct. 15, 1930), 400.

48. *DT,* Sept. 4, 1930.

49. *DT,* Aug. 26, Sept. 1, 4, 5, 8, 1930; *DN,* Aug. 27, 30, Sept. 1-4, 1930; *DLN,* Sept. 5, 1930; FM speech [Aug. 26, 1930], FM Papers; Reichmann to FM, Aug. 23, 1930, James Blandiun to FM, Aug. 25, 1930, Saverio Sdao to FM, Aug. 27, 1930, A. Vogt to FM, Aug. 27, 1930, Ida Elzea to FM, Aug. 28, 1930, FM to Noone, Aug. 28, 1930, Marcel E. Figlock to FM, Aug. 31, 1930, High to FM, Sept. 1, 1930, ibid.

50. *DT,* Aug. 29, 1930; *DLN,* Sept. 5, 1930; *DN,* Aug. 29-31, Sept. 1, 8, 9, 1930; Lovett, "Detroit's Recall Election," p. 731.

51. *DT,* Aug. 21, Sept. 4, 1930; *DN,* Aug. 24-28, 30, 31, Sept. 1, 3-9, 1930; *DFP,* Aug. 23, 28, 29, Sept. 2, 5-8, 1930; *DSN,* Aug. 30, 1930; Akron *Beacon-Journal* [Sept. 11, 1930], MSB.

52. Rothman, "Detroit Elects a Liberal," p. 401; *DT,* Sept. 8, 1930; *DN,* Aug. 31, Sept. 1-6, 8, 9, 1930; Mead interview, p. 5.

53. *DN,* Sept. 9, 10, 13, 1930; *DT,* Sept. 9, 1930; Richard W. Reading to FM, Sept. 13, 1930, FM Papers.

54. FM to White, Sept. 13, 1930, FM Papers. The official precinct-by-precinct returns are enclosed with Reading to FM, Sept. 19, 1930, ibid. Solomon, "Participation of Negroes," pp. 146, 153-55, and the vote for Cecil Rowlette in the 1929 Recorder's Court election are useful in locating the black precincts in Detroit.

55. FM to Leonard L. Schemanske, Sept. 17, 1930, FM to L. A. Koscinski, Sept. 19, 1930, FM to Magyar Hirlap, Sept. 22, 1930, FM Papers; *DT,* Sept. 10, 1930. The demographic data were derived from Bureau of the Census, *Fifteenth Census of the United States: 1930, Population,* III, Part 1 (Washington, 1932), 1183. The mayoralty vote for John Sosnowski in 1931 (*DN,* Oct. 7, 1931) helps one to identify some of Detroit's Polish precincts. For the size of the Polish community of Detroit in 1930, see Lois Rankin, "Detroit's Nationality Groups," *Michigan History Magazine,* XXIII (Spring 1939), 178.

56. *DN*, Sept. 10, 1931; Rothman, "Detroit Elects a Liberal," p. 401.
57. Haber, "Fluctuations in Employment," p. 144; James Schermerhorn to FM, Sept. 10, 1930, FM Papers; *DSN*, Sept. 13, 1930; Edward C. Banfield and James Q. Wilson, *City Politics* (Vintage Book; New York, 1966), pp. 159-60, 166. According to the federal census of unemployment of January, 1931, 11 percent of the native-born white population of Detroit, 17.2 percent of the foreign born, and 32.1 percent of the blacks were unemployed. Bureau of the Census, *Fifteenth Census of the United States, 1930, Unemployment,* II (Washington, 1932), 371.
58. Bureau of the Census, *Religious Bodies: 1926* (Washington, 1930), I, 408, 410; Bureau of the Census, *Religious Bodies: 1936* (Washington, 1941), I, 502, 504.
59. *DT*, Sept. 10, 1930.
60. Joseph Weisman to FM. Sept. 10, 1930, ——— to FM, Sept. 11, 1930, FM Papers.
61. Louis S. Cohane to FM, Sept. 10, 1930, John A. Reynolds to FM, Sept. 10, 1930, John W. Mulford to FM, Sept. 10, 1930, Upson to FM, Sept. 10, 1930, Edward O'Connor to FM, Sept. 10, 1930, Dorothy Detzer to FM, Sept. 10, 1930, Arthur B. Spingarn to FM, Sept. 10, 1930, Agnes Abbs to FM, Sept. 10, 1930, Alvan Macauley, Jr., to FM, Sept. 10, 1930, B. E. Hutchinson to FM, Sept. 10, 1930, John C. King to FM, Sept. 10, 1930, A. K. Burrows to FM [Sept. 10, 1930], Percival Dodge to FM, Sept. 11, 1930, Earl F. Wilson to FM, Sept. 12, 1930, Leon Fram to FM, Sept. 12, 1930, S. Centille to FM, Sept. 11, 1930, Keller to FM, Sept. 27, 1930, Andrews to FM, Sept. 30, 1930, Jouett Shouse to FM, Oct. 6, 1930, Villard to FM, Oct. 27, 1930, Harold M. Kingsley to FM, Oct. 31, 1930, ibid.; Rothman, "Detroit Elects a Liberal," p. 401; (New York) *Daily Mirror,* Sept. 12, 1930, MSB.
62. Muller to FM, Oct. 12, 1930, HE Papers.
63. *DT*, Sept. 10, 1930; *DN*, Sept. 10, 1930; FM to Fram, Sept. 12, 1930, FM Papers.

CHAPTER X

1. *DN*, Sept. 15-17, 23, 1930; Bowles to Richard W. Reading, Sept. 15, 1930, FM Papers; *DLN*, Oct. 3, 1930.
2. DBGR, *Detroit's New Charter* (Detroit, 1918); Harlan M. Holt, "The Government of Detroit" (M.A. thesis, Wayne State University, 1935), pp. 53-54. Members of the Civil Service Commission could be removed only for cause.
3. *Civic Searchlight,* Dec. 1930; William P. Lovett to Mayo Fesler, Dec. 15, 1930, Lovett to Alvan Macauley, Jr., Jan. 19, 1931, Lovett to T. P. Myers, June 30, 1931, Lovett to Henry J. Richmond, June 27, 1931,

DCL Papers; FM to Macauley, Feb. 3, 1931, MOR; *DN*, Apr. 1, 1931; *DFP*, June 16, 1931; Mabel L. Walker, "Rating Cities . . . ," *American City*, XLI (July 1929), 134.

4. Edward C. Banfield and James Q. Wilson, *City Politics* (Vintage Book; New York, 1966), pp. 46, 139; FM to Lee Kreiselman [July 1932], MOR; FM to Davie Davis, June 4, 1933, FM to Joseph T. Finnegan, Sept. 29, 1934, FM Papers; *DLN*, Apr. 8, 1932; Wichita *Beacon*, July 23 [1932], MSB; *Journal of the Common Council*, Jan. 13, 1931, p. 8; FM radio speech [1931], FM Papers; Shannon, *The American Irish* (New York, 1963), p. 344.

5. FM radio speech [1931], FM Papers; FM statement for WMBC [1933], ibid.; William L. Stidger to FM, Aug. 1, 1939, ibid.; FM to Jack Burkhart, Nov. 18, 1931, MOR; [*Border Cities Star*, Jan. 16, 1932], MSB; unidentified Boston newspaper, Nov. 24, 1931, MSB; "The Labor Governors," *Fortune*, XV (June 1937), 138; Carl Muller, "Frank Murphy: Ornament of the Bar," *Detroit Lawyer*, XVII (Sept. 1949), 182.

6. Cleveland *Plain Dealer*, June 5, 1931, MSB; Detroit *Mirror*, Apr. 7, 1931, MSB; New Orleans *Item-Tribune*, Sept. 17, 1939, MSB; Edward M. Levine, *The Irish and Irish Politicians* (South Bend, 1966), pp. 39, 47, 51, 80-88, 91-94, 134-39, 155-61, 171-78, 183-84; Thomas W. Brown, *Irish-American Nationalism, 1870-1890* (Philadelphia, 1966), p. 133; Nathan Glazer and Daniel Patrick Moynihan, *Beyond the Melting Pot* (Cambridge, Mass., 1963), pp. 224-29; Shannon, *American Irish*, pp. 64-65, 343; FM speech [Mar. 17, 1933], MOR.

7. FM to MBM, Dec. 18, 1922, JFM Papers; *DT*, Oct. 20, 1930; FM to Brigid McKenna, Sept. 19, 1932, FM to IM, Dec. 3, 1935, FM Papers; Washington *Star*, Jan. 8, 1939, clipping in ibid.

8. *DT*, Sept. 14, 1930; *DN*, Sept. 11, Oct. 3, 14, 15, 1930, Jan. 4, 1931, July 20, 1949; FM to Frank Oldfield, July 8, 1932, FM to Charles E. Jones, Sept. 2, 1932, JG to L. J. Rengers, May 27, 1931, MOR; EMB to GM, May 1, 1945, GM Papers; FM to Caroline Parker, July 12, 1934, FM Papers; Washington *Star*, Jan. 8, 1939, clipping in ibid.; Mauritz A. Hallgren, "Detroit's Liberal Mayor," *Nation*, CXXXII (May 13, 1931), 527; Interview with Martin S. Hayden, Oct. 6, 1964, pp. 6, 21, MHC; Interview with Carl Muller, Oct. 6, 1964, p. 21, MHC.

9. *DN*, Oct. 16, 1930; *DSN*, Nov. 1, Dec. 27, 1930; Couzens to FM, Aug. 1, 1934, FM Papers; Interview with Harry Mead, Aug. 5, 1963, pp. 15-16, MHC.

10. Bowles to Mills, Nov. 6, 1930, Joseph E. Mills Papers, BHC; typed biography, undated, in ibid.; Mills to Milan Vukmonovicz, Jan. 7, 1931, MOR; *DN*, Jan. 16, 17, 1932; [*Philippines Herald*, Apr. 7, 1934], MSB.

11. *DN*, Jan. 10, 11, 1931; *DSN*, Dec. 6, 1930, Jan. 17, 1931; Interview with Norman H. Hill, Aug. 21, 1963, p. 9, MHC; Muller interview, p. 32; Mead interview, p. 9; Blair Moody, "High Commissioner to

Manila," *Survey Graphic*, XXIV (Dec. 1935), 631; Memorandum, Mar. 22, 1932, ACLU Archives, Vol. 575.

12. *DT*, Apr. 21, 1929; *DN*, July 19, 1930, Jan. 11, 1931; *DSN*, Dec. 6, 1930; *DFP*, Jan. 12, 1931; Giles Kavanaugh to Franklin D. Roosevelt, Aug. 29, 1932, DNC Records, FDRL; G. H. Roosevelt to F. D. Roosevelt, Sept. 12, 1930, Governor Papers, ibid.; JG to Walter S. Vose, Jan. 19, 1933, MOR; Mead interview, pp. 11-12.

13. *DN*, Oct. 23, 1930, Jan. 23, 1931, Jan. 17, 20, Nov. 29, 1932; Lovett to H. W. Dodds, Apr. 10, 1931, DCL Papers; *Civic Searchlight*, Jan. 1932; Charles S. Kennedy to FM, Oct. 22, 1930, FM Papers.

14. Hallgren, "Detroit's Liberal Mayor," p. 527; *DN*, Dec. 1, 1930, May 22, 1931, Jan. 27, 30, 1932, Sept. 14, 1933; *Central Press Association*, Aug. 29, 1932, MSB; *DSN*, Nov. 14, 1931; JG to Dale M. Belmont, June 13, 1932, JG to Frank Payne, June 15, 1932, JG to Corwin Dale Wilson, July 6, 1932, JG to Helen Hitchcock Miller, July 11, 1932, JG to Vene Smeltzer, July 18, 1932, MOR.

15. *DN*, Nov. 18, Dec. 27, 1930, Feb. 4, 1931, Jan. 27, Feb. 15, 24, Nov. 18, 1932; *DLN*, Sept. 19, 26, 1930, Feb. 6, 1931, Jan. 29, Apr. 8, Nov. 18, 1932; *DSN*, Dec. 27, 1930, Feb. 7, 1931; *DFP*, Nov. 9, 1932.

16. Dancy to Russell Cowan, Mar. 17, 1933, and attached statement, DUL Papers; John C. Dancy, *Sands against the Wind: The Memoirs of John C. Dancy* (Detroit, 1966), 104-5; Malinda L. Wells to FM, Apr. 3, 1932, Fred W. Fuller to FM, Mar. 18, 1933, FM to Roxborough, Mar. 13, 1931, Bradby to FM, May 27, 1931, FM to Bradby, Dec. 26, 1931, Apr. 6, 1932.

17. FM statement to press [1931], MOR; Mayor to Common Council, Mar, 22, 1932, FM to Desiderius Nagy, Mar. 9, 1933, MOR; Detroit *Jewish Chronicle*, Dec. 26, 1930, MSB; Carl Suesser to FM, May 6, 1933, FM Papers.

18. Washington *Star*, Jan. 8, 1939, clipping in FM Papers; Wilcox to FM, Oct. 19, 1932, Mills to FM, Jan. 30, 1932, MOR. See also Wilcox to FM, Mar. 27, 1933, ibid.

19. William P. Lovett, *Detroit Rules Itself* (Boston, 1930), p. 163. Cf. Maurice S. Ramsey, "Some Aspects of Non-Partisan Government in Detroit, 1918-1940" (Ph.D. thesis, University of Michigan, 1941), p. 37.

20. Banfield and Wilson, *City Politics*, pp. 214-16; *DN*, Sept. 25-29, Oct. 2, 1930, Feb. 8, Apr. 9, May 5, Oct. 6, Dec. 8, 1931, Jan. 5, Dec. 18, 19, 1932; Minutes of the Meeting of the Board of Street Railway Commissioners . . . , Sept. 29, 1931, MOR; FM to Mills, Jan. 4, 1933, MOR.

21. *DN*, Sept. 28, 1930, Jan. 18, 22, Feb. 8, 10-14, Mar. 18, 1931, Jan. 12, 1932; *DSN*, Feb. 7, 1931.

22. *DN*, Feb. 4, 8, 12, Sept. 17, 1931, July 21, 1932, Mar. 13, 1938; Mead to Taylor, Nov. 16, 1931, MOR; Minutes of the Meeting of the

Committee on Operating Efficiency, Oct. 2, 1931, MOR; Mead interview, p. 15.

23. *DN,* Feb. 11, 1931, Jan. 27, 1933; Hill interview, p. 35; Lenhardt to Taylor, June 17, 1932, FM to C. J. Plagens, Dec. 31, 1931, Plagens to FM, Jan. 7, 1932, MOR.

24. *DN,* Nov. 12, 18, 1930, Jan. 4, 28, 30, Sept. 26, 1931; *DT,* Jan. 30, 1931; Robert G. Brand to FM, Oct. 18, 1930, Leo F. Burke to FM, Nov. 1, 1930, FM to J. Hopkins, Feb. 8, 1932, FM to Edward D. Smith, Jr., Aug. 19, 1932, FM to department heads, undated, MOR; FM to Rowland W. Fixel, Jan. 28, 1931, Burke to Taylor [Jan. 1931], Ralph T. O'Neil to FM, Oct. 7, 1931, Jerry McCarthy to FM, Oct. 9, 1931, Leonard S. Coyne to FM, Jan. 6, 1930 [1931], FM Papers.

25. Bureau of the Census, *Religious Bodies: 1926,* I (Washington, 1930), 408, 409; Bureau of the Census, *Religious Bodies: 1936,* I (Washington, 1941), 502, 503; *DN,* Nov. 3, 1930; Detroit *Jewish Chronicle,* Jan. 23, 1931, MSB; FM speech on Jewish Radio Forum [1932], MOR; FM radio address [1931], ibid.; FM to O'Neil, Mar. 6, 1931, Philip Slomovitz to FM, Mar. 9, 1931, FM to Aaron De Roy, May 2, 1932, FM Papers; W. J. C. Kaufmann to FM, Mar. 30, 1933, FM to Kaufmann, Mar. 31, 1933, Henri Gressitt to FM, Feb. 7, 1933, FM to Gressitt, Feb. 23, 1933, MOR. Italics supplied.

26. FM address, Jan. 29 [1933], MOR; FM to Joseph Wedda, Dec. 10, 1931, Wedda to FM, Jan. 30, 1933, MOR; FM release, Jan. 24, 1933, MOR; Lois Rankin, "Detroit Nationality Groups," *Michigan History Magazine,* XXIII (Spring 1939), 178.

27. Interview with Beulah Carter, May 17, 1972; *DT,* Oct. 19, 1930; draft of NAACP release, Oct. 24, 1930, File G-96, NAACP Papers; Memorandum from the Acting Secretary, Dec. 12, 1930, File A-21, ibid.; Detroit *Daily,* Mar. 11, 1931, MSB; Roy Wilkins to FM, June 24, 1932, MOR.

28. *DN,* Feb. 15, 1931; *DFP,* Feb. 14, 1931, MSB; *DSN,* Feb. 21, 1931; Flint *Journal,* Feb. 16, 1931, MSB; Fred J. Schumann to FM, Mar. 19, 1931, MOR.

29. Beulah Young to FM, Jan. 7, 1930 [1931], FM Papers; [Moses L. Walker] to Dear Member, Apr. 24, 1933, DUL Papers; inscription on plaque, Apr. 1933, in Murphy home, Harbor Beach, Michigan.

30. FM to Martel, Sept. 11, 1930, Wayne County AFL-CIO Papers, ALHUA; *DLN,* Oct. 3, 1930.

31. FM to Woll, June 22, Sept. 9, 1931, MOR; FM address [Apr. 5, 1932], MOR; *DLN,* Mar. 20, Sept. 11, Oct. 2, 1931, Mar. 25, Apr. 8, 1932; *International Fire Fighter,* XV (Mar. 1932), 21.

32. *DLN,* Oct. 10, 17, 24, 31, 1930, Dec. 9, 1932; *DN,* Oct. 5, 29, Dec. 3, 10, 1930, Feb. 6, 1933.

33. *DLN,* Apr. 10, 17, 1931; *DN,* Apr. 7, 8, 1931; Resolution recommended by Executive Board, Division #26, Mar. 17, 1932, MOR.

34. *DN,* Jan. 20-23, 1931; *DLN,* Feb. 6, 13, 20, 1931.

35. *DN,* May 21, June 30, 1931; *Detroiter,* XXII (July 6, 1931), 5; E. S. Evans to FM, and enclosed confidential reports, FM to W. R. Angell, June 17, 1931, FM to R. L. Martin, July 1, 1931, MOR; C. C. McGill radio talk, June 14, 1931, ibid.

36. *DN,* Nov. 13, 17, Dec. 6, 8, 1930, Jan. 28, 1931; FM to Harry Riseman, Feb. 21, 1931, FM to Clarence S. Dill, Feb. 23, 1931, FM to Abraham Epstein, Apr. 3, 1931, JG to Pearl Mason, June 12, 1931, Epstein to Officers and Members of Advisory Council, Feb. 24, 1933, MOR; *Old Age Security Herald,* V (May 1931); FM speech [1933], HE Papers; Isadore Pastor, "Public Old Age Assistance in Michigan" (M.A. thesis, Wayne State University, 1937), pp. 32, 38-40.

37. *DSN,* Sept. 26, 1931; William Bailey to Taylor, Oct. 6, 1931, MOR. Taylor declined the offer lest it set a precedent. Taylor to Bailey, Oct. 8, 1931, ibid.

38. *DLN,* Apr. 28, 1933; FM to Martel, Apr. 22, 1933, FM Papers.

39. *DSN,* Oct. 25, Nov. 15, 29, Dec. 27, 1930, Jan. 3, 24, 1931; *Civic Searchlight,* Dec. 1930; *DN,* Jan. 12, 1932; FM statement, June 11, 1931, MOR; FM to Patrick J. Hurley, undated, MOR.

40. *DN,* Oct. 15, 19, 1930; FM to Harry Bitner, Jan. 22, 1932, FM Papers; FM to Roger M. Andrews, Mar. 4, 1932, Andrews to FM, Mar. 9, 1932, FM to Moody, Aug. 17, 1932, MOR; FM to GM, Dec. 13, 1944, GM Papers; *DT,* Apr. 27, 1931; *DFP,* Nov. 7, 1931; *DSN,* Feb. 14, 1931; Bright to FM, Apr. 14, 1934, FM Papers; Muller interview, p. 27.

41. FM to Carson, Apr. 4, Oct. 26, 1931, FM to J. M. Patterson, Oct. 12, 1931, FM to Editor, Detroit *Mirror,* Nov. 4, 1931, Carson to FM, Apr. 13, 1932, John J. Gorman to FM, July 27, 1932, MOR; FM veto message [Aug. 2, 1932], MOR; Carson to FM, Sept. 19, 1933, FM Papers.

42. Young to FM, Sept. 14, Nov. 24, 1930, Jan. 7, 1930 [1931], Suesser to FM, May 6, 1933, FM Papers; Hill to FM [Dec. 1932], MOR; FM to Nagy, Mar. 9, 1933, MOR.

43. *DN,* May 5, Nov. 6, 1931, Feb. 24, June 7, 1932, [Jan. 1971]; *DSN,* Nov. 14, 1931; Ann Arbor *News,* Jan. 5, 1971; Hill interview, pp. 6-7; Taylor to FM, Sept. 28, 1932, FM Papers.

44. *DN,* Sept. 24, 26, Oct. 15, 1930; GM to William Walker, Nov. 17, 1930, GM Papers.

45. City of Detroit Payroll . . . , Mar. 31, 1933, MOR; *DN,* Dec. 30, 1930, Nov. 6, 1931; Hill interview, pp. 12-13; Richard D. Lunt, "The High Ministry of Government: The Political Career of Frank Murphy" (Ph.D. thesis, University of New Mexico, 1962), pp. 51-52; J. Weldon Jones to Sidney Fine, Jan. 29, 1966.

46. *DN,* Sept. 26, Oct. 15, 1931, Mar. 27, 1931; Hallgren, "Detroit's Liberal Mayor," p. 526; The Reminiscences of Roger N. Baldwin (1953-1954), I, 252, Columbia University, New York, New York; FM to Elise

Sendelbeck, Feb. 21, 1933, JG to Winifred Lockhart, Dec. 31, 1931, MOR; FM to Finnegan, Sept. 29, 1934, FM Papers.

47. Interview with Hilmer Gellein, Aug. 21, 1963, p. 18, MHC; Couzens to FM, Apr. 27, 1931, Norton to Couzens, Nov. 16, 1931, CF Papers, Box 10, MHC.

48. *DN*, Sept. 28, 30, Nov. 20, 1930, May 4, 1931; *Civic Searchlight*, May 1931; Clyde Burroughs to FM, May 4, 1931, C. E. Brewster to FM, May 4, 1931, and attached executive order of same date, Hill to Dear Sir, Oct. 11, 1932, MOR.

49. *DN*, Oct. 15, 1930; *DT*, Oct. 20, 1930; Lovett to Charles B. Van Dusen, Oct. 4, 1930, Lovett to H. W. Dodds, Sept. 29, 1930, DCL Papers; Kennedy to FM, Oct. 22, 1930, John A. Dodds to FM, Oct. 22, 1930, Dorothy Kemp Roosevelt to FM, Apr. 19, 1933, Kathleen McGraw Hendrie to FM [Apr. 4, 1931], FM Papers; "Our New Leader" [1930], ibid.; Thomas D. Buick to FM, June 4, 1932, J. G. Riordan to FM, Apr. 26, 1932, M. I. J. to FM, Jan. 7, 1932, MOR.

50. Holt, "Government of Detroit," pp. 45, 47; Lovett, *Detroit Rules Itself*, p. 119; Banfield and Wilson, *City Politics*, p. 166.

51. Banfield and Wilson, *City Politics*, p. 95; *DSN*, Sept. 19, 26, 1931; *DN*, Aug. 14, 1931; Lovett to Richmond, Aug. 5, 1931, DCL Papers; Ramsey, "Non-Partisan Government," pp. 93, 95, 97–102, 106.

52. *DN*, Oct. 7, Nov. 4, 1931; *NYT*, Nov. 8, 1931; Lovett to Clarence E. Ridley, Nov. 25, 1931, DCL Papers; Ramsey, "Non-Partisan Government," pp. 95, 100–102, 106; Lovett, "Detroit Voters Show Discriminating Judgment," *National Municipal Review*, XX (Dec. 1931), 741; JG, in *DFP*, Mar. 12, 1972.

53. Robert H. Salisbury, "Urban Politics: The New Convergence of Power," *Journal of Politics*, XXVI (Nov. 1964), 780–81; Ramsey, "Non-Partisan Government," pp. 115–23, 134–35; Banfield and Wilson, *City Politics*, p. 263; Lovett, *Detroit Governs Itself*, pp. 158–60.

54. Ramsey, "Non-Partisan Government," pp. 136, 138–40, 143–46; Lovett to Dodds, Sept. 10, 1930, May 25, 1931, Lovett to Mayo Fesler, Sept. 26, 1930, DCL Papers; *DN*, Oct. 17, 1930; Salisbury, "Urban Politics," p. 787.

55. Irving Bernstein, *The Lean Years: A History of the American Worker, 1920–1933* (Boston, 1960), p. 300; FM to Paul Ohman, May 25, 1932, MOR; Wilson, "The Despot of Dearborn," *Scribner's Magazine*, XC (July 1931), 25.

56. Bureau of the Census, *Fifteenth Census of the United States: 1930, Unemployment*, I (Washington, 1931), 500, II (Washington, 1932), 371; William Haber, "Fluctuations in Employment in Detroit Factories, 1921–31," *Journal of the American Statistical Association*, XXVII (June 1932), 147–49; Eric Kocher, *Physical Growth of Detroit* (n.p., 1935), p. 79; *DN*, Nov. 11, 1930, Mar. 21, 1931; Harold Ross, "Social Consequences of the Business Cycle," *Sociology and Social Research*,

XXIII (Jan.-Feb. 1932), 204; IM to Hill, Nov. 17, 1932, FM Papers; Allan Nevins and Frank Ernest Hill, *Ford: Expansion and Challenge, 1915-1933* (New York, 1957), p. 687. Haber uses the wrong figures in calculating the unemployment as of October, 1930.

57. Kocher, *Growth of Detroit,* pp. 61, 77; DBGR, *Accumulated Social and Economic Statistics for Detroit* (Detroit, 1937), pp. 14, 17, 18; Selwyn D. Collins and Clark Tibbits, *Research Memorandum on Social Aspects of Health in the Depression* (New York, 1937), p. 91; House Committee on the Judiciary, *To Amend the Bankruptcy Act . . . Hearing on HR 1670 . . . ,* 73 Cong., 1 Sess. (Washington, 1933), p. 92; Addams, "Social Consequences of Depression," *Survey,* LXVII (Jan. 1932), 371; Robert C. Ferguson to FM, May 11, 1932, Kenneth J. McCarren to Hill, Feb. 7, 1933, MOR; *DN,* May 23, 1937.

58. DBGR, *Social and Economic Statistics,* p. 3; Ross, "Social Consequences," p. 204; *DN,* Sept. 24, 1932, May 23, 1937; Department of Health, Monthly Statement to Controller's Office, Mar. 1932, MOR; *Journal of the Common Council,* Jan. 12, 1932, p. 6.

59. Ross, "Social Consequences," p. 204; DBGR, *Social and Economic Statistics,* p. 15; *DN,* Dec. 28, 1930; Department of Health, Monthly Statements, Dec. 1930, Dec. 1931, Jan., Dec. 1932, MOR; Vaughan to FM, Apr. 11, 1932, MOR; Vaughan, "Unemployment—Its Effect on Health," Apr. 8, 1932, MOR; *DN,* Dec. 28, 1930, Feb. 26, Apr. 9, 1931; Collins and Tibbits, *Social Aspects of Health,* pp. 11, 13, 14, 25-26.

60. Robert S. and Helen Merrell Lynd, *Middletown in Transition* (New York, 1937), p. 400; Alice Stenholm, Report on Field Trip, Nov. 10-13, 1931, State Files, POUR Records; James H. Williams, *Human Aspects of Unemployment Relief . . .* (Chapel Hill, 1933), p. 64; Department of Health, Monthly Statement, Nov. 1931, MOR; "The Extent of Underweight Children in Detroit" [1932], ibid.; IM to Hill, Nov. 17, 1932, FM Papers; *DT,* Nov. 1, 1932.

61. Mayor's Unemployment Committee survey [Sept. 1932], MOR; *DN,* Sept. 23, 1932.

62. *DN,* Oct. 6, 1930; Civil Works Administration in the State of Michigan, Nov. 17, 1933-Mar. 31, 1934, A Report . . . , p. 22, CWA Central Files, RG 69, NARS; Dancy to Walter Nelson, Dec. 18, 1930, IM to T. Arnold Hill, Nov. 13, 1931, Dancy to F. A. Jackson, Dec. 7, 1931, Dancy to C. E. Nicholson, Jan. 28, 1933, Dancy to Forrester B. Washington, Jan. 26, 1933, Dancy to T., A. Hill, Apr. 18, 1933, DUL Papers; Department of Health, Monthly Statement, May 1931, MOR.

63. Oral History Interview of Merlin D. Bishop, Mar. 29, 1963, p. 1, MHC; *DT,* July 10, 1931; *DN,* Mar. 28, 1933; Report of Addresses . . . , Dec. 10, 1932, FM Papers; Carl M. Weideman to Jesse Jones, Mar. 31, 1933, RFC Records; Hallgren, "Grave Danger in Detroit," *Nation,*

CXXXV (Aug. 3, 1932), 99; Williams, *Human Aspects,* pp. 35–36; *Journal of the Common Council,* Jan. 12, 1932, p. 6.

64. Mrs. Addison Caler to FM, Sept. 10, 1930, T. E. La France to FM, May 26, 1932, Mrs. Andrew L. Wilson to FM, July 14, 1932, MOR.

65. Mrs. Frank De Pasqualin to FM, Aug. 18, 1932, Emma Thies to FM, Sept. 26, 1932, Mrs. Boyd to FM, Oct. 3, 1932, MOR.

66. Mr. and Mrs. E. Molinaro to FM, Sept. 19, 1932, Zelda M. Brandon to George W. Trendle, Dec. 7, 1932, MOR.

67. Brandon to Trendle, Dec. 7, 1932, Pansy Mageles to FM, Apr. 5, 1931, MOR.

68. Evan H. May to FM, May 19, 1931, Michael Hoar to FM [Apr. 1932], W. Kirby Schaefer to FM, Dec. 27, 1932, Abraham H. Jaffin to FM, Mar. 31, 1933, MOR.

69. FM to Jack Burkhart, Dec. 4, 1931, FM to Vincent H. Conlogue, Nov. 14, 1932, JG to E. R. Zalewski, Apr. 8, 1932, MOR; To the Members of the Detroit Municipal Employees Club, Dec. 8, 1932, MOR; Tugwell, *The Democratic Roosevelt* (Penguin Book; Baltimore, 1969), p. 177; FM to John Ballenger, Dec. 27, 1934, FM Papers; Monroe *Evening News,* Sept. 27, 1930, MSB.

70. *DN,* Sept. 29, Nov. 19, 1931, Feb. 6, 1933; FM to James P. Kirby, July 3, 1931, FM Papers; AFL, *Report of Proceedings of the Fiftieth Annual Convention, 1930* (Washington, 1930), p. 179; Brightmoor *Journal,* Jan. 22, 1931, MSB; Ionia *Sentinel-Standard,* July 27, 1931, MSB; Martin Frances Owens, "Gentleman, Scholar, Humanitarian," Detroit *Merry Go-Round,* Feb. 1933, FM Papers; FM radio address, Oct. 31, 1931, MOR; *DT,* June 9, 1932.

71. AFL, *Proceedings, 1930,* p. 179; *Journal of the Common Council,* Jan. 10, 1933, p. 1.

72. Seymour Martin Lipset, "Religion and Politics in the American Past and Present," in Robert Lee and Martin E. Marty, eds., *Religion and Social Conflict* (New York, 1964), p. 113; David J. O'Brien, *American Catholicism and Social Reform: The New Deal Years* (New York, 1968), p. 46; *DN,* Mar. 21, 1932; (Buffalo) *Echo,* May 19, 1932, MSB; *Michigan Catholic,* Feb. 23, 1933, MSB; "A Mayor's Interpretation . . ." [Nov. 20, 1932], MOR; FM, "The Moral Law in Government," *Commonweal,* XVII (May 19, 1933), 64.

73. Charles Tull, *Father Coughlin and the New Deal* (Syracuse, 1965), pp. 1–14; Shannon, *American Irish,* pp. 297–303; Interview with IM, July 30, 1964, pp. 11, 13, MHC; *DT,* Apr. 23, 1933; FM to Coughlin, Oct. 13, 1930, Coughlin to FM, Oct. 13, 1931, Grenville Vernon to FM, June 29, 1940, and enclosed MS, FM Papers; EG notes on interview with GM, 1949, EG Papers.

74. Wilson, "The Mayors vs. the Cities," *Public Interest,* No. 16 (Summer 1969), pp. 29–30.

75. Detroit *Mirror,* Apr. 7, 1931, MSB; *DFP,* June 2, 1931; FM to Roger

N. Baldwin, Sept. 13, 1932, MOR; MM, My Trip Abroad book, Apr. 1933 entry, MM Papers.

76. Detroit *Mirror,* Apr. 7, 1931, MSB; Harding to FM [Oct. 1932], Theodora McManus to FM [May 1933], FM to Katherine Cornell, Dec. 16, 1932, Mrs. William D. Henderson to FM, Apr. 8, 1933, FM to Russell B. Porter, Feb. 26, 1939, FM Papers; FM to Wanda Ropele, Jan. 4, 1933, MOR; *DT,* Apr. 14, 1932; *La Defensa,* July 22, 1933, Norman H. Hill Scrapbooks, MHC.

77. *DN,* May 13, 1933; FM to John Brennan, Jan. 3, 1933, FM Papers; IM to Mrs. D. T. Roots, Dec. 11, 1933, IM Papers; San Francisco *Chronicle* [May 20, 1933], MSB.

78. Flint *Journal* [Mar. 15, 1931], MSB; FM to Sherry Sherwood, July 24, 1931, FM to Davie Davis, June 4, 1933, FM Papers; (New York) *Daily Mirror,* May 20 [1933], clipping in ibid.

CHAPTER XI

1. *Journal of the Common Council,* Sept. 23, 1930, pp. 2441-42.

2. Edward Ainsworth Williams, *Federal Aid for Relief* (New York, 1939), pp. 8-10; Irving Bernstein, *The Lean Years: A History of the American Worker, 1920-1933* (Boston, 1960), p. 240; Josephine Brown, *Public Relief, 1929-1939* (New York, 1940), pp. 3-4, 8-10.

3. American Federation of Labor, *Report of Proceedings of the Fiftieth Annual Convention . . . , 1930* (Washington, 1930), p. 178; *DT,* Mar. 21, 1931; FM message attached to document dated Apr. 18, 1932, MOR.

4. *DN,* Sept. 28, Oct. 2, 13, Dec. 4, 1930, Jan. 7, Nov. 19, 1931; FM to Jacob Segal, Jan. 13, 1932, FM to Perrini Palmer, July 5, 1932, MOR; *Journal of the Common Council,* Jan. 12, 1932, p. 7.

5. *DN,* Oct. 13, Nov. 6, 1930; *Journal of the Common Council,* Jan. 12, 1932, p. 6.

6. *DN,* Nov. 6, 1930, May 3, 4, 1931, Feb. 13, 1933; FM radio addresses [Nov. 2, 1931], 1931, MOR; FM to Mabel Ford, Dec. 5, 1947, FM Papers; *Central Press Association,* Aug. 29, 1932, MSB; [Baltimore *Sun,* Mar. 13, 1931], MSB; *Detroit Merry-Go-Round* [1933], MOR.

7. FM to Carl Weideman, Feb. 20, 1933, MOR; *DN,* Nov. 6, 1930; FM to Joseph T. Finnegan, Sept. 29, 1934, FM Papers; Interview with Mary Lutomski, May 17, 1972; Subcommittee of the Senate Committee on Manufactures, *Unemployment Relief. Hearings on S. 174 and S. 262,* 72 Cong., 1 Sess. (Washington, 1932), p. 278.

8. DBGR, *Outdoor Relief as Administered by the Detroit Department of Public Welfare* (Detroit, 1930), pp. 45-47; Joanna C. Colcord, *Cash Relief* (New York, 1936), pp. 87-89; William J. Norton, "The Relief Crisis in Detroit," *Social Service Review,* VII (Mar. 1933), 9-10; "City Physician's Division," accompanying J. F. Kilroy to FM, Mar. 14,

1930, FM Papers; FM to Fred J. Hart, Feb. 10, 1933, MOR; Irma Unruh, "Detroit's Nursery School," *Survey,* LXIV (Apr. 15, 1930), 81; *DSN,* June 14, 1930.

9. Norton, "Relief Crisis," p. 8; *DLN,* Oct. 3, 1930, July 10, 31, 1931; *DN,* June 14, 1931; *DT,* July 8, 1931; *DFP,* June 2, 1931; Blain to A. C. Williams, June 24, 1931, MOR.

10. *DSN,* June 7, 1930; *DN,* May 17, 1938; Sophie T. Cole to FM [June 13, 1931], FM Papers; Interview with IM, July 30, 1964, p. 44, MHC; Interview with William J. Norton, undated, p. 6, MHC.

11. *DN,* Sept. 13, 24, Oct. 15, 1930, Feb. 22, May 10, Aug. 2, 1931, Dec. 8, 1932, Feb. 8, 1933; Frank D. Adams to James Couzens, Oct. 13, 1932, MOR; FM to EGK, Nov. 9, 1932, EGK Papers.

12. *DN,* Oct. 5, Dec. 2, 1930; *Proceedings of a Conference of Progressives* . . . , Mar. 11, 12, 1931, p. 112, George W. Norris Papers, LC; Norton to Couzens, Apr. 25, 1931, CF Papers, Box 10; Gertrude Springer, "The Burden of Mass Relief," *Survey,* LXV (Nov. 15, 1930), 201.

13. JG, "Employment Situation in Detroit," with JG to Guy A. Matlock, Jan. 13, 1931, MOR; Beulah Amidon, "Detroit Does Something about It," *Survey,* LXV (Feb. 15, 1931), 540; *DN,* Sept. 16, 17, Oct. 22, Nov. 4, 6, 1930; Interview with Larry S. Davidow, May 12, 1967, p. 12, MHC; *DLN,* Sept. 19, 26, 1930; Outline of Organization, Activities and Program of the Mayor's Unemployment Committee (MUC) . . . to . . . Nov. 10, 1930, DUL Papers; Dancy et al. to E. E. Kramp, Oct. 9, 1930, ibid.; Organization, Activities, and Program of the MUC, Jan. 31, 1931, MOR.

14. *DN,* Sept. 25, Oct. 2, 8, 16, 25-31, Nov. 1-3, 7, 9-11, 14, 15, 22, 23, 25, 27, Dec. 8, 9, 15, 20, 1930, Jan. 18, Feb. 1, Oct. 29, Nov. 7, 8, 22, 23, 25, 1931, July 5, Nov. 6, Dec. 11, 1932, Feb. 8, 12, Mar. 1, 8, Apr. 30, 1933; Outline of MUC, Nov. 10, 1930, DUL Papers; Accomplishments of MUC, Sept. 16, 1930-Apr. 7, 1931, GM Papers; Edward J. Hickey to Felix Holt, Mar. 15, 1933, FM to Dear Friend, Apr. 24, 1933, MOR.

15. *DN,* Mar. 25, May 10, 24, July 21, Aug. 2, 4, Oct. 8, 10, Nov. 6, 1932, Feb. 8, 1933; Lewis to FM, June 19, 1931, MOR; undated typed sheet [1931], MOR; Report of Addresses . . . , Dec. 10, 1932, FM Papers.

16. *Proceedings of a Conference of Progressives,* p. 112, Norris Papers; Organization of MUC, Jan. 31, 1931, MOR; *DN,* Sept. 20-22, 24-26, 28, 1930.

17. William Haber, "Fluctuations in Employment in Detroit Factories, 1921-31," *Journal of the American Statistical Association,* XVIII (June 1932), 148; *DN,* Oct. 6, 11, 1931; Amidon, "Detroit Does Something," p. 540.

18. *DN,* Oct. 10, Dec. 27, 1930, Jan. 31, 1931; Outline of MUC, Nov. 10, 1930, DUL Papers; Robert S. Wilson, *Community Planning for*

Homeless Men and Boys: The Experience of Sixteen Cities in the Winter of 1930-31 (New York, 1931), p. 91.

19. *DN*, Sept. 26, 27, Oct. 1, 7, 21, Nov. 11, 1930; Outline of MUC, Nov. 10, 1930, DUL Papers; IM interview, pp. 40-41.

20. *DN*, Oct. 21, 1930, Sept. 9, Nov. 19, 20, 22, 1931; Organization of MUC, Jan. 31, 1931, MOR; Adams to Couzens, Oct. 13, 1932, MOR; Nina K. Perrin, Activities of the MUC for Oct. 1, 1930 to June 30, 1933, Aug. 5, 1933, MOR.

21. *DN*, Sept. 29, 30, Oct. 4, 6, 7, 14, Nov. 8, Dec. 10, 14, 16, 21, 27, 1930, Jan. 13, 23, Feb. 10, Oct. 4, 18, Dec. 3, 4, 1931, July 4, 1932; FM radio address [1931], MOR; JG, "Employment Situation," MOR; Outline of MUC, Nov. 10, 1930, DUL Papers; Perrin, Activities of MUC, Aug. 5, 1933, MOR.

22. *DN*, Sept. 26, Oct. 2, 13, 1930; JG, "Employment Situation," MOR; Organization of MUC, Jan. 1, 1931, MOR; Accomplishments of MUC, Sept. 16, 1930-Apr. 7, 1931, GM Papers; Norton to Couzens, Oct. 10, 1932, James L. Couzens Papers, LC.

23. *DN*, Sept. 24, 26, 28, Oct. 28, 30, 31, Nov. 11, 15, 19, Dec. 12, 1930, Apr. 26, May 7, 1931; Organization of MUC, Jan. 31, 1931, MOR.

24. *DN*, Sept. 26, 1930; Organization of MUC, Jan. 31, 1931, MOR.

25. *DN*, Nov. 5, Dec. 5, 1930; *DLN*, Nov. 7, 1930. For a taxpayers' suit regarding the legality of the Board of Education decision, see *DN*, Nov. 24, 1930.

26. Outline of MUC, Nov. 10, 1930, DUL Papers; Organization of MUC, Jan. 31, 1931, MOR; *DN*, Oct. 1, 1930.

27. *DN*, Oct. 9, 1930; *NYT*, Dec. 14, 1930.

28. *DN*, Oct. 13, 17, 26, Nov. 1, 5, 8, 15, 17, Dec. 1, 3, 12, 16, 23, 26, 28, 30, 1930, Jan. 2, 9, Feb. 19, Mar. 29, Apr. 12, 18, May 3, June 15, Aug. 21, Nov. 15, Dec. 3, 1931, Jan. 7, Feb. 7, 1932; J. Walter Fay, . . . Progress Report of Educational Museum . . . , undated, MOR; Fay statement, Jan. 15, 1932, CF Papers, Box 4; JG to Fay, Feb. 24, 1932, MOR; Perrin, Activities of MUC, Aug. 5, 1933, MOR.

29. *The Memoirs of Herbert Hoover: The Great Depression, 1929-1941* (New York, 1952), p. 195; *DN*, Nov. 8, 19, 20, 23, 24, Dec. 30, 1930, Jan. 5, 1931; Adams to Couzens, Oct. 13, 1932, MOR; Perrin, Activities of MUC, Aug. 5, 1933, MOR.

30. Terry Hamburg, "The Depression in Detroit: The First Year, October, 1929 to September, 1930" (MS, 1968), pp. 47-50, in my possession; S. H. Rhoads to FM, Jan. 9, 1931, FM to Common Council, Mar. 27, 1933, MOR; *DN*, July 23, 1931; J. Joseph Hutmacher, *Senator Robert F. Wagner and the Rise of Urban Liberalism* (New York, 1968), pp. 61-62; Bernstein, *Lean Years,* pp. 239-40; Detroit Department of Public Welfare, *Annual Report for the Calendar Year of 1930* [Detroit, 1931], p. 8; Lutomski interview.

31. *DN*, Sept. 26, Oct. 1, 2, 4, 5, 25, 1930, July 24, Aug. 4, 1931; JG,

"Employment Situation," MOR; FM to Common Council, Mar. 27, 1933, Hickey to Frank Couzens, May 15, 1933, J. E. McDermott et al. to Mayor and Common Council, June 27, 1933, MOR.

32. *DN*, Dec. 2, 5, 9, 10, 1930; *DT*, Dec. 2, 1930.

33. *DN*, Jan. 6, 8, 9, 21, 22, 25, 27-31, Feb. 17, 22, Mar. 18, July 23, 1931; Rhoads to FM, Jan. 9, 1931, FM to Rhoads, Jan. 14, 1931, John L. Boer to FM and Common Council, Jan. 31, 1931, FM to Samuel Beattie, Feb. 12, Mar. 7, 1931, Beattie to FM, Feb. 16, 1931, FM to Wilber M. Brucker, Apr. 9, 1931, JG to W. N. Doak, Aug. 28, 1931, Haber to Adams, Nov. 2, 1932, MOR; Report of the Conference . . . [Jan. 29, 1931], MOR.

34. *DN*, Oct. 4, 1930; McDermott et al. to Mayor and Common Council, June 27, 1933, JG to Hollingshead, June 27, 1932, FM to Common Council, Mar. 27, 1933, MOR; McDermott statement [Feb. 27, 1933], MOR; Perrin, Activities of MUC, Aug. 5, 1933, MOR.

35. *DN*, Oct. 1, 1930; Outline of MUC, Nov. 10, 1930, DUL Papers; Organization of MUC, Jan. 31, 1931, MOR; Mary McComas Edgar to Roy D. Chapin, Nov. 6, 1930, Feb. 10, 1931, Roy D. Chapin Papers, MHC.

36. *NYT*, Feb. 15, 1931; Wilson, *Community Planning*, pp. 91-92; *DSN*, June 28, 1930; *Community Fund News*, Mar. 1930; *DN*, Oct. 2, 23, Nov. 7, 1930.

37. *DN*, Sept. 24, Oct. 23, Nov. 15, 1930, July 22, 1931; Norton interview, p. 7; Norton to Couzens, Apr. 25, 1931, CF Papers, Box 10; Norton to Couzens, Oct. 10, 1932, Couzens Papers; JG, "Employment Situation," MOR.

38. *DN*, Oct. 23, 24, 28, Nov. 5, 25, Dec. 3, 23, 27, 1930; Wilson, *Community Planning*, pp. 92-93, 94.

39. *DN*, Oct. 23, 24, Nov. 2, 4, 6, 7, 11, 22, Dec. 1-3, 23, 27-29, 1930; Wilson, *Community Planning*, pp. 93-94.

40. E. F. Fisher to FM, Dec. 11, 1930, Oct. 25, 1932, MOR; *DN*, Dec. 8, 12, 13, 21, 23, 1930, Jan. 9, 13, 17, 21, Feb. 23, Mar. 3, 1931.

41. *DN*, Jan. 1, May 19, 1931; JG, "Employment Situation," MOR; Fred W. Jurgensen to Commanding Officer, 1st Precinct, Oct. 15, 1932, MOR.

42. *DN*, Jan. 14, Feb. 27, 1931; *DT*, Jan. 15, 1931.

43. *DN*, Jan. 9, Feb. 3, 5, 10, 23, 1931; Wilson, *Community Planning*, p. 95; *DSN*, Apr. 4, 1931; Charles R. Walker, "Down and Out in Detroit," in Charles A. Beard, ed., *America Faces the Future* (Boston, 1932), p. 77; *NYT*, Feb. 15, 1931; Albert S. Norris to FM, Feb. 4, 11, 1931, FM to Norris, Feb. 16, 1931, Joseph Lambert et al. to FM, June 9, 1932, MOR.

44. Wilson, *Community Planning*, pp. 95-96; FM to Common Council, June 23, 1931, MOR; Report of Voluntary Labor Performed by Homeless Single Men . . . , undated, MOR; *DN*, Mar. 15, 31, Apr. 18, 1931.

45. Wilson, *Community Planning*, p. 95; Kilroy to Public Welfare Commission, Mar. 9, 1931, MOR.

46. *DSN*, Apr. 4, 1931; *DN*, Dec. 9, 1930, Jan. 13, Feb. 11, 1931; JG statement, July 17, 1931, MOR.

47. Ralph K. Trix to FM, Apr. 20, 1931, MOR; *DN*, May 19, 31, June 17, 19, July 14, 1931.

48. Opal V. Matson, *Local Belief to Dependents* (n.p., 1933), pp. 24-29; *DN*, Feb. 27, June 5, 1931, Jan. 1, 1932; FM to Common Council, June 23, 1931, MOR; PWC Proceedings, Nov. 18, 1932. Of the 2,900 inmates at Eloise in July, 1931, only 272 were able-bodied unemployed persons. *DN*, July 10, 1931.

49. *DN*, June 5, 17, 19, 24, 25, 30, 1931; *DT*, July 7, 1931; Gilchrist to FM, June 23, 1931, FM to Common Council, June 23, 1931, MOR; PWC Proceedings, June 24, 30, 1931.

50. *DT*, July 3, 5, 7, 1931; *DFP*, July 4, 1931; *DN*, June 24, July 1-3, 6, Aug. 5, 1931. Murphy's close relationship with Martel may explain the preferential treatment accorded the DFL kitchen.

51. *DN*, July 6, 1931; *DT*, July 6, 8, 1931; Reynolds to FM, July 9, 1931, MOR.

52. *DN*, June 30, July 7-10, 1931; *DT*, July 8, 10, 1931; *DFP*, July 9, 1931; *DLN*, July 10, 1931; PWC Proceedings, July 7, 1931.

53. *DN*, May 12, July 9, 11, 12, 14, Sept. 2, 1931; Manistee *News-Advocate*, July 11, 1931, MSB; PWC Proceedings, Aug. 11, 1931, May 31, 1932; FM to William Chenay, Aug. 28, 1931, T. K. Gruber to JG, July 11, 1932, MOR. By July 28, 818 men had been admitted to Eloise from the lodges. PWC Proceedings, Aug. 11, 1931.

54. *DN*, July 12, 14, 21, Aug. 4, Sept. 2, 10, 11, Nov. 3, 4, 6, 11, Dec. 3, 1931; FM to Albert Fleming, Aug. 21, 1931, J. J. McLeod et al. to FM [Nov. 1931], MOR; JG statement, July 7, 1931, MOR; PWC Proceedings, Dec. 8, 1931. The lodgers met part of the cost of their maintenance by a wood-cutting program. *DN*, Dec. 3, 1931.

55. PWC Proceedings, May 26, 31, June 7, 1932; *DN*, May 31, June 1, 8-10, 13, 14, 1932; M. [?] J. Kennedy to FM, June 9, 1932, enclosing Lambert et al. to FM, June 9, 1932, MOR.

56. Roy E. Duquette to Taylor, Mar. 16, 1932, William Reese to FM, Nov. 18, 1932, MOR; *DN*, June 16, July 7, Oct. 18, 25, Nov. 2, 1932; Dos Passos, "Detroit: City of Leisure," *New Republic*, LXXI (July 27, 1932), 281.

57. James K. Watkins to FM, Nov. 16, 1932, Henry Vaughan to FM, Oct. 28, 1932, MOR; PWC Proceedings, Oct. 25, Nov. 18, 29, 1932; *DN*, Oct. 18, 1932.

58. *DN*, Oct. 19, 23, 26, Nov. 11, 13, 18-20, 22, 30, 1932; Ballenger to Public Welfare Commission, Nov. 18, 1932, MOR; PWC Proceedings, Aug. 30, Nov. 18, 29, 1932; Recommendation of the Welfare Commission [Nov. 29, 1932], MOR.

59. *DN*, Dec. 2, 8, 9, 1932, Jan. 5, 1933; PWC Proceedings, Jan. 4, 1933.

60. *DN*, Jan. 5, 1933, Aug. 12, Sept. 11, 1942.
61. JG, "Employment Situation," MOR; Norton to Couzens, Oct. 10, 1932, Couzens Papers; *DN*, Dec. 10, 11, 28, 1930, Feb. 4, 1932; Organization of MUC, Jan. 31, 1931, MOR; Accomplishments of MUC, Sept. 16, 1930 to Apr. 7, 1931, GM Papers; JG to Julia Carter, Nov. 18, 1932, MOR; PWC Proceedings, Aug. 11, Dec. 15, 1931; Wilson, *Community Planning*, p. 99n; FM, "The Detroit Plan," *Plain Talk*, Oct. 1932, p. 37.
62. *DN*, Dec. 4, 11, 1930, Mar. 17, Oct. 18, Nov. 13, 1931, Jan. 6, 1932; FM to Detroit . . . Relief Committee, Dec. 13, 1930, Frank Cody to Adams, Oct. 16, 1931, MOR; Memorandum from Social Service Committee to District Principals . . . , Jan. 13, 1932, CF Papers, Box 11; Perrin, Activities of MUC, Aug. 5, 1933, MOR.
63. Harry Barnard, *Independent Man: The Life of Senator James Couzens* (New York, 1958), pp. 187-88; William C. Richards and William J. Norton, *Biography of a Foundation: The Story of the Children's Fund of Michigan, 1929-1954* (n.p., 1957), pp. 129, 152; Scott M. Cutlip, *Fund Raising in the United States* (New Brunswick, 1965), pp. 58, 221; Norton interview, pp. 1-2.
64. Board of Trustees Minutes, Jan. 14, 1931, Jan. 14, 1932, Jan. 18, May 4, 1933, CF Papers, Box 1; A. N. Henningar to Norton, May 6, 1932, Jan. 27, June 6, 1933, ibid.; Memorandum to District Principals, Jan. 13, 1932, ibid., Box 11; L. A. Wiles to Norton, June 6, Sept. 29, 1932, ibid.; Report of Material Relief Program, May 1, 1931–Sept. 1, 1932, ibid.; *DN*, Dec. 11, 1930, Oct. 18, Nov. 13, 23, 28, 1931, May 28, July 6, 1932; PWC Proceedings, Mar. 7, 1933. The New York City Board of Education began to finance a school-lunch program in the fall of 1930, and the Philadelphia Committee for Unemployment Relief initiated a school-breakfast program soon thereafter. Bernstein, *Lean Years*, p. 295; Bonnie R. Fox, "Unemployment Relief in Philadelphia, 1930-1932: A Study of the Depression's Impact on Voluntarism," *Pennsylvania Magazine of History and Biography*, XCII (Jan. 1969), 100.
65. Percival Dodge to Couzens, Oct. 22, 1932, Couzens Papers; FM, "Detroit Plan," p. 37; Catlin, *The Story of Detroit* (Detroit, 1926), pp. 615-17; FM to Martin S. Hayden, Aug. 27, 1934, FM Papers; Melvin G. Holli, *Reform in Detroit: Hazen S. Pingree and Urban Politics* (New York, 1969), pp. 70-73; *DN*, Mar. 2, 3, 1931.
66. FM to James E. Devoe, Mar. 24, 1931, FM to H. J. Callahan, Mar. 21, 1931, JG to W. W. Arnett, Jr., Apr. 2, 1931, MOR; Henry A. Johnson, Report of the Detroit Thrift Gardens . . . [Jan. 22, 1932], Central Files, POUR Records; *DN*, July 10, 1932.
67. *DN*, Mar. 17, 22, 24, 27, 31, Apr. 18, 22, 29, 1931; FM to Bethune D. Blaine, Mar. 23, 1931, James M. O'Dea to FM, Apr. 28, 1931, MOR.
68. Johnson Report, POUR Records; *DN*, Mar. 13, 20, July 16-18, Oct.

1, 1931; JG to Ada L. Barrett, Jan. 19, 1933, MOR.

69. Adams to Olga A. Jones, Jan. 11, 1931 [1932], Central Files, POUR Records; Johnson Report, ibid.; Department of Public Welfare and Detroit Thrift Gardens Committee, Annual Report of the Detroit Thrift Gardens for the Garden Year Ending Oct. 31, 1933, FM Papers; Norton to F. W. Brooks, Apr. 29, 1932, Norton to Alice E. Robison, June 25, 1932, CF Papers, Box 11; Johnson to Committee Member, May 9, June 22, 1932, JG to Clara Swieczkowska, May 9, 1932, MOR.

70. *DN*, Jan. 25, Apr. 4, 1933; PWC Proceedings, Feb. 14, 21, 28, Mar. 21, 28, 1933; Report of Bureau of Markets, Mar., Apr. 1933, MOR; DPW to Welfare Clients, Mar. 23, Apr. 23, 1933, Joe Brown Collection, ALHUA; FM to Dear Friend, Apr. 24, 1933, MOR; Report of Thrift Gardens Committee, Oct. 31, 1933, CF Papers, Box 11; Hickey to Couzens, June 17, 1936, ibid. The Thrift Gardens Committee charged its gardeners fifty cents per garden.

71. Report of Thrift Gardens Committee, Oct. 31, 1933, CF Papers, Box 11; Gardeners of Field #12 to FM, undated, with Johnson to FM, Aug. 4, 1931, MOR.

72. Johnson Report, POUR Records; Report of Thrift Gardens Committee, Oct. 31, 1933, CF Papers, Box 11; *DN*, Apr. 24, 1932; Joanna C. Colcord and Mary Johnston, *Community Programs for Subsistence Gardens* (New York, 1933), pp. 43-44.

73. Joseph Takacs and family to FM, Sept. 18, 1931, MOR.

74. Colcord and Johnston, *Subsistence Gardens,* pp. 7, 9-10, 52-53; Department of Commerce, *Subsistence Gardens* (Washington, 1932).

75. *Crisis*, XXXVIII (Dec. 1931), 414; Roosevelt to D. W. Wade, Oct. 30, 1930, Dancy to T. Arnold Hill, Dec. 4, 1930; IM to Hill, Oct. 27, 1931, with Dancy to Hill, Nov. 13, 1931, Dancy to F. A. Jackson, Dec. 7, 1931, Dancy to Walter White, Mar. 9, 1932, DUL Papers; FM to Ballenger, Jan. 9, 1932, Ballenger to FM, Jan. 13, 1932, MOR.

76. Citizen of Detroit to Re-Finance [*sic*] Corporation of America, Aug. 1, 1932, RFC Records; Report of an Investigation of the Welfare Department of the City of Detroit, July 27, 1932, MOR; P. A. W. Fitzimmons to B. E. Hutchinson, July 30, 1932, DCL Papers.

77. Hickey to F. Couzens, May 15, 1933, MOR.

78. *DN*, Nov. 4, 11, 18, 25, 27, 29, Dec. 1, 2, 1930, July 17, 1931; *DT*, Nov. 30, 1930; *DLN*, Nov. 14, 21, 28, 1930; Norton to Couzens, Apr. 25, 1931, CF Papers, Box 10.

79. The Canadian labor issue seems to have been sidetracked.

80. *DT*, Nov. 29, Dec. 2, 1930; *DN*, Dec. 2, 9, 1930; *DLN*, Dec. 5, 12, 1930; *DFP*, Dec. 10, 1930; *NYT*, Dec. 14, 1930.

81. *DN*, Dec. 2, 4, 8, 1930; *DLN*, Dec. 5, 1930; William P. Lovett, "Detroit Feeds Its Hungry," *National Municipal Review*, XX (July 1931), 404; *Michigan Manufacturer and Financial Record*, XLVI (Dec. 6, 1930), 16; *DFP*, Dec. 1, 3, 1930; *Civic Searchlight*, Dec. 1930; *DSN*, Dec.

6, 1930; *NYT*, Oct. 12, Dec. 14, 1930.

82. *DN*, Jan. 18, 20, 27, Feb. 22, 25, Mar. 1, 8, May 24, June 2, Sept. 9, Oct. 8, Nov. 19, 1931, Jan. 7, Apr. 7, June 11, Sept. 9, 23, Oct. 22, Nov. 2, 3, 1932; Norton to Couzens, Nov. 16, 1931, CF Papers, Box 10; Adams to Joseph J. Majeske, Jan. 7, 1931 [1932], Adams to Taylor, Mar. 1, 1932, Adams to JG, Mar. 16, 1932, and enclosed document, Adams to Couzens, Oct. 13, 1932, JG to Fay, Feb. 24, 1932, JG et al. to Committee Member, Mar. 30, 1932, MOR; FM to EGK, Nov. 9, 1932, EGK Papers.

83. *DN*, Mar. 31, May 10, 12, 24, 27, 30, 31, June 2, 3, 7, 8, 10–12, 16, 23, July 5–7, 28, 1931, Mar. 25, 1933; *DLN*, Apr. 17, June 12, 1931; Adams to EGK, July 21, 1931, EGK Papers; Report of the Sub-Committee Studying the Milk Problem for Indigent Families, undated, MOR; Cole to G. V. Branch, May 8, 1931, Douglas Dow to Dolan, June 16, 1931, Adams and JG to Hoover, July 29, 1931, MUC to Wilcox, May 2, 1932, MOR; PWC Proceedings, June 15, 24, 1931.

84. *DN*, June 14, July 17, 1931, Dec. 23, 1932; *DLN*, July 31, 1931; Adams to FM, Nov. 21, 1932, Hickey to FM, Jan. 5, 1933, MOR.

85. *DN*, May 12, 19, 30, July 28, Aug. 4, 1931, Nov. 3, 1932, Jan. 3, Feb. 8, 1933; *DLN*, Aug. 7, 14, 1931; Report of Committee on Labor, May 17, 1931, Adams to EGK, Aug. 20, 1931, EGK Papers; Fram to FM, Aug. 11, 20, 1931, FM to Fram, Aug. 19, 1931, Hickey to F. Couzens, May 15, 1933, MOR.

86. *DN*, Feb. 8, 1933; Norton to F. Couzens, May 22, 1933, F. Couzens to Norton, May 31, 1933, CF Papers, Box 11; Hickey to F. Couzens, May 15, 1933, McDermott et al. to Mayor and Common Council, June 27, 1933, MOR; PWC Proceedings, Sept. 19, 1933; Detroit newspaper clipping, July 25, 1933, in FM Papers; FM to George R. Treble, Nov. 10, 1933, ibid.

87. See Fox, "Unemployment Relief," pp. 86–108. The Philadelphia committee provided direct relief, work relief, shelter for homeless men, breakfasts for indigent school children, and a revolving loan fund.

88. Joanna C. Colcord, "Unemployment Relief, 1929–1932," *Family*, XIII (Dec. 1932), 271; Davidow interview, p. 15; *DT*, Dec. 24, 1930; *DN*, Oct. 24, 1930, Jan. 27, Aug. 2, 1931; New York *World Telegram*, Mar. 13, 1931, MSB.

89. See, for example, Williams, *Federal Aid for Relief*, p. 17; and Charles Hathaway Trout, "Boston during the Great Depression" (Ph.D. thesis, Columbia University, 1972), pp. 181–84.

90. Norton, "Relief Crisis in Detroit," p. 10; *Community Fund News*, Nov. 1930, Feb., June, Sept. 1931, Jan., Apr. 1932; James H. Norton, "A History of the Detroit Community Fund and the Council of Social Agencies of Metropolitan Detroit, 1917–1938" (M.A. thesis, University of Michigan, 1940), pp. 78–80; *DN*, Feb. 23, June 17, Nov. 5, 14, 23, 1931, July 19, 1932; Minutes of the Meeting of the Executive

Committee, Advisory Relief Council, Nov. 23, 1931, CF Papers, Box 11; A Relief Program for Detroit . . . , Dec. 17, 1931, DUL Papers; Alice E. Stenholm, Report on Field Trip, Nov. 10–13, 1931, State Files, POUR Records; Norton to Couzens, Oct. 10, 1932, Couzens Papers.

91. *DN*, Feb. 27, Nov. 17, 1931, Sept. 4, Dec. 24, 1932, Jan. 22, 1933; Detroit *Jewish Chronicle*, Nov. 21, 1930, MSB; Hill to L. G. Lenhardt, June 14, 1932, Lenhardt to Joseph E. Mills, June 16, 1932, Mrs. James S. Fisher to FM, June 22, 1931, Madonna Guild to FM, Nov. 11, 1931, MOR; McGregor Institute, *Forty-First Annual Report, 1931* (n.p., n.d.); Relief Program for Detroit, Dec. 17, 1931, DUL Papers.

92. *DN*, Dec. 16, 1930, Apr. 24, 1931, Dec. 24, 1932; Annual Report of Detroit Attendance Department, 1931–1932, with Hennigar to Norton, Aug. 22, 1932, Hennigar to Norton, June 6, 1933, CF Papers, Box 11.

93. *DN*, Sept. 27, Oct. 10, 1930, Jan. 15, Feb. 12, Sept. 27, 30, 1932; Detroit Police Department, *Sixty-Fifth Annual Report, 1930* (Detroit, n.d.), p. 3; Detroit Police Department, *Sixty-Sixth Annual Report, 1931* (Detroit, n.d.), pp. 3, 6.

94. Harry L. Hosmer to FM, Jan. 11, 1932, MOR; *DT*, Jan. 12, 1932; *DN*, Dec. 4, 11, 25, 1931, Jan. 6, 7, 10, 17, 25, Feb. 8, 15, 23, Aug. 24, 1932; Board [of Health] Minutes, Jan. 22, 1932, MOR; PWC Proceedings, Dec. 15, 28, 1931, Sept. 6, 1932; Robert M. Warner, *Profile of a Profession: A History of the Michigan State Dental Association* (Detroit, 1964), pp. 170–71; *Bulletin of the Wayne County Medical Society*, XXIII (Jan. 12, 1932), 9.

95. Minutes of the Board of Trustees, Dec. 10, 1930, Jan. 14, Nov. 12, 1931, Jan. 14, June 22, Sept. 19, Nov. 10, 1932, Jan. 18, May 4, 1933, CF Papers, Box 1; Norton to Couzens, Jan. 8, 15, 1931, Nov. 21, 1932, Oct. 25, 1933, ibid., Box 10; Annual Report of Attendance Department, 1931–1932, ibid., Box 11; Report of Material Relief Program, May 1, 1931–Sept. 1, 1932, ibid.; Wiles to Norton, Sept. 29, 1932, and enclosed Summer Feeding Centers, Statement of Expenditures, June 27–Sept. 5, 1932, ibid.; *DN*, Nov. 28, 1931, May 1, 1933; Richardson and Norton, *Biography of a Foundation*, pp. 59–60, 132–33.

96. FM to Chapin, Sept. 25, 1930, Chapin Papers; *DN*, Sept. 27, 30, Oct. 10, 1930, Feb. 10, 1931, Jan. 10, May 13, 1932, Feb. 15, 1933; *DT*, Apr. 26, 1931, Apr. 2, 1933; *NYT*, Feb. 15, 1931; FM to C. E. Smith, May 25, 1932, Lovett to FM, Jan. 27, 1932, MOR; Raymond C. Miller, *Kilowatts at Work: A History of the Detroit Edison Company* (Detroit, 1957), pp. 337–38; Subcommittee of Senate Committee on Manufactures, *Unemployment Relief*, pp. 282, 285–86; *Michigan Manufacturer and Financial Record*, XLVIII (July 11, 1931), 10.

CHAPTER XII

1. *DN*, Apr. 5, 1931.
2. In the election of November 4, 1930, the voters agreed to increase the general public-improvement bonding limit from 4 to 4-1/2 percent but to decrease the street-railway limitation by the same percentage. *DN*, Nov. 5, 1930.
3. Egbert S. Wengert, *Financial Problems of the City of Detroit in the Depression*(Detroit, 1939), pp. 7–10, 12, 35; DBGR, *Accumulated Social and Economic Statistics for Detroit* (Detroit, 1937), p. 5; *DN*, Sept. 26, Nov. 5, 1930, May 3, 1931, July 17, 1932; *NYT*, May 17, 1931.
4. On this point, see *DN*, June 7, 1931, and *Journal of the Common Council*, Jan. 12, 1932, p. 3.
5. Wengert, *Financial Problems,* pp. 14–15, 32, 44–45; Ralph Stone to Mayor and Common Council, Jan. 7, 1931, MOR; *DN*, Dec. 6, 8, 1930, May 28, 29, 31, July 8, 1931.
6. Carl H. Chatters, "Municipal Finance," in Clarence E. Ridley and Orin F. Nolting, eds., *What the Depression Has Done to Cities* (Chicago, 1935), p. 2; Virginia Eyre, *A Study of Tax Delinquency in the Second Ward of Detroit* . . . (Detroit [1933]), pp. 3–4; Sidney G. Tickton, *An Analysis of Tax Delinquency* (Detroit, 1932), pp. 13–14; Wengert, *Financial Problems,* pp. 35–36; DBGR, *Just a Minute, No. 129,* Dec. 10, 1932; Stone to Mayor and Common Council, July 7, 1931, MOR.
7. Beyer, "Financial Dictators Replace Political Boss," *National Municipal Review,* XXII (Apr. 1933), 162–63, 165, (May 1933), 232–33; Ralph Stone, "Detroit, Practises Economy," *Review of Reviews,* LXXXV (June 1932), 26–28; FM radio address, undated, MOR; FM speech draft [Apr. 6, 1932], MOR; *DLN*, Apr. 8, 1932.
8. Beyer, "Financial Dictators" (May 1933), p. 234; Henry Hart, "The Decline, Fall and Resurrection of the Credit of the City of Detroit," *National Municipal Review,* XXV (June 1936), 349; Interview with JG, May 17, 1972.
9. *DN*, Dec. 5, 6, 12, 1930, Jan. 7, 1931; *Journal of the Common Council*, Jan. 13, 1931, p. 5.
10. Executive Orders Nos. 1, 3, 5, 7, 8, 12, Jan. 23. 28, Feb. 18, May 23, 1931, and undated, MOR; *DN*, Jan. 25, Mar. 9, May 23, 1931.
11. Wilcox to FM, June 2, 1931, R. G. Brand to Department Heads, May 19, June 3, 1931, Douglas Dow to FM, May 20, 1931, MOR; Memorandum Report from Roosevelt to Dow [June 23, 1931], MOR; *DN*, May 23, June 1, 1931.
12. *DN*, Dec. 13, 15, 19, 31, 1930, Feb. 20, June 19, 1931; *Journal of the Common Council,* Jan. 13, 1931, p. 5; Stone to FM, Jan. 2, 1931, Stone to Common Council, Jan. 2, 1931, FM to Stone, Jan. 2, 1931, FM to Hart, Jan. 13, Feb. 19, 1931, MOR.

13. *DN,* Feb. 2, 28, Mar. 1, 17, May 2–4, 8, 11, June 19, 1931; *NYT,* May 17, 1931; Wengert, *Financial Problems,* p. 48. Detroit's tax rate as of August, 1930, was the eighth highest among the thirteen largest cities in the nation. *DN,* Dec. 22, 1930.

14. *DT,* Mar. 2, 1931; *DN,* Mar. 11, 1931; C. C. McGill talk, Mar. 15, 1931, FM Papers; Chatters, "Municipal Finance," p. 2.

15. *DN,* Mar. 7–9, 11–14, Apr. 3, 1931; *DFP,* Mar. 11, 13, 1931; *Detroiter,* XXII (Mar. 16, 1931), 10; *Civic Searchlight,* Mar. 1931.

16. *DN,* Apr. 26, May 12, 18, 28, 1931; Wengert, *Financial Problems,* p. 12.

17. Wengert, *Financial Problems,* vi; *DN,* May 30, 31, June 7, 9, 12, 15–18, 25–27, 29, 30, July 1, 1931; *DFP,* May 19, 1972.

18. The estimates of the number of persons per case range from 4.2 to 4.7. Ballenger used the 4.5 figure.

19. *DN,* Oct. 1, 1930, Mar. 9, 1931; Dolan to FM, Sept. 29, Oct. 26, Dec. 5, 30, 1931, Jan. 27, 1931 [1932], Mar. 1, Apr. 4, 1932, MOR; William J. Norton, "The Relief Crisis in Detroit," *Social Service Review,* VII (Mar. 1933), 4; IM to FM, Apr. 23, 1931, FM Papers; Interview with IM, July 30, 1964, pp. 40–42, MHC.

20. Detroit Department of Public Welfare, *Annual Report for the Calendar Year of 1930* [Detroit, 1931], pp. 5–6; Norton, "Relief Crisis," p. 4; IM to FM, Apr. 23, 1931, Sophia T. Cole to FM [June 13, 1931], FM Papers; [Pence Committee] to FM, Feb. 3, 1931, MOR; Dolan to FM, July 21, 1931, MOR; *DSN,* Feb. 7, 1931; *DN,* June 14, 1931; Gertrude Springer, "The Burden of Mass Relief," *Survey,* LXV (Nov. 15, 1930), 199; Beulah Amidon, "Detroit Does Something about It," ibid., Feb. 15, 1931, p. 540; ibid., LXVI (July 15, 1931), 405.

21. Cole to FM [June 13, 1931], FM Papers; *DN,* Dec. 27–30, 1930, Jan. 17, 20, 23, 29, Feb. 6, June 10, 1931; Norton to James Couzens, Apr. 25, 1931, CF Papers, Box 10; Norton, "Relief Crisis," p. 4; [Pence Committee] to FM, Feb. 3, 1931, MOR.

22. *DN,* Feb. 6, 18, Mar. 3, 24, Apr. 12, 17, 18, May 10, 13, 1931; Norton to Couzens, Apr. 25, May 2, 1931, CF Papers, Box 10.

23. *DT,* Apr. 16, 27, 1931; *DLN,* May 15, 22, 1931; *DFP,* Apr. 24, 1931; *DN,* Mar. 20, Apr. 22, 23, May 3, 1931; McGill radio talk, May 10, 1931, MOR; Lovett to FM, May 1, 1931, and enclosed resolution, MOR; Norton to Couzens, Apr. 25, May 2, 1931, Couzens to FM, Apr. 27, 1931, CF Papers, Box 10.

24. *DN,* Apr. 27, May 3, 4, 1931; *DT,* Mar. 21, 1931; FM to George W. Trendle, Apr. 29, 1931, MOR.

25. *DN,* Apr. 5, 7, 14, 17, 18, May 12, 1931; Report of the Food Committee [May 1931], MOR. See also Visiting Housekeeper Association, Scale for Estimating Minimum Budget for Dependent and Independent Families, Nov. 15, 1930, May 15, 1931, DUL Papers.

26. *DN,* Apr. 26, May 7, 10, 19, June 3, 16, 26, July 8, 1931; Queen,

"What Is Unemployment Doing to Family Social Work?...," *Family*, XII (Feb. 1932), 300; Charles Hathaway Trout, "Boston during the Great Depression, 1929-1940" (Ph.D. thesis, Columbia University, 1972), pp. 179-81.

27. Employment in Detroit area factories rose from 174,250 in February to 184,980 in May and then fell to 171,550 in June. William Haber, "Fluctuations in Employment in Detroit Factories, 1921-31," *Journal of the American Statistical Association*, XXVII (June 1932), 144.

28. Dolan to FM, July 21, 1931, MOR; Council of Social Agencies, "A Brief Summary of Historical and Current Data on the Detroit Department of Public Welfare," Jan. 1933, p. 69, MOR; Edward Ainsworth Williams, *Federal Aid for Relief* (New York, 1939), p. 17; Department of Public Welfare, *The Department of Public Welfare, 1930 to 1940* (Detroit, n.d.), p. 84; *DN*, Nov. 6, 30, 1930; Oliver P. Baker to Harvey Campbell, Nov. 21, 1932, and enclosed document, MOR; James Joseph Hannah, "Urban Reaction to the Great Depression in the United States" (Ph.D. thesis, University of California at Berkeley, 1956), pp. 104-6; Arthur Edward Burns, "Federal Emergency Relief Administration," in *The Municipal Year Book, 1937* (Chicago, 1937), p. 388; Department of Public Welfare, Schedule of Case Loads and Expenditures, July 1, 1929-June 30, 1933, EGK Papers; FM to Joseph T. Finnegan, Sept. 29, 1934, FM Papers; Emma A. Winslow, *Trends in Different Types of Public and Private Relief in Urban Areas, 1929-35* (Washington, 1937), pp. 72-85.

29. Norton, "Relief Crisis," p. 4; *DN*, June 9, 10, 1931; *DFP*, June 10, 1931.

30. *DSN*, June 20, 1931; *DN*, June 11, 12, 1931; *DFP*, June 11, 13, July 20, 1931. Cf. *Detroiter*, XXII (June 29, 1931), 10.

31. Jim Lee to FM, June 14, 1931, FM Papers; Lovett to H. W. Dodds, June 13, 1931, DCL Papers.

32. Only 65 of the 529 DPW employees, nearly all of whom were on the county payroll, were not on civil service. *DN*, June 17, 1931.

33. *DN*, June 11, 13, 14, 1931; *DT*, June 14, 1931.

34. *DN*, June 10, 13, 15, 16, 19, July 7, 14, 15, Aug. 4, Sept. 11, 16, 1931, Nov. 28, 1937; Touche, Niven and Co. to Toy, July 10, 1931, MOR. The other investigations were conducted by Roosevelt, Ballenger, and the police.

35. FM to L. W. Cunningham, May 13, 1931, MOR; *DN*, Feb. 6, 10, Mar. 10, Apr. 9, 21, 26, June 16, 1931; *DT*, Apr. 26, 1931.

36. *DN*, June 12, 13, 1931.

37. *DN*, June 12, 14-18, 21, 23, 1931.

38. *DN*, June 17, 19-27, 29, July 2, 1931; Samuel M. Levin, "The Ford Unemployment Policy," *American Labor Legislation Review*, XXII (June 1932), 107.

39. Ten men to FM, June [?] 16, 1931, Ward to FM, June 24, 1931,

FM to Ward, June 25, 1931, FM Papers.

40. See, for example, Marshall *Evening Chronicle,* Oct. 1, 1930, MSB; Akron *Times-Press,* Oct. 15, 1930, MSB; Cleveland *News,* Oct. 18, 1930, MSB; and New York *World-Telegram,* Mar. 13, 1931, MSB.

41. "Detroit's Duel over Doles," *Literary Digest,* CX (July 11, 1931), 11; Washington *Post,* June 23, 1931, MSB; Kansas City *Star,* June 24, 25, 1931, MSB; Springfield (Missouri) *Leader,* June 26, 1931, MSB; Chicago *Tribune,* July 5, 1931, MSB.

42. FM to James F. Murphy, Mar. 10, 1932, FM to W. A. S. Douglas, July 8, 1931, MOR; Stone, "Detroit Practises Economy," p. 27.

43. Stone to Mayor and Common Council, July 7, 1931, Upson to FM, Dec. 31, 1931, MOR; *DN,* July 7, 8, 13–15, 24, 1931; C. E. Rightor to Arthur F. Lederle, Dec. 12, 1933, EGK-BHC Papers, Box 15.

44. *DN,* June 7, Aug. 3–7, 13, 28, Nov. 3, 8, 20, 22, 1931, Nov. 29, 1932; *DT,* Aug. 13, 1931; Wengert, *Financial Problems,* pp. 12, 16; Stone to FM, July 16, 1931, Mar. 23, 1932, FM to Bankers Co. of New York, Aug. 13, 1931, Stone to Common Council, Jan. 22, 1932, MOR; Lovett to Mayo Fesler, Dec. 15, 1931, Lovett to Howard A. Coffin, Mar. 23, 1932, DCL Papers.

45. *DN,* July 5, 8, Aug. 12, 13, Oct. 15, 16, Nov. 18, Dec. 4, 30, 1931; Upson and R[ightor] document, Nov. 17, 1932, MOR; Committee on Efficiency and Economy to FM, Dec. 22, 1931, Roosevelt to FM, Jan. 29, 1932, MOR; First Detroit Co., How Detroit Is Keeping Its Expenditures within Its Actual Cash Income, Mar. 8, 1932, MOR.

46. *DN,* July 8, Dec. 14, 28, 31, 1931, Jan. 3, 5, 6, 10, 11, 13, 15, 16, 19, 21, 27, Feb. 1, 12, 24, 26, 1932; *DSN,* Mar. 5, 1932; *DFP,* Jan. 7, 1932; FM to Andrew Biddle, Aug. 22, 1931, E. S. Evans to FM, Jan. 25, 1932, MOR; Report of the Committee on Accounting and Business Procedure [Dec. 1931], MOR; McGill speech, Jan. 31, 1932, MOR.

47. Roosevelt to Common Council, Mar. 21, 1932, FM to Stone, Mar. 22, 1932, Stone to FM, Mar. 23, 1932, FM to E. F. Dustan, Mar. 28, 1932, MOR; *DN,* Mar. 22–24, 31, 1932.

48. Roosevelt to FM, Mar. 29, 1932, MOR; *DN,* Mar. 29, 31, 1932.

49. *DN,* Feb. 3, Mar. 9, 25, Apr. 1, 2, 1932; *DT,* Apr. 4, 1932; FM to Stone, Sept. 30, Nov. 19, 1931, MOR; FM address [Apr. 3, 1932], MOR; Lovett to William S. Gilbreath, Apr. 6, 1932, DCL Papers.

50. *DFP,* Apr. 3, 1932; *DT,* Apr. 4, 1932; *DN,* Apr. 5, 1932; Stone to FM and Common Council, Apr. 4, 1932, FM Papers; Stone statement [Apr. 4, 1932], MOR; Stone to Clark C. Brooks, Ralph Stone Papers, MHC.

51. *DT,* Dec. 21, 1931; *DN,* Apr. 6–8, 13–19, 21, 1932; *Detroiter,* XXIII (Apr. 11, 1932), 8; Stone to Roy Chapin, Apr. 7, 1932, Roy Chapin Papers, MHC; Charles M. Kennedy to Stone, Apr. 4, 1932, Harry B. Seldon to Stone, Apr. 4, 1932, Lester C. Batdorf to Stone, Apr.

4, 1932, Ralph B. Wilkinson to Stone, Apr. 5, 1932, E. S. Clarkson to Stone, Apr. 5, 1932, Stone Papers.

52. FM to Common Council, Apr. 22, 1932, MOR; *DN,* Apr. 22-30, May 1, 3, 5, 10, 11, 18, 27, June 2, 7, 12, 14, 25, 1932; *DT,* Apr. 25, 1932. The salary reductions did not apply to salaries below $25 a week, and salaries between $25 and $50 were reduced to $25.

53. Mauritz A. Hallgren, "Grave Danger in Detroit," *Nation,* CXXXV (Aug, 3, 1932), 100; *DSN,* Apr. 23, 1932; *DN,* Apr. 23, 1932; Stone to A. Mitchell Palmer, Apr. 28, 1932, Stone Papers.

54. Executive Orders Nos. 15, 25, 29, July 9, Nov. 13, 1931, Feb. 16, 1932, MOR; Committee on Efficiency and Economy to FM, Dec. 22, 1931, Dow to Roosevelt, Jan. 2, 1932, Dow to Common Council, Jan. 15, 1932, MOR; *DN,* Aug. 13, Oct. 19-23, Nov. 2, 20, 1931, Jan. 11, Apr. 5, 1932.

55. Frank W. Herring, "Public Works," in Ridley and Nolting, eds., *Depression,* p. 33; Minutes of the Meetings of Committee on Operating Efficiency, Oct. 2, Nov. 6, Dec. 4, 1931, Jan. 29, Feb. 5, 1932, MOR; Mills to Wilcox, June 10, 1931, Mills to FM, Oct. 31, Dec. 24, 1931, Lenhardt to FM, Feb. 17, Dec. 29, 1932, MOR; Total Expenditures, Department of Public Works [1932], MOR; Department of Public Works, Annual Report, Calendar Year 1932, p. 2, MOR; *DN,* June 7, 1932.

56. *DN,* Dec. 4, 8, 16, 21, 27, 1931, Jan. 10, Feb. 1, Apr. 5, May 3, 27, 1932; William P. Frost and John S. Foley to FM, Apr. 21, 1932, FM Papers; Joseph R. Young, "A History of Public Lighting in Detroit" (M.A. thesis, Wayne State University, 1937), pp. 80-81; L. J. Schrenk, "Street Lighting and Fatal Traffic Accidents in Detroit," *American City,* XLIX (May 1934), 101.

57. C. E. Brewer to FM, Mar. 9, 17, 1932, FM to Leon Fram, Jan. 7, 1932, FM to James Cash, Feb. 27, 1932, FM to Roosevelt, June 10, 1932, H. W. Busch to Common Council, Mar. 8, 1932, Alvan Macauley, Jr., to FM, Jan. 8, 1931, Sidney D. Waldon to FM, Sept. 9, 1932, and attached draft of interview with FM, MOR; Department of Parks and Boulevards, Annual Report for . . . , 1931, MOR; Mayor's Port Commission, Minutes, Oct. 3, 1932, MOR; *DN,* Oct. 30, Nov. 3, 10, Dec. 13, 1930, Jan. 8, 9, Feb. 15, 1932; *Journal of the Common Council,* Jan. 13, 1931, p. 2.

58. *DN,* July 5, Aug. 12, 21, 25, 1931, Jan. 7, 11, 16, 18, Feb. 4, Apr. 13, May 13, June 12, 1932; John F. Thomas to FM, Jan. 25, 1932, JG to Eleanor Schelke, Feb. 3, 1932, FM to Jane Hammer, Apr. 25, 1932, Helen M. Crane to FM, Apr. 25, 1932, JG to I. M. Raupp, May 2, 1932, Clyde H. Burroughs to FM, Jan. 6, May 5, 1932, MOR; R. L. Duffus, *Our Starving Libraries* (Boston, 1933), pp. 12-26; Detroit Library Commission Proceedings, Feb. 16, 1932, MOR; Detroit Library Commission, *Sixty-Sixth Annual Report, 1930-1931* (Detroit, n.d.), p.

10, *Sixty-Seventh Annual Report, 1931–1932* (Detroit, n.d.), pp. 4, 8, *Sixty-Eighth Annual Report, 1932–1933* (Detroit, n.d.), pp. 7–8; Address of Clyde H. Burroughs, May 12 [1932], MOR.

59. *DN*, Jan. 7, 1932; Board Minutes, Jan. 22, 1932, MOR; Henry F. Vaughan to FM, Feb. 5, 1932, MOR.

60. *DN*, Dec. 1, 3, 1931, Jan. 1, 8, 11, 15, 22, 27, 31, Feb. 9, Mar. 9, 1932; *DSN*, Mar. 19, 1932; Watkins Statement to the Press, Jan. 7, 1932, MOR; H. D. Baker to FM, Jan. 27, 1932, Watkins to FM, Feb. 4, 1932, Watkins to William Curran, June 13, 1932, MOR; Detroit Police Department, *Sixty-Seventh Annual Report, 1932* (Detroit, n.d.), p. 4.

61. Helen E. Phillips, "History of the Fire Department of the City of Detroit" (M.A. thesis, Wayne State University, 1941), pp. 53–54; *DN*, Jan. 9, 20, Feb. 26, Mar. 12, Apr. 12, 1932; Joseph A. Reed to All Members of Department, Jan. 14, 1932, C. Hayward Murphy to FM, Jan. 21, Feb. 5, 1932, MOR; Minutes of the Meeting of Board of Fire Commissioners, Mar. 10, 1932, MOR; Percy Bugbee, "Fire Service," in Ridley and Nolting, eds., *Depression*, p. 37.

62. *DN*, Jan. 21, 24, 26, Mar. 25, July 10, 1932; *Journal of the Common Council*, Jan. 12, 1932, p. 4; Stone to Common Council, Jan. 22, 1932, FM to Common Council, Mar. 8, 1932, MOR.

63. *DN*, Feb. 21, 28, Mar. 9, 12, 25, 29, Apr. 12, 13, 22, 28, 29, June 19–21, 28, July 22, 1932; Stone to FM, Apr. 21, 1932, FM to Common Council, Mar. 8, Apr. 26, 28, 1932, Lenhardt to FM, Dec. 29, 1932, MOR; Roosevelt Memorandum to FM, May 27, 1932, FM Papers; Roosevelt statement, June 17, 1932, MOR; *DLN*, May 27, 1932.

64. J. A. Burns to FM, July 1, 1932, MOR; *DN*, May 5, June 30, 1932.

65. *DN*, Oct. 7, 29, Dec. 6, 9, 1931, Jan. 28–31, Feb. 2, 3, 8, Mar. 21, 22, Apr. 19–22, May 8, 11, June 7, 8, 15, 23, 24, 1932; Eyre, *Tax Delinquency*, p. 3.

66. *DN*, Dec. 13, 1931, Mar. 22, 1932; FM to William Mills, Feb. 17, 1932, MOR; City of Detroit, General City Tax Bill [1931], FM Papers.

67. The 1931–32 budget included $200,000 for family relief, $200,000 for hospitalization of the needy, and $175,000 for rent. *DN*, July 7, 1931. See also *DN*, July 6, 8, 14, Aug. 21, 25, 26, 1931; and Dolan to Common Council, Aug. 25, 1931, MOR.

68. *DN*, July 1, 2, 3, 7, 8, 12, 1931; *DT*, July 7, 1931; FM to Harold Titus, July 1, 1931, FM Papers; FM to Douglas, July 8, 1931, MOR; *Time*, XVIII (July 20, 1931), 17.

69. Report of the Relief and Social Service Division [July 1931], MOR; PWC Proceedings, July 8, 17, 1931; Report of an Investigation of the Welfare Department of the City of Detroit, July 27, 1932, MOR.

70. Norton, "Relief Crisis," p. 5; PWC Proceedings, July 7, 8, 17, 24, 1931; Whalen to Public Welfare Commission, Aug. 20, 1931 (with Dolan to Common Council, Aug. 25, 1931), DPW to Executives of

Detroit Social Agencies, Oct. 6, 1931, MOR; *DN*, July 10, 14, 18, 25, 28, 1931.

71. PWC Proceedings, July 17, 1931; *DN*, July 18, 1931.
72. PWC Proceedings, July 24, Sept. 15, 1931; Whalen to Public Welfare Commission, Aug. 20, 1931, Dolan to FM, Sept. 29, 1931, MOR; Report of Welfare Aid Committee, Sept. 30, 1931, EGK Papers; *DN*, July 25, 29, 31, Aug. 4, 20, 26, 27, Sept. 16, Dec. 3, 1931.
73. Report of Welfare Aid Committee, Sept. 30, 1931, EGK Papers.
74. PWC Proceedings, July 17, 24, 1931; Whalen to Public Welfare Commission, Aug. 20, 1931, MOR; *DN*, July 30, Aug. 2, 16, Oct. 24, 1931; *DT*, Nov. 19, 1931; Eric Kocher, *Economic and Physical Growth of Detroit, 1701–1935* (n.p., 1935), p. 79.
75. *DT*, July 10, 1931; *DN*, July 19, 28, 30, Aug. 1, 1931; Whalen to Public Welfare Commission, Aug. 20, 1931, MOR.
76. For the starvation controversy, see the folder of material on the subject in the Joe Brown Collection, ALHUA; *New Republic*, LXVIII (Oct. 7, 1931), 192; ibid., LXIX (Nov. 25, 1931), 30; *Labor News*, Sept. 9, 1931; C. H. McLean to FM, Aug. 28, 1931, MOR; *DN*, Oct. 21, 22, 29, 1931; PWC Proceedings, Oct. 20, 1931; FM to Merlin [Merle] Thorpe, Oct. 28, 1931, Harvey Campbell to Thorpe, Oct. 30, 1931, Central Files, POUR Records; McGill talk, Nov. 1, 1931, MOR; typed excerpt from *Pravda*, MOR; IM interview, p. 39.
77. *DN*, July 30, Aug. 14, 1931; Report of Welfare Aid Committee, Sept. 30, 1931, EGK Papers.
78. Wilhelmina Luten, "A Survey of 1200 Families, Detroit Department of Public Welfare," *Family*, XIII (June 1932), 127–30; *DN*, Oct. 13, 1931; Subcommittee of Senate Committee on Manufactures, *Unemployment Relief. Hearings on S. 174 and S. 262*, 72 Cong., 1 Sess. (Washington, 1932), p. 280. The findings in a study by the Philadelphia Community Council of 400 families cut off from relief in that city in 1932 are strikingly similar to the results of the Detroit survey. See Ewan Clague, "When Relief Stops What Do They Eat?," *Survey*, LXVIII (Nov. 15, 1932), 583–85.
79. PWC Proceedings, July 7, 24, 1931, Jan. 12, 26, Feb. 16, May 12, 1932; *DN*, July 8, 9, 12, 18, 21, 25, Aug. 4, 5, Sept. 16, Dec. 4, 29, 1931, Jan. 27, Feb. 17, Mar. 1, 11, June 15, 1932; Norton, "The Situation in Detroit" [Sept. 1931], CF Papers, Box 11; William Gutman et al. to Welfare Department, Feb. 29, 1932, and enclosed report, MOR; Welfare Investigation Report, July 27, 1932, MOR; Rowland Haynes to F. C. Croxton, Dec. 16, 1931, State Files, POUR Records; Lovett to Upson, Aug. 5, 1931, DCL Papers.
80. PWC Proceedings, July 14, 24, Nov. 24, Dec. 8, 1931; *DFP*, June 2, 1931; *DN*, July 9, 15, Aug. 5, 12, 1931, Jan. 14, 21, Feb. 2, 18, Mar. 4, Aug. 16, 1932; W. J. Cassidy to FM, Aug. 13, 1931, Mildred Sheldon to City Welfare Commission, Jan. 26, 1932, Annie L. Bryant

to JG, Apr. 25, 1932, Dolan to FM, June 30, 1932, MOR; *Community Fund News,* Sept. 1931.

81. Sophia T. Cole, "We Dip Into Farm Placement," *Family,* XIII (May 1932), 79–81; FM to Frank E. Kelsey, Feb. 23, 1932, JG to Julia Thomas, Mar. 23, 1932, JG to William R. Gunning, Apr. 22, 1932, JG to Kelley C. Cater, May 18, 1932, FM to Ray Herbert, May 6, 1933, MOR; PWC Proceedings, Oct. 20, 27, 1931; Report of the Municipal Bureau of Markets, Feb. 1933, MOR; notice of meeting on Mar. 23, 1933, MOR; *DN,* Oct. 21, 22, Nov. 4, 17, 1931.

82. PWC Proceedings, July 7, Aug. 11, Sept. 2, 15, Dec. 8, 1931, Apr. 5, 1932; *DN,* July 21, 25, 26, 28, Aug. 5, Sept. 16, Dec. 7, 9, 1931, Feb. 11, Aug. 31, Oct. 11, 18, 1932. The DPW had spent about 5.5 percent of its 1931–32 budget for rent as of May, 1932, as compared to 15 percent in 1930–31. Dolan to FM, July 21, 1931, MOR; *DN,* May 23, 1932.

83. PWC Proceedings, July 8, 14, Aug. 4, 1931; T. J. Moppins et al. to Ballinger [*sic*], Dec. 30, 1931, G. V. Branch to Public Welfare Commission, Aug. 4, 1931, Virginia Alfano to FM, July 28, 1932, FM to James W. Ames, July 11, 1932, MOR; Welfare Investigation Report, July 27, 1932, MOR; *DN,* Apr. 21, June 24, July 8, Aug. 5, 1931; Joanna C. Colcord, *Cash Relief* (New York, 1936), pp. 18–19; "Welfare Cafeterias Out," *Survey,* LXIX (Jan. 1933), 39.

84. Welfare Investigation Report, July 27, 1932, MOR; PWC Proceedings, June 21, Nov. 9, 1932, June 7, Aug. 8, 1933; *DN,* July 8, 15, 1931, Jan. 15, Apr. 12, 28, June 20, July 4, 12, Aug. 2, 3, Nov. 7, 1932; *Survey,* LXVIII (Aug. 15, 1932), 370; "Welfare Cafeterias Out," p. 39.

85. PWC Proceedings, July 14, Aug. 4, 1931, Feb. 9, 1932; Branch et al. to Public Welfare Commission, Aug. 4, 1931, MOR; *DN,* July 15, 1931, Feb. 10, 11, July 10, 1932.

86. PWC Proceedings, Mar. 8, 1932, July 11, 1933; *DN,* Feb. 10, Mar. 9, 10, 13, Apr. 2, 1932; Luten, "Survey of 1200 Families," p. 128; Welfare Investigation Report, July 27, 1932, MOR; "No One Has Starved," *Fortune,* VI (Sept. 1932), 80.

87. *DN,* Dec. 25, 1931, Jan. 7, 9, 14–16, Feb. 28, 1932; "Nutrition in Hard Times," *Survey,* LXVII (Mar. 15, 1932), 691; Welfare Investigation Report, July 27, 1932, MOR; Minutes of Board of Trustees, Jan. 14, 1932, CF Papers, Box 1; ——— to Norton [Jan. 14, 1932], CF Papers, Box 17.

88. A work-relief program had been put into effect briefly by the Bowles administration. Carol A. Horne, "Detroit: The First Year of Depression, 1929–1930" (MS [1966]), pp. 37–38, in my possession.

89. *DN,* Nov. 19, Dec. 12, 1930, Jan. 29, Apr. 21, July 6, 24, 28, 1931; Dolan to FM, July 21, 1931, MOR; Wills, *Nixon Agonistes* (Signet Book; New York, 1971), p. 489; Joanna C. Colcord, "Unemployment

Relief, 1929-1932," *Family,* XIII (Dec. 1932), 271-72; Joanna C. Colcord et al., *Emergency Work Relief . . . 1930-1931 . . .* (New York, 1932), pp. 12, 20, 26-30, 225-28, 246.

90. Mills to FM, July 27, 1931, MOR; PWC Proceedings, Aug. 18, Oct. 27, 1931; Minutes of Committee on Operating Efficiency, Aug. 24, 1931, MOR; Welfare Investigation Report, July 27, 1932, MOR; *DN,* Aug. 4, 7, 12, 14, 30, 1931.

91. PWC Proceedings, Aug. 18, Sept. 15, 1931, May 3, June 3, July 5, 1932; FM, "The Detroit Plan," *Plain Talk,* Oct. 1932, p. 36; Public Welfare Commission to Common Council, May 12, 1932, Hill to FM, Feb. 8, 1932, MOR; Minutes of . . . Department of Public Works, June 10, 1932, MOR; Department of Public Works, Annual Report, Calendar Year 1932, p. 9, MOR; Welfare Investigation Report, July 27, 1932, MOR; *DN,* Aug. 15, 16, 25, Sept. 11, 27, 1931, June 3, 1932.

92. Colcord, "Unemployment Relief," p. 272; Couzens to FM, Aug. 21, 1931, FM to Couzens, Aug. 24, 1931, FM to Mrs. Alfred G. Wilson, Oct. 2, 1931, Alvan Macauley to FM, Oct. 8, 1931, Matilda Wilson to FM, Oct. 16, 1931, MOR; FM to Fred A. Alger et al., Oct. 1, 1931, Norton to Couzens, Oct. 5, 1931, CF Papers, Box 10; Report of Visit of Rowland Haynes to Michigan, Nov. 10, 1931, State Files, POUR Records; Alice E. Stenholm, Report on Field Trip, Nov. 10-13, 1931, ibid.; *DN,* Aug. 22, 23, 25, 27, Sept. 12, Oct. 13, 14, 1931; *DSN,* Aug. 29, 1931; Harry Barnard, *Independent Man: The Life and Times of James Couzens* (New York, 1958), p. 203. Couzens indicated that he was willing to consider some other amount if the sum he had proposed was too large or too small.

93. Couzens Memorandum, Oct. 30, 1931, James Couzens Papers, LC; FM to Charles Fisher, Nov. 4, 1931, MOR; Norton to FM, Nov. 6, 1931, and enclosed statement, Norton to Couzens, Nov. 16, 1931, CF Papers, Box 11; PWC Proceedings, Dec. 28, 1931; *DN,* Nov. 10, 12, 1931.

94. *DN,* Nov. 5, 8-16, 20, 1931; FM to Mrs. Henry Sheldon, Nov. 2, 1931, JG to Sheldon, Nov. 24, 1931, MOR; Norton to Couzens, Nov. 16, 1931, CF Papers, Box 11.

95. Norton to Couzens, Nov. 16, 1931, Norton to FM, May 12, 1932, CF Papers, Box 11; *DN,* Nov. 13, 17, 18, 28, Dec. 22, 30, 1931, Jan. 3, Feb. 13, Mar. 21, Apr. 21, May 1, 5, 1932; *DT,* Aug. 26, 1931; Public Welfare Commission to Common Council, May 12, 1932, MOR; Interview with William J. Norton, undated, pp. 5, 7, MHC.

96. PWC Proceedings, Dec. 28, 1931, Mar. 15, Apr. 19, 1932; Dolan to FM, May 2, June 14, Oct. 14, 1932, MOR; Welfare Investigation Report, July 27, 1932, MOR; *DN,* Nov. 13, 19, Dec. 1, 13, 20, 1931, Mar. 1, 16, 31, Apr. 6, 7, 21, May 1, 5, 1932; Subcommittee of Senate Committee on Manufactures, *Unemployment Relief,* p. 282.

97. *DN,* Mar. 4, Apr. 21, 22, 26, 27, May 1, 12, 16, 23, 25, 29, June 3, 6-8, 18, 22, 30, July 1, 11, 17, 26, 1932; PWC Proceedings, Mar. 15, Apr. 26, May 10, 24, 26, June 7, 21, July 26, 1932; Public Welfare Commission to Common Council, May 12, 1932, MOR; Haynes to Croxton, Mar. 29, 1932, Central Files, POUR Records; Welfare Investigation Report, July 27, 1932, MOR.
98. PWC Proceedings, June 27, July 12, 1932; Guy Durgan to FM, June 27, 1932, MOR; *DN,* June 24, 27-30, July 3, 12-14, 29, Aug. 14, 1932.
99. JG to Paul Jones, Mar. 23, 1932, District Committee, Communist Party to FM, Aug. 3, 1932, MOR; *DN,* July 2, 6, 22, 25, 26, 29, 31, Aug. 1-7, 1932; Hallgren, "Grave Danger in Detroit," p. 99; "No One Has Starved," pp. 22-24, 28, 80-84; Colcord, *Cash Relief,* p. 132; Albert U. Romasco, *The Poverty of Abundance: Hoover, the Nation, the Depression* (New York, 1965), pp. 166-69.

CHAPTER XIII

1. Opal V. Matson, *Local Relief to Dependents* (n.p., 1933), pp. 9, 11, 13, 19; William Gutman et al. to Welfare Department, Feb. 29, 1932, and enclosed report, MOR; *DN,* Apr. 9, June 25-30, July 2, 13, Oct. 3, 8, 13, 1931, Jan. 5, 6, Mar. 16, Sept. 1, 1932.
2. Norton to Couzens, Apr. 3, 1933, CF Papers, Box 10; Alice E. Stenholm, Report on Field Trip, Nov. 10-13, 1931, State Files, POUR Records; Brucker to Herbert Hoover, Aug. 21, 1931, Records of Walter S. Gifford, ibid.; Brucker statement [1931], confidential source; *DN,* Aug. 22, Oct. 27, 1931, May 5, 1932; Richard Theodore Ortquist, Jr., "Depression Politics in Michigan, 1929-1933" (Ph.D. thesis, University of Michigan, 1968), p. 156.
3. FM statement to press, Mar. 4, 1931, MOR; Report by Rowland Haynes, June 1, 1931, General Records of the Assistant Director, POUR Records; J. Walter Drake to Walter S. Gifford, Nov. 18, 1931, Central Files of PECE, ibid.; Francis J. Plym to Editor, Nov. 6, 1931, Central Files, ibid.; Brucker to Hoover, Aug. 21, 1931, Gifford Records, ibid.; Stenholm Report, States Files, ibid.; Ortquist, "Depression Politics," pp. 113-14, 142-44; *DN,* Aug. 22, 1931.
4. L. Laszlo Ecker-R, "Revenues for Relief," *State Government,* VII (Nov. 1934), 243; Haynes Memorandum to Fred Croxton, Mar. 27, 1933, FERA Central Files, Records of the Work Projects Administration, RG 69, NARS; Stenholm Report on Michigan Field Trip, Oct. 2, 1931, State Files, POUR Records; Drake to Gifford, Nov. 18, 1931, Central Files of PECE, ibid.; Plym to Editor, Nov. 6, 1931, Central Files., ibid.; *DN,* Oct. 18, Nov. 28, 1931; Ortquist, "Depression Politics," p. 145.
5. Norton, "The Situation in Detroit" [Sept. 1931], CF Papers, Box 11; Couzens to Brucker, Sept. 24, 1931, Couzens to Norton, Sept.

25, 1931, ibid., Box 10; Report of visit of Rowland Haynes to Michigan, Nov. 10, 1931, State Files, POUR Records; Drake to Gifford, Nov. 18, 1931, Central Files of PECE, ibid.; FM to Brucker, Mar. 12, 1932, G. Hall Roosevelt to Brucker, Mar. 10, 28, 1932, MOR; *DN*, Jan. 24, 26, 27, Feb. 9, 17, Mar. 8, 9, 18, 25, Apr. 2, 8, 1932.

6. *DN*, Mar. 29, 30, Apr. 1, 2, 8, 30, May 6-8, 17, 1932; *DT*, Apr. 30, 1932; FM radio address [Apr. 7, 1932], MOR; FM to Elmer E. Mains, May 26, 1932, MOR; Ortquist, "Depression Politics," pp. 115-21.

7. FM to Brucker, June 15, 1932, Roosevelt to Brucker, July 7, 1932, MOR; *DN*, July 10, 26-28, 1932.

8. Paul V. Betters et al., *Recent Federal-City Relations* (Washington, 1936), pp. 3-4. For an account of the problems faced by two other big cities at this time, see Bonnie R. Fox, "Unemployment Relief in Philadelphia, 1930-1932: A Study of the Depression's Impact on Voluntarism," *Pennsylvania Magazine of History*, XCII (Jan. 1969), 86-108; and Alex Gottfried, *Boss Cermak of Chicago* (Seattle, 1962), pp. 276-77.

9. Irving Bernstein, *The Lean Years: A History of the American Worker, 1920-1933* (Boston, 1960), pp. 287, 302-7; Edward Ainsworth Williams, *Federal Aid for Relief* (New York, 1939), pp. 24-28; Albert V. Romasco, *The Poverty of Abundance: Hoover, the Nation, the Depression* (New York, 1965), pp. 145-49; Harold Buttenheim to FM, Jan. 6, 1931, FM to Clarence C. Dill, Feb. 23, 1931, MOR; *DN*, Jan. 7, June 2, 1931.

10. Richard Lowitt, *George W. Norris: The Persistence of a Progressive, 1913-1933* (Urbana, 1971), pp. 509-10; Norris to FM, Mar. 5, 1931, Robert La Follette, Jr., to FM, May 1, 1931, FM to La Follette, Jr., May 5, 1931, MOR; *DN*, Mar. 6, 1931; *Proceedings of a Conference of Progressives . . . , Mar. 11 and 12, 1931* (n.p., n.d.), pp. 115, 159-60, George W. Norris Papers, LC.

11. *DN*, May 12, June 2, 23, July 3-5, 7, 28, Oct. 15, 1931; Frank D. Adams and JG to Hoover, July 29, 1931, Central Files, POUR Records; Marsh to FM, Sept. 22, 1931, FM to Marsh, Sept. 26, Dec. 24, 1931, MOR. The MUC letter to Hoover was opposed by 38 of 130 MUC members.

12. Williams, *Federal Aid*, pp. 30-35; Romasco, *Poverty of Abundance*, pp. 163-65; Stanley C. Barker to Gifford, Aug. 26, 1931, Central Files, POUR Records.

13. Jordan A. Schwarz, *The Interregnum of Despair: Hoover, Congress, and the Depression* (Urbana, 1970), pp. 146-54; Bernstein, *Lean Years*, pp. 464-65; Williams, *Federal Aid*, pp. 36-41; Subcommittee of the Senate Committee on Manufactures, *Unemployment Relief. Hearings on S.174 and S.262*, 72 Cong., 1 Sess. (Washington, 1932), pp. 277-87.

14. Schwarz, *Interregnum of Despair*, pp. 91-92; FM to Couzens, Jan.

11, 1932, Couzens to FM, Jan. 12, 1932, James Curley to FM, Jan. 18, 1932, MOR; FM to Dudley Field Malone, Jan. 12, 1932, FM Papers; *DN*, Jan. 12, Feb. 17, 19, 1932.

15. Williams, *Federal Aid*, pp. 140-42; *DN*, Mar. 11, 26, 29, 31, May 15, July 5, 9, Aug. 2, 31, 1932; PWC Proceedings, Apr. 18, 1933.

16. *DN*, Nov. 1, 1930, July 25, 1931, May 10-12, 14-17, 1932; *DT*, Nov. 1, 1930, July 25, 1931; Marsh to FM, July 14, 1931, FM to H. Wirt Newkirk, May 14, 1932, MOR; Schwarz, *Interregnum of Despair*, p. 164.

17. The Proceedings and Transactions of a Conference of Mayors . . . , May 18, 1932, MOR; FM et al. to Hoover, May 23, 1932, Official File (hereafter OF) 264-B, Herbert Hoover Presidential Library, West Branch, Iowa; *DN*, May 19, 1932; *DT*, May 19, 1932.

18. Stone to Common Council, May 20, 1932, FM to Carl F. Clarke, May 23, 1932, MOR; *DN*, May 21, 22, 25, 29, 1932.

19. Proceedings of a Conference of Mayors, May 18, 1932, pp. 13, 23, 25, 73-76, MOR; Conference of Mayors of the United States, June 1, 1932, p. 22, MOR. The May 18 conference had also resolved that the Michigan mayors should be organized into a permanent body, but nothing came of this decision.

20. Daniel J. Elazar, "Urban Problems and the Federal Government: A Historical Inquiry," *Political Science Quarterly*, LXXXII (Dec. 1967), 505-25; Paul V. Betters, *Federal Services to Municipal Governments* (Washington [1931]), pp. 5, 93, et passim; Suzanne G. Farkas, *Urban Lobbying: Mayors in the Federal Arena* (New York, 1971), pp. 35, 37-38; Glen Leet to FM, June 2, 1932, and enclosed clipping, MOR.

21. Walker to FM, May 20, 1932, FM to Welsh, May 26, 1932, FM to G. E. Kellogg, June 4, 1932, FM to Malone, undated, MOR; *DN*, May 20, 31, June 1, 1932.

22. Conference of Mayors, June 1, 1932, MOR; FM to Hoover, June 6, 1932, and enclosed resolutions, MOR; *DN*, June 1, 2, 1932; *DT*, June 2, 1932; Rolland B. Marvin to Hoover, June 2, 1932, OF 264-B, Hoover Library.

23. Farkas, *Urban Lobbying*, p. 36; *DT*, May 15, 17-19, 25, 31, June 1, 2, 9, 1932; *DN*, June 3, 1932; *DFP*, June 1, 3, 1932; *DSN*, May 21, June 4, 1932; Eugene Criswell to Hoover, June 4, 1932, OF 264-B, Hoover Library; Lovett to H. W. Dodds, July 13, 1932, DCL Papers.

24. FM to Darwin J. Meserole, June 2, 1932, MOR; *DN*, June 7, 8, 1932; Schwarz, *Interregnum of Despair*, pp. 166-67; Bernstein, *Lean Years*, p. 467; *NYT*, June 8, 1932.

25. Conference of Mayors, Feb. 17, 1933, p. 32, MOR; *NYT*, June 9, 1932; Bernstein, *Lean Years*, pp. 467-69; Betters et al., *Federal-City Relations*, pp. 4-5; Farkas, *Urban Lobbying*, p. 48. The Garner bill

provided $100 million for direct relief, $1 billion for RFC loans to states, cities, corporations, and individuals, and $1 billion for federal public works. The Wagner-Garner bill provided $1.5 billion for loans to public bodies, corporations, and individuals, $300 million for relief, and $300 million for public works.

26. Williams, *Federal Aid,* pp. 43–45; Romasco, *Poverty of Abundance,* p. 223; Betters et al., *Federal-City Relations,* pp. 7–10; *DN,* July 29, 1932.

27. Betters et al., *Federal-City Relations,* p. 6; Williams, *Federal Aid,* p. 49; Subcommittee of the Senate Committee on Manufactures, *Federal Aid for Unemployment Relief. Hearings on S.5125,* 72 Cong., 2 Sess. (Washington, 1933), pp. 204–7; Norton to Brucker, July 30, 1932, Brucker to Murphy, July 29, 1932, MOR; Brucker to RFC, July 29, 1932, RFC Records; *DN,* July 30, 31, Aug. 5, 1932.

28. *DN,* Aug. 1, 3, 5–7, 9, 11, 28, Sept. 23, 1932; RFC Release, Aug. 4, 1932, RFC Records; Jarvis to Leach, Sept. 23, 1932, ibid.; Guy Durgan to FM, Aug. 8, 1932, MOR; PWC Proceedings, Aug. 8, 1932; *DT,* June 2, 1932. The RFC loan was for a period of two years with the privilege of renewal.

29. See Chapter XII, n. 67.

30. Department of Public Welfare, *The Department of Public Welfare, 1930 to 1940* (Detroit, n.d.), p. 84; Council of Social Agencies, "A Brief Summary of Historical and Current Data on the Detroit Department of Public Welfare" [Jan. 1933], MOR; Emma Winslow, *Trends in Different Types of Public and Private Relief in Urban Areas, 1929–35* (Washington, 1937), pp. 72–85.

31. Roosevelt statement, June 17, 1932, MOR; FM to George E. Miller, June 30, 1932, MOR; *Journal of the Common Council,* July 5, 1932, pp. 1161–63; William P. Lovett to C. B. Van Dusen, July 7, 1932, DCL Papers; *DN,* June 28, Sept. 18, 19, 1932. The Hutchinson committee was technically a subcommittee of a Committee of Industrialists organized earlier in the year by GM's Alfred P. Sloan, Jr. Egbert S. Wengert, *Financial Problems of the City of Detroit in the Depression* (Detroit, 1939), p. ii.

32. *DN,* July 6, 11, 1932; *Journal of the Common Council,* July 5, 1932, pp. 1164–66; *Civic Searchlight,* July 1932; C. C. McGill radio talk, July 13, 1932, MOR.

33. *DN,* July 6, 19, 1932; Lovett to Tracy W. McGregor, June 30, 1932, DCL Papers; FM to Divie B. Duffield, July 8, 1932, Harry B. Earhart to FM, July 29, 1932, MOR; McGill talk, July 13, 1932, MOR; *Detroiter,* XIII (July 18, 1932), 8; Mauritz A. Hallgren, "Grave Danger in Detroit," *Nation,* CXXXV (Aug. 3, 1932), 100.

34. *DN,* Feb. 9, 17, Mar. 25, 31, May 5, 7–8, 11, June 11, 24, 29, 1932.

35. *DN,* Feb. 9, Mar. 1, 25, 31, May 31, June 26, 27, 29, July 1, 20, 22, 27, Aug. 3, 5, 7, 8, 1932; FM speech [Aug. 8, 1932], MOR;

K. J. McCarren to FM, Feb. 5, 1932, John Taylor to W. C. Bernardi, Aug. 8, 1932, Norman H. Hill to Sherman Brown, Oct. 13, 1932, MOR; "A Few Simple Facts," "A Desperate Dodge," "Mr. Average Home Owner!," handbills in MOR; Sidney G. Tickton, *An Analysis of Tax Delinquency* (Detroit, 1932), p. 12; Richard D. Lunt, *The High Ministry of Government: The Political Career of Frank Murphy* (Detroit, 1965), p. 62.

36. *DN,* June 27, July 1, 2, 27, 29, 1932.

37. "Pull Detroit out of the 'Murphy Muddle' . . . ," handbill in MOR; Victor C. Doherty to FM, July 21, 1932, Taxpayer to FM, July 29, 1932, George W. Trendle to FM, July 28, 1932, and enclosed letter, MOR.

38. *DN,* July 11, 20, 22, 1932; Minutes of the Meeting of the Committee on Operating Efficiency, July 1, 29, 1932, MOR; C. E. Brewer to FM, July 25, 1932, MOR.

39. *DT,* July 12, 1932; *DN,* July 19, 21, 24, 27, 30, 31, Aug. 1, 4–6, 8, 1932; *DFP,* Aug. 6, 8, 1932; *DLN,* July 22, 1932; *Civic Searchlight,* July 1932; *Detroiter,* XXIII (Aug. 15, 1932), 8; Jack R. C. Cann to FM, July 12, 1932, Committee on City Finances to Voters of Detroit, July 29, 1932, MOR. Stone thought that the suggestion of a $61 million tax limitation had had a good effect on "the Councilmanic mind," but he attempted to head off the actual filing of the petitions. Stone to Louis E. Palmer, Apr. 20, 1932, Ralph Stone Papers, MHC.

40. *DN,* June 26, July 17, 20–30, Aug. 1, 3–5, 8, 1932; *Civic Searchlight,* July 1930; FM to Moody, Aug. 17, 1932, Blair Moody Papers, MHC. There is a synopsis of the $61 million budget in *DN,* July 19, 1932.

41. *DN,* July 15, 19, 20, 1932; *DT,* July 20, 1932; Upson to FM, July 18, 1932, MOR; Joseph H. Creighton, "Frank Murphy—Off the Record," Part Two (MS [Aug. 1938]), pp. 15–16, FM Papers.

42. Hutchinson to FM, July 20, 1932, Stone to FM, July 20, 1932, Macauley to FM, July 20, 1932, Franklin to FM, July 20, 1932, Joseph Murphy to FM, July 20, 1932, MOR. Cf. Chester L. Weaver to FM, July 21, 1932, MOR.

43. Jim Lee to FM, July 9, 1932, Hill to JG, undated, FM to R. L. Bradby, July 30, 1932, FM to the Reverend Mr. Williams, July 29, 1932, MOR.

44. *DN,* Aug. 7, 9, 10, 15, 1932; FM speech [Aug. 8, 1932], MOR; FM to McCarren, Aug. 10, 1932, MOR; *DLN,* Aug. 12, 1932.

45. *DN,* July 8, 9, 11, 13, 14, 19, 20, 24, 28, Aug. 6, 10, Dec. 18, 1932, Jan. 15, 16, 1933; Detroit Police Department, *Sixty-Eighth Annual Report, 1932* (Detroit, n.d.), p. 4; Detroit Police Department, *Sixty-Ninth Annual Report, 1933* (Detroit, n.d.), p. 4; Board of Fire Commissioners of the City of Detroit, Annual Report, 1932, p. 1; ibid., 1933, p. 4; Trendle to FM, July 11, 30 (two letters), 1932, FM to Wilcox, Aug. 3, 1932, Joseph F. Creed to FM, Feb. 25, 1933, Frank Martel

to FM, Sept. 8, Nov. 14, 1932, FM to Martel, Sept. 12, 1932, E. T. Olsen to John Ballenger, Nov. 23, 1932, MOR.

46. Stone to Roosevelt, July 27, 1932, FM to Malcolm W. Bingay, Dec. 23, 1932, MOR; FM to Arthur F. Lederle, Jan. 15, 1934, FM Papers; *Journal of the Common Council,* Jan. 10, 1933, p. 2; Senate Committee on the Judiciary, *Uniform System of Bankruptcy, Hearing on S.5699,* 72 Cong., 2 Sess. (Washington, 1933), p. 4; *DN,* July 21, Aug. 17, 1932, Jan. 4, 22, 1933; *Civic Searchlight,* Jan. 1933.

47. *DN,* July 21, 24, Aug. 3, Sept. 7, 9, 10, 15, Nov. 8, 20, 29, 1932, Jan. 29, Feb. 6, 15, 1933; Stone to Roosevelt, July 27, 1932, Roosevelt to FM, Sept. 1, 1932, Hal Smith to Charles H. Williams, Nov. 30, 1932, Smith to FM, Dec. 15, 17, 23, 1932, Jan. 8, 1933, Hutchinson to FM, Jan. 13, 1933, MOR; C. E. Rightor to Lederle, EGK-BHC Papers, Box 15; Wengert, *Financial Problems,* p. 36.

48. *DN,* Aug. 2-4, 9, 1932; Committee on City Finances to Common Council, Sept. 9, 1932, MOR.

49. *DN,* Sept. 11, 13-16, 19, 20, 1932.

50. Hutchinson to FM, Oct. 10, 1932, Roosevelt to George Bailey, Oct. 18, 1932, Mills to FM, Nov. 16, 1932, FM to Brucker, Dec. 7, 16, 1932, Brucker to FM, Dec. 14, 1932, MOR; *DN,* Dec. 5, 6, 9, 10, 15, 17, 1932.

51. *DN,* Dec. 25, 27-29, 1932, Jan. 1, 3, 4, 11, 13, 14, 1932; *DT,* Dec. 28, 1932; Hutchinson to FM, Jan. 13, 1933, MOR; Wengert, *Financial Problems,* p. 14.

52. *DN,* Aug. 2, Sept. 23, 1932, Jan. 25, 26, Feb. 5, 1933; Conference of Mayors, Feb. 17, 1933, pp. 19-20, MOR.

53. Betters to FM, Sept. 23, Nov. 19, 1932, Jan. 30, Feb. 8, 1933, Betters to Mabel Ford, Nov. 23, 1932, FM to Hoan, Jan. 19, 1933, Hoan to FM, Jan. 23, 1933, Betters to Upson, Jan. 21, 1933, Upson to FM, Jan. 25, 1933, FM to Anderson, Feb. 7, 1933, FM to Mayors, Feb. 11, 1933, MOR; "C. E. Rightor, Dec. 1, 1932," MOR; *Journal of the Common Council,* Jan. 10, 1933, pp. 2-3; *DN,* Feb. 2, 6, 8, 10-12, 17, 1933.

54. Conference of Mayors, Feb. 17, 1933, MOR; FM to John F. Forward, Jr., Feb. 21, 1933, MOR; *DN,* Feb. 18, 1933.

55. FM to Forward, Jr., Feb. 21, 1933, Betters to FM, Feb. 27 (and enclosed document), Apr. 3, 1933 (two letters), Betters to Mr. Mayor, Apr. 4, 1933, MOR.

56. Murphy had been able to reduce his earlier estimate of the fixed charges that would have to be serviced in the 1933-34 budget because Detroit industrialists had expressed a willingness to defer payments due that year until 1934-35. *DN,* Feb. 8, 12, 26, Apr. 19, 1933; FM to Mayors, Feb. 11, 1933, MOR.

57. *DN,* Feb. 18-20, 1933; *DT,* Feb. 19, 1933; FM to Charles P. Gillen [Apr. 11, 1933], MOR.

58. *DN*, Aug. 24, 25, 31, Dec. 4, 1932, Jan. 12, 1933; DPW, *The Department of Public Welfare 1930 to 1940*, p. 84; Thomas E. Dolan to FM, Oct. 14, 1932, Feb. 7, 1933, Dolan to F. Couzens, June 6, 1933, MOR. Cf. Croxton Memorandum for Charles A. Miller, Jan. 11, 1933, RFC Records, and DPW, City Cases, July 1, 1932-Apr. 30, 1933, MOR, for the city's own expenditures. The total RFC amount given in the DPW's summary report for the 1930s appears to understate the actual figure by more than $489,000.

59. See, for example, Arthur M. Schlesinger, Jr., *The Age of Roosevelt: The Crisis of the Old Order, 1919-1933* (Boston, 1957), p. 241; William E. Leuchtenburg, *The Perils of Prosperity, 1914-1932* (Chicago, 1958), p. 258; Bernstein, *Lean Years*, pp. 470-73; and Romasco, *Poverty of Abundance*, p. 227. Cf. Williams, *Federal Aid*, pp. 56-57; and James S. Olson, "Gifford Pinchot and the Politics of Hunger," *Pennsylvania Magazine of History and Biography*, XCVI (Oct. 1972), 520.

60. Conference of Mayors, Feb. 17, 1933, p. 11, MOR; Betters to Mr. Mayor, May 17, 1933, MOR.

61. State of Michigan, Detroit, Application for Funds to RFC [Sept. 1932], MOR; FM to Brucker, Sept. 30, 1932, Clarence E. Page and William J. Curran to FM, Oct. 21, 1932, MOR; Croxton Memorandum to RFC, Oct. 24, 1932, Croxton to Brucker, Oct. 28, 1932, Croxton to Directors, Jan. 4, 1933, Ballenger Memorandum to William S. Carpenter, Feb. 25, 1933, Croxton Memorandum for the Directors, May 16, 1933, RFC Records; RFC Request, Mar.-Apr. 1933, ibid.; PWC Proceedings, May 16, 1933; *DN*, Sept. 23-27, Oct. 11, 25, 28, 29, Nov. 18, Dec. 18, 20, 21,.31, 1932, Jan. 6, Mar. 8, 9, 21, Apr. 8, 12, 1933; *DT*, Apr. 9, 1933; Subcommittee of the Senate Committee on Manufactures, *Federal Aid for Unemployment Relief. Hearings on S.5125*, 72 Cong., 2 Sess. (Washington, 1933), p. 209.

62. *DN*, Sept. 16, 18, 20, 22, Oct. 28, 1932, Jan. 13, 1933; *DT*, Sept. 23, 1932; Betters to FM, Sept. 23, 1932, MOR; Application for Funds [Sept. 1932], MOR.

63. *DN*, Sept. 22, Oct. 18, 1932; *DT*, Sept. 22, 23, 1932; Brucker to Henry B. Joy, July 23, 1935, Henry B. Joy Papers, MHC.

64. *DN*, Sept. 23-27, 30, Oct. 1, 7-11, 13, 14, 25, Nov. 18, 29, 1932; MUC report [Sept. 1932], EGK Papers; FM to Brucker, Sept. 30, 1932, Betters to FM, Oct. 5, 19, 1932, MOR. Of the approximately $280 million loaned by the RFC for relief, only $19.6 million was loaned directly to the political subdivisions of the states. Josephine C. Brown, *Public Relief, 1929-1939* (New York, 1940), p. 126.

65. *DN*, Sept. 18, Oct. 31, Dec. 16, 1932, Jan. 5, 6, Feb. 8, 1933; *DT*, Oct. 23, 1932; Norton to Couzens, Dec. 29, 1932, Couzens to Norton, Dec. 31, 1932, CF Papers, Box 10.

66. Haynes Memorandum to Croxton, Feb. 17, 1933, FERA Central Files,

RG 69; *DN*, Feb. 17, Mar. 21, 25, 26, 28, 29, 1933; Norton to Couzens, Mar. 14, 1933, CF Papers, Box 10; FM to GM, Sept. 29, 1934, FM Papers; John H. Hamilton to Carl M. Weideman, Mar. 27, 1933, Carl M. Weideman Papers, MHC.

67. Haynes Memorandum to Croxton, Mar. 27, 1933, FERA Central Files, RG 69; Norton to Couzens, Mar. 31, 1933, Norton to Howard Hunter, Apr. 7, 1933, CF Papers, Box 12; *DN*, Apr. 5, 6, 8, May 17, 1933; *DT*, Apr. 9, 1933.

68. PWC Proceedings, Oct. 11, Dec. 9, 1932; *DN*, Aug. 14, Oct. 8, 24, Dec. 10, 21, 1932, Jan. 7, 10, 11, Feb. 14, 1933; Hill to Claude F. Perry, Mar. 8, 1933, JG to James H. Pleuss, Apr. 13, 1933, MOR; "Rent Survey" [1933], RFC Records; Joanna Colcord, *Cash Relief* (New York, 1936), p. 88. Monthly rent checks were generally reduced from a maximum of $20 to a maximum of $10.

69. *DN*, Oct. 31, Dec. 19, 1932; *Journal of the Common Council*, Jan. 10, 1933, p. 6; FM to H. M. Richey, Nov. 25, 1932, FM to Hutchinson, Nov. 22, 1932, Ballenger to La Follette, Jr., Jan. 15, 1933, MOR; FM to Lacy, Nov. 23, 1932, FM to GM, Sept. 17, 1934, FM Papers; Creighton, "Murphy," Part Two, pp. 11-14. For the task-force report, see Report on Investigation of the Welfare Department of the City of Detroit, July 27, 1932, MOR.

70. JG to Harold Chesser, Oct. 28, 1932, MOR; IM to Hill, Nov. 17, 1932, FM Papers; *DN*, Dec. 19, 1932, Mar. 6, 1933. For comparative welfare figures, see *DN*, Dec. 19, 1932.

71. *DN*, Aug. 12, 16-17, Nov. 2, 6, 11, 13, Dec. 7, 29, 1932, Mar. 16, 1933; FM to Guy A. Durgan, Mar. 14, 1933, MOR; PWC Proceedings, May 9, 1933; Louisa Wilson to Harry L. Hopkins, Nov. 24, 1934, Harry L. Hopkins Papers, FDRL.

72. *DN*, July 3, 6, 8, Aug. 17, 22, Sept. 5, Nov. 10, 11, 19, Dec. 28, 1932, Jan. 25, 1933; PWC Proceedings, Aug. 23, Oct. 25, Nov. 9, 18, 22, 1932.

73. *DN*, Dec. 21, 1932, Jan. 6, 8, 15, 18, 19, 21, Feb. 3, 1933; *DFP*, Jan. 15, 1933; PWC Proceedings, Dec. 27, 1932, Jan. 17, 24, 31, Feb. 21, Mar. 7, 1933; Ed Thal to Common Council, Jan. 19, 1933, FM to Thal, Jan. 31, 1933, JG to Mary Beland, Feb. 14, 1933, William Reynolds to FM, Feb. 1, 1933, FM to Reynolds, Feb. 16, 1933, MOR; Frank Martel to Ballenger, Feb. 21, 1933, Wayne County AFL-CIO Papers, Box 23, ALHUA; *DLN*, Feb. 3, 10, 1933; *Detroit Hunger Fighter*, I (Mar. 1, 1933), 1.

74. Hart, "The Decline, Fall and Resurrection of the Credit of the City of Detroit," *National Municipal Review*, XXV (Jan. 1936), 350; *NYT*, Feb. 14, 1933.

75. Jones (with Edward Angly), *Fifty Billion Dollars: My Thirteen Years with the RFC* (New York, 1951), pp. 54-65; Harry Barnard, *Independent Man: The Life of James Couzens* (New York, 1958), pp. 213-17;

Susan Estabrook Kennedy, *The Banking Crisis of 1933* (Lexington, 1973), pp. 77-96; John T. Flynn, "Michigan Magic: The Detroit Banking Scandal," *Harper's,* CLXVIII (Dec. 1933), 1-11; Ruth Donna Roth, "Nightmare in February" (M.A. thesis, Wayne State University, 1956); *Business Week,* Feb. 22, 1933, p. 5; *DN,* Feb. 14, 1933.

76. FM to Julia S. Hotchkiss, Apr. 5, 1933, MOR; *DLN,* Mar. 17, 1933; Chicago *Tribune,* Mar. 5, 1933. For the legal outcome of the indictments the federal government brought against the Detroit bankers, see *DN,* June 9, 1937.

77. *DT,* Mar. 23, 1933; Memo for [Marvin] McIntyre, Mar. 23 [1933], President's Personal File 2338, FDRL; McIntyre Memorandum for Louis Howe, Mar. 27, 1933, ibid.; FM to Raymond Moley, Mar. 20, 1933, Raymond Moley Papers (in Mr. Moley's possession); FM to Dorothy H. Parker, Mar. 31, 1933, FM to Willard M. Lemon, Apr. 5, 1933, FM to Louis B. Ward, Mar. 21, 1931 [1933], MOR; MM Diary, Mar. 27-29, 1933, MM Papers; Grenville Vernon to FM, June 30, 1940, and enclosed draft of manuscript, FM Papers; Charles J. Tull, *Father Coughlin and the New Deal* (Syracuse, 1965), pp. 24-25; Kennedy, *Banking Crisis,* pp. 98-102, 193-95.

78. *DT,* Mar. 15, 1933; *DN,* Mar. 15, 1933.

79. *DN,* Feb. 14, 15, Mar. 13, Apr. 23, 1933.

80. *DN,* Aug. 18, 19, Sept. 10, Dec. 4, 1932, Feb. 5, 19, Mar. 7, 11, 12, Apr. 16, 19, 27, 30, 1933; JG to Edgar Gault, Apr. 6, 1933, MOR; PWC Proceedings, Mar. 28, Apr. 25, May 2, June 27, 1933; Bernstein, *Lean Years,* pp. 416-19.

81. Lemon to FM, Mar. 24, 1933, Doris Palolsjean to FM, Mar. 28, 1933, IM to FM, Feb. 14, 1933, MOR; John Dancy to Virgil and Theodore Spaulding, Apr. 13, 1933, DUL Papers; Eric Kocher, *Economic and Physical Growth of Detroit, 1701-1935* (n.p., 1935), p. 79.

82. *DN,* Feb. 15, 17, 26, Mar. 1, 4, 6, 7, 9, Apr. 25, 26, 1933; Jones, *Fifty Billion,* p. 66.

83. *DN,* Mar. 4, 8, 18, 19, 21, Apr. 25, 1933.

84. *DN,* Feb. 24, Mar. 5, 10, 12, 21, 24, 26, Apr. 9, 1933.

85. Earl N. Parker, Statement of Facts, undated, RFC Records; Memorandum from Croxton to the Directors, Mar. 15, 1933, ibid.; PWC Proceedings, Mar. 7, 14, Apr. 11, 1933; Percival Dodge to Couzens, Apr. 15, 1933, James Couzens Papers, LC; Norton to Couzens, Mar. 14, 31, 1933, CF Papers, Box 10; *DN,* Mar. 3, 8, 9, 15, 17, 26, 1933; Norton, "Deflation Where Is Thy Sting? . . . ," *Survey,* LXIX (May 1933), 184-85.

86. IM to FM, Feb. 14, 1933, MOR; *DN,* Feb. 15, 24, 26, Mar. 5, 9, 17, 26, 28, Apr. 7, 12, 1933; *DT,* Apr. 9, 1933; PWC Proceedings, Mar. 21, Apr. 4, 1933; Weideman to Jones, Mar. 31, 1933, RFC Records.

87. *DN,* Feb. 15, Mar. 5, 9, 10, May 10, 1933; *Business Week,* July 22, 1933, p. 13; Lovett to FM, Mar. 6, 1933, MOR.

88. *DN*, Mar. 3, 5-13, 1933; Hill to Clarence R. Lahr, Mar. 15, 1933, MOR; Isbey statement, Mar. 10, 1933, FM Papers; Public Announcement on Detroit City Scrip [Apr. 1933], MOR.

89. *DN*, Mar. 9, 10, 15, Apr. 3, 6, 9, 10, 14, 15, 21-23, 25, 26, 28, May 4, 7, 13, 1933; FM radio speech, Apr. 14, 1933, MOR; Hart to Stone, Mar. 15, 1933, Stone Papers.

90. *DN*, Mar. 8, May 3, 1933; F. Couzens to William J. Serlin, May 11, 1933, MOR; *Business Week*, July 22, 1933, p. 13; Wengert, *Financial Problems*, p. 19. The Council resolution of May applied to the first $10 million in scrip, dated April 27, 1933. The remaining $8 million, dated July 10, 1933, was later made redeemable as of November 10, 1933. City Treasurer to All America Garment Co., June 8, 1933, MOR.

91. *DN*, Feb. 20, 23, 26, 28, 1933; Senate Committee on the Judiciary, *Uniform System of Bankruptcy*, pp. 3, 17; Betters to FM, Feb. 28, 1933, MOR.

92. *DN*, Mar. 2, 1933. The terms of the McLeod bill are set forth in Senate Committee on the Judiciary, *Uniform System of Bankruptcy*, pp. 1-3.

93. *DN*, Mar. 12, 18, 19, 21, 24, 31, Apr. 3, 1933; Betters to Hill, Mar. 9, 1933, FM to Edward Zimmerman, Mar. 30, 1933, MOR; FM to Moley, Mar. 21, 1933, Moley Papers; Betters et al., *Recent Federal-City Relations*, p. 15.

94. *DN*, Mar. 12, 19, 24, Apr. 3, 27, 1933; Sander Shanks, Jr., to Hart, Mar. 17, 1933, Zimmerman to FM, Mar. 28, 1933, FM to Homer Cummings, Apr. 19, 1933, MOR; Hart to Stone, Mar. 15, 1933, Stone Papers.

95. *DN*, Mar. 1-4, 1933; Norris to Matthew W. Neely, Mar. 1, 1933, Norris Papers; FM to Mayors, undated, MOR; Senate Committee on the Judiciary, *Uniform System of Bankruptcy*, pp. 3-10, 31, 40, 45.

96. Zimmerman to Royal McKenna, Feb. 16, 1938, FM Papers; FM to Moley, Mar. 21, 1933, Moley Papers; Clarence J. McLeod to FM, Mar. 10, 1933, FM to Wilcox, Mar. 8, 1933, FM to Claris Adams, Mar. 15, 1933, Ward to FM, Mar. 9, 17, 1933, FM to Hearst, Mar. 11, 1933, FM to Lewis Marcus, Mar. 22, 1933, FM to Harry T. Hartwell, Mar. 24, 1933, FM to Betters, Mar. 27, Apr. 29, 1933, FM to C. Nelson Sparks, Apr. 1, 1933, FM to Arthur H. Vandenberg, Apr. 5, 1933, FM to Hoan, Apr. 5, 1933, FM to Zimmerman, Mar. 21, 24, 1933, FM to John C. Lehr and Joseph Hooper, Mar. 28, 1933, FM to Homer Cummings, Apr. 19, 1933, MOR; McIntyre Memo for the President, Apr. 1, 1933, OF 259, FDRL; *DN*, Mar. 12, 18, 19, 21, 31, Apr. 1, 3, May 3, 1933; House Committee on the Judiciary, *To Amend the Bankruptcy Act . . . Hearing on H. R. 1670 . . .*, 73 Cong., 1 Sess. (Washington, 1933), p. 32.

97. House Committee on the Judiciary, *To Amend the Bankruptcy Act,* pp. 84–88, 92–113, 122–24; Hart to Stone, Mar. 15, 1933, Stone Papers; *DN,* Mar. 31, 1933.
98. *DN,* Mar. 24, 31, Apr. 3, 5, 13, 27, 30, May 1–5, 9, 1933; Zimmerman to FM, Apr. 14, May 1, 1933, Betters to FM, Mar. 28, 1933, MOR; FM to Standish Evans, June 28, 1934, Zimmerman to McKenna, Feb. 16, 1938, FM Papers; House Committee on the Judiciary, *To Amend the Bankruptcy Act,* p. 141; Betters et al., *Recent Federal-City Relations,* pp. 16–18.
99. *DN,* Apr. 6, 7, 18, 20, 27, 1933; Lovett to Harold D. Smith, Apr. 19, 1933, Upson to Rightor, Apr. 20, 1933, DCL Papers; *Business Week,* May 24, 1933, p. 20.
100. *DN,* Mar. 1, Apr. 4, 6, 8–10, 15–21, 28, 1933; Upson to Rightor, Apr. 5, 1933, DCL Papers; FM to Cummings, Apr. 19, 1933, MOR; Wengert, *Financial Problems,* p. 21.
101. Wengert, *Financial Problems,* pp. 22–25; Hart, "Decline of the Credit of Detroit," p. 351; Rightor to Lederle, Dec. 12, 1933, EGK-BHC Papers, Box 15.
102. *DN,* Jan. 22, Feb. 10, Mar. 15, 30, Apr. 6, 7, 11, 12, 25–26, 28, 30, 1933; FM to Common Council, Mar. 14; 1933, MOR; Wengert, *Financial Problems,* p. 24; DBGR, *Accumulated Social and Economic Statistics for Detroit* (Detroit, 1937), pp. 5, 17.
103. FM to Ballenger, May 5, 1933, FM Papers; Norton, "The Relief Crisis in Detroit," *Social Service Review,* VII (Mar. 1933), 8.

CHAPTER XIV

1. *Journal of the Common Council,* Jan. 13, 1931, p. 3; FM to Heinrich Pickert, Apr. 25, 1934, FM Papers.
2. Wilson, *Varieties of Police Behavior* (Cambridge, Mass., 1968), pp. 227–33.
3. *DN,* Sept. 26, Oct. 7, 30, 31, 1930, Jan. 10, 11, 1931; *DSN,* Dec. 27, 1930; Detroit *Daily,* Jan. 10, 1931, MSB; William P. Lovett to Charles B. Van Dusen, Oct. 28, 1930, DCL Papers; Ralph S. Moore to FM, Sept. 11, 1930, Cyril Arthur Player to FM, Jan. 15, 1931, Joseph S. Apelman to FM, Jan. 17, 1931, FM Papers; Hugh Chalmers to FM, Nov. 14, 1930, FM to Chalmers, Nov. 15, 1930, R. N. Holsaple to FM, Jan. 7, 1931, MOR; Memorandum, Mar. 22, 1932, ACLU Archives, Vol. 575.
4. *DN,* Jan. 2, 11, 12, Sept. 17, 1931; FM to Holsaple, Jan. 10, 1931, MOR; "Detroit Court Solves Bail Problem," *JAJS,* XVI (Feb. 1933), 149; Parker to Baldwin, Feb. 2, 1931, ACLU Archives, Vol. 488.
5. *DN,* Sept. 26, 27, 1930, Jan. 11, 1931, Jan. 14, 1932; FM to John D. Dingell, Apr. 27, 1931, MOR; FM radio speech [Oct. 1, 1931], MOR; Pickert to FM, Apr. 14, 1934, FM to Pickert, Apr. 25, 1934,

FM Papers; Interview with Nathaniel H. Goldstick, Dec. 9, 1963, p. 6, MHC.

6. FM to Flora L. Robinson, Jan. 5, 1931, JG to Patrick J. O'Grady, Oct. 16, 1931, MOR.

7. *DN*, Feb. 1, Apr. 19, Sept. 1, 2, 1931; FM radio speech [Oct. 1, 1931], MOR; *Journal of the Common Council*, Jan. 13, 1931, pp. 3-4, Jan. 12, 1932, p. 8; Parker to FM, Feb. 4, 1932, FM to Parker, Feb. 27, 1932, Watkins to Parker, Feb. 29, 1932, MOR; Charles Rhodes to Watkins, Mar. 17, 1933, Watkins to Parker, May 8, 1933, Parker to Baldwin, May 11, 1933, ACLU Archives, Vol. 661.

8. Bruce Smith, "Police Service," in Clarence E. Ridley and Orin F. Nolting, eds., *What the Depression Has Done to Cities* (Chicago, 1935), pp. 30-32; Detroit Police Department, *Sixty-Fifth Annual Report, 1930* (Detroit, n.d.), p. 3; Detroit Police Department, *Sixty-Seventh Annual Report, 1932* (Detroit, n.d.), p. 4; *Journal of the Common Council*, Jan. 12, 1932, p. 8; Police Department report [Sept. 1931], MOR; *DN*, Feb. 8, 1931; "Detroit Court Solves Bail Problem," p. 149. The *total* police force dropped from 3,758 in 1930 to 3,541 in 1933 and the number of patrolmen from 3,133 to 2,935. DBGR, *Accumulated Social and Economic Statistics for Detroit* (Detroit, 1937), p. 11.

9. *DLN*, Oct. 24, 1930; *DN*, Dec. 7, 1930, Jan. 14, 1932; *Journal of the Common Council*, Jan. 13, 1931, p. 4, Jan. 12, 1932, p. 8; FM to K. T. Keller, Sept. 23, 1931, MOR; FM radio speech [Oct. 1, 1931], MOR.

10. National Commission on Law Observance and Enforcement, *Report on Lawlessness and Law Enforcement* (Washington, 1931), pp. 120-23; Ernest Jerome Hopkins, *Our Lawless Police* (New York, 1931), pp. 24, 129; Police Department report [Sept. 1931], MOR; *DLN*, Nov. 20, 1931; *DN*, Sept. 6, 1932; FM to Watkins, Sept. 9, 1932, MOR; Parker to Baldwin, Feb. 8, 1932, ACLU Archives, Vol. 575.

11. Parker to Baldwin, Feb. 8, 1932, ACLU Archives, Vol. 575; ACLU, "'*Sweet Land of Liberty*,'" *1931-1932* (New York, 1932), p. 41; "Detroit Court Solves Bail Problem," p. 149; *JAIS*, XVI (Feb. 1933), 133; *DSN*, Sept. 3, 1932. For instances of police brutality while Murphy was mayor, see Hopkins, *Our Lawless Police*, pp. 38, 48; *DN*, Sept. 6, 1932; Statement of Karapeet Mkretichan, June 3, 1932, MOR; and Resolution of Protest . . . , Feb. 27, 1932, MOR.

12. *DN*, Nov. 21, 22, 1930, Apr. 19, 30, May 4, 1931, Feb. 19-21, 1932; FM to Keller, Sept. 23, 1931, MOR; Watkins to FM, Feb. 19, 1932, and enclosed draft on release of prisoners, MOR; *Journal of the Common Council*, Jan. 13, 1931, p. 4; Orders by Commissioner James K. Watkins, June, 1932, ACLU Archives, Vol. 575; Parker to Baldwin, June 24, 1932, Baldwin to FM, June 27, 1932, ibid.

13. ACLU (Detroit Branch), *Report of Activities for the Year 1930* (n.p., n.d.), p. 8; *DN*, Oct. 31, Nov. 16, 1930, May 1, 1933; *Journal of the*

Common Council, Jan. 13, 1931, p. 4; Police Department report [Sept. 1931], MOR.

14. *DN,* Nov. 15, 1930; Hopkins, *Our Lawless Police,* pp. 139–40. For the enforcement of prohibition by Detroit officials before Murphy became mayor, see Larry Daniel Engelmann, "O, Whisky: The History of Prohibition in Michigan" (Ph.D. thesis, University of Michigan, 1971), pp. 547–67.

15. *DN,* Nov. 15, 16, 23, 29, Dec. 26, 1930, Jan. 27, Mar. 15, 1931, Oct. 21, 1932; *DSN,* Nov. 29, 1930, Jan. 31, 1931; *Journal of the Common Council,* Jan. 13, 1931, p. 4; Police Department report [Sept. 1931], MOR.

16. *DN,* Jan. 27, 29, Mar. 4, 15, 20, 21, 28, Apr. 4, 9, July 22, 31, Aug. 25, 1931, Jan. 3, 14, 21, Feb. 26, 28, 29, Mar. 1, 1932; Engelmann, "O, Whisky," pp. 542–44.

17. *DN,* Sept. 24, 1931, May 15, June 14, 15, Sept. 27, Nov. 11–13, 1932; *DFP,* Nov. 14, 1932; FM to M. V. MacKinnon, May 3, 1932, FM to Hoyt E. Morris, June 18, 1932, FM to Loren O'Brien, June 24, 1932, MOR; FM statement [1932], MOR; FM radio speech, Oct. 8, 1932, MOR.

18. *DN,* Nov. 30, Dec. 28, 1930, Jan. 26, Feb. 24, Mar. 22, Oct. 21, 1932; *DFP,* Jan. 2, 1931; FM to Chalmers, Nov. 15, 1930, MOR.

19. Leon Radzinowicz, "Economic Pressures," in Radzinowicz and Marvin E. Wolfgang, eds., *Crime and Justice,* 3 vols. (New York, 1971), I, 433; Thorsten Sellin, *Research Memorandum on Crime in the Depression* (New York, 1937), p. 25; Detroit Police Department, *Sixty-Sixth Annual Report, 1931* (Detroit, n.d.), p. 3; Detroit Police Department, *Sixty-Eighth Annual Report, 1933* (Detroit, n.d.), pp. 12, 32; *DT,* Sept. 12, 1931; *DN,* Sept. 29, Oct. 23, 1932; Watkins to FM, Dec. 19, 1931, FM Papers; Police Department report [Sept. 1931], MOR. The larceny figures on pp. 12 and 32 of the 1933 police department report are slightly at variance. Auto thefts decreased substantially between 1929 and 1932, perhaps because of the smaller number of autos in use. The reported cases of robbery (larceny of property from the person) decreased from 2,029 in 1929 to 1,823 in 1932.

20. Parker to Baldwin, Oct. 1, 1930, ACLU Archives, Vol. 425; *DT,* Oct. 1, 1930; ACLU (Detroit Branch), *Report for 1930,* pp. 6–7. Cf. the Boston record as depicted in Charles Hathaway Trout, "Boston during the Great Depression, 1929–1940" (Ph.D. thesis, Columbia University, 1972), pp. 121–22, 172–73.

21. Ionia *Sentinel-Standard,* Mar. 7, 1931, MSB; *DN,* Oct. 13, 1930, Aug. 24, 1931; *Journal of the Common Council,* Jan. 13, 1931, pp. 4–5; FM to Walter M. Nelson, Apr. 24, 1931, FM to Joseph M. Gray, June 12, 1931, FM to Wilson Critzer, Aug. 7, 1931, FM to Ralph B. Gehring, Mar. 30, 1931, FM to Joseph T. Clark, Apr. 13, 1931, [FM] to Crofoot, Aug. 14, 1931, FM to Charles E. Boyd, Aug. 21, 1931, FM to William

H. Chenay, Aug. 28, 1931, FM to Carmen Peck, Sept. 8, 1931, FM to Ludwell Denny, July 29, 1932, MOR.

22. *DN*, Oct. 13, 1930, Mar. 24, 31, Apr. 4, 1931; *DT*, Apr. 1, 19, 1931; *Journal of the Common Council*, Jan. 13, 1931, p. 5; JG to Harold Buttenheim, Apr. 2, 1931, D. J. Goodwin to FM, Nov. 5, 1930, A. G. Mezerik to FM, Nov. 5, 1930, MOR; Frank D. Adams to FM, Mar. 30, 1931, FM Papers; Lovett to Henry Ling, Mar. 23, 1931, Lovett to Adams, Mar. 25, 1931, DCL Papers; Parker to Baldwin, Apr. 3, 4, 1931, Baldwin to FM, Apr. 7, 1931, ACLU Archives, Vol. 488.

23. Dana Ingalls to FM, Apr. 13, 1931, ACLU Special Committee to FM, July 30, 1931, MOR; Parker to Baldwin, June 28, 1931, ACLU Archives, Vol. 488; *DT*, July 11, 29, 1931; *DN*, Aug. 26, 1931.

24. *DN*, Aug. 26, Dec. 3, 1931; *DT*, Aug. 26, 1931; Boyd to FM, Aug. 20, 1931, Chenay to FM, Aug. 27, 1931, Watkins to Parker, Sept. 7, 12, 1931, Parker to Watkins, Sept. 10, 1931, City Clerk to Watkins, Sept. 5, 1931, Cohn Shops to FM, Oct. 7, 1931, FM to David K. Niles, Nov. 27, 1931, MOR; Parker Memorandum, Sept. 26, 1931, ACLU Archives, Vol. 488; Police Department report [Sept. 1931], MOR.

25. House Special Committee to Investigate Communist Activities in the United States, *Investigation of Communist Propaganda. Hearings Pursuant to H. Res. 220*, 71 Cong., 2 Sess., Part IV, I (Washington, 1930), 185; *DN*, Oct. 25, 1930, July 8, Aug. 21, 22, 1931, Mar. 10, 1932; Unemployed Councils of Detroit handbill [Oct. 1930], MOR; Unemployed Councils of Detroit, "Program for Relief . . ." [Feb. 1933], MOR; Milton Derber and Edwin Young, eds., *Labor and the New Deal* (Madison, 1957), pp. 87–90.

26. Unemployed Councils of Detroit handbill [Oct. 1930], MOR; *DN*, Oct. 25, 1930; *DFP*, Aug. 3, 1941; Parker to Baldwin, Oct. 26, 1930, Forrest Bailey to Parker, Oct. 30, 1930, ACLU Archives, Vol. 425.

27. *DN*, Oct. 29, Dec. 4, 1930, Feb. 26, 1931; *DT*, Apr. 17, 19, 1931; Parker to Bailey, Jan. 6, 1931, Parker to Baldwin, May 1, 1931, ACLU Archives, Vol. 488; Parker notes, Feb. 13, 27, 1931, ibid.; Philip A. Raymond and Alfred Goetz to FM, Apr. 2, 1931, MOR; Edmund Wilson, "The Despot of Dearborn," *Scribner's*, XC (July 1931), 26; ACLU, *The Fight for Civil Liberty, 1930–1931* (New York, 1931), pp. 21, 34; Cleveland *Press*, July 1, 1931, MSB; Ionia *Sentinel-Standard*, Mar. 7, 1931, MSB.

28. *DN*, July 8, Nov. 23, 25, 26, 28, 29, Dec. 3, 4, 28, 1931; *DT*, July 8, Nov. 26, 28, 1931.

29. *DN*, Nov. 26, 29, 1931; *Daily Worker*, Dec. 7, 1931; Trade Union Unity League et al. handbill [Dec. 1931], MOR; Detroit ACLU Resolution, Dec. 1, 1931, MOR; FM to Niles, Nov. 27, 1931, FM to Oswald Garrison Villard, Dec. 3, 1931, FM to Harry Slavin, Dec. 3, 1931, MOR.

30. ACLU, " '*Sweet Land of Liberty*,' " p. 41; *DN*, Dec. 4, 1931; draft

of Special Order, Dec. 1, 1931, MOR; ———— to Watkins, Dec. 1,
1931, Watkins to FM [Dec. 1931], Baldwin to FM, June 27, 1932,
G. O. Ohlsson to FM, Mar. 17, 1932, John Meyering to FM, Aug.
2, 1932, Cohn Shops to FM, Sept. 23, 1932, William Abramsohn to
FM, July 28, 1932, MOR; Parker to Baldwin, May 11, 1933, ACLU
Archives, Vol. 661. Before the December 4 regulations were adopted,
Baldwin rated Detroit the sixth "freest" city in the nation (after
Baltimore, San Francisco, St. Louis, Cleveland, and New Orleans).
R. L. Duffus, "Civilization in American Cities," *Scribner's*, XC (Oct.
1931), 357.

31. FM to Baldwin, Mar. 9, 1932, MOR.
32. Memo by W. P. Lovett, Mar. 8, 1932, with Lovett to Wilber Brucker,
Mar. 8, 1932, Lovett to Howard A. Coffin, Mar. 21, 1932, DCL Papers;
DN, Mar. 8, 1932; "Protest against the Bloody Ford Massacre," handbill
in MOR.
33. The account of the march is based on *DN*, Mar. 8, 9, 15, July 1,
1932; *NYT*, Mar. 8, 1932; *Daily Worker*, Mar. 8, 9, 19, 1932; *DT*,
Mar. 8, 1932; Lovett Memo, Mar. 8, 1932, DCL Papers; Oakley Johnson,
"After the Dearborn Massacre," *New Republic*, LXX (Mar. 30, 1932),
172; Maurice Sugar, "Bullets—Not Food—for Ford Workers," *Nation*,
CXXXIV (Mar. 23, 1932), 333-35; Felix Morrow, "Class War in Detroit,"
New Masses, VII (May 1932), 13-14; Harry Bennett, *We Never Called
Him Henry* (as told to Paul Marcus; New York, 1951), pp. 91-94;
"The Massacre of the Ford Hunger Marchers," *New Force*, I (Mar.-Apr.
1932), 7; Young Communist League, *The Youth and the Ford Hunger
March* [Detroit, 1932], pp. 3-9; Irving Bernstein, *The Lean Years:
A History of the American Worker, 1920-1933* (Boston, 1960), pp.
432-34; Keith Sward, *The Legend of Henry Ford* (New York, 1948),
pp. 231-38; Allan Nevins and Frank Ernest Hill, *Ford: Decline and
Rebirth, 1933-1962* (New York, 1962, 1963), pp. 32-34; Alex Baskin,
"The Ford Hunger March—1932," *Labor History*, XIII (Summer 1972),
335-42; Rowland Haynes to Fred C. Croxton, Mar. 14, 1932, State
Files, POUR Records; and Watkins to FM, Mar. 9, 16, 1932, MOR.
34. Undated and unsigned document in ACLU Archives, Vol. 575; "Statement of Eye-Witness . . . ," undated, ibid.; *DN*, Mar. 8, 1932; *DFP*,
Mar. 8, 1932; *DT*, Mar. 8, 1932; *NYT*, Mar. 8, 1932; *Daily Worker*,
Mar. 11, 1932; Johnson, "After the Dearborn Massacre," p. 174; Watkins
to FM, Mar. 16, 1932, MOR.
35. *Daily Worker*, Mar. 9-12, 14, 15, 19, 28, Apr. 4, 1932; *DN*, Mar. 12,
14, 15, 1932; *New Force*, I (Mar.-Apr. 1932); "Some Questions for
Ford's Mayor Murphy," undated, MOR; Young Communist League,
Youth, pp. 9-10; *Protest Resolution against Ford Massacre* [Mar. 1932],
MOR; Morrow, "Class War," pp. 14-15; Robert L. Cruden, *The End
of the Ford Myth* (New York, 1932), pp. 13-15.
36. Baskin, "Ford Hunger March," pp. 348-50; *DT*, Mar. 13, 1932; *DN*,

Mar. 11, 13, 1932; FM to Baldwin, Mar. 18, 1932, MOR; JG to FM [June 1949], FM Papers. There are dozens of wires and letters of protest from Communist-front groups in the MOR.

37. *Daily Worker,* Mar. 18, 28, 1932; *New Force,* I (Mar.-Apr. 1932); Cruden, *Ford Myth,* p. 12; Jerry H. Bacon to Baldwin, Mar. 21, 1932, ACLU Archives, Vol. 575; Baskin, "Ford Hunger March," pp. 352-56; *DN,* Mar. 8, 9, 11, 14, 15, July 1, 1932. On the participation of Ford personnel, see Helen V. Barnes, "Frank Murphy and the Ford Hunger March of 1932" (MS, 1952), pp. 25-26, in my possession.

38. Baldwin to FM, Mar. 8, 1932, FM to Baldwin, Mar. 9, 1932, Watkins to FM, Mar. 9, 1932, MOR. Italics supplied.

39. ACLU Release, Mar. 11, 1932, ACLU Archives, Vol. 575; Baldwin-Nelson statement, Mar. 12, 1932, ibid.; *DN,* Mar. 8, 11-13, 1932.

40. Watkins to FM, Mar. 16, 1932, Baldwin to FM, Mar. 17, 19, 1932, FM to Baldwin, Mar. 18, 1932, MOR; Baldwin to FM, Mar. 22, 1932, Baldwin to Nelson, Mar. 19, 1932, Watkins to Baldwin, Mar. 24, 1932, ACLU Archives, Vol. 575.

41. In the end, the ACLU had to abandon the idea of civil suits because evidence directly linking agents of the Ford Motor Company or Dearborn to the case was "wholly lacking." Baldwin to William L. Patterson, Oct. 10, 1933, ACLU Archives, Vol. 661.

42. Russell E. Golden to Baldwin, Mar. 21, 1932, Nelson to Baldwin, Mar. 24, 1932, Baldwin to Nelson, Mar. 28, 30, 1932, Baldwin to Sugar, Mar. 28, 31, 1932, Sugar to Baldwin, Mar. 29, 30, 1932, ibid., Vol. 575; Baldwin to FM, Mar. 30, 1932, MOR.

43. FM to Baldwin, Apr. 5, May 10, 1932, Watkins to FM, Apr. 13, 20, 1932, Baldwin to FM, May 3, 1932, FM to E. T. Olsen, May 7, 11, 1932, Olsen to FM, May 9, 18, 1932, FM to Guy A. Durgan, May 11, 1932, William C. Markley to FM, May 13, 1932, Bessie Bavley et al. to FM, Apr. 12, 1932, JG to Carl Brooks, May 10, 1932, JG to Fred J. Drexel, May 12, 1932, MOR; Affidavit by William L. Lewis, May 16, 1932, MOR; Johnson, "After the Dearborn Massacre," p. 174. Watkins later conceded that some of the wounded prisoner patients had been turned over to the Dearborn police at the latter's request. Watkins to FM, Apr. 20, 1932, MOR. Italics supplied.

44. Baldwin to FM, Mar. 30, Apr. 7, 12, 1932, FM to Baldwin, Apr. 11, 1932, MOR.

45. Baldwin to FM, June 16, 1932, Sugar to Baldwin, June 14, 1932, FM to Baldwin, June 24, 1932, ACLU Archives, Vol. 575; *DN,* June 6, 7, 1932; Mauritz A. Hallgren, "Grave Danger in Detroit," *Nation,* CXXXV (Aug. 3, 1932), 49.

46. FM to Baldwin, June 24, 1932, Baldwin to FM, June 27, 1932, Fred J. Schumann to Baldwin, July 26, 1932, ACLU Archives, Vol. 575.

47. *DN,* June 8, Nov. 25, 1932, Feb. 23, 1933; Goodwin to FM, Nov. 5, 1930, JG to Buttenheim, Apr. 2, 1931, JG to Guy C. Weed, May

27, 1932, Harry Riseman to FM, July 13, 1932, Unemployed Councils of Detroit to FM, Oct. 7 [1932], Committee to FM, Apr. 17, 1933, Ballenger to Norman H. Hill, Apr. 26, 1933, MOR; Hallgren, "Grave Danger," pp. 100–101; *DT,* Feb. 27, July 10, 1931; *Civic Searchlight,* Nov.–Dec. 1931, Mar. 1932; Lovett to T. F. Meyers, Dec. 3, 1935, DCL Papers; Lovett Memorandum on Communism and the Detroit Citizens League, Mar. 4, 1936, ibid.

48. Murphy was not disposed to make an issue of the censorship powers exercised by the police, who revoked the licenses of certain burlesque houses and stopped the sale of books that exploited the interest in crime and glorified criminals. The mayor himself, it will be recalled, stopped the showing of *The Birth of a Nation. DN,* Feb. 18, 1931, Nov. 16, 1932; Schumann to FM, Mar. 19, 1931, Watkins to FM, Oct. 18, 1932, MOR.

49. Parker to Bailey, Oct. 30, 1930, ACLU Archives, Vol. 425; HFW [Harry F. Ward] to Nelson, Dec. 8, 1930, Parker to Baldwin, Oct. 8, 1931, Baldwin to FM, Oct. 9, 1931, Mar. 30, 1932, ibid., Vol. 488; Nelson to Baldwin, Jan. 4, 1932, ibid., Vol. 575; *DN,* Nov. 28, 1930.

50. For an ugly confrontation between police and pickets in a strike of metal polishers against the Motor City Plating Co. soon after Murphy became mayor, see *DLN,* Oct. 3, 24, 31, Nov. 7, 1930.

51. Oral History Interview of Josephine Gomon, Dec. 22, 1959, p. 15, MHC; *NYT,* Jan. 29, 1933; JG to Mrs. Clarence Darrow, Feb. 11, 1933, MOR.

52. Mauritz A. Hallgren, *Seeds of Revolt* (New York, 1933), pp. 107–8; "The Briggs Waterloo Strike" [Jan. 1933], Henry Kraus Papers, ALHUA; "Strike at Brigg's [sic] Vernor Highway Plant," Joe Brown Collection, ibid.; Report of the Mayor's Non-Partisan Committee on Industrial Disputes (the Fact-Finding Committee), In the Matter of the Strike . . . at the Briggs Manufacturing Co., Feb. 21, 1933, pp. 31–32 (hereafter cited as Fact-Finding Report); *Auto Workers News,* Jan. 27, 1933; *Daily Worker,* Jan. 12, 16, 30, 1933; *DLN,* Jan. 20, 1933; *DN,* Feb. 10, 1933; Phillip Bonosky, *Brother Bill McKie* (New York, 1953), p. 89; Samuel Romer, "That Detroit Strike," *Nation,* CXXXVI (Feb. 15, 1933), 167; *Industrial Worker,* Jan. 24, 1933; Phil Raymond, "The Briggs Auto Strike Victory," *Labor Unity,* VIII (Mar. 1933), 21–24; James R. Prickett, "Communists and the Automobile Industry in Detroit before 1935," *Michigan History,* LVII (Fall 1973), 199–200.

53. Fact-Finding Report, pp. 2–20, 42–48, 55; Sidney Fine, *The Automobile under the Blue Eagle* (Ann Arbor, 1963), pp. 27–28; *DLN,* Jan. 27, 1933; *Auto Workers News,* Jan. 27, 1933; "Brigg's [sic] Strike," undated, Brown Collection; *DN,* Jan. 24, 26, 27, 29, Feb. 7–9, 21, 22, 1933; Harry H. Brown to Franklin D. Roosevelt, Feb. 3, 1933, DNC Records, FDRL; Pilkington to H. L. Kerwin, Jan. 28, Feb. 2, 7, 1933, File 170-7752, Records of the Federal Mediation and Conciliation Service,

RG 280, NARS (hereafter cited as CS File); [John F. Hamilton] to William A. Comstock, Mar. 4, 1933, Carl M. Weideman Papers, MHC; checks of Briggs workers, in ibid.; Bonosky, *McKie*, p. 88; *Forbes*, XXI (Feb. 15, 1933), 11–13; Jim Piekarniak to FM, Feb. 26, 1933, MOR; Sward, *Legend*, p. 221; Ralph Janis, "The Briggs Strike" (MS, 1967), p. 17, in my possession.

54. Report of Proceedings before the Mayor's Non-Partisan Committee on Industrial Disputes, Feb. 2, 1933, pp. 140, 145, Frank Marquardt Papers, ALHUA (hereafter cited as Fact-Finding Proceedings); *DN*, Jan. 27, 31, Feb. 2–7, 1933; *Auto Workers News*, Jan. 27, 1933; Fact-Finding Report, pp. 21, 32; *DLN*, Feb. 17, 1933; *Business Week*, Feb. 15, 1933, p. 7; Prickett, "Communists and the Automobile Industry," pp. 200–205. See the Statements taken . . . Feb. 11, 1933 in the Office of Larry S. Davidow, pp. 1, 7, 11, 14, 22, EGK Papers.

55. *DN*, Feb. 8, 1933. For the Communist reaction to this decision, see *Auto Workers News*, Feb. 13, 1933, and "Some Lessons of the Strike Struggle in Detroit," *Communist*, XVII (Mar. 1933), 200–201.

56. *DN*, Jan. 28, 31, Feb. 1, 2, 7–9, 21, 1933; Pilkington to Kerwin, Feb. 2, 7, 1933, CS File 170-7752; Fact-Finding Proceedings, Jan. 31, 1933, p. 487, Feb. 2, 1933, p. 139; Fact-Finding Report, pp. 29, 37, 50; *Business Week*, Feb. 15, 1933, p. 7; *Automotive Industries*, LXVIII (Feb. 11, 1933), 175.

57. *DN*, Jan. 26, 27, 30, 31, Feb. 1–3, 7–11, 13, 1933; *Business Week*, Feb. 15, 1933, p. 7; *Industrial Worker*, Feb. 7, 1933.

58. Pilkington to Kerwin, Jan. 28, 1933, CS File 170–7752; *DN*, Jan. 27, 1933; *NYT*, Jan. 31, 1933; *DLN*, Feb. 3, 1933; *Business Week*, Feb. 22, 1933, p. 10; Sward, *Legend*, pp. 220–21; W. J. Cameron to Lovett, Feb. 15, 1933, DCL Papers.

59. *DN*, Jan. 28, 30, 31, Feb. 1–4, 7, 9, 11, 12, 21, 1933; Pilkington to Kerwin, Feb. 27, Mar. 20, 1933, CS File 170-7752; Fact-Finding Report, p. 36; *DLN*, Feb. 3, 17, Mar. 10, 1933; Detroit *Leader*, Feb. 11, Mar. 4, 1933; *Industrial Worker*, Feb. 14, 28, Mar. 7, 14, 1933; [Hamilton] to Comstock, Mar. 4, 1933, Weideman Papers.

60. Fact-Finding Proceedings, Feb. 6, 1933, p. 400; *DN*, Feb. 6, 21, 22, 1933; Pilkington to Kerwin, Feb. 21, 1933, CS File 170-7752; *DLN*, Apr. 7, 1933; Oral History Interview of John W. Anderson, Feb. 17–May 21, 1960, p. 18, MHC.

61. FM to Brian McCluskey, Feb. 3, 1933, FM to Piekarniak, Mar. 1, 1933, MOR; *DN*, Jan. 27, Feb. 6, 12, 1933; Fact-Finding Proceedings, Feb. 2, 1933, pp. 185–86; JG to FM, Dec. 11, 1947, FM Papers.

62. Minutes of the Meetings of the Board of Street Railway Commissioners, Feb. 3, 7, 1933, MOR; undated item, ibid.; *DN*, Feb. 6, 1933.

63. *DT*, Jan. 27, 1933; *DN*, Jan. 28, 31, Feb. 9, 1933; [*Central Press Association*, Jan. 1933], MSB; FM to Higgins, Feb. 27, 1933, MOR.

64. Fact-Finding Proceedings, Jan. 31, 1933, pp. 487, 492–94, 495, 497–98; [*Central Press Association*, Jan. 1933], MSB; *DN*, Feb. 6, 1933; FM

to L. W. Wickson, Mar. 23, 1933, MOR.

65. Fact-Finding Report, pp. 37-39; Fact-Finding Proceedings, Jan. 31, 1933, p. 500, Feb. 2, 1933, pp. 151, 337, 349, Feb. 3, 1933, pp. 380-82, 387, Feb. 6, 1933, p. 502, Feb. 8, 1933, pp. 503, 506-7; *DN*, Jan. 31, Feb. 1, 4, 7, 8, 10, 12, 1933; Pilkington to Kerwin, Feb. 7, 1933, CS File 170-7752.

66. Fact-Finding Report, pp. 51-57; *DN*, Feb. 23, 1933.

67. FM to Higgins, Feb. 27, 1933, MOR.

68. *DN*, Feb. 4, 9, 1933; *NYT*, Feb. 4, 1933; Interview with Larry S. Davidow, May 12, 1967, pp. 13-14, MHC; Detroit *Leader*, Feb. 11, 1933; Fact-Finding Proceedings, Jan. 31, 1933, p. 492, Feb. 6, 1933, p. 485.

69. [Report of the Committee on Labor and Legal Problems, Mar. 1933], Joseph A. Labadie Collection, Harlan Hatcher Graduate Library, University of Michigan, Ann Arbor, Michigan; *DT*, Mar. 2, 1933; Detroit *Leader*, Mar. 4, 1933.

70. Briggs hired some private police to serve at the Mack Avenue plant, but their role appears to have been minimal. Fact-Finding Report, p. 36.

71. *DN*, Feb. 2-5, 7, 9, 13, 1933; *NYT*, Feb. 2, 1933; Watkins to FM, Feb. 7, 1933, MOR; Fact-Finding Proceedings, Feb. 2, 1933, p. 347; *Industrial Worker*, Feb. 14, 21, 1933; JB's [Joe Brown] Field Notes, Briggs Strike, Mar. 7, 1933, Brown Collection.

72. Oksen Mirrakian et al. to FM, Feb. 3, 1933, Briggs Strike Defence [*sic*] Committee to FM and Watkins, Feb. 6, 1933, Watkins to FM, Mar. 7, 1933, MOR; Fact-Finding Proceedings, Feb. 2, 1933, pp. 327-28, 337, 345, Feb. 3, 1933, pp. 383-84; Fact-Finding Report, p. 41; *DN*, Jan. 30, Feb. 2-5, 7, 8, Mar. 3-5, 1933; *DLN*, Mar. 3, 10, 1933; sheet headed "10940 Mack Ave. . . . ," Mar. 20, 1933, Brown Collection; Pilkington to Kerwin, Jan. 28, 1933, CS File 170-7752.

73. Fact-Finding Proceedings, Jan. 31, 1933, pp. 496-97, 500, Feb. 2, 1933, p. 339, Feb. 6, 1933, pp. 484-85; FM to George McKenzie, Feb. 2, 1933, FM to McCluskey, Feb. 3, 1933, FM to Otto Freund, Feb. 7, 1933, FM to . . . Polish Chamber of Labor, Feb. 7, 1933, FM to John Wasilewski, Feb. 9, 1933, FM to Polish-American Political Club . . . , Feb. 27, 1933, MOR; *DN*, Jan. 27, Feb. 6, 7, 1933; *DLN*, Mar. 10, 1933; JB's Field Notes, Mar. 7, 1933, Brown Collection.

74. Fact-Finding Report, p. 56; *DLN*, Feb. 3, 1933; FM to Polish-American Political Club . . . , Feb. 27, 1933, Baldwin to FM, Mar. 30, 1932, MOR.

CHAPTER XV

1. *DLN*, Jan. 1, 1932.

2. Harry Dahlheimer, *Public Transportation in Detroit* (Detroit, 1951), pp. 8-17; Harry Barnard, *Independent Man: The Life of Senator James Couzens* (New York, 1958), p. 126-33.

3. William P. Lovett, *Detroit Rules Itself* (Boston, 1930), pp. 119-20, 125-26; *DN*, Sept. 11, Oct. 13, Dec. 15, 1930, Jan. 27, 31, Feb. 1, 1931, July 21, 1932.
4. *DN*, Sept. 24, 27, Oct. 3, 13, 1930; E. J. Lunt to FM, undated, with William M. Hauser to FM, Sept. 19, 1930, Nick J. Schorn to FM, Sept. 20, 1930, FM Papers.
5. *DN*, Oct. 2, 3, 1930, Mar. 18, May 6, 1931, Jan. 12, 15-17, Mar. 3, July 20, Dec. 6, 1932, Mar. 26, 1933; *Journal of the Common Council*, Jan. 13, 1932, pp. 1-2.
6. *DN*, Mar. 26, Apr. 9, 1933.
7. *DN*, Sept. 29, Oct. 2-4, 1930, Jan. 27, 31, Feb. 1, 6, July 29-31, Aug. 4-5, 1931; *DT*, July 30, 1931; *DLN*, July 31, 1931; FM to Frank Couzens, June 26, 1931, MOR; FM message, Jan. 17, 1931 [1932], FM Papers; Dahlheimer, *Public Transportation*, p. 18.
8. *DN*, Feb. 1, 6, Mar. 2, 28, 31, Apr. 28, May 23, Dec. 23, 1931; Frank Martel to Henry Montgomery, Mar. 13, 1931, Wayne County AFL-CIO Papers, Box 3, ALHUA.
9. *DN*, June 6, July 8, Aug. 27, Sept. 1, 15, 18, Oct. 1-4, 28, Dec. 8, 14, 16, 21-24, 29, 1931; *DLN*, Sept. 25, Dec. 25, 1931; FM to Robert O. Lord, Jan. 4, 1932, MOR; FM reply to "Committee of 51" questionnaire, undated, MOR.
10. *DN*, Dec. 26, 28-30, 1931; *DLN*, Jan. 1, 8, 1932; Caroline Parker to Roger N. Baldwin, Apr. 3, 1932, ACLU Archives, Vol. 575.
11. *DN*, Dec. 23, 1931, Jan. 1-4, 1932.
12. G. Hall Roosevelt to FM, July 27, 1932, FM to Frank P. Book, Sept. 22, 1932, FM to James I. Williston, Dec. 13, 1932, MOR; George H. Fenkell, Information Re Water Department, Nov. 14, 1932, ibid.; City of Detroit, Department of Water Supply [Dec. 1932], ibid.; *DN*, Feb. 16, Mar. 13, Nov. 17, Dec. 7, 1932; Department of Water Supply, Annual Report for the Year Ended June 30, 1933, p. 4.
13. Melvin G. Holli, *Reform in Detroit: Hazen S. Pingree and Urban Politics* (New York, 1969), pp. 74-94; Michael B. Staebler, "From the Progressive Era to the New Deal: A Study of Three Detroit Reform Mayors" (MS, 1966), p. 40, in Mr. Staebler's possession; Raymond C. Miller, *Kilowatts at Work: A History of the Detroit Edison Company* (Detroit, 1957), pp. 37-38, 199-203, 206-7; Thompson to Martel, Apr. 2, 1931, Wayne County AFL-CIO Papers, Box 14; Thompson to FM, Apr. 2, 8, Aug. 6, 1931, FM to Thompson, Apr. 3, 9, 1931, MOR.
14. John Bauer, "Public Utilities," in Clarence E. Ridley and Orin F. Nolting, eds., *What the Depression Has Done to Cities* (Chicago, 1935), p. 44; FM to Harry Bitner, Jan. 22, 1932, FM Papers; FM to C. L. Weaver, May 18, 1932, MOR; *DN*, Jan. 28, Feb. 25, 1932; *DLN*, Apr. 8, 1932.
15. FM to Bitner, Jan. 22, 1932, FM Papers; *DT*, Feb. 22, 1932; *DLN*, Mar. 18, 1932; *DN*, Sept. 20, 27, 1931, Jan. 28, Feb. 24, 25, Mar. 7, 1932; Wilcox to FM, Nov. 29, 1932, MOR.

16. *DN*, Jan. 28, Feb. 14, 21, 24, Mar. 4, 11, 20, 22, 31, 1932; FM to J. D. Richardson, Mar. 25, 1932, FM to Fitzpatrick, Dec. 21, 1932, Arthur F. Lederle to Wilcox, Nov. 28, 1932, MOR; Raymond J. Kelly to FM, June 2, 1937, FM Papers.

17. *DT*, Jan. 25, 1932; Thompson to FM, Aug. 7, 1931, MOR; Holli, *Reform in Detroit*, pp. 83-85; *DLN*, Feb. 12, 1932; *DN*, Mar. 9, 16, 1932; *DFP*, Mar. 11, 1932; Miller, *Kilowatts at Work,* pp. 38, 44, 194, 239.

18. *DN*, Feb. 17, Mar. 6, 10, 12, 16, Apr. 2, 7, May 4, 5, Aug. 20, Nov. 3, 13, 1932; James H. Lee to Wilcox, Nov. 28, 1932, MOR; Miller, *Kilowatts at Work,* pp. 330, 332; William H. Lane, *A History of Electric Service in Detroit* (Detroit, 1937), pp. 82-83.

19. Thompson to FM, Aug. 6, 7, 1931, Louis J. Schrenk to FM, Mar. 2, 1932, MOR; *DN*, Feb. 24, 25, 1932.

20. *DN*, Feb. 14, Mar. 30, Apr. 25, May 19, June 2, 10, 16, Aug. 10, 1932; Smith to Elizabeth Gilley, Aug. 30, 1932, Oil and Gas Producers Association of Michigan to FM, Mar. 19, 1932, William J. Woolfolk to FM, Apr. 21, 1932, John L. Lovett to FM, Apr. 23, 1932, Woolfolk to Common Council, July 30, 1932, enclosing Lovett to William P. Bradley, Apr. 23, 1932, Haswell Grant to Dear Mr. ———, June 15, 1932, MOR.

21. *DN*, Mar. 5, 6, 8, 9, 13, 15-19, 30, Apr. 2, May 8, 1932; Woolfolk to FM, Apr. 2, 1932, MOR; *DT*, Mar. 21, 1932.

22. *DN*, May 13, 18, 23-25, 28, June 1, 7-9, 15, 21, 1932, Jan. 10, 1933; *DT*, Mar. 8, 1933; Woolfolk to Common Council, July 11, 1932, John Atkinson and Wilcox to FM, Nov. 28, 1932, MOR; F. Couzens to FM, Apr. 26, 1937, Kelly to FM, June 2, 1937, FM Papers.

23. *DN*, July 21, Aug. 4, 10, Nov. 9, 1932; Ralph Stone to FM, Aug. 11, 1932, and enclosed Memorandum re Charter Amendment . . . [Aug. 7, 1932], Roosevelt to FM, Aug. 5, 1932, MOR.

24. Bauer, "Public Utilities," p. 45; FM to Thompson, Apr. 9, 1931, MOR; FM to Clement A. Norton, Aug. 3, 1935, Loren N. O'Brien to FM, Apr. 11, 1932, FM Papers; O'Brien to FDR, Mar. 15, 1932, DNC Records, FDRL.

CHAPTER XVI

1. *DN*, Apr. 12, May 22, 1931; *DT*, Sept. 2, 1931.

2. *DN*, Aug. 9, 11, 14, 30, 31, Sept. 4, 6, 11, 12, 17, 1931; C. V. Fenner to FM, Aug. 1, 1932, MOR.

3. *DN*, Aug. 11, 21, 22, 30, Sept. 9, 13, 18, 27, Oct. 2, 5, 1931; *DT*, Sept. 13, Oct. 3, 1931; Raul H. Rice to FM, Nov. 22, 1931, FM Papers; G. Hall Roosevelt to Louis Howe, Aug. 12, 1931, DNC Records, FDRL; EGK notes on J. Woodford Howard MS [June 20, 1959], EGK Papers.

4. *DN*, Sept. 4, 9, 11, 12, 17, 18, 20, 25-30, Oct. 1-5, 1931; statement to press [1931], MOR.

5. Mead to M. L. Walker [Nov. 3, 1931], Moses L. Walker Papers, MHC;

C. E. Brewer to FM, June 1, 1931, and enclosed order, MOR; *DN,* Aug. 30, Sept. 13, 15, 1931, June 10, 17, 18, 1932; *DFP,* Sept. 12, 15, 1931, June 11, 1932; *DT,* Sept. 15, 17, Oct. 7, 1931; *DSN,* May 30, June 6, 1931; Lillian G. Durgan to FM, Nov. 6, 1931, FM to Niebuhr, Nov. 9, 1931, Peter A. Quinn to FM, May 10, 1932, FM to GM, Feb. 15, 1936, enclosing FM to A. R. Johnson, Feb. 15, 1936, FM Papers; GM to Byron Foy, Oct. 15, 1931, GM Papers.

6. *DN,* Sept. 16–19, 26, 27, 29, 30, Oct. 1, 2, 4, 5, 1931; *DT,* Oct. 3, 1931; *DLN,* Oct. 2, 1931; FM radio address [Oct. 1, 1931], MOR; FM reply to "Commitee of 51" questionnaire, undated, MOR; *Frank Murphy What He Has Done! . . . ,* FM Papers.

7. *DN,* Sept. 19–22, 26, 28–30, Oct. 1, 3, 5, 1931; *Legion News,* Oct. 2, 1931; Donald J. Graham to FM, Sept. 23, 1931, FM Papers; Allen Bibb to FM, June 13, 1932, MOR. See "Reported Meetings Attended by Mayor Murphy" and the many invitations to attend meetings of ethnic groups in FM Papers, BHC.

8. *DN,* May 22, 24, Sept. 20, 1931; *DT,* Oct. 3, 1931; statement to press [1931], MOR; Alex E. Black to FM, May 28, 1931, T. J. Maloney to FM, Sept. 7, 1931, Charles Kessler to FM, Sept. 30, 1931, Cermak to Miles B. Geringer, Oct. 1, 1931, Geringer to Cermak, Oct. 2, 1931, M. Nicholson to FM, Oct. 3, 1931, FM Papers; G. G. Lopez to Norman H. Hill, FM Papers, BHC; extract from *Italian Federation Political News* [Oct. 1931], MOR; Frank Martel to FM, Sept. 24, 1931, Wayne County AFL-CIO Papers, ALHUA; *DLN,* Sept. 18, Oct. 2, 1931.

9. *The Reminder,* Oct. 4, 1931, FM Papers; Fred C. Zimmer to FM, Oct. 3, 1931, Coughlin to FM, Oct. 7, 1931, Mother Patricia to FM, Oct. 17, 1931, ibid.; *Frank Murphy What He Has Done! . . . ,* ibid.

10. William Randolph Hearst to FM, Oct. 19, 1931, FM Papers; [Detroit *Mirror,* Sept. 9, 1931], clipping in ibid.; G. H. Roosevelt to Howe, Aug. 12, 19, 1931, DNC Records; FM to J. M. Patterson, Oct. 12, 1931, FM to Editor, Detroit *Mirror,* Nov. 4, 1931, MOR.

11. Starrett received 21,928 votes; Sosnowski, 11,543; Hanna, 7,370; Schmies, 5,085; and Gover, 711. *DN,* Oct. 7, Nov. 4, 1931; *DT,* Oct. 7, 1931.

12. For the precinct returns in the primary, see Canvass of Votes Cast in the Primary, Oct. 6, 1931, FM Papers. The analysis of the returns is based on *DN,* Oct. 7, 1931; Thomas R. Solomon, "Participation of Negroes in Detroit Elections" (Ph.D. thesis, University of Michigan, 1939), pp. 55, 89, 119, 146, 153–55; Donald S. Hecock and Harry A. Trevelyan, *Detroit Voters and Recent Elections* (Detroit, 1938), Foreword, pp. 45–62; Bureau of the Census, *Fifteenth Census of the United States: 1930, Population,* III, Part 1 (Washington, 1932), 1183; and Raymond E. Wolfinger, "The Development and Persistence of Ethnic Voting," *American Political Science Review,* LIX (Dec. 1965), 896. The Solomon study pinpoints black precincts, and the Hecock

and Trevelyan work is useful in identifying precincts with large concentrations of the foreign born.

13. FM to Villard, Oct. 9, 1931, FM Papers; *Nation*, CXXXIII (Oct. 21, 1931), 418; Mrs. Donald H. Bacon to *Time*, Oct. 9, 1931, MOR; *DFP*, July 24, 1931.

14. *How and Why Are You Voting November 3rd* [Oct. 1931], FM Papers; *DN*, Nov. 4, 1931.

15. *DN*, Oct. 28, 31, Nov. 2, 4, 1931; *DT*, Oct. 31, 1931; *DSN*, Oct. 17, 31, 1931; William Tuns [?] to FM, Oct. 29, 1931, FM Papers; William P. Lovett, "Detroit Voters Show Discriminating Judgment," *National Municipal Review*, XX (Dec. 1931), 741.

16. *DN*, Oct. 28, 31, Nov. 4, 1931; *NYT*, Nov. 8, 1931; Charles B. Williams to FM, Oct. 27, 1931, Mary O'Leary to FM, Oct. 29, 1931, Kathryn L. Tice to FM, Nov. 2, 1931, James J. Widdifield to FM, Nov. 3, 1931, FM Papers; Mr. and Mrs. Stephen J. Cherry to FM, Oct. 30, 1931, John Erler to FM, Oct. 28, 1931, Robert Laws to FM, Oct. 29, 1931, A. Wunderle to FM, Oct. 29, 1931, Anthony J. Lamach to Citizens Fact Finding Committee, Oct. 28, 1931, MOR.

17. *DN*, Oct. 20, 22, 28, 30, 31, Nov. 1, 2, 4, 1931; William Vollmer to FM, Oct. 16, 1931, Ambrose A. Hudwick to FM, Oct. 22, 1931, James C. Traylor and Thomas J. Ormsby to FM, Oct. 23, 1931, M. L. Black to FM, Oct. 26, 1931, FM to Vincent Guiliano, Oct. 26, 1931, James Novick and Paul Malis to FM, Oct. 28, 1931, Michael J. Topalov to FM, Oct. 31, 1931, P. E. Mayrand to FM, Oct. 31, 1931, John D. Dingell to FM,. Nov. 4, 1931, FM Papers; Sandor Engel to FM, Oct. 20, 1931, Robert J. Peretto to FM, Oct. 24, 1931, FM Papers, BHC; Harold M. Owen to FM, Oct. 15, 1931, MOR; *DLN*, Oct. 30, 1931; *DT*, Oct. 15, Nov. 2, 1931; Hill notes on FM radio address [Nov. 2, 1931], FM Papers.

18. *DN*, Nov. 4, 1931; *DT*, Nov. 4, 1931; Solomon, "Participation of Negroes," p. 146; Hecock and Trevelyan, *Detroit Voters*, pp. 45–62; Bureau of the Census, *Fifteenth Census, Population*, III, Part 1, 1183. Murphy received 87 percent of the vote in Ward 3, 92.8 percent in Ward 5, and 93.1 percent in Ward 7—the three black wards—as compared to 54.5 percent in Ward 2, 53.5 percent in Ward 4, and 45.3 percent in Ward 22, all predominantly native-born white wards. Emmons defeated Murphy 110 to 47 in the wealthy Precinct 15 of Ward 1, 526 to 428 in the Palmer Woods district, and 262 to 213 in the Indian Village–Whittier Hotel precincts.

19. Raymond J. Kelly to FM, Nov. 4, 1931, Leon Fram to FM, Nov. 6, 1931, Niebuhr to FM, Nov. 6, 1931, Samuel Levin to FM, Nov. 6, 1931, William L. Stidger to FM, Nov. 6, 1931, William Murphy to FM, Nov. 6, 1931, Martha Gross to FM, Nov. 4, 1931, Mrs. Cornelius Georgette to FM [Nov. 1931], FM Papers; Lovett, "Detroit Voters," p. 741; *Michigan Catholic*, Nov. 5, 1931; Detroit *Mirror*, Nov. 4, 1931,

MSB; *DT,* Nov. 6, 1931; *NYT,* Nov. 8, 1931; *DSN,* Nov. 7, 1931; Lovett to Hal W. Hazelrigg, Nov. 14, 1931, DCL Papers.

20. Detroit *Mirror,* Nov. 4, 1931, MSB; F. D. Roosevelt to FM, Nov. 12, 1931, FM Papers.

21. FM to Chairman, Wayne County Republican Convention, Sept. 16, 1930, Roscoe B. Huston to FM, Jan. 25, 1932, FM Papers; *DT,* Oct. 20, 21, 1930; *DN,* Oct. 8, 11, 13, 1930; Abbott to Comstock, Oct. 5, 1930, William A. Comstock Papers, MHC; Richard Theodore Ortquist, Jr., "Depression Politics in Michigan, 1929-1932" (Ph.D. thesis, University of Michigan, 1968), pp. 71-73.

22. *DN,* Feb. 22, Mar. 5, 6, 14, Apr. 12, 1931; Alpena *News,* Mar. 13, 1931, MSB; Arthur A. Ekirch, Jr., *Ideologies and Utopias: The Impact of the New Deal on American Thought* (Chicago, 1969), pp. 70-71; FM to Howard Y. Williams, Jan. 5, May 22, 1931, Dewey to FM, Jan. 15, 1931, Williams to FM, May 18, 1931, MOR; Richard Lowitt, *George W. Norris: The Persistence of a Progressive, 1913-1933* (Urbana, 1971), pp. 509-10.

23. Greenville (Michigan) *Daily News* [Jan. 1932], clipping in MOR; Couzens to FM, Mar. 18, 1931, Stidger to FM [Apr. 1931], FM Papers; Merrick M. Hill, in [Lansing *Capital News*], undated, MSB; Flint *Sunday Journal* [Mar. 15, 1931], MSB; Alpena *News,* Mar. 15, 1931, MSB; *DT,* Mar. 15, 1931; "The Progressives' Bid for Power," *Literary Digest,* CVIII (Mar. 28, 1931), 7-8.

24. Hallgren, "Detroit's Liberal Mayor," *Nation,* CXXXII (May 13, 1931), 526-28; Wilson, "The Despot of Dearborn," *Scribner's,* XC (July 1931), 26; (New York) *Daily Mirror,* Sept. 9, 1931, clipping in FM Papers; *DN,* Nov. 19, 1931; Kennedy, "City of Hope," *Collier's,* LXXXIX (Apr. 30, 1932), 20, 50; FM to Kennedy, Dec. 22, 1932, FM Papers.

25. FM to Charles W. Casgrain, Aug. 15, 1932, Lee Kreiselman to FM, June 29 [1939], FM Papers; Interview with Lee Kreiselman Jaffe, Nov. 13, 1964; Interview with Jack Manning, Dec. 4, 1964, p. 5, MHC; Czar Dyer to FM, Feb. 24, 1932, EMB Papers; *DN,* July 4, 1932; George Q. Flynn, *American Catholics and the Roosevelt Presidency* (Lexington, 1968), pp. 7-10; Richard T. Ortquist Interview with Harry Mead, June 8, 1964, p. 7, MHC. Cf. Interview with Carl Muller, Oct. 6, 1964, p. 34, MHC.

26. *DN,* Feb. 22, 24, 1931; *DFP,* Feb. 22, July 13, 1931; *DSN,* Feb. 28, Mar. 14, 1931.

27. *DN,* Apr. 12, 1931, Jan. 4, 1932; [*Border Cities Star,* Jan. 16, 1932], MSB; FM to Walter White, Feb. 11, 1932, MOR; FM to Dyer, Feb. 27, 1932, EMB Papers; GM to Farley, Mar. 31, 1932, GM Papers; William J. Davitt to FM, Apr. 2, 11, 1932, FM Papers.

28. G. H. Roosevelt to F. D. Roosevelt, Sept. 12, 1930, Governor Papers, FDRL; G. H. Roosevelt to Howe, Aug. 12, 19, Dec. 2, 1931, [Howe] to G. H. Roosevelt, Nov. 16, 1931, DNC Records; *DN,* June 7-8, 1931.

29. *DN*, Jan. 4, 8, Feb. 28, 1932; *NYT*, Jan. 3, 1932; F. D. Roosevelt to FM, Dec. 29, 1931, FM to FDR, Dec. 30, 1931, FM Papers. Murphy's influence is misjudged in Frank Freidel, *Franklin D. Roosevelt: The Triumph* (Boston, 1956), pp. 284-85, and Earland Irving Carlson, "Franklin D. Roosevelt's Fight for the Presidential Nomination, 1928-1932" (Ph.D. thesis, University of Illinois, 1956), p. 334.

30. *DN*, Mar. 31, Apr. 1, 13, 14, June 5, 13, 1932; *DT*, Mar. 31, Apr. 1, 14, 16, 1932; GM to Farley, Apr. 1, 1932, GM Papers; O'Brien to FDR, Apr. 18, 1932, DNC Records; FM to Davie Davis, June 14, 1933, FM to GM, Sept. 17, 1934, FM Papers; Interview with Harry Mead, Aug. 5, 1963, p. 12, MHC; Ortquist interview with Mead, pp. 6-7.

31. *DN*, Mar. 17, Apr. 10, 14, 15, May 27, 1932; *DT*, Mar. 17, 1932; Interview with James A. Farley, Nov. 11, 1964, pp. 1-2, MHC; Ortquist interview with Mead, p. 10; G. H. Roosevelt to F. D. Roosevelt, Apr. 19, 1932, Roland S. Phillips to FDR, Apr. 10, 1932, DNC Records; FM to Picard, Mar. 9, 1932, Farley to FM, Apr. 11, 1932, FM Papers; Farley to GM, Apr. 11, 1932, GM Papers; FDR to Abbott, Apr. 29, 1932, Abbott to F. D. Roosevelt, May 9, 1932, Horatio J. Abbott Papers, MHC; Carlson, "Roosevelt's Fight," p. 334.

32. GM to Howe, Feb. 9, 1932, GM to Farley, Apr. 16, 1932, Farley to GM, Apr. 21, 1932, GM Papers; G. H. Roosevelt to F. D. Roosevelt, Feb. 20, Mar. 7, Apr. 19, 1932, F. D. Roosevelt to G. H. Roosevelt, June 3, 1932, DNC Records; Farley to FM, May 3, 1932, FM Papers; Freidel, *Triumph*, p. 285. George Murphy and Hall Roosevelt were obviously relaying advice received from Frank.

33. *DN*, June 19, 24, July 3, 1932; *DSN*, June 18, 1932; Comstock to Joseph E. Stringham, Apr. 18, 1932, Comstock Papers.

34. The platform advocated the extension of federal credit to the states for relief when state resources were inadequate and, also, the expansion of federal public works. Henry Steele Commager, ed., *Documents of American History*, 6th ed. (New York, 1958), II, 418.

35. *DT*, June 26-28, 30, 1932; *DN*, June 27, July 4, 1932; Ortquist, "Depression Politics," p. 184.

36. *DN*, June 29, 30, July 1-4, 1932; *DT*, July 1, 3, 1932; *DSN*, July 9, 1932; *DFP*, Nov. 13, 1932; Ortquist, "Depression Politics," p. 188; Gloria Winden Newquist, "James A. Farley and the Politics of Victory, 1928-1936" (Ph.D. thesis, University of Southern California, 1966), pp. 417-18; GM to Ernest K. Lindley, July 7, 1932, GM Papers; Kreiselman to FM, June 29 [1939], FM Papers.

37. Ortquist interview with Mead, p. 9; FM to W. J. Niederpruen, Aug. 12, 1932, FM to Casgrain, Aug. 15, 1932, FM to Frederic C. Howe, Sept. 23, 1932, FM Papers; Jordan A. Schwarz, *The Interregnum of Despair: Hoover, Congress, and the Depression* (Urbana, 1970), p. 199.

38. *DN*, Oct. 3, 1932; Flynn, *Catholics and Roosevelt*, p. 17.

39. Stokes, *Chip Off My Shoulder* (Princeton, 1940), pp. 304-5. Cf. *DN,* Oct. 23, 24, 1932. See Theodore G. Joslin, *Hoover Off the Record* (Garden City, 1934), pp. 320-21, and FM to J. R. Wilson, Jan. 21, 1933, for allegations that Communists instigated the demonstration against Hoover. Murphy was on the campaign trail when Hoover visited Detroit.

40. GM to George E. Manting, Oct. 12, 1932, Kinnane to William F. Connolly, Oct. 27, 1932, GM to Elliot Coupland, Oct. 28, 1932, GM Papers; G. H. Roosevelt to Howe, Oct. 24, 1932, GM to Howe, Oct. 24, 1932, and enclosed clipping from (Marquette) *Daily Mining Journal,* Oct. 22, 1932, GM to Howe, Oct. 19, 1932, and enclosed clipping, Mrs. John Roach to FDR, Nov. 1, 1932, DNC Records; Stanley L. Bullivant to Hill, Oct. 25, 1932, Richard Quick to FM, Oct. 27, 1932, James Hammond to FM [Nov. 8, 1932], FM to GM, Sept. 17, 1934, FM Papers; *DN,* Dec. 18, 1932.

41. Clipping with GM to Howe, Oct. 19, 1932, (Marquette) *Daily Mining Journal,* Oct. 22, 1932, with GM to Howe, Oct. 24, 1932, DNC Records; *DT,* Oct. 30, Nov. 4, 1932; *DN,* Oct. 26, Nov. 1, 1932.

42. G. H. Roosevelt to Howe [Sept. 1932], FM to Howe, Oct. 20, 28, 1932, DNC Records; *DT,* Oct. 20, 26, 30, 1932; *DN,* Oct. 20, 1932; Parker to Roger N. Baldwin, Oct. 29, 1932, ACLU Archives, Vol. 575; Ortquist, "Depression Politics," pp. 192-93.

43. Ortquist, "Depression Politics," pp. 205-7; Del Smith to FM, Nov. 9, 1932, FM to Benjamin Comfort, Nov. 15, 1932, MOR; Thomas A. Hyland to FDR, Nov. 9, 1932, DNC Records; FM to Brigid McKenna, Nov. 15, 1932, Vincent J. Toole to FM, Jan. 19, 1933, enclosing Toole to Farley, Dec. 28, 1932, FM Papers; Edward H. Litchfield, *Voting Behavior in a Metropolitan Area* (Ann Arbor, 1941), p. 39. Litchfield's figures for the black and foreign-born vote are based on the vote for governor.

44. Martel to FM, Nov. 17, 1932, FM to J. Pomfret, Jan. 2, 1933, MOR; Toole to Farley, Dec. 28, 1932, with Toole to FM, Jan. 19, 1933, FM Papers. See also Ira Altschuler to FM, Nov. 19, 1932, Kelly to FM, Nov. 9, 1932, MOR; Marguerite Meagher to F. D. Roosevelt, Nov. 8, 1932, and J. P. Hayes to F. D. Roosevelt, Dec. 16, 1932, DNC Records.

45. Flynn, *Catholics and Roosevelt,* pp. 50-53; Frank J. Markey to FM, Oct. 5, 1932, FM to Raymond F. Kernan, Jr., Nov. 14, 1932, Kernan to FM, Nov. 22, 1932, R. S. Cuddihy to FM, Nov. 21, 1932, Frank Flynn to FM, Apr. 8, 1933, FM Papers; James F. Drought to F. D. Roosevelt, Apr. 7, 1933, Allan F. Lillis to F. D. Roosevelt, Apr. 10, 1933, Murphy Personal Record, Records of the Bureau of Insular Affairs, RG 350, NARS; L. E. McGivena to James Fitzgerald, Dec. 6, 1932, MOR. There is a copy of the speech in ibid.

46. G. H. Roosevelt to F. D. Roosevelt [Feb. 15, 1933], President's Personal

File 285, FDRL; G. H. Roosevelt to F. D. Roosevelt, Mar. 12, 1933, FM File, 1933–36, Alphabetical File, FDRL; GM to Coughlin, Mar. 16, 1933, GM Papers; *News-Week,* V (Mar. 16, 1935), 17; *DN,* Oct. 18, 1936; Interview with Martin S. Hayden, Oct. 6, 1964, p. 16, MHC; Sheldon Marcus, *Father Coughlin* (Boston, 1973), pp. 48–49. Cf. Charles Tull, *Father Coughlin and the New Deal* (Syracuse, 1965), p. 24.

47. *DN,* Nov. 23, Dec. 11, 18, 1932, Mar. 3, 4, Apr. 8, 1933; *DT,* Mar. 3, Apr. 8, 9, 1933; *Philippine Free Press,* Jan. 26, 1935, MSB; FM to Moley, Jan. 18, Feb. 10, 1933, Raymond Moley Papers, in Mr. Moley's possession; Raymond Moley, *After Seven Years* (New York, 1939), p. 124; Raymond Moley, *The First New Deal* (New York, 1966), pp. 77–78n; Moley to Sidney Fine, Jan. 12, 1967; Jaffe interview; *NYT,* Mar. 3, 1933; "Lay Bishop," *Time,* XXXIV (Aug. 28, 1939), 15. The Walsh appointment was not announced until the end of February. *NYT,* Mar. 1, 1933. Roosevelt at one point had considered appointing Murphy head of the Veterans Bureau. Frank Freidel, *Franklin D. Roosevelt: Launching the New Deal* (Boston, 1973), p. 138.

48. Stimson Diary, Mar. 28, 1933, Henry L. Stimson Papers, Sterling Library, Yale University, New Haven, Conn.; Max Freedman, annotator, *Roosevelt and Frankfurter, Their Correspondence, 1928–1945* (Boston, 1967), pp. 111, 122, 124; note concerning Comstock in FM File, 1933–36, Alphabetical File, FDRL; Guy H. Jenkins to George C. Booth, July 29, 1935, Guy H. Jenkins Papers, MHC; *NYT,* Apr. 8, 1933; *DN,* Apr. 7, 8, 1933.

49. *DN,* Apr. 8, 9, 26, 30, May 10, 1933; *NYT,* Apr. 9, 1933.

50. *Legion News,* Apr. 28, 1933, MSB; *DT,* Apr. 15, 20, 1933; R. M. Kennedy and A. P. Dueweke to Dear Sir and Brother, Apr. 17, 1933, Wayne County AFL-CIO Papers; *DLN,* Apr. 28, 1933; *DN,* Apr. 21, 1933.

51. James M. O'Dea to Dear Friend of FM, Apr. 15, 1933, Henry Joy Papers, MHC; *DT,* Apr. 22, 1933; *DN,* Apr. 22, 1933.

52. EGK to Chase S. Osborn, Feb. 3, 1932, Chase S. Osborn Papers, MHC; Chapin to Mrs. C. P. White, Apr. 10, 1933, Roy D. Chapin Papers, MHC; "The Mayor's Job," *Detroiter,* XXIV (May 15, 1933), 3.

53. EGK to Osborn, Feb. 3, 1932, Osborn Papers; Fram to FM, Apr. 10, 1933, W. D. and Robert Henderson to FM, Apr. 8, 1933, FM Papers. See also H. Ralph Higgins to FM, Apr. 8, 1933, Parker to FM, Apr. 8, 1933, and Dorothy Roosevelt to FM, Apr. 19, 1933, ibid.

54. Norton to FM, Apr. 15, 1933, FM Papers.

55. Roy E. Duquette and the Residents of the Fisher Lodge to FM, Apr. 10, 1933, John T. Kitchen et al. to FM, Apr. 15, 1933, Mrs. Joe Hartman to FM, Apr. 8, 1933, Florence Manillo to FM, May 9, 1933, ibid.

56. Sarainne Andrews to FM, Apr. 21, 1933, Beulah Young and Josephine E. Belford to FM, Apr. 17, 1933, R. L. Bradby to FM, Apr. 20, 1933,

Coughlin to FM, Oct. 13, 1931, Mother Patricia to Mother Prioress, Apr. 15, 1933, ibid.; Gallagher to Michael J. O'Doherty, May 12, 1933, EMB Papers.

57. John J. Brennan to FM, Apr. 7, 1933, ibid.
58. For Pingree, see Melvin G. Holli, *Reform in Detroit: Hazen S. Pingree and Urban Politics* (New York, 1969), pp. 23-30, 41-52, 68-124, 135-36, 147-48, 153. For Couzens, see John M. T. Chavis, "James Couzens: Mayor of Detroit, 1919-1922" (Ph.D. thesis, Michigan State University, 1970), passim, and Harry Barnard, *Independent Man: The Life of Senator James Couzens* (New York, 1958), pp. 123-33. The three mayors are compared in Michael B. Staebler, "From the Progressive Era to the New Deal: A Study of Three Detroit Reform Mayors" (MS, 1966), in Mr. Staebler's possession.
59. Mead interview, pp. 10-11; *Civic Searchlight,* Apr.-May 1933; Lovett to William H. Phelps, Nov. 10, 1936, DCL Papers; William Anderson to FM, Apr. 13, 1933, MOR; Hill to Dan Cochrane, Sept. 10, 1936, Adam Strohm to Osborn, Mar. 18, 1940, EMB to William Skrzycki, Jan. 4, 1943, FM Papers.
60. *DN,* May 10, 15, 1933; *DT,* May 10, 15, 1933; Eliot ——— to FM, May 16, 1933, ——— to FM (two letters) [May 1933], Montgomery to FM, Jan. 26, 1933 [1934], FM Papers.

Bibliographical Note

No attempt has been made in the following pages to list all the works that have been cited in the footnotes or to include sources that are relevant only to Frank Murphy's career after 1933. Comment has been reserved for unpublished and published materials of particular value or interest for this study.

Manuscript Sources

The most important single collection for the study of the life and times of Frank Murphy is the Frank Murphy Papers, in the Michigan Historical Collections, Ann Arbor, Michigan. This unusually rich collection has been added to substantially since it was first acquired by the Michigan Historical Collections in 1961. Murphy apparently did not begin to save his correspondence in any systematic manner until he became governor-general of the Philippines in 1933, but there is nevertheless a substantial amount of material in the Frank Murphy Papers pertaining to the pre-1933 period of Murphy's life. The Michigan Historical Collections also contains a considerable number of manuscript collections that supplement and complement the Frank Murphy Papers. For the period before 1933 the most significant of these collections is the John F. Murphy Papers, which include the crucially important letters that Frank wrote to his mother after he left Harbor Beach in 1908 until her death in 1924; these letters are particularly abundant for the period of Frank's military service in World War I. There is also material of consequence relating to Frank Murphy in the papers of Marguerite Murphy, George Murphy, Harold Murphy, and Irene Murphy. The numerous Frank Murphy items in the Eleanor M. Bumgardner Papers could just as well have been a part of the Frank Murphy Papers.

There is some very valuable material pertaining to Frank Murphy's youth in Harbor Beach in the Eugene Gressman Papers, also in the Michigan Historical Collections. One or two items concerning Frank Murphy's histrionic career while he was at the University of Michigan are in the J. Fred Lawton Papers. The Henry M. Bates Papers and the Harry Burns Hutchins Papers provide some insights into requirements and curricular developments in the Law Department while Murphy was pursuing his legal studies. The context for Murphy's service as a night school teacher in Delray in 1914–15 is made evident in the Americanization Committee of Detroit Papers. The massive Arthur J. Tuttle Papers reflect the career of the federal judge for the Eastern District of Michigan while Murphy was a United States attorney in that district, but the Tuttle Papers shed little light on Murphy's activities during this period of his life.

The Children's Fund Papers, in the Michigan Historical Collections, are invaluable for information on welfare problems in Detroit while Murphy was mayor. The Detroit Urban League Papers include significant material on the plight of blacks during the Great Depression and contain quite a few items pertaining to the Mayor's Unemployment Committee. There is additional material concerning the Mayor's Unemployment Committee as well as other relevant Murphy items in the Edward G. Kemp Papers. There is scattered correspondence pertaining to Murphy or events with which he was associated in his Detroit years in the Horatio J. Abbott Papers, the Roy D. Chapin Papers, the William A. Comstock Papers, the Henry B. Joy Papers, the Chase S. Osborn Papers, the Ralph Stone Papers, the Moses L. Walker Papers, and the Carl M. Weideman Papers, all in the Michigan Historical Collections.

The decisions of the University of Michigan law faculty concerning Frank Murphy's academic status in the Department of Law are contained in the Department of Law Faculty Records, in the University of Michigan Law School. The Joseph A. Labadie Collection in the Harlan Hatcher Graduate Library of the University of Michigan includes a few items relevant to Murphy's mayoralty.

The indispensable manuscript source for Murphy's mayoralty is the difficult-to-use Mayor's Office Records, in the Burton Historical Collection of the Detroit Public Library. The Burton Collection also contains a small Frank Murphy collection pertaining to the 1931 mayoralty campaign. There are a substantial number of handwritten letters from Murphy that help to illuminate his life and career in the 1920s in the Hester Everard Papers. The Detroit Citizens League Papers, a splendid collection, contain significant material pertaining to Murphy's service on the Recorder's Court and as mayor of Detroit. The portion of the Edward G. Kemp Papers in the Burton Historical Collection, valuable primarily for Murphy's governorship, includes a few items relevant to his mayoralty. There is some material pertaining to the Detroit Street Railways in the Joseph E. Mills Papers, in the Burton Historical Collection.

The Wayne County AFL-CIO Papers, located in the Archives of Labor History and Urban Affairs of Wayne State University, Detroit, Michigan, serve, among other things, to document the relationship of Frank Murphy and the Detroit Federation of Labor. There is some material on the Briggs strike as well as on other aspects of the depression in Detroit in the Joe Brown Collection. The Frank Marquardt Collection, in the Archives of Labor History and Urban Affairs, contains the minutes of the proceedings of the Mayor's Non-Partisan Committee on Industrial Disputes, an important source for Murphy's role in the Briggs strike.

The National Association for the Advancement of Colored People Papers, in the Library of Congress, Washington, D.C., are indispensable for the Sweet cases. There is also some Sweet material in the Arthur Barnett Spingarn Papers and the Clarence Darrow Papers. The James Couzens Papers, which are incomplete, contain some correspondence relevant to Murphy's mayoralty. There is material on the National Progressive Conference in the George W. Norris Papers, in the Library of Congress.

The Records of the Department of Justice (Record Group 60), in the National Archives and Records Service, Washington, D.C., are valuable for Murphy's career as a United States attorney. Washington's view of the relief problem in Detroit and Michigan while Hoover was president is reflected in the Records of the President's Organization on Unemployment Relief (Record Group 73). Detroit's dependence on emergency relief loans from the Reconstruction Finance Corporation in the fiscal year 1932–33 is documented in the Records of the Reconstruction Finance Corporation (Record Group 234). There is an important file on the Briggs strike in the Records of the Federal Mediation and Conciliation Service (Record Group 280).

The Democratic Party National Committee Records, the Governor Papers, the Alphabetical File, and the G. Hall Roosevelt Personal File, in the Franklin D. Roosevelt Library, Hyde Park, New York, shed light on the relationship of Frank Murphy and Franklin D. Roosevelt and especially on Murphy's role in the 1932 campaign. There are a few items pertaining to the May 18, 1932, conference of Michigan mayors and the Conference of Mayors of June 1, 1932, in Official File 264-B in the Herbert Hoover Presidential Library, West Branch, Iowa. The American Civil Liberties Union Archives at Princeton University, Princeton, New Jersey (there is a microfilm copy of the Archives in the New York Public Library), are a major source for police and civil-liberties issues while Murphy was mayor. There are a few items pertaining to Murphy's quest for a moratorium on municipal debts in the Raymond Moley Papers, recently acquired by the Hoover Institute, Stanford University, Stanford, California.

Interviews

Interviews with the following persons proved helpful in my effort to reconstruct the career of Frank Murphy up to 1933: John V. Brennan, Beulah Carter, Thomas F. Chawke, Larry S. Davidow, James A. Farley, Hilmer Gellein, Nathaniel Goldstick, Josephine Gomon, William Haber, Mrs. Joseph R. Hayden, Martin S. Hayden, Norman H. Hill, Alexander Holtzoff, Lee Kreiselman Jaffe, J. Fred Lawton, Mary Lutomski, Lucille Malcolm, Jack Manning, Harry Mead, Carl Muller, Brigid Murphy, George Murphy, Irene Murphy, William Norton, Frank Potts, and Nell D. Wilson. Transcripts of most of these interviews are in the Michigan Historical Collections. The Eugene Gressman Papers, in the Michigan Historical Collections, contain notes on interviews Gressman conducted with Marguerite and George Murphy shortly after Frank's death. There are transcripts

of interviews conducted by Alex Baskin with some of the principals of
the Sweet trials in the Michigan Historical Collections. J. Weldon Jones,
Hilmer Gellein, Josephine Gomon, Brigid Murphy, Irene Murphy, and
Raymond Moley generously responded in writing to my inquiries about
Frank Murphy.

Newspapers and Periodicals

The Frank Murphy Scrapbooks that arrived at the Michigan Historical
Collections along with the Frank Murphy Papers cover only the post-1933
phase of Murphy's career. The Michigan Historical Collections, however,
has compiled two additional Frank Murphy Scrapbooks that include
clippings pertaining to his entire career and has also acquired the scrapbooks
that Murphy's staff compiled during the first year of his mayoralty, from
September 5, 1930, to September 28, 1931. There are, in addition, numerous
newspaper clippings scattered throughout the Frank Murphy Papers. There
are notes on Harbor Beach newspaper items relevant to Frank Murphy's
youth in the Gressman Papers. The *Michigan Daily* makes it possible
to recreate Murphy's years as a student at the University of Michigan.
The Arthur J. Tuttle Scrapbooks are useful for some of the cases with
which Murphy dealt as a United States attorney.

The Detroit *Times,* the Detroit *News,* the Detroit *Free Press,* and the
Detroit *Saturday Night* are indispensable for the study of Murphy's Detroit
career. Among these newspapers, the Detroit *Times* provides the fullest
coverage of Murphy as a criminal-court judge, and the Detroit *News* is
the most valuable for Murphy's mayoralty. There is a substantial amount
of Murphy biographical material in the Souvenir Section of the Detroit
Times of April 23, 1933. There is no available file of the Detroit *Mirror,*
but clippings from this short-lived newspaper are preserved in the Murphy
Scrapbooks and the Frank Murphy Papers. The *Daily Worker* is a convenient
source for the Communist reaction to Murphy and for the Communist
version of such events as the Ford Hunger March. The importance of
Murphy's mayoralty is attested to by the attention that it received in the
New York *Times.*

The Detroit *Labor News,* the organ of the Detroit Federation of Labor,
took special note of Murphy's activities beginning in 1923. The views
of the Detroit Citizens League were reported in *Civic Searchlight* and
those of the Detroit Board of Commerce in the *Detroiter.* The *Journal
of the American Judicature Society* is a major source for the study of
judicial reform in the 1920s in general and for the Detroit Recorder's
Court in that decade in particular. The *Journal of the American Institute
of Criminal Law and Criminology* also contains some articles on the
Detroit court in the 1920s. Developments in Detroit while Murphy was
a judge and the city's chief executive form the basis for several articles
in the *National Municipal Review.* The *Community Fund News* appeared
irregularly in Detroit during the depression.

Miscellaneous Unpublished Sources

Fred Yonce, "The Big Red Scare in Detroit, 1919-1920" (MS, 1963), in my possession, is the fullest account of that topic. The mayoralty of James Couzens is the subject of John M. T. Chavis, "James Couzens: Mayor of Detroit, 1919-1922" (Ph.D. thesis, Michigan State University, 1970). Eugene Strobel, "Frank Murphy: Crusading Judge, 1923-1930" (MS, 1962), in my possession, surveys Murphy's career on the Detroit Recorder's Court. The race-relations background of the Sweet trials is set forth in David Allan Levine, "'Expecting the Barbarians': Race Relations and Social Control, Detroit, 1915-1925" (Ph.D. thesis, University of Chicago, 1970), and, in a more limited way, in Norman Frederic Weaver, "The Knights of the Ku Klux Klan in Wisconsin, Indiana, Ohio and Michigan" (Ph.D. thesis, University of Wisconsin, 1954). The police file on the Sweet cases (Homicide File #1074) is in Police Headquarters in Detroit, and what survives of the official court record of the two cases is contained in Recorder's Court File Nos. 60317-60318, in the Frank Murphy Hall of Justice. There are two incomplete transcripts of the Sweet trials in the Burton Historical Collection; no complete transcript survives. Alex Baskin compiled a notebook on the Sweet cases, presently in my possession, that includes a miscellany of information on the affair. There are accounts of the cases in Charlotte Goodman, "'Dear God! Must We Not Live?'" (MS, 1963), and in a similarly entitled paper by Alex Goodwin, written in 1966, both in my possession.

Maurice M. Ramsey, "Some Aspects of Non-Partisan Government in Detroit, 1918-1940" (Ph.D. thesis, University of Michigan, 1940), is the best available study of the characteristics of nonpartisan government in Detroit. The same subject is treated in David Greenstone, "A Report on the Politics of Detroit" (Cambridge, Mass., 1961). The impact of the depression on the two-party system in Michigan is described and evaluated in Richard Theodore Ortquist, Jr., "Depression Politics in Michigan, 1929-1933" (Ph.D. thesis, University of Michigan, 1968); the structure of the two major parties in nonpartisan Detroit during Murphy's Detroit years is treated in John W. Lederle, "Political Party Organization in Detroit—1920 to 1934" (MS [1934]), a copy of which is in the Bureau of Government Library of the University of Michigan. Thomas R. Solomon, "Participation of Negroes in Detroit Elections" (Ph.D. thesis, University of Michigan, 1939), is a useful introduction to the voting habits of Detroit's blacks in the 1930s. Franklin D. Roosevelt's efforts to win the Michigan delegation in 1932 are considered in Earland Irving Carlson, "Franklin D. Roosevelt's Fight for the Presidential Nomination, 1928-1932" (Ph.D. thesis, University of Illinois, 1955), and Gloria W. Newquist, "James A. Farley and the Politics of Victory, 1928-1936" (Ph.D. thesis, University of Southern California, 1966).

The history of prohibition enforcement in Detroit is one of the subjects treated in Larry Daniel Engelmann, "O, Whisky: The History of Prohibition in Michigan" (Ph.D. thesis, University of Michigan, 1971). The most satisfactory account of the recall of Charles Bowles is Lawrence Veenstra, "The Recall of Mayor Charles Bowles of Detroit" (MS, 1963), in my possession. The impact of the depression on the cities across the nation is sketchily explored in James Joseph Hannah, "Urban Reaction to the Great Depression in the United States, 1929-1933" (Ph.D. thesis, University of California, Berkeley, 1956). The Boston experience, in particular, is developed in Charles Hathaway Trout's well-researched "Boston during the Great Depression, 1929-1940" (Ph.D. thesis, Columbia University, 1972). The manner in which Detroit reacted to the depression in the year before Murphy became the city's mayor is set forth in Terry Hamburg, "The Depression in Detroit: The First Year . . ." (MS, 1968), in my possession.

The Proceedings of the Public Welfare Commission, in the Burton Historical Collection (there is a microfilm copy for the years 1929-33 in the Michigan Historical Collections), are an invaluable source for the understanding of Detroit's welfare problems during Murphy's mayoralty. Rachel Ganapol, "Public Welfare Relief Activities in Detroit, 1802-1930" (Detroit, 1946), is an excellent history of public relief in Detroit before Murphy became mayor. The response of the Detroit Community Fund to the depression is treated in James H. Norton, "A History of the Detroit Community Fund and the Council of Social Agencies of Metropolitan Detroit, 1917-1938" (M.A. thesis, University of Michigan, 1940). The Report of the Mayor's Non-Partisan Committee on Industrial Disputes (the Fact-Finding Committee) in the Matter of the Strike of the Workers at the Briggs Manufacturing Company . . . (1933), is available in the Michigan Historical Collections.

Hilmer Gellein, "United States Supreme Court Justice Frank Murphy . . ." (MS, n.d.), in the Hilmer Gellein Papers in the Michigan Historical Collections, is most useful for the period of Murphy's service on the Recorder's Court. Myles M. Platt, "Frank Murphy: Detroit's Liberal Mayor (1930-1933)" (MS, 1954), in the Michigan Historical Collections, is based almost entirely on newspaper sources. Joseph H. Creighton, "Frank Murphy—Off the Record," Part Two (MS [Aug. 1938]), in the Frank Murphy Papers, contains some valuable information about the life of Frank Murphy. Detroit's three most important mayors since the Civil War are compared in Michael B. Staebler, "From the Progressive Era to the New Deal: A Study of Three Detroit Reform Mayors" (MS, 1966), in Mr. Staebler's possession.

Published Sources

The two principal published biographies of Frank Murphy are Richard D. Lunt, *The High Ministry of Government: The Political Career of Frank Murphy* (Detroit, 1965), and J. Woodford Howard, *Mr. Justice Murphy: A Political Biography* (Princeton, 1968). Lunt's book all but ignores

Murphy's career before he became mayor and concludes with his appointment to the Supreme Court. The research for the book was completed before the Frank Murphy Papers became available. The well-crafted Howard biography focuses on Murphy's service on the Supreme Court; only about 12 percent of the text is devoted to Murphy's life and career before 1933. Although Howard made effective use of the Frank Murphy Papers, the collection was far from complete when he consulted it, and a substantial number of other manuscript collections were unavailable to him or escaped his attention. There are important insights into Murphy and his career in Blair Moody, "High Commissioner to Manila," *Survey Graphic*, XXIV (Dec. 1935), 610-11+, and "The Labor Governors," *Fortune*, XV (June 1937), 78-81+. The chapter on Murphy in William L. Stidger, *The Human Side of Greatness* (New York, 1940), is especially valuable for Murphy's youth.

Murphy's Irish-American heritage can be gleaned from Thomas N. Brown, *Irish-American Nationalism, 1870-1890* (Philadelphia, 1966); George W. Potter, *To the Golden Door: The Story of the Irish in Ireland and America* (Boston, 1960); William V. Shannon, *The American Irish* (New York, 1963); and Andrew M. Greeley, *That Most Distressful Nation: The Taming of the American Irish* (Chicago, 1972). The extent to which Murphy departed from the stereotype of the Irish politician in America is evident from the analysis in Edward M. Levine, *The Irish and Irish Politicians* (South Bend, 1966).

Charles Moore, *History of Michigan* (Chicago, 1915), II, includes a short biography of John F. Murphy. There is material on Sand Beach, Harbor Beach, and Huron County in *Biographical Album of Huron County* (Chicago, 1884); Ladies Aid Society of the Presbyterian Church, *Souvenir of Sand Beach Michigan, 1898* (Sand Beach [1898]); and Chet Hey and Norman Eckstein, *Huron County Centennial History, 1859-1959* (n.p., 1959). Frank Murphy's favorite high school teacher is the subject of Lura Lincoln Cook, *The Book of Esther* (New York, 1962).

Howard H. Peckham, *The Making of the University of Michigan, 1817-1967* (Ann Arbor, 1967), contains the best picture of the University of Michigan while Murphy was a student there. There is a good deal of factual information concerning the Law Department of the university in Elizabeth Gaspar Brown, *Legal Education at Michigan, 1859-1959* (Ann Arbor, 1959). Christian A. Bach and Henry Noble Hall, *The Fourth Division. Its Services and Achievements in the World War* (n.p., 1920), provides an account of the occupation of Germany by the division that Murphy joined as the fighting ended in World War I. The American involvement in the struggle for Irish independence, to which Murphy lent his support, is set forth most satisfactorily in Alan J. Ward, *Ireland and Anglo-American Relations, 1899-1921* (London, 1969); Charles Callan Tansill, *America and the Fight for Irish Freedom, 1866-1922* (New York, 1957); Joseph P. O'Grady, "The Irish," in O'Grady, ed., *The Immigrants' Influence on*

Wilson's Peace Policies (Lexington, 1967); and John B. Duff, "The Versailles Treaty and the Irish-Americans," *Journal of American History*, LV (Dec. 1968), 582-98.

There is, lamentably, no satisfactory history of Detroit in the twentieth century. William P. Lovett, *Detroit Rules Itself* (Boston, 1930), is a history of municipal reform in Detroit from the perspective of the Detroit Citizens League. Harry Barnard, *Independent Man: The Life of Senator James Couzens* (New York, 1958), deals much too briefly with the Couzens mayoralty. There is a good deal of miscellaneous information about Detroit in Clarence M. and M. Agnes Burton, eds., *History of Wayne County and the City of Detroit, Michigan*, 5 vols. (Chicago, 1935), George B. Catlin, *The Story of Detroit*, 2d and rev. ed. (Detroit, 1926), and Robert Conot, *American Odyssey* (New York, 1974), and a good brief account in Leo Donovan, "Detroit: City of Conflict," in Robert S. Allen, ed., *Our Fair City* (New York, 1947). Data on Detroit's ethnic groups are provided in Lois Rankin, "Detroit Nationality Groups," *Michigan History Magazine*, XXIII (Spring 1939), 129-205. Reinhold Niebuhr, *Leaves from the Notebook of a Tamed Cynic* (Chicago, 1929), includes some interesting observations on Detroit in the 1920s. The status of the prohibition experiment in Michigan and Detroit shortly before Murphy became mayor is presented in sensational terms in Walter W. Liggett, "Michigan—Soused and Serene," *Plain Talk*, VI (Mar. 1930), 257-73. Robert L. Duffus, "Utopia on Wheels," *Harper's*, CLXII (Dec. 1930), 50-59, presents an unduly optimistic picture of Detroit at the beginning of the depression. Edward C. Banfield and James Q. Wilson, *City Politics* (Vintage Book; New York, 1966), is studded with insights that help one to appraise Murphy's Detroit career.

The essential statistics pertaining to Detroit's development are conveniently brought together in Detroit Bureau of Governmental Research, *Accumulated Social and Economic Statistics for Detroit* (Detroit, 1937), and Eric Kocher, *Economic and Physical Growth of Detroit, 1701-1935* (n.p., 1935). The voting behavior of different ethnic, racial, and income groups in Detroit is analyzed in Edward H. Litchfield, *Voting Behavior in a Metropolitan Area* (Ann Arbor, 1941). Donald S. Hecock and Harry A. Trevelyan, *Detroit Voters and Recent Elections* (Detroit, 1938), provides statistics on the country of origin of Detroit's registered foreign-born voters, precinct by precinct, as of February 1, 1938.

There is a superior account of A. Mitchell Palmer's administration of the Department of Justice in Stanley Coben, *A. Mitchell Palmer* (New York, 1963). Information on the Red Scare in Detroit is provided in Subcommittee of the Senate Committee on the Judiciary, *Charges of Illegal Practices of the Department of Justice*, 66 Cong., 3 Sess. (Washington, 1921); Louis F. Post, *The Deportations Delirium of Nineteen-Twenty* (Chicago, 1923); Robert K. Murray, *Red Scare* (Minneapolis, 1955); Max Lowenthal, *The Federal Bureau of Investigation* (New York, 1950); Frederick R. Barkley, "Jailing Radicals in Detroit," *Nation*, CX (Jan. 31, 1920), 136–37; and Barkley, "Improving on the Czar," *Nation*, CX (Apr. 10, 1920), 458–59.

The annual reports of the Detroit Recorder's Court, valuable for the statistical information that they contain, are available in the Detroit Public Library. Raymond Moley, *Our Criminal Courts* (New York, 1930), is a penetrating study of the criminal courts of the United States as of the end of the third decade of the twentieth century. Mark H. Haller, "Urban Crime and Criminal Justice: The Chicago Case," *Journal of American History*, LVII (Dec. 1970), 619–35, contrasts the advocates of punitive and reformative justice. There is a history of the Detroit Recorder's Court in Michigan Historical Records Survey Project, *Inventory of the Municipal Archives of Michigan: Detroit Recorder's Court* (Detroit, 1942). Murphy's sentencing plan is lauded in J. A. Fellows [Josephine Gomon], "Detroit's Crime Clinic," *Nation*, CXXX (May 14, 1930), 568–70.

There is an abundant literature on the Sweet cases, among which the following published works are noteworthy: Marcet Haldeman-Julius, *Clarence Darrow's Two Great Trials* (Girard, Kansas, 1927), which includes two articles on the trials previously published in the *Haldeman-Julius Monthly*; Kenneth G. Weinberg, *A Man's Home, a Man's Castle* (New York, 1971); Clarence Darrow, *The Story of My Life* (New York, 1932); Irving Stone, *Clarence Darrow for the Defense* (Garden City, New York, 1943); Arthur Garfield Hays, *Let Freedom Ring* (New York, 1937); Walter White, *A Man Called White* (New York, 1948); Eugene Levy, *James Weldon Johnson* (Chicago, 1973); Paul E. Baker, *Negro-White Adjustment* (New York, 1934); David E. Lilienthal, "Has the Negro the Right of Self-Defense?," *Nation*, CXXI (Dec. 23, 1925), 724–25; Walter White, "The Sweet Trial," *Crisis*, XXXI (Jan. 1926), 125–29; and James Weldon Johnson, "Detroit," *Crisis*, XXXII (July 1926), 117–20. Kenneth T. Jackson, *The Ku Klux Klan in the City, 1915–1930* (New York, 1967), is the best study of the Klan in Detroit. Mayor's Inter-racial Committee, *The Negro in Detroit*, 2 vols. ([Detroit] 1926), contains the results of the study by the committee appointed by Mayor John Smith following the attack on the Sweet home.

Mayor Bowles is defended and Gerald M. Buckley attacked in Cash Asher, *Scared Cows: A Story of the Recall of Mayor Bowles* (Detroit, 1931), and Cash Asher, *The Real Buckley Tragedy* (Detroit, 1931). Charles T. Haun, "Bloody July: The Buckley Case—1930," in Alvin C. Hamer, ed., *Detroit Murders* (New York, 1948), is a police reporter's account of the Buckley murder. R. Rothman, "Detroit Elects a Liberal," *Nation*, CXXXI (Oct. 15, 1930), 400–401, is favorable to Murphy, as is Mauritz A. Hallgren, "Detroit's Liberal Mayor," *Nation*, CXXXII (May 13, 1931), 526–28. Hallgren had second thoughts about Murphy, however, criticizing him from a left-wing perspective in "Grave Danger in Detroit," *Nation*, CXXXV (Aug. 3, 1932), 99–101, and *Seeds of Revolt: A Study of American Life and the Temper of the American People during the Depression* (New York, 1933). Murphy is the hero of John B. Kennedy, "City of Hope," *Collier's*, LXXXIX (Apr. 30, 1932), 20+.

The relief problem in the nation between 1929 and 1933 and the response of the Hoover administration are treated in Irving Bernstein, *The Lean Years: A History of the American Worker, 1920-1933* (Boston, 1960); Josephine C. Brown, *Public Relief, 1929-1939* (New York, 1940); Albert U. Romasco, *The Poverty of Abundance: Hoover, the Nation, the Depression* (New York, 1965); Jordan A. Schwarz, *The Interregnum of Despair: Hoover, Congress, and the Depression* (Urbana, 1970); and Edward Ainsworth Williams, *Federal Aid for Relief* (New York, 1939). Unemployment in Detroit can be compared with unemployment elsewhere in Bureau of the Census, *Fifteenth Census of the United States: 1930, Unemployment*, I (Washington, 1931), and *Unemployment*, II (Washington, 1932). Detroit's relief expenditures as compared to the relief expenditures of other cities are set forth in Glen Steele, "Cost of Family Relief in 100 Cities, 1929 and 1930," *Monthy Labor Review*, XXXII (Apr. 1931), 20-28; Anne E. Geddes, *Trends in Relief Expenditures, 1910-1935* (Washington, 1937); Emma A. Winslow, *Trends in Different Types of Public and Private Relief in Urban Areas, 1929-35* (Washington, 1937); and Arthur Edward Burns, "Federal Emergency Relief Administration," *The Municipal Year Book, 1937* (Chicago, 1937). Some demographic effects of the depression in Detroit and Wayne County are indicated in Harold Ross, "Social Consequences of the Business Cycle," *Sociology and Social Research*, XXIII (Jan.-Feb. 1939), 203-10.

The following articles and books make it possible to compare the Detroit welfare program while Murphy was mayor with the experience of other communities: Stuart A. Queen, "What Is Unemployment Doing to Family Social Work? . . . ," *Family*, XII (Feb. 1932), 299-301; "No One Has Starved," *Fortune*, VI (Sept. 1932), 19-29+; Joanna C. Colcord, "Unemployment Relief, 1929-1932," *Family*, XIII (Dec. 1932), 270-74; Colcord, *Emergency Work Relief as Carried Out in Twenty-Six Communities, 1930-31* . . . (New York, 1932); Colcord and Mary Johnston, *Community Programs for Subsistence Gardens* (New York, 1933); Colcord, *Cash Relief* (New York, 1936), an especially valuable work; Robert S. Wilson, *Community Planning for Homeless Men and Boys: The Experience of Sixteen Cities in the Winter of 1930-31* (New York, 1931); and Bonnie R. Fox, "Unemployment Relief in Philadelphia, 1930-1932: A Study of the Depression's Impact on Voluntarism," *Pennsylvania Magazine of History and Biography*, XCII (Jan. 1969), 86-108.

Opal V. Matson, *Local Relief to Dependents* (n.p., 1933), outlines the administrative structure for the dispensing of general and categorical relief in Michigan. There is important statistical information on both unemployment and relief in Detroit during the 1920s and in the first two years of the Great Depression in William Haber, "Fluctuations in Employment in Detroit Factories, 1921–31," *Journal of the American Statistical Association*, XXVII (June 1932), 141–52. The manner in which relief was administered in Detroit and the status of the Department of Public Welfare near the end of the Bowles administration are set forth in Detroit Bureau of Governmental Research, *Outdoor Relief as Administered by the Detroit Department of Public Welfare* (Detroit, 1930). Helen Hall describes the early impact of the depression on Detroit in "When Detroit's Out of Gear," *Survey*, LXIV (Apr. 1, 1930), 9–14+. The response to unemployment in Michigan during the initial years of the depression is surveyed in Richard T. Ortquist, "Unemployment and Relief: Michigan's Response to the Depression during the Hoover Years," *Michigan History*, LVII (Fall 1973), 209–36.

The Detroit Department of Public Welfare published annual reports for 1929 and 1930 but not for the years 1931–39, surveying its activities for the 1930s in Detroit Department of Public Welfare, *The Department of Public Welfare, 1930 to 1940* (Detroit, n.d.). The welfare reports are available in the Detroit Public Library. William J. Norton, "The Relief Crisis in Detroit," *Social Service Review*, VII (Mar. 1933), 1–10, is a superb summary of Detroit's welfare record during Murphy's mayoralty. Among many contemporary articles concerning welfare and unemployment in Detroit while Murphy was mayor, the following are of special interest: Beulah Amidon, "Detroit Does Something about It," *Survey*, LXV (Feb. 15, 1931), 540–42; William P. Lovett, "Detroit Feeds Its Hungry," *National Municipal Review*, XX (July 1931), 402–6; Sophia T. Cole, "We Dip into Farm Placement," *Family*, XIII (May 1932), 79–81; Samuel M. Levin, "The Ford Unemployment Policy," *American Labor Legislation Review*, XXIII (June 1932), 101–8; Wilhelmina Luten, "A Survey of 1200 Families, Detroit Department of Public Welfare," *Family*, XIII (June 1932), 127–30; Charles R. Walker, "Down and Out in Detroit," in Charles A. Beard, ed., *America Faces the Future* (Boston, 1932); John Dos Passos, "Detroit: City of Leisure," *New Republic*, LXXI (July 27, 1932), 280–82; and Frank Murphy, "The Detroit Plan," *Plain Talk* (Oct. 1932), pp. 36–37. United States Department of Commerce, *Subsistence Gardens* (Washington, 1932), focuses on Detroit. William C. Richards and William J. Norton, *Biography of a Foundation: The Story of the Children's Fund of Michigan, 1929–1954* (n.p., 1957), surveys the activities of the Children's Fund during the Great Depression.

Murphy's testimony before congressional committees concerning Detroit's welfare and financial problems is included in Subcommittee of the Senate Committee on Manufactures, *Unemployment Relief. Hearings on S. 174 and S. 262*, 72 Cong., 1 Sess. (Washington, 1932); Senate Committee on the Judiciary, *Uniform System of Bankruptcy. Hearing on S. 5699*, 72 Cong., 2 Sess. (Washington, 1933); and House Committee on the Judiciary, *To Amend the Bankruptcy Act . . . Hearing on H.R. 1670 . . .*, 73 Cong., 1 Sess. (Washington, 1933). Paul V. Betters explained the shortcomings of the Emergency Relief and Construction Act in Subcommittee of the Senate Committee on Manufactures, *Federal Aid for Unemployment Relief. Hearings on S. 5125,* 72 Cong., 2 Sess. (Washington, 1933).

The indispensable published source for Detroit's financial problems while Murphy was mayor is Egbert S. Wengert, *Financial Problems of the City of Detroit in the Depression* (Detroit, 1939). The principal analyses of the city's critical tax-delinquency problem are Sidney G. Tickton, *An Analysis of Tax Delinquency* (Detroit, 1932), and Virginia Eyre, *A Study of Tax Delinquency in the Second Ward of Detroit . . .* (Detroit [1933]). Ralph Stone, "Detroit Practises Economy," *Review of Reviews,* LXXXV (June 1932), 26–28+, and Henry Hart, "The Decline, Fall and Resurrection of the Credit of the City of Detroit," *National Municipal Review,* XXV (June 1936), 347–53, are accounts of Detroit's fiscal policies in the Murphy years written by bankers who participated in the shaping of those policies. The clash between "financial dictators" and the political leadership in cities like Detroit during the depression is analyzed in William C. Beyer, "Financial Dictators Replace Political Boss," *National Municipal Review,* XXII (Apr. 1933), 162–67+, and (May 1933), 231–34+. The origins of the Michigan banking holiday are considered in the aforementioned Barnard biography of Couzens, in Susan Estabrook Kennedy, *The Banking Crisis of 1933* (Lexington, 1973), and in Jesse H. Jones, with Edward Angly, *Fifty Billion Dollars: My Thirteen Years with the RFC (1932–1945)* (New York, 1951).

The deliberations of the Common Council while Murphy was mayor can be followed in the *Journal of the Common Council,* a set of which is in the Burton Historical Collection (there are scattered issues in the Murphy Papers). Clarence E. Ridley and Orin F. Nolting, eds., *What the Depression Has Done to Cities* (Chicago, 1935), contains appraisals by thirteen authorities of the depression's impact on the principal municipal activities. The depression's effect on the departments of the city of Detroit is reflected in the annual reports of these departments, copies of which are available in the Detroit Public Library. The relationship of a mayor to his police department is one of the subjects treated in James Q. Wilson's informative *Varieties of Police Behavior* (Cambridge, 1968). Ernest Jerome Hopkins, *Our Lawless Police* (New York, 1931), and National Commission on Law Observance and Enforcement, *Report on Lawlessness in Law Enforcement* (Washington, 1931), provide some evidence of lawless behavior by the Detroit police at the beginning of the Murphy administration. The high standing with civil libertarians of Mayor Murphy's Detroit is attested to in American Civil Liberties Union, *The Fight for Civil Liberty, 1930–1931* (New York, 1931), and American Civil Liberties Union, *"'Sweet Land of Liberty,'" 1931–1932* (New York, 1932).

Alex Baskin, "The Ford Hunger March—1932," *Labor History,* XIII (Summer 1972), 331–60, is the best-researched account of the Ford Hunger March. There are several interesting contemporary articles on the same subject, including Maurice Sugar, "Bullets—not Food—for Ford Workers," *Nation,* CXXXIV (Mar. 23, 1932), 333-35; Oakley Johnson, "After the Dearborn Massacre," *New Republic,* LXX (Mar. 30, 1932), 172-74; and Felix Morrow, "Class War in Detroit," *New Masses,* VII (May 1932), 13-17. The entire issue of *New Force,* I (Mar.-Apr. 1932), published by the John Reed Club of Detroit, is devoted to the Ford Hunger March. Samuel Romer, "That Detroit Strike," *Nation,* CXXXVI (Feb. 15, 1933), 167-68, deals with the Briggs strike. The place of the Briggs strike in the history of industrial relations in the automobile industry is assessed in Sidney Fine, *The Automobile under the Blue Eagle* (Ann Arbor, 1963). The role of the Communists in the strike is stressed in James R. Prickett, "Communists and the Autombile Industry in Detroit before 1935," *Michigan History,* LVII (Fall 1973), 185-208.

Detroit is one of ten cities studied by R. L. Duffus in his *Our Starving Libraries* (Boston, 1933). There is a brief consideration of the controversy surrounding the public ownership of the street railway in Detroit in Harry Dahlheimer, *Public Transportation in Detroit* (Detroit, 1951). The essential information concerning public and private electric service in Detroit is provided in William H. Lane, *A History of Electric Service in Detroit* (Detroit, 1937), and Raymond C. Miller, *Kilowatts at Work: A History of the Detroit Edison Company* (Detroit, 1957).

The change in the relationship between city governments and the federal government that Mayor Murphy helped to initiate is reflected in American Municipal Association, *Proceedings . . . 1931-1935* (Chicago, 1936; Paul V. Betters et al., eds., *Recent Federal-City Relations* (Washington, 1936); and Suzanne G. Farkas, *Urban Lobbying: Mayors in the Federal Arena* (New York, 1971). Frank Freidel, *Franklin D. Roosevelt: The Triumph* (Boston, 1956), exaggerates Murphy's role in winning the Michigan delegation for Roosevelt in 1932. Charles J. Tull, *Father Coughlin and the New Deal* (Syracuse, 1965), provides some information on the Murphy-Coughlin relationship, as does Sheldon Marcus, *Father Coughlin* (Boston, 1973). The interrelationship of Catholicism and the New Deal, of consequence for Murphy's career in the 1930s, is considered in George Q. Flynn, *American Catholics and the Roosevelt Presidency* (Lexington, 1968), and David J. O'Brien, *American Catholics and Social Reform: The New Deal Years* (New York, 1968).

Index